FFION HAGUE was born in Cardiff. A native Welsh-speaker, she was educated through the medium of Welsh and took her first degree, in English Literature, at Jesus College, Oxford. She became interested in the Celtic-inspired work of Thomas Gray and spent two years in further research into his work and that of Welsh poets in the mid-eighteenth century, culminating in an MPhil from the University of Wales.

Latterly, Ffion has worked as a policy civil servant, a director of a national charity and, since 2000, has been a head-hunter specialising in main board appointments and board evaluation. She holds a number of advisory positions in the commercial and not-for-profit sectors.

Ffion is married to William Hague and lives in Yorkshire.

From the reviews of *The Pain and the Privilege*:

'Hague's light touch and deft handling of abundant letters and diaries makes for a riveting examination of the dynamic between a man, his mistress, his wife and his daughter. Played out behind the doors of Downing Street, it throws light on the depth of ambition of one of the 20th century's great political machinators'   *The Times*

'This well written and intelligent book . . . tells an involving, multifarious and often poignant tale. It describes to a tee in the process a particular type of man – egomaniacal, brilliant, sexually unscrupulous and crazily risk-taking – frequently found in politics'   *Spectator*

D1348038

THE PAIN AND THE PRIVILEGE

*The Women who Loved
Lloyd George*

FFION HAGUE

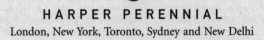

HARPER PERENNIAL
London, New York, Toronto, Sydney and New Delhi

Harper Perennial
An imprint of HarperCollins*Publishers*
77–85 Fulham Palace Road, Hammersmith, London w6 8jb

www.harperperennial.co.uk
Visit our authors' blog at www.fifthestate.co.uk
LOVE THIS BOOK? WWW.BOOKARMY.COM

This Harper Perennial edition published 2009
1

First published in Great Britain by Harper*Press* in 2008

A catalogue record for this book is available from the British Library

ISBN 978-0-00-721950-6

Set in Minion with Linotype Didot display by
Palimpsest Book Production Limited, Grangemouth, Stirlingshire

Printed and bound in Great Britain by Clays Ltd, St Ives plc

Mixed Sources

Product group from well-managed
forests and other controlled sources
www.fsc.org Cert no. SW-COC-1806
© 1996 Forest Stewardship Council

To four remarkable families:
Lloyd George, George, Longford – and my own

CONTENTS

ILLUSTRATIONS

Highgate, the cottage in Llanystumdwy to which Betsy George fled as a young widow with the two-year-old Lloyd George. *(By permission of the National Library of Wales)*

Betsy George. *(By permission of the National Library of Wales)*

William George, Lloyd George's father. *(By permission of the National Library of Wales)*

Lloyd George, aged two, with his sister Polly.

Criccieth in 1880.

Lloyd George, aged around sixteen. *(© Hulton Archive/Getty Images)*

Margaret Owen. *(Lady Olwen Carey Evans Archive)*

Lloyd George soon after his election as MP for Caernarvon Boroughs in 1890. *(By permission of the National Library of Wales)*

Margaret Lloyd George soon after her marriage.

The Owen and Lloyd George family with friends c.1895.

Lloyd George with his youngest daughter Megan in about 1905. *(© National Portrait Gallery, London)*

Margaret surrounded by her children. *(© Hulton Archive/Getty Images)*

Margaret, Lloyd George, Mair and Megan in the garden of their London home c.1904. *(© Hulton Archive/Getty Images)*

Mair with Lloyd George. *(© Hulton Archive/Getty Images)*

Mair's grave in Criccieth. *(Photograph by Dai Noble)*

Lady Julia Henry. *(© National Portrait Gallery, London)*

Frances Stevenson c.1910.

Lloyd George as Chancellor of the Exchequer. (© *Gwynedd Archives Service*)

The family in 11 Downing Street in about 1910. (© *Hulton Archive/Getty Images*)

Uncle Lloyd and Lloyd George in Downing Street. (© *Hulton Archive/Getty Images*)

Dick's wedding to Roberta McAlpine. (*Lady Olwen Carey Evans Archive*)

Olwen marries Tom Carey Evans.

Margaret on the platform with Lloyd George at the 1917 Birkenhead Eisteddfod. (© *Illustrated London News*)

Lloyd George inspecting the troops in the trenches in France. (*By permission of the National Library of Wales*)

Frances at her desk. (© *National Portrait Gallery, London*)

Frances in evening dress.

Frances and Megan in Paris during the 1919 Peace Conference.

The portrait of Frances which Lloyd George always carried, disguised to look like a pocket book.

Lloyd George at the Peace Conference with Italy's Vittorio Orlando, France's Georges Clemenceau and US President Woodrow Wilson. (© *Bettmann/Corbis*)

Lloyd George, Margaret and Megan at Chequers c.1921, with French Prime Minister Aristide Briand, Marshal Foch, Frances and Philippe Berthelot. (*By kind permission of Owen Lloyd George. Original print photographed by Dai Noble*)

Chequers in 1921. (© *Illustrated London News*)

Megan and Lloyd George at Chequers. (© *Bettmann/Corbis*)

Cartoon by David Low first published in the *Evening Standard* 9 March 1929. (*Reproduced by kind permission of the British Cartoon Archive, University of Kent. © Solo Syndication Ltd*)

Brynawelon, the house Lloyd George and Margaret built in Criccieth in 1908.

Bron-y-De. (*By kind permission of Owen Lloyd George. Original print photographed by Dai Noble*)

Lloyd George, the foremost orator of his generation. *(© Hulton Archive/ Getty Images)*

Margaret became an accomplished political campaigner. *(By permission of the National Library of Wales)*

Megan became a star broadcaster after entering Parliament in 1929. *(© Hulton Archive/Getty Images)*

Frances, Nanny and Jennifer bound for a family holiday in Portugal in 1934. *(By permission of the National Library of Wales)*

Jennifer with Lloyd George. *(By permission of the National Library of Wales)*

Frances with Thomas Tweed.

Lloyd George and Tweed.

11 December 1932: Margaret arrives in Churt with Olwen, Tom and Megan to tell Lloyd George that Frances has been unfaithful. *(© Associated Newspapers)*

Jennifer and Lloyd George at Bron-y-De.

Jennifer with Frances on her first day at school in 1941.

Dame Margaret Lloyd George. *(© Caernarvonshire Record Office)*

Megan with Philip Noel-Baker. *(Photograph by D.L. Carey Evans)*

Margaret's funeral in January 1941. *(© Associated Newspapers)*

The celebratory lunch for Lloyd George's eightieth birthday, January 1943. *(© Hulton Archive/Getty Images)*

Lloyd George and Frances on their wedding day, 23 October 1943. *(© Popperfoto/Getty Images)*

Lloyd George's coffin leaves his Llanystumdwy home on 30 March 1945. *(From Amgueddfa Lloyd George Museum)*

Frances, Countess Lloyd-George of Dwyfor.

Megan Lloyd George MP. *(Photograph by Brian Seed. © Time & Life Pictures/Getty Images)*

The Prince of Wales and the Duchess of Cornwall unveil a statue of Lloyd George in Parliament Square on 25 October 2007. *(© AFP/Getty Images)*

INTRODUCTION

No one who grows up in Wales can escape the long shadow cast by David Lloyd George. In a country that loves heroes, the 'Welsh Wizard' and his mythology are still a potent force. 'Lloyd George knew my father,' runs the old song, '. . . and my mother,' goes the unspoken second line, with a wink. To Conservative politician Lord Boothby, Lloyd George was 'an artist expressing himself through the medium of politics . . . the greatest creative force I have ever come across'.[1] Women found him compelling in a different way: 'He could make anyone a friend of his. He had all the gifts and he could get his charm over to anybody and they would, as you know, worship him,' according to his mistress.[2]

Intrigued though I am by Lloyd George, I have always found his first wife, Margaret, equally compelling. Maggie Owen was raised a God-fearing, Calvinistic Methodist, a Welsh-speaker and patriot. My original intention was to write a biography of this Welshwoman, to explore and understand how she made the journey from rural North Wales to Downing Street. I wanted to know if she felt overawed by her aristocratic and royal acquaintances, if she enjoyed her role in public life, if she regretted leaving Wales, and, above all, what price she paid for spending her life with an extraordinary man.

I was prepared to admire Margaret: it is difficult not to. She was a woman who took every opportunity to serve her beloved Criccieth and the wider community she came to represent during the country's darkest hour. She was in some ways a conservative woman. Raised during the reign of Queen Victoria, she claimed home and hearth as her natural territory. In the early years of marriage she considered raising her children to be her career, and she was a late convert to the cause of female suffrage. Yet because of the man she married Margaret was presented with opportunities that took her far beyond the life she had anticipated for herself. She became immersed in her husband's political career, and proved herself to be a formidable campaigner and speech-maker. When she found herself propelled into 10 Downing Street, this daughter of a North Wales farm had the wisdom and confidence to interpret her role anew, making it her own and, in the words of her brother-in-law, 'showing the world what a home-loving wife of a Prime Minister could do'.

In undertaking the initial research for the book, I discovered that Margaret's story would be incomplete without considering the other major player in her marriage: her husband's mistress, Frances. Frances was as English (or, at least, non-Welsh) as Margaret was Welsh. She was a young Edwardian girl with nothing, it seemed, in common with Lloyd George. How could he share his life with two such fundamentally different women? As I learned more about Frances, I realised that she too had lived an extraordinary life. I began to appreciate that it had taken considerable courage for her to put her love of Lloyd George above conventional respectability, and to live her life according to her own interpretation of freedom and emancipation. Frances was a groundbreaking woman too. She gained a degree in Classics, became the first female Private Secretary to a British Prime Minister, was an eyewitness to some of the most momentous events of the twentieth century and the confidante of a great statesman.

To my initial surprise, I found that I had empathy with Frances too. When I joined the Civil Service in 1991 as a fast-stream graduate entrant I took it entirely for granted that I could, potentially, rise to the top of my profession. I wondered what it had been like for Frances when she started working at the Treasury. She became the most senior woman in Downing Street – not entirely through her professional efforts, it must be said – but she proved to be more than capable, and was offered a permanent position as a civil servant when her 'Chief' left office. Frances was absolutely right when she wrote of her role as Private Secretary, 'There is perhaps no other profession in which there are so many occasions when a woman might let her employer down . . . If she makes a mistake, it is probably her employer who will suffer.' [3] Her job involved keeping a lot of secrets, which Frances was supremely well-equipped to do. She was a brave woman too. It took courage for her not to opt for the safe option of marriage and children in her twenties, and yet more courage for her to have a child at the age of forty, when she was still unmarried. I wanted to know how she had coped with her earlier abortions – what medical help was available to a woman in her situation – and whether late motherhood had fulfilled her expectations.

Frances paid a heavy price for her place in Lloyd George's life. She endured loneliness, bitterness and trauma before becoming the second Mrs Lloyd George for the last seventeen months of his life, and like Margaret she never looked back. But their love of the same man meant that they could never be friends. Their rivalry injected poison into the lives of many others, and inspired a feud that outlived them both.

Lloyd George's two wives were opposites in almost every sense, and he was faithful to neither; but as I discovered more about them, it became easier to understand why he needed them both. He loved Margaret, and she, to him, embodied Wales. She kept him in check, outwardly at least conforming to the principles of nonconformism and temperance. Margaret was intelligent in an instinctive way, but her mind was untrained and undisciplined. Her letters and articles betray her incomplete education: they are written in English but often adopt complex Welsh syntax which, when transposed directly from her first language make her style seem wordy. She moves seamlessly from English to Welsh and back again, on paper as in life, and refreshingly brings all political issues back to the same homespun common sense. Frances, by contrast, was both clever and trained – Lloyd George described her as having a 'woman's susceptibility with a man's brain',[4] which he intended as a compliment, and in his work he could rely on her educated and discreet mind. Her instincts were not as in tune with his as Margaret's. She was of a different generation, and did not share his empathy with small nations and international underdogs. But Frances was able to share his work in a way that Margaret could not. She was utterly loyal where her 'Chief' was concerned, and had a sixth sense about the people around him – Lloyd George once told Lord Riddell that Frances would be in his ideal Cabinet to 'suss out the rogues'. He relied on Frances' judgement when it came to politicians and statesmen, but if he wanted to speak to the general public, to convince them he had not lost touch, it was to Margaret that he turned.

This story could not have been written if the women in Lloyd George's life had not preserved and bequeathed or sold their letters, diaries and memoirs to public libraries. I make no apology for shining a spotlight on some private matters, for it was their intention that the story should be told. Nowhere does Lloyd George's masterly understanding of the women in his life show better than in these papers. His letters to Margaret are different in tone and language to his letters to Frances. He speaks plainly to Margaret, combining Welsh and English as freely as she does, and his expressions of affection are natural without seeming sentimental: it is the language of a long-married couple who have found a way of accepting and accommodating each other's weaknesses. Lloyd George and Frances, on the other hand, write to each other using extreme romantic language, even after more than twenty years as lovers. Frances' daughter, Jennifer, who was privy to many of their daily conversations, finds their letters cloying and sentimental: it is not the language of everyday life, and Frances adopts a much more realistic tone in her diary.

Was the tone of these letters genuine? Commentators have taken them as proof that the passion that inspired Lloyd George to take a permanent mistress lasted for the rest of his life. It is true that the connection between him and Frances was strong and durable to the end, but it is equally possible that Lloyd George was playing the romantic hero in his letters, in full knowledge that Frances needed to feel that she was necessary to him if she was to endure her precarious and unequal position. Frances sought romance, passion and a cause to believe in, which is precisely what Lloyd George gave her in his letters. They may not have been written in the language of their day-to-day relationship – which may be why they sound false to Jennifer – but that was necessary if he was to keep Frances at his side. With an eye to posterity, Lloyd George may also have intended the letters to excuse and justify his adultery. Let the reader be the judge.

From being intrigued by Margaret and Frances it was a short step to extending my research to the other women in Lloyd George's life. Mair, Olwen and Megan, his daughters, were important players in the life of their brilliant father, from whose spell they never fully broke free. Megan is the subject of an excellent biography by Mervyn Jones, and her groundbreaking career as female MP and political broadcaster deserves greater attention than it has been possible to give in this book. Other women, of whom there were many in Lloyd George's life, make their appearance in the narrative but exert less influence on the man and are not permanent features in his life. Rebecca Llwyd, Betsy George and Polly – his grandmother, mother and sister – are the exceptions: profound in their influence even though they fade out of the story at an early stage.

I have become convinced that Margaret was one of the most successful Prime Minister's wives of all time. She became famous for her dignity and her dedication. She achieved an immense amount for charity, and took to public life with ease. It was fascinating to me to reflect, not for the first time, on the ambiguous position of women married to men in public life. Margaret Lloyd George never put a foot wrong. During wartime she worked harder than anyone around her, eschewing social glitter for austerity and public service. She played a supporting role to Lloyd George in public, but never lost her own sense of identity. She was politically active, yet she never embarrassed or publicly contradicted her husband. She was a steadfast friend and a formidable foe. By the time she died she was famous throughout the world, but she remained a Criccieth girl at heart. I cannot think of a better role model for those who find themselves in this most difficult of situations. Yet she has been overlooked for reasons that are unfathomable to me, unless it is because of the fact that her voice was not preserved in a memoir or diary.

Our story begins in rural North Wales, among working men and women who suffered hardship, persecution and injustice. From this voiceless class and this unforgiving environment, one man had the talent and the opportunity to find his voice and to help shape the course of the twentieth century. His community and his family devoted their scarce resources to nurturing his talent. They were the first people to experience the pain and the privilege of smoothing the path of David Lloyd George. While his life provides the structure of this book, it is not primarily about him or about the politics he lived and breathed: I would encourage readers who wish to know more about both to read the work of John Grigg and Kenneth Morgan, whose expertise in political history far exceeds mine.

The writing of this book has been a pain and a privilege in itself. I have learned a vast amount about my country and my heritage. The nineteenth-century Wales I describe in the early chapters shaped the late-twentieth-century Wales in which I grew up. I have always been conscious that there is a different social structure in Wales to that in England: a meritocracy based on education and culture which can be baffling to those who are used to social structures largely determined by wealth and birth. Calvinistic Methodism, nationalism, education and poetry are all vitally important factors in my Wales. Margaret, I am sure, would have shared my outrage at the nineteenth-century *Encyclopaedia Britannica* which baldly states, 'For Wales – see England.'

Finally, it has been my privilege to get to know members of three families: the Lloyd George, George and Longford families. I could not have undertaken this book without their help, and their friendship is the principal reward of writing it.

Ffion Hague
April 2008

1

Hewn from the Rock

THE SMALL VILLAGE OF Llanystumdwy lies on the south side of the Llŷn Peninsula in North Wales. From the hills behind, the bay of Criccieth comes into view, with a far-distant prospect of the hills of Eifionydd. On a clear day, the outline of Harlech Castle can be seen in the distance guarding the coastline. The village is a mile and a half inland and about the same distance to the west of the coastal town of Criccieth. The fast-moving river Dwyfor emerges from the woods to meander between its houses and lanes, and is crossed by an arched stone bridge that provides the village with its focal point to the present day. On those arches, nearly 150 years ago, a schoolboy carved his rough initials: D LL. They are there still, a reminder that the village gave Wales her most famous and successful statesman.

The main village street runs parallel to the coast. Opening directly onto its narrow pavement, stands a stone cottage half-covered in ivy. It is a simple two-up, two-down structure with a scullery at the back and a single-storey extension on the left-hand side to accommodate a small, two-roomed workshop. The cottage is called Highgate, and it now bears a plaque that marks it as the boyhood home of David Lloyd George.

The cottage is entered from the road through a small, narrow passageway. To the right is the parlour, a formal room furnished with care and kept for serious activity: study and Sunday best. To the left lies the largest room, running from the front of the house to the back and containing a large hearth with table and chairs for family meals and for making the most of the dying embers on winter evenings.

Behind the living room, a small scullery houses the pots and pans and leads to the back door and the garden beyond, where the earth closet sits at the furthest possible point from the house.

A wooden staircase rises from the front hall to the upper level, where the space is similarly divided into two rooms. The stairs spill out directly into the largest of the two, to the left and directly above the living room below, while the smaller bedroom, reserved for the head of the household, is enclosed and to the right above the parlour. Space is cramped, the ceilings and doorways are low and the solid stone walls form an impenetrable barrier to both wind and sun. It is a long road from Highgate to No. 10 Downing Street, yet the journey was staged in only two generations.

Llanystumdwy lies between the sea and the slate-grey rocks of Snowdonia. In the early nineteenth century its inhabitants bore a strong resemblance to the surrounding landscape: hard, weathered and stoic. The villagers belonged to the lowest of the social classes of rural Wales. They were the unlanded working class, as distinct from the landed gentry and the professional classes, entry to which could be achieved only through wealth or education; and opportunities for either were hard to come by in North Wales. The few born into wealth left, bound for expensive schools and colleges. They returned as landlords on the large estates or, in the case of younger sons, as Anglican clergy. These men formed the judiciary, owned the slate quarries and shipping companies, and elected members of their own class to Parliament. They were seen by the villagers as oppressors, people from a different ethnicity and culture.

Those who could not pay for education and who did not have any land to inherit worked on the land, dug slate or coal out of the ground, became domestic servants, or worked as fishermen, tradesmen, craftsmen and labourers in the docks of Porthmadoc and Caernarvon. The adventurous sailed away on the majestic ships that appeared from over the horizon to empty their holds and restock. There was nothing much to tempt those who remained to travel overland, since the roads were no more than rough turnpike tracks, and the railways that would bring industry and tourism to the area did not reach the north-west coast of Wales until 1867. The lucky few with aptitude and access to education rose to the top of the unlanded society, escaping manual work by becoming lawyers, doctors and teachers. Still, the social divide between them and the gentry was unbridgeable, underlined by the fact that the latter did not commonly speak the Welsh of the people, preferring English. Within the same square mile they spoke different languages and lived in different worlds.

Elizabeth Llwyd, known as Betsy, was born in Highgate in 1828. Her parents, Dafydd Llwyd and his wife Rebecca, were pillars of village society. Dafydd Llwyd, the highly skilled village shoemaker, was a tall, fair-haired man, profoundly religious and with an air of natural nobility. He had broad shoulders and a straight back, and spoke in a quiet but dignified manner.[1] Dafydd was born in the parish of Llanystumdwy, and belonged to a generation of craftsmen who served a seven-year indentured apprenticeship with an established cobbler, made their own tools, and perfected their craft with years of patient toil. His son Richard was to carry on the trade, but he would be the last shoemaker in the family as the use of machine tools replaced their handiwork and produced cheaper products for a mass market.

Dafydd earned his living from making shoes, but regarded himself primarily as a man of religion. Religion was of paramount importance in Wales during the nineteenth century, with tensions between the established Anglican Church and the dissenting followers of Calvin, Wesley and the Baptists reaching a climax in 1811. In that year, Thomas Charles and his followers parted company with the Church of England to establish the nonconformist Church of the Methodistiaid Calfinaidd (Calvinistic Methodists), the only new Church ever to be established in Wales. A frenzy of chapel-building followed: between 1801 and 1851 it is thought that on average a chapel was completed in Wales every eight days. By the middle of the century there were over 2,800 nonconformist chapels in Wales, serving a total population of only 1,163,139, giving rise to a multitude of itinerant preachers. Men like John Elias, Christmas Evans and William Williams conducted preaching tours within Wales, speaking to mass congregations of hundreds if not thousands of the faithful.

Dafydd and Rebecca Llwyd were unusual in their community in being Baptists. More unusually still, they were Scotch Baptists. Baptists were most commonly found in South Wales, but even there were outnumbered by the Calvinistic Methodists and the Congregationalists, or Independents (Annibynwyr), who were numerous throughout Wales, particularly in the north and the west. The Established (Anglican) Church formed part of the archdiocese of Canterbury, and was to be the only official form of worship in Wales until the Disestablishment Act was finally implemented in 1920. This caused great tension in communities where devout nonconformists could not legally be married and buried in their own places of worship according to their own rites.

Naturally enough, since freedom of conscience was one of the reasons why the nonconformists broke away from the Church, Baptists placed a considerable emphasis on individual interpretation of gospels. This led to the breaking away of smaller groups. One of these was the Scotch Baptists, followers of the Scottish theologian Archibald McLean. Scotch Baptist chapels, scattered across a broad area, had tiny congregations: Rhuthun had only six members, Llanufydd twenty-five, Llanfairalthaiarn thirty-six and Llaneilian twelve. Members believed in living life as simply as possible according to the teachings of the primitive Church, and like the Quakers they did not have full-time ministers or priests. They differed from mainstream Baptists in two respects: they met to break bread in Holy Communion every Sunday rather than every month, and they placed a greater emphasis on baptism by total immersion, which generally happened at fourteen or fifteen years of age. The faithful were expected to attend services at least twice on a Sunday, sometimes three times. Dafydd Llwyd led the small Scotch Baptist community who worshipped in the simple stone chapel called Capel Ucha (High Chapel) in Pen-y-Maes, Criccieth. He was ordained in 1830, and for the rest of his life he served the small congregation there while working daily in his shoemaking workshop.

Dafydd married Rebecca Samuel in 1824, when he was twenty-four and she was twenty-one. Rebecca was a practical, hard-working and capable woman, the perfect foil to her husband, who was an intellectual and a bit of a dreamer. They shared the same religious outlook; indeed, it is highly likely that their religion brought them together since it was uncommon to marry interdenominationally, the consequences of which could be as harsh as total exclusion from chapel and community life. Their daughter Elin was born in 1826, Betsy two years later. Each birth was proudly inscribed in the family Bible, as was that of Rebecca and Dafydd's only son, Richard, in 1834.

Rebecca Llwyd had exceptional strength of character and was known for her independence of mind, her fierce protection of her family and her strict, almost puritanical views on religion. She was the matriarch, and took care of the practical, day-to-day care of the family. She believed in hard work, discipline and self-improvement, as did her husband. Dafydd set his family a stern example, putting in long hours at his shoe-making by day and sitting up until the early hours working on his sermons by candlelight. In 1820, Dafydd and his fellow local intellectuals set up a debating society in Criccieth. The 'Cymreigyddion' (the Welsh Scholars) gathered regularly to discuss religious and political issues.

Dafydd and Rebecca were devout, patriotic Welsh citizens, part of the largely self-educated, chapel-going, economically depressed but intellectually ambitious elite of mid-nineteenth-century Wales. Dafydd Llwyd may have been a working-class man who made shoes for a living, but at the same time he was a leader within his community by virtue of the fact that he was a minister and a man of learning.

Rebecca and Dafydd could not afford to indulge their children. They lived their lives in hope of reward in the next world. Rebecca's faith was put to the test when in 1839, with Betsy only eleven years old, Dafydd fell seriously ill. He had been suffering from a stomach complaint periodically, but this time it was to prove fatal. With no money to pay for medical help, Dafydd tried to treat himself with 'Morrison's Universal Medicine' pills, as advertised in one of his periodicals, but to no avail. He died on 25 October at the age of thirty-nine, and was buried in the tiny cemetery bordering Capel Ucha.

Dafydd's death was both an emotional and a practical tragedy for Rebecca. Left alone with three small children, she could not afford to grieve for long. This determined and resourceful woman refused to accept the fate of many widows, who sold their possessions to settle mounting bills before going into service or accepting charity. She chose instead to take on her husband's shoemaking business herself. Richard was only five years old, and Rebecca knew that she would have to carry the burden alone for many years, but she had courage and stamina. Until her son was old enough to take over she employed two cobblers, Robert and Richard Morris, who lived with the family in Highgate. The overcrowding was slightly eased by the fact that Elin had left home to work as a maid at a nearby farm, but life was still hard. Rebecca rose early to set the journeymen to work and supervised their labour during the day, walking a twelve-mile round trip to the neighbouring coastal town of Pwllheli if necessary to buy materials. Late at night when the family were asleep, she would work by candlelight preparing accounts which she would deliver on foot to neighbouring houses and farms the following day, walking for miles over open countryside. Her efforts alone could not sustain the whole family, so Betsy had to leave school. After a period at home helping her mother, she followed her sister into service.

As a young woman, Betsy was a mild character, a devout Baptist like her parents, bright like her father, and attractive. She was described by her youngest son William as 'a good looking woman of medium height, fair complexion, very dark hair and bright brown eyes giving a most winning expression to her thoughtful face'.[2] She had a kind and gentle nature, in contrast with Rebecca's rather stern manner. Betsy suffered from episodes of asthma throughout her life, and she was never physically strong. Hard work from an early age, coupled with poor sanitation and rudimentary medical care, frequently led to some kind of chronic complaint, and her condition was not unusual.

At around sixteen Betsy found a place as a maid and lady's companion in Pwllheli. The ports of North Wales were becoming significant centres of commerce as large sailing ships carried passengers and goods between Britain and the rest of the world. Pwllheli was a bustling, lively town. Betsy became a regular attender at the Pwllheli Baptist Chapel, and there, when she was approaching thirty years of age, she met a teacher who led an adult class in Sunday School. He was an eloquent, well-educated widower by the name of William George.

Eight years Betsy's senior, William was handsome, with dark hair and striking blue eyes. He was a sensitive, driven man who was a good teacher and a would-be intellectual. Of average height and broad-shouldered, he was described by his youngest son as 'well knit together with a somewhat thin pale face surmounted by a thick crop of dark hair, a high broad forehead, large lively eyes indicating a quick percep-tive mind, a heart full of sympathy and tenderness, and all his move-ments quick but firm and determined'.[3] His pupils would remember him as a passionate Baptist who was never beaten in debate.

William George was born in North Pembrokeshire in 1820, the son of staunch Baptists David and Mary George, who had a large farm called Trecoed. David died when William was very young, and the children were raised by Mary and her second husband, Benjamin Williams. From an early age William showed more interest in books than in animals. Life in an urban environment appealed to his hunger for experience and advancement, so he left home at seventeen to seek his fortune in the town of Haverfordwest.

William may have been intelligent and ambitious, but he lacked firm purpose and direction in life. First apprenticed to a pharmacist and then to a draper, he drifted from position to position, recording in his diary his dreams of becoming a great intellectual. He could not settle in any trade because he was determined to continue his studies, often reading late into the night, which made him tired and inefficient by day. His determination to study stemmed from the fact that any opportunity to improve his lot could be obtained only through education. Indeed, he had been lucky to attend school to the age of sixteen, since education would not be provided by the state until 1833.

The level of education in Wales was poor even by the standards of the nineteenth century. Children who spoke nothing but Welsh were taught in English, often by teachers who barely spoke the language themselves, and in appalling conditions. The overwhelming majority of the general population were nonconformists, but only members of the Anglican Church could become pupil-teachers. The Baptist William George nevertheless decided that teaching would be his profession, which meant that he would have to study full-time to gain a qualification.

At around the age of twenty-one William plucked up the courage to move to London and enrol in the Battersea Teachers' Training Institute. For the first time he experienced intellectual fulfilment as he finally found the guidance he had been searching for. He described the experience as the most useful year of his life, 'the means by which he was brought from a *miserable*, useless life to . . . a happy one and not altogether destitute of usefulness to others'.[4] After qualifying as a teacher he went on to hold several short-term teaching positions in London, recording in his diary his agonising internal debate over what he would do with his life: 'I am still very unsettled in my mind as to my future plans and prospects. I cannot somehow make up my mind to be a schoolmaster for life . . . I want to occupy higher ground sometime or other. I want to increase the stock of my attainments but hardly know how to set about it.'[5]

This 'higher ground' was William's secret desire to try his hand at writing. Spurred on by his ambition, he arrived in Liverpool around 1846. By then he had spent so much time away from his native land that he had all but forgotten its language. 'I wished to say a few words to you in Welsh,' he wrote to his mother, ' – but I am sorry that I cannot do so, although Welsh is my mother tongue – and I knew very little English until I was nine years of age – but I have used English ever since. The English language has done with me what the English people have done with our country – taken possession of the richest and largest part of it.'[6]

The latter half of the nineteenth century was an age of emigration from rural North Wales, with the decline in agriculture driving young men and families away from their homes to seek employment in the coalfields of South Wales, the metropolis of London and, increasingly, the cities and towns of North-West England, which came to form the largest concentration of Welsh people outside Wales. Those who left often found better educational prospects and more lucrative employment. With prosperity came a new breed of Welshman – middle-class, confident and socially ambitious. In Liverpool, Welsh industrialists and philanthropists like David Hughes and Owen Elias were responsible for building large parts of the city, and the entrepreneurial industrialist Sir Alfred Lewis Jones also made his fortune there. When William George arrived, around 20,000 of Liverpool's citizens were Welsh-born, and he found a welcoming home among the Welsh diaspora. He felt at home among his professional compatriots and made the acquaintance of fellow intellectuals, some of whom, like the lawyer Thomas Goffey, were to remain his friends for life. He also met the famous Unitarian preacher James Martineau, one of the governors of the school in which he taught, who encouraged him to further extend his intellectual horizons.

But a nineteenth-century city was no utopia, and there were outbreaks of contagious diseases in the new suburbs that threatened all but the most robust. Eventually, fears for his health forced William to move back to Haverfordwest, where he opened his own school in Upper

Market Street in April 1854. On 11 April 1855 he married the thirty-five-year-old Selina Huntley, whose family owned a Bond Street engraving and printing business. It is not known how they met, but she was suffering from tuberculosis, and it is likely that she, like William, was in Pembrokeshire for her health. The marriage took place in Hanover Square, London, and on the marriage certificate the bride and groom's residence is, puzzlingly, given as Bond Street. They must have returned to Pembrokeshire after the wedding, for on 4 December Selina died there of consumption.

At the same time, William had to accept that his school had failed. Prompted by his lack of professional success, by his bereavement, or both, he decided to leave Pembrokeshire. In 1857 he responded to an advertisement for a schoolmaster to teach at the British School at Troed-yr-Allt in Pwllheli. He took up his position in 1858, and joined the Baptist chapel, where he met the attractive, dark-haired Betsy Llwyd. They were married in St Peter's, the parish church in Pwllheli, on 16 November 1859, Betsy's brother Richard acting as a witness.

After the wedding, Betsy left her domestic position to keep house for her husband. William was badly paid even by the standards of the day, and it is likely that they could not afford to run their own household. They moved back to Highgate, from where William walked or rode on horseback daily to school. William and Richard shared the same intellectual disposition, and quickly became firm friends; the fact that William was a Baptist no doubt pleased the fervently religious Rebecca.

Highgate was also home to the son of Betsy's elder sister Elin, who had married William Jones, a Criccieth farmer. Finally free of the upkeep of her two daughters, Rebecca had decided to ease her elder daughter's burden by taking in one of her children. This was a fairly commonplace arrangement at a time when resources were strained and large families were the norm. The boy was named David Lloyd Jones, his Christian names the anglicised version of Dafydd Llwyd in memory of his grandfather. For Rebecca, the young David was more than another mouth to feed. He was an intelligent, bookish child who from an early age was marked out as the gifted member of the family. Rebecca devoted all her spare time to his development, much as she would to Betsy's talented son in future years. In both name and upbringing, David Lloyd Jones was to be the precursor of his later, famous cousin. The young David was undoubtedly bright, but he was a sickly, delicate child, and William George doubted whether he had enough drive to find his way in the world. Nevertheless, he took him under his wing and acted as his mentor and teacher, encouraging him to read and take notes from his own small library of precious books. Space in the confined household was found for him to study, and candles allocated to his late-night study. As he read, others did his share of the household chores, and pennies were found to pay for paper, ink and other essentials.

When Betsy returned to Highgate after an absence of fifteen years, she took some of the burden of caring for the household from her mother's shoulders. It was hard work: water needed to be carried daily from the village pump for cooking and washing, and the earth closet had to be tended with noisome regularity. Life did not progress smoothly for Betsy and William. William was experiencing difficulty in relearning the Welsh language, which disadvantaged him in a wholly Welsh-speaking area. Language issues apart, Llanystumdwy did not provide him with enough intellectual stimulation, and it seems that he was not entirely happy in his school in Pwllheli either. Betsy quickly fell pregnant, but the daughter born to them did not live long enough to be named. It was a crushing disappointment, and when Betsy discovered that she was pregnant again, fears of another tragedy in the cramped accommodation of Highgate were enough to drive the couple to seek better fortune elsewhere. William secured a teaching position in Newchurch, a small town near Blackburn in Lancashire, twenty miles or so from Manchester, and in 1861, only two years into their marriage, they took the stage-coach from Pwllheli to Caernarvon, from where they could travel by steamer to Liverpool. The fourteen-year-old David went with them, in the hope and expectation that he would qualify as a teacher under William's watchful eye.

As soon as they reached their destination, Betsy and William summoned a doctor to examine David. He warned them that the boy was in danger of becoming consumptive, confirming their worst fears and reminding them of the threats to their own health. As the months passed, the restless William became increasingly disenchanted with life in Newchurch. The one piece of good news was the birth of a daughter, Mary Ellen (called Mary or Polly), in November 1861. By the following year, William had managed to get himself a temporary position in a mill-school in Manchester. The move would mean a return to unhealthy urban life, but William was desperate to leave Newchurch. He wrote to Richard Lloyd:

> The place itself we could do with very well – though cold and rather damp, it is healthy – the air is much purer there than at Manchester, and neither of us could hold out long without pure air. It was the Newchurch *school* and the people connected with it that did not suit me; and I need not say that I did not suit them. Nearly all the 'Directors' are rough working men who had not the means to act liberally even if disposed to do so, – and besides my temper is such that I would rather be the master of work people than their servant.[7]

The little family moved to take up lodgings at 5 New York Place, Chorlton-upon-Medlock, but this time David did not go with them. Aged fifteen, he was on the brink of independence, and William remembered the wrench of leaving home himself at a similar age. He sympathised, but he knew that David would have to make his own way. William hardened his heart and left the boy behind.

The Manchester school better suited William's temperament, but his health deteriorated and he reluctantly concluded that he would have to give up his position and go back to the country. He could not act on this decision immediately, because Betsy was in the late stages of pregnancy, which meant that on 17 January 1863, Wales' most famous politician was born in England. The new baby was named David Lloyd after his grandfather and his cousin.

Betsy was not strong, and her recovery from her third labour was slow, not helped by the difficulty of getting clean water to drink. William had decided to give up teaching altogether in favour of farming. He consoled himself with the thought that at last he might have time to fulfil his ambition of writing a book that would make his name. He still dreamed of becoming one of the foremost scholars of his generation. Sadly, like all his other dreams, it was not to be.

The family settled in South Pembrokeshire, a more naturally English-speaking area of the county, and from Bullford, a smallholding near Haverfordwest, William continued to watch over the career of the elder David. He involved his Liverpool friend Thomas Goffey in his attempts to get the boy a place as a schoolmaster, but by then David's threatened consumption had taken hold, and his family's hopes of a glittering career were dashed only a few years later, when he died at the age of twenty.

In the meantime, a different tragedy had engulfed the family. The move had failed to strengthen William George's health. At the end of May 1864 he spent a day out in the fields attending to the hay harvest, and caught a chill. His condition quickly deteriorated, and Betsy took the unusual and expensive step of calling the doctor. There was nothing to be done. Pneumonia had set in, and on 7 June William died, at the age of forty-four.

Betsy was heartbroken. She was left alone with the financial burden of a smallholding as well as two small children to support. She might also have suspected, even at that early stage, that she had another baby on the way. The family's small capital, amounting to only £640 (about £56,000 at today's values), was invested in a Liverpool building society, but the interest was not enough to provide for their day-to-day needs. Betsy was effectively destitute. She gathered enough strength to send a telegram to her brother: 'Tyrd Richard' (Richard, come!). The two-word message summed up her helplessness and despair.

Richard set off at once. A journey that would take a few hours today took two and a half days, and when he reached Pembrokeshire he found his sister in a state of shock. Numbed by grief, Betsy had been unable to demonstrate any emotion since her husband had succumbed to his illness. When she saw the familiar face of her brother again, though, she dissolved into tears and threw herself into his arms. Richard immediately took the little family under his wing: he was to be their protector and guardian for the rest of his life.

Betsy was not altogether friendless in Pembrokeshire, and between them, Richard and Benjamin Williams of Trecoed made the funeral arrangements and disposed of the smallholding's lease. The natural, and possibly only, option for Betsy was to take her children back to Llanystumdwy, and she wrote a pitiful letter to her husband's Liverpool friend Thomas Goffey, mingling expressions of grief with requests for advice on winding up William's affairs.

Dear Mr Goffey,

I am greatly obliged by your kind letter received the 18th inst. Indeed I cannot tell you what a source of consolation it has been to me in my deep affliction – Well I may believe that my dear husband was your 'dearest friend' and that he was highly esteemed by all his friends there, for such he always considered you and his respect for all his friends in Liverpool was very much. It is a comfort to me to think how much he was beloved by all his numerous friends. Oh! What a dear husband I have lost . . .

I cannot tell you now when I leave the South – We are trying to find a person to take the place that will pay me something for the lease – and to take the crop under valuation . . . Some months ago my dear husband thought he was going to lose me – When I recovered he said – I was walking about without knowing what to do. If that would be the case I was determined to leave the place at once – I couldn't stop on a day here but it was me that was to stay and how hard it is upon me to be here after him.[8]

William George was laid to rest in Trewrdan Cemetery. A few days later Betsy packed up the family's home, and a sale of surplus furniture was held to raise funds for the journey north. Betsy's feelings on seeing her belongings dispersed and her home broken up ran so deep that she would never be able to discuss that period in her life. As they grew up, her children learned not to ask about Pembrokeshire or their father, in order to spare their mother's feelings. One thing she did reveal was that the two toddlers, Polly and David, aged only three years and eighteen months respectively, were nevertheless old enough to share her grief. As neighbours and friends carried pieces of furniture out of the front door and down the path to the gate, the two children took the heaviest stones they could lift and rolled them across the path in a futile attempt to block the way. It was the best they could do to keep their home and possessions from disappearing.

The journey back to Criccieth was nightmarish. The family – Richard, Polly, David and a now obviously pregnant Betsy – carrying their entire worldly goods, travelled by rail as far as Caernarvon, and then journeyed on to Llanystumdwy by carriage. Betsy had to decide which possessions to leave behind, but one thing was certain: she was not going to give up her husband's treasured book collection. The little library was carefully packed up, carried all the way to Highgate and put back in the parlour they had left only three years previously. Physically weakened and emotionally distraught, Betsy sank back onto the family hearth, lucky to have avoided the workhouse misery of many other widows.

It soon became apparent that young David had all the talent of the first David Lloyd, and added to it his father's dreams of greatness. He also had a robust constitution, and this time Rebecca, Richard and Betsy were determined that the story would not end in tragedy. The tale of David Lloyd George's upbringing, and his family's nurturing of his prodigious talent, was to be one of the most remarkable of any politician of his time.

2

The Cottage-Bred Man

HOME AGAIN IN LLANYSTUMDWY, Betsy finally gave way to grief and ill-health. She had been deeply in love with her husband, and although she had been concerned about his health, there had been no major alarms to prepare her for his sudden death. The change in her circumstances overwhelmed her sensitive nature and rendered her physically and emotionally incapacitated. After a few months her second son was born, and was named William after his father. Betsy was too weakened to share the burden of housework or even to look after her baby: William recalled being bathed by his grandmother in a large earthenware basin on the kitchen floor because his mother was too ill to look after him.[1]

Into the breach stepped the redoubtable Rebecca. She was already running the household and the shoemaking business, which she had kept going during her son's four-month mercy dash to Pembrokeshire. Now she took on the care of her invalid daughter, two young children and a newborn. Fortunately, Rebecca had enough practicality and stamina for all of them. She also understood what her daughter was going through, since she too had been widowed at an early age and had struggled to make ends meet. Rebecca was over sixty by this time, but she kept the reins firmly in her capable hands, and remained the head of the household until the day she died.

In order to provide for her family Rebecca had to make a success of the shoemaking business, and at times she surprised her family with her diplomatic skills. She would often take her young grandson David

Lloyd George with her on long walks in the hills surrounding Llanystumdwy, and he inherited her love of walking, together with her belief in fresh air as the cure for all ills. They would often call at remote farms where, not entirely coincidentally, a shoemaking account was overdue. Rebecca would never mention it herself, but the embarrassed farmer's wife inevitably did. A copy of the bill would then be produced from Rebecca's pocket, where it had lain, by chance of course, and the account would be settled with friendly relations maintained.

Living quarters were cramped in the small cottage. Rebecca took Betsy and little Mary Ellen to sleep with her in the larger of the upstairs rooms, while Richard shared his quarters with David and William, who slept together in a narrow wainscot bed. The small inheritance that Betsy had invested in the Liverpool building society gave her a modest, fluctuating income of up to £46 (£4,039 today) a year. She could at least pay her way – for now. This was important to bolster her pride, for dependence on family was only one step away from charity, and both her upbringing and her religion, with their emphasis on self-reliance, led her to shrink from accepting handouts.

Eventually Betsy grew stronger, and she was able to take over more of the running of the house, with its never-ending demands of fires to tend, rooms to clean and bread to bake. She had not been well for very long, though, when a second unexpected blow took away her main support. In 1868, Rebecca died at the age of sixty-five. The head of the family, whose unwavering faith and unrelenting self-discipline had been its bedrock, followed her husband to the grave after twenty-nine years of widowhood. The family rallied round once more – indeed, they had very little choice. Richard took charge of the business, and Betsy ran the house. All three children were deemed old enough to take on their share of the chores, and life took on a new rhythm.

Although she suffered throughout her life from ill-health, Betsy always seemed able to summon up a reserve of strength when her children were in need. Following Rebecca's death she held the family together, and was by all accounts a skilful and resourceful housewife. Highgate was rented from David Jones, the village shopkeeper, who lived by a simple creed, 'The rent is mine, the house is yours,' and refrained from carrying out even the most basic repairs to his properties. For a rent of £7 per annum (£547 today) Betsy and Richard were left to their own devices in maintaining the fabric of the crumbling cottage. Betsy had to turn her hand to household repairs as well as the washing and baking. The latter was a particular challenge, since the ancient oven at Highgate was on its last legs. Every week Betsy would patch up the holes in its sides with brown paper, and pray that her handiwork would last until the bread was baked.

Betsy established an unvarying routine: Monday was washing day, Thursday was baking day. Chores and social obligations filled the other four working days of the week. Sunday was reserved for three chapel services, with a three-mile round trip to each one. This might have seemed like an additional chore to a less devout person, but it was Betsy's main comfort in a life of unrelenting hard work. She gave no sign that she ever considered remarrying. Perhaps the strength of her feelings for her late husband prohibited it. In any case, there were not many eligible men in the village at a time when ambitious young men headed for towns or ports to earn a living.

Betsy spent her forties raising three children, keeping house for her brother, and thanking God that she was not completely alone in the world. She had matured into a kind, sympathetic and attractive woman, rather small, according to her elder son, but with a good figure and a soft, sweet voice.[2] 'She was a fine character,' he wrote in a memoir, ' – gentle, unselfish and courageous. She never complained and never spoke of her struggles. It was not till long after that her children fully appreciated how much they owed to her, and how fine her spirit had been in the hard task of bringing up her fatherless family.'[3] Her widowhood had left its mark, and although Betsy could sometimes enjoy a joke, she was a serious woman. She was also proud, refusing to let her sons join their friends in weed-picking for sixpence a time. Rebecca had taught her to be a disciplined housekeeper, a 'mistress of method' in the home, a good cook and generous in giving hospitality.[4] She allowed herself few pleasures, but one exception was her fondness for flowers. She grew a rose vine to cover the front of the house. Its flowers bloomed in a splendid display through the summer months, and it was not unusual for the family to overhear strangers on the road outside exclaiming at their beauty.

Betsy inherited Rebecca's independence of spirit, if not her strength of character, and her gentle demeanour masked a strong adherence to her parents' beliefs and values. She was proud to be part of the same Welsh-speaking, chapel-going class. The ladies of Trefan, the nearby estate, were often driven past Betsy's door by their uniformed coachman, but Betsy did not envy them, nor did she feel inferior, and she made sure that her children took pride in their position in life too. When they were older, David and William were both offered positions as pupil-teachers in their school, one of the few ways a bright village lad could get on in the world and escape a life of manual labour. But the offer carried a sting in its tail. Because the school was sponsored by the Anglican Church, pupil-teachers were required to join the Church and renounce their nonconformism, a condition that most, willingly or under duress, fulfilled. When the idea was discussed in Highgate, Betsy exclaimed that she would rather see her boys growing up to break stones on the roadside than turn their backs on the little chapel at Pen-y-Maes. The issue was never broached again.

In common with other nonconformists of the period Betsy was a firm follower of the temperance movement, and regarded alcoholic drink as an evil influence on society. Richard Lloyd was of the same view, although, with characteristic modesty, he rarely spoke his mind on the matter or criticised others. His influence locally was such, however, that many years later, when he was helping out at his nephews' law practice in Criccieth, the firm's landlady was obliged to evict them. She reluctantly revealed that the public house opposite had complained that thirsty customers were afraid to enter by the front door in case Richard Lloyd spied them through the window of his office. Betsy and Richard's influence was so strong on Lloyd George that he never set foot in a public house until adulthood, and although he drank wine and whisky in moderation in later life, he hated drunkenness, and regarded with contempt anyone who drank to excess. With Betsy though, principle would not stand in the way of kindness, and she would invite the village drunk, William Griffith, into the house to sober up by the fire before sending him home.

The shoemaking business and Betsy's savings provided enough of an income for the family to live on. They were certainly not well off, but the children did not want for anything either. 'Comfortable, but thrifty and pinched' was Lloyd George's description of Highgate.[5] The children never had both butter and jam on their bread – it was one or the other – and the great treat on Sundays was half an egg each at breakfast. The family only felt the sting of real hardship after moving to Criccieth in 1880, when Richard had to give up the shoemaking business and the financial demands of giving the boys a good start in the world increased. At Highgate, Betsy's careful husbandry made sure that there was enough to go around. She would spend hours mending the children's clothes or altering her elder son's cast-offs for William. Her pride demanded that her children were well dressed, and she was rewarded when Mrs Evans, the well-born wife of the local schoolmaster, remarked that 'William George and his brother are the best-dressed children in school.'[6]

Even in these years, however, the family encountered hard times when Betsy's investment income fluctuated or the shoemaking business dipped. These difficulties were enough to drive the already highly-strung Betsy to despair. Her asthmatic attacks were often severe, terrifying her young children, who watched helplessly as their mother struggled for breath. Richard knelt by her side rubbing her hand and muttering soothing words, but comfort came only in the form of religion. Once, Betsy was in tears after failing to make ends meet, when she caught sight of an article in a periodical. The transformation that came over her face was so striking that more than half a century later, William set out to see what it contained. The article, by one D. Morris, was headed 'The Bible, the Destitute and the Widow', and listed thirty passages from the Bible offering hope and comfort to those in Betsy's situation. Her faith had come to her rescue yet again.

Betsy's strength and vitality were slowly sapped by years of raising children under the constant shadow of financial hardship. She was never a strong woman, and her health held out just long enough for her to see her family grow to maturity. The children were in their teens before she became too ill to carry on. From then on the main responsibility for guiding her children was passed to Richard Lloyd, who, fortunately, was temperamentally and intellectually ideally suited to the task. Richard Lloyd was a stern taskmaster who earned his nephews' obedience and respect, but like many men of the time, he left the task of disciplining the children to Betsy. She could never bring herself to punish David Lloyd. She spoiled him: he was never made to dress himself or even find his own socks, something that had 'a *marked* effect' on him in later life, according to his mistress.[7] He grew to rely on his mother's approval and unconditional love, and took an interest in every detail of her daily life even when he was married and living largely in London. Lloyd George's last letter to her, two days before she died in 1896, reveals his anxious concern:

> My dearest Mother,
>
> . . . What you ought to do as long as the heat lasts is to take absolute rest . . . You must not try to be housekeeper, housemaid, cook and maid of all work in one. Just you sit down in the coolest room of the house and boss the lot of them. Give orders. I know they will all be pleased to obey and if they do not just you give them that tongue a bit of which your eldest son has inherited from you . . . Go out in the cool of the evening but don't walk in this hot weather. It is more than anyone can do with any comfort. Let them get you a bathchair with Woodhart or someone else to wheel it. The approach to [the house] is so steep that it is most tiring for anyone, even in the best of weathers to walk it. You should not do so on any account as long as this terrible heat lasts. I am sure William will see to that . . .
>
> It is a good thing that you have such a store of pluck to bear you up . . . I will back my good old Mother against the whole lot of them . . .
>
> Your fond boy,
> Dei[8]

As an invalid, Betsy would play an increasingly marginal role in her son's life, but she was still able to take pride in his achievements, and in particular his growing fame. 'I am glad that 'rhen wraig [the old woman] got some satisfaction from her parentage of her eldest son,' Lloyd George wrote to his brother in 1895. 'She had a good deal of trouble with him in his younger days & I know of no one who made a braver & a more heroic fight to bring up her children respectably & to give them a fair start. She deserves all the feeling of elation which a contemplation of their success affords her.'[9] Betsy lived to see Lloyd George elected to Parliament three times before her death at the age of sixty-eight.

The circumstances of her life and the age in which she was born led Betsy to live her life for and through her children. She accepted her situation stoically and, like Rebecca, kept her eyes firmly fixed on the rewards of the next life. Betsy inspired great devotion among those who appreciated her gentle, kind nature. She doted on her children, and indulged them as far as she could within the limits of her resources. They loved her deeply in return. In later life, Lloyd George prized liveliness and independence of mind in his female companions, yet he looked for different things in his domestic life: comfort, serenity and steadfastness. Betsy was the first woman who provided him with the domestic nurturing and adoration he needed.

Betsy succeeded on the whole in keeping her cares and worries from her children, and the three young Georges had a happy existence in Highgate. They adapted quickly to their new surroundings, which Lloyd George found 'picturesque, beautiful and inspiring'.[10] Their games were those of country children: catching songbirds in the hedgerows, playing soldiers in the woods and throwing sticks in the fast-flowing river. Climbing trees was a favourite activity, especially if it was rewarded with cherries or apples from a neighbour's orchard. Novelty was provided by the sight of four steaming horses pulling heavy cartloads of building materials through the village to the site where the local squire, Sir Hugh Ellis-Nanney, was building his new mansion, Gwynfryn. Treats included walking to Criccieth to fetch two pennyworth of treacle in a tin can and sampling a little on the way home, and, on baking day, soaking chunks of newly baked bread in buttermilk and anticipating the delights of rice pudding.

Household chores were divided up between the children. Polly helped her mother with the housework, learning to bake, clean and attend the washing, while William was sent daily to fetch a large bucket of water from the village well. David, known as Davy or Davy Lloyd, preferred to be outdoors, and his task was to tend the garden. He had inherited his mother's green fingers, and loved to find rare plants on his long country walks to plant in the plot of land behind the cottage. One such find was a rare 'royal fern'. It flourished at Highgate, and was so highly prized that it was dug up and transplanted to the garden of Morvin House when the family moved to Criccieth.

Davy was also in charge of gathering firewood for the household, a task in which he took immense pride. Among the many factors that made him one of the most successful orators of his time was his ability to use details from his childhood to illustrate a point, enabling him to form a point of contact with his audience. In a defiant speech defending his controversial 1909 budget, he recalled: 'I am not afraid of storms. It wasn't in a period of fine weather that we used to go to the woods to gather firewood when I was a boy. Not at all; we went after a big storm had struck the wood and littered the ground with broken branches. I'm telling you that after this storm has passed, there will be plenty of firewood to warm the hearths of old people and to brighten the lives of the poor.'[11]

The children had a secure childhood, protected by their uncle and indulged by their mother. Yet they could not entirely escape the manifestations of injustice in the social order. Even in the quiet backwater of Llanystumdwy, landlords wielded their near-absolute power over tenants with harrowing consequences. For the children, this meant that a walk through the woods involved avoiding the estate gamekeepers at all costs. The owners of Trefan were kind individuals who allowed local children to play on the estate's land as long as they respected the livestock and did not disturb nesting birds. Their keepers, and those of Sir Hugh Ellis-Nanney, were a different breed altogether. The George brothers escaped their clutches by a hair's breadth on numerous occasions. They knew that a widow in the village had had to send her son away for good to escape dire punishment after being caught with a hare killed on private land.

The benign presence of the Trefan ladies in the village, and the fact that the Ellis-Nanney family sponsored the local school, did not disguise the extent of the landlords' power. In effect, the village was controlled by the squire and the parson, two all-powerful figures whose intervention could at a stroke destroy a lifetime's work for tenants or parishioners. In 1868, when Davy Lloyd George was five years old, that power had banished some of his schoolmates from the village in an outrageous and vindictive act of revenge. The cause was the general election of that year, when the electorate dared return a Liberal candidate, the Welsh-speaking nonconformist Love Jones-Parry, instead of the local landowner Baron Penrhyn's son, George Douglas-Pennant. Since the ballot was public, not secret as it became in 1872, disobedient tenants were easily identified. Flying in the face of democracy, compassion and common sense, the landlords retaliated. Families were turned out of their homes and robbed of their livelihoods as farms, shops and workshops had to be left behind. It was said that eighty men who worked in the Penrhyn slate quarry lost their jobs. For a family thrown out on the streets the only options were to rely on charity – something no proud nonconformist would willingly accept – or to move away to seek employment elsewhere. Thus, at an impressionable age the young George children saw some of their playmates in Llanystumdwy forced to leave the village, their families rendered destitute by the landlords. It was an injustice that burned into their consciousnesses, and one that Lloyd George never forgot.

At the age of three, Polly was the first of the George children to leave the hearth and join the procession of girls and boys marching daily to the village school. In September 1866 she was joined by her brother Davy Lloyd, with William following in 1868. The Llanystumdwy National School was established in 1851, in a two-roomed building next to the church. The majority of the pupils were from nonconformist families and spoke nothing but Welsh, but in school they adhered to Church rituals and learned to speak and write only in English.

Girls and boys of all ages were taught together by David Evans, an excellent teacher, able to bring his subjects to life and to excite young minds, and his staff of two pupil-teachers. There were seven standards, ranging from infants upwards, and school inspectors decided when each child was ready to progress to the next. After a year in the seventh standard, at around the age of fourteen most pupils were considered ready to leave school, but for especially gifted pupils David Evans offered a year's further teaching, which he called standard 7X. The chosen ones would sit at a table close to Evans' own desk, and would often be offered the chance to become pupil-teachers at the end of the year.

The curriculum consisted of the three 'R's plus geography, history and, for the brightest, a little algebra. Naturally for a school in a coastal area, a number of school leavers went to sea each year, so navigation was taught as an extra subject for recently-departed pupils bound for the ports of Porthmadoc and Pwllheli. David Evans also indulged his own interest in jurisprudence, which opened the eyes of at least a few of his pupils to the possibilities of a career in law. Reading was encouraged, but literature was available only to the lucky few like the George children who had books at home.

Welsh literature or history played no part in children's formal education. They were given, in effect, the same education as their contemporaries in England, with no attempt to teach them about their own country or to connect with their community. The prevailing attitude among the (English-speaking) school authorities was that the Welsh language should be beaten out of children and replaced with the English of the Empire. It did not occur to them that the English language might not be of much use to children who would grow up to be farmers, shopkeepers, craftsmen and labourers in a wholly Welsh-speaking area, or that bilingualism was in itself a good thing. Instead, the use of Welsh was fiercely discouraged, and the use of severe force to punish children caught speaking their natural language was widespread. Polly and her brothers did not have to leave their home to hear of one: Richard Lloyd had been caught speaking Welsh to a schoolmate one day at school. The teacher struck him on the side of the head with such force that he permanently lost the hearing in one ear.

In addition to the National Schools, Sunday Schools were run by both churches and chapels. The nature and quality of the instruction given was very different. Church Sunday Schools were attended mainly by children, and concentrated on scriptural study. Inspired teaching could make these sessions enjoyable and rewarding, but in most places they descended into mere rote-learning. The Welsh-language, nonconformist Sunday Schools were attended by the whole congregation, either after the main morning service or in a separate afternoon session. They began with Bible readings, hymns and prayers before the congregation divided into classes, each occupying a separate area among the pews in chapel. Classes were sometimes single-sex, and were divided according to age. Each had its own teacher, and although these were occasionally professional teachers, like William George senior, they came mostly from the ranks of the better-educated adult members. Teachers would read passages of the Bible and discuss doctrinal issues like 'The Fall of Man' and 'The Universality of the Flood', according to the age and understanding of class members. Children were taught more than the Bible in these sessions: they were taught to read, to debate, to sing sol-fa and to engage in question-and-answer sessions with the adults. Sessions would close with a simultaneous catechising of the whole congregation, prayers and hymn-singing. For those without any other access to education, Sunday Schools provided a level of basic skills that was, literally, a godsend.

The importance of Sunday Schools emerged even in the government's disastrous review of education in Wales in 1847. The review was prompted by Welshmen like William Williams MP who were concerned about standards, and three commissioners were appointed to investigate and report. The commissioners – none of whom was Welsh or had ever lived in Wales – reported that the conditions in which Welsh children were taught were 'dreadful' even by contemporary standards: only just over half of Welsh bridegrooms could sign their names. In some areas Sunday Schools were the only form of education available. The report was coloured throughout by the commissioners' lack of understanding. It neglected to point out that children who spoke only Welsh received their entire education through the medium of English, which even their teachers barely spoke. Such was the travesty of the report that it came to the conclusion that nonconformism encouraged immorality. As anyone with even a passing acquaintance with Calvinistic Methodism could attest, nothing could have been further from the truth.

The furore over the report increased the sectarian and linguistic differences between English- and Welsh-speakers. Thirty years later, the obvious disconnect between the Welsh nonconformist chapels and the English-language, Church-ritualised school in Llanystumdwy still jarred. Torn between the two, the pupils were close to open rebellion. In the young Davy Lloyd, they found their natural leader.

The occasion was the visit of the school inspectors, regarded as an opportunity for the schoolmaster to demonstrate the good behaviour and academic prowess of his charges. The inspectors, the Misses Evans of Trefan and Sir Hugh Ellis-Nanney, visited the school every year. The children were marched in single file in front of them, and made to recite the catechism in English, but in 1875 the twelve-year-old Davy Lloyd decided that the event would not go smoothly. He had been brought up at the knee of a Baptist preacher in a devout and proud family. Nonconformists had fought hard to be allowed to worship according to their faith: it was not long since persecution had been commonplace, with dissenters forced to attend church services or face dire consequences.

Young Davy Lloyd was already a leader among his schoolmates, one of whom remembered him as a child of three or four standing on the stairs at home, 'preaching' to his assembled friends below. For a determined, independent boy, it made no sense to have to memorise and recite the Church text. Furthermore, it was an insult to have to pretend to be an Anglican, and worst of all for a Baptist boy, to have to attest that he was given his name at christening, which was against the most specific teaching of his denomination. Having suffered the indignity every year, he now decided to organise a rebellion, and persuaded every child in the school to turn mute when invited to recite the catechism. When Mr Evans stepped forward and indicated to the children that it was time to begin, his prompt was met with stony expressions and silence. The utterly bewildered schoolmaster tried again. 'I believe . . .' he repeated hopefully, but to no avail. It was a tense moment, for the visitors behind him were not only inspectors but also his employers. Finally, after what seemed like an age, William George could not bear to see the well-liked Mr Evans get into trouble, and shouted 'I believe!' One by one his classmates joined in, and the catechism was given in full.

This incident is rightly famous, and much has been made of the evidence it provides of the young Lloyd George's precociousness and refusal to conform. The protest was entirely successful: the children were never again asked to recite the catechism at school, and while legend has it that Davy gave his brother a good thrashing afterwards – which William George always denied – there is no record of the ringleader himself having been punished at all. It may be that Mr Evans never came to know who had led the rebellion, but it certainly proved that Davy Lloyd George was a boy who got away with things. He had guts and a great deal of charm, and he used both to the full. This combination, even during his school years, was particularly effective with women, and got him out of all kinds of trouble. One of many incidents occurred when an Irish labourer working on the Ellis-Nanney mansion took offence at the way in which a group of village boys were teasing his daughter. He was a big man, and known to have a violent temper. As he approached the boys, they wisely scattered and he grabbed at the nearest, who happened to be Davy. 'Not that one!' cried the little girl anxiously, 'Not that one!' Davy was spared a thrashing because of a susceptible female supporter. He also had two adoring female supporters at home in Rebecca and Betsy, both of whom indulged and spoiled him. He grew up to expect the admiration of women and to rely on their loyalty.

As their three charges grew from children to teenagers, Betsy and Richard were determined to give them the best start possible in life. It was assumed from early childhood that Davy would be the outstanding one of the three, but the other two were also encouraged to 'get on', although with the clear understanding that they would play a supporting role in Davy's life if he needed them.

This was perhaps most understandable in the case of Polly. She left school at the age of fourteen, and was not invited to stay on for an extra year. Schools were not designed to provide the same education for girls and boys. Boys needed to make their way in the world; girls needed only enough instruction to be useful wives and mothers. An educationalist wrote as late as 1911 that 'boys needed instruction in courage, self-control, hard work, endurance and protection of the weak. Girls needed to be taught gentleness, care for the young and helpless, interest in domestic affairs and admiration for the strong and manly character in men.' Without her uncle's financial support Polly would have had to choose between going into service and staying at home to help her mother, but Richard Lloyd enrolled her in Miss Wheatley's private girls' school in Criccieth. The school took boarding pupils from better-off local families for a year or two to teach them deportment and other useful subjects. A private education was a real advantage to a young woman. It enhanced her marriage prospects, and would enable her to get a better position as a governess or lady's companion if she did not marry.

Polly was expected to stay at the school for two or more years, but she had been away for only two terms when Betsy's health gave way. The family could not afford to pay for help to look after her younger brothers and to keep house for her mother and uncle: there was no choice but to bring Polly back. Any chance she had of building a different life for herself disappeared as she returned to Llanystumdwy, although it was not immediately apparent that Polly could not continue her studies and pursue a career: in 1884 her brother David Lloyd wrote in his diary that he was determined that Polly should train as a doctor: 'I contemplate with absolute contempt and disgust the husband-waiting for, the waiting-for-someone-to-pick-me-up policy of the girl of the period . . . Why shouldn't [Polly] go in for being a doctor? The idea struck me with great force today. She shall.'[12] Despite his good intentions the family's income could not stretch that far, and Polly's ambitions were sacrificed for those of her brothers.

For the boys, it was to be very different. If they could not be teachers, David Lloyd and William needed some other profession, and Mr Evans with his love of jurisprudence, or perhaps the memory of Mr Goffey in Liverpool, brought to mind a career in law. For William it meant a steady career with good money to be made. For Davy, whose brilliant mind and natural leadership qualities had already marked him out, the law was a respectable way to embark on a career in public life.

William's role in supporting David's political career is widely (and justly) acknowledged. He did not seem to resent the universal assumption that his brother was destined for greater things, nor did he demand the kind of attention that flowed David's way. Described by his daughter-in-law as 'the kindest man I ever met',[13] William was different from his brother David in almost every respect. Devout, truthful and patient, he resembled both his father and Richard Lloyd. He accepted without demur that he needed to work to support the entire family while his brother pursued his (unpaid) political career, and he even denied himself the prospect of marriage and children for many years while all his income was needed to support Betsy, Richard, Polly and his brother's family. A truly remarkable man, he lived his life in his brother's shadow with exceptionally good grace; only David's colourful private life ever caused more than an occasional coolness between the two.

As for Davy Lloyd, Richard Lloyd believed that he had a prodigy on his hands. 'This boy will be famous!' he exclaimed, and the whole family set about making it happen. The Lloyd/George family turned itself into an organisation to support David, and every resource at its disposal was unhesitatingly put to use. Richard Lloyd discussed his nephew's progress with Mr Evans the schoolmaster, and watched over his studies at home. The young Davy combined natural aptitude with a love of reading. His favourite subjects were geography and history, and he had a good head for figures. In later life he told his son, only half-jokingly, that he had realised he was a genius while reading Euclid at the top of an oak tree. But, genius or not, he would have to pass his preliminary law examination before he could get on the first rung of the ladder by persuading a firm of solicitors to take him on as an apprentice. The examination required a specific programme of study, and Davy used his extra year in school to prepare himself, aided by the willing Mr Evans.

Davy Lloyd was fortunate in his broad-minded and scholarly teacher, but he was equally fortunate in his uncle and mentor. Richard Lloyd – known fondly within the family as 'Uncle Lloyd' – was no ordinary cobbler: he was a craftsman who could turn his hand as easily to a pair of high-topped boots trimmed in yellow wash leather for the Trefan coachman as to repairing a working man's boots. He was as devout as his father before him, and had followed in his footsteps to become the ordained minister of Capel Ucha, as a result of which his workshop was the gathering place for village intellectuals. He was renowned for the care he took of his congregation and the wisdom of his advice, readily given to those who dropped by during the day. He kept a scrap of paper or a piece of discarded leather in a niche in the wall by his side as he worked so that he could jot down a thought or a phrase to use in his sermons.

In 1841 the congregation of Capel Ucha had broken off from the Scotch Baptists to join 'The Disciples of Christ', the followers of Baptist preacher Alexander Campbell. They clung to an even more literal interpretation of the Bible, with an emphasis on simple living and an almost puritanical modesty. The denomination was even smaller than the Scotch Baptists, but was then, as now, strongest in the United States, where three Presidents – Garfield, Johnson and Reagan – were baptised into its ranks. There was a narrow but clear doctrinal difference between the Disciples of Christ and the Baptists, and they remain a separate denomination in the USA, although in the UK they joined the Welsh Baptist Union in the 1930s.

The Disciples of Christ were a modest and unassuming denomination. Richard Lloyd would painstakingly explain that they did not claim that they *alone* were disciples of Christ, rather that they were disciples of Christ alone. As well as adhering to a literal interpretation of the Bible, they believed that it was unlawful for Christians to treasure wealth on earth by putting it aside against future times. They believed that fasting and prayer were essential, and that it was a Christian's duty to marry within the faith. They dressed modestly at all times, and it was deemed obscene for women to wear gold, jewels or expensive clothes, or even to plait their hair. Likewise, it was considered an affectation for preachers to wear black: the Disciples' preachers wore their Sunday best in the same way as their congregations.

In February 1875 Davy and his sister Polly were baptised in the small stream that ran past Capel Ucha. Uncle Lloyd conducted the ceremony, but did not record why his nephew was baptised at the unusually early age of twelve, rather than fifteen, as was customary. The boy's precocity had always prompted special treatment, and perhaps there is no more to it than that. Baptism was a serious matter to the Lloyds and the Georges. It was a solemn ceremony that signified acceptance of the faith of the Church, and rebirth through total immersion in water as an adult member of the congregation.

It would have been cold as Richard Lloyd dammed the stream to form a pool of water for the baptism. Nevertheless, he waded into the water as he did for each baptism ceremony, and stood waist-high to receive the candidates who waited on the bank. When it was Davy's turn, Uncle Lloyd asked him solemnly if he believed in God, Father, Son and Holy Ghost, and then if he would promise, with the help of Jesus Christ, to love and serve God for the rest of his life. The boy answered with the customary 'I do!' and waded out to join his uncle in the cold flowing water. Richard Lloyd baptised David Lloyd George in the name of the Father, the Son and the Holy Spirit, and then, supporting his nephew in his strong arms, plunged him momentarily under the surface of the water. Dripping wet, Lloyd George made his way back to the waiting congregation before taking his first communion inside the chapel. It was to be a turning point in his life, not because of its religious significance, but because he decided from that day onward to adopt the 'Lloyd' in his name as a second surname, in tribute to the man who raised him. He was no longer Davy Lloyd, but David Lloyd George.[14]

The religious intensity of the ceremony, however, was too much for the independent-minded Lloyd George. That night as he lay in bed he experienced a dramatic anti-conversion. It occurred to him suddenly, with perfect clarity, that everything he had been taught about religion, and even the Bible itself, was nothing more than unfounded imaginings. He saw an image of his family's deepest-held beliefs collapsing around him like a building falling into ruin.[15] He sat bolt upright in bed and shouted out loud that God and all the things he had been taught were but a dream.

Lloyd George fully realised the significance of the revelation. He tried to pray, but when he closed his eyes he heard only his own voice echoing in the emptiness. He had a sleepless night, but kept his feelings to himself for some time before tentatively confessing to Uncle Lloyd. Demonstrating the wisdom for which he was renowned, Richard Lloyd reacted calmly. He told the boy that it was natural to doubt, and that his faith would return in due course. Lloyd George was not so sure. Religion had lost its hold on him. He continued to obey the rules of his upbringing, when his family were around at least, but more to appear respectable than out of conviction. He continued to attend, and even to enjoy, chapel services with his family, but he experienced them as a spectator rather than as a believer. He loved the 'theatre' of religion, relished a good sermon, but seemed to pick up more tips on public speaking than on saving his soul. He would listen avidly to the best pulpit performers, and would critique them later in his diary, noting how a good preacher held his audience by using his voice to create dramatic emphasis, or by gesturing with his arms to mark an emotional climax. Special praise was always reserved for Uncle Lloyd, whose sermons he admired, even if he was not convinced by their content. Throughout his life he continued to enjoy nonconformist services with their fervent hymn-singing and dramatic preaching, but he lived according to his own, very different, rules.

Richard Lloyd was a well-read and highly self-educated man. He took a close interest in his nephews' and niece's reading, and made good use of William George's library. These books were treasured by the whole family, and were kept in a glass-fronted cabinet in the parlour.

They included Shakespeare's plays, Green's *History of England*, Burnet's *History of the Reformation* (six volumes), *The Pictorial History of England* by Charles Knight (eight volumes), a complete set of the *Penny Encyclopaedia*, *Webster's Dictionary*, *The Journals of George Fox*, *Arnold's Life and Correspondence* (two volumes), Hallam's *Constitutional History*, Guizot's *History of the English Revolution* and many language texts and books on education as well as classic works of literature.

In order to pass his law exam, Lloyd George needed to study Latin as well as a second language (Welsh, needless to say, did not count). Mr Evans could teach him some rudimentary Latin, but there was no one in the village who knew French. Uncle Lloyd was not to be deterred: a French primer had been among the first David Lloyd's possessions, together with a copy of Aesop's fables in French, and every evening, after a hard day's labour in the workshop, Uncle Lloyd bent his head over a candle to teach himself French before passing on his knowledge to his nephew. In this way, often staying only one lesson ahead of his pupil, he succeeded in getting Lloyd George up to the required standard. He also painstakingly worked alongside the boy as they tackled the first volume of Julius Caesar's *De Bello Gallico* and Sallust's *Catiline*. The cost to his health and strength must have been enormous. Not only did he work hard into the evening, but also long into the night when the rest of the family was in bed, reading texts and preparing the sermons he delivered every Sunday to his congregation. But nothing was too much trouble for the boy he regarded as a son.

In October 1877 Uncle Lloyd accompanied his nephew to Liverpool, the longest journey of his life, to sit the preliminary examination, and on 8 December Lloyd George heard that he had passed. He was to look back on the day the postman bore the good news to Highgate as the most memorable day of his life. 'On that day,' recorded his mistress many years later, 'he was treading on air, the future was heaven, everything seemed possible.'[16]

Lloyd George was now ready to serve his articles with a law firm, if one could be persuaded to take him on. Through dogged enquiries and a lot of string-pulling by friends of the family, Randall Casson, of the firm Breese, Jones & Casson in Porthmadoc, agreed to give the boy a place as an articled clerk, with an initial six-month trial period. Betsy's precious capital was raided to find the £100 (£8,000 at today's values) needed to pay for his indenture, and a further £80 in stamp duty was found from the family's barely adequate funds. David Lloyd George, aged fifteen, was finally on his way. Ahead lay fame, if not fortune, and the glittering career his family confidently expected. More immediate was the heady freedom of living away from his family for the first time in his life, and the opportunity it afforded to explore the worlds of politics – and girls.

3

Love's Infatuated Devotee

IN JULY 1878 DAVID LLOYD GEORGE packed his scant belongings and left Highgate for the wider world beyond Llanystumdwy. At fifteen, he was too young to be fully independent, and it was arranged that he should lodge in Porthmadoc during the week, returning home on Sundays. But his ambition was limitless, and his family urged him on, despite the daunting cost of his training and the sacrifices they would have to make to support him. Lloyd George's success was their dearest ambition, their collective life's work, and he could count on receiving the lion's share of the family's resources.

While he headed for Porthmadoc and all the stimulation that the world of work could offer, his sister Polly had returned home to Highgate and a life without prospects. She accepted her fate calmly, but a recurring illness over the next few years suggests that all was not well with her. In Richard Lloyd's diary he records her poor health with deep sympathy. On one occasion, after she had been confined to bed for three weeks, he voiced his frustration at not being able to help her as he had helped her brother: 'Would feel greatly relieved in mind were it in my power to put her in a respectable position in life, in a way of business, or some other occupation to suit her disposition and abilities. But for the present we must both in her and Wil Bach's [Little William's] case try and learn to labour and to wait.'[1]

There is an intriguing suggestion here that Polly, unlike Betsy, was no home-bird, and would have been better suited to an occupation other than looking after the family in Highgate. She was quite different from her mother – the family thought she had inherited some of her traits from the formidable Rebecca. But she was needed at home, and even the limited career options that were possible for a young Victorian woman were closed to her. Any potential that lay in her for other achievements was unfulfilled, since unlike her younger brother William, who was to follow David into the law, Uncle Lloyd never did succeed in getting a better deal in life for Polly.

Polly did not complain. She seemed to channel any frustration she felt into promoting her brother's ambitions. Her role was mainly domestic, caring for Betsy and Uncle Lloyd, and later becoming a second mother to her nieces and nephews. Her oldest nephew, Dick, remembers her as 'a strong character, definitely uncompromising'. She might have been 'narrow-minded in religious matters', but she was open-hearted when it came to her nieces and nephews: 'Everything we wanted her lavish, generous hand gave us.'[2] Polly looked after the family well. She kept an eye on Richard Lloyd's diet, and was capable of launching a 'devastating counter-attack' if he dared help himself to a second slice of apple tart.

After a few sleepless nights, the young Lloyd George began to settle down. He lodged with Mrs Owen and her husband in a house on Porthmadoc High Street, paying ten shillings a week for his bed and board out of the small cash allowance that Betsy gave him. He would get up early, between six and seven, and make himself useful at the office of Breese, Jones & Casson all day, carrying messages, copying documents and taking dictation. He worked hard, keen to persuade Mr Casson to take him on permanently. If he was lucky he could supplement his allowance with commission earned by collecting insurance premiums from Porthmadoc householders. At the same time, he did not neglect his studies. He had further law exams to take if he was to be successful, and he continued the habit that Uncle Lloyd had instilled in him of setting a daily reading target, taking notes as he went. He was spurred on by ambition, and also by competitiveness: 'I feel I must stick to reading,' he wrote in his diary on 17 September 1879, 'or my time will be wasted and I shall be no better than the clerks and I am determined to surpass (DV).'[3] This kept him out of trouble on the whole, although Mrs Owen had occasional cause to show him the rough side of her tongue for staying out late.

Lloyd George was bursting with ambition and youthful ideals. Primed

by both temperament and upbringing to believe that he was capable
of great things, he could not wait to make his mark on the world. His
diary is striking in its similarity to that of his late father at the same
age. But the son shows more steel. Perhaps because of the innate self-
belief which was one of his strongest characteristics, or because of the
firm guidance he received from Uncle Lloyd, Lloyd George never
doubted his ability to 'get on'. His diary records his advice to himself
and sets out his goals as he entered his articles:

Q. Your chief ambition? A. To promote myself by honest endeavour
   to benefit others.
Q. The noblest aim in life. A. (1) To develop our manhood. (2) To do
   good. (3) To seek truth. (4) To bring truth to benefit our fellows.
Q. Your idea of Happiness. A. To perceive my own efforts succeed.

To 'perceive his own efforts succeed' was to be the driving factor of
Lloyd George's life. He put success in his work above all else, and never
allowed love, illness or even bereavement to distract him for long. That
said, leaving Highgate meant an end, temporarily at least, to his family's
close scrutiny of his leisure time. At sixteen years old he was experiencing the usual hormonal turmoil, and in essence Lloyd George had
a country boy's attitude to sex, no matter how hard his mother tried
to restrain him with chapel decorum.

The practice among farming people and servants at the time was to
allow a courting couple to meet at night for 'caru gwely' (bed-courtship).
This was – in theory and probably in practice – a lot more innocent
than it sounds. A young girl in domestic service would have limited
opportunities to meet local boys. When she did, say at an evening chapel
gathering, if she wanted to extend the encounter beyond a walk home,
she could invite her beau to her room as a way of saving candles and
fuel on cold nights. The bedroom was unlikely to be hers alone, but
that did not seem to deter young lovers, and they would spend a few
hours together in bed, fully dressed to avoid temptation.

This may seem extraordinarily permissive given the stern view of
premarital sex taken by the nonconformists, but sex was not meant to
be part of the deal. It was expected that the young lad would behave
himself and not get his sweetheart in trouble. She, for her part, was

not the innocent creature that her upper-class contemporary was raised to be, and not only knew the facts of life from an early age (living on or near farms meant that these mysteries were easily unravelled), but knew only too well the consequences of allowing things to go too far. If a girl became pregnant she would be drummed out of society, lose her chance of catching a good husband, and unless her family took her in, would have to fend for herself and her baby. This knowledge, it seemed, was quite an effective contraceptive.

Bed-courtship was normally confined to the labouring classes, and not to devout intellectuals like the George family, but Lloyd George, never one to let class considerations stand in the way of an exciting encounter, extended his experience of the world in this way at least once. In company with a Porthmadoc friend, Moses Roberts, he attended a Pentecostal dance at which they were 'sorely tempted by two Irish girls'.[4] Caru gwely followed, and his studies were forgotten for one night at least.

Betsy, Polly and Uncle Lloyd would have been aghast at such behaviour. Lloyd George kept them firmly in the dark, but they were still concerned at the degree of freedom he was enjoying. He had begun to forget the strict ways of home, and one Sunday was enjoying himself digging in the garden when his mother gave him a sound telling-off, shocked at the sight of him breaking the Sabbath. She had good reason to be worried: her son was not growing up to be a faithful Disciple of Christ at all.

Taking pains to avoid Uncle Lloyd's disapproval was something of a George family habit. Lloyd George and William had to find plausible excuses even to go and hear a good sermon in another chapel, and no grumbling at the three walks to Capel Ucha on a Sunday was tolerated, even after a hard week's work. Uncle Lloyd's reprimands were mild, and he never forced his family to conform to his views, but they never forgot how much they owed him, and were loath to disappoint him. But now Lloyd George was free for six days a week to ignore the rules and indulge his fancy. Away from the moral influence of Uncle Lloyd he explored his new environment to the utmost. In Porthmadoc he found a heady combination of work, politics and sex.

Lloyd George's first priority, even as a sixteen-year-old, was his work. His uncle had hung a portrait of Abraham Lincoln above the fireplace in Highgate to inspire the young boy, who never forgot the story of the self-taught lawyer who had by his own endeavours become President of the United States. It took rare confidence for a village boy in Llanystumdwy to believe that he too was capable of such a feat. Having decided that the law was to be the starting point for his career, he worked diligently, and after persuading Randall Casson to take him on as an articled clerk, the next hurdle was to pass his intermediate law examination. He received little support for his studies from the firm, apart from access to law books and periodicals, but Uncle Lloyd devised a rigorous programme for both him and William, who had passed his preliminary examination in 1880. With typical thoroughness, Lloyd George rejected the easy option of cramming just enough information to scrape through from a primer in favour of reading texts from cover to cover. Every book, every chapter, even note-texts and footnotes were read, and notes taken.

Uncle Lloyd was able to supervise his nephew's studies more closely after the family left Highgate and took up residence in Criccieth in 1880. Even though the move brought them only a mile closer to Porthmadoc, it was no longer deemed necessary for Lloyd George to lodge near the office, and he began to walk the ten-mile daily round trip from Criccieth. He undoubtedly benefited from the extra discipline that Uncle Lloyd imposed on his studies. By 1881 he felt ready to take his next examination, and travelled to London where it was held. He felt the weight of expectation on his shoulders as he recorded his feelings after the exam: 'There has been a mixture of hope and fear – hope predominating. I must now abide the result. If the verdict be adverse, I scarcely know what to do – to face friends and others who are so sanguine and seem to have no doubt about the result will be terrible. I can scarcely conceive really the consequences of an adverse verdict. I will be disgraced – lowered in the estimation of my friends and gloated over by mine enemies.'[5]

While he waited anxiously in London for the result he took the opportunity to see the sights, visiting Madame Tussaud's and the Law Courts. With great excitement he went to Charing Cross station to see for himself the new phenomenon of electric light, noting that it was 'a sort of pale blue – melancholy – but unquestionably stronger than gas'. Later, he was contemplating the statue of Demosthenes in the British

Museum when to his surprise he was hailed by Mr Lloyd, the Tremadoc parson. But the highlight of the trip was to be his first visit to the House of Commons:

> Sat 12 Nov. Went to the Houses of Parliament – very much disap-pointed with them. Grand buildings outside but inside they are crabbed, small and suffocating, especially House of Commons. I will not say but that I eyed the assembly in a spirit similar to that in which William the Conqueror eyed England on his visit to Edward the Confessor as the region of his future domain. Oh, vanity. [6]

Even as he took the next step towards a career in law, the young David Lloyd George was regarding the House of Commons as his 'region of future domain'.

There was no inherent contradiction between Lloyd George's pursuit of a law qualification and his desire, ultimately, to make his name in politics. MPs were not paid a salary until 1911, so it was very difficult for someone without money to enter Parliament. An aspiring politi-cian needed either a private income or a profession that was flexible enough to combine with a parliamentary career. Law was ideal, and men like Herbert Asquith, Edward Carson and Rufus Isaacs had all used it as a stepping-stone to a career in public life.

It was necessary to have an ongoing source of income when in full-time politics, and it seems that Lloyd George had a plan from the very beginning. He needed training within an established law firm, and Breese, Jones & Casson fitted the bill perfectly, but he never seri-ously considered staying with the firm beyond the initial five years of his articles. After he had passed his final examinations as well, to become a fully-qualified solicitor in 1884, Randall Casson would ask him to supervise the firm's new Dolgellau office. It was a good offer, but Lloyd George was impatient to be his own master.[7] He left the firm and set up on his own, working from the back room of the family home in Criccieth. His plan was neat and unashamedly self-serving. Randall Casson had taken William George on as an articled clerk, and Lloyd George only had to wait until William too was qualified before his brother could join his own firm and take over the donkeywork. In the meantime, while he built up the practice, he concentrated on the real love of his life, and the only mistress to whom he was completely faithful: politics.

David Lloyd George came to believe very early in life that he was destined for a career in politics. There was no sudden moment of realisation: politics was in his nature, and he was raised to believe that public life was the highest possible calling for a man of talent – apart from religion, which for him was never a serious option. Richard Lloyd encouraged his ambition, and introduced him at an early age to political debate to encourage his confidence and independence of mind. There was always plenty of debate around the workshop in Llanystumdwy, and there was also scope for extending Lloyd George's education at the 'Village Parliament', a debating society that met in the smithy to discuss religious and philosophical topics, providing an intellectual outlet for the working men of Llanystumdwy. Highgate too was not a typical village cottage, in that practically every periodical published in Wales, some twenty-eight of them, was delivered to its door. In this way the young Lloyd George absorbed the issues of the day, and although he lived in a remote part of North Wales, he was connected to the debates and topics of the wider world by a chain of ideas.

Lloyd George's upbringing, his uncle's political views and his nonconformist background all made him a natural Liberal, but in Porthmadoc he came into contact for the first time with radical ideas such as the need for social reform and the disestablishment of the Church in Wales. He found a mentor in John Roberts, a prominent member of the Porthmadoc Baptist community who often held political debates in his candle-making workshop. In his diary Lloyd George described his new friend as 'a socialist and an out and out one',[8] and Roberts held views that went far beyond the accepted orthodoxy of the Liberal Party. He was a fierce opponent of the extravagance of the upper classes, especially the royal family, and spoke passionately about justice for the poorer people in society.[9]

This was socially and politically risky. There had been a time when the Calvinistic Methodists, the largest group of nonconformists, had mostly supported the Conservative Party, which chimed with their belief in self-reliance, independence from the state and individual determination. Although their unease at the widening division in Wales between the landlords and the working classes had eventually aligned them with the Liberal Party, they strongly disapproved of its more radical fringes. When the young Lloyd George found himself at the heart of a group of radicals in Porthmadoc, he risked alienating the Welsh-speaking chapel-goers who would be his natural political support base.

Nevertheless, he put his toe in the water by joining the Liberal campaign in Criccieth during the general election of March 1880. He was put to work checking the register of voters, which in view of his legal apprenticeship he was well qualified to do. Nationally, the election resulted in a victory for the Liberals under William Gladstone.* The Liberal Party won all but four seats in Wales, including Caernarvon Boroughs, the constituency that included Criccieth, where Watkin Williams defeated George Douglas-Pennant, Lord Penrhyn's son, who had captured it for the Conservatives in 1874.

Later that year, as he gained confidence in his political views, Lloyd George tried his hand at journalism. The general election was followed in December by a by-election in Caernarvonshire, caused by the appointment of Watkin Williams as a High Court judge, which meant he had to resign his seat as an MP. Using the pseudonym 'Brutus', Lloyd George sent an article to the *North Wales Express*. His subject was the Tory Party, soon to undergo a change of leadership from Disraeli to Lord Salisbury, and much to his delight it was published on 5 November. He was sufficiently encouraged to write a second piece, this time a response to an address by the Tory by-election candidate, his old Llanystumdwy adversary Hugh Ellis-Nanney. This too was published, albeit with one particularly aggressive passage omitted. Over the next few weeks 'Brutus' appeared several times in the press, and Lloyd George was even able to see his 'Address to the Electors' printed in large characters on *North Wales Express* posters around the town.

Lloyd George wrote on both local and national issues with precocious boldness. His literary style was slightly awkward and over-elaborate, mimicking the convoluted syntax and long words of the worthy

---

* The outcome was a political shock, since the election had been called early in order to deliver a renewed mandate for the Conservatives. The final result was Liberals 350, Conservatives 245, Home Rulers (Irish Nationalists) fifty-seven.

but antiquated books in the Highgate library. Nevertheless, English was his second language, a language for reading and writing, but not for everyday speaking, and it was an extraordinary achievement for him to write so fluently in what was to all intents and purposes a foreign language.

On 1 December 1880 Lloyd George savoured his second electoral victory of the year as the Liberal candidate, William Rathbone, defeated Ellis-Nanney, although with a reduced majority. Still, victory was sweet, and Brutus was content.

Between law, chapel and politics, the waking hours of the young Lloyd George were filled to bursting. There was always time for a little recreation, though, and his favourite hobby was flirtation. He had grown to an average height for his place and time, around five feet five inches, but he had a good, upright figure, and he had inherited the striking looks of his father. He emphasised these by growing a dashing moustache and by taking great care of his clothes and general appearance. His reputation as a local genius and 'young man on the make' also made it easy for him to attract the attentions of young ladies. The three Sunday services at Capel Ucha and frequent evening meetings during the week were perfect opportunities for him to practise his flirting skills on local girls, and he made the most of his chances.

At first, with the burden of fulfilling his uncle's expectations weighing heavily on his shoulders, Lloyd George professed himself to be intent on behaving decorously, but before long he had begun his first relationship with a young Baptist girl. Jennie Evans, one of the prettiest girls in the area, was a friend of Polly's. A flirtatious, teasing relationship developed between her and the teenage Lloyd George, and their encounters were faithfully recorded in his diary: 'A very lively singing meeting ... Sitting in the middle of girls – in the arm of Jennie ha-ha!'[10]

Lloyd George was very conscious of the danger of becoming distracted from his work. He was also being watched over by every member of his family, even his younger brother, who reproved him for signs of 'fast behaviour', although William's words mostly fell on deaf ears:

Good singing meeting. Went up with Jennie about 5. I was rather dry with her tonight for many reasons. I was determined to be so, because if I went on to court her as I have done I would soon fall in love with her and really I have gone further than I thought . . . Jennie has been flirting with other boys. I must stick to my lessons. It was not right for me to carry on flirting with her, as WG my brother says. All the same I mean to carry on with her. I am a fool![11]

The relationship continued, but by March 1880, when he had just turned seventeen, his family's concerns had begun to take effect:

Fri. 26. Dull . . . To Caerdyni. Annie & Jennie came there. I went to Criccieth with John. Saw the girls afterwards. Was reserved with Jennie. I want to get rid of her – we are being talked about. Uncle knows it this long time!

Mon 29. Fine . . . Jennie here; avoided her . . . It costs me some trouble to get rid of that girl, but in flirting with her, I have everything to lose and nothing to win. This shall be regarded as proof of my pluck. If I cannot resist this, how do I expect to gain other things, which require a good deal more determination. She attempted to tease me by flirting with others – bastards.[12]

He was not able to keep from flirting for long. His brother's counsel had had no effect whatsoever, and soon Uncle Lloyd and Polly pitched in as well. On 15 June he was on the receiving end of a stern talk from Uncle Lloyd, who 'told me I was becoming the town talk, that I must mend my ways in this matter at least, or else it would ruin my chances of success'.[13] Two days later he wrote with great seriousness in his diary:

My sister gave it me rather solemnly for flirting with Jennie etc. Indeed I am rather seriously disposed to give up these dealings – this I know – that the realization of my prospects, my dreams, my longings for success are very scant indeed unless I am determined to give up what without mistake are the germs of a 'fast life'. Be staunch and bold and play the man. What is life good for unless some success, some reputable notoriety be obtained – the idea of living for the sake of living is almost unbearable – it is unworthy of such a superior being as man.[14]

Throughout the summer and autumn of 1880 Lloyd George was caught between the attractions of flirting with Jennie and his family's disapproval. Occasionally the latter won, and he was particularly indignant when his good behaviour was not acknowledged: 'Out with John Caerdyni – on top of Dinas. Splendid view. Feel quite as happy without being troubled as to whereabouts of any girls, though I have not courted with any of them. On good terms with all. It is when I have occasional fits of total abstention from girls that I am sometimes attacked!!'[15]

This does not sound as if he means to make his 'occasional fits of total abstention' more permanent, and his Christmas Day diary entry in 1880 reveals that he was back to his old ways: 'In the afternoon went with a gang of girls towards Llanystumdwy. I had many kisses on the road, especially of Jennie. Such a fool I am! At 6 went to a Literary Meeting here – a wretched affair if I had not had a lot of girls by my side.'[16]

Finally, in his diary entry of 31 December, he acknowledges that he has lost the fight: 'To my lasting shame be it said – Love can fairly record me amongst its infatuated, brain-skinned devotees.'[17]

Perhaps Lloyd George thought his genius invincible, but his family were growing ever more concerned that he was being distracted by his flirting. Having failed to get him to stop seeing Jennie by direct appeal, the shrewd Polly resorted to more subtle tactics. She began to widen the circle of his female acquaintance by bringing more friends home. She organised little trips: a walk to a local beauty spot, or after-service singing sessions at which teenage boys and girls could mix. Faced with a greater choice of companions, Lloyd George concluded that he should not get so serious with Jennie. He began to take his evening walks with several different girls, and eventually the references in his diary to Jennie disappear entirely.*

*

---

* Jennie remained in Criccieth until her death in 1930. She never married, and was generally thought to have pitched her expectations too high to be satisfied with her local suitors.

The family's move from Llanystumdwy to Criccieth in 1880 had been prompted by a number of factors: Uncle Lloyd's health broke at the age of forty-five, and he was not strong enough to keep up his shoe-making as well as his preaching. His congregation were so anxious not to lose him prematurely that they arranged for him to have Morvin House, a small terraced house in the shadow of Criccieth Castle, at a peppercorn rent, enabling him to retire from his daily grind. At the time, it was not thought likely that he would ever recover his strength, a perfectly reasonable expectation given the premature deaths of his father, Dafydd, aged thirty-nine, and his brother-in-law William, aged forty-four. In the event, after a few years of ill-health he recovered, and lived to the age of eighty-two.

The logic of the move was inescapable. Although modest, Morvin House offered far more space and privacy than the cramped rooms at Highgate. Betsy was struggling to make ends meet, and in addition she had to find £180 (£14,965 in today's money) to pay for her younger son's articles. Practical considerations aside, the whole family was aware of the rumours of 'fast living' surrounding Lloyd George, and it would suit very well to have him back home, where they could keep an eye on him. In May the family packed up its possessions, including the precious collection of books, Betsy and Lloyd George dug up their favourite plants from the garden, and they moved a mile down the road to Criccieth. They left Llanystumdwy in a positive frame of mind, their financial worries eased for the present. Lloyd George wrote in his diary: 'Left Llanystumdwy without one feeling of regret, remorse nor longing.'[18]

But the move to Criccieth was to herald their bleakest years as a family, and their financial difficulties, far from being over, were about to get much worse. Disaster struck when the building society in which Betsy had invested her capital collapsed, taking her remaining savings with it.* The family was left with virtually no capital, and little income

---

* Accounts differ as to when this happened. There is a suggestion that it was this that prompted Polly's return from Criccieth in the mid-1870s, but since Betsy managed to pay a considerable sum to cover her sons' articles, it is more likely that it was after 1882, a period when there is more evidence that the family were in financial difficulties. By 1892 they were on a stronger financial footing, and William George was able to build a substantial house, Garthcelyn, in Criccieth for himself, his mother, his uncle and sister.

beyond the minimal earnings of the young Lloyd George on which to live.

For proud people like Betsy and Richard, this was a bitter blow. They had survived many hardships without asking for help, but this time there was simply no option. Richard was forced to swallow his pride and ask a neighbour to lend him some money, but these occasional 'loans' barely kept the family afloat. Richard Lloyd mended and re-mended Polly and Betsy's shoes, and Lloyd George records in his diary how Polly was unable to attend a festival in Caernarvon for want of the four-shilling fare until he managed to scrape it together for her. Betsy's health suffered under the strain, and Lloyd George helped care for her as best he could while keeping up his punishing schedule of studying. In 1883 he recorded in his diary: 'Mother had a very bad attack of asthma this morning prevented my going to my books until between 10 and 11. Reading few pages of Middleton's Settled Estates & Statutes had to get candle at 7 tho' I had my head out through the garret window.'[19]

Finally, desperate to bring in a little money, it was decided that they would offer room and board at Morvin House to tourists during the summer months. This seemed like an indignity to Lloyd George, conscious of his status as a budding lawyer and more mindful of his own comfort than his siblings, but in the end he had to agree to the inconvenience, and he was a little mollified when he discovered that one of their early visitors was H. Rider Haggard, the author of *King Solomon's Mines*.

While Polly and Betsy struggled to keep house and home together, Lloyd George's mind was on other things. He had been raised by one of the best pulpit speakers in the district, and under Uncle Lloyd's tutelage he began to speak at Baptist services in the area, sometimes even preaching. He was keen to practise his speaking skills: he needed to become a good public speaker if he was to fulfil his dreams of a political career. Among the chapels he visited regularly was that in Penmachno, near the famous beauty spot of Betws-y-Coed. Unbeknownst to his family, he had a second motive for his frequent visits there, for among the congregation was a young girl called Kate Jones.

During the summer of 1882 Lloyd George walked the twenty miles to Penmachno a good deal more frequently than was strictly necessary. Kate, then aged eighteen, lived with her parents in a house called Glasgwm Hall. Lloyd George would have had plenty of opportunities to see her, for her father was an active Liberal and would become the first Liberal member of the new Caernarvonshire County Council when it was formed in 1889. Politics and religion combined to bring the two young people together, and soon Lloyd George was smitten. This time it was no mere flirtation. He was only nineteen and yet, without his family to intervene to keep things light, he seemed serious enough about Kate to consider marriage for the first time. The young girl was certainly a 'catch': she was from a respectable family and from the same Liberal, Baptist stock as Lloyd George himself. Best of all, she lived at a distance from Criccieth, and for a while was blissfully unaware of his reputation as the town flirt. Her innocence in that respect could not possibly last. However well he played the part of faithful suitor, in a close-knit society, people talked. The seriousness of his love did not extend to fidelity – it never would – and he was simultaneously courting a girl in Porthmadoc. This second affair was not significant enough for him to record it in his diary, but relying on geographic distance alone to keep his two girlfriends in ignorance of each other was bound to end badly, and the news of Lloyd George's other girlfriend soon reached Kate.

This might not necessarily have been a terminal blow to the relationship, except that at the same time, a rival suitor came on the scene. The most eligible bachelor in Penmachno, the local doctor, Michael Williams – old enough to be established, but not too old to court an eighteen-year-old – took a shine to Kate. She was torn between the two for a while, and continued to see Lloyd George whenever he could arrange to speak in chapel. He in turn became more ardent in his suit, and wrote her long letters to impress her with his brilliance. Unfortunately, these backfired spectacularly, as Kate found his thoughts to be 'far too independent' for her liking. In November 1882 she gave in to her parents, who preferred their neighbour and friend to the struggling young lawyer from Criccieth, and accepted Williams' proposal. She wrote to Lloyd George to tell him of her engagement and in his diary he recorded his stoic acceptance: 'Well – I am not sorry. I think it is better she should stick to a man who is in a position to give her a comfortable position and not to an unthinking stripling of 19.'[20]

The reasonableness of her decision was obvious, and Lloyd George could see that she had had a better offer. But he had regarded himself as a serious contender for her hand, much more than a casual sweetheart. Whether this stemmed from genuine love or from the competition posed by his rival, we shall never know. The rather glum tone of his diary would suggest the former, and shortly after Kate's engagement was announced he wrote her some verses. These prove that the world of politics did not rob the world of poetry of its brightest flame, but they do smack of true feeling:

> I'm told there's so bright a land
> Beyond this night of sores
> That neither pain nor cruel bond
> Shall trample its happy shores.
>
> If this be true – God grant it be –
> Where no souls shall part
> Fond heart from fond heart –
> That is the world for you and me. [21]

Lloyd George was not trying to win Kate back, but he needed to express his feelings. He consoled himself with recording in his diary that Kate had let slip to a mutual friend, 'Lord knows I prefer [Lloyd George] to anyone I have ever been with.' But however much she might have liked Lloyd George, she stuck to her decision, and married Dr Williams in February 1883.

Deeply held feelings at the age of nineteen are often short-lived, and by the time of the wedding Lloyd George had recovered his sense of humour: 'John Roberts only just come home from Penmachno – Brought me a piece of wedding cake Dr and Mrs Williams left with Miss Vaughan by Miss Jones to give me!!!'[22]

His affair with Kate had inspired Lloyd George to think of marriage for the first time, and had given him bitter experience of losing to a rival in love. It also taught him that he needed to be well established in his career before he could approach a girl with serious intentions, ·

and also perhaps made him determined never again to lose a girl because of the intervention of her parents. These were all valuable lessons which were not forgotten.

Thus far, Lloyd George's fledgling relationships had ended before he became fully entangled, but the next one was different. It was to have serious repercussions, nearly derailing his later courtship of Maggie Owen and laying down a lifetime's habit of sailing close to the wind in matters of the heart. This time the object of his affections was a dark-eyed brunette called Lizzie Jones.

Young people in rural Wales were encouraged to meet and mingle in chapel. In this way they could get to know their future spouses under the protective gaze of the chapel elders, avoiding too much intimacy and the social and ideological complications of an inter-denominational marriage. This was not just a means of keeping affairs respectable and young girls out of trouble: interdenominational rivalry ran high, and a cross-chapel marriage was socially troublesome. For nonconformists like Lloyd George and his family, chapel membership was a serious, lifelong commitment. The congregation acted as an extended family and an early form of social services, with each chapel looking after its own sick and elderly and members clubbing together to meet shared expenses. Each chapel had its own ceremony to accept new members and bind them for life, and the Calvinistic Methodists and other denominations took their 'cwrdd derbyn' (confirmation service) very seriously indeed. Members were expected to play a part in the chapel community, attend services faithfully and pay a subscription each week to meet expenses. Interdenominational, even same-denomination, inter-chapel rivalry meant that relationships that crossed the boundaries were heavily discouraged.

This caused practical difficulties within the broader community. How could married partners belong to different congregations when membership was, in effect, a subscription to a large family? Husbands and wives would have to inhabit different social circles. In which faith would children be raised, and what about the financial contribution that families were expected to make? They could hardly afford to pay two. It was just not feasible. Admittedly, marrying into a different noncon-formist denomination was better than marrying Church, but only just.

It was better to make sure that young people married within their own faith, and it was thus hardly surprising that Lloyd George should have first set eyes on Lizzie Jones in chapel. In fact, the first thing that attracted him to her was not her appearance, but her rich contralto voice. He himself was developing a pleasant tenor voice, and an interest in attending local singing festivals quickly followed his discovery that they were good places to meet young ladies. In 1883, just as he was recovering from his disappointing affair with Kate, he began to notice an attractive addition to the voices of the choir in chapel, and quickly matched it to the sparkling brown eyes of Lizzie Jones. She was a talented singer in a community of good singers, and had ambitions to train professionally as an opera singer. Lizzie was in demand to perform at events and eisteddfodau throughout Caernarvonshire and Merionethshire. This made her less available, and Lloyd George considerably keener:

> Sun 25 Nov. A miserable Sunday in all respects for me . . . My feet wet all day owing to leaky shoes . . . L. went to Beddgelert on Friday to sing in an Entertainment there and in spite of my earnest request that she would not go, but the little Jezebel has stayed there over Sunday which has given me unutterable pain throughout the day. In earnest I do not know what to do with the girl. I wish to God I had never meddled with her, but I am afraid it is too late now. She has acquired a wonderful mastery over my idiot-heart.[23]

For once in his life, Lloyd George had met his equal in flirtation. Lizzie seems to have led him a merry dance through the spring of 1884, and in June he records his frustration at not being able to make progress with her: 'I wish to God she would keep away altogether. I might feel it, keenly perhaps, for a while, but I'd sooner get over it by not seeing her at all than by being compelled, as I am now, to see her and <u>hear her voice</u> twice a week.'[24]

A few days later came another tantalising encounter: 'Lizzie Jones sang some song with the burden "Oh, where is my boy tonight?" When she sang the last line, "<u>I love him still he knows</u>" – she gave me a glance.'[25]

Her singing talent was clearly matched by a talent for teasing, and

Lloyd George was most willing to play the game. Their liaison was cut short when Lizzie came down with diphtheria and was put in isolation. Even this did not deter Lloyd George, and although he was squeamish throughout his life when it came to illness, he insisted on visiting her sickbed. This gave the local gossips a field day, especially when Lloyd George suffered a sore throat shortly afterwards:

> March 23rd 1885: After dinner strolling about the garden with Eliza Caerdyni [his cousin, daughter of Betsy's sister Elin] – she makes excellent company, an agreeable girl; if anything, rather too much of a puritan. She told me how Mrs Owen Mynydd Ednyfed had been telling her that I got my sore throat from my 'cariad' [sweetheart]. Blast these malicious gossips.[26]

Alas for Lloyd George, this particular 'malicious gossip' was to become his mother-in-law, but not before he had had to work hard to mend his reputation.

Soon afterwards Lizzie ended the relationship, leaving Lloyd George wounded but philosophical. She went on to marry a schoolmaster called Lloyd Williams and, as we shall see, was to make one last, devastating, appearance in Lloyd George's life a few years later. After they parted on this occasion, he consoled himself again with the thought that he was better off without her: 'it would cost between £200 & £300 to train in the Royal Academy of Music . . . It is not likely that I shall be in a position to do this for her for many a year yet.'[27]

Lloyd George richly enjoyed his flirtations. He recorded every encounter and played the game with relish, but he also felt genuine affection for each girl. He was not just playing the field; quite the opposite. His diaries reveal a young man who despite good intentions fell in love rather too easily. He would become overwhelmed by his emotions, but thus far at least they ran pretty shallow. He got over each lost love quickly, and consoled himself with reasons why it would not have worked out before moving on to the next with equal sincerity.

By now Polly was seriously worried. Not only was Lloyd George proving himself to be highly resourceful in escaping the family's supervision, but he also seemed to catch the eye of every pretty girl in the district. The family at Morvin House was only too aware that their hopes and all Lloyd George's dreams of greatness could be utterly derailed if he got a girl pregnant. Not even Richard Lloyd could save his reputation then. A change of approach was called for. Polly decided that rather than try to hold back the tide, she would find him a suitable girlfriend and encourage him to settle down. Suitable meant a chapel girl, and that, she trusted, would keep him out of the worst kind of trouble. In this operation Polly was to show herself to be the equal of her brother in resourcefulness.

4

Maggie Owen

POLLY SET ABOUT HER CAMPAIGN immediately and with energy by arranging evening singing sessions in chapel for the younger members, social events that the elders could not object to, and inviting her friends to call at Morvin House. It required more planning to extend her brother's social circle to include girls from other chapels, since there were fewer excuses for getting together outside the chapel walls. Polly therefore arranged trips to local places of interest along the coast, and invited young people from neighbouring chapels to make up the numbers. One such outing took place on 13 July 1885, when she organised a day trip by steamer to Bardsey Island, two miles west of the tip of the Llŷn Peninsula. Sixteen young men and women left Criccieth that morning in an excitable state, looking forward to spending a day together without the constant, spirit-dampening supervision of the chapel authorities. They were expecting a day of sunshine, picnicking and perhaps some mild flirting, but for two of them at least it was to be a life-changing adventure.

Bardsey was a well-known beauty spot, but local tradition also maintained that 20,000 saints or pilgrims were buried on the island. In the sixth century St Cadfan began to build a monastery there, and the island later hosted an Augustinian abbey whose ruins are still to be seen. Such was Bardsey's spiritual significance in the early Middle Ages that three pilgrimages to it were the equivalent of one to Rome. Even the most puritanical chapel elders could not object to a day trip to such a holy spot. The Criccieth party left Porthmadoc aboard the steamer *Snowdon*, and on arrival they soon split up into groups of two or three, clambering up the steep slopes to find sunny spots to eat their picnic lunches. Lloyd George found himself in a group of three with Polly and one of her friends. In his diary entry for the day he records how much he enjoyed the company of a certain Miss Owen: 'I was with Miss Owen, Mynydd Ednyfed, mostly. MEG (my sister) with us – Enjoyed myself immensely.'[1] Polly had scored a bull's-eye.

Margaret Owen, known as Maggie, was the only child of Mr and Mrs Owen of Mynydd Ednyfed (Mount Ednyfed) farm. She was eighteen years old, and had returned to Criccieth from Dolgellau, where she had been attending Dr Williams' boarding school for young ladies. It was highly unusual for a girl to be educated beyond the age of fourteen, and the Owens' decision to send Maggie away to finish her instruction was a clear signal of their devotion, as well as a sign that they wanted the best in life for her. Lloyd George had noted her in his diary before – he commented on virtually all the girls he bumped into during the course of his day – but not in a way that suggested any particular attraction. In June 1884 he commented that Maggie Owen was 'a sensible girl without fuss or affectation about her'. The following spring there was another reference: 'May 1885 [Criccieth Debating Society soirée] A really 1st class affair – the victualling part as excellent as the entertainment – playing forfeits and the like games until 11.30. About 30 present. Took Maggie Owen home a short way – her mother waiting for her in some house.'[2]

It was not typical of Lloyd George to take girls home the short way, but Mrs Owen was one step ahead of any glad-eyed youth, and was determined to make sure that her daughter got home promptly. By the time he had encountered Maggie Owen a few more times he noted that she 'Seems to be a jollier girl as you get on with her.'[3]

Maggie Owen appeared not really to be the kind of girl to catch Lloyd George's eye. She was not flirtatious or showy, but she had a grace and a quiet confidence that set her apart. She was pretty, with lively blue eyes, but was not considered a beauty so much as a good catch, and she had at least two other serious suitors in Criccieth. But she had been absent during Lloyd George's adolescence, and was not as familiar to him as the girls he had grown up with. She now appeared in his life with all the allure of novelty just as he was getting over Lizzie

Jones. As they wandered around Bardsey Island together, a mutual attraction grew between them.

On the face of it, there were major obstacles to a match between Lloyd George and Maggie Owen. For a start, she was far from ideal in Uncle Lloyd's eyes for the simple reason that she was a Calvinistic Methodist. Indeed, Maggie's family was almost as far removed from the Lloyds socially as was possible within the narrow confines of a small town like Criccieth. For their part, the Owens would have equally strong reasons to rule out Lloyd George as a potential match for their daughter.

Richard Owen, Maggie's father, was a well-to-do farmer and a pillar of the Calvinistic Methodist community of Capel Mawr (Great Chapel) in Criccieth. As the prosperous proprietor of the hundred-acre Mynydd Ednyfed farm he was wealthy enough to invest some capital in the Porthmadoc fleet, to educate his daughter privately, and on his retirement in 1891 to build a pair of fine semi-detached stone houses looking out over Criccieth bay. He was not a member of the landowning class – he was a nonconformist, and he and his family spoke Welsh as their first language – but he was economically in a different class to the Lloyds, and indeed to most of the inhabitants of Criccieth. When he died he left an estate of £1,558.2s.6d (£131,000 in today's currency) to his wife. Not without reason, Richard Owen and his wife considered themselves to be a cut above the Lloyds and the Georges.

Richard Owen could trace his ancestry back to Owen, the twelfth-century Prince of Gwynedd. The power and the land belonging to this class had long since been superseded, but pride remained. Richard Owen might work for a living, but he took his place at the top of Criccieth society, with the natural authority of those born to rule. He was a strong, well-built man even by the standards of the mountain farmers of Llŷn, and his reputation for physical feats was matched by respect for his sound judgement. He spoke slowly, was not easily roused to anger, and had deep-set eyes in a calm, serene face. His physical courage was legendary: he had once been charged by a bull, but had stopped it in its tracks by grasping it by the horns. This and other examples of his strength had earned him the respect of the whole community. He was often asked to adjudicate in disputes between his neighbours, some of whom had known him for decades yet still addressed him as 'Mr

Owen'. On market days he had his own wooden bench on the green in Criccieth that no one dared sit on unless by his invitation.

Richard's local status was further enhanced by his election as head deacon of Capel Mawr, where he sat in authority next only to the Rev. Jones. The deacons together with the minister visited the sick, educated the young, and led and encouraged the faithful. They were also responsible for judging and punishing any member who strayed. Their ultimate sanction was to cast out a member from the congregation, and in so doing take away the sinner's place in society. It followed that deacons were expected to lead exemplary lives themselves, and they carried great moral and social authority. As head deacon of Capel Mawr, Richard Owen would sit in judgement on any member of chapel who married out of the faith. For his own daughter to do so would humiliate him in the most public way possible.

Naturally enough, Richard had chosen his own bride from another ancient Welsh family: Mary Jones of Tyddyn Mawr could trace her ancestry to the tenth-century South Welsh King Hywel Dda, whose laws set the pattern of Welsh society for centuries. Mary Jones was typical of the strong-willed Welsh 'mam'. She was a slightly-built woman whose husband towered over her, but she was as feisty as he was placid, and bustled from one task to the next with indefatigable energy. In her youth she was famous throughout the district as a fine horsewoman, and she was also renowned for her ferocious rages. When she was roused her diminutive frame would shake with anger and her flashing eyes would signal danger as she unleashed a 'veritable Niagara of indomitable force', according to her grandson Dick.[4] Even when she was calm, her pursed lips and sharp gaze warned anyone nearby not to cross her, and she was quick to judge those who failed to live up to her high standards. Mary too was conscious of the natural dignity of her ancestry, and despite the fact that lack of education meant that she was unable to write she was much in demand as chairman and secretary of local societies.

Mynydd Ednyfed occupied a hundred acres of land high on the mountain behind the town of Criccieth, and it was there, on 4 November 1866, that Richard and Mary's only child was born. Richard was a loving, indulgent father who doted on Maggie from the very first. Mary too demanded only the best for her daughter. Country people know that the most valuable stock comes from pure bloodlines, and Richard and

Mary Owen, both proud of their noble ancestry, passed a double dose of pride to their daughter. Indeed, ancestry left its physical mark on Maggie, who was born with 'bys yr Eifion' (Eifion's finger) – a crooked little finger on her right hand that, tradition has it, marks those descended from a fourteenth-century knight called Hywel y Fwyall (Howell of the Axe), whose crooked finger gave him a strong grip which helped to make him the best axeman in Wales. At least one member of each generation of Richard Owen's family bore the telltale finger, and Maggie delighted in bearing the physical mark of her nobility. She was as Welsh as the hills on which she was born.

Maggie had a happy, easy-going nature. She spent her childhood in and around Criccieth, and occasionally caught sight of the young Lloyd George, dressed in his knickerbockers, walking alongside Betsy and Uncle Lloyd on their frequent journeys to and from Capel Ucha.

Richard Owen, along with most of the Calvinistic Methodists, was a supporter of the Liberal Party, which had succeeded in becoming the party of the Welsh nonconformists in their battle for religious recognition (through disestablishment) and equality. Nonconformists had suffered considerable persecution by agents of Church and state in the previous century, and the widening social gap between rich landowners and struggling tenant farmers and miners increased the alienation between the wealthy English establishment and the Welsh dissenting middle and working classes. The spiritual gulf between Church and Chapel, and the cultural barrier between English- and Welsh-speakers, made any politician who challenged the Tory establishment a natural friend to the nonconformist.

1885 and 1886 were turbulent years politically. In 1885 the Liberal Prime Minister, William Gladstone, resigned after losing a crucial vote in the House of Commons. The Tory Lord Salisbury took over as caretaker PM, but after Parliament rose in August, electioneering began in earnest, and went on until an election was eventually called at the end of November. By then Lloyd George had stepped up his political activities, was becoming a regular speaker at political meetings, was even being hailed by some activists as a future MP. The election in November/December, which resulted in a minority Tory administration led by Salisbury, was followed by a split in the Liberal Party between supporters of Gladstone's 'Home Rule' policy in Ireland and those of Joseph Chamberlain's New Radical

Union with its 'unauthorised programme' of federalism as the solution to the Irish problem. Wales remained staunchly behind Gladstone, who with his Welsh wife and family base in Hawarden in North Wales rightly considered the Principality to be a stronghold. Following the defeat of Gladstone's Home Rule Bill in Parliament in June 1886, a second election followed in July, in which Gladstone won thirty out of the thirty-four Welsh seats, although elsewhere he did not do so well. With the Liberal Party divided, Salisbury held on to office, shored up by an alliance with Chamberlain and the Irish national MPs. It was to be the beginning of a rift in the Liberal Party between the moderate mainstream and the radicals.

In Wales, moderate men like Richard Owen wanted religious freedom and the right to earn a fair living on the land. He was a mainstream Liberal, naturally conservative, and with no time for those on the more radical fringes of his party who talked of social reform, the separation of the Church in Wales from the state, and even of Home Rule for Wales. David Lloyd George was a natural radical who had expressed admiration for Chamberlain, but the prevailing political wind in Wales carried him into the Gladstonian camp.

Richard and Mary Owen wanted Maggie to marry a Calvinistic Methodist, preferably a Liberal with conventional views, who was well established in life and able to offer her a comfortable future. From the elevated perspective of Mynydd Ednyfed, Lloyd George's prospects did not look good. Before he had even begun to court Maggie, Mr and Mrs Owen regarded him as socially inferior and wholly unsuitable: he was a Baptist, and a political radical who was not yet firmly established in his profession. Worse still, Mrs Owen had her ears pressed well to the ground and regarded him as 'fast', a flirt who 'walked out' with too many local girls. To the Owens, Lloyd George seemed neither reliable nor respectable. Maggie could not have chosen anyone from her limited circle of acquaintance more likely to raise objections from her parents, and in the summer of 1885 these seemed insuperable. Nevertheless, with the time-honoured inevitability of such situations, the attraction between Lloyd George and Maggie grew with each meeting.

During the weeks following the Bardsey Island trip, Lloyd George took every opportunity to put himself in front of Maggie and her family.

He had few excuses to visit Mynydd Ednyfed, but he made use of what little connection he had with Richard Owen's political activities. At first, Mr Owen accepted Lloyd George's sudden interest in establishing a Liberal club in Criccieth at face value, but he was no fool and he soon realised that the young man's visits had more to do with Maggie than with politics. Lloyd George was promptly banned from Mynydd Ednyfed and told, firmly, to leave Miss Owen alone. This served only to increase his interest, but, temporarily defeated, he retired from the field to consider his tactics.

Mr Owen was seriously alarmed: not only did he and his wife disapprove of Lloyd George, they also had the ideal husband for their beloved child already picked out. His name was John Thomas Jones, and he was a deacon at Capel Mawr. To add to his qualifications the thirty-four-year-old Jones was financially well-off, having made a small fortune in Australian goldmines before returning to his native North Wales. He lived in a newly-built, substantial house overlooking Criccieth, and he was the very opposite of 'fast'. He was rather uncouth and brusque of manner, but that was a minor disadvantage compared to the facts that he was the right denomination and had excellent prospects. The Owens were delighted when he started courting their daughter, but Maggie was not impressed. She resisted all attempts by her parents to persuade her to accept his proposals, and did not even mention his existence to his younger rival until well into their relationship.

Meanwhile, Lloyd George decided that if he could not court Maggie openly, he would take every opportunity of doing so covertly instead. He wrote to her frequently, and they conspired to meet at local social events. The first note from Lloyd George that Maggie kept is dated 30 December 1885, and was addressed respectfully to 'Dear Miss Owen':

I enclose tickets for our Societys entertainment. The meeting commences at 7.30 p.m. punctual.

Young ladies need not arrange for any escort home after the meeting, as the Society provides efficient protection for them in that respect!

Kindly recollect this so as to avoid troubling anyone to wait for you from the meeting.

Yours sincerely

D. Lloyd George[5]

The formal tone of the note was perhaps intended to be proof against prying eyes, and belies the clear understanding between them that security on the way home would be provided by one D. Lloyd George, personally.

A week later, Lloyd George's diary records that he lay in wait for Maggie, hoping for a private meeting: 'Very glad I waylaid Maggie Owen; induced her to abstain from going to the Seiat [evening service] by showing her by my erratic watch that she was too late, then for a stroll with her up Lôn Fêl.'[6]

Maggie fell for these none-too-subtle tactics several times over the next few weeks, and in turn her quiet charms grew steadily on him:

4 Feb. At 6 p.m. met Maggie Owen by appointment on the Marine Parade. With her until 7. I am getting to be very fond of the girl. There is a combination of good nature, humour and affection about her.[7]

Three days later, Lloyd George confessed to his brother his growing interest in Maggie, with an acknowledgement of the difficulty of courting a Calvinistic Methodist against the wishes of her parents: 'After dinner with W.G. along Abereistedd and thence to chapel. Mentioned my predicament with regard to love affairs. He does not disapprove.'[8]

With characteristic speed, Lloyd George was falling in love:

9 Feb. At 5.45 attended Burial Board meeting, thence to an appointed rendezvous by 6.30 at Bryn Hir gate to meet Maggie Owen; took her home by round-about way, enjoyed the stroll immensely and made another appointment. It looks as if I were rapidly placing myself in an irretrievable position. Doesn't matter. I don't see that any harm will ensue. Left her at 7.45.[9]

He paused to throw a backward glance at the memory of Lizzie Jones only to reassure himself of the superior qualities of his new love:

15 Feb. (After concert) I then waylaid Maggie Owen to take her home. Never felt more acutely than to-night that I am really in deep love with girl. Felt sorry to have to leave her. I have I know gradually got to like her more and more. There's another thing I have observed in

connection with this, that my intercourse with L. rather tended to demoralize my taste; my fresh acquaintance has an entirely different influence. She firmly checks all ribaldry or tendency thereto on my part. [10]

Lloyd George was getting serious. Maggie Owen was in a different class to the girls he had flirted with in the past. It was not only her background – Lizzie, for example, was the daughter of the local fishmonger – but also her character. From the outset Maggie set high standards of behaviour, and without making herself a killjoy, seemed to make him behave better in return. She was not a girl to be toyed with or treated badly. Her natural dignity and fixed moral compass demanded respect. In the young Maggie Owen's 'checking' effect on the flirtatious Lloyd George we see the essence of their mature relationship. It was her strength of character too that was in due course to inspire admiration and love throughout Wales and beyond.

By late spring 1886 Lloyd George was committed, announcing in his diary that he had made his choice, but all the evidence suggests that Maggie felt less sure. While she was happy to slip out from Mynydd Ednyfed to meet him in the early days of their courtship, when he pressed his case in earnest she began to have doubts. He continued to waylay her at every opportunity, but he waited nearly a year after the Bardsey Island trip before daring to use an endearment for the first time:

> 27 June. After making a feint of running for the train, envelope in hand, started via sea-wall and Turnpike, Criccieth, for the hills. M. expecting me. M. asked me what I would tell them at home if they wanted to know where I'd been. I replied: 'I'd say I'd been to see my sweetheart.' This is the second time I've called her so. She likes it. I am now quite committed. [11]

Matters came to a head in July when he confided in Polly: 'Told my sister M.E.G. to-night about M. She is well-pleased and thinks a lot of her, says I may mention the matter [of marriage] to M. shortly but that it would not do to marry for about five years at least.' [12]

Polly could see that a long engagement was the only sensible way forward, given the fact that Lloyd George was far from established in his career, and that his family could not give him any financial help. She would not have been blind to the other obstacles in the way of the young couple, and her advice was perhaps also coloured by the fact that Lloyd George would have to convince not one but two families to agree to the match.

This raises the question, why *did* Lloyd George's devout Baptist siblings approve of the interdenominational match? The answer surely lies in the fact that they could see the advantages to their brother. Polly knew Maggie very well, and respected the strength of her character. Lloyd George would need a strong woman as a wife, both to support his limitless ambitions and to keep him in check, and Maggie appeared more than equal to the task. There were clear social advantages to the match: Lloyd George would benefit from his association with the well-to-do Owen family, which might be useful to him in building his law practice. Politically too, Lloyd George could not make a better match. A Baptist politician lacked a natural power base, since there were comparatively few Baptists in the area. A Baptist with no other recommendation would be seen as an outsider by both the church-going Tory voters and by the dominant nonconformist group, the Calvinistic Methodists. By marrying into a prominent Calvinistic Methodist family like the Owens, Lloyd George the future political candidate would be gaining a significant advantage.

Maggie was the catch of the district, and Lloyd George always deserved – and got – the best. It was true that there were issues to resolve before the marriage could take place, but Polly knew her brother supremely well, and never underestimated his determination to get what he wanted. She gently supported his campaign, speaking well of Maggie to those whose objections needed neutralising, encouraging Lloyd George to think of marriage, and keeping Uncle Lloyd out of his way. On the Owens' side, however, there were no apparent advantages to a relationship between their daughter and Lloyd George. He was not marriage material in their eyes, and they doubted his ability either to support Maggie or to make her happy. On both counts they were eventually to be proved right.

Despite the dark stormclouds on the horizon, Lloyd George felt that all was well as he prepared to take a short trip to London over the August bank holiday weekend in 1886. His absence gave Maggie time to think, and she confided to a friend that she feared Lloyd George would let her down if she gave him her heart, although she confessed that she was very fond of him.[13] With typical self-confidence, when this reached his ears Lloyd George rejoiced in the second admission without dwelling too much on the first. He regarded Maggie's fears as a challenge, and he was sure enough of her affection to take the next step, and to propose to her.

Lloyd George chose his moment with care. Maggie had relatives living at Bodfan in Llanwnda, fourteen miles from Criccieth, and at the end of August she went to stay there for a few days. Lloyd George guessed that this would be his best chance of catching her alone, away from the baleful influence of her mother, and he followed with his plan of action worked out. His diary gives the story in detail:

25 Aug. Left Caernarfon per 4.40 train – dropped down at Llanwnda. Wrote at the Inn at Llanwnda a note for her . . . marched right up to the door [where she was staying], asked if Miss Owen was in, told the girl at the door that I was desired by her father Richard Owen to give her a note in passing! Eventually I saw her. It appears Miss Jones had read the note, M. being too excited to open it. She had to go to a party that evening, but promised to try and return by 8, and to meet me by the gate; I gave her a bouquet I had brought with me . . . I returned at 8 to Bodfan – but had to wait until 9.45 until the girls returned.

We can imagine his agony of suspense as he waited an hour and three quarters for his sweetheart to appear, but Maggie did finally arrive: 'M came with me for a long drive in carriage (I had brought from Llanwnda). Here I proposed to her. She wanted time to consider, but admitted her regard for me. Although, when I write this, I have not been formally accepted, I am positive that everything is all right so far as the girl is concerned. I left her about mid-night. M. has some of the "coquette" about her – she did not like to appear to jump at my offer.'[14]

His confidence in Maggie's regard was unshakeable, but he was mistaken in interpreting her genuine hesitation as mere coquetry. The truth was that she was disturbed by the gossip her mother and friends had passed on to her about Lloyd George's reputation as a ladies' man, and was not about to jump into a hasty engagement. She was also close to her parents, and was reluctant to go against their wishes.

Lloyd George knew when to press his advantage, and followed his appearance at Llanwnda with a letter on 28 August. '. . . Write me your answer to the question I gave you on Wednesday evening (or Thursday morning – I am not sure which it was!). Do, that's a good girl. I want to get your own decision up on the matter. The reason I have already given you. I wish the choice you make – whatever it be – to be really yours & not anyone else's.'[15]

Maggie's religion had been the subject of gentle teasing between the lovers from the beginning, with Lloyd George trying to distract her from her regular attendances at Capel Mawr and avoiding his own duties at Capel Ucha as often as possible. The fact that Maggie did not object, and in fact seems to have enjoyed the fun as much as he, strongly belies the theory put forward by William George in later life that her hesitation was due to the religious difference between them. In October, after keeping Lloyd George waiting nearly six weeks for an answer, Maggie finally explained why she continued to hold back. He recorded the conversation in his diary:

1 Oct. To Mynydd Ednyfed & Mr and Mrs Owen having gone to Ty Mawr. I remained until 1 a.m. I pressed M. to come to a point as to what I had been speaking to her about [his proposal of marriage]. She at last admitted that her hesitation was entirely due to her not being able implicitly to trust me. She then asked me solemnly whether I was really in earnest – I assured her with equal solemnity that I was as there is a God in Heaven. 'Well then,' she said, 'if you will be as true and faithful to me as I am to you, it will be allright.' She said nothing about her Mother's frivolous objection to my being a Baptist nor as to her own objection to my sceptical vagaries – for I told her emphatically the other day that I could not even to win her give them up & I would not pretend I had – they were my firm convictions.[16]

It seems that their different denominations were not an insurmountable difficulty for Maggie. Neither did she mind Lloyd George's 'sceptical vagaries', his radical political convictions – in which case she would have done well to note that his courageous defence of them contained a warning: he would not give up his beliefs – or his political ambitions – for her or for anyone else. In this, he was to remain constant until the day he died.

While Maggie was considering whether or not to accept Lloyd George as a husband, her doubts with regard to his fidelity cropped up repeatedly, but she had no doubts at all about his professional success. Lloyd George was a man who would 'get on'. What was not specifically discussed between them though was the future career he had in mind. Lloyd George was beginning to make a name for himself locally as a promising young lawyer, but he was also getting more and more involved in politics.

The swift changes of government in 1885–86 made for exciting times for the political activist in Morvin House. Most Liberals in Caernarvon Boroughs were Gladstonians. There is some evidence that Lloyd George's natural political sympathy lay with Chamberlain, and but for a mix-up with the dates of a crucial meeting in Birmingham he might have openly declared his support for Gladstone's rival. It was politically canny, though, given the views of Welsh Liberals, for him to present himself as a Gladstonian, which is what he did.

Lloyd George's political reputation had grown so rapidly by 1886 that he was shortlisted as the Liberal candidate for that year's general election in the neighbouring constituency of Merioneth, but he soon regretted his candidacy. He withdrew, ostensibly to allow his friend T.E. Ellis to gain the Liberal nomination, but his diary reveals that he had been carried away by the enthusiasm of his supporters, and soon realised that he had neither the financial means nor the political experience to make a success of becoming an MP at such an early age: 'When alone and calculating the possible consequences . . . I would not be in nearly as good a position as regards pecuniary, oratorical or intellectual capacity to go to Parliament now as in say 5 years hence. Now I would put myself in endless pecuniary difficulties – an object of contempt in a House of snobs.'[17]

During the election the Liberal candidate in Caernarvon Boroughs, Love Jones-Parry, made a mess of his campaign, first alienating his supporters by denouncing Home Rule, and then having a last-minute change of mind. He was defeated by his Conservative rival Edmund

Swetenham. Nationally, support for Gladstone was not as strong as it was in Wales, and Salisbury returned to power with a majority of over a hundred seats.

Lloyd George was heavily involved in the local campaign despite the fact that he had decided not to stand for Parliament himself. His political activities could not have escaped the notice of his sweetheart. Indeed, it was during the years of their courtship that he became seriously committed to a political career and began to plan his way out of the law. His attitude towards his profession changed subtly: what was previously a source of pride became more a means to an end, a way of earning a living while developing his reputation as a political activist and speaker.

As Maggie wondered whether she could trust her young lover, did she fully understand what future life he was offering? Lloyd George's diary records that their conversations were mainly about things they had in common: chapel, Criccieth society, her family's disapproval, his legal clients. He did not seem to talk to her much about politics: she was not interested in the subject at this stage of her life, and he possibly regarded it as his own domain, and not a subject for feminine conversation. He would also have wanted to emphasise his professional successes to Maggie and her family, to prove that he could support a wife and family. His involvement in local politics would not necessarily have signalled his wider ambitions to Maggie. After all, her father was a leading local Liberal too, but he did not have any ambitions to enter politics professionally. Also, while with hindsight Lloyd George's progress in politics seems the most significant development during this period, at the time much more attention was paid to his growing reputation as a lawyer. This may explain why Maggie was able later to claim that she did not regard his political career as a certainty when she was considering whether to marry him, despite all the evidence to the contrary.

Throughout the rest of 1886, Maggie was losing her heart, if not her head, to her insistent suitor, and on 11 November Lloyd George triumphantly records: 'Never on better terms. First time she ever gave me a kiss. She gave it in exchange for a story I promised to tell her.'[18] Lloyd George and Maggie had been courting for over a year, and had been discussing marriage since August, but Maggie had been brought up as a respectable chapel girl, and did not even kiss her lover until November. The increased intimacy was cautiously acknowledged by Lloyd George as he addressed letters thereafter to 'My dearest Miss Owen', rather than the simple 'My dear Miss Owen' he had previously been using. He did not yet dare use her Christian name.

Maggie's reluctance to commit herself was understandable, for the rumours of Lloyd George's flirting were not all in the past. Only two days after their kiss, he records in his diary: 'Rather strong rebuke from M. for having condescended to gabble at all with Plas Wilbraham girls. I foolishly let out somehow that I had done so – she let me off – dismissed me – in disgrace.'[19]

Given her mother's views, Maggie was very sensitive to suggestions that Lloyd George was flirting with other girls, and he would have been well advised to steer clear of any potential or former girlfriends while he was waiting for her answer. This was to prove quite beyond him, and he saw no reason to mend his ways either before or after his engagement, trusting in his wits and in the strength of Maggie's feelings to get him out of trouble. Both were to be tested to breaking point in the weeks leading up to their engagement as his old flame Lizzie Jones made her final destructive appearance in his life, and his determination to ignore the local rumour mill very nearly derailed his new relationship.

Regarding himself as engaged – unofficially at least – Lloyd George had been pressing Maggie to face up to her parents. They were still so opposed to the relationship that the lovers had to communicate secretly, leaving letters in a niche in the stone wall on the lane near Mynydd Ednyfed, which they referred to as 'the post office'. They met behind the Owens' back whenever Maggie could sneak away, but Lloyd George upbraided Maggie constantly in his letters for keeping him waiting, or for letting him down. He had obviously reached the end of his tether by November 1886. On Friday the nineteenth, he signed his letter to Maggie 'Yours (hyd y ffrae nesa' ac wedyn) D Lloyd George' [Yours (until the next quarrel, and beyond) D Lloyd George][20] – and four days later he wrote an angry missive in a furious scrawl following yet another disappointment:

Wednesday morning,

Thanks for another sell – with regard to what you suggest about this evening I am not inclined to abandon my work at Porthmadoc any more upon the mere <u>chance</u> (as you term it) of your being able successfully to cheat your mother. You failed to do so <u>last</u> night & you may fail tonight. Letting alone every question of candour & duty it would be far more expedient in my humble opinion to tell your mother where you want to go. You have more than once vetoed the project of my discussing matters with her. However one of us will have to do it. As I told you before I disdain the idea of lurking like a burglar about premises when I merely seek to obtain an honest interview with my sweetheart & I have the same contempt for myself when I have been kicking my heels on the highway & lying in ambuscade like a footpad for half an hour or less vainly expecting the performance of a definite promise of a stroll with my girl.

If you can meet me for a certainty at the usual time & place on Thursday evening (5.30 by Parkia Gate) kindly drop me a note at the post office today so that I may get it tomorrow. But should you propose making your promise contingent upon your mother's passing humour then the project had better be deferred until you have been more thoroughly steeled.[21]

He had made his point, and Maggie wrote immediately to soothe him with the promise of a meeting by Criccieth cemetery, a secluded spot on the lane between Criccieth and Mynydd Ednyfed:

Dearest Lloyd George,
    I will be by the cemetery this evening at 7 p.m. without fail.
    Yours with love,
    Maggie[22]

More significant than the message was the way in which she signed her Christian name and wrote her love. It was a capitulation.

The following month, Lloyd George persuaded Maggie to confront her mother over her continuing refusal to allow him to visit Mynydd Ednyfed, and followed up his argument with a letter:

I trust you will have something to report to me tomorrow of the result of an interview with your mother. As I have already intimated to you it is but of trivial consequence to me what your mother's views of me may be – so long of course as they do not affect yours. All I wish for is a clear understanding so that we may afterwards see for ourselves how we stand.

You will appreciate my anxiety to bring the matter to an issue with your mother. I somehow feel deeply that it is unmanly to take by stealth & fraud what I am honestly entitled to. It has a tinge of the ridiculous in it, moreover.

This being done, you will not be troubled with any more lectures & I am confident I shall be thereby encouraged to act in such a way as will ensure your requited Confidence.

Yours in good faith,

D Lloyd-George[23]

The pattern of their relationship was set: Lloyd George would coax, persuade and tease Maggie to take the next step along the road to marriage. She would resist, caught between the twin forces of her mother and her suitor until he lost his temper. Forced to choose, she would give in, and so their relationship progressed, step by step. Lloyd George's next goal was to become officially engaged, which meant getting Maggie to accept a ring. As she hesitated, unable to conquer her misgivings about his fidelity, matters took a turn for the worse.

By the start of 1887, despite Maggie's parents' opposition and Lloyd George's mother and uncle's ignorance of the situation, the couple were acknowledged sweethearts, even if they could not yet be openly betrothed. Maggie was still conscious of her lover's bad reputation, and acutely aware of the damage a scandal could cause. In other words, this was not a good time for Lloyd George to be associating publicly with Criccieth girls who had caused tongues to wag in the past, since it would only reinforce Mrs Owen's objections. He, as usual, felt immune from danger. As 1886 drew to a close, he was asked to act in a professional capacity in a breach of promise case. These suits, usually brought by a jilted fiancée whose reputation had been compromised by her lover's change of heart, were commonplace, and Lloyd George had already handled several. This time, though, the parties were known to him, for the claimant was Ann Jones, sister of his former girlfriend Lizzie.

As fellow members of Capel Ucha, it was natural for Ann and Lizzie to turn to Lloyd George when Ann sued her former fiancé, John Jones of Caerdyni Farm – or it would have been, if Jones was not Lloyd George's friend and first cousin.* Given the delicate condition of his courtship of Maggie Owen, not to mention the family relationship involved, it would have been prudent for Lloyd George to refuse the case, but he did no such thing. Perhaps he preferred to face down his critics, or perhaps it went against the grain to refuse any case when his family needed the money so badly.

Oblivious to danger, Lloyd George seemed sure that his engagement was imminent, writing confidently to Mr R. Bonner Thomas, a Porthmadoc jeweller, on 26 January 1887 to order a ring for Maggie:

> I enclose your finger card – the size of the rings I require is no. 7 on the card – I have matched it – send off for a few today without fail – I want them by Friday.
>
> The prices might range between 7 & 15 guineas – get one or two with emeralds in as well as diamonds – but the majority I would prefer to be with diamonds alone.[24]

Yet Maggie was not ready to accept his ring in defiance of her parents' wishes, emeralds and diamonds notwithstanding. A quarrel followed, and Lloyd George's next letter to her refers to 'the heat of last night's rancoure [sic]', and is signed rather brusquely, 'Yours D Ll G', with a curt postscript: 'It is time you should cast off your swaddling clothes.'[25]

A second remonstration proved necessary as Maggie continued to prevaricate and to cancel meetings. This second letter is an extraordinary testament to his view of the world, and shows how clearly Lloyd George saw the path ahead, even at the age of twenty-four. Using all his powers of advocacy, he expresses his impatience with the slow progress of their courtship, and spells out the priority his work has in his life and will always have in future. He begins by berating her for

---

* John Jones was the son of Elin, Betsy George's sister.

keeping him waiting in vain – not because he missed her company, but because it inconvenienced him in his business dealings:

My dearest Miss Owen,

Without any preamble or beating about the bush, let's straight to the topic. Here I am under the very disagreeable necessity – through no fault of my own you must admit – of addressing you for the hundredth time during a not very protracted courtship in a remonstrative spirit. Appealing to the love I have for you or that you have professed for me seems to be but vanity itself in your sight. I am now going to appeal to your sense of fairness & commiseration. I have repeatedly told you how I am steeped to the lips in an accumulation of work – that I am quite entangled & confounded by my office arrears – that I have to work late every evening & then get up early the following morning to effect some measure of disentanglement. You know how important it is for a young fellow starting in business that he should do his work not only efficiently but promptly. Another thing you have been told is that clients from Criccieth & the surrounding districts can only see me in the evenings & that they generally ask me to make appointments with them beforehand. And yet notwithstanding that you have been fully & emphatically acquainted with all these considerations the only assistance you give me is this – that in the course of a <u>week</u>'s time you have disappointed in <u>three</u> appointments made by you, that at the last moment, when my business arrangements had been made to suit those appointments, that moreover you kept me on Friday evening to loiter about for about 30 minutes before you even took the trouble to acquaint me with your intention to make a fool of me at your mother's nod. Now letting love stand aside for the nonce – even a general sense of philanthropy might dictate to you that such conduct is scarcely kind on your part. I am sure you will recognise that it is not in keeping with your usual kindliness of spirit. I must really ask you for a little sympathy in my struggles to get on.

It becomes clear that his vanity has also been wounded:

Another thing – you well know how you lecture me about my lack of self respect. Well how is it you conduce to this quality to me? By

71

showing me the utmost disrespect. You stick me for half an hour in a conspicuous spot to wait for you & having made an exhibition to all passers by, you coolly send word that it is your mother's pleasure I should go home to avoid another disappointment.

Having engaged her sympathy and made her feel that she is in the wrong, he turns up the heat and forces her to make a decision:

Now once for ever let us have an end of this long standing wrangle. It comes to this. My supreme idea is to get on. To this idea I shall sacrifice everything – except I trust honesty. I am prepared to thrust even love itself under the wheels of my Juggernaut, if it obstructs the way, that is if love is so much trumpery child's play as your mother deems courtship to be. I have told you over and over that I consider you to be my good angel – my guiding star. Do you not really desire my success? If you do, will you suggest some course least objectionable to you out of our difficulty? I am prepared to do anything reasonable & fair you may require of me. I can not – earnestly – carry on as present. Believe me – & may Heaven attest the truth of my statement – my love for you is sincere & strong. In this I never waver. But I must not forget that I have a purpose in life. And however painful the sacrifice I may have to make to attain this ambition I must not flinch – otherwise success will be remote indeed . . .

Write me your views candidly & in as good & honest a spirit as I impart mine to you.

With fondest love

From your sweetheart D. Ll.G.[26]

This is an extraordinary letter, and is highly revealing as to the psychology of both author and recipient. It is a lawyer's, not a lover's letter. Love is secondary to business – no suitor ever made that clearer. Lloyd George will 'thrust even love itself under the wheels of [his] Juggernaut' if necessary to advance his career. It is in order to 'get on' that he needs Maggie by his side, and yet even in this frank letter he refrains from spelling out for her that he is referring to his political ambitions, not simply to his career as a rural attorney. Although the language he uses betrays the scale of his ambition, he draws back from telling her directly that he intends to make his mark on the national stage: that would have to wait until she was fully committed. His career would always come first, but he softens the blow a little by calling her his 'guiding angel'. She is necessary to him, if only to achieve his ambitions.

There is no doubt that Lloyd George wrote sincerely and from the heart, but the letter is also a clever attempt to bend Maggie to his will. He appeals to her deep-rooted sense of duty, and the work ethic that was both a feature of her faith and a strong characteristic of her family. Maggie was raised to believe in hard work and obligation. Lloyd George knew this well, since it was her unyielding sense of duty to her parents that had frustrated him for so long. Appealing to her emotions would be like trying to persuade a river to leave its course: she would always place her duty first. In writing this letter he showed how well he understood her character, and how readily he would use that knowledge to manipulate her. His skill was to make it seem as if she had an equal duty to help him in his career. It was his strongest card, and he played it supremely well.

The letter must have given Maggie considerable food for thought, and while she was digesting it her concerns about his breach of promise case grew stronger. Unable to persuade him to drop the case, she wrote to him to air her views – it is one of the first letters from her that he kept.

My dear Mr George,
I have begged them to let me come to Portmadoc this evening, but father has utterly refused to let me go. I am sure I don't know why, therefore I must submit to his will and stay at home . . . I am returning you the girl's letter. After reflecting upon what you told me yesterday I must tell you that I should much prefer your leaving it to some one else to take up; not because of your relationship to the man nor to let him go unpunished by any means for he really deserves it, but for your own sake. All the old stories will be renewed again. I know there are relatives of mine at Criccieth, and other people as well, who will be glad to have anything more to say to my people about you, to set them against you and that will put me in an awkward position. I know this much, I shall not be at my ease while the thing is on, if you will be

taking it up. If she were a stranger to you, and you took her case, people would wonder why on earth you took it against your cousin, knowing that your relations were against your doing so; but now they will draw different conclusions – that you are on friendly terms with these people while your duty is to do all that is in your power to make them forget that you ever were on friendly terms with them & taking up this case will not help you in the least to do it.

Let some one else do it. You can get plenty of excuses; <u>one</u> that your people are against you doing it and recommend some other lawyer. Should your reputation depend on it, as you said, that would only be from a professional point of view, not from any other point of view, I can assure you.

Yours faithfully,
M. Owen.[27]

The formal way in which she addresses him and the plaintive tone of the letter betray her anguish at the thought of the renewed contact between Lloyd George and Lizzie Jones. But even faced with this highly convincing case, Lloyd George bafflingly dug in his heels, choosing to face the opposition of his family and his sweetheart and to risk his personal reputation by prosecuting his cousin on behalf of his former love's sister. He does not explain his reasons in his diary, nor in any letter that survives, but financial considerations must have been among them, as well as sheer stubbornness and perhaps a desire not to allow Maggie to dictate to him which cases he should take and which drop.

When Maggie tried again to persuade him not to take the case, with a threat to end their engagement, he came out fighting. He wrote her a second carefully crafted letter designed to make her accept him on his own terms, using every means at his disposal to end her indecision once and for all:

My dearest Maggie,
Your ultimatum to hand & here I launch my protocol in reply.

What I wish to make clear is this. That whatever course you may think fit in your unfettered discretion to adopt has not been necessitated or even occasioned by any dishonourable or disgraceful proceeding on my part.

What is the gravamen of your charge? Simply this – that I have deigned to permit myself to be entertained with a little harmless music by a couple of girls whom a bevy of dried-up dessicated [sic] & blighted old maids object to. I am not sure whether their objection is not a recommendation. And can you give me anyone whom they don't object to? Miss R: Bronygadair objected even to you. I might plead guilty if I only knew the charge. My calls upon the girl were of a purely professional character – as witness the fact that prior to this breach of promise affair I was not on speaking letting alone visiting terms with her.

Again, his tone is legal: he is writing a protocol, an early version of a treaty between them. In other words, he is setting out his terms, which Maggie must accept or reject him altogether. He knew that he was on firm ground, since Maggie had given away the fact that she was jealous of the time he spent with his former girlfriend. Knowing that her love for him was strong, he chose not to promise an end to such behaviour. Instead, he decided again to appeal to her sense of duty by arguing, not entirely successfully, that his professional duty required him to socialise with clients:

– Now I could give you good reasons for my not objecting to a little music to finish up the consultation. I aim to please all my clients & thus make them as much as possible personal friends & were an Italian organ grinder to put anything in my way I would probably endeavour to please him at the risk of a little personal discomfort by asking him to display the musical qualities of his infernal machine. Now Miss Jones is to me a really good client – for if her case is fought out as it may (& as it would but for my regard to your anxiety for a settlement) my bill of costs would be a matter of between £50 and £100. There is moreover the notoriety of advertisement involved in the case which is in actual fact more valuable to me. Well such a client, to begin with, is worth trying to please. Moreover whilst music is as innocent a recreation as you could possibly indulge in it always affords me unlimited pleasure.

Then, with breathtaking nerve, he justifies his behaviour on religious grounds, and accuses Maggie of snobbery in her disapproval of the Jones sisters:

Furthermore the girls are members of the same chapel as I am and one of the few religious dogmas of our creed I believe in is – fraternity with which you may couple equality. My God never decreed that farmers & their race should be esteemed beyond the progeny of a fishmonger & strange to say Christ – the founder of our creed – selected the missionaries of his noble teaching from amongst fishmongers. Do you really think that the Christ who honoured & made friendship with Zebedee the fishmonger's son would disdain the acquaintance of a poor toiling fishmonger's daughter . . . To tell you plain truth I thought there was more humanity in you than to be led away by such silly notions.

My preference for you rather than for those girls arises not from any social distinctions – these I have the utmost contempt for – but it arises entirely from your superiority in many endearing qualities.

He goes on to criticise her debating tactics, demolishing her arguments as if he was facing a particularly inept prosecutor in court:

And now, honestly, don't you think you have chosen the most inopportune moment for your outburst . . . even if it were a very improper & wicked thing to listen to the song of a fishmonger's daughter – it is now about a month since I heard the chime of her voice – except in chapel. You are like Blucher of Waterloo – you only appear on the field when the enemy has fled . . . I will admit your letter is a clever piece of special pleading. You have picked up disjointed tit-bits from one story and shown that in conjunction with a rag from another story it bears such & such a colour. You have been mixing colours & then accuse me with being responsible for the hideousness of the resulting picture. Very clever you know but scarcely candid.

Then comes the most crucial passage in all the letters of Lloyd George and Maggie's long courtship. He lays out in an entirely unambiguous way what he expects of her as his wife, the terms on which their future lives are to be lived, and his ambition as both lawyer and politician:

You very fiercely suggest that possibly I have committed a blunder in my selection. Well, I do make mistakes often, but as a rule it does not take me two years to find them out. And besides . . . my ideas as to the qualifications of a wife do not coincide with yours. You seem to think that the supreme function of a wife is to amuse her husband – to be to him a kind of toy or plaything to enable him to while away with enjoyment his leisure hour. Frankly, that is simply prostituting marriage. My ideas are very different – if not superior – to yours. I am of opinion that woman's function is to soothe & sympathise & not to amuse. Men's lives are a perpetual conflict. The life I have mapped out will be so especially – as lawyer & politician. Woman's function is to pour oil on the wounds – to heal bruises of spirit received in past conflicts & to stimulate to renewed exertion. Am I not right? If I am then you are pre-eminently the girl for me. I have a thorough belief in your kindliness and affection.

With stunning clarity and disarming honesty, Lloyd George outlines his firm, lifelong philosophy for Maggie to accept or reject: her role would be to 'soothe and sympathise', to be the companion of his hearth and to heal his wounds after each battle. She need not worry about amusing him: his words contain just a hint of a suggestion that he could – and would – find his playthings elsewhere.

With all the facts laid out, he challenges Maggie to make her decision:

As to setting you free, that is a matter for your choice & not mine. I have many times impressed upon you that the only bond by which I have any desire to hold you is that of love. If that be lost then I would snap any other bond with my own hand. Hitherto my feelings are those of unflinching love for you & that feeling is a growing one.

You ask me to choose – I have made my choice deliberately & solemnly. I must now ask you to make your choice. I know my slanderers – those whom you allow to poison your mind against me. Choose between them & me – there can be no other alternative.

He concludes his case with the confidence of an advocate whose victory is assured, but his anxiety as to her answer shows, if only in the pleading postscript:

May I see you at 7 tomorrow? Drop me a note will you. I would like to have a thorough talk with you. We must settle this miserable squabble once & for all.[28]

This time, after deploying all his courtroom eloquence, the field was his, and Maggie finally accepted a diamond cluster ring as a formal token of their betrothal.

When she allowed Lloyd George to place the ring upon her finger she accepted more than just his word that he was faithful to her: she accepted his definition of her role as his wife. This was to be a defining moment in Maggie's life, but it is far from clear how well she understood the deal she was accepting. She can have been in no doubt as to the strength of Lloyd George's ambition, for he literally spelled it out for her, but even so, did she really understand how far he wanted to go, and in which direction? In later life she was to acknowledge her naïvety in this respect in an interview: 'I thought I was marrying a Caernarvonshire lawyer. Some people even then said he was sure to get on, but it was success as a lawyer that they had in mind. I am sure neither of us guessed then what lay before us.'[29]

Most commentators have interpreted her words as retrospective self-justification for her refusal to leave Criccieth for London – if she did not know at the outset that he was set on becoming a politician, she could not be accused of subsequent unreasonableness or lack of support for her husband. But in view of the rift that beset their marriage later, it is worth pausing to consider exactly what future Maggie thought she was accepting.

Maggie must have known of Lloyd George's ambition to become a Member of Parliament, for as we have seen, he briefly considered becoming a candidate in the 1886 election. This does not necessarily mean, though, that she understood what being the wife of an MP involved. Maggie Owen led a sheltered life at Mynydd Ednyfed, and her knowledge of politics was filtered through either her father or her fiancé, neither of whom was very keen to talk to her about such matters. She could not have known much about what being married to an MP was like. Furthermore, the nature of the job itself was changing at that very point in history, with MPs who regarded their parliamentary roles as status-enhancing, albeit unpaid, sinecures giving way to a more professional political class.

In 1887 that change was only beginning to show in North Wales, and local MPs had hitherto managed to keep a fairly constant presence in Caernarvonshire as well as to carry out their parliamentary duties. Surely it was reasonable for Maggie Owen to assume that she would continue to live in Criccieth while her husband pursued his ambition and 'got on' in Westminster? There is no evidence in their letters that they ever discussed the details of their future life, or that she ever gave him an undertaking that she would leave Criccieth for London. Also, if Maggie failed to anticipate how high her husband would climb, she was not alone, since his eventual success was unprecedented. If in the full flush of her first serious love affair she chose not to look too far ahead, and to take the future on trust, how far is she to be blamed?

From her rare public comments, it seems that Maggie never envisaged leaving her beloved Criccieth for good. It would have been entirely out of character for her to do so, and would make her later behaviour inexplicable. But she did accept the wifely role that her future husband described. She would help him through the 'perpetual conflict' of his life. It was an essentially submissive role: she was to be the companion of his hearth, the comfort to which he returned each night. For better or worse, she would be Mrs Lloyd George.

5

Mrs Lloyd George

Persuading Maggie to accept his ring was one thing, but getting her mother to accept their relationship was quite another, as Lloyd George was to discover. In the early months of 1887 the outlook was indeed bleak. Lloyd George was not allowed near Mynydd Ednyfed, and the lovers still had to meet in secret. The situation in Morvin House was no better: Lloyd George did not dare tell his mother about the relationship, and to confide in Uncle Lloyd was out of the question. But Lloyd George was not easily deterred. Throughout his life he had found that if he worked hard and used his head, the things he wanted tended to fall into his lap, and although he was frequently frustrated at the slow progress of his courtship, he never once admitted the possibility of defeat.

As a boy, Lloyd George was fond of reading military history. He saw each challenge in his own life as a battle to be won, and, as befits a future war leader, his long campaign to be married to Maggie Owen was planned and executed with determination and precision. In his diary, he reveals his strategy: 'Find I can always work much better for an immediate defined object than for a remote possible one – so think it advisable to have fixed time.'[1]

Since the previous summer Lloyd George had concentrated on winning Maggie's heart. Now, in the next phase of the campaign, he was intent on winning her hand. His goal was to persuade Richard Owen to give him permission to marry his daughter, who, still only twenty years old, could not legally marry without her parents' consent.

Maggie loved her parents dearly, and was in all respects a dutiful daughter. Lloyd George knew that it would cause her great unhappiness to go against their express wishes in a matter as important as marriage. For that reason also he needed their agreement to the match, and he knew that the main problem was not likely to be the doting father, but his fiercely judgemental wife.

The breach of promise case involving Ann and Lizzie Jones had indeed caused all the local rumours about Lloyd George to resurface, as Maggie had predicted. On 22 March he wrote gloomily in his diary: 'It appears that Misses Roberts of Bronygadair and Ystwellgu have been reviling me to Mrs Owen – tllg her that they are surprised how I could stand in my shoes [with Maggie] when I had been courting "merch Nansi Penwaig" [Nancy Herring's daughter].' But he turned the situation to his advantage, taking the opportunity to move towards his next goal: 'Told her that if her parents continued to nag at her in that style that the only way to put an end to it was to get married.'[2]

Maggie was not to be manipulated so easily: her mother's objections hit home, especially since she was already worried about Lloyd George's flirting. Lloyd George knew that he needed to win over the disapproving Mrs Owen, and since he was not allowed to approach her himself, he would have to rely on impressing people close to her who could plead his case.

His first and most devoted advocate was Maggie herself, and Lloyd George had for many months been coaching his sweetheart on how to manage her mother. Back in November the previous year he had been half-jokingly feeding her excuses to slip out to meet him, and had even felt in a strong enough position to poke fun at Mrs Owen's obstinacy: 'I send you herewith a formal ticket of invitation to the lecture . . . You can square your mother by reminding her that Mr Williams is one of the etholedigion [the elect – i.e. a Calvinistic Methodist] & that Griffydd ap Cynan was an eminent Methodist divine who flourished before Christ & in fact initiated him into the true principles of Calvinism. That ought to propitiate her.'

Again, when he had received letters from T.E. Ellis, his friend who had been elected MP for Merioneth in 1886 and who was a respectable Methodist, he wrote:

I enclose the two last letters I received from T. Ellis. It would do your mother good to read these letters as it will bring home to her mind that it is not perhaps essential to even good Methodism that you should taboo other sectarians. Darllenwch nhw i'ch mam bendith tad i chi [Read them to your mother, for goodness' sake]. She'll pull as wry a face as if she were drinking a gallon of assafatida [a popular but pungent herbal remedy]. Did you tell her what a scandal she has created about us throughout Lleyn?[3]

Lloyd George's humorous tone was becoming tinged with exasperation; he was not used to facing opposition as determined as this, and in Mrs Owen he very nearly met his match. But he had no equal in persistence. Shortly after giving Maggie her ring, when he was called to London at short notice he set her a tricky task to accomplish during his absence:

Remember to behave in my absence 'fel pe byddwn bresenol yn y corph' [as if I were present in the flesh] as I shall be 'yn yr ysbryd' [in spirit]. Redeem your faithful promise to show your mother the token of our engagement. You may also should you deem it prudent (this I leave to your discretion) arrange an appointment for me to discuss matters with your father mother or any or either or both of them.

That's a good week's work (for you) – I have cut out for you.

With sincerest love . . .

It seems that Maggie did not find the courage to approach her parents during his absence – or decided that there was no point in doing so – and it was to be many months before she and Lloyd George could even meet at her home, let alone have her parents' blessing to marry.

A few pages later in the carbon letter-book in which lie copies of all Lloyd George's letters is a draft letter to Miss Roberts, Ynysgain, urging her despite her illness to keep an engagement for tea at Mynydd Ednyfed. Dorothy Roberts was a cousin of the Owens, and Lloyd George had been courting her good opinion almost as assiduously as he had courted Maggie's. Miss Roberts lived some way outside Criccieth, and was therefore less influenced by the gossip surrounding Lloyd George's love life. Despite being well established in middle age, she was in an excellent position to advise Maggie. The two were great friends, and Maggie confided her innermost feelings to her cousin. Miss Roberts was a frequent visitor to Mynydd Ednyfed, and could help soften Mrs Owen's opposition to the match, so Lloyd George decided to launch a full-blown charm offensive.

He began to call on Miss Roberts frequently as he attempted to persuade her of the strength of feeling between himself and Maggie. Before long, Dorothy Roberts had fallen for his charm, and not only spoke favourably of him to Mary Owen, but also helped shore up Maggie's courage as she faced her parents' disapproval. According to Lloyd George and Maggie's eldest son, Dick, 'It was her aunt [i.e. Dorothy Roberts] who stiffened her backbone and helped her to follow the dictates of her heart in the face of her parents' violent opposition.'[4] Dorothy advised Maggie to put love ahead of family, chapel and politics. This might sound excessively romantic, but it was based on thorough knowledge of the characters involved, and was of course exactly what Maggie wanted to hear.

Another of Lloyd George's supporters was also female. For some time, Lloyd George had found the 'post office', where he and Maggie left notes for each other, troublesome. The problem was that they could not be sure that the notes would reach their recipient quickly. When Maggie could not get away, or Lloyd George's work sent him on an unexpected journey, letters often failed to reach them in time, and Lloyd George's frustration grew with each mishap. He needed a go-between, someone who had access to Maggie, and so he began to work his charm on the Mynydd Ednyfed maid, Margiad.

Margiad was a steadfast but canny character whose devotion to her mistress, Mary Owen, was surpassed only by her fierce loyalty to Maggie, whom she had helped to raise. In the early stages of the courtship she was sent out to the lane by Mrs Owen to tell Lloyd George not to wait around for Maggie, and she also carried the message that he was not a welcome visitor to Mynydd Ednyfed. Lloyd George knew exactly how to get around a country girl like Margiad, though, and soon the two were conspiring together to persuade Maggie to slip away from under her mother's nose. It was quite a feat to transfer Margiad's loyalty from her employer to himself: Lloyd George's attractiveness to women, it seems, was nearly universal – only his future mother-in-law remained impervious.

As the year wore on, Lloyd George made little progress. Maggie had got over the breach of promise case, but her jealousy was sharpened, and Lloyd George was frequently admonished for his flirtatious behaviour: 'Got a lecturing from Maggie very strong about Tymawr girls. Wrote her a long reply in evening.' And again: 'long altercation . . . made up in the end as usual. "Love quarrels oft in pleasing concord end" quite true, fortunately, Mr Milton.'[5]

At the same time, Lloyd George was making sure that he had the support of his own family – at least, of those members of it in whom he could confide. This was vitally important, since he was relying on the Morvin House family to support him financially when, as he fully expected, his political career took off. The first step had been to persuade William to leave Breese, Jones & Casson to join Lloyd George's fledgling practice. William had asked Mr Casson for permission to leave in 1886, but Casson saw no reason to help a rival firm, and refused. This was perhaps just as well. The atmosphere at work was difficult for William since his brother had started competing with his employer for cases, but without access to the firm's legal textbooks he would have been hard pressed to pass his finals. He took his final examinations in May 1887, and there was much celebration in Morvin House when he passed with first class honours.* After qualifying William was released from his articles and promptly left to join his brother. The plaque on the door of Morvin House was changed to read 'Lloyd George & George', and from that point onwards Lloyd George had a diligent and tireless business partner in his younger brother.

Polly too had to be kept on side, since Lloyd George would have to tell his mother and Uncle Lloyd about his relationship with Maggie sooner or later, and he would need her as an ally. He confided in her regularly, and in April told her of his plans to marry before waiting the five years she had advised, providing he could pay off his debts to Uncle Lloyd:

Walked after dinner MEG past Ynysgain Fawr. Told her my ideas as to getting married, that I wanted to pay Uncle his £200 first and then

---

* Lloyd George, distracted by his political activities, had managed only a third class honours degree.

directly I am remunerated another £300 – told her that if I were to complete matters in hand, I should probably get about £500 for them, and that W.G. could collect them in about 6 months. She didn't in any way dissuade me but approved of the amount I had fixed so that perhaps after all my impulse had directed me wisely – persons most likely to disapprove don't do so . . . owing to other reasons the sooner I get married the better – it will steady me.[6]

Lloyd George's sums did not allow for the fact that he and Maggie had nowhere to live. This made it even more important to get the Owens' approval: he knew they would not allow their daughter to go without a roof over her head.

Through the spring of 1887 and into summer, Lloyd George continued to flirt, Maggie continued to upbraid him, and Mrs Owen continued to disapprove. Things could not go on as they were, and the month of August was to bring with it a few summer storms that would force matters to a head.

Given the strength of feeling of their families there was no question of either Maggie or Lloyd George converting to the other's denomination, so they had to find a compromise. They decided that it would be perfectly possible to maintain their own denominational loyalties within the marriage. In the spring they had started to attend services together at Capel Mawr, and Lloyd George soon realised it was not a happy place. Tension had been simmering under the surface for some time, caused by a proposal to offer services in English during the summer months for the benefit of the visitors to Criccieth. This led to a disagreement between those who equated the Calvinistic Methodist faith with Welsh-speaking patriotism and those who felt it was their duty to evangelise and reach out to those who came to join their community, even temporarily. The controversy widened to include all manner of other issues, and erupted into a full-blown crisis in August 1887, when the congregation divided into two implacable camps. The national governing body of the Calvinistic Methodist Church was eventually called in to adjudicate. Its decision was to allow a group of disaffected members, including the Rev. Owen, to establish their own separate chapel in Criccieth.

Maggie and her family found themselves in the middle of this painful wrangle. It was extremely difficult for Richard Owen to face the fact that the congregation was irretrievably divided, but when the time came he cast his lot with the Rev. Owen. Such was the strength of feeling among the dissenters that the considerable expense of a new building was borne rather than attempt a reconciliation with Capel Mawr. The whole family transferred their membership to the new chapel, Seion.

Political battles of this kind were irresistible to the young Lloyd George. As a non-member at Capel Mawr he was not able to participate directly, but he was not slow to spot an opportunity to use the row to his advantage. By publicly supporting the Rev. Owen, he was able – finally – to gain some currency with Richard Owen. This emboldened him to wonder if he should press his advantage and formally ask for Maggie's hand:

30 August. Bye the bye I am in a very queer state of mind upon this question [of marriage]. My urge is strong for a marriage straight away – say in [an] hour. On the other hand I am anxious that it should not come off until the spring at the earliest. Maggie I believe to be in a very similar state of mind but on the whole I think she wd. prefer the earlier date. However my present view is that prudence dictates spring as the date & I rather imagine that the event will be postponed to that season. I shd however like to be in a position to ask the old folks consent now. One very good reason for postponement is that there is no available house for one's residence – except Cefniwrch which neither of us cares for. The only thing to be said for it is this, that if it so be let furnished for a short period we might have another house by the end of that period. It is when I am with Maggie that I find myself most anxious for marriage. Her society has a wonderful charm for me & I believe she now much prefers me to her parents. She will tell me so occasionally.[7]

There is no doubt that Lloyd George was charmed by Maggie's company – but trouble still occurred when he was out of her sight. Through the summer she still found reason to take him to task for flirting with other girls, and the subject became a constant source of friction between them. In July, Lloyd George wrote to Maggie from Trefriw near Llanrwst, where he was staying with a friend:

> Don't imagine angry things about me, – that's a pet. I shall redeem all misbehaviour yet. Believe me, though I am bodily in the coffee room of the Belle Vue Hotel Trefriw with Parry Pwllheli by my side assiduously inditing a letter to one of his numerous sweethearts I am in mind at M[ynydd Ednyfed] with my sweetheart by me. I swear by the pen which I now hold in my hand that I shall not flirt nor even wink improperly at a girl. Parry is my surety as to that.[8]

Maggie was unlikely to be reassured by the fact that Parry, with his 'numerous sweethearts', was responsible for keeping Lloyd George in line, but neither did she realise the full, obvious implication of his continual flirting: while she was with him he resisted casual flirtations, but when they were apart he was unable to be faithful.

In a letter from the same period, there is a tantalising hint that Maggie may have tried to bring Lloyd George to heel with a little flirting of her own. This was disastrous. He retaliated triumphantly that she had now given him an excuse for all his indiscretions: 'Your letter . . . will justify all my flirtations for the past – and future [these two words were added as an afterthought] – and teach me how to gloss them over when caught.'[9] She could not say she had not been warned.

The Capel Mawr controversy had a special resonance for the Owen family because Richard and Mary Owen had at one time hoped that Capel Mawr's young minister would eventually be their son-in-law. Lloyd George was not aware of this at first, but over the summer Maggie confessed to him that she had received three offers of marriage, and that one of her suitors was the Rev. Owen. Secure in her affection, Lloyd George felt that this showed becoming modesty in his future wife, and recorded proudly in his diary: 'Cannot help admiring the honour and lack of brag which caused the girl not to show these letters to me ere this.'[10]

After a lull of many months Lloyd George was back on track and escalating his campaign to get a wedding date fixed. Having gained a strategic advantage with the Owens at last, he pressed his case. The first objective was to be allowed to visit Maggie openly, for, six months into their engagement, Mrs Owen would still not allow him across the threshold of her house, nor would she give Maggie permission to meet him elsewhere. The couple had to meet in the dead of night, which must have been tiring as well as somewhat ridiculous. Lloyd George's midnight roving had not gone unnoticed at home. Uncle Lloyd was still in the dark with regard to his nephew's relationship with Maggie, but he had noticed his night-time excursions. Suspecting the worst, Richard Lloyd had taken to wandering the streets of Criccieth asking if anyone had seen him, so it was more important than ever for Lloyd George to be able to meet Maggie during civilised hours. In the meantime he did the best he could by hiding his uncle's boots before leaving the house so that the old man could not follow.

Feeling more confident now that he was on better terms with Mr Owen, Lloyd George chose to go on the offensive and bully Maggie into confronting her mother:

> Long talk as to my night visits. Told her that I was not enamoured of them especially as my uncle seemed to feel them so sorely – but they were our only resource since her mother was not civilized enough to permit my visiting her during decent hours. I suggested that she shd. tell her mother that I intended to come up at 8 every evening & she said that she had been thinking of the same thing, that she was thoroughly tired of our midnight meetings as they involved a sense of transgressing respectable rules. She finally promised to tell her mother on Monday without fail. She may do so.[11]

Lloyd George was not absolutely sure that she would go through with it, but Maggie was not lacking in courage, and she resented the indignity and the impropriety of the midnight meetings too. She was also getting thoroughly tired of being caught in the middle between her mother and her lover: 'My parents are angry with me one day and you another. I am on bad terms with one or the other continually . . . Well I am very miserable, that is all I have to say, Dearest Dei,* and I hope things won't be long as they are now.'[12]

---

* Maggie variously addressed Lloyd George in writing as 'D', Dei, or 'Die', all abbreviations of 'David'.

This time, perhaps feeling short of friends as a result of the Capel Mawr rift, or perhaps responding at last to their daughter's pleas, the Owens relented. Mrs Owen made a half-hearted attempt to limit Lloyd George's visits to three a week, but she must have known that she had been utterly defeated. With Lloyd George comfortably ensconced in her parlour from eight till ten each evening, it was only a matter of time before she would have to agree to a wedding.

By October, the issue was not *if* Lloyd George and Maggie would be married, but where and how. Lloyd George turned his mind to how to announce his engagement to his own mother and uncle. The denominational difference was likely to be an even greater obstacle to his own family than it was for the Owens, since even the strict rules of the Calvinistic Methodists did not live up to the puritanical standards of the Disciples of Christ. The prospect of their Davy, the golden boy of the family, marrying into another denomination was bound to cause a great upset. Lloyd George's regard and respect for his uncle's judgement was still strong, and he wrote in his diary in October: 'We had a good talk about marriage. We arranged to get married soon – provided my uncle did not upon my talking the matter over with him show good cause to the contrary.'[13]

November 1887 came, and with it a significant milestone. On the fourth Maggie reached her twenty-first birthday, and her parents could no longer legally prevent her from marrying, although they could still withhold their blessing. They could only ask the young couple to respect their wishes, arguing that there were still practical reasons why the wedding could not take place yet. Lloyd George wrote in his diary on 1 November:

> I then had a talk with Mr & Mrs Owen – they pleaded for delay – that they had made up their minds not to stay at Mynydd Ednyfed . . . but that they could not get anything like a good price for the stock these bad times . . . that if they sold their things under value it would be our loss in the end – they wished us to wait for a yr. or so – that we were quite young &c . . . I thought the old man very cunningly tried to persuade me to delay by showing me it was in my own interest . . . I told them when [Richard Owen] said something about money that

I wanted no money as I had of course before coming to that point seen that I wd. have sufficient myself without any extraneous aid (I am not sure whether it would have been better to plead poverty – but I wanted to show them that I took no commercial views of my engagement). The interview ended by their asking me to reconsider the matter & see them again about it.[14]

With matters having reached this advanced stage, it was time for Lloyd George to steel himself to tell his invalid mother that he would soon be leaving home. He was careful to make sure that Polly was on hand with plenty of praise for Maggie, but this was not enough to soften the blow, and he recorded in his diary how upset Betsy was on hearing the news: 'the poor old woman cried and said she felt my leaving very much. She then gave me some very good advice about being kind to Maggie, never saying anything nasty to her when I lost my temper, to be attentive to her if & when she was ill, that sort of thing. She praised M. very much from what she had heard from M.E.G. [Polly].'[15]

In her weakened, dependent state Betsy could not bear the thought of either of her sons marrying. She would have been upset even if Lloyd George were marrying a Baptist, but he knew that it would not be as easy to gloss over the chapel issue with Uncle Lloyd. For the meantime therefore he decided to say nothing to the old man until the very last minute, when all the arrangements for the wedding were in place.

At the end of November the Owens were still refusing to give the couple their blessing, but they finally gave in to Maggie's pleading over Christmas – the denominational mismatch was such a serious matter that they had to formally consult Seion's deacons before acknowledging the engagement. They began to bargain with Lloyd George over the location and form of the ceremony. Richard Owen would not hear of his daughter being married in a Baptist chapel, and Lloyd George knew that his uncle would not countenance a Methodist wedding. Two things were clear: a compromise would have to be found, and since neither family would be in a mood to celebrate, the wedding had better take place at a distance from Criccieth. Lloyd George argued strongly for Capel-y-Beirdd, a Baptist chapel three miles away, but Richard Owen had been defeated on every count thus far, and insisted on having his way with regard to the location. Lloyd George's diary records his frustration: 'The old folk still very adverse [sic] to going to Capel y Beirdd. Their hostility due in a great measure to a silly pride quite as much as to religious bigotry. I am inclined to get stiff about the matter. I would not care a rap where to get married, were it not that I am going out of my way to cater for sectarian pride and bigotry.'[16]

Richard Owen finally decided that the wedding should take place at the Calvinistic Methodist chapel at Pencaenewydd, and would brook no opposition. Lloyd George knew when to give in gracefully, and at last a date was set. Maggie and he would be married on 24 January 1888.

Pencaenewydd is a tiny hamlet hidden in the hills five miles inland from Criccieth. It is about as obscure a location for a wedding as could be found – hardly the natural choice for the popular Criccieth belle Maggie Owen. Richard Owen was signalling his disapproval as clearly as he could.

Finally, the time had come for Lloyd George to tell Uncle Lloyd that he was to be married, and to present him with the *fait accompli* of the wedding arrangements. He waited until 9 January, only two weeks before the ceremony he hoped his uncle would conduct, and, balking at witnessing the reaction of his guardian and mentor, he asked Betsy to break the news. Disappointing Richard Lloyd was one of the hardest things that Lloyd George had had to do in his life: he had never forgotten how much he owed his uncle, and marrying a non-Baptist was a poor way to repay him. He did not usually shirk difficult tasks, and his diary entries betray his nervous feelings as he approached this, the last hurdle of all: 'Mam told Uncle today that I propose getting married in a fortnight – he seemed to feel it but said nothing except that he hoped we would go through the business without any fuss.'

Uncle Lloyd's love for his nephew overcame his disappointment, and by the following day good relations were restored: 'Told Uncle my reasons for not telling him before – he took it very well . . . He said that everyone told him my little girl was a charming and sensible lassie. He told us to learn steadiness, domesticity and unselfishness etc; warned me that I was entering in to a new family, and must adapt myself to its proclivities – excellent advice – feel much relieved after telling him.'[17]

Richard Lloyd had only a passing acquaintance with Maggie, but he could see that Lloyd George was quite determined, and whatever his private feelings, he accepted the match. In his diary he wrote that evening: 'Mae pawb yn dweud ei bod yn eneth fwyn, synhwyrol ac yn eneth ddefnyddiol' (Everyone says that she is a lovely sensible girl, and a practical girl).[18] He agreed to conduct the ceremony, only stipulating that he would prefer the wedding to be as simple and unshowy as possible. In this respect, he was at one with Richard and Mary Owen.

When the news of the impending marriage became known, Maggie and Lloyd George were at last able to formalise their courtship. Given its clandestine nature, he had not had a chance to get used to acknowledging such a serious relationship in public. In addition, they had only a few days in which to make the wedding arrangements. On 19 January Lloyd George went to Pwllheli to take out a marriage licence, and it was then that the importance of the commitment he was about to enter hit him: 'Never felt so queer. It was then I began to thoroughly realize what I was doing and I felt quite stunned tho' without an atom of repentance or regret.'[19]

He was seemingly in the same frame of mind when he went away with some friends for a half-hearted stag weekend: 'Drove to Rhyl with Howell Gee and Alun Lloyd – either I was in an extra serious mood owing to coming events or the company indulged in hilarity which I did not appreciate, for I did not enjoy myself – They drank, smoked and played billiards, and flirted with giddy barmaids.'[20]

It was with trepidation that Lloyd George finally approached his wedding day.

West of Llanystumdwy, a narrow road snakes its way inland into the heart of the Llŷn Peninsula, passing through the quiet hamlet of Pencaenewydd before meandering onwards. The village consists of a few farms and cottages and a pair of solid, semi-detached houses separated from the road by their well-kept gardens. Set further back from the road is a Calvinistic Methodist chapel, a plain, unremarkable stone building with a pair of tall, narrow arched windows overlooking the road. It is now a private residence but still bears a simple slate plaque with the words 'Pencaenewydd M.C. 1822' inscribed upon it.

It was there that David Lloyd George and Richard Lloyd made their way on the cold morning of Tuesday, 24 January 1888. They set off early, leaving Criccieth on the 7.15 train to Chwilog, five miles away. There they were met by Myrddin Fardd (the poet John Jones), a long-standing family friend, and they breakfasted with him before walking the three miles to Pencaenewydd. As they approached, a heavy mist shower began, as if to further dampen the mood. No other family members joined them for the ceremony. This was principally out of respect for Uncle Lloyd's request for a quiet wedding. Whatever their private feelings on the matter, Betsy, Polly and William went about their business as usual on this momentous day.

At 10.15 the bridegroom entered the chapel and waited for his bride. He had just turned twenty-five years old, and had grown into a handsome young man, slim and carefully turned out, with a fashionable handlebar moustache adorning his upper lip. He wore the long frock-coat of the period, a waistcoat and a tie beneath a starched wing collar. His most striking features were his lively, intensely blue eyes, which on that morning could be forgiven for wearing a rather anxious expression. Maggie at twenty-one was very attractive; pretty rather than beautiful, but with calm blue eyes in a rounded face, compact features and a trim figure. They would make a good-looking couple.

The bride and her father arrived in the Mynydd Ednyfed carriage, accompanied by the Rev. John Owen. Maggie's former suitor was there at Richard Owen's insistence, for, notwithstanding any possible awkwardness, he had been asked to jointly preside over the ceremony, adding just a little bit more Methodism to placate the bride's family.* A second carriage drew up containing members of the Owen family – Mary Owen almost certainly, and perhaps Dorothy Roberts too – and they took their places inside the small chapel. The ceremony was conducted by Richard Lloyd, with prayers and a reading by John Owen. It went without a hitch, and the newlyweds were pelted with rice as they left in a carriage, bound for a short honeymoon in London.

---

* The Rev. Owen's feelings about the day's proceedings are not recorded, but he later returned a postal order that Lloyd George sent him in recognition of his services, with a generously worded letter saying: 'I never accept anything for marrying and burying people, nor for christening children, and I certainly would not break the rule with a couple of friends. Should either of you feel desirous of being properly buried I shall stick to my rule, or should any christenings be unavoidable in your family the terms will be the same . . . Wishing you both long life and real happiness, and with my kindest regards to Mrs George and yourself . . .'

At long last the deed was done, and Lloyd George and Maggie were married. Later that day he wrote in his diary: 'I am very glad the whole business is over – Never felt so anxious.'[21] Richard Lloyd's comment in his diary was simply: 'May Heaven make it to Dei and his Maggie a very bright <u>red letter day</u>.'[22]

6

From Wales to Westminster

Uncle Lloyd and Richard Owen may have wanted minimal fuss over the wedding, but Criccieth was determined to celebrate. As the newlyweds sped by train to London a bonfire was lit, fireworks set off and the whole town draped in bunting and flags to mark the wedding of two of its most popular young citizens. The greyness of the skies failed to deter the organisers, and although the suggestion was made that they should postpone celebrations until the couple returned from honeymoon this was rejected, since it was equally likely that the weather would be unfavourable then.

Lloyd George and the new Mrs Lloyd George spent a week enjoying the sights of London, no doubt relieved that the long-anticipated wedding had finally happened. But even on honeymoon, Lloyd George's ambition did not allow him to stop working. He wrote a letter to D.R. Daniel, a political associate, from his London hotel, failing even to mention the wedding. What is yet more astounding is that this letter followed one that he had written on his actual wedding day, presumably before setting out from Morvin House at daybreak. He did at least make a passing reference to the significance of the day in that letter, but only in a brief and very oblique way: 'yr ydwyf am gychwyn i wlad bell – gwell hefyd, disgwyliaf' (I am about to set off for a far distant land – and a better one too, I expect).[1]

Lloyd George did not neglect Maggie, though, and together they made the most of the opportunities London offered, seeing a varied selection of the theatrical entertainment on offer – *Hamlet, Puss in*

Boots and Gilbert and Sullivan's *HMS Pinafore*. The only incident that marred an otherwise happy time was an altercation between Lloyd George and a cab driver over a fare. The two nearly came to blows, but Maggie intervened.

Mr and Mrs David Lloyd George arrived safely back in Criccieth on 3 February to an enthusiastic welcome from a crowd of well-wishers. Mr Owen's carriage was waiting at the station, and in a scene that would have been unimaginable only a few months previously, Lloyd George was borne back to Mynydd Ednyfed – where it had been decided that the couple would live at first – not as a guest, but as a member of the family. The disputes that had threatened the engagement were put aside, and Lloyd George's diary entry for the night of their return shows his relief at the warm reception he received: 'Mrs Owen very pleased to see us. Felt very awkward this first night at Mynydd Ednyfed. Both Mr. and Mrs. O were however very kind and assisted us to feel as homely as possible.'[2]

For Maggie, this arrangement was ideal. She was able to resume life with her beloved parents and almost-as-beloved maid, Margiad. She lived, as before, in her childhood home, but with the welcome addition of her handsome husband. Her parents made every effort to get on with the new member of the family, and having forgiven him for winning their daughter's hand, quickly came to appreciate the qualities that appealed to her so strongly. Whenever Maggie was with Lloyd George in London over the following years, Richard Owen wrote a weekly letter with all the news from Mynydd Ednyfed, addressed affectionately to 'Annwyl Blant' (Dear Children), and at home he worked hard to promote his son-in-law's political career. Had he realised how quickly Lloyd George would put aside his marriage vows, and how soon his political activities would give him the opportunity to stray, perhaps the welcome would not have been so warm.

The first months of marriage were golden for Maggie. She was a good-humoured young woman, naturally disposed to be happy, and had been very distressed by the endless quarrels of the previous months. Now she could live again as the pampered daughter of Mynydd Ednyfed while at the same time enjoying married life. To add to her happiness, she took pride in the professional success of her new husband. Each time he won a case or achieved public praise for his oratory she would carefully cut out the press reports and paste them in a scrapbook. A letter she wrote to him soon after the wedding is full of affection and contentment:

> My dearest Die,
> ... I was very glad to hear that the case was partly heard yesterday & I fully trust that you will be able to return home Sunday morning. I will stop at home to expect you, so come up straight, will you? ... Mother & I were at Morvin House last night, we had a cup of coffee before going home. You didn't relish the going away without a few minutes with your Mag, so I was told. Well neither did I. If it had been possible I would have been at the station in no time, but there was no chance.[3]

Living with her parents may have appealed strongly to Maggie at the time, but it was probably not the wisest start to the young couple's married life. A more definitive separation from her family might have given Maggie a better chance of learning about being a wife. At Mynydd Ednyfed, Mary Owen ran the household. Maggie was allowed to avoid all but the tasks she truly enjoyed: mainly gardening, which was a life-long passion. She had never embraced the traditionally feminine skills: her school reports confirm that although she was a very good student in all other subjects, she was only 'fair' when it came to domestic science and simple sewing.[4] She was neglectful of the more mundane aspects of housekeeping, and never seemed to get the hang of daily tasks such as lighting fires. This did not matter at Mynydd Ednyfed, where Mary and the servants attended to such things, but it became a bigger issue between Maggie and her husband later on.

Lloyd George was as fond of his creature comforts as Maggie was careless of them. He had been raised by extremely capable women whose first priority had been his comfort and welfare. Lloyd George and Maggie were raised in an age when it was considered a wife's first duty to care for her husband and children. Maggie would prove to be superb at the latter, but she did not always attend as assiduously to the former. Lloyd George upbraided her from time to time for her lack of expertise in sewing and cooking, and they would often quarrel if he came home to an unlit hearth or an empty larder. But in the early days of their marriage it was not a cold hearth that awaited Lloyd George at the end of the day. His diary records his contentment when he returned home late one night to find that 'Maggie was lying on the hearth waiting for me,'[5] and in the summer following their wedding, Maggie found that she was expecting their first child.

The whole family rejoiced at the news, and Maggie was happy and contented during her pregnancy, which passed without complication. Her husband was working hard, and her letters to him while he was away on business or speaking at political gatherings are full of love:

> Your letter to hand this morning & many thanks to you for writing, as I did not expect a letter this morning till tomorrow & it was all the sweeter for that reason.
>
> I am afraid you won't come home till Thursday, will you? Unless Mr Meek says you must which would be a good thing from my point of view . . .
>
> I have no more to tell you, only that we are all alive and kicking here <u>all</u> of us mind you, hoping your cold is better. Let me know when to expect my sweetheart home, will you?
>
> Best love
> From your loving child* [&] wife
> Maggie

Maggie did not have to wait long for her faith in Lloyd George's ability to be justified. Only weeks after their wedding he took on a legal case that would put him on the first rung of the political ladder and make his name famous throughout Wales. He was asked to act in it partly because of his growing reputation for impressive performances in court, and partly because it coincided neatly with his political views, which were also becoming well known. The case concerned a prime example of the discrimination and injustice suffered by Welsh nonconformists at the hands of the English establishment; Lloyd George could not have devised a more appropriate peg on which to hang his political career.

The story began in 1864 when the parish church of Llanfrothen, a

---

* The word 'child' was added as an afterthought by the expectant mother.

village eight miles east of Criccieth, received the gift from a Mr and Mrs Owen of a small adjoining strip of land to be an extension of the graveyard. It was walled in, consecrated and used for burials over the following years. At the time all burials on church ground had to be held according to Anglican rites, a rule that was bitterly resented by nonconformists. In 1880, after a decade of fruitless attempts, the Liberal MP for Denbighshire, George Osborne Morgan, succeeded in passing an Act to allow nonconformists to conduct funerals in parish church-yards according to their own rites. The law was changed, but the Church of England was not going to give up its monopoly on burials without a fight.

The vicar of Llanfrothen was Rev. Richard Jones, a dyed-in-the-wool conservative who deeply resented the new Act and was determined to prevent its implementation, in his churchyard at least. Rev. Jones exam-ined the paperwork closely, decided that the Owens' land had not been properly transferred in 1864, and persuaded Mrs Owen to re-convey her gift to the Church, specifying that only Anglican burials were to be permitted in it. This meant that nonconformists in the parish either had to submit to being buried according to Church rites or be buried in a scrap of land used for the graves of suicides and other undesirables.

The situation came to an explosive head in April 1888, when Robert Roberts, an old quarryman and a nonconformist, died. He had speci-fied in his will that he wished to be buried next to his daughter, who had previously been buried in the Llanfrothen churchyard extension. The family arranged for a nonconformist funeral to be held, and to prevent this from happening, the Rev. Jones locked the churchyard gates and ordered the grave which had been prepared to be filled in. In desperation, Evan Roberts, the deceased's brother, turned to Lloyd George for advice. Lloyd George came to the conclusion that, since the churchyard extension had been used for burials since 1864, it was subject to the 1880 Burial Act, and therefore the Rev. Jones was acting illegally. He confidently advised the family to return to Llanfrothen, prise the gates open by force and conduct the funeral according to the deceased's wishes. Such open defiance of the Church was virtually unprecedented, and the case attracted widespread publicity.

The Rev. Jones was incensed, and sued the Roberts family for tres-pass. The case came before Porthmadoc County Court in May 1888, with Lloyd George acting for the defence. A jury of local people found in favour of the Roberts family, but in a breathtaking example of bias, the judge inaccurately recorded their verdict and ruled for the Church. Lloyd George refused to be beaten, and encouraged the family to appeal. The case came before the High Court in London in December 1888. Amid triumphant scenes that were reported widely in newspapers and celebrated throughout the length and breadth of Wales, the Lord Chief Justice overturned the previous judgement, awarded the family their costs and, for good measure, reprimanded the Porthmadoc judge for his conduct.

The commentators were virtually unanimous: Lloyd George had single-handedly challenged the persecutors of nonconformism and won justice for his people against the English-speaking establishment. The young lawyer from Criccieth was a hero.

Maggie was proud of her husband, who had proved to the world that he was principled, courageous and eloquent. Had she realised the full consequences of his notoriety, though, she might not have been so happy. The Liberal Party in Caernarvon Boroughs was selecting a candidate for the general election presumed to be forthcoming in 1892. Ten days or so after the Llanfrothen triumph they made their decision. Their candidate was Lloyd George, the hero of the hour.

Though he lived in a rural area of North Wales, the constituency which Lloyd George was to represent in Parliament for fifty-five years was comprised of the urban populations of six townships: Criccieth, Pwllheli, Nevin, Caernarvon, Bangor and Conway. It had around 4,000 registered voters out of a total population of nearly 29,000. The naturally Liberal populations of Criccieth, Pwllheli and Nevin were counterbalanced by the Church-dominated, largely Tory-voting citizens of the cathedral city of Bangor. The constituency could sometimes confound expectations, as had happened in the general election of 1886. The Liberals and their erstwhile colleagues the Liberal Unionists had swept the board in Wales, winning twenty-eight of the thirty-four parliamentary seats, but, presented with an unpopular Liberal candidate, Caernarvon Boroughs had elected the Tory Edmund Swetenham.

There is an element of luck in every successful political life, and it was Lloyd George's good fortune that there was an opportunity for him to be selected as a candidate in his home constituency so early in his career. He had worked hard to be in a position to be a credible candidate, serving as Secretary of the local Anti-Tithe League and launching a Liberal newspaper, *Udgorn Rhyddid* (Freedom's Trumpet) with some friends. Financially he was worse off after marrying than before, but perhaps his Llanfrothen victory had given him confidence that he could make a success of his law practice, or perhaps he simply could not bring himself to refuse an opportunity that might not come again for years. Having stood aside in 1886 he was not about to do so again, and after winning the nomination he prepared to wait – at least two years, he thought – for the next general election.

This was not at all to Maggie's liking. As she prepared for the birth of her first child, she might have been able to ignore Lloyd George's increasing preoccupation with politics, but when he accepted the candidacy for a seat that was winnable at the next election she could no longer do so. She tearfully tried to dissuade him from accepting, arguing that it was impractical for him to take on an unpaid job in London when they were expecting a baby and did not even have a house of their own. This was not unreasonable. A less ambitious man might have preferred to secure his family financially before launching himself into national politics. But Lloyd George had been raised to go as far as he could as early as he could. He took the view that his family would always provide for him, and he received encouragement from Morvin House. It was left to William George to worry about how the newly formed two-man legal practice could support two families with Lloyd George, at best, a part-time partner.

Lloyd George and Maggie's first child, Richard (known as Dick), was born on 15 February 1889 in the room in which Maggie herself was born. His parents' excitement was matched by his grandparents' delight. Richard and Mary Owen loved children and would play a large part in their grandchildren's lives, often taking care of them for weeks while their parents were in London. In happy anticipation of many more new arrivals, Richard Owen decided to retire from farming, and after realising his assets he built a pair of tall, semi-detached stone houses in Criccieth overlooking the bay. He and Mary would live in one, and Maggie and her family would be close at hand, next door.

This new arrangement was much more to Lloyd George's taste. Despite his improved relationship with his in-laws, there were signs that he was missing his personal freedom, and he was finding reasons for spending evenings away from Mynydd Ednyfed. This was, to an extent, justifiable, since as he was the Liberal candidate he needed to make himself known, and he was also working hard to build up his legal practice. He did not see the two as separate activities: to place himself in the best possible position at the time of the next general election, he had to develop his reputation as a public speaker, and following the Llanfrothen case, his court addresses were often reported in the press. During 1889 his law and political careers progressed in harmony, his success in court adding to his reputation as a rising political star. As an advocate he displayed the eloquence, the debating skill and the remarkable independence of mind that were to characterise the mature politician. He was at his best championing the rights of the people he had grown up with against the landowners, and he became famous for his audacious and aggressive challenges to any display of prejudice from the bench.

The impact of Lloyd George's behaviour was all the greater because the local JPs and judges would have expected a local solicitor to show due deference not only to their legal authority over him, but also because the landowners had grown accustomed to getting their own way where nonconformists were concerned. It might have been wise for Lloyd George to be a little less antagonistic towards the bench, but he had already left behind the thought of a career in law, and was playing to a wider audience than that in the courtroom. His clashes with the magistrates attracted valuable publicity, and his reputation as defender of the working man's rights helped his political career. He had nothing to lose in attacking the pompous, class-prejudiced magistrates who presided in court. They in turn did not know how to deal with the fearless young attorney who simply would not let them ride roughshod over the rights of the Welsh people.

Maggie was delighted by Lloyd George's growing fame as a lawyer, speaker and people's champion, but he was also becoming more established in the Liberal Party in Caernarvonshire, which was less to her liking. She did not join in any of his political activities, but she faithfully wrote to give him the political gossip during his business trips.

Early in 1889 she wrote: 'I am sorry to inform you that the most zealous person on the side of Cebol at Mynydd Ednyfed has turned round to canvass for Mr Graves. She is going to see these persons instead of Father. Old Cebol is very ill, poor fellow. Father thinks that if he gets in, he will jump out of bed like a shot, and should he lose will die poor fellow.'⁶

Maggie was referring to the local elections of January 1889, when, following the 1888 Local Government Reform Act, county councils were formed for the first time. The elections were the cause of much celebration in Wales, representing as they did the first wholesale transfer of local power from squires and magistrates to elected politicians. The voters of Caernarvonshire were not slow to take advantage of their opportunity. The Liberals were determined to maximise their representation on the new council, and took control with a handsome majority. Indeed, the Liberals took every county in Wales, with the exception of Brecon in the south. Naturally Lloyd George had been seen as a potential candidate, but his eyes were on the greater prize of Westminster. Nevertheless, he campaigned energetically throughout the county with the message that electing Liberal, Welsh-speaking nonconformists to the councils was a vital step along the road to self-government for Wales.

At the age of twenty-six, Lloyd George was already seen as one of the most able and prominent politicians in North Wales, and the newly formed council co-opted him to the position of Alderman, usually reserved for senior Councillors.* The co-option of the 'Boy Alderman' was widely reported; there was no doubt that Lloyd George's star was in the ascendancy.

In welcoming the results of the county elections, Lloyd George spelled out his desire for self-determination in Wales. As ever, he was at the forefront of the radical wing of the Liberals, stating in a speech in Liverpool in 1889: 'Those elections afforded the best possible test of the growth in Wales of the national movement, which, after all, is but a phase of the great Liberal movement.' The growing confidence of the

---

* Lloyd George's brother William would be elected Chairman of Caernarvonshire County Council in 1911, and in 1917 he too was co-opted as Alderman, a position he held until his death in 1967.

new political class in Wales was creating momentum for a campaign similar to that which Irish MPs were pressing for Home Rule. The young Lloyd George and his fellow radicals were impatient for self-determination, tired of having Wales' claims to Home Rule treated less seriously than those of Ireland. To the South Wales Liberal Federation in February 1890 he declared:

> Welsh Home Rule alone can bring within the reach of this generation the fruits of its political labours. Now it surpasses my imagination to conceive how persons who are ardent advocates of Irish Home Rule can discover any plausible reason for objecting to Welsh Home Rule ... For my own part, I cannot help believing that the prospects of Wales would be brighter and more promising were her destinies controlled by a people whose forefathers proved their devotion to her interests on a thousand battlefields with their hearts' blood, and a people who, despite the persecutions of centuries, have even to this very hour preserved her institutions and her tongue, and retained the same invincible love for her hills.[7]

With so many calls upon his time, one might have expected Lloyd George to save his leisure hours for his wife and young son. But the parlour of Mynydd Ednyfed was less attractive to him than the meetings of the local amateur dramatic society, where the company was congenial and he could indulge his love of oratory. He became a regular attendee at the society's private parlour meetings, and was able to indulge his love of female company at the same time. His son Dick later claimed that Lloyd George had an affair during this period with a widow in Caernarvon. The lady was identified only as 'Mrs J', a well-known Liberal activist and a popular member of Lloyd George's social circle. If this is true, his marital fidelity to Maggie lasted only a few months.

The revelation that Mrs J and Lloyd George were on intimate terms was apparently prompted by the sensational discovery that she was pregnant, which soon came to the attention of the leaders of the Liberal Association. Faced with the potential ruin of all his political hopes, Lloyd George had to ensure both that the scandal was ended before he could be deselected, and that Maggie did not find out about it. With Mrs J's cooperation, he succeeded on both counts. Dick writes that she accepted an annuity for life with the condition that no documentary evidence or photographs of the child ever came to light.

Dick's colourful account of his father's love life has been rightly viewed with a degree of scepticism, since he had reason to be angry with his father. When the book was published in 1960 Lloyd George was long dead, and a rift between them had led to him disinheriting his firstborn. Furthermore, Dick was by then a sick man who needed money, and some say he was well remunerated for his sensational material, and that the book was actually ghost-written. The book contains many rumours of affairs. Dick concluded that his father was 'probably the greatest natural Don Juan in the history of British politics', and that 'With an attractive woman he was as much to be trusted as a Bengal tiger with a gazelle.'[8]

But the story of the affair with Mrs J gains credibility from Lady Olwen Carey Evans, Lloyd George's third child, who mentions the Caernarvon widow in her own autobiography. Olwen was in her nineties when her memoir (also ghost-written) was published in 1985, but unlike Dick she had maintained a good relationship with her father. More to the point, she was a sensible and level-headed woman who neither worshipped nor reviled her father. To a greater extent than any of his other children, she was immune to the glamour of his personality, and was better able to judge his strengths and weaknesses. Her book deals with his womanising in a matter-of-fact way, describing his lifelong weakness for women while emphasising also the strength of his marriage: 'Although it was not until after I married that Mother ever mentioned Father's infidelities to me, I was aware from an early age that there were other women in his life . . . I believe Father started having affairs with other women very soon after my parents were married.'[9]

Given the lack of hard evidence for many of Lloyd George's rumoured affairs, it has been suggested that there is an element of myth in his reputation as a womaniser. It is true that he covered his tracks well, and no indisputable evidence has been uncovered to link him with any illegitimate offspring. No mistress has confessed publicly to a liaison apart from his second wife, Frances, and during his life he won every court case involving his personal life. But everyone who knew Lloyd George well acknowledged this side of his character, and the testimony of his closest confidants, his family and his political colleagues must carry significant weight. From the wives of his parliamentary colleagues to secretaries in his office, his conquests, it seems, were many and varied. If he did not in fact live up to his reputation, he must surely be among the most unfairly maligned figures in history.

It is not surprising that so little hard evidence exists. Lloyd George carried out his liaisons with women who had a great deal to lose and nothing to gain by exposing him. Either from preference or from deliberate calculation, he also often favoured women who did not keep diaries or make demands of one of the country's most eminent politicians. Those who did were swiftly cut out of his life. He also won the loyalty of his mistresses because, in his own way, he genuinely loved women. He did not deceive them with promises of a future together, and he tended to leave behind goodwill, not enmity, at the end of a liaison. Such appears to have been the case with Mrs J, who remained on good terms with him for many years.

It was thanks to the good nature of his lover, and perhaps also to William George's legal skills, that the young Liberal candidate survived to fight his first general election. Domestic harmony was also preserved, although the family later 'tacitly acknowledged', as Olwen put it, that they had a half-brother living in Caernarvon. Dick made extensive enquiries when he first heard the rumours as an adult, and concluded that the story was true. He avoided being seen with his half-brother in public because the physical resemblance between them was so strong. Due to the speed with which the settlement was arranged, Maggie never came to hear the rumours. As Olwen commented, she was spared this time, but was not to be so fortunate in the years to come.

Unaware of her husband's behaviour, Maggie continued to play little part in Lloyd George's professional and social worlds. Her life revolved around her baby, and she was preparing to leave Mynydd Ednyfed to move to the new house in town. She was also pregnant again, with Dick barely nine months old.

On 20 March 1890 Maggie had arranged to meet Lloyd George at Criccieth station. He had gone to Porthmadoc early in the morning on business, and the two of them planned to spend the rest of the day together in Caernarvon. As she arrived on the platform Maggie was handed a telegram addressed to 'Lloyd George'. Assuming that it was for her, she opened it and read the four-word message that was to change her life: 'Swetenham died last night.' Maggie was thus the first to receive the shocking news that Edmund Swetenham, Caernarvon Boroughs' Conservative MP, was dead of a heart attack at the age of sixty-eight. Maggie knew what the news meant: there would be a by-election in Caernarvon Boroughs, and instead of enjoying the next two years quietly with his wife, Lloyd George was facing the first major battle of his political life immediately, and with no time to prepare.

Struggling to take in the unexpected news, Maggie did not know what to do and held back from buying her ticket to Caernarvon in case Lloyd George wanted to cancel the trip. But when he arrived on the Porthmadoc train they decided to go ahead as planned, perhaps sensing that this would be their last outing together for the foreseeable future. They did not have a happy time. As Maggie later put it, 'The sunshine seemed to have gone from the day . . . The shadow of the coming election spoiled everything.'[10]

Lloyd George was not the only one to be caught out by Swetenham's death. The Conservatives had to find a new candidate at once, and luckily for Lloyd George, the best candidate they could field at such short notice was the Llanystumdwy squire, Hugh Ellis-Nanney. There was rich irony in the battle between the Highgate lad and the living embodiment of the social system he hated so much.

As the campaign began, the outcome was far from certain. Lloyd George was in many ways the perfect candidate for the constituency: local born, Welsh-speaking and eloquent. He had also been making himself known to the electorate for over a year. Ellis-Nanney on the other hand was affable, well-meaning and an experienced candidate, having stood for Caernarvonshire Division in 1880, and for South Caernarvonshire Division in 1885. But he had lost both times, and was not in good health when he was persuaded to try again in 1890. He was also not Welsh-speaking, which was becoming more of an issue with the electorate. With little time to prepare, Ellis-Nanney played the strongest card in his hand, depicting his opponent as a radical fire-brand and, less advisedly, as a young man who was more interested in the wider world than in Caernarvon Boroughs. The slurs only empha-sised the unflattering contrast between the squire and his brilliant young opponent.

Lloyd George had two tireless campaigners at his side in Uncle Lloyd and his brother William. The three set out to attend to every possible detail during the election period, and Lloyd George consulted them on his every move, even enlisting his brother's help in writing his election address. In it, he held back his most radical views in order not to frighten off the more moderate Liberal voters. His address 'To the Free and Independent Electors of the Carnarvonshire District Boroughs' was resolutely Gladstonian. He declared early on: 'I come before you as a firm believer in and admirer of Mr. Gladstone's noble alternative of Justice to Ireland,' before making a brief reference to Wales' own claims, not to Home Rule, since that was still controversial, but to the disestablishment of the Church in Wales, which would end the dominance of the Church over the Welsh nonconformist majority, and which was the Liberals' main campaign in the late 1880s and 1890s. He said:

> I am deeply impressed with the fact that Wales has wants and aspirations of her own which have too long been ignored, but which must no longer be neglected. First and foremost among these stands the cause of Religious Liberty and Equality in Wales. If returned to Parliament by you, it shall be my earnest endeavour to labour for the triumph of this great cause. Wales has for many a year yearned in her heart for the attainment of that religious equality and freedom which is impossible whilst the English Church as by law established is imposed upon us as the National Religion of Wales, and is maintained by Welsh national endowments, and whilst clerical bigotry dominates over our Churchyards.[11]

The reference to churchyards was a none-too-subtle reminder of the candidate's personal triumph at Llanfrothen.

The Tories bitterly opposed Welsh disestablishment, and William George described in his diary how fierce the battle became: 'We are in the thick of the fight. Personal rather than party feeling runs high. The Tories began by ridiculing D's candidature; they have now changed their tune. Each party looks upon it as a stiff fight . . . The struggle is not so much a struggle of Tory v Liberal or Radical even; the main issue is between country squire and the upstart democrat.'[12]

Lloyd George was not afraid of being tagged 'an upstart democrat'.

He rejoiced in being a new breed of politician. By virtue of his education and legal qualifications he belonged more truly to the professional middle classes than to the 'gwerin' or peasant class, but he emphasised his humble origins in a speech that came to be recognised as prophetic:

> I see that one qualification Mr Nanney possesses . . . is that he is a man of wealth, and that the great disqualification in my case is that I am possessed of none . . . I once heard a man wildly declaiming against Mr Tom Ellis as a Parliamentary representative; but according to that man Mr Ellis's disqualification consisted mainly in the fact that he had been brought up in a cottage. The Tories have not yet realised that the day of the cottage-bred man has at last dawned.[13]

Indeed it had.

On 10 April 1890 the 4,000 voters in Caernarvon Boroughs went to the polls. Lloyd George spent the day with his supporters in Pwllheli before meeting up with Uncle Lloyd at Avonwen. The following day he made his way to the Guildhall in Caernarvon, where the votes were being counted. It was going to be a close-run thing. The votes piled up in two equal-looking heaps, and then Lloyd George was given the bad news: he had been defeated. But the returning officer had spoken prematurely. Lloyd George's supporters had been primed to be on the lookout for any irregularity or skulduggery, since they (rightly) suspected that their opponents would do anything to secure victory. At the eleventh hour, Lloyd George's electoral agent, J.T. Roberts, spotted a sheaf of twenty Liberal votes in the Conservative pile. He demanded a recount, and the result was overturned. By the skin of his teeth – only eighteen votes – Lloyd George had been elected to Parliament.

A large crowd was waiting as he emerged onto the balcony of the Guildhall, his brother at his side, and it greeted the new Member with half-crazed enthusiasm. After making a short speech in Welsh, Lloyd George travelled to Bangor, where he hailed the result as 'a victory of democracy over the aristocracy'[14] before dashing off a telegram to Uncle Lloyd. His message combined the rhetoric of victory – 'Have triumphed against enormous influences' – with engaging practicality: 'home six; they must not engage band as rumoured, illegal; ask Maggie down'.[15]

Uncle Lloyd was overjoyed. He was not an excitable man, nor one given to exaggeration, but he wrote in his diary that night that the result was 'almost a miracle'[16] – a word he did not use lightly. At 6 p.m. the newly elected Lloyd George returned to Criccieth, where he was greeted by crowds, bonfires and bunting – but no wife. Five months pregnant and with a fourteen-month-old baby to nurse, Maggie had decided that it was not sensible to leave Mynydd Ednyfed, despite her husband's request. Lloyd George was rather prone to make unreasonable demands of her, ignoring her physical condition when she was pregnant and the practical difficulties of looking after young children. Although she occasionally ignored his pleas, it did not cause much friction between them, at this stage at least.

The celebrations in Criccieth lasted well into the night, and when, finally, Lloyd George was escorted home by an elated and noisy crowd he was met, not by an adoring and excited wife, but by a furious nursemaid charged with looking after the infant Dick. The new MP was brought quickly down to earth. He was subjected to a stern telling off, and his supporters were ordered to stop their shouting immediately for fear of waking the baby. It was a sharp reminder of his wife's priorities.

7

Kitty Edwards

WHEN MARGARET HEARD THAT HER husband had been elected to Parliament, she wept. Lloyd George later recalled that they were 'tears of regret for the ending of her hopes for a quiet, untroubled existence in the country'.[1] However unrealistic her expectations of a quiet country life had been when she married, they were, it seems, genuine, and were now dashed to pieces.

The result of the Caernarvon Boroughs by-election attracted extensive coverage in the Welsh press and nationally. This was partly due to the name the successful candidate had already made for himself, but also because Lloyd George had overturned the Conservative majority of the previous general election, and, then as now, such upsets attracted a lot of comment. Lloyd George's arrival at Westminster also received far more attention than it would have done if he had been elected amid a throng of others at a general election.

David Lloyd George MP took his seat on budget day, 17 April 1890, and his wife added the newspaper reports to her scrapbook:

It was a striking sight, the closely packed benches, the Chancellor of the Exchequer [George Goschen] with many little volumes of notes, bracing himself up for a grand effort; while immediately below the venerable figure of Lord Cottesloe stood the young M.P. for the Caernarvonshire Boroughs, nearly seventy years his junior, pale with excitement and the thoughts of the career opening before him.[2]

Maggie did not accompany her husband to London: amid the excitement following the election, Lloyd George had no time to find accommodation, and when he was in the capital he stayed with Criccieth friends or at the National Liberal Club, according to his circumstances. But she was not far from his thoughts, and he took the first possible opportunity to write to her, during the budget speech itself. His pride and sense of achievement in getting into Parliament, the 'region of his future domain', is tangible: 'This is the first letter which I write as an introduced member of the House of Commons and I dedicate it to my little darling. I snatch a few minutes during the delivery of Goschen's budget to write her. I was introduced amid very enthusiastic cheers on the Liberal side.'[3] The next day, he wrote to his brother with the bemusement of a new Member of Parliament: 'My first division last night. I voted against Bi-metallism, but I couldn't tell you why.'[4]

As Lloyd George was finding his feet at Westminster, Maggie was wondering how they would manage now that her husband was an unsalaried MP with little or no time to spend on building his business. Unlike Lloyd George, who was not practical by nature, both she and William George could see the financial difficulty his election had placed them in as a family, and William's diary betrays the sleepless nights the situation caused him: 'For the village lad to have beaten the parish country squire is a (great) honour. Two practical questions present themselves: (a) How is D to live there? (b) How am I to live down here?'[5]

The law practice, now mainly run by William George, would have to provide for all: Lloyd George, Maggie and their growing family as well as Uncle Lloyd, Betsy and Polly. The firm was doing reasonably well as a result of some hard work by William, and had moved to premises in Porthmadoc. Uncle Lloyd helped out as an office clerk, but the family's income would be spread thinly for some years to come. As late as 1894, William George recorded in his diary that his supper consisted of a cupful of hot water with some bread and butter. The first of many requests for financial help came from London when Maggie paid her husband a visit:

Dei wished me to ask you to send him £5 by return please. He has been using some of my money. If he doesn't get it your dear sister

can't return home on Saturday without leaving her husband quite
penniless in this great city . . . He also wants you to send him a few
blank cheques. For goodness sake don't send him many. They are such
easy things to fill in and then the slashing signature of D. Lloyd George
put to them – which I fear you would not be too glad to see.[6]

Maggie was as careful with money as Lloyd George was extravagant.
Every penny was precious, and she formed money-saving habits that
remained with her for life. Unfairly perhaps, they gave her a reputation for being tight-fisted. In her defence, she never enjoyed spending
money on herself, but even Polly, who was perfectly aware of their
financial situation, commented on her meanness to William George
while on a visit to London in 1891:

> You will be anxious perhaps to know whether your P.O's came to hand
> safely. I may say that they are in the strictest sense of the word. Mag
> pounced upon them directly & no one has seen a scrap of them since
> or ever will . . . A rare one for keeping money is my little sister-in-law.
> She is a very kind little hostess and we get on very nicely together, it
> is when it comes to spending that she shows her miserliness, she will
> borrow a penny to pay the tram sooner than pay for you herself.[7]

During the first few weeks after his election, Lloyd George immersed
himself in national politics and London life. He was anxious to find a
place to live so that Maggie could join him, and did not seem to see
the impracticality of this plan. In June 1890 he entreated her to make
the eighteen-hour round trip from Criccieth by train so that they could
spend Sunday house-hunting – not a prospect that would entice many
women who were seven months pregnant.[8] His pleading was all the
more extraordinary because Maggie's second pregnancy had not been
straightforward. Her letters to Lloyd George, though trying to reassure
him, are full of fear that she might lose the baby: 'This afternoon we
are going to Dwyfor Villa to tea, the walk will do me good if I do it
slowly & rest at Criccieth. I'm going and coming back. Much more
good than a drive that shakes me so much.' And again: 'I don't feel very
well today don't be alarmed if you find an unease in the family when
you come down. I am in good spirits. Mag.'[9]

Lloyd George was worried, and despite his efforts to cheer her up, Maggie was clearly having a hard time. She wrote:

> I am longing dreadfully after you today. After being home for a flying visit you seem to have gone from my sight without hardly having seen you, & it may seem very silly on my part but I go to every room in the house today to find a trace of your having been occupying it, & I find but little traces of you, but when I do I relieve myself in tears, but I shall be alright when I get a letter tomorrow morning.
> . . . send me a loving letter tomorrow & I shall be happy & make haste home on Saturday if you cant come before. I feel that I must see you once more before I am taken ill.[10]

There was great joy when Mair Eluned Lloyd George was born without complication on 2 August 1890, although the proud father was not at home to witness the event. He was told of the birth of his first daughter by his brother in a telegram, and caught the mail train to Criccieth for a flying visit before returning to London.

Lloyd George naturally wanted to participate in full in his first parliamentary session, but when the House rose in mid-August his family expected him to return to Criccieth to nurture his constituency, to help his brother with the law practice, and to spend time with his wife and new baby. Maggie was clearly looking forward to having her husband back, but he had other ideas: to Lloyd George politics was a full-time occupation, and when Parliament was not sitting he gave speeches across the country and travelled abroad with his political friends, a fact that his wife and brother eventually had to accept.

This was hard for Maggie. She could not see the attraction of London for her husband, and resented the time he spent there when he could be with his family. On one occasion soon after Mair's birth Lloyd George announced that he was staying in London for the weekend to prepare a speech instead of coming home. Maggie had been looking forward to a visit, and her disappointment was sharpened when he mentioned casually that he had been distracted from his work by his friend and fellow Welsh Liberal MP, S.T. Evans, who she felt was a bad influence on him. On the Sunday, the two had taken a bus to Kew Gardens and had failed to attend chapel. Maggie was incensed:

Well I don't approve of the way you spent your Sunday & I am sure by the way my old Dafydd put it that he knows I don't. Thanks to you all the same for being honest in telling your Maggie. Tell her everything will you always never keep anything from her. If you were at home now & wanted to make a speech & your old Mag asked you to come with her to Chapel for 2 hours you would at once say well I can't come I can't go to such and such a place unprepared & make a fool of myself & that I must be responsible for the result if you come with me, but S T Evans turns up & asks you to go with him to waste a day you consent I am sure with a bright smile & no conditions as to responsibility. I shall remember last Sunday in future.

Maggie chose to believe that Lloyd George was a reluctant participant in the day trip, and blamed his friend for the episode:

I can't bring myself to like S T Evans after what you told me. He is not teetotller (I am sure that is not spelt properly) for one thing & other things [i.e. his flirting] that you've told me, which I always dislike in men, that he must be rather fast. Perhaps I am mistaken. Tom Ellis [nonconformist MP for Merioneth] would be the man I should like to see you friendly with. I don't think there would be any danger of your being any the worse for being in his company. I am not so sure about STE.

Her idea of a well-spent Sunday was not at all the kind that appealed to Lloyd George: 'Buasai yn llawer gwell i ti fod yn Grassgarth hefo Davies yn cadw cwmpeini iddo fe. Gallset neud dy speech tra buasai Davies yn y capel ond iti fynd yno hefo fo unwaith' (It would be far better for you to be at Grassgarth with Davies* keeping him company. You could prepare your speech while Davies was in Chapel, if you only went with him once).[11] Maggie's outburst did not change her husband's behaviour, but it did make him more careful to conceal his pleasure trips from her.

---

* R.O. Davies, a Criccieth acquaintance and chapel-goer, was a successful London draper. He and his family lived in Grasgarth, a comfortable house in Acton with a large garden and a tennis court.

Lloyd George's entry into the world of national politics took place during a period of great change. Irish Home Rule was dominating the political headlines, supporters of female suffrage were beginning to attract attention to their cause, and demographic and social changes in densely populated industrial areas were leading inexorably to the formation of a new political force as the Independent Labour Party was formed in 1893 under the chairmanship of Keir Hardie. Simultaneously, the dominance of the landed gentry in Parliament was giving way to men with 'new' money or from the professions, although in 1890 the average Conservative MP still had roughly twice the personal income of the average Liberal Member. The House of Commons reflected the habits and lifestyle of the aristocracy, creating a potentially hostile and threatening atmosphere to a working-class MP. But it was not intimidating to Lloyd George. He soon grasped the ways of the House, taking to it as naturally as if he had been born to it.

The change of character in the membership of the House meant that in the general election of 1892, Lloyd George was joined by more men of similar backgrounds. He himself increased his majority from the wafer-thin eighteen votes of the by-election two years previously to 196, despite facing the well-liked Tory candidate Sir John Puleston, Constable of Caernarvon Castle and veteran of the American Civil War. Of the thirty-four Welsh Members returned, thirty-one were Liberals, and over twenty were Welsh-born. Significantly, the group contained six village-school-educated men, fourteen lawyers, fourteen businessmen and twenty-two nonconformists. The Liberals, led by Gladstone, were not so successful elsewhere, and with a reduced Liberal majority of only forty, if they banded together as a group the Welsh Members to some extent held the balance of power. They were not slow to take advantage of the fact. Courted by the government, the Welsh MPs were determined to secure the great prize: a Bill for the disestablishment of the Welsh Church which would end the state-maintained dominance of the Anglican Church in Wales and give religious equality – at last – to nonconformists.

Maggie was not politically aware when she married, but she could see that these were important battles, and that her husband's participation in Westminster politics at this time was crucial to the future of her own country, denomination and way of life. She could not see though why he had to be away from her when Parliament was not in session. He in turn could not understand why she did not want to follow him to London to look after him there.

Lloyd George wanted his family with him in London – 'I don't know what I would give now for an hour of your company. It would scatter all the gloom & make all the room so cheerful,' he wrote in June 1890[12] – but the unpleasant reality was that he could not afford to set up a second household on his income. At first he stayed in Acton with the Davies family, who became close friends and welcomed Maggie whenever she could visit London. But she now had two children under two years old to take care of, and also had plenty to occupy her at home, packing up at Mynydd Ednyfed and preparing to move to the new house in December 1890. It would have been difficult for her to spend more time in London even if the succession of temporary digs had been satisfactory, and they clearly were not.

The Lloyd Georges' first home in London was a set of rooms in Verulam Buildings, Gray's Inn, which they took on a lease of £70 (£6,147 at today's values) a year early in 1891. The rooms were serviced, and there was a porter at the gate and two housekeepers on the premises, but the lease was surrendered at the end of the 1892 parliamentary session. That winter they took a six-month lease on a set of rooms at 5 Essex Court in the Temple, and in late autumn 1893 Lloyd George took a flat, No. 30 Palace Mansions in Addison Road, Kensington, for £90 a year which was to be their London home for six years. For the most part, however, Maggie stayed in Criccieth, resigning herself to the long absences that came to characterise her relationship with her husband at this time.

There has been much speculation about Maggie's attitude towards living in London. Her visits there were so infrequent during 1894, when she was expecting their fourth child, that Lloyd George arranged for the flat to be let for six months, and it was again sub-let in 1896, when she was pregnant a fifth time (the pregnancy ended in a miscarriage). It does not appear that she was in London very often during the remainder of 1896, in 1897 (although she was there when she suffered another miscarriage in the spring) or 1898, until, finally, with the marriage at crisis point, she consented to let their Criccieth home and move to a family house near Wandsworth Common. Even then she delayed making the move for as long as possible.

The overwhelming consensus among Lloyd George's biographers is that Maggie simply preferred Criccieth to London. In this way, the blame for the difficulties in their marriage has been divided between the philandering husband and the absent wife. The evidence, though, strongly suggests that, her preference apart, Maggie's decision not to join Lloyd George in London at the beginning of his parliamentary career was based on practical considerations. After all, when the children were older she did – albeit reluctantly – move to London, and she was mostly at her husband's side through his years as Chancellor and Prime Minister.

The conventional view is largely based on Lloyd George's pleas in his letters home for Maggie to join him, although the possibility exists that he was exaggerating his loneliness to divert attention from his active socialising in her absence. Nevertheless, the love between him and Maggie was strong, and he was clearly anxious to have his family with him more often during these early years. This was the first time in his life that he had had to fend for himself without women to take care of his needs, and he did not enjoy it. He was not temperamentally equipped to look after himself. He had been spoiled as a child by the devoted Betsy and Polly, and cared for latterly by the servants at Mynydd Ednyfed. For the pampered young man, who to the end of his life was never able to tie his own shoelaces, it was a shock to the system to come home to an empty room with no food to eat and no clean collars for his shirts. In some ways, as we shall see, his solitary existence in London suited him, and he made the most of the opportunity to enjoy his new social circle, but the loneliness was not entirely faked, and his domestic helplessness was a real problem.

Lloyd George was not a systematic man, especially when it came to correspondence. Despite writing regularly and frequently to Maggie, William George and Uncle Lloyd, he never kept track of the letters he received, and the majority of theirs to him have been lost. Consequently, Maggie's views on living in London and her reasons for her undisguised preference for Criccieth have not received similar attention.

There are many facts that would have affected her decision. Travel between Criccieth and London involved an uncomfortable and expensive nine-hour train journey via Bangor, Shrewsbury and Crewe. Money was desperately short, and when Lloyd George was elected, the twenty-three-year-old Maggie had a baby of fourteen months with another on the way. When Mair Eluned was born the practical difficulties doubled. It was far from clear in 1890 that Lloyd George would hold on to his seat for more than a couple of years, when the next general election was expected. Also, in the 1890s the parliamentary timetable was less regular and less frantic than it is now: sessions ran, typically, from January to late summer, with a short break at Easter, but Members were then free to return to their constituencies for the rest of the year, unless they were in office with government departments to run. Life as a backbencher involved having one foot in Westminster and the other in the constituency. It may have seemed utterly reasonable to Maggie that she and the family should stay where they were, with Lloyd George returning as often as he could.

The family's health was another major factor. Lloyd George wrote to Maggie in June 1890:

> You can't imagine how glad I was to get such a long and interesting letter from you. I read it with avidity and delight. I went out for a stroll before breakfast to the Embankment Gardens & read your letter there. It made me quite happy. There is a sort of pleasure even in 'hiraeth' [homesickness] itself. I am sorry that they are cutting the hay so soon. Were it next week I might come then. I would so like to scent the hay. It would be such a contrast to this infernal sooty stinky [city].[13]

London was not a healthy place to live in the 1890s. Country people had long feared the contagion and 'bad air' of the rapidly growing cities – one of the reasons for Betsy and William George's return to Wales from Lancashire in 1864. In subsequent years things had got worse. Some of the richest men in London were brewers, who provided an alternative to drinking the city's dirty water, which posed a very real danger: a House of Commons cleaner died of cholera as late as 1893. City doctors were widely mistrusted, especially with regard to childbirth: infant mortality in the cities was 30 per cent higher than in the country. Maggie was happy to visit London before she became a mother, but with young children it was a different matter. The prospect of looking after two babies in a cramped set of rooms was a real deterrent. No wonder she thought it best for the children to stay in their comfortable house by the sea in Criccieth, with her parents on hand and servants to look after them.

In later life, Maggie declared with seeming sincerity that 'a wife must put her husband first, her children second, and herself last. That is the way to take couples happily to their golden wedding.'[14] It is difficult to reconcile that view though with her actions when her children were young. From the moment she first fell pregnant in 1888, the children filled her world, and although she loved her husband passionately, there is not much evidence to support the view that she put his needs above theirs. All in all, this was the worst time in her life to ask Maggie to live for long periods in London. During the first seven years of their marriage, she was pregnant for a total of thirty-six months, gave birth four times,* and assuming she nursed each child for six months after birth (a conservative estimate for the period), there were only fourteen months during the years 1888–95 when she was not either pregnant or nursing. After 1895 Maggie's health was not strong, and she miscarried twice before giving birth to the couple's last child, Megan Arvon, in April 1902.

Maggie's life was centred around her children, her family and chapel. In London, she had none of the support systems she needed to make a home. Her social circle was small and scattered across the city, and getting about with small children was not easy. Lloyd George was wholly preoccupied with the intoxicating world of politics, and kept highly irregular hours. Yes, it was her duty to look after her husband, but did she not have an equal duty to look after her children? In the years ahead, this question was to cause increasing tension between them.

In the early 1890s, however, their relationship was warm and close, and Lloyd George's affection for the children fills his letters: 'When am I going to get little Dickie's photo? I want it badly. I can't stand this solitude much longer.'[15] But while he was missing Maggie, he was not missing Criccieth. He had found life there, with gossips monitoring his

---

* Following Dick and Mair, Olwen was born in 1892 and Gwilym in 1894.

movements, too confining and he never grew to like the town. He complained about the weather (very wet), and the fact that as his fame grew he was never left in peace. As the years wore on he came to regard time spent in Criccieth as a matter of duty, not respite. Early on in his parliamentary career he was making excuses to Maggie instead of returning to the family home at weekends. The truth was that, in his early thirties, he was relishing his freedom and enjoying the more cosmopolitan life in London. Maggie's absence gave him plenty of time, and the incentive, to make the most of the social opportunities that were open to a young star in the Welsh Liberal Party. He made friends with his fellow Welsh MPs and with members of the flourishing Welsh community in the capital.

There has been a flow of people from Wales to London as far back as records exist, and the numbers grew to a torrent in the nineteenth century, forming a large, socially mixed group of immigrants. Then, as now, the Welsh in London did not feel a pressing need to gather protectively together. They spread themselves out across the city, with a slightly denser concentration in the west and north-west around Paddington and Euston, the two great gateways to Wales. Many of the migrants came from farming communities, and they made two farming-based trades their own: dairy and drapery. The sight of a Welsh dairy or draper's shop was a familiar feature of Victorian London, and the great Welsh retailers' names are still visible, Peter Jones, Dickins and Jones and D.H. Evans among them. These establishments, and countless smaller ones, attracted more Welshmen and women to work as dairy maids, shop assistants and domestic servants. They intermarried freely with native Londoners, lived above the shop or in the houses they served, and built up a community life around the numerous Welsh-language chapels and churches they built in the city. Some did well: two nineteenth-century Lord Mayors of London were Welsh, and when the National Eisteddfod was held in the Albert Hall in 1887, royalty attended.

The prosperous Welsh in London readily opened their doors to Lloyd George, who enjoyed their lively social gatherings. He got to know them – and their wives – and there was enough evidence of flirting to make Maggie suspicious. In a letter written soon after Mair's birth, she sounded a warning: 'I am glad you have not seen any girl you should like better than poor me, but are you sure that you have not seen anyone to flirt with. Remember to be careful in that line as I will soon find out.'[16]

As early as 1893–94, in an undated fragment, Lloyd George had to defend himself against the same charge: 'Am y reception [As for the reception]. I behaved very modestly. I am sure Mrs Gwynoro hardly saw me *speaking* even to any ladies – at least very casually.'[17] He evidently felt he needed to make it clear to Maggie that his companion on this occasion was not physically attractive: 'I dined that evening at Wynford Phillips & took his wife, a black thin skinny bony Jewess whom you could not squeeze without hurting yourself. This lady I took to the reception & left her there directly he arrived.' He then lists all the women he met at the event, some of whom were clearly known to Maggie, and others whom he took care to describe in highly unflattering terms: 'I met Mrs Evans of Llanelly (formerly Miss Hughes) Belle Vue, Miss Griffith Springfield, Miss Jones (hogan goch & spectols) [a red-haired girl with spectacles] & Mrs Dr. Price, Mrs Dr. Parry & a few more whose names even I do not recollect.'[18]

Dick recalls that this was a typical tactic of his father's. Maggie was quick to confront her husband with evidence of any inappropriate behaviour. She had inherited a little of her mother's temperament, and could be fierce when roused. Lloyd George believed that attack was the best form of defence: when accused he would come out fighting, disarming Maggie with a teasing response or a forthright denial. Their letters, though warm and affectionate, are littered with accusations and denials, some jocular, others less so. In November 1895, Lloyd George wrote: 'Oh yes, Miss Jones. She is lovely. Twenty-one, charming & so jolly. It is a perfect delight to spend Sunday in the same house. Dyna i ti rhen Fagi! [There you are, old Maggie!] Love, fond & warm from your sweetheart.'[19] Again, in February 1896: 'You are a jealous little creature! Miss May is not there. As a matter of fact I have not seen her for months.'[20] And from Rome, where he was holidaying with two colleagues, he addresses a letter to 'My dear suspicious old Maggie':*

---

* Lloyd George often refers to his wife as 'old Maggie'. In Welsh, particularly in North Wales, the word 'hen', which literally means 'old', is used as an endearment. A more accurate translation would be 'little Maggie' or 'dear Maggie'.

'Mrs Blythe is a widow – young, pretty and genial. *Are you scared stiff to hear this, old Maggie? Well, you needn't be.* She worships the memory of her dead husband and can think of nothing else.'[21]

Hardly reassuring. He went on to deploy another favourite tactic, suggesting that another member of his party was misbehaving, making himself look angelic in comparison: '*They all know how fond I am of my Maggie. They see me writing letters when that is difficult . . . Gilchrist never talks of his wife and children, but I do often.*'[22]

Lloyd George genuinely considered himself to be a good husband and family man.* He was certainly a regular and enthusiastic correspondent, and he took a close, affectionate interest in his children. But left to his own devices in London, there were plenty of women who were more than happy to offer him the comfort of their parlours, posing a threat to the distant Maggie. An undated letter written to Lloyd George in the 1890s spells out the danger:

My Dear Mr Lloyd George
I have just returned from Birmingham. Went there yesterday and now I am back here in my flat [and my maids]. If you are going no where else tomorrow afternoon come up here and have some music. I shall be staying here now for a while so hope to see you.
    In haste, yours etc
    RFL[23]

Again, from 1899 comes the distraught voice of a lady friend who wanted more attention than Lloyd George was able to offer:

My Dear Lloyd
Do please answer my letters. I never knew whether you got the one I sent you before you went abroad wishing you 'bon voyage'. I am on

---

* In 1895 he wrote to Maggie: 'Ellis Griffith [MP for Anglesey] & I were comparing notes the other day & we both said that if we were asked on a future great occasion in what capacity we would like to be tried before the Judgement seat we would answer "As a husband if you don't mind." We both thought we would fare pretty well if we had to stand or fall by our merits or demerits as husbands.'

[illegible] in case they do not reach you safely. Come & see me one
<u>Evening</u> this week only let me know then I shall be in. I am dying for
a <u>long talk</u> with you. <u>Now do not fail</u> to answer this <u>letter</u>.

Ys in haste,

Kate[24]

Scribbled across the top of the letter, which is on black-edged mourning
paper, is the instruction:

Read & tear it up at once but mind and <u>write me</u>. I have <u>news</u> for you
too. <u>A surprise</u>.

We do not know what happened next, but the end of the story emerges
in a telegram sent to Lloyd George at the Liberal Club. It seems that
he had used the time-honoured way out of a tedious correspondence
by continuing to ignore her letters:

I do think you unkind – you might put me out of my misery & acknowledge the receipt of my letters. I shall never write again unless you
answer this. Will you come here or meet me tomorrow night – <u>Friday</u>?
K[25]

It is possible that Lloyd George was innocent of any wrongdoing in
this case – there is no concrete evidence of indiscretion. But he was
at the very least unwise to behave in such a way as to invite emotional
letters of this kind. He was alone in London, at the height of his
attractiveness. He was a popular and entertaining guest, and was as
free as a single man to enjoy some music and female company once
the business of the House was over for the day. From the start, he
had redrawn the rules of marital fidelity to exclude sex from the deal.
Maggie had his first loyalty, his love and his name. Anything she could
not provide – including companionship and sex when they were apart
– he felt free to take from others. Maggie had every reason to fear the
worst.

The one thing Maggie did not have to fear was divorce. Quite apart
from the fact that he loved her, Lloyd George was not going to leave

his wife, for before he had served his first full session in Parliament he had witnessed at close quarters one of the most calamitous divorce scandals of the age. The affair between the leader of the Irish National Party, Charles Stewart Parnell, and Mrs Katharine O'Shea rocked the political establishment to its core. It made the young Welsh MP even more determined to put ambition before love, and political success above all else.

Katharine O'Shea, the wife of a captain in the 18th Hussars, met the charismatic Parnell in 1880, and they were soon living together in London and Brighton. She became closely involved in his political work, nursed him through his frequent periods of illness, and was often consulted by British and Irish politicians alike as Irish Home Rule became a more pressing issue. Her home was the first port of call when Gladstone or his lieutenants wanted to speak to Parnell, who was rapidly becoming one of the most prominent politicians of the day. He was worshipped in Ireland, and as the leader of the Irish Nationalists in the House of Commons, he held the balance of power.

It was perhaps inevitable that the chink in his armour, his relationship with Mrs O'Shea, with whom he had three children, would be used against him. The long-absent Captain O'Shea, who had seemed wholly unperturbed by his wife's living arrangements, was persuaded by Parnell's enemies to sue for divorce in 1889, citing Parnell as co-respondent. Parnell refused to fight the case, relying on his personal reputation to help him ride out the crisis, but he lost the support of Gladstone, and with it the leadership of his party. It was the end of his career, and also the end of the campaign for Irish Home Rule which was his life's work. He and Mrs O'Shea were eventually married in June 1891, and he died a little over three months later. He was forty-five.

The sheer scale of the scandal surrounding the O'Shea divorce case is difficult to imagine today. 'Kitty' O'Shea was reviled in the press, and Lloyd George attributed the loss of a by-election in Bassetlaw in December 1890 to the scandal. Parnell's fellow MPs were amazed and appalled that he could have sacrificed the great Irish cause for the sake of a woman, no one more so than Lloyd George. He wrote: 'The Irish party are now upstairs discussing Parnell's future. I saw him just now in the tea-room looking as calm & as self-possessed as ever. But it is a serious business for him. Here he is quite a young man having attained the greatest career of this century, dashing it to pieces because he couldn't restrain a single passion. A thousand pities. It is a still worse business for some of us fellows holding doubtful seats . . .'[26] A few days later he referred to Parnell as 'a base selfish wretch':

> Everyone is so preoccupied about Parnell. Well it appears that fellow persists in brazening it out. The situation is getting very serious & acute & no one knows what will become of it. If Parnell sticks & his party stick to him it is generally conceded that Home Rule is done for. Isn't he a rascal. He would sacrifice even the whole future of his country too.[27]

Parnell was universally condemned for having put personal happiness ahead of his duty to his country.

What did Lloyd George glean from this episode? It was an early lesson in the ways of high society. Queen Victoria was still on the throne, but the Prince of Wales, heading the fast 'Marlborough set', was establishing new rules when it came to combining public life with private happiness. The Parnell affair elicited a strange mix of old attitudes and new ones.

Prince Edward, who became Edward VII in 1901, was the ultimate playboy prince. He had earned himself the nickname of 'Edward the Caresser' with a series of affairs which scandalised his parents and enthralled the nation. Indeed, it was during a visit to his son's college in Cambridge in the wake of an incident involving a popular actress called Nellie Clifden that Prince Albert contracted his fatal dose of typhoid, and Queen Victoria never forgave her son for being the indirect cause of her widowhood. In an attempt to regularise his private life, Prince Edward was married off to the beautiful and virtuous Princess Alexandra, but that did not curb his behaviour for long. Soon he and his intimate circle, the so-called Marlborough House set, were developing a code of practice that allowed them to indulge in serial affairs without upsetting the social order. The rules of the game were simple, and designed to keep the players out of the divorce courts. Affairs were confined to women of the same, aristocratic social class. Single women were out of bounds, as were married ones until they had had two or three children, including the necessary heir. But after family obligations

Highgate, the cottage in Llanystumdwy to which Betsy George fled as a young widow with the two-year-old Lloyd George. Her brother Richard's shoemaking workshop is on the left.

Left Betsy George in old age, 'a fine character, gentle, unselfish and courageous' – the mother who adored and indulged David Lloyd George.

Right William George, Lloyd George's father, who died at the age of forty-four, leaving his young family virtually destitute.

Lloyd George aged two with his sister Polly. She kept a watchful eye over him, and was 'a second mother' to his children.

Criccieth in 1880, the year Lloyd George and his family moved to Morvin House, a small terraced house in the shadow of the castle.

Lloyd George and Margaret Owen, both aged around sixteen. He was the town flirt, she was the 'catch' of the district. Their courtship began in 1885, and was fiercely opposed by her parents.

David and Margaret Lloyd George soon after their marriage and his election as MP for Caernarvon Boroughs in 1890.

The Owen and Lloyd George family with friends, c.1895. Richard and Mary Owen lived next door to their daughter in one of a pair of tall houses overlooking Criccieth bay, and doted on their grandchildren. Left to right: Richard Owen, Olwen, Mair, D.R. Daniel, Dick, Herbert Lewis, Margaret (holding Gwilym), Lloyd George and Mary Owen.

The adoring father – especially when it came to his daughters: Lloyd George with his youngest, Megan, in about 1905, the year he was appointed President of the Board of Trade.

Above Putting the family first: Margaret surrounded by her children, in about 1905.

Left Margaret, Lloyd George and Mair (holding Megan) in London c.1904, after Margaret had reluctantly agreed to leave Criccieth in 1899.

The favourite: Mair Eluned Lloyd George with her father... and her image carved on the grave in Criccieth where she was buried, aged seventeen, in 1907. Her last words, 'He is just and merciful,' are carved on the headstone.

Lady Julia Henry, society hostess wife of Liberal MP Sir Charles Henry. She was 'quite mad on' Lloyd George, and fled to America when he dropped her: 'That was my misfortune that we ever met & that he admired me…', she wrote to her husband. 'I can never face England again.'

Frances Stevenson c.1910, a graduate of Royal Holloway College, looking far younger than her age (twenty-one). She would meet Lloyd George in 1911, when he engaged her as Megan's governess.

David Lloyd George, Chancellor of the Exchequer 1908–15.

The family in 11 Downing Street in about 1910: Margaret, Lloyd George and Megan. Megan became the pet of Downing Street, her home from the ages of six to twenty.

The guardian and mentor: Uncle Lloyd with his protégé in Downing Street.

had been fulfilled, gentlemen and married ladies could conduct discreet affairs during country-house Saturday-to-Monday parties or long afternoon visits in town while husbands were at their clubs. House-party hostesses would understand what was expected of them in arranging bedroom accommodation for their guests. In this way immoral behaviour was cloaked in respectability, and scandal averted. Young girls' marriage prospects were not ruined by affairs with older men, and elaborate rules involving chaperones were devised to make sure that everyone obeyed the code.

After making the proper kind of dynastic marriage, providing their aristocratic husbands with heirs, and transferring their children's care to nannies, well-born women would find themselves at leisure. They were often bored, and played the game as enthusiastically as their husbands. Society colluded to keep everything discreet, even when prominent ladies gave birth to 'late' children who looked nothing like their husbands. The only threat to this happy arrangement, the thing to be avoided at all costs, was the public scandal of the divorce courts. Then the gloves came off, and the losers – usually women – were reviled in the press and excluded from society.

As an illustration of this code of conduct, there could be no better example than the Parnell affair. Everyone who knew Parnell and Mrs O'Shea, from the Prime Minister himself to the chambermaids who served them, treated Mrs O'Shea as Parnell's lawful wife, and no one seemed to trouble themselves about the morality of the situation. But the fateful intervention of Captain O'Shea removed Parnell's private life from the realm of the Marlborough House set rules, and cast it firmly into the public arena, where such things could not be accommodated. Thus Gladstone, who had been perfectly happy to acknowledge the affair in private, could not risk supporting Parnell through a public scandal. This may seem like utter hypocrisy – it seemed so to Mrs O'Shea at the time – but it was a reflection of the fact that the middle and working classes expected their national leaders to keep out of such scandals.

This was the world in which Lloyd George found himself when he entered Parliament, and this was the context to his own behaviour during the years that followed. The Parnell affair had lessons to impart in terms of both his marriage and his career, and he learned them well.

Within his marriage, he was able to keep transient flirtations and affairs separate from the love and commitment he offered Maggie. While expecting total fidelity from his wife, he indulged in relationships with other women and was never faithful to any of them, making full use of the prevailing silence of the press in such matters. This was a million miles away from the attitudes in Criccieth, but then, Lloyd George *was* far away from Criccieth. Such was the impact of the Parnell affair on Lloyd George that he would give Frances Stevenson a biography of Parnell when he asked her to be his mistress. The warning was implicit: there would be no divorce in his case. There would be no scandal. His career came first.

However clear in his mind Lloyd George was on this point, the story of the gallant Irish politician who sacrificed his career for love sent a very different message to others of his acquaintance. One of them was Catherine Edwards, the wife of a respectable doctor in Cemmaes, Merioneth, who by fancying herself as the Welsh Kitty O'Shea caused the first major scandal of Lloyd George's parliamentary career.

By the summer of 1896, Maggie's life had settled into its uneven split between Criccieth and London, and since Lloyd George had maintained his majority in the general election of 1895, she could be confident that her life as an MP's wife was likely to continue. She was thirty, and her brood now numbered four chicks, with Dick aged seven, Mair six, Olwen four, and the youngest, Gwilym, eighteen months. She was pregnant for the fifth time, and as usual she intended to stay in Criccieth until the birth. She and Lloyd George were still spending long times apart. He was making a name for himself as a backbencher and leader within the Welsh Parliamentary Group, and had taken several long holidays with political friends, while she stayed behind in Criccieth, which seemed to suit them both.

Money was still a problem. In his struggle to keep the family financially afloat, Lloyd George was apt to be tempted into unwise business dealings, and in 1893 the prospect of a quick return on a goldmine in far-distant Patagonia had been too attractive to resist. The consequences were disastrous, and in an attempt to turn the situation around he decided to take a trip to Argentina during the 1896 parliamentary recess, leaving on 21 August and returning on 27 October. He also needed a holiday, for his mother had died on 19 June. She was sixty-eight, and had been an invalid for many years. Lloyd George returned to Criccieth for a small, private funeral, and was so upset that Richard Lloyd sent him back to London so that politics could distract him from his grief. Maggie was too unwell to attend Betsy's funeral, and during his trip – or possibly just before his departure – she lost the baby. While she was recovering from this setback, unbeknownst to her a child was being born to a cousin of hers, Catherine Edwards. This child was going to cast a shadow over her life for the next three years.

Catherine Edwards, or 'Kitty' as she was (ironically) known, was a 'pretty, pert, amiable young woman'[28] who lived with her daughter and her husband, the local doctor, near the village of Mathafarn. In August 1896 her husband realised that she was pregnant, which was a surprise to him since the couple were estranged and had occupied separate bedrooms since 1894. What happened next came within a whisker of destroying Lloyd George's political career.

Kitty later claimed that on 10 August her husband used physical violence to induce her to sign a statement written in his hand. It read:

> I, Catherine Edwards, do solemnly confess that I have on 4th of February, 1896, committed adultery with Lloyd George MP, and that the said Lloyd George is the father of the child, and that I have on a previous occasion committed adultery with the above Lloyd George.[29]

Dr Edwards denied using violence against his wife, but he did throw her out of the house, and just over a week later she gave birth to a child at a temperance hotel called The Tower in Penygroes, near Caernarvon. At the time it was claimed that the baby was born near its full term, but the date of the confessed adultery, together with Dr Edwards' ignorance of his wife's condition until August, lend credence to a later doctor's report that the child was born substantially premature, weak and sickly at just over four pounds. The child did not survive to adulthood.

Naturally, within a small community, news like this could not be kept quiet, and Lloyd George's political enemies made sure that the gossip persisted. While Lloyd George was abroad the rumours reached the ears of his brother William. To his credit, William never entertained the notion that his brother could be guilty as charged, but he recognised the gravity of the situation, recording gloomily in his diary: 'The event that has overshadowed everything else in my little world during the last two days is the charge which is being made against D in connection with Mrs Dr Edwards . . . I hope to God that neither Uncle nor Maggie will hear anything of this slander until D returns when, of course, he will be in a position to deal with the "affair" effectively.'[30]

William knew that the scandal would end Lloyd George's career if he was not able to defend himself adequately, a fear that was reinforced the next day when he received a letter from R.O. Roberts, Lloyd George's election agent, containing the sombre message: 'The story is in everybody's mouth here, and naturally enough, people are shocked whether it be true or not. If true, then D's days are numbered; if untrue then it is a most devilish trick to blacken a man in his absence.'[31]

William immediately set about discovering the facts in order to mount a defence, taking care that Maggie heard nothing of the matter. He wrote a letter to Lloyd George with the bare bones of the accusation and sent it to Southampton to await his return. Having consulted Uncle Lloyd's diary, which faithfully recorded Lloyd George's whereabouts every day, he satisfied himself that his brother was innocent, and proceeded to do everything he could to keep a lid on the story. However, he did not know the date of the alleged adultery. He must have counted back nine months from the birth of the child rather than check the date in Kitty's 'confession', because Uncle Lloyd's diary clearly showed that Lloyd George *did* spend the night of 4 February at Dr Edwards' house. Edwards had been called out during the night, and had not returned until morning, leaving his wife and Lloyd George alone in the house. This did not mean that Lloyd George was guilty, but William was premature in celebrating his brother's innocence.

Dr Edwards was a Liberal supporter, and Lloyd George had got to know him when he campaigned for the Liberal candidate in Montgomeryshire in an 1894 by-election. A letter written to Lloyd George by Kitty suggested that he had also got to know Mrs Edwards rather well:

I am addressing this to the Club and the minute you have read it please commit it to the fire, I shall not expect an answer until you write to tell me you are going to spend a few days with us again . . . No more news, you may expect some trout from me in April, I shall send as many as I catch to Maggie and you and if my basket is not sufficient to supply your larder the Dr must help.

Excuse such an untidy letter and with my kind regards

Believe me

Yrs very sincerely

Kitty Edwards[32]

Kitty Edwards was a young, flirtatious, bored wife, and it later emerged that not one but two other men were also in the frame as the possible father of her second child. Nevertheless, for some reason, under the pressure of her husband's interrogation, she named Lloyd George as her lover, and for a short time this was believed by Dr Edwards.

In late October, Lloyd George returned home to Criccieth to find political uproar awaiting him, with all except his wife and his uncle in the know. He denied the charge and, advised by his brother, wrote to Dr Edwards to protest his innocence. The brief correspondence between them suggests that Edwards by then accepted that his wife had lied, but the doctor put the matter in the hands of his solicitor. Sooner or later with all this activity going on Maggie was bound to find out, and find out she did. She was not told about the affair by her husband, but discovered it when she read a letter that was addressed to him. It provoked a violent quarrel between them. Maggie was understandably distressed, but she came to believe in his innocence, and remained stalwart in her support for him through the whole, drawn-out affair.

In March 1897 Dr Edwards finally sued for divorce, and was promptly counter-sued by Kitty on the grounds of his cruelty. Lloyd George was not cited as co-respondent (that dubious honour went to Edward Wilson, the stationmaster at nearby Cemaes), but the libel of Kitty's confession had circulated so widely that the judge asked Lloyd George if he wanted to join the suit so that he could clear his name publicly on oath. This presented Lloyd George with a dilemma. Maggie was insistent that to appear in court in connection with such a sordid business would inevitably lead to more gossip. Mud sticks, she felt, even if he was found not guilty. On the other hand, refusing to clear his name could also lead to more rumour. Eventually, strongly advised by his brother (who consistently gave him excellent, impartial legal advice),

Lloyd George decided to keep his name out of the proceedings.

If Maggie ever doubted her husband in this matter, she did not show it. On the contrary, whatever her private feelings, she maintained a philosophical, almost nonchalant attitude, writing to William George:

> PRIVATE:* Is it not a great nuisance to have this old story risen up again? I trust it will be over on Monday for Die's sake – he is worrying about it. This world is a very cruel one, don't you think so? The innocent must suffer in order to shield the culprits. There are several persons in this matter who are left out of it altogether, who no doubt are guilty of misbehaving with this woman.[33]

In November 1897, by which time the scandal had been circulating for a full fifteen months, a court date was set. Shortly before then, a deal was reached between Dr and Mrs Edwards: she dropped her claims of cruelty in return for his withdrawing the charge against Edward Wilson. The reason for this deal became apparent later, and was connected with the discovery of indiscreet letters written by Mrs Edwards to a third man, known only as 'Gillet', which exonerated the stationmaster. But this did not emerge at the time and the judge proceeded to grant Dr Edwards a decree nisi on the grounds of his wife's adultery 'with persons unknown'.

Clearly this did not satisfactorily address the rumours concerning Lloyd George, so the judge took it upon himself to read out Kitty's confession in court, adding: 'I have no hesitation in saying that I think no case whatever has been made out against Mr Lloyd George – I think it was in the interests of Mr Lloyd George himself that the written confession has been brought forward and dealt with fully.'[34]

The relief to Lloyd George and his family must have been considerable. The only cloud on the horizon was that since the proceedings would be reported in the press, Uncle Lloyd had to be told about the affair. He wept and was thoroughly upset, but still, Lloyd George's name had been cleared.

---

* This was intended to signal to William that the note was for his eyes only, not to be read to the rest of the family.

And so the matter would have rested had not the divorce been interrupted in a most unfortunate manner. During the then compulsory six-month period between the granting of decree nisi and decree absolute, the man who employed Kitty as his secretary – Dr Beddoes of Aberystwyth – contested the decree nisi on the grounds that Dr Edwards had forced his wife to sign the confession. This dug up the scandal all over again, and led to a second court hearing in June 1899. The strain on Lloyd George and his family was compounded as further details of the affair came to light. Kitty's confession was reprinted in the press, and when the court hearing came around, the whole business descended to near farce. Kitty's letters inviting Gillet to visit her when her husband was away were exposed. She had also written to Dr Edwards begging him to let her return to the marital home, acknowledging, 'I know I have sinned, but I have repented bitterly . . . I cannot expect you to receive me home yet, and of course the child shall never come,'[35] which hardly backed up her claim that the child was her husband's all along. Lloyd George referred to the resurrection of the case as 'another dose of purgatory', and it weighed heavily on both him and Maggie. His political opponents made the most of his discomfort, and the matter only ended when the judge unhesitatingly granted Dr Edwards his decree absolute.

There is no definitive answer to the question of whether Lloyd George did or did not have a relationship with Kitty Edwards, but given the evidence of her letter it seems most likely that there was a flirtation, if not a sexual relationship, between them. The two court cases and William George's investigative work focused on identifying the father of the child, but fathering the baby was only the first of two charges Kitty made against Lloyd George in her confession. The second was that she had 'on a previous occasion' committed adultery with him, a charge which was more difficult to disprove. It may well be that a relationship existed between them in 1894, a relationship that may even have caused the rift between Kitty and Dr Edwards, but that by 1896 she had taken another lover who was actually the father of her child. We shall probably never know for certain.

Despite her unflinching loyalty, Maggie was troubled by this episode. Even so, the mounting evidence of Lloyd George's tendency to stray did not persuade her to move the family base to London. It took a far more serious affair of his to persuade her not to leave him alone in the city. The two affairs were not unconnected, since it was when the Edwards case was at its height, and Lloyd George was under great pressure, that he felt the need for some comforting female companionship in London. With his career on a knife-edge and his wife still based in Criccieth, he needed support and he readily found it from another quarter.

8

Mrs Tim

Visiting the homes of Welsh friends was a normal Sunday-afternoon activity for the Lloyd Georges in London. When Dick was about eight years old, he and his father went to pay a social call in Putney, finding the lady of the house alone. Returning home, Dick ran to find his mother and excitedly told her of his adventures. He had seen Tada (Father) and the lady playing a game. 'He was eating her hand,' he said.[1] Maggie knew what that meant: Lloyd George was having an affair with Elizabeth, wife of his friend Timothy Davies. A row followed, the first of many over 'Mrs Tim'.

Elizabeth Davies was twenty-six in 1897, fourteen years younger than her husband. She lived in Oakhill Road, Putney, in a house named Pantycelyn,* within walking distance of the Lloyd Georges. Her life was comfortable if not exciting, with a rather dull husband and three children. Timothy Davies was a solid member of the London Welsh community, who Lloyd George rather unkindly held up to Maggie as a kind of 'insipid, wishy washy fellow'.[2] On his letterhead he styled himself a 'General Draper, Silk Mercer, Ladies Outfitter, Carpet and a furnishing warehouseman', and he owned a number of premises in Walham Green in Fulham. He was President of the Welsh Presbyterian Association and a Liberal who shared the same radical views as Lloyd George. He married Elizabeth (known as 'Lizzie' to her husband, 'Mrs Tim' to the Lloyd

* After one of the foremost Welsh hymn-writers.

George family) in 1893. She became an accomplished hostess, popular among the London Welsh, and Tim soon began to bring Lloyd George home. After making a success of his commercial ventures, Davies concentrated on politics, serving on London County Council, becoming Mayor of Fulham in 1901 and, with Lloyd George's active support, Liberal MP for Fulham from 1906 to 1910 and for Louth from 1910 to 1920. Before then, his home had become a refuge for the lonely young Lloyd George, a haven of good meals, blazing fires and political conversation.

The two men struck up a friendship, travelling abroad together at least twice without their wives – to Rome in December 1897 and on a cruise at the end of 1898. Perhaps Timothy Davies was oblivious to the growing attraction between Lloyd George and Lizzie, or perhaps he decided to follow the lead of the Prince of Wales' set and ignore the relationship. Either way, as Mrs Tim embarked on an affair with Lloyd George that was to last many years, her husband looked the other way.

Dick described Mrs Tim as 'a lively, attractive creature, rather loquacious, very stylish, perhaps a little flamboyant'.[3] She wore a scent that reminded him of a basket of carnations, and she went out of her way to charm the little boy. As for his father, Mrs Tim became the first woman to occupy a regular place in Lloyd George's life since his marriage to Maggie.

It was inevitable that this relationship would hurt Maggie. She could be certain that Lloyd George would not risk the major scandal of divorce, but it irked her that he should spend his time with another woman, especially a woman she considered inferior to herself in all but housekeeping ability. This tension shows in her letters. In May 1897 she upbraided Lloyd George for giving Mrs Tim a ticket for the Queen's Diamond Jubilee festivities, instead of the more worthy Davies family he had stayed with in Acton as a new MP. In reply, he came out fighting:

What a jealous little wife I have got to be sure! Now let me prove to her how groundless her suspicions are – as usual. So much was I in agreement with her as to the prior claims of the [Acton] Davies's, that I offered them my extra seat last night – but they had already received as many as eight seats elsewhere. I then told the Morgans, having got the Davies's out of the way, that I had an available seat – but they also had 'excellent seats' in another quarter. So poor Mrs Tim only comes third or even fourth. But still I don't wish her to occupy even that back seat if you object. Is there anyone else you would like me to hand my seat to?[4]

Lloyd George believed in brazening out any embarrassing situations, both in politics and in his personal life. His mistress, unlike Kitty Edwards, was not the type to risk her own comfortable situation, and Lloyd George trusted her not to expose their affair or to make excessive demands on him. Far from trying to keep the families apart, Lloyd George encouraged social contact between them. As the relationship between him and Mrs Tim flourished, his whole family was drawn into their social arrangements. Dick recalls being taken often to Pantycelyn, and going for long walks on which he and the Davies children would be sent ahead, allowing his father and Mrs Tim to have a leisurely tête-à-tête. Finally the penny dropped that this woman was making his mother unhappy, and although Mrs Tim was friendly and generous towards him, Dick turned against her with a fierce 'childish hostility'.*

Other members of the family also realised that there was more to their father's visits to Putney than social duty, including Olwen, who already had a reputation for being outspoken. She recalls playing a guessing game with her father, her siblings and Maggie, who had made her husband a present of a pen. Lloyd George held the pen aloft and invited his children to guess who had given it to him. 'Is it a lady?' he was asked. 'Oh yes!' 'Is it someone you kiss?' asked Dick. 'Well, yes!' came the reply. Then, in her innocence, Olwen dropped the bombshell. 'Is it Mrs Timothy Davies?' The embarrassed silence that followed opened her eyes for the first time to her father's infidelity.[5]

In the spring and summer of 1897, tension simmered between Maggie and Lloyd George. Maggie was jealous of Mrs Tim, and they were both feeling lonely as they continued to spend long periods apart. At the end of May, Maggie wrote from Criccieth chiding her husband once more for not spending enough time with his family. He, always on the lookout for ways of increasing his income, was about to start up a law practice in London, at 13 Walbrook in the heart of the City. His partner,

---

* Dick claimed that one of Mrs Tim's children was in fact Lloyd George's, but there is no corroborating evidence.

the Anglesey lawyer Arthur Rhys Roberts, was expected to do the work, while Lloyd George, with his store of London contacts, provided the clients. Money, he replied to Maggie, was the reason he needed to stay in London. Her dismissive response provoked him to set out a few home truths:

> You say you would rather have less money and live in a healthy place. Well, hen gariad [little love], you will not forget that you were as keen about my starting as I was myself. Then you must bear in mind that we are spending more than we earn. I draw far more than my share of the profits [of the North Wales practice] though I don't attend to 1/10th of the work. This is neither fair nor honourable & feel sure you do not wish it to continue.

For all their sakes, he argued, it was time for his family to join him on a permanent basis:

> Now you can't make omelettes without breaking eggs & unless I retire from politics altogether & content myself with returning to the position of a country attorney, we must give up the comforts of Criccieth for life in England. As to attending to the business during sessions & running away from it afterwards your good sense will show you on reflection that it is impossible. No business could be conducted successfully on those terms. You are not right, however, that this presupposes living entirely in London. If you prefer, we can take a home somewhere in the suburbs – say Ealing or Acton, Ealing for choice. There the air is quite as good as anything you can get in Wales as it is free from the smoke of the great city. Or if you prefer we could go still further out & live say in Brighton as Clifton does . . . Think of it, old pet, & think of it with all the courage of which I know you capable.[6]

Maggie would not budge, and by August Lloyd George's sympathy was wearing a little thin: 'How infinite your self-pity is! Poor lonely <u>wife</u>. You are surrounded by all who love you best – father, mother, children, Uncle Lloyd & all. But can't you spare some sympathy & compassion for the poor lonely husband who is surrounded on all hands by wolves who would tear him – did they not fear his claw?'[7]

A few days later he wrote Maggie a loving letter, but the teasing, affectionate tone of the correspondence between them was about to be rudely interrupted. They were still under pressure from the Edwards divorce case, but the incident that sparked their most serious quarrel yet was Maggie's decision not to accompany her husband on a trip to Llangadog in Carmarthenshire, presumably on political business. On 13 August Uncle Lloyd recorded in his diary that both Maggie and William George had received strong letters from Lloyd George: 'Mag heard from D.Ll.G – fully expecting her to go to Llangadock. Pity he made his mind so – as she is unable to go. W.G. had letter today also, it seems.'[8] His tone is sympathetic towards Maggie – at least, he does not seem to blame her for not going. He and William George often thought Maggie's decision to stay in Criccieth far more reasonable than Lloyd George allowed. They were in a position to see the practical difficulties of moving a young family between Criccieth and London, and tended to take Maggie's side.

Not so Lloyd George. His letter to William was angry and vengeful. He decided to force Maggie to join him in London permanently by giving up their house in Criccieth:

My wife declines to go out of her way to spend Sunday with me at Llangadock. She makes the kids an excuse. Becca [Owen, a cousin] would be only too glad to take up her quarters at Bryn Awel* for a few days to look after them. I have made up my mind to give up the Criccieth house altogether. M. is giving notice today. She has failed to let it furnished, and even if she succeeded I shall want the furniture for a house up here [in London]. I mean to let the flat and take a small house in the suburbs. You can't keep kids in a flat. Can't you let Bryn Awel for me unfurnished?[9]

Lloyd George's peremptory tone and unilateral decision-making might have brought some wives to heel, but not Maggie. It was one thing for him to ask her to join him in London, quite another for him to give up the house her father had built for their use without her agreement. Maggie wrote a furious and destructive letter threatening her husband

* 'Breeze Hill', their Criccieth home, sometimes referred to as Brynawelon. Brynawelon was also the name they gave to the house they built in Criccieth in 1908.

with a public scandal. It has not survived, and we do not know if she was alluding to his relationship with Mrs Tim, some other personal matter, or, since Lloyd George was under pressure from his constituents because of the infrequency of his visits, a political exposure. The gist of her threats can be deduced from Lloyd George's reply. In a cold, cruel letter he hit back, targeting her own weak spot: her failure as a wife:

> When next you discuss your relations with your husband with the servants you may tell Jane – since you quote her views as having so much weight – that the marriage vow was not one-sided. You have worried me to distraction about my share of it. What about yours? You have <u>wilfully</u> disobeyed your husband – in a matter he was enti-tled to obedience – yes in a matter any other wife would have been only too delighted to obey him in.
>
> You threaten me with a public scandal. Alright – expose me if that suits you. One scandal the more will but kill me the earlier. But you will not alter my resolution to have neither correspondence nor commu-nication of any sort with you until it is more clearly understood how you purpose to guide your course for the future. I have borne it for years & have suffered in health & character. I'll stand it no longer come what may.[10]

He does not deny that Maggie has the ammunition to cause a scandal. Instead he argues that it is all her fault. Her neglect is responsible for his defects of both 'health' and 'character'. Instead of reassurance, she received an ultimatum: he would not write or talk to her again until she agreed to join him in London. Her reply, unfortunately, is also lost and the trail of letters is difficult to follow, since in the heat of the argu-ment they wrote to each other more than once a day,* but it seems that it was an angry one. This drew a curt and equally unconciliatory letter back from Lloyd George: 'What colleague do you allude to? You

---

* The letters between Maggie and Lloyd George are unreliably dated at best during this period. Both sometimes put the wrong date on letters, and Maggie frequently gives no date, or just the day of the week. Some of the dates given are from postmarks, others are based on the information available and on the letters' internal evidence.

are still at your old trick of innuendo. You say this business is childish. You may yet find it is more serious than child's play.'[11]

Maggie must have sent another letter the same day containing an apology, for Lloyd George wrote again later in a softened tone, and although he returned to the ongoing quarrel, he also sent a gift of fruit: 'I would much rather see you express sorrow for your refusal to comply with your husband's earnest desire to see you than defend yourself as you do. It was a wilful act of disobedience. Of course I did not command. That is what no husband cares to do to his wife but I did entreat – for the last time.'[12]

Maggie, though, was not quite ready to let the matter rest. It seems she sent another intemperate letter – or perhaps their letters crossed – followed immediately by an apologetic and capitulatory telegram. Sensing victory, Lloyd George wrote back pressing his advantage to secure his goal of getting Maggie to agree to move to London:

My sweet but stupid Maggie

That telegram just saved you. Your letter this morning made me wild – there was the same self-complacent self-satisfied Pharisaism about it as ever. You had done no wrong. Even now there is a phrase in it that I cannot pass by unnoticed. When did I ever suggest in the faintest measure that you were a burden to me? Have I not always complained rather that you 'burdened' me too little with your society? You have no right to make these charges. What I have said I neither withdraw nor modify how grave soever the implication may be – nor do I wish to retract a syllable of what I told you in London about my being even happier when you & the kids are around me. A wise woman who loved her husband well & who knew herself well-beloved by him, would not write foolish letters arguing out the matter with him & doing that badly – she would rather put these things together, ponder them well & resolve at all costs to redeem the past.

He then goes for the kill.

Be candid with yourself. Drop that infernal Methodism which is the curse of your bitter nature & reflect whether you have not rather neglected your husband. I have more than once gone without breakfast. I have scores of times come home in the dead of night to a cold dark & comfortless flat without a soul to greet me. When you were surrounded by your pets.

Next comes the nearest thing to a confession Lloyd George ever made:

I am not the nature either physically or morally that ought to have been left thus. I decline to argue & you will mortally offend me if you attempt it. I simply ask you in all sincerity of soul – yes, & as a message of true love I supplicate you to give heed to what I am telling you now – not for the first time. I shall then ask you how you would like to meet your Judge if all this neglect led me astray. You have been a good mother. You have not – & I say this now not in anger – not always been a good wife. I can point you even amongst those whom you affect to look down upon – much better wives. You may be a blessing to your children. Oh Maggie annwyl [darling] beware lest you be a curse to your husband. My soul as well as my body has been committed to your charge & in many respects I am as helpless as a child.[13]

As an argument of defence, the letter is masterful. It would not sound out of place as a sermon, delivered in solemn tones from the pulpit of Seion. How well Lloyd George knew his wife. In asking her to abandon her Methodism he plays on it for all he is worth, conjuring up the Calvinistic exhortation to reflect on sin, and encouraging her to take on the responsibility and guilt for his own moral lapses.

The row was over, and the correspondence between them swung back into its previous comfortable rhythm, but a powerful message had been delivered to Maggie. She did not dismiss Lloyd George's covert warning that her absences were leading him into temptation. While she was in Wales the despised Mrs Tim had a clear field, and with the children growing older, she had less reason to cling on to Criccieth. Nevertheless, the bonds were difficult to break, and it was not until the end of 1898 that she finally agreed to join her husband in the city she hated.

With peace restored – somewhat precariously – between Maggie and Lloyd George, a happier period ensued. Indeed, for a family commuting between North Wales and London, theirs was a remarkably stable home life, due to Maggie's unblinking focus on her children. The elder children, Dick, Mair and Olwen, had happy memories of growing up in Criccieth, largely cared for by Richard and Mary Owen and watched over by Uncle Lloyd in Garthcelyn, the house William had built for the family. With Maggie dividing her time unevenly between Criccieth and London, Dick remembers her as an occasional visitor during his infancy, with longer spells at home before a new brother or sister arrived. As a young child he missed his mother very much, and he may have exaggerated their periods of separation. His early memories may also have been coloured by the fact that he was sent back to Criccieth to attend school during the Boer War which broke out in 1899, and lived apart from his family for large parts of the year. Mair left no diary or memoir to speak for her, but Olwen, three years younger than Dick, writes of growing up in London with only extended holidays spent in Criccieth. The truth probably lies in between: the family was firmly based in Criccieth in the early 1890s, but as time went on pressure grew on Maggie to spend more time in London. She usually took the youngest member or members of the family with her, leaving the elder children behind, which would account for the different recollections of Dick and Olwen.

Dick was a sensitive boy who inherited his mother's love of North Wales but did not possess his father's brilliance and ambition. His restless energy found an outlet in mischief, especially during endless sermons in chapel, and he was made to sit with Richard Owen in the 'set fawr', the front pew reserved for deacons, on more than one occasion to put a stop to his antics. He had a gift for mimicry, and when he began to acquire some English he found he could deflect his mother's anger by assuming an exaggerated accent and declaring 'Oh I say!', reducing her to helpless laughter. He was very close to Maggie, whom he worshipped, and as the first grandchild in either the Owen or the Lloyd family, he was secure in the attention of both.

As a child growing up by the sea in Criccieth, Dick was enthralled by the sight of the hundred-ton schooners moored to the stone jetty under the castle rock waiting their turn to load up with Porthmadoc slate. He watched their sails unfurl as they left the shelter of the bay for the open sea, and listened to the tales of weather-hardened fishermen on the seafront. The 'maes' (village green) gave yet more scope for entertainment as farmers and stockmen compared notes with Richard Owen presiding. Here, though, young Lloyd Georges had to behave or risk the displeasure of Uncle Lloyd, who frequently sat on a bench overlooking the maes. As the eldest child, Dick was more aware of the tension between his parents than were his siblings, and he was badly affected by their heated rows.

With regard to religion, a compromise was reached despite the entrenched attitudes of the older generation. Dick was raised a Baptist, and attended Berea, the handsome new chapel which replaced Capel Ucha in 1886, with Uncle Lloyd every Sunday; Mair was christened a Methodist like Maggie; Olwen was a Baptist; and Gwilym a Methodist. Only Megan, the youngest, bucked the pattern by becoming a Methodist too. When Maggie was at home she would take all the children with her to Seion, but when she was away Dick would sometimes take Megan to the Baptist service on Sunday mornings, and both would go to the Methodist service in the evening. This was all highly irregular, but not, it seems, confusing to the children, who were loyal to their own denomination while being perfectly at home in the other.

Mair Eluned's arrival in August 1890 brought great joy to the family. Lloyd George had longed for a daughter, and he doted on the little girl. Mair was a special child who inspired great love from the beginning. She was beautiful and intelligent, and had a gentleness about her that led her brother and sister to use words like 'saintly' and 'angelic' to describe her, without ever implying that she was priggish or dull. The only musical child of the family, she loved to play her father's favourite hymns on the piano.

Olwen, next in line, was born in 1892, and could not have been more different in looks or personality. While Mair had dark hair, Olwen was the fairest of all the children, earning herself the nickname 'Llwydyn' (little pale one). Outspoken, determined and independent, she was 'magnificently formidable' according to Dick. What she lacked in academic ability she made up for in common sense, and she shared Maggie's uncomplicated view of the world, her patriotism and her religious steadfastness.

Gwilym, born in 1894, was for seven years the baby of the family. Peaceable and slow to anger, he could nevertheless be a bit of a handful when in the mood for mischief. He, far more than his elder brother, inherited Lloyd George's interest in politics, and took every opportunity to accompany his father to the House of Commons. There he would solemnly shake the hand of every policeman he saw, believing that they were on the lookout for naughty children, and that by befriending them he would be safe from censure.

By the time Megan Arvon arrived in 1902 to complete the family, Gwilym was already in school, leaving the new arrival to soak up the attention of the adults. Megan more than made the most of her opportunity. From the beginning she was, as Dick says, 'the Personality'. Vivacious and quick-witted, she played to the audience at every opportunity, and entertained her father with her sharp sense of humour. By the time Megan was born Lloyd George was a successful politician, and she took for granted the attention lavished on her father and, by extension, on his family. The limelight that engulfed the family was as natural and desirable to Megan as it was uncomfortable to the older children, and the family's view was that if Megan had not pursued politics as a career she could have been a successful actress.

Life in Criccieth was full of adventure for the children, even if their freedom to roam around the town and neighbouring farms was counterbalanced by strict discipline at home, where the threat of the birch rod, wielded by Maggie or Mary Owen (never by their husbands) was ever-present. Whenever they returned to Criccieth from London Lloyd George would get the whole family to give a loud cheer on rounding the corner on the Porthmadoc road and catching their first glimpse of the castle. The children got on well together, spending their days in the pine-clad nursery at the top of Bryn Awel with its magnificent views of the castle and across Criccieth Bay, running next door to visit the Owens, or venturing further afield to be spoiled by Betsy and Polly at Garthcelyn.

Polly became even more devout than her mother. Denied the chance of a career, she devoted herself instead to chapel life and the community in which she lived, and took charge of the spiritual as well as the physical wellbeing of her younger brothers. She was the housekeeper, hostess and female head of the household during her brothers' bachelor years, and lived at Morvin House and then at Garthcelyn until she died prematurely in August 1909 at the age of forty-seven. Such was her devotion to the family that she did not leave even when she married. Her husband, Philip Davies, was a sea captain who spent months away at sea, and Polly was needed at home to look after the ageing Betsy, Richard and the bachelor William. She sometimes accompanied her husband on short voyages, however, and her letters home reveal that her horizons were not as limited as has sometimes been assumed, since she spent time with him in Rotterdam, Paris and Liverpool in 1898 and 1899. Polly was thirty-five when she married, and she never had children of her own. Instead, she took an active interest in her nieces and nephews. Although she was strict with them, and a fierce keeper of the Sabbath, she liked to take them on outings to Tripp Farm overlooking the sea, with games on the beach and a huge spread to follow, or to Beddgelert, a nearby beauty spot.

The biggest excitement of all, however, was when Lloyd George made an appearance in Criccieth. Olwen recalled that 'Tada's' presence created a whirlwind of activity: 'When I think of my father, I remember more than anything else the feeling of excitement every time he came home. We always knew when he was there. There was a kind of electricity running through the house. You felt something was going to happen. When he arrived unexpectedly, everything would suddenly become alive.'[14]

Lloyd George had a special affinity with children, and whatever shortcomings he may have had as a husband, he was a loving and attentive father. He wrote to Maggie in 1896 after cancelling a visit to Criccieth: 'I am so sorry to have to disappoint you . . . Don't forget that it is very much worse for me than for you. You've got the youngsters around you. Every little one I see toddling around reminds me of one or other of the hen byttia bach [little tots]. I get quite depressed about it occasionally.'[15] His letters home are peppered with anxious enquiries about the children, and he saw reminders of them everywhere: 'The Mediterranean as blue as Wil [Gwilym] bach's eye – and as sparkling as Llwyd [Olwen] bach's . . .'[16]

When his schedule allowed him to get back to Criccieth he would bring presents for the children – usually boxes of fruit bought at Victoria Station, but sometimes more exotic gifts. At the end of 1897, returning from Rome where he had had a Papal audience, he gave Olwen some sweets that the Pope himself had blessed. He had been given a second packet for Tim Healy and John Dillon, two leading Irish politicians, as a symbolic gesture to bring peace.[17] Olwen, by her own admission, was a greedy little girl, and to Lloyd George's dismay she polished off both packets. By doing so, he claimed, she delayed peace in Ireland for years.

Lloyd George was keen to give his children the same nurturing and encouragement that he had received from his family. The older children received their early education in Criccieth, with Welsh as their first language. Their mother ensured that they were familiar with Welsh history and legends, but none was as keen a reader as their father, and he came to feel that they were behind in their familiarity with the classics. His remedy was entertaining and highly effective. He always had a book on the go himself, often a novel by Dickens or a Dumas thriller. On Sunday evenings in London before the children went to bed they would gather in the drawing room and he would act out whatever he was reading. Dick recalls:

> Even in those early days, my father was rapidly becoming for me a sort of wonder man, a mesmerist, a story-teller who could enact the roles of six different characters from Monte Christo or David Copperfield ... Thus I wept bitterly over Mr Murdstone's cruelty to poor helpless David. And when Jean Valjean put his mighty shoulder under the shaft of the broken cart to release the guard slowly being pulverised beneath it, I held my breath until my face turned scarlet in sympathy with the strain; and my father would have to terminate the performance abruptly to prevent me having convulsions.[18]

The children pleaded with him to continue, but he would send them to bed, saying that he had only read that far, and that they would have to wait until the following week to see what happened.

Occasionally Lloyd George would take the children to the House of Commons. He described one such visit in a letter to his brother in 1898:

> Dick and Gwilym on Terrace yesterday. I had been telling Dick the story of Oliver Cromwell and Charles 1. How the former fought for the Capelwrs [chapel-goers] against the Eglwyswrs [church-goers] ... Dick got quite excited and so did Wil bach ... Dick wanted to see the

death warrant of Charles 1 – the spot where he stood when he was tried and the place of his execution. He regarded with great interest the signature of John Jones the Regicide.[19]

If Lloyd George was loved by his children, Maggie was worshipped by them. Like Mary Owen before her, she was engrossed and fulfilled by her family. Whatever criticism she might incur as a wife, her ability and commitment as a mother were not in doubt. She took charge of discipline within the family, and was only a little more liberal than her own mother, but this did not make her a stern or killjoy parent. She was as ready as Lloyd George to enter into games, as Olwen recalled: 'Mother liked being out of doors and she liked games. She enjoyed playing cricket with the boys, and sometimes sent the ball into other people's gardens. She used to send Gwilym, the youngest boy, to fetch it. Eventually we had to stop her because she was losing too many balls.'[20] Maggie also made sure that family celebrations were memorable. She made a great fuss of birthdays, and held a big family party at Christmas. Once, when the gas range broke on Christmas morning, she cooked and served a feast in the cellar, where the range was still hot, and the whole family ate by candlelight, to their great delight.

The children were too small to register the fluctuations in their parents' relationship, but Christmas 1893 was the first that Lloyd George chose to spend away from his family. This was partly because he disliked the Criccieth climate, which was at its most unpleasant in December and January. He often headed abroad in search of warmth instead, a fact that Maggie grew to accept.

Naturally, the children absorbed their mother's love of Criccieth, with its freedom to roam and aunts and uncles to fuss over them. Olwen says that she hated being in London, where she had to be looked after every minute of the day. Her only freedom was walking in the park with her nursemaid, Kate, whose hands were always unpleasantly hot to hold. How much of this attitude was genuine and how much of it inherited from the adults in Criccieth is not clear. Maggie was not the only one who desperately wanted the family to stay in North Wales. Olwen recalls: 'Grandfather used to take us along the sea wall, and we loved running up and down it. There was a song he used to sing in

Welsh as I ran: "Little Olwen and I were going to London, but the way is far and the water is wet, so we are going to stay where we are." '[21] It was understandable for Richard Owen to want to keep his daughter and grandchildren near him: that was why he had built twin houses for them. Whether it was helpful for the children to have their mother's dislike of London reinforced by their grandparents, however, is questionable.

Maggie spent most of the first half of 1895 in Criccieth, following the birth of Gwilym the previous December. Her mother was not well, which gave her an additional reason for staying at home, and with a general election looking likely, Lloyd George would have been spending more time in his constituency than usual. He had won a reputation as a firebrand radical in Parliament, and to no one's surprise he was not always in agreement with his party's leadership. He was also much taken up with a movement called Cymru Fydd* during this period. Under the auspices of the Calvinistic Methodist minister and leading Welsh nationalist Thomas Gee, and Lloyd George's friend Tom Ellis, Cymru Fydd, which had begun as a group of Welsh nationalists based in London, campaigned for a Welsh legislative assembly and provided a focus for an emerging Welsh national consciousness.

Lord Rosebery had succeeded Gladstone as Liberal Prime Minister in 1894, and by the following year his administration was in serious trouble, and it was a case of when, not if, its credibility would be put to the test. During the course of 1895 Lloyd George and his Welsh colleagues were preoccupied by the passage of the Welsh Church Bill. Lloyd George, who had particularly strong views on disestablishment and was impervious to any attempt by the government to bring its backbenchers into line, organised a rebellion against a contentious clause in the Bill, with the Tory party's gleeful cooperation. In the event, on 21 June, before the rebels had their moment, Rosebery lost a parliamentary vote of censure on cordite supplies and, fatally weakened, resigned. Salisbury took his place, embarking on his third term of office, and a general election followed.

* The name is difficult to translate, but carries the meaning of both 'Future Wales' and 'Wales-Will-Be'.

In Caernarvon Boroughs, Lloyd George's opponent was once again Hugh Ellis-Nanney, but this time he was vulnerable because he was open to the charge of helping to bring down the Liberal government with his well-publicised guerrilla campaign to amend the Welsh Church Bill. Lloyd George faced his critics down. If he was a thorn in the side of a Liberal government, he audaciously asked, how much more so would he be to a Conservative administration? He retained his seat with an unchanged margin of victory on 22 July, but nationally Salisbury secured a Tory majority of 152. It was the beginning of a decade in opposition for Lloyd George. He was not comfortable as an establishment figure, and opposition quite suited him. Over the next ten years he would be transfigured from prominent Welsh politician to national political leader.

Following the election, Lloyd George took over as the parliamentary leader of Cymru Fydd, to the resentment of some MPs who feared he was building up a personal power base. At first the movement gained momentum from his leadership, and he campaigned tirelessly across Wales. His hopes of a unified national structure were boosted when the North Wales Liberal Federation merged with Cymru Fydd, but to his intense frustration the South Wales Federation rejected a merger in a stormy meeting in Newport in January 1896. By 1900 Cymru Fydd was moribund, having failed to attract Wales-wide support.

The strain of his continuous campaigning was bound to show, and on 26 July 1895, while speaking at an event in Amlwch, Lloyd George had a minor breakdown. He was brought home to Maggie, and stayed in her care for a fortnight – an unusually long period of time for them to spend together, particularly in Criccieth. His collapse was part physical, part emotional, but it did no lasting damage. Maggie was at her best when looking after her sick husband. Calm, soothing and gentle, she was the perfect nurse, and his two-week recuperation was a happy period for the couple. The following year he wrote fondly, if not entirely convincingly: 'I always come back with a sensation of restful delight to Brynawelon. I only wish I could get such a fortnight there as I enjoyed immediately after my election collapse. In spite of my complete physical prostration I never enjoyed my life as I did then. I felt perfectly happy.'[22]

*

In February 1896 Maggie was showing no sign of spending more time in London, and the old familiar subject cropped up again in their correspondence. She charged Lloyd George with neglecting their home in Wales, and received a reminder in return that it was not his fault that the family was separated for long periods of time: 'You know very well that the pressure to bring us together invariably comes from me. I have led a very strenuous and anxious life for the past five years, & it is beginning to tell upon me. That has had a good deal to do with my apparent indifference to my home.'[23]

It was true that Lloyd George's London lifestyle was unsatisfactory. In Maggie's absence he looked after himself as best he could, and his letters are full of descriptions of domestic disharmony, intended no doubt to inspire sympathy and guilt in his absent wife: 'My bread is now so hard that I could hardly cut it with a knife,' he wrote in July 1896;[24] more alarmingly, he wrote the following year: 'you can't leave me in town alone. That would be an act of desertion which I know you are too noble to contemplate . . . Besides Heaven knows what it might not eventually lead me to.'[25]

Maggie was with Lloyd George in London before he left on his business trip to Argentina in August 1896, and sometime during this period – possibly as soon as the family finances could stretch to it – she engaged a Welsh servant to look after him. This put an end to his plaintive letters for a while.

At the end of 1896 Maggie discovered she was pregnant again. In February 1897, while the Kitty Edwards affair was causing tongues to wag vigorously in North Wales, she went to visit Lloyd George in London, and on 1 March he telegrammed his sister Polly asking her to come in haste to London, where Maggie was laid up 'as last summer'. It was her second miscarriage in twelve months. Lloyd George was normally squeamish when it came to physical illness. He was as dismissive of others' ailments as he was over-anxious about his own, but during Maggie's recovery he was a tender and loving husband. He wrote to her later in the year that he and a colleague 'were talking about our respective wives last night & we both said that the affection of a man for his wife was a much tenderer & carer & deeper feeling than any passing fancy of the hour. I said that I had discovered that when you were ill.'[26]

Lloyd George's plans to set up a family home in London in 1897 resulted from his confident expectations of the London law practice together with yet another business investment, this time in the Dorothea slate mine in North Wales. By the end of August that had fallen through, and the pressure on Maggie to give up Bryn Awel gradually receded. They could not afford a house in the London suburbs even if they had both wanted one. The whole family was feeling the financial pressure. In January 1898 William George recorded in his diary:

D and M have only just left . . . I consider the question of accounts a serious one, and I wanted to arouse D's anxiety about it. I think I succeeded in doing so, much to the disturbance of his peace of mind, I am sorry to say, and to the subsequent breach of the family concord. But it cannot be helped. All the extravagance will have to be stopped and 2 or 3 years of the strictest economy practised . . . D takes a very sensible view of things but Margaret doesn't I am afraid. It is natural she should kick a bit, but when she brings that strong common sense of hers into play everything will be set to rights, in a very short time, I fancy.[27]

Maggie's common sense did come into play when it became clear that in order to make ends meet, Lloyd George had to spend more time building up his legal business in London. With financial pressure forcing her hand, and with the evidence mounting that Mrs Tim was all too eager to look after her husband in her place, Maggie finally gave notice to her father in April 1898 that she would be leaving the house later that year. The decision must have cost her dearly. After ten years of marriage and four children, she was giving up the idea that her home was in Criccieth. For the foreseeable future at least, when she returned there it would be as a guest in her parents' house. It would be ten years before she would again have a home in North Wales.

Maggie's decision was sure to please her husband, and the correspondence between them was warm and affectionate through the first half of 1898. She had intended to leave Criccieth in November of that year, but it was to be another year before the family moved into their new home in Trinity Road, Wandsworth. Maggie had been obliged to follow Betsy's lead and take in visitors as paying guests, which strongly suggests that a shortage of money was the reason for the delay. But her decision to postpone their reunion did not prevent Maggie from becoming more and more jealous of the time her husband spent in Mrs Tim's parlour. With the Kitty Edwards court case dragging on, she was especially sensitive on the subject of her husband's fidelity, and she made him promise that while she was in Criccieth he would not go to Putney or see Lizzie Davies. Lloyd George must have given his word, whether or not he intended to keep it. But in August came the confirmation that Maggie had been dreading. She wrote an emotional letter, confronting him directly with her suspicions:

I had your letter & your message re Conway. I will come there to meet you & bring your things if urgent business calls you back to town & you cannot spend Sunday with the children here. Perhaps after you read what I have to say you would rather that I should send your things rather than meet you. Wire me early whether I am to come or not.

I was very much upset this morning when Kate [the children's nurse-maid in London] casually told me of a very early visitor you had at Palace Mansions one morning there by arrangement at about nine a m, & you ready and drove off with them. I suppose I find out one of these meetings accidentally. How many more of which I know nothing, I cannot say. They naturally make me very unhappy & doubtful & this grieves me terribly to waver in my faith of <u>one</u> I would not for the world mistrust in the least.

The evidence appeared incontrovertible: Lloyd George was still seeing Mrs Tim, even if he had kept his promise not to visit her house without his wife. Maggie quotes from his letters to prove that he set out to deceive her:

I have been reading today your letters dated July 25th & here is an extract, 'Herbert I failed to see so I went to Club. Intended going Castle St instead went to Park. Lovely music. Sat it out till after nine.' Is not that written to convey to my mind an impression that you had kept your promise to me. I care not in what form I had written of it as visiting their house or otherwise it matters not to me. I would rather a short curt note were it <u>straight</u> than a most affectionate letter planned to mislead me. If I treated you so I know what you would think of me.

Maggie's discovery that he had been lying was devastating. Her emotions raw, she pleaded piteously with him to stay true to her, for the sake of their marriage as well as his career:

> This business I tell you comes between <u>you and me</u> more so than you imagine & is growing, & you know it & yet you cannot shake it off. It pains me to the quick, & I am very unhappy. If you must go on as at present I don't know where it will end. And yet you assure me. I want to know what I am to believe. I can't write more. I wish I could go somewhere & cry to relieve myself. I have your own view of other men & that is that they can't stop at the place they may desire. Beware. Don't give place for any scandal for the sake of your own personal self and your bright career.
> Yours very sorrowfully,
> M[28]

This was the closest Maggie ever came to losing faith in her husband. For the first and possibly only time in their marriage she had proof that he was lying to her. It was an unusual slip for Lloyd George to make, and he reacted in an uncharacteristic way, mollifying his wife instead of fighting back. Fortunately for him he saw Maggie three days later, presumably at the Conway meeting she alluded to in her letter. It was a fleeting encounter, but it was long enough for Lloyd George to work his charm. With an eyewitness to his meeting with Mrs Tim there was little he could do but confess to it, but he claimed that it had been at her request, to escort her to catch an early train. After parting, Maggie wrote from Caernarvon: 'Our meeting passed off (I mean ours you & I) much calmer than I had dreamt, alright dont you go escorting any more to stations will you & we shall be friends. I am much happier tonight. Paid ti a gadael i neb beri anghydfod rhyngom ni. [Don't you let anyone cause disharmony between us.] I wish I had more of your company. It seems to have slipped away so quickly . . .'[29]

Maggie had forgiven him, but he had more work to do before she would forget his transgression, and for a few days he was on his best behaviour: 'I know you would stick up for me – on all occasions,' he wrote two days later. 'I would trust you with my life & honour. There is no one – except my dear old uncle – whom I place such implicit unquestioning confidence in. You will, I feel certain, pardon my placing him on a level even with my hen Faggie [dear Maggie]. Won't you hen gariad [dear love].'[30] For a while Maggie was showered with attention: 'Well I was surprised this morning when I got *three* letters all together from you,' she wrote. '. . . I am glad you are pleased with your hen Fagi for standing out for you. Mrs M. said that I was a brick of a wife, over & over again. I never thought myself so till she told me.' She was back on Lloyd George's side, affronted that Mrs Tim should have the presumption to ask him to act as her escort:

> It is not saying what a nice little woman she is, I would not mind that, but things much more tangible than that, is the cause of my being a prey to the green eyed monster. I am very angry with Mrs T. for persevering so much with you. Fancy coming over to a man like you, so superior to her Tim, and thinking it was an honour to you to see her off. I am very disgusted to tell you the truth. The idea. I am more angry than ever with her for her presumption. I would not dream of going to any friend to expect anything of the sort. Mi rodd o yn swydd rhy sal o lawer i ti. [It was far too poor a job for you.] She had no business to do such a thing, and if I see any inclination on her part to make you <u>cheap</u> I shall some way or another make her understand that I will not have it . . . I feel exactly the same with you as you do with me if someone does not show me every respect.
>
> Yours in true love
> Kisses without end
> Maggie[31]

There is just a hint in her words that she objected to Mrs Tim's vulgarity. Maggie had a fixed view of the world, in which everyone knew their place, and something about Mr and Mrs Timothy Davies raised her hackles. A few days later she found another reason to criticise her:

Fancy Mrs Tim not telling her husband where she is. She is not fit to have married any man . . . Caiff helynt gyda hi ryw ddydd [He'll have trouble with her some day]. Mae ei hen gariad Mrs Captain Howard yn Criccieth. Mae hi yn llawn [his old sweetheart Mrs Howard is in Criccieth. She is fully] as nice looking as Mrs T, & more . . . but she thought Tim too goody-goody for her, ond cafodd e golled maen diawn [but he suffered a loss, for sure].[32]

With Lloyd George in a penitent mood, Maggie could not hold back. But it was not to last long. Unwisely, a few weeks later she attacked him fiercely for preferring Pantycelyn to their flat, which prompted a hurtful response from her husband: 'So would anybody. Mrs T with all her defects – and these I am not blind to – is at least fairly interesting. By the way I hear she is seriously ill. T. just been on the telephone wanting me to go for a drive with him this afternoon. Says Mrs T. rather bad. Has to undergo an operation. What it is I don't know. He had just seen the Doctor and was rather despondent. That will please you I suppose.'[33]

Maggie's pride was wounded, and she took the moral high ground in return:

I am surprised that you should think I would be pleased to hear of Mrs Tim's illness. I am never pleased to hear of people's misfortune however much I might dislike them. I suppose you were too despondent to sleep after hearing it, that's the state you are in no doubt. I am just as sorry for her as I would be for any other woman I know, I am not like you that I treat her as I would any other person, but to you she is different. You sneer at me when you say she is ill. I can't help it. I wish I could suffer in her place, to relieve all round.[34]

He had hit a nerve, and she became suspicious that he was still seeing Mrs Tim. Three days later she went too far, demanding to know what he was doing with his time. It was more than he could stand, and she had to swallow her words: 'I will apologise for what I asked you about your evenings & I am very glad to know that you are able to keep from being too often in company with the one I mentioned.'[35]

But she was still offended, and the exchange that followed shows how easily misunderstandings occurred when they were separated for long periods of time, especially on long-sensitive subjects like visits to London. A letter from Maggie prompted another chilling, legalistic response:

> I am very disappointed with your letter. I had been thinking very fondly of you all day yesterday. I had been drawing pictures of your coming to the office to fetch me at 4 – of our going to tea together – then spending the evening either in the Parks or some place of amusement & this morning as I woke I looked forward with a sense of anticipatory joy to receiving an affectionate warm letter from my old Maggie. But when I read it! How it chilled me. 'If you wish me to come' let me know – I'll obey if you command. I thought in my foolish heart you might not be displeased at the idea of having any excuse for seeing your Dei after five weeks of separation. I am to go here but not there. I am to see these people, but not those. This is the tenor of my recent correspondence. It won't do. I should have thought bitter experience had taught you I am not to be directed by letter. However as you will.[36]

Maggie was in no mood to quarrel this time, and wrote quickly to explain herself:

> My Dearest Dei,
> You have quite misunderstood my letter. What I meant was to know clearly whether you could come or not. Yr Hen Ddafydd, yr wyt yn rhy barod i fy nrwgdybio bob amser, a'r tro yma yr wyt yn gwbl oddi ar y track [Dear David, you are always too quick to suspect me, and this time you are completely off the track]. My letter was written when my mind was full of the sweetest thoughts possible of you, & indeed I will dearly enjoy coming up to you for a fortnight, till the end of the month.

She goes on to explain that her summer visitors prevented her from coming to London straight away, chides him gently for the tone of his letter and, teasing him a little perhaps in view of her famous dislike of housework, describes in loving detail how she plans to look after him (translated from Welsh): 'You were nasty today, but I shall see you soon, and all will be well. Don't think that I don't like coming to you, whatever. We'll go to the flat, the two of us, to sleep and I'll make us both breakfast, and wash the dishes, and I'll make our bed and Mrs White will come to scrub the kitchen and clean the parlour and the Hall for us, yes? Living for a while without a maid, see how I would like it!'[37]

She seemed to be ready to travel to London, but five days later she was still at home, and forced to explain away yet another misunderstanding between them. This time the cause is not apparent – perhaps a business deal of some kind – but it is evident that their relationship was still tense:

My Dearest Dei

Your letter of yesterday astounded me beyond anything & yours of today was nothing but a [illegible] note. I mentioned that matter to you, not in order to worry you or give you trouble, or to satisfy my own selfishness as you say but because I was asked to do so, by one who is as much affected by it as you are . . . Uncle Lloyd has been kept in ignorance of it . . . ond beth bynnag a ddigwyddo a phwy bynnag fydd yn gyfrifol am bethau o'r fath fe fydd y cerydd yn sicr o ddisgyn arnaf i . . . ond does dim i'w wneud ond ei gymryd yn ddistaw [but whatever happens and whoever is responsible for things like this, the censure will surely fall upon me . . . but there is nothing to be done except to accept it quietly]. You thank me today in the most sneering way for my instructions to you to come over here. I think Dei that it is both absurd & wrong to suggest such a thing. You know very well and so do they all here that I have been expecting a wire to come up to town . . . Now I am told to stay where I am. That I am not wanted . . . However now you have my explanation I have nothing more to offer.

Yours in sorrow

M[38]

Her explanation was accepted, and the affectionate tone was reinstated in their correspondence.

Whatever lay behind this particular quarrel, it was unlikely to be Mrs Tim. The relationship between Lloyd George and Lizzie Davies had settled back into a flirtatious friendship, although he never severed the connection entirely. He remained good friends with both Lizzie and her husband, and there are several more references to her in his letters. She saw Lloyd George and his brother off on an overseas trip in 1905, and even played a vital role in saving Lloyd George's life: while she was visiting him after an operation to remove his tonsils he began haemorrhaging, and her prompt action in sending for a doctor forestalled a potentially life-threatening situation. On another occasion, the lawyer and newspaper proprietor George Riddell was summoned to give Lloyd George advice on a troublesome libel case only to find him 'lying on a settee, his brow being mopped by . . . Mrs Timothy Davies'.[39] Mr Tim was the unwitting (or witting) go-between, even visiting Lloyd George when he was Prime Minister in 1918 to mend a quarrel between him and Lizzie and to apologise for his wife's 'rudeness' some months earlier.[40]

By early 1899 Lloyd George was seeing far less of Mrs Tim, and was able to refer to her husband freely in his letters. 'You have more brains than all those women put together,' he wrote to Maggie in January, 'but you don't always think it worth your while to exert them. T. [Timothy Davies] was telling me the other day very emphatically "I always consider Mrs. George a woman of very strong common sense" . . . You are worth a luggage train packed full of the women you mention. And especially *for me* if you only knew it. You are just fitted.'[41]

Maggie's jealousy of Mrs Tim did not prevent her from using Timothy Davies' services to move the family's furniture from Criccieth to London – or perhaps she did so to make a point. The size of the bill emphasises the practical cost of Lloyd George's insistence that they should move to join him. Having received an estimate, Maggie wrote indignantly in haste, totally forgetting her grammar: 'Timothy Davies has sent estimates for removing furniture from here to London & from Pal Mal to Wandsworth Common. I told you it would be £30 [£2,700 today] & you said no nothing of the kind & we went to Tim if you remember that Sunday, he said no only a few pounds, well the estimate is £28.10 & he remarks that it is exceptionally high, so you see that you can rely upon me for some things at any rate.'[42]

By the end of 1899 the house in London was ready, the furniture packed, the children's schooling arranged, and finally Maggie said her goodbyes in Criccieth. A grateful husband waited for her: 'I have never loved you so deeply and truly as I have during the past few years & you know that hen gariad annwyl [dear little darling]. You know that

I am fond of you & of your society. I never get tired of it. On the contrary the longer I am with you the less do I wish to part with you.'[43]

The family's move to the capital marked the start of a period when they were together more often than ever before. But their strength was about to be tested to the limit by war, public demonisation and personal tragedy.

9

Mair

LONDON IN THE EARLY 1900S was a rapidly expanding city at the heart of a seemingly invincible empire. As Margaret unpacked her furniture and arranged the rooms at 179 Trinity Road near Wandsworth Common, few could have imagined how much change she would witness over the next two decades. The seeds were already sown: in Osborne House on the Isle of Wight, the old Queen was failing after sixty-three years on the throne. The longest-serving head of state in British history had reigned over a period of imperial expansion and had imparted a sense of self-confidence to the nation, and with it a sense of racial superiority. The succession of Edward VII in January 1901 brought a change of style – the new King was far more dependent on his ministers and advisers than his mother had been – and an unleashing of so-called 'modern' values, embodied in the corpulent person of the fun-loving, loose-moralled King.

Technology was advancing. Edward, then Prince of Wales, declared in 1898 that a motor car would soon become 'a necessity for any English gentleman',[1] and by 1902, 23,000 cars were registered in Britain. Vast ocean liners were making Atlantic crossings in less than six days. For those who could not afford such luxurious forms of travel, bicycling became a passion and a way for those trapped in the expanding suburbs of the big cities to enjoy the great outdoors. The penny-farthings and boneshakers of the Victorian years gave way to the safety bicycle with its lightweight frame, and the new inventions of the last quarter of the nineteenth century – electric lighting, the telephone and the typewriter – became staples of social and business life.

Industry was thriving, and having a direct impact on the old, formerly impregnable class structure. The wealthiest men in society were no longer invariably the scions of landed families, but captains of industry: William Hesketh Lever, Thomas Lipton and George Cadbury became the new aristocrats. Their wealth was built on the everyday commodities of modern life: soap, tea and chocolate. They built new towns for their workers, founded charities and hobnobbed with royalty, combining extraordinary wealth with philanthropy and effectively supplanting the old guard.* They competed to build huge country houses which even King Edward himself felt obliged to keep up with. Edwin Lutyens designed the houses and Gertrude Jekyll transformed the gardens of the super-wealthy as the gap between rich and poor reached obscene dimensions.

The decline in British agriculture in the late Victorian period in favour of cheaper foreign imports had resulted in a redistribution of the population. Whole families moved to the cities, and produced more and more children. The resulting population growth, accompanied by the hasty construction of mass housing, was a recipe for public health disaster and social instability. Victorian politicians had turned a blind eye, allowing philanthropists to provide for the 'deserving poor' and the workhouses to soak up the rest. Edwardians thought differently, gradually acknowledging the social consequences of unemployment and responding to the growing pressure for state intervention. Improvements in public health led to an 18.5 per cent fall in the death rate between 1901 and 1913, while the introduction of readily available contraception contributed to a 15.5 per cent decline in the birthrate.[2]

Whether this made the population stricter or looser in terms of morality is difficult to say. There was a perceptible shift in behaviour among the upper classes, as we have seen, with adultery being expected, only divorce being shocking. King Edward himself set the tone: his love affairs with society beauties were followed by his citizens with as much interest as they would be today.

While divorce could topple politicians like Charles Stewart Parnell, anything short of divorce was acceptable as long as the proprieties were

---

* Edward VII's close friend Sir Thomas Lipton entertained the King at Cowes, provoking the disparaging aside from the Kaiser: 'My uncle has gone sailing with his grocer.'

observed. King Edward risked public scandal several times, appearing as a witness in two divorce cases, which was unprecedented for a member of the royal family. His mistresses and their husbands 'played the game' discreetly, while the Crippen murder case, which illustrated, among other things, the middle class's horror of divorce, gripped the nation's imagination.*

The erosion of Victorian social structures that opened the way for Lloyd George's election as an MP was also his political focus. In 1900 only 58 per cent of adult males were entitled to vote, and there was a powerful vested interest in maintaining the status quo.† Lloyd George chipped away at the bastions of privilege, with campaigns on land reform and on disestablishment and self-determination for Wales, and skilfully coordinated opposition to the 1902 Balfour Education Act, which strengthened the position of Church schools. Following the collapse of Cymru Fydd the fire under the cauldron of Welsh nationalism was temporarily extinguished, and as he became a more experienced back-bencher, Lloyd George's interests broadened. He mounted a spirited defence of free trade against Joseph Chamberlain's tariff reform, which would transform the British Empire into a united trading bloc, persuading the young Winston Churchill to cross the floor to join the Liberals in the process, and to the delight of his nonconformist constituents he threw his weight behind the campaign to oppose the 1904 Licensing Act.

The loosening of the rigid class system opened up opportunities for men of talent, and gradually for women too. Edwardian women were

---

* Rather than divorce, Crippen killed his wife, unsuccessfully attempted to dissolve her body in acid and hid it beneath the floorboards of their suburban house.
† Only male ratepayers were entitled to vote, which ruled out most working-class men. Lloyd George acknowledged the issue in a speech in Cardiff on 4 February 1890 as 'that vast social question which must be dealt with in the near future. There is a momentous time coming. The dark continent of wrong is being explored, and there is a missionary spirit abroad for its reclamation to the realm of right.' He further attacked this limited version of democracy in a speech in Newcastle in April 1903: 'There are about six million electors in this land at the present day, and yet the Government is in the hands of one class. They have so manipulated Parliament that it is all in the hands of that one class ... It does not matter up to the present which Party is in power, you have practically the same class governing the country. There is no democratic country in the world where such a state of things exists.'

better off than their Victorian mothers: they could own property, be granted a divorce and retain custody of their children. They could vote in local elections and be appointed to a limited number of public posts, for instance as churchwardens or parish councillors. But theirs was still a life full of restrictions. Most universities admitted women, but parents were often reluctant to let their daughters attend them. Women could not practise law or accountancy, and there were significant barriers to other professions like medicine, dentistry and horticulture. Educated women could do only three things easily: marry, teach or nurse; and working women earned significantly less than their male counterparts.

In Manchester, Emmeline Pankhurst qualified as a lawyer but was unable to practise. British campaigners for 'Votes for Women' were encouraged as women were given the vote in New Zealand in 1893 and in Australia in 1902, and in 1903 Mrs Pankhurst and her daughters Christabel and Sylvia formed the Women's Social and Political Union (WSPU). Female suffrage, they believed, would be the first step towards a more equal society, where the plight of working-class women as well as the more affluent could be addressed.

Margaret Lloyd George, steeped in traditional values, did not welcome Mrs Pankhurst's campaign, and came to bear a personal animosity towards suffragettes in subsequent years, when they targeted her husband with violence. It has been said that she opposed giving women the vote because of her essentially Victorian outlook, in contrast with Frances Stevenson's Edwardian enthusiasm for female suffrage.* But Margaret did support Votes for Women in principle. In a rare article for the *Daily Chronicle* she explained:

> The original policy advocated by the Suffragettes, the Pioneers of Votes for Women, was to grant it only to the single woman of property, or to a widow. As a result I, being a married woman, was precluded which alienated me accordingly, and it was not until the Bill was modified, and the admittance of married women as voters included, that I became a supporter. I was never a supporter though of their militant tactics.[3]

---

* Frances described herself as 'an ardent suffragist', and attended meetings addressed by Mrs Pankhurst.

By 1927, when Margaret wrote the article, women over thirty had been able to vote for many years, and her words were slightly disingenuous, since there is not much evidence that she had been bothered about married women getting the vote at the time. (Lloyd George, by contrast, abstaining from voting in 1892, wrote in a letter home: 'The Women's Franchise Bill is before the House & the Division is now taking place. As I am not in favour of enfranchising widows & spinsters without giving a vote to married women at the same time, I take no part in trotting round the lobby at all. I am in favour of the general principle.'[4]) Margaret was a traditional soul, and believed that marriage and mother-hood was a woman's natural 'career'. She disapproved strongly of the suffragettes' use of violent tactics, believing that they were counter-productive and unladylike. How on earth, she would ask, did putting vitriol in a pillarbox help anyone get the vote? Such acts only empha-sised the campaigners' irresponsibility, and alienated those who were in a position to help them.

In the winter of 1899–1900, Margaret had more pressing worries than female suffrage: the Boer War was about to change her husband's standing from that of rising Liberal radical to national hate-figure.

Moving to London meant a great upheaval for Margaret and the children. Dick was enrolled in Dulwich College, while Mair finished her primary education before attending Clapham High School. Olwen, aged only seven, started at a London Board School where her lack of English made it difficult at first for her to indulge her usual chatterbox tendency, but she soon caught up. The five-year-old Gwilym was the only child at home, and had a nursemaid to look after him.

Margaret presided over a household that was as similar to her beloved Bryn Awel as she could make it. She employed only Welsh servants, hiring them all in Criccieth. One of these, the dragon-like housekeeper Sarah Jones, known as 'Lally' (for 'Sally'), was to play an active part in the family's domestic life for over fifty years. Her stern discipline perfectly complemented Margaret's rather sloppy housekeeping; Lally was the only woman, it is said, of whom Lloyd George was afraid. The family spoke nothing but Welsh together, and ate the familiar combination of meals (breakfast, luncheon and an unfashionable combination of tea and supper) that would remain the routine even in 10 Downing Street.

Socially, they sought out the London Welsh community, and visitors would often find them grouped around Mair at the piano, singing Welsh hymns. In addition to the live-in servants, Margaret often had workers and craftsmen from Wales to stay, for she preferred to pay carpenters, painters and decorators to come down from Criccieth rather than trust their London counterparts. This had the added benefit of keeping her closely in touch with Criccieth news.

Members of the family were regular visitors: Margaret's mother, Mary Owen, often came to London, especially after the death of Richard Owen in 1903. Polly was another popular visitor, and her letters home offer an insight into Lloyd George and his family's life in London. She was amused to observe that the children had inherited some of their parents' views on the aristocracy:

> It is very hot here these days, too hot for the children to sleep last night. The Queen is trying to make up for her coolness towards the House of Commons by inviting them to Windsor next Saturday, with their wives. But Mag most indignantly refused to go with David. She is not willing to be treated like a sulky child, she says, it is too infra dig. D. asked Dick this morning if he would not rather go to see the Queen at Windsor than go to the Zoo on Saturday. But Dick shook his head all the time, altho his Father pressed him very hard, describing the glories of Windsor etc.
>
> 'A mae'n well gen ti weld mwncwns y Zoo, 'ngwas i, na'r Frenhines?' medda D. 'Ydi', medda Dic yn emphatic iawn. ['So you prefer to see the Zoo monkeys, my boy, than the Queen?' said D. 'Yes', said Dick, very emphatically.][5]

The children thrived in the nurturing atmosphere of their extended family. They regarded it as normal to divide their time between London and Criccieth, and barely registered the extent to which their father's profession affected their everyday lives – that is, until the Boer War began.

In 1899 Lloyd George was a member of a fact-finding tour to Canada at the invitation of the Canadian government, which was trying to encourage immigration from Britain. While he was away, clumsy diplomatic efforts to avert an armed conflict between the Dutch Boers in

South Africa and the British Uitlanders* failed. He returned hastily, and was outspoken in his opposition to the war, despite its popularity at home. Lloyd George was not anti-war as such: in this case his views sprang from his empathy for small nations and his ardent conviction that social reform could not wait while an expensive war was fought. Like the Welsh, he felt, the Boers were right to want self-determination, and it was wrong to throw the full might of the British Empire against them. During the Carmarthen by-election campaign in November 1899 he made an explicit comparison between the Boers and the Welsh: 'Even if I leave Carmarthen to-morrow without a friend', he insisted, he would demand 'fair play for a little country whose population is less than Carmarthenshire – the British Empire against Carmarthenshire!' It was outrageous, he continued,

> to wrong a little, poor, weak state – [sounds of dissent from the audience] – Yes, weak in spite of what they are doing now! – to trample on them is cowardice. This is a war which we will live, most of us, to be ashamed of . . . we are fighting for a franchise in the Transvaal which we do not give our own subjects at home . . . These men [the Boers] are god-fearing men: they are the kind of men who are a simple type of the old Welsh Covenanters. They might be right or wrong, but they are finer men and godlier men than those whom we are fighting for. We have had to put a hundred thousand men in the field – we, who have an Empire on which the sun never sets; we who have forty millions in these islands, and scores of millions abroad, to crush a hundred thousand men, women and children.[6]

Lloyd George was acutely conscious of the fact that the war was costing an enormous amount of money, which could have paid for measures to tackle poverty at home. In the same speech he claimed that there was not a shell which burst on the African hills that did not carry away an old-age pension. 'What is the satisfaction? Oh, it killed two hundred Boers – fathers of families, sons of mothers, who wept for them. Are you satisfied to give your old-age pensions for that?'

---

* British subjects who had emigrated to South Africa in the hope of making their fortune from diamond mining, and who were demanding full citizenship rights.

Speeches like these, which were in sharp contrast to the jingoistic attitude of the majority of the population, brought him to national attention, and his notoriety spread far beyond Wales and Westminster. He became a thorn in the side of the Tory government, and the butt of pro-war propaganda. In Wales he was in the minority too, but a bigger one that included a large number of nonconformists, so his opposition to the war did not seem unpatriotic to his family and inner circle. But there was no doubt how unpopular his stance was as the situation in South Africa worsened and the conflict extended, eventually claiming over 29,000 British lives.

Her husband's unpopularity hit home to Margaret when it began to affect the children. One day she had cause to upbraid Dick for the umpteenth time for losing his school cap. He took his reprimand like a trooper, but seemed miserable, and eventually broke down and revealed that he was constantly being set upon by gangs of boys at school who attacked him physically, called him a 'dirty pro-Boer' and stole his cap. He later recalled that there was 'a kind of hysteria' directed against his family. Margaret was used to hearing her husband called names, but this was an entirely different matter. She pursed her lips and said quietly, 'This simply won't do. I won't have it.' Dick was immediately taken out of Dulwich College and sent to live with Uncle Lloyd, William George and Polly in Garthcelyn, attending Porthmadoc Grammar School. He was never bullied again.

Dick was not the only one to feel the strain. In Criccieth there was such anger directed against those who opposed the war that effigies of William George – and even Uncle Lloyd – were burned on a bonfire, and Lloyd George was physically attacked as he made a speech in Bangor in his own constituency. The younger children were not as badly affected as Dick, but even they felt the pressure of being members of an 'unpatriotic' family. Olwen recalled: 'It was an awful period for us children ... It felt like being a traitor.'[7]

When the besieged British garrison at Mafeking was relieved in May 1900, the whole country rejoiced. Every house in Trinity Road was decorated with flags except No. 179, where Lloyd George had banned them on principle. That evening Margaret was in the parlour when he returned home from Parliament, his face black with rage. He demanded to know who had decorated the house. Margaret did not know what he was talking about, but on investigation saw that there were indeed flags waving from the upstairs windows: the youngest children, who were too small to understand their father's politics, had felt so badly left out that they had spent their pocket money on flags. Fortunately, Lloyd George only laughed.

During the war, Margaret and Lloyd George became much closer. The fact that they now lived together most of the time, and Margaret's support for him in the face of his public revilement, strengthened the affection between them. The war was also having an adverse effect on their already scant income, as clients boycotted Lloyd George's law firm. In despair, he told Margaret, 'I will have to live in an attic and you will have to go home to North Wales.' This may have been the only time in her life that Margaret refused the chance to go home, for she staunchly replied, 'If you live in an attic, I will live in it with you.'

In 1901, when Margaret was visiting Criccieth, Lloyd George wrote a letter that perfectly illustrated their domestic contentment: 'My own sweetheart. So disappointed when I got home last night not to find a wire from you awaiting me and this morning I woke up at quarter to eight and got up expecting to find a letter. Ond dim gair oddi wrth Margaret [but not a word from Margaret]. Actually left the house at 9.30 – do you think that would have happened had my round little Margaret been by my side to tumble and towzle about?'[8]

In a further sign of their renewed closeness, Megan, their fifth child, was born in the final month of the war, on 22 April 1902. Margaret returned to Criccieth for the birth, and her husband missed her more than ever: 'I have come finally to the conclusion that I cannot live happily without yr hen Fagi [little Maggie]. My hiraeth is getting worse & worse. Not the slightest symptom of convalescence. Tyrd yn dy ol, hen gariad [Come back, little love].'[9] And a few weeks after Megan's birth: 'I was never more unhappy by your absence – cold coffee, cold grape nuts & eternal ham help to make you much more popular. I want to turn out the present ministry at Trinity Rd & bring back the old Prime Minister. Tyrd gynta gallwch chwi, hen gariad annwyl [Come as soon as you can, dear little love].'[10] He may have carried the analogy between the Boers and the Welsh a little too far when he wrote the next day: 'Why the poor Boer women had often to trek on waggons through sun & rain over open rough country for days when baby was only a fortnight or 3 weeks old. I am not so hard as that. But the concentration camp on Wandsworth Common does need your presence.'[11]

The biggest crisis of the war for the family came on 18 December 1901. Lloyd George's opposition to the war had brought him into conflict with the imperialist Colonial Secretary, Joseph Chamberlain, whose radical politics he had admired in previous years.* Lloyd George compounded the quarrel by accusing Chamberlain of profiting from the war through his brother's firm Kynoch & Co., which supplied war materials to the government. The row rumbled on through the general election of 1900,† and relations between the two politicians were at an all-time low when the following year Lloyd George was engaged to speak at the town hall in Birmingham.

Birmingham was Chamberlain's political heartland. He had been the city's popular mayor before entering Parliament, and he still carried tremendous influence there. As the date drew nearer, the atmosphere in Birmingham was getting tenser by the day. Pro-Chamberlain newspapers stirred up resentment against Lloyd George, labelling him 'this most virulent anti-Briton' and gleefully forecasting a riot,[12] and the Lord Mayor provocatively issued Lloyd George's Liberal Association hosts with a public reminder that they had accepted responsibility for any damage done to the town hall at the meeting. It was clear that there would be serious trouble, but Lloyd George would not be persuaded to cancel even to save his own life.

Margaret, who was five months pregnant, waited anxiously in London for events in Birmingham to unfold. Telephones were not yet commonplace, so she could not rely on receiving prompt news if anything went wrong. A friendly journalist, Harold Spender, arranged for a Fleet Street runner to take any news to Trinity Road as soon as it was received. In the meantime Margaret waited, not knowing if her husband was dead or alive.

At midnight, the messenger finally arrived with news: there had been

---

* Joseph Chamberlain, as leader of the Liberal Unionists, formed an alliance with the Conservative Party in 1886 and was rewarded with the post of Colonial Secretary in Salisbury's Cabinet. He was responsible for British policy during the Boer War.
† Lord Salisbury's Conservative government was returned, but Lloyd George and some other anti-war candidates in Wales increased their majorities.

a riot in Birmingham. Lloyd George had arrived early at the town hall without encountering any trouble, but before the meeting began a crowd of up to 30,000 had surrounded the building, the vast majority of them angry protesters. Three hundred and fifty policemen were sent to keep the peace, but as the meeting opened the sound of the hall's organ playing 'Men of Harlech' was drowned out by the noise of the mob outside. Lloyd George's enemies had infiltrated the audience, and it became clear that he would not be allowed to speak. He stood on the platform, calmly waiting for a silence that never came, until a hail of stones came from outside, breaking every window in the hall. The *Daily Argus* report gives a flavour of what happened next:

> Still the shouting and whistling went on, and still Mr. Lloyd George doggedly sought to make himself heard. But he was soon brought to a sensational stop. Without any warning a very ugly rush was made for the platform. Practically all on the floor of the hall came with a sweep for the front, knocking over forms, tumbling over each other. The reporters fled, and an attempt was made by the crowd to climb by way of the raised press-table to the platform. Mr. Lloyd George suddenly disappeared, an army of constables mounted the table and battled with those who struggled to reach the platform. To the accompaniment of the constant crashing of glass, the boom of the bricks dropping here and there on the floor, and the battering of doors the platform quickly emptied.[13]

Police surrounded Lloyd George and shuffled him into a back room. He escaped with his life only by donning a policeman's helmet as a disguise. A protester died, two policemen were injured, and the crowd had to be charged with batons before they dispersed.[14]

The older children were able to understand that this was serious, but little Gwilym took an entirely different message from the incident, saying to Olwen, 'I wish Father was a policeman. I would much rather he was a policeman than a politician.'[15]

In the years after the Boer War, Margaret was naturally preoccupied with the new addition to the family. When Megan Arvon was born, the next youngest child, Gwilym, was seven, and Margaret had suffered two miscarriages. Her joy at having a baby in the nursery again was shared by her daughter-besotted husband. Megan was raised in very different circumstances to her older siblings, all of whom were largely independent by the time their father's career reached its pinnacle. For Megan, one of only a handful of children to be raised in Downing Street, nothing could compare with the excitement of life at the centre of the political world.

At the time of her birth her father had been a backbench MP, albeit a prominent and influential one, for twelve years. A career in politics is heavily influenced by timing, and Lloyd George's was no exception. In 1895, before he had amassed the experience and seniority to join the government, his party was overthrown in favour of the Unionist administration of Lord Salisbury and his successor from July 1902, Arthur Balfour. Lloyd George had an outsider's aptitude for opposition politics, and enjoyed causing the government difficulties, but every opposition party longs for a chance to govern, and it was frustrating even for a natural rebel like him to sit out the whole ten years of the Liberal Party's exile from power.

Eventually it became clear that Balfour could not hold on to power for the duration of the Parliament. He resigned in December 1905, and the Liberal leader Henry Campbell-Bannerman was sent for by Edward VII and asked to form a government (the following year he would win his mandate from the country in a landslide election victory). Naturally this produced excited anticipation in the Lloyd George household, and finally Margaret received a telegram which read:

> Llywydd y Bwrdd Marchnad, reit hapus. Cariad D [President of the Board of Trade. Quite happy. Love D][16]

It was quite a leap from the backbenches to the Cabinet in one bound, but Lloyd George's stature within the Liberal Party meant that his was an essential, if controversial, appointment. Margaret shared his joy for a very practical reason: a ministerial post commanded a salary of £2,000, the equivalent of £168,000 in today's money. For the first time in fifteen long years her husband would be earning a living from his political career, a considerable relief to her and the whole family. She would be the wife of a Cabinet Minister for the next seventeen years, and for fourteen of them her address would be Downing Street.

It was as well for Margaret – as for Lloyd George – that they could not see into the future, for the circumstances of his next promotion were very different. In three years' time Lloyd George would take up one of the great offices of state, as Chancellor of the Exchequer. On that occasion he trudged home in the rain, tears pouring down his cheeks because there was one fewer child waiting to share his news. Mair, his beautiful, adored daughter, was dead.

Criccieth cemetery is set on a hillside above the town. Margaret's birthplace, Mynydd Ednyfed farm, stands above it on the steep mountainside. Below, the town is masked by trees, and the onlooker's eyes are directed instead to the sea and the mountains of Eifionydd across the bay. It must be one of the most captivating views from any such place in Britain. Here, close to the lane along which Lloyd George was borne in triumph after his first electoral victory, Margaret and her distraught husband laid to rest their daughter. Her monument is marked by a fine sculpture of the seventeen-year-old girl, her face to the sea and her eyes, unsmiling but serene, gazing on the mountains where she wandered as a child. The sculpture was executed by Sir Goscombe John, supervised closely by Margaret to get the likeness exact. Mair's last words, 'He is just and merciful,' are carved on the stone, together with the simple commemoration 'Er Cof am Mair Eluned, annwyl ferch David a Margaret Lloyd George, Brynawelon, Criccieth. Ganwyd 2 Awst 1890, bu farw 29 Tachwedd 1907' ('In memory of Mair Eluned, beloved daughter of David and Margaret Lloyd George, Brynawelon, Criccieth. Born 2 August 1890, died 29 November 1907').

The tragedy of Mair's death occurred at a time when the Lloyd George family was enjoying a period of rare stability and contentment. Margaret was happiest when she had a child at home, and Megan had grown into a cosseted and engaging five-year-old. Lloyd George was proving an efficient and successful minister, to the extent that he was seen as a leading contender for the position of Chancellor if the incumbent, Henry Asquith, succeeded the physically ailing Sir Henry Campbell-Bannerman as party leader and Prime Minister. His stock was rising, and he had scored a significant political triumph when he settled a damaging railway strike. He proudly recorded in a letter to his brother that he had been clapped on the shoulder at a reception by the Prince of Wales, and then, 'before I said two words in answer to his congratulations the Emperor [of Germany] left the P.M., held out his hand to me and congratulated me on my settlement of the Railway Strike'.* The family was bathed in his success, and the children were getting a fair bit of publicity themselves: 'The King congratulated me and so did the Queen and said that she had seen such a nice photograph of me with my little girl. I wonder where she saw it? Was it Mair or Megan?'[17] He wrote the letter on 13 November 1907; by the end of the month, Mair would be dead.

Mair, at the age of seventeen, had lost none of her capacity to charm, and was emerging as the most beautiful, musical and academically gifted child of the family. It is testament to her sweet nature that she did not attract any resentment from her siblings. Olwen ruefully noted that Mair was obedient, gentle and conscientious, whereas she herself was the exact opposite, but the two sisters were firm friends. Dick too wrote that Mair was unlike the other children, far less boisterous and noisy.[18] Allowance must be made for their rose-tinted recollection of a dead sister, but the evidence from others who knew Mair is remarkably consistent. D.R. Daniel, a frequent visitor, called her 'Y Fair serchog brydferth o gorff a bywiog o feddwl' (gracious Mair, beautiful of body and lively of mind), [19] and W. Watkin Davies in his 1939 biography of Lloyd George describes her as 'famed for her beauty, her mental abilities, her exquisite charm and her loveable disposition'.[20] It is possible that her academic excellence was slightly exaggerated, since her Clapham High School report described her as only 'satisfactory', but the school had high standards, and Mair was hoping to read Mathematics at Cambridge, which suggests that she was no ordinary scholar. She was in demand at school to coach less able pupils, among them the young Frances Stevenson. Frances recalled that Mair was 'a gentle and charming personality . . . she was good at mathematics: I

---

* Lloyd George was not unreservedly loved by Edward VII: he was rebuked by the King in 1906 for a particularly hard-hitting attack on the House of Lords, then in the process of amending the Education Bill. Lloyd George said: 'If the House of Lords persists in its present policy, it will be a much larger question than the Education Bill that will come up for consideration. It will be the issue of whether this country is to be governed by the King and the peers, or by the King and his people.'

was not, and she was always ready to explain away my problems. I liked her very much.'[21] Her view in later years, influenced by hindsight and by her close relationship with Lloyd George, was that Mair was 'a very sweet and gentle girl, and clever too – much loved by all at school. But there was always a certain sadness in her face, & a thoughtfulness beyond her years.'[22]

Mair shared Margaret's sense of fun and they seemed more like sisters than mother and daughter as they conspired to get their own way with Lloyd George: 'The reason why I did not write on Saturday was because the girls dragged me immediately I breakfasted to buy furniture,' wrote Lloyd George to his brother in 1891, '– which I did to the tune of £125 – £9.10 of which is yours. The girls helped each other to increase my bill. I could have managed Margaret fairly well but when she was reinforced by Mair I surrendered at discretion or rather compromised.'[23] Mair's relationship with her mother was very close, the more so because they shared the same faith. The family often worshipped together at the Baptist chapel in Eastcastle Street in central London, but Mair and Margaret's spiritual home in London was the Calvinistic Methodist chapel in Beauchamp Road, Clapham Junction. Mair played the organ at its services, and the temperance movement became a shared cause between them. Only a fortnight or so before her death, Mair and her chapel friends took part in a service in a temperance mission in the East End. After her death the *South Wales Daily News* wrote: 'Warm-hearted to a degree, she made friends wherever she went, and was of incalculable assistance to her mother in entertaining visitors, whilst she was simply adored by her father.'[24]

Mair loved going to the theatre and to parties with her parents. Lloyd George had begun to treat her as a political confidante, appreciating her quick brain as well as her uncritical devotion, which he did not always get from his wife. He was proud of his good-looking daughter, and liked to show her off to his friends. A letter on 18 September 1906 from Lloyd George to Mair enclosed a newspaper cutting reporting her success in passing her Oxford and Cambridge Higher Certificate Examination: 'There you are Mair George – your achievements chronicled amongst those of the great. At the same time you might have remembered your old father by sending him a letter. If your mother doesn't care to have a three days ride from London to Wales would you?' Mair would often be called upon to play the piano when Welsh gatherings, as they frequently did, ended in singsongs.

Since 1903 the family had been living in Routh Road, a little closer to Wandsworth Common than their previous home, and in the autumn of 1907 Mair had been studying hard for her matriculation exams. She began to suffer a pain in her side, but not wishing to cause any worry, she did not mention it to her mother. Eventually, on 25 November, the pain became agonising, and she fell ill at school. Mrs Woodhouse, the headmistress, telephoned Margaret and sent Mair home in a cab. It was clear that she was seriously ill. Margaret summoned a doctor at once, and then asked for a specialist to examine her daughter. The doctor insisted that there was no need for alarm, but Mair's condition deteriorated steadily.

Lloyd George was worried to the point of distraction. As soon as he heard of Mair's illness he sent an 'alarming' telegram to William George in Criccieth. Under normal circumstances he would have asked Polly to set off for London immediately to help Margaret, but Polly had been ill herself for some time, and was unable to travel. Instead he decided to engage a nurse, and by chance he secured the services of Anita Williams, a Welsh-speaker from Pembrokeshire who was a nursing sister at the Royal Northern Hospital in London.*

On the morning of Friday, 29 November a specialist, Mr Harry Fenwick, was called at last. He diagnosed a burst appendix, and recommended an immediate operation which, according to the custom of the day, would be carried out at home. Margaret set about converting Lloyd George's study into an operating theatre for the afternoon's ordeal, and sent word to him to come home at once. When he received the message, Lloyd George telegrammed his brother begging him to set off for London immediately. Why he did so is not clear, as it is unlikely that William George could offer any practical assistance. But Lloyd George had been used to having his family around him in times of crisis all his life, and it was his natural instinct to want his brother at hand. Perhaps also, with the sixth sense of a parent, he feared the worst,

---

* Anita was in due course engaged to nurse Polly through her last illness, became a friend of the family and, much to their delight, married William George in 1910.

and knew that his brother's presence would be both a comfort and a rock in the days to come.

The telegram reached William while he was in court, but such was the fame his brother now commanded that Mair's illness had been reported in the press, and he only had to show the telegram to the Chairman of the Bench to be immediately excused. He took the first train to London, arriving at Routh Road late at night, to be told that the worst had already happened: Mair had undergone the operation and had come round from the anaesthetic. But the operation was carried out too late. Still fully sensible, she asked if she was going to die. Anita Williams, a wise and experienced nurse, knew better than to give her false assurances. Mair uttered her last words, 'He is just and merciful,' before passing away. For Margaret and Lloyd George, waiting in the drawing room downstairs, it was a blow from which neither would ever fully recover.

William George took his brother back to his Whitehall office to get him out of the house while Margaret dealt with the distressing task of having Mair's body removed. He later recalled the black day that followed, with Lloyd George 'distraught with grief, pacing up and down the corridor in his darkened room in the Board of Trade offices'.[25] Sympathetic officials made every effort to distract him with news and work, as, in her own way, Margaret filled the day with funeral arrangements and family communication.

Over the next few hours the news reached Dick, newly arrived at Cambridge, Olwen, who was away at school in Dolgellau, and Uncle Lloyd and Polly in Criccieth. The suddenness of Mair's death as well as its untimeliness added to the shock. For once in his long lifetime, Uncle Lloyd halted his daily record of events. The four days following 30 November 1907 have been left empty in his diary, save for a single sentence written across them: 'This filled by our inexpressible sorrow in Mair bach's decease.'[26]

As the news spread, friends, acquaintances and well-wishers joined the family in their grief. On 30 November the Caernarvon Town Council was meeting to consider giving Lloyd George the freedom of the borough when it received the news. The meeting was immediately cut short, with the Mayor expressing his disbelief and sorrow: he had been the Lloyd Georges' guest less than a week previously, and had seen Mair in apparently robust health. Among the shocked recipients of the news was Frances Stevenson:

> The first term in college was marred by the news which reached us of the death of Mair Lloyd George. I think it was the first time I had experienced the death of someone of my own age. I was shocked and shattered and found it difficult to realise that one with whom I had sat in class such a short time ago had been cut down in the flower of her youth. Her father, David Lloyd George, had lately obtained Cabinet rank when the Liberals came into office. I thought of him, and the cruel destiny that had given him high office, the realisation of his ambition, with one hand, and taken away his beloved child with the other.[27]

Little did she imagine that the news was to have such impact on her own life in years to come.

Arrangements were made for the funeral in Criccieth on Tuesday, 3 December. The railway company placed special carriages at Lloyd George's disposal, and Mair's oak coffin was laid in one and the grieving family travelled in another. As they left Euston a crowd of London Welsh gathered on the platform to see them off and to pay their last respects to Mair. People thronged every station along the route to catch a glimpse of the sad procession. Lloyd George, immersed in his grief, could not face them, but sent a message thanking them for their sympathy. He sat, inconsolable, the carriage windows shrouded in heavy black blinds. The only cheerful face was five-year-old Megan's. Too young to comprehend what had happened to her sister, the child occasionally lifted the blinds to smile at the people gathered outside.[28]

As the family arrived in Criccieth, squalls of rain added to the bleak atmosphere. Mair's body lay overnight in Garthcelyn, and at 11 o'clock the following morning the family was joined by a handful of close friends for a private service. The weather was calmer, cold but with occasional gleams of sunshine, as the funeral procession left the house towards midday. Mair's coffin lay in a glass-panelled hearse covered in wreaths of lilies and stephanotis, among them wreaths from Clapham Junction Sunday School and Clapham High School sixth form. As it passed through the town on its way to the cemetery, every business closed its doors, houses had their blinds closed and flags on public buildings flew at half mast. The hearse was followed by the bearers and chief mourners, Lloyd George 'a pathetic figure leaning on the arm of his Uncle',[29] Dick, Gwilym and William George.

The funeral was of the utmost simplicity. Margaret was absent: according to custom, women did not attend the graveside. The service was conducted by John Owen, who had married Lloyd George and Margaret, and who had travelled to London to confirm Mair as a member of the Calvinistic Methodist Church. Friends, townspeople and the press formed a great crowd: 'All eyes were turned in tender sympathy to the central figure of this affecting drama of human suffering – Mr Lloyd George, leaning brokenheartedly on his aged uncle's shoulder,' wrote one journalist. 'I have witnessed many an impressive and affecting graveyard spectacle, but none which appealed more strongly than this to every heart present.'[30] Lloyd George could not conceal his emotion as he watched his daughter's coffin being lowered into a grave dug beside the family vault.*

After the funeral the family assembled in Garthcelyn, where they were joined by a handful of friends and political colleagues. Letters of condolence were received from as far afield as Capetown in South Africa, and messages arrived from the King, the Cabinet and leading politicians from around the world. The Queen, clearly moved by the Lloyd Georges' bereavement, sent a separate telegram: 'Feel most deeply for you and your family in this terrible loss you have sustained,' she wrote, 'know how devoted you are to your children. Alexandra.'[31]

Later in the day Lloyd George's friend and fellow MP Herbert Lewis took him for a six-mile walk to distract him. He succeeded in lifting Lloyd George's spirits a little, and they spent the evening together, as he recorded in his diary: 'Spent the evening at Garthcelyn in conversation that sought to divert the current of L.G.'s thoughts. Laughter and tears were very near one another, and in the midst of it all he had to leave us for a while. He returned and kept us all amused and interested with a brilliant flow of literary, historical and reminiscent talk.'[32]

---

* The decision to bury Mair next to the vault was taken by William George, who made the funeral arrangements. Lloyd George described his distress at seeing her buried in what looked like 'a pauper's grave', and she was later re-interred in the family vault.

Mair's funeral was widely reported in the next day's newspapers. The journalists inevitably focused on the grieving father, who cut such a tragic figure at the graveside: 'In his great loss the President of the Board of Trade must feel comforted by the knowledge that a whole nation shows its grief, even though it does not obtrude its sympathies on the sacredness of his sorrow.' Towards the end of the lengthiest report of all was the simple statement, 'Mrs Lloyd George is reported to be bearing very bravely the great tribulation that has befallen her, and her great patience and calmness of spirit are a source of much comfort and strength to her husband.'[33]

Margaret did not emerge from Garthcelyn to face the reporters. With her family around her, she did not need to write any letters, so we have no record of her grief other than her children's recollection that she was calm, immersing herself in practical matters by way of distraction. Her quiet suffering contrasted with Lloyd George's raw emotion. D.R. Daniel met Lloyd George two weeks after Mair's death, and felt that his grief was threatening his sanity: 'the tugging of his heartstrings were tortuous, bordering on madness'.[34] Lloyd George himself believed that he was only pulled back from the brink by a vision of Mair that appeared to him in a dream. Writing to William George after the death of his and Anita's twenty-month-old son in 1914, he said:

> I can speak from a painful experience, which is even now often renewed, symptoms of you [sic] pressing the spear to a wounded breast. You feel as if it were disloyal to the dear little departed to dismiss them from your thoughts when they present themselves to you. It is quite the reverse. It is unkindness to worry about them when they have passed from the zone of danger to that of rest. Do you know what helped to cure me of it? Little Mair appeared one night to me in a dream and told me I was distressing her and begged me not to do so. I then exerted my will power when the spasms of anguish returned and turned my thoughts deliberately to other things, and if these things are in themselves exalted and beneficient [sic], you thus doubly honour the dead.[35]

Lloyd George's initial reaction, however, was so violent that it was clear he could not return to Routh Road. It was arranged that he would escape to the South of France with Dick and Gwilym, while Margaret stayed behind with Olwen and Megan to break up their London house and find a place where they could make a fresh start. The need for a large garden and clean air was not as great with the children growing older, so Margaret took a lease on 5 Cheyne Place in Chelsea, within walking distance of Westminster and Whitehall.

From Manchester on the day after the funeral, Lloyd George had written Margaret a touching letter:

> I am so pleased to think you are joining me up in London tomorrow night darling. Your placid, brave spirit has a soothing effect on my turbulent & emotional nature. And, as John Owen so truly said, there is not a trace of the morbid about you. That is more than I can say of myself. I have always been disposed towards morbidity. We must help each other not to brood. Take warning from the sad example of poor Mr & Mrs Robert Thomas [acquaintances, presumably, who had suffered a similar bereavement] who were always towing each other out into the breakers. We did our best.

He then writes, chillingly, given that war in Europe was already on the horizon, that they must remember that others suffered in a similar way:

> It was the decree of fate which millions besides ourselves are now enduring. What right have we to grumble? More than that I have a profound conviction that cruel as the blow may appear & purposeless as it may now seem it will prove to be the greatest blessing that has befallen us & through us multitudes whom God has sent me to give a helping hand out of misery and worry a myriad worse than ours. I can see through the darkness a ray of hope. I am not sure yet what it will reveal but I am certain of its presence & promise.

His attempt to make sense of the senseless does not ring quite true; perhaps it is an attempt to console Margaret in words that would mean more to her than to him. Finally, he pays a well-deserved tribute to his brother and the household at Garthcelyn for their support: 'How nobly the Garthcelynites have all behaved. Whilst I know the tragedy was wringing their hearts they spent no sympathy on themselves but spared it all for us.'[36]

It was later suggested by Frances and others that Mair's death drove Margaret and Lloyd George apart. Frances writes in her autobiography:

> From what L.G. told me, after Mair's death they had drifted apart. They each had their poignant grief but could not go to each other for sympathy and understanding – there was no sharing of the trouble, both blaming each other, perhaps, for what went wrong, the delay in calling the doctor, the carrying out of an emergency operation without a highly skilled staff and hospital amenities. The gap of incompatibility which had always been there became emphasised and more difficult to bridge.[37]

The truth was more complex. In the short term Margaret lost herself in practicalities, while Lloyd George turned to friends and politics to keep his mind occupied. There is no evidence that either blamed the other for the tragedy. 'Don't brood over what could have happened if some other course had been followed,' wrote Lloyd George to his brother. 'That is the most tormenting, and, at the same time, the most futile of all exercises.'[38] But with the passing of time the differences in their personalities and in their outlooks on life were highlighted by their loss, and this proved difficult for their relationship to overcome. Olwen, always a shrewd and relatively impartial commentator on her parents' marriage, later reflected that Margaret and Lloyd George could not share their grief because they were too different as people. This is not to say that one felt less than the other, rather that the manifestations of their grief were so different that they did not know how to console each other.

They clearly did turn to one another in the immediate aftermath of the bereavement, and although they spent Christmas apart, they corresponded daily and were reunited in London in the New Year. On his return journey to England from the South of France, Lloyd George wrote another affectionate letter: 'Three weeks without your gentle and soothing influence have been very trying & often heart-breaking. I would rather have you – jealous old Margaret as you sometimes are – I would rather see you near me in my trouble than anybody else – you & Uncle Lloyd. You don't mind my bringing him in, do you?'[39]

As time passed, Margaret resumed the rhythm of daily life in their new London home. Her grief became less discernible, whereas her husband's was still raw months, even years later. This led him to conclude that she had recovered from the blow more easily. In fact, Margaret was better equipped to deal with a crippling emotional blow than her husband, for she had a deep and sustaining faith. She had also suffered bereavement only eighteen months before Mair's death when her much-loved mother had died, and knew from experience that time and faith healed even the deepest sorrow. Her quiet acceptance was stoic rather than unfeeling, as a letter she wrote in June 1906, shortly after her mother's death, shows:

> My own dearest Dei
> Thank you so much for your loving letters & telegrams. They cheered me up very much indeed. You are so kind & loving to me & I shall never forget how thoughtful you have been all through & I thank Providence for a kind husband & dear children . . .
>   Don't worry about me cariad [darling]. I shall be alright & I will try & eat as much as I can. The doctors thought my voice was affected by the shock more than a cold . . . I am glad I am not there tomorrow in a way. I don't think I could bear a service after poor mother . . . Megan told me today that she was very sorry Nain [Granny] had gone & she said 'Mae hi hefo Iesu Grist' [She is with Jesus Christ] she has not said anything before at all . . .

Margaret's faith helped her cope with bereavement because she truly believed that every loss on earth, however senseless and unjust it might appear, had a providential purpose. This, coupled with a firm belief in the reunion of the dead in heaven, worked over time to blunt the sharp edge of her grief. Her husband was not only devoid of such faith, but had never experienced a serious loss or significant setback in his life. He had lost both his parents, but he was too young to grieve for his father, and he recovered fairly easily after Betsy's death in 1896. His outlook was centred on self-determination. He believed that with hard work and dedication he could not only achieve greatness in his life, but bend others to his will. This philosophy was powerless to help him make sense of the sudden loss of someone he depended upon. It was an event beyond his control, and was unfathomable to him. His friend

D.R. Daniel recorded his struggle to make sense of the loss: ' "Some hand from the darkness" had stolen away his heart's beloved, and to him, she simply "was not" any more. "She has gone" were his words, and to him there was not the slightest enjoyment in trying to follow her in his imagination . . . her light had been extinguished, leaving only darkness.'[40]

This fundamental difference in outlook was at the heart of the disconnection between husband and wife. Margaret's 'infernal Methodism' was her crutch and her consolation, while for Lloyd George Mair's death was 'an ever open wound'.[41] This showed in the way in which they later offered comfort to others who had been similarly bereaved. Lloyd George's concern was for those left behind. Immediately on hearing of the death of his brother's infant son, he wrote to William George:

> When the blow fell, it all seemed so wantonly cruel. Fate seemed to me to have inflicted torture without any purpose. I had just settled a great Railway Strike which had threatened untold misery and it all seemed to me to be a piece of blind fury. I know now what it was for. It gave me a keener appreciation of the sufferings of others . . . I am never sorry for the dead. My grief is all for the living . . . Another maxim I found comfort in was given me by Winston, 'Never press the spear to your breast', which means, don't brood unnecessarily and dwell incessantly on the details of the catastrophe and travel over its burning surface again and again.[42]

Margaret's faith shone through when she met a man whose child had recently died. In the words of her son Dick:

> Everyone in Criccieth except my mother and the object of her sympathy was profoundly relieved by the death of a motherless imbecile child. But the father was inconsolable in his grief. It was worse than useless to try to show him how much better it was – for him as well as for the baby – that an all-wise God had cut short its wretched life. Such well-meaning attempts to lessen his grief having proved unavailing, Criccieth left the poor man to grieve alone. And it was then my mother stepped into the breach.

'You see,' Margaret said,

> 'I can sympathise with you because I, too, lost a child of mine – a blow which it was not easy to believe could be struck by a just God. But in the years that have passed since then I have come to realize God moves in a mysterious way His wonders to perform, and it is not for us to question the wisdom of His ways. At least your baby is safe in His keeping now, and for you life still holds much that is good.'

And that marked the end of the father's grieving.[43]

Lloyd George was able to offer advice on how to lessen grief's pain; Margaret was able to cure it.

Margaret and Lloyd George were fortunate to have a large and sympathetic network of friends to help them through bad times. D.R. Daniel, for instance, realising that the anniversary of Mair's death was upon them, went out of his way to call on them to make sure that they had a diversion from their memories. He recalls in his diary:

> I thought a lot about [Lloyd George] and his family today, and thought I would call in the evening. I arrived at around 7pm. In answer to my card, I was asked to go up. I heard Megan's sweet voice and laughter echoing as I was on the stairs. I found the three, the father, the mother and the little one, by the fire in the drawing room. Megan and her father were playing enthusiastically with a toy bear, and both were deriving great enjoyment from the game. I suspected that the game was full of meaning for the father and that the noise drowned out the sound of memories that today were knocking at the door of the heart and mind. He squeezed my hand. I sat down to talk to Mrs George . . .[44]

In truth, neither Lloyd George nor Margaret was ever able to forget the tragedy, or to free themselves entirely from their memories. To a lesser extent, neither could their children. In the early years of the twentieth century there was a prevailing theory that mental exertion could result in physical illness, and that this was particularly dangerous for women. Mair's death occurred after she had been studying particularly hard, and this convinced Lloyd George of the theory's veracity. He became obsessively protective of his children's health, his daughters in partic-ular. Olwen was taken out of her Dolgellau school and sent to Roedean on the south coast of England so that the fresh sea air could cure her persistent sore throats. During her time there her father never allowed her to take an examination. Megan was educated rather haphazardly by governesses at home until she was nine years old, and when she was fourteen a bout of measles caused her parents near-hysterical anxiety. Neither Olwen nor Megan attended university although both their brothers graduated from Cambridge. In fairness, neither seemed to have Mair's academic ability, and it was still far from the norm for women to take degrees, but they were also discouraged from serious study on health grounds by their over-anxious father.

The long-term effect of the bereavement on Margaret manifested itself in a more subtle way. Throughout the rest of her life, she detested and feared the colour green. No member of the family was allowed to purchase a green motor car, and she herself did not possess a single green item of clothing. Mair's favourite dress at the time of her death was green, and anything that reminded her mother of it brought back painful memories.

The after-effects of his grief never fully left Lloyd George either, and those closest to him were careful not to remind him of Mair's death. He never returned to the house in Routh Road, and for the rest of his life would avoid driving through the area if he could. In April 1908, when Herbert Asquith took over the premiership from Henry Campbell-Bannerman, he offered Lloyd George the position of Chancellor of the Exchequer as 'a well-deserved tribute to your long & eminent services to our party, and to the splendid capacity which you have shown in the administration of the Board of Trade'.[45] On his arrival at the Treasury on 6 April 1908 Lloyd George ordered black-edged mourning paper for his correspondence, and he did not sing his favourite Welsh songs at home again until the 1920s, when the memories had faded.

As time went on, however, life resumed its normal tempo. Both Margaret and Lloyd George had much to distract them. Margaret was overseeing the building of a new house in Criccieth, set on the hill behind the town with fine views of the castle and the bay. There, closer to Llanystumdwy and his boyhood haunts, Lloyd George would have more privacy during his infrequent visits to the town, and she would be able to indulge her love of gardening on a larger scale. The new house, named Brynawelon like their earlier Criccieth home, was ready by 1908, and Margaret, who hated house-moving, supervised the move. She had already moved twice in London that year, firstly from Routh Road to Cheyne Place under intensely difficult circumstances, and then, following her husband's promotion to Chancellor, to one of the most famous addresses in the country: No. 11 Downing Street. Margaret set about making herself and her family as comfortable as possible in the grand surroundings of the Chancellor's residence. For her, comfort meant all things Welsh, and she promptly moved her own Criccieth staff into the servants' quarters. 'Duw Annwyl!' (Dear God!) exclaimed the housekeeper Lally on seeing the vast kitchens with their array of pots and pans. 'And what ever am I going to do with all these things?'[46]

From that point onwards, Lloyd George had distractions aplenty as he took up his place at the heart of government. He also found solace and companionship in his daughter Megan, who was able to fill Mair's place in his life and in his heart much more than the absent Olwen. Megan was closer to her father than any of the other children, since she was still at home during the Downing Street years when they lived, literally, above his office. In addition, they shared many characteristics, including a natural love of the limelight. Indulged by her father in every way, she adored him in return.

Lloyd George's absorption in politics in part shielded him from a second blow in the summer of 1909. Polly, older sister, friend and companion, had been diagnosed with cancer, and died in Criccieth on 9 August, at the age of forty-seven. Lloyd George received the news as he was preparing to present his first budget. He was affected, but not incapacitated by grief. Later, sitting on the benches of the House of Commons, he said to his political colleague Charles Masterman: 'How death alters things. All this seems to me like the chattering of apes!'[47]

Life was not the same for Lloyd George after losing Mair. She had provided him with unconditional love and admiration, and despite his extraordinary talent, he needed the appreciation of those closest to him. Margaret, although she understood him better than anyone else, either did not see this need, or gradually tired of being his uncritical cheerleader. When they were first married she wrote admiring notes after his speeches and her letters were full of praise, but as time wore on her focus turned to her children. Without Mair to fill the gap, Lloyd George was dangerously vulnerable to other female admirers. As luck, or fate, would have it, Megan was to be the means of bringing into his life a young woman who not only had her intelligence, her soft charm and her sympathetic nature, but who had known Mair, and could share his memories of her. This young woman, Frances Stevenson, was to be his companion for the rest of his life.

10

Frances

EASTCASTLE STREET, A NONDESCRIPT London street of mainly commercial buildings, lies on the north side of Oxford Street. Tightly hemmed in between two office blocks stands an ornate late-Victorian red-brick chapel on the façade of which is carved the words 'Capel Bedyddwyr Cymreig' (Welsh Baptists' Chapel) and the date 1889. This was a brand new building when the Lloyd George family started attending services there, and it reflects the strength and wealth of the London Welsh community that such chapels were being erected in large numbers at the turn of the century. Inside, the wooden pews form a semi-circle in front of a raised pulpit, in traditional Welsh chapel style. These pews were packed and the gallery filled to bursting on a hot Sunday in June 1911 for one of the most popular events in the chapel's calendar. This was 'Lloyd George Sunday', when the man himself would address the congregation.

Those in attendance, dressed in Sunday best, were more Wales than London, with prosperous merchants and their wives rubbing shoulders with milk traders from Carmarthenshire, civil servants, teachers and the housekeepers who served them. Every class was represented, apart from the Anglican church-going gentry. But there was one member of the congregation that evening who did not understand a word of the language spoken around her, and who had never been to Wales in all her twenty-two years.

Frances Stevenson had been invited to the service by the Welsh housekeeper of Allenswood School in Wimbledon, where she was teaching. She had at least one close Welsh friend, another teacher, but had no other connection with Wales. It might therefore seem strange that she should want to sit through a Baptist service in Welsh. But the attraction was not religion, it was the opportunity to hear Lloyd George in action.

It had become Lloyd George's habit to address the congregation at Castle Street, as the chapel was known, on the last Sunday of June. He had acquired near-legendary status among London's Welsh community, partly because of the personal charisma and eloquence that made him the focal point of any gathering, but also because he had outstripped all other Welsh politicians with his appointment as Chancellor of the Exchequer in 1908. His fame had spread far beyond Wales, with his spirited and courageous opposition to the Boer War followed by his success in averting the threatened rail strike in 1907. His 'People's Budget' of 1909–10 had strengthened his reputation as a champion of social reform. It was, he declared, 'a war budget . . . for raising money to wage implacable war against poverty and squalidness'.[1] To fund his war, Lloyd George proposed raising over £13 million more in taxes, partly to pay for eight heavily armoured warships to counter the rise in German naval strength. The rich would pay more income tax, inheritance tax would be increased, and drinkers and smokers would pay more for their pleasures. But the most radical proposal was a system of land taxes.

Lloyd George's land taxes were intended to address the overpowerful position of the landlords, beginning to right a wrong he had witnessed at first hand. The first tax, on the difference between the present value of land and its value at the point of sale or death, would hit landlords whose land was improved by workers, but who refused to make or fund improvements. A second tax was to be levied on undeveloped sites whose owners refused to let them go until a high price was offered. The third was a 10 per cent reversion duty on any benefit to lessors at the end of a lease. Only around £500,000 would be raised by these taxes in the short term, but the amount would increase as time went on. More to the point, the government would finally be addressing the injustices Lloyd George had been fighting all his life.

At last, after twenty years as an MP, Lloyd George had the power to put into action the ideas and ideals he had cherished as a young man. Opposition to his measures was fierce among those who had much to lose, particularly the landed gentry who made up the majority of members in the House of Lords. There was no precedent in modern times for the Lords to oppose a financial measure proposed by the Commons, but the relationship between the two chambers had become increasingly prickly as the government pressed ahead with social reform. It was clear that there would be a fight, and Lloyd George campaigned vigorously to win popular support for his proposals. In a speech given to 4,000 people in Limehouse in East London in June 1909, he spelled out his philosophy: 'We are placing burdens on the broadest shoulders. Why should I put burdens on the people? I am one of the children of the people. I was brought up amongst them. I know their trials; and God forbid that I should add one grain of trouble to the anxieties which they bear with such patience and fortitude.'[2]

The battle raged through the summer of 1909, and Lloyd George made another highly charged attack on his opponents in a speech in Newcastle on 9 October. He enraged the Lords (and the King) even further by pointing out that 'a fully-equipped duke costs as much to keep up as two Dreadnoughts, and they are just as great a terror, and they last longer'. He railed against the dominance of the House of Lords which dared oppose his budget. 'The question will be asked,' he thundered, 'whether five hundred men, ordinary men chosen accidentally from among the unemployed, should override the judgement – the deliberate judgement – of millions of people.'[3]

Lloyd George was not surprised when the Lords rejected his Finance Bill by 350 votes to seventy-five. Asquith condemned their actions as 'a breach of the constitution and a usurpation of the rights of the Commons', but Lloyd George knew that the moral victory was his. The greed of the Lords had been exposed. 'We have got them!' he declared. A general election followed, and Asquith returned to power but with a much-reduced majority. Henceforth the Liberals were dependent on the votes of the Irish Nationalist and Labour MPs. The 'People's Budget' was finally passed in May 1910,* and Lloyd George sent a copy back to Criccieth inscribed 'To Uncle Lloyd, the real author of this Budget, with his pupil's affectionate gratitude.'[4]

As he stood in the pulpit of Castle Street chapel that evening in June 1911 the Chancellor was in his forty-ninth year, and age was beginning to show in the lines on his forehead, but not yet in his dark hair, barely tinged with grey at the temples. He dressed well, often with a flower in his buttonhole, and his handsome profile together with the breadth of his shoulders made him appear a tall man, even though he was of only average height. He had a magnetic presence, and was a master of oratory who could forge a connection with any audience, using many of the tricks he had learned from the nonconformist preachers of his youth. He would start softly, making his listeners strain to hear his words, and would slowly build up volume and pace. He was adept at reading his audience, and woe betide anyone who was foolish enough to heckle – the rapier-sharp Lloyd George wit would demolish his opponent in a trice.[†] By the time he reached the climax of a speech he was roaring out his emotive phrases, often half-singing in the style of a Welsh preacher, the audience in the palm of his hand. This was the 'Welsh Wizard' who had become a familiar figure for lampoonists in the press, the 'cottage-bred man' who had made his home in Downing Street, the outsider at the heart of the English establishment. No wonder Frances Stevenson wanted to hear him speak.

She was not disappointed. She recalled: 'There for the first time I came into contact with the Welsh Chancellor of the Exchequer and

* The constitutional crisis deepened when Edward VII died suddenly before the general election. The new King, George V, cooperated with the government, and his threat to create enough new Liberal peers to force through the budget finally brought the Upper House to heel. Nevertheless, it took seventy days of parliamentary debate and 554 divisions for the Finance Bill finally to be enacted. This titanic struggle between the Upper and Lower House led to the Parliament Act of 1911, a measure designed to prevent, among other things, the House of Lords from blocking finance Bills.

† In a speech during the Home Rule campaign, Lloyd George expressed his view that if Ireland should have Home Rule, then so should Wales: 'Home Rule for Ireland, Home Rule for Wales, and yes, Home Rule for England too!' 'Home Rule for hell!' shouted a heckler. 'Agreed,' responded Lloyd George at once. 'Let every man speak for his own country!'

instantly fell under the sway of his electric personality. I listened to his silver voice, observed his mastery over his audience. He seemed to establish a personal relationship immediately with every member of it, and although he spoke almost entirely in Welsh, I felt myself in some mysterious way drawn in to the orbit of his influence.'[5]

She would remain within that orbit for the rest of her life.

Louise Frances Stevenson was born in Kennington, South London, on 7 October 1888. Her parents were a happy couple, but mismatched in almost every respect.* John Stevenson was fair-haired, tall and good-looking, a Celt of Scottish ancestry. His father, a strict Presbyterian of the same stamp as Uncle Lloyd, was raised in Lanarkshire, moved to London and died young. As a result, John learned responsibility early in life and, showing great enterprise, took a position in France, learning French to a high standard. Back in Britain he became secretary to a firm of French import agents, a job he enjoyed despite its modest remuneration.

According to his daughter, John Stevenson was an honest and courageous man who made up for his lack of worldly ambition with steadfastness and a strong sense of personal morality. He was more relaxed than his family on denominational issues, and at the age of thirty-four he decided to marry a Catholic. Family outrage followed. His choice of bride was Louise Augustine Armanino, Augustine to her husband but Louise to everyone else. Olive-skinned and dark-haired, she was John's opposite in almost every respect. Her Italian father, Leopold, chose to pursue a career as an artist, and while studying in Paris he met and married his French wife. In the run-up to the siege of Paris in 1870 they fled to London on the last train before the rails were torn up by the advancing Prussian army. They settled near the Kennington School of Art, and raised a family. Somehow, probably through mutual French connections, their daughter Louise met John Stevenson, and

---

* There were some striking parallels between the Lloyd Georges and the Stevensons. Both couples were socially and religiously mismatched, and their families had tried to separate them. Both had five children, had their last child in 1902 after a gap, and both suffered traumatic bereavements of a beloved child. None of these things was particularly unusual, but they do help to explain how Frances fitted in so easily to the Lloyd George family, and how she quickly came to understand its dynamics.

they married when she was only nineteen years old. Louise was as fiery, artistic and temperamental as her husband was calm. She could be quick to take offence, but she was also intelligent and loyal.

Unpromising as this blend of characters would seem, Louise and John lived happily together and raised five children in a Kennington house that was large enough to accommodate the ageing Armaninos too, with a studio for Leopold on the top floor. Their first child was christened Louise Frances, but was known as Frances, and in adult life usually signed her name 'F.L. Stevenson'. A second daughter, Janet, followed, then another, Ninette, and then a much-cherished son, Paul. After a gap of some years, a fifth and last child, Muriel, was born in 1902, when Frances was thirteen years old.

In the light of her unconventional life, much has been made of Frances' 'bohemian' upbringing, but the evidence for this is somewhat scant. It is true that she was raised in the same house as her artist grandfather, but by the time she was born he earned his living producing lithographs for commercial advertisements. Although his studio was at the top of the house, it was hardly a garret. The Armaninos used to throw parties, rolling up the carpets for dancing, but this seems to have been the extent of the bohemianism in the Stevenson household. Always quick to suspect a slight, Louise was determined to prove to her snobbish middle-class neighbours and her in-laws that she was respectable. Her house was furnished with fashionable, dark pieces of wooden furniture and her children were impeccably turned out, with hand-embroidered underclothes and immaculate, if oft-mended, navy-blue-and-white sailor suits. Frances' mother was the very opposite of a free-thinking, rebellious artist. She held up the little Princes at Windsor Castle as examples for her children, and read the works of her favourite author E.F. Benson over and over again. She was the model of a conventional Victorian mother in her insistence on plain dress for her daughters and her horror of newfangled inventions like bicycles.

Yet there was still something fundamentally un-English in Frances' upbringing. She picked up her mother's love of outward respectability, but also her grandparents' broader view of the world and their catholic (and Catholic) tastes. Her grandparents taught her to speak French fluently and to debate politics vigorously at the kitchen table. One of their early topics was the rights and wrongs of the Boer War, with Frances and her grandfather on the side of the Boers (and thus of Lloyd George) and her father loyally siding with the British Empire. Frances was also taught to play the piano by her grandmother, who had run a school in Montmartre with her sister and was a strict taskmaster. Mistakes as she practised were marked by a knock on the floor with a cane from her grandmother's room above.

There was not much in the way of formal religion in the Stevenson household. Louise, having converted to the Church of England, arranged to have her older children confirmed, but took little interest beyond that. If John Stevenson had been as strict a Presbyterian as his father he would have insisted that the children followed his faith, but in this, as in all other respects, he was easy-going. Frances did come into contact with her father's Presbyterian roots when she spent time with her Scottish grandmother, who she remembered as very strict. She was the first to take her to church as a child, where Frances was thoroughly bored, made her say her prayers morning and evening, and would not allow her to play music other than hymns and religious pieces on Sundays.

Frances was indulged at home by her extended family, and was generally a happy child, with an optimistic but somewhat emotional and romantic nature. As a little girl she told her mother that she wanted to play with the little Princes and write a book, and the sight of an almond tree in full blossom sent her into pre-adolescent raptures. Her home was not poor by any standards – the children recalled teas with toast and dripping, or butter and jam, and large Sunday breakfasts, and the adults usually had a bottle of wine on the table – but money was never in abundance. Although her childhood was more comfortable than Lloyd George's, Frances was very aware of her family's financial constraints. While Frances was still young they moved from Kennington to Aldebrook Road near Clapham Common. Frances was educated to the age of thirteen at a local school, but with the arrival of Muriel in 1902 there was not enough money for school fees, and Frances and her older siblings were sent to council schools, much to the chagrin of the status-conscious Louise. It was expected that at least some of them would win scholarships to better schools; Frances quickly did so, and was enrolled at Clapham High School.

At the turn of the century Clapham High School was one of the leading girls' schools in South London. Frances was understandably nervous on her first day, but was delighted by the physical beauty of her new surroundings: 'I thought it the most beautiful building I had ever been in, with its polished floors and staircases, its lovely central hall in which stood a statue of the Venus de Milo; the reproductions of Old Masters on the walls, and, above all, its opportunities for friendships with both girls and mistresses.'[6] She also appreciated that the school could be her gateway to university, a comparatively unusual experience for a girl still, and eventually to a career of her own.

The headmistress, Mrs Woodhouse, was a clever and assertive woman who encouraged her pupils' ambitions. Frances showed plenty of promise: she passed her matriculation examination a year early, and excelled in Classics, although whether that was through natural talent or her fervent admiration of the Classics teacher, Miss Trenerry, is hard to tell. As we have heard, she met and formed a friendship with Mair Lloyd George, but Frances was a year ahead of Mair, and they were parted at the end of the summer term of 1907 when Frances, again a year early, left for university. Encouraged by Miss Trenerry, she had dreamed of reading Classics at Girton or Newnham, the only Cambridge colleges that admitted women. Mrs Woodhouse had other ideas. Perhaps sensing that Frances, though bright, was not academically strong enough for Cambridge, she persuaded her to apply instead to the University of London. She won a generous scholarship, and having been persuaded that her parents could not afford to send her to Cambridge, she somewhat reluctantly accepted a place at Royal Holloway College, one of the university's two colleges for women, situated nineteen miles west of London in Surrey.

Founded in 1879 by the millionaire philanthropist Thomas Holloway, the college occupied a large, highly ornate building set around two quadrangles and filled with Victorian art. By 1907 Royal Holloway was making a name for itself as a pioneer in women's higher education. Emily Wilding Davison, the suffragette who was killed after throwing herself under the King's horse at the 1913 Derby, was a graduate, as were Helen Cam, who went on to be the first female professor at Harvard, and the novelist Ivy Compton-Burnett.

Frances was a lively and popular young woman. Her excellent

grounding at Clapham High School meant that she was ahead of her fellow students, which left plenty of time for bicycle rides through Windsor Great Park – 'we must have looked very prim with our long skirts, our stiff collars and our boaters, but there was no primness in our hearts'[7] – music, tennis parties and amateur dramatics. She went on walking trips with her fellow students and dabbled with suffrage politics, though without getting seriously entangled. She may have loved the freedom of her new life a little too much, since she was warned by her tutors at the end of her first year that she needed to work harder if she wanted to sit for an honours degree. She took the warning to heart, but graduated with a third in 1910. She received her degree from the former Prime Minister Lord Rosebery, and noted that he was 'a dignified, handsome figure'. It was her first contact with a great statesman.[8]

Frances' options were limited when she left university, but she was keen to exploit any opportunity that came her way. Regarding herself as an emancipated woman rebelling against the bustle-and-corset restrictions of her mother's generation, she joined a suffrage organisation and, pursuing her interest in social reform, heard George Bernard Shaw lecture at the Fabian Society while she looked around for a suitable position. Unmarried women usually chose one of the accepted 'female' careers – teaching, looking after children, nursing, librarianship and the like – and gave up work when they married. Despite having a degree, Frances was still expected to devote her life to a husband and children. But she was no militant suffragette: marriage and children was precisely what she expected and wanted for herself. Her grandmother predicted that she would marry a country clergyman and have ten children, a life that would have suited her well. Slightly tongue-in-cheek, Frances herself wrote in her memoir: 'I knew that the most wonderful thing in the world would be to marry a *good* man – preferably a clergyman – and to devote my life to good works.'[9]

In the meantime Frances tried to obtain a job in journalism, visiting the offices of various newspapers without success. In the end she was obliged, like many young women in her situation, to turn to teaching. Rather than take a position as a private governess, she applied to various schools, and even tried for a post in Calcutta, much to her parents' distress. Young for her age in both character and looks, it is doubtful whether she would actually have gone through with it had she got the post, but it came to nothing. She was relieved in the end to be offered a residential position at Allenswood, a girls' boarding school in Wimbledon.

Allenswood was not as academically rigorous as Clapham High School. Its aim was to 'polish' rather than to educate young ladies of good families, and the focus was on socially useful subjects such as French and music. Pupils were taught to 'correct' their regional or foreign accents in the interests of social advancement. The older girls were barely younger than Frances, so she was put in charge of younger pupils who were around the same age as her younger sister Muriel. To begin with Frances hated teaching, and on her first visit home she sobbed on her mother's shoulder. But after a short while she settled down, and found friends among her fellow teachers. As the oldest of a family of five, she was used to being around younger girls, and she became a mentor to many of her pupils. She felt, however, that she was not a good teacher: 'I was not nearly strict enough: I saw the children's point of view too well and too easily. To the young ones I was a good story-teller, preferring to teach them their history and literature in this way. To the older ones I was a confidante.'[10]

At Allenswood she confided to a fellow teacher that she 'completely renounced religion'.[11] In truth, she had never been very firm in her convictions. She had initially accepted a relaxed religious orthodoxy gleaned from church and school. This early faith was more romantic than deep, and led to a brief desire to be a Christian martyr after reading the bestseller *Quo Vadis*. Her beliefs were first challenged at the age of eleven or twelve when her beloved grandfather fell seriously ill. Despite her ardent prayers he died, and she began to question the existence of a benevolent and indulgent God. Her eventual renunciation of formal religion was not the traumatic experience it had been for Lloyd George. It did not seem to matter much at the time, although it was to prove fortuitous in later life that she had already decided to forgo conventional morality.

Frances at twenty-two was a pretty, vital young woman, eager to experience the world. Her fair hair had darkened only slightly as she matured and was thick and wavy, often escaping her attempts to tame it. She was slightly above average height at five feet five inches, and had a good figure. Her oval face, gentle blue-grey eyes, small mouth and round chin made for a pleasing, attractive whole. Frances' romantic aspirations were still strong, and she was by now craving 'a little male company'.[12] Her mother had taught her to dress plainly in order to attract a good man who would love her for herself alone and put her on a pedestal, but Frances soon rejected this advice: she did not want to be put on a pedestal. She tried to dress attractively, but she was not a naturally stylish person: later, when she began to attend international conferences, a colleague took her aside and advised her that she really ought to visit Mr Worth, the foremost London fashion designer, for some help. Frances subsequently became an elegant dresser with a classic style.

As a young woman, Frances' character lacked depth. She was not grounded in faith or creed like Margaret Lloyd George, and her mother's teaching had placed perhaps too great an emphasis on maintaining appearances rather than on solid values. She showed a tendency to be easily led, as when she allowed her headmistress to persuade her to study at Royal Holloway, but she was at least aware of her susceptibility to powerful characters, writing later in life: 'I found the greatest difficulty in setting up any real genuine enthusiasm for the suffrage movement at college, keen as I am on votes for women, though I have no doubt that if I knew Mrs Pankhurst I should be devoted to her and through her to the cause.'[13] She dreamed of romance and of travelling the world, but did not have the opportunity or the force of character to make these things happen by herself.

Even in her early twenties there was a strangely paradoxical quality to Frances. Her friends, of whom there were many, responded to her loyalty, her sympathetic nature and her generosity of spirit – she was accused by her mother of being too ready to 'forget and forgive'.[14] She was popular with both sexes because she was a lively companion, had 'enough nerve for anything',[15] was not too clever or bookish, and had a positive and optimistic outlook on life. At the same time, Frances was at heart a rather unfocused, emotionally charged young woman who longed to find a cause to which she could devote her life. For such a cause she would be prepared to break all the rules.

Frances' character had two distinct layers. At her core she was as self-centred as a teenager, with a romantic view of life and a determination to experience as much as she could of it, without knowing quite how to go about doing so. But she also craved approval and love, which she had been raised to expect. She developed a quietly charming, accommodating outer layer, with pleasing manners and an ability to put people at their ease. As Megan Lloyd George later put it, Frances seemed 'like a thick pile carpet into which one's feet sank gratefully'.[16] Megan's sister Olwen, a better judge of character, saw through the outer shell: 'she seemed meek and mild, but underneath she was as hard as nails'.[17] Frances displayed the occasional flash of spitefulness, mainly directed in later life at the other women in Lloyd George's life, and she was a world-class keeper of secrets. She was as subtle and difficult to read as a Siamese cat. The girls of Allenswood who nicknamed her 'Pussy' hit the mark with precision.

This then was Frances Stevenson at the age of twenty-two, sitting in her pew at Castle Street chapel in June 1911 at what was the beginning of the most important relationship of her life.

Frances was impressed by the politician she saw that day, but it was pure chance that brought her into closer contact with him. In the summer of 1911, at the age of forty-four, Margaret Lloyd George was settling into middle age, and her brood was beginning to fly the nest. Dick, twenty-two, was embarking on a career in engineering after graduating from Cambridge; Olwen, nineteen, had just returned from Germany where she had spent a year learning the language; and Gwilym, sixteen, was preparing to go up to Jesus College, Cambridge. Although the family had recovered outwardly from the loss of Mair four years earlier, the after-effects of the bereavement remained, not least in the fact that Megan had not yet been sent to school.

But Megan's freedom was about to come to an end. In the autumn of 1911 her parents decided that she should attend a boarding school. Margaret and Lloyd George were over-cautious when it came to the health of their children, and a standard bout of tonsillitis had been enough to make them cancel Megan's lessons for the whole summer term of 1911. This meant that she was falling behind in her education, and it was felt that she needed some extra tuition over the summer to help her catch up. They decided to find a tutor to join the family in Criccieth for the whole of August and September, and, not knowing where else to turn, Margaret wrote to Mrs Woodhouse at Clapham High School:

> You will be surprised to hear from me. I have dear little Mary's [i.e. Mair's] photo for you and Miss Lees but I have never sent them to you. I hope to do so when you return from your holidays. My object in writing today is to ask if you know of any nice girl that would be suitable for a temporary governurse [sic] during the Holidays for my little girl. We want one to teach her music & French, one that can talk French well. She had a governurse in the mornings for 2 years but during this last term she had no lessons at all because she suffered from enlarged tonsils. I fear she will forget all unless she has some lessons during August & September. If you know of any one would you let me know ...[18]

At first Mrs Woodhouse recommended a girl who it turned out had already made plans for the summer, but then she thought of Frances Stevenson. Frances was perfectly qualified for the job. Not only was she fluent in French, but she played the piano well, was accustomed to teaching girls of Megan's age, and had not made any plans for the long summer holidays apart from a two-week trip in August. Lack of funds was perhaps the reason, and if Mrs Woodhouse suspected that Frances might welcome the chance to escape the family home for a few weeks, she was not mistaken. Frances promptly wrote to Margaret, who having decamped by then to Criccieth, delegated the job of finding a suitable girl to her husband and Olwen.

Olwen telephoned Frances, but finding that she would not be available for the whole summer, she concluded that they would have to look elsewhere. She expressed her regret, 'as otherwise I'm sure you would satisfy us'.[19] Frances' holiday plans were hastily dropped and she was invited to an interview on 29 July at 11 Downing Street. She described herself as 'nervous and pale' as she waited in the large drawing room. When Lloyd George appeared, she had a second chance to form an impression of the famous statesman. She wrote in her memoirs:

> His image as I saw him then is graven on my mind: the sensitive face, with deep furrows between the eyes: the eyes themselves, in which were

all knowledge of human nature, grave and gay almost simultaneously – which, as they scrutinised yours, convinced you that they understood all the workings of your heart and mind, sympathised with all your difficulties, set you in a place apart. The broad brow, the beautiful profile – straight nose, neat insolent chin, and a complexion as young and fresh as a child's. (He was very proud of his skin.)

Lloyd George was both handsome and powerful: he was bound to impress the young Frances. But 'there was something more even than this which distinguished him from all other men I had ever met – from all whom I ever did meet thereafter – a magnetism which made my heart leap and swept aside my judgement, producing an excitement which seemed to permeate my entire being. I was strung to the utmost point of awareness by this strange encounter, which meant so much for me, then and for ever after.'[20]

How much Frances later inflated the significance of this first face-to-face encounter is difficult to judge. She did not record that Olwen was present at the interview, nor that she was in competition for the post with another girl, 'a nice German-Swiss – simple, straight, kind-looking but not good looking'.[21] Olwen preferred the other candidate, but Lloyd George, probably noting how pretty Frances looked in her little flowered hat, overruled her on the grounds that Frances was more intelligent and that her French was better. Frances, ever the romantic, wrote: 'I left Downing Street under the impression that I was a free and independent person: in truth, I was enslaved for the rest of my life.'[22]

She was told that she would be collected the following Tuesday, just three days hence, at 11.30 a.m., taken to Downing Street for lunch, and then to Paddington to catch the train to Wales. The invitation to lunch might well have been the action of a concerned father wanting to get to know the new governess a little better before putting his daughter in her care, but one wonders if the plain Swiss girl would have received similar attention. For Frances, this was an adventure. She had never travelled in a private car before, and she had certainly never sat down to lunch with the Chancellor and the Attorney General, Sir Rufus Isaacs, discussing the issues of the day. She drank up the experience as if it would never be repeated.

In Criccieth, Frances was made welcome by Margaret and treated as one of the family. Margaret was quite used to having house guests during their holidays in Wales. Lloyd George had for years been in the habit of inviting his political friends to join him to provide some extra stimulation during his obligatory stays there. The spacious new house, Brynawelon, was built at the top of a hill to the west of Criccieth, giving it a spectacular view over the bay while remaining fairly private – or as private as possible, since when Lloyd George was at home tourists would try to catch a glimpse of him through the trees. It was surrounded by a large garden which was Margaret's delight. It was only a mile or so over the hills to Llanystumdwy and Lloyd George's boyhood haunts, and was within easy walking distance of Garthcelyn. Originally built with six bedrooms, two more were added to accommodate visitors, and at times even the staff cottages at the bottom of the garden were commandeered as guest bedrooms.

Frances, at twenty-two, was virtually the same age as Dick and Olwen, and she blended in easily with the family and their friends. On the night she arrived Megan, the spoiled pet of the family, insisted on staying up to meet her new governess, and after Frances had been thoroughly scrutinised they became fast friends. They fell into a comfortable round of lessons in the mornings and games, trips and fun with the other young people in the afternoons. In an interview given in 1970, Frances described their routine: 'I taught her a little bit of arithmetic, some reading, we used to read and then I gave her things to write out and we had a little music. She was very fond of singing and she used to sing Welsh songs in the intervals and I played the piano for her and then we used to go out for walks together. It was a very, very happy time I had up there.'[23]

Lloyd George, detained by his duties in London, was kept abreast of the new teacher's progress. In a letter to Megan he wrote:

I am glad that you like your new companion, & that you get on so well together. I knew you would. I want you to learn French & music so that you can talk French like a petite Parisien [sic] and play the piano like Paderewski.

I am so looking forward to seeing your bright face.
Tada[24]

Whatever the other members of the family subsequently thought of Frances (Olwen rather cattily recalled that she was regarded as 'dull'), that summer they all became friends. Olwen would keep in touch with Frances when she returned to Allenswood, writing to her from Paris in the fondest terms: 'My dear Frances, Thanks very much for your long letter which you wrote in spite of your busy life – my dear don't you work too hard or there will be nothing of you left by the time I come home.'[25]

The household in Criccieth was transformed by the arrival of Lloyd George, accompanied by his ministerial colleague Charles Masterman and his wife Lucy. 'Thereafter the tempo of the household was considerably enlivened,' wrote Frances. 'The atmosphere was electric . . . The atmosphere at Brynawelon glowed.'[26] She could not help but notice how much energy Lloyd George brought with him: 'When L.G. was present anywhere all attention was necessarily focused on him. He would always hold the initiative, whether in great things, or small – a political campaign or a picnic party. The tempo of a household would change when he entered it from one of quiet and order to something exciting and almost feverish. Everything naturally, it seemed, revolved around him, and nobody else.'[27]

Lloyd George was sitting for a portrait by an artist called Christopher Williams that summer, an experience he always found irksome.* This gave Frances and Megan an excuse to abandon lessons and entertain him instead. In the afternoons Lloyd George organised excursions to local beauty spots, picnics by the river Dwyfor or drives in the countryside. He was on incorrigibly good form, and for once seemed to enjoy his summer 'duty visit' to Criccieth. One morning he roused the household before daybreak to walk up Snowdon, the highest peak in Wales, to see the sunrise, only to be frustrated by mist. At other times he showed off his physical agility by wading across mountain springs (displaying, Frances unprimly noted, a shapely calf), and dared his companions to climb to the top of a tree with him, a challenge only Lucy Masterman accepted.

---

* Williams, a well-known portrait artist from Maesteg in South Wales, painted three portraits of Lloyd George. The one in question showed him in his robes as Chancellor of the Exchequer.

It may be fanciful to suggest that these hi-jinks were evidence that Lloyd George was over-conscious of the presence of a pretty newcomer in the midst of his family. He had other reasons for feeling buoyant: he had pulled off a significant coup in July by organising the investiture of the young Prince of Wales at Caernarvon Castle, bringing the entire royal family to his constituency. Still, in Frances' recollection many years later, the hot summer of 1911 was when the attraction between her and Lloyd George started to grow: 'That summer did so much to me and for me. It was 1911, the summer of perpetual sunshine: sea, sun and mountains – such a combination of beauty I had never before experienced.'

She was not exaggerating when she described a 'summer of perpetual sunshine'. 1911 remained the hottest summer on record until 2006. By 20 July there had been twenty consecutive days without rain – even in Wales. Grass and hedgerows withered, *The Times* ran a regular column on 'Deaths from Heat', and temperatures remained sky high until 11 September.

Frances was an easy and popular guest, and was a hit with the whole family. By the end of September it had been agreed that Megan would return to Allenswood with her, to be enrolled at the school as a weekly boarder. This arrangement meant that Frances stayed in touch with Lloyd George. The busy Chancellor took every opportunity to drive to Wimbledon to see his youngest child, and to check on her progress with the attractive Miss Stevenson. He would sometimes invite Frances to Downing Street for Sunday tea, and she was also occasionally invited there by other members of the family. She soon noticed that Margaret 'never took the initiative in matters either great or small: her life was made for her, and she accepted it all. The visitors to the house in Downing Street were her husband's visitors, sometimes her children's, scarcely ever her own. She was, in effect, a visitor in her husband's house – except at Criccieth, where he was a visitor in hers.'[28] Frances' views on Margaret are understandably biased, but they contain a grain of truth: Margaret's domain was Criccieth, while Lloyd George dominated in London.

Frances' popularity with the whole family meant that no excuse was needed for including her in parties and excursions, and Lloyd George probably did not question himself too closely as to why her company was so delightful to him. She was only too eager to break the monotony of life at Allenswood with visits to Downing Street. On at least one occasion she accompanied the family to chapel, and she played the piano after supper while they sang hymns. In this way she began to fill the void left in Lloyd George's life when Mair died.

But Frances was not Mair, and, rightly or wrongly, Lloyd George began to take an altogether unfatherly interest in her. At first she could not bring herself to believe that the famous Chancellor of the Exchequer felt anything for her, and imagined the attraction she felt for him to be entirely one-sided. In any case, the situation seemed hopeless as far as she was concerned, since he was a married man. Nevertheless, she could not stop her feelings from developing, and began to share her innermost thoughts with the sympathetic Lloyd George. She confided in him her desire to stop teaching as soon as possible, and he began to involve her in his work.

At Easter 1912, Lloyd George was planning the next stage of his land campaign, in which he would press for a court system to adjudicate on fair rents and tenure for agricultural land and fair valuation of leases, and for tribunals to fix agricultural wages. He asked Frances to translate a French book on the subject for him, and she did such a good job that he was encouraged to give her more work. 'At present I am learning German & shorthand,' she wrote to an Allenswood colleague, 'as Mr Lloyd George has promised to find me something to do as soon as I know shorthand. Meantime I am doing some work for him for his Land Bill. It is awfully interesting – I started it in the summer, you know, & he wants me to go on with it in my spare time.'[29]

The relationship between Frances and the Lloyd George family was gradually supplanted by a relationship between Frances and Lloyd George alone. It was professional rather than personal, through most of 1912 at least, but she was beginning to recognise the depth of her feelings for him: 'I remember going to the House of Commons to see him for some instructions on the work I was doing for him one summer's evening before the House rose for the recess. He was very tired and his eyes were red-rimmed with late-night sittings. "I have to flog myself, otherwise I could not go on," he said to me. My heart went out to him, and I wanted more than anything to help him.'[30]

In the summer of 1912 Lloyd George was working hard on implementing the National Insurance Act,* the land campaign and the long-awaited introduction of the Welsh Disestablishment Bill. He was also facing the most serious threat yet to his political career.

On 17 April, two days after the sinking of the *Titanic*, he had been offered a 'sure thing' on the stock market. Although he was financially better off than before,† there was no guarantee that his position, and thus his salary, would continue. He was therefore as susceptible as ever to the lure of a quick profit, although he was still as inept in business matters.

The crisis in Lloyd George's affairs that was to become known as the Marconi affair began when the Attorney General, Rufus Isaacs, offered Lloyd George and Alexander Murray, the Liberal Chief Whip, the chance to buy shares in the American telegraph company Marconi. The shares were not generally available – Isaacs had prior access to them through his brother Godfrey, one of Marconi's directors – but they were due to begin trading on 19 April, so Lloyd George did not have much time to stop and think. Notwithstanding his criticism of Joseph Chamberlain for his interest in Kynock & Co. during the Boer War, he took a thousand shares at £2 each, while Murray took 3,500, together, crucially, with five hundred on behalf of the Liberal Party itself. The shares came on the market at a price of sixty-five shillings each. By the end of the day they had risen to £4.

Lloyd George may or may not have benefited from information supplied by Rufus Isaacs that the shares would increase in value. But that was not all. The English Marconi company had a stake in its American sister company, although the arrangement was not reciprocal – the American company did not own any part of the English one. But there was a close relationship between them, illustrated by the fact that

* Lloyd George was the architect of the National Insurance Bill, the foundation of the welfare state, which would, in his words, 'relieve untold misery in myriads of homes', and which would for the first time make workers eligible for sick and maternity pay.
† As Chancellor of the Exchequer Lloyd George was paid £5,000 (worth £416,000 today) a year, £3,000 more than he had received as President of the Board of Trade. To put this in perspective, just after the Boer War he had been paid a fee of a thousand guineas by George Cadbury for negotiating the purchase of a newspaper. This, wrote his son Gwilym, enabled the whole family to live comfortably for five years.

Godfrey Isaacs was a director of both. On 7 March 1912 the English Marconi had been awarded a highly lucrative contract to build a series of wireless stations throughout the British Empire.* The contract was so significant that it could not be signed until it had been tabled in Parliament, and when that happened on 19 July, rumours started circulating that government ministers had profited from the company's shares.

The press began to hint that there had been favouritism at work in awarding the contract to Marconi, and that there had been insider dealing in the company's shares. Neither claim was entirely true: the contract had been fairly negotiated by the Postmaster General, Herbert Samuel, who was not one of the ministers involved in the share purchase. Furthermore, the shares traded were in the American company, not the British one, and the American Marconi would not – directly, at least – benefit financially from the contract. But it was bound to increase the value of the English Marconi, and it was likely that the share price of the American company would rise by association, at least temporarily. Government ministers would have known about the contract, and were in a position to vote for it in Parliament. They should surely have taken the view that it was inappropriate for them to benefit in any way, however indirect, from either Marconi.

Samuel was certainly aware that this was an issue since he informed the Prime Minister of the ministers' share purchases in June. Asquith did not act on the information, perhaps hoping that nothing would come of the matter, but if so he was mistaken. In August there was a parliamentary debate on the issue, during which Samuel had to defend the awarding of the contract to English Marconi, and Asquith was forced to agree to an inquiry into the conduct of his Chancellor, Chief Whip and Attorney General. A Select Committee was convened with a Liberal majority, but the matter would not go away. In October, during another parliamentary debate, Rufus Isaacs denied on record that he had dealt in shares in English Marconi, linking Lloyd George (but not Murray) to his actions. His failure to mention the fact that they *had* dealt in the shares of American Marconi was an error they were to regret.

---

* The potential of the telegraph technology was demonstrated in a compelling way in April 1912, when it was the means of communicating the fate of the *Titanic* to the world.

From the beginning, Lloyd George and his ministerial colleagues had decided against suing the press over the allegations, something else that was later held against them. It is possible they thought that the rumours would die down of their own accord, although that would have been unlikely when such senior ministers were involved. It is also likely that Lloyd George at least did not fully appreciate the extent of the problem he was facing. Despite having been President of the Board of Trade he was vague at best about the mechanics of business, and he never made much, if any, money from his commercial dealings. Indeed, he even managed to make a loss on his Marconi shares, after buying some more when the price slumped. In his defence, the deal had been suggested at a particularly busy time and by a trusted source. As Attorney General, Rufus Isaacs was the highest law officer in the land, and could surely be trusted not to propose any improper or illegal dealings. But if he had thought it through, it should perhaps have been clear to Lloyd George that the Chancellor of the Exchequer, who was responsible for administering the country's economy, should not be chancing his arm on the stock market while in office.

Either way, the summer and autumn of 1912 was an anxious time for Lloyd George. He was used to fighting his political battles openly and vigorously. This time, as he waited for the Select Committee to deliver its verdict, he could only hope that the Prime Minister's support would not evaporate. Margaret was doing her best to be supportive, writing on 13 October from Criccieth: 'My Dearest D, So glad of yesterday and today's letters & that you squashed those who are trying all they can to get something against (you specially) & the government. I am thinking of you all the time. I was never so loathe to leave you.'[31] It was during these months that he fell in love with Frances Stevenson.

Frances and Lloyd George had been seeing each other regularly while he was in London under the paper-thin guise of the work she was doing for him, but neither seemed in a hurry to bring matters to a head. Frances 'hovered between doubt and longing, dread and desire',[32] hardly daring to hope that her feelings were returned, while Lloyd George seemed uncharacteristically hesitant to put his famed talent for seduction into action. This time it was different. Seducing a young, single girl was an altogether more serious business than enjoying a fling with a safely married woman. His previous affairs had been with women who had as much to lose from exposure as he did, and who were unlikely to make difficult demands of him. Married women also had the advantage of being able to conceal accidental conceptions under a cloak of respectability: a big consideration in days when contraception was difficult to obtain and generally unreliable. An affair with Frances Stevenson was not to be embarked on casually, even for Lloyd George.

While he hesitated, Lloyd George spent a great deal of time with Frances, often taking her out after his weekly visits to see Megan, and meeting during school holidays to discuss the work assignments he gave her. The mutual attraction grew but was not expressed, although Frances must have wondered at the frequency of Lloyd George's visits and the interest he showed in her. Then, on the first Sunday of July 1912, when they had known each other for nearly a year, Lloyd George travelled down to Allenswood to see Frances, and they acknowledged their feelings openly for the first time. She wrote in her diary in 1921: 'D. said it was the same road . . . he took the Sunday years ago . . . when both of us realised for the first time that something serious was happening – when I asked him to come to the garden party the following Saturday & he said he would. From then we never lost touch with each other & events marched more or less rapidly.'[33]

In fact it took another six months for their relationship to be established permanently. Furthermore, Frances maintained in her memoirs that she did not make up her mind whether to commit to the relationship until December 1912, although she was probably nearer the mark when she said she had lost her heart at that very first meeting in Downing Street in July 1911.

It was not unusual for Lloyd George to flirt, and seek to sleep, with a pretty woman. But this was more than a casual fling. From the beginning there was a caution in his actions that suggests he knew his feelings for Frances were deeper and more complex than those for his other conquests had been. Given the dangers inherent in forming a relationship with a young, unmarried woman, he needed a plan if he was to bring the affair to fruition. Frances was both attractive and intelligent. She could speak French and was a graduate, trained to research and process information. Furthermore, she was bored with her teaching position, feeling 'cribbed, cabin'ed and confined', and was actively looking for a different career.[34] Lloyd George reached the conclusion that she might be useful to him in a professional capacity, which would also conceal and facilitate their personal relationship.

By the end of July or the very beginning of August, he had discussed with Frances the possibility of her taking a position as his secretary at the Treasury. Frances had taken a few days' holiday at the beginning of August at Budleigh Salterton in Devon, from where she corresponded with Lloyd George formally and politely about work. On her return she continued to mull over the thought of working for him, while he in turn kept feeding her odd tasks to test her skills and to provide reasons for keeping closely in touch. He became certain that he wanted Frances as both his secretary and his mistress. He had come to trust her discretion, to respect her intelligence, and above all to love her enough to feel confident that he would marry her if he was ever free to do so. Nothing less would be fair recompense for involving Frances in a long-term adulterous relationship.

With characteristic determination, Lloyd George decided on his course of action and then used every atom of his understanding of Frances' character to manipulate her into agreeing to it. Having already put it to her in the summer that she should resign her post at Allenswood and work for him as his secretary, he went on to explain that if she did so, she would need to be his mistress also. They could not work together unless it was on his terms.

Frances had only just realised that her feelings for Lloyd George were reciprocated. The romantic in her rejoiced at being in love, even as she realised that she had to make the biggest decision of her life. To reject his offer would surely mean the end of their friendship, and a return to a life of tedium with no hope of escape from teaching except through marriage to somebody considerably less exciting than Lloyd George. But to accept would be to risk scandal and disgrace if they were exposed. She would have to conceal her feelings from even her closest friends, and accept a life of deception. Above all, she would have to give up any thoughts of making a respectable marriage and of having children of her own. Lloyd George offered her no firm prospect of marriage. In fact, in a move that recalled his brutal honesty with Margaret more than twenty-five years previously, he underlined the fact that there would be no official place for her in his life by giving her a biography of Parnell. Even in the first ardent throes of love, Lloyd George was adamant that no statesman had a right to sacrifice a great cause for his private happiness. As ever, his career came first. To his credit, he never sought to mislead Frances on this point, and since Margaret was younger than he and in good health, Frances could not realistically entertain any hope of a change in his circumstances.

Frances gave notice at Allenswood at the end of the autumn term of 1912. Her headmistress, who had noted with disapproval the arrival of almost daily letters from Lloyd George,* exploded: 'The man has upset me enough with his Insurance stamps and now he takes away one of my staff.'[35] It was not until December, however, that Frances accepted that she could not work with Lloyd George without being his mistress, 'on his own terms', as she put it, 'which were in direct conflict with my essentially Victorian upbringing'.[36]

At first she had refused, leaving Lloyd George one night in the House of Commons after saying she could not agree to his proposal. They spent Christmas apart, with their families. Frances made plans to visit friends in Dundee over New Year, and to think things over very carefully, away from his influence. She left for Scotland on 30 December, without giving Lloyd George her answer. He had no intention of allowing a lull in his campaign at this critical point, and they wrote to each other almost daily.

Then the unexpected happened: in Scotland, Frances encountered an old flame. Stuart Brown, the brother of a college friend of hers, was a Cambridge graduate and a rising star in the India Office. Frances described him as 'in every way a desirable "*parti*", highly intelligent, musical, a civil servant with a future',[37] and was flattered by his attention. He renewed his suit, asking her once again to be his wife. His proposal neatly underlined to Frances what she would give up by agreeing to be Lloyd George's mistress. She was not in love with Brown, but if she married him she would be his legal wife and could bear his children. In confusion, she wrote to Lloyd George telling him what had happened.

---

* The letters have not survived, seemingly because Lloyd George and Frances decided to burn them on receipt; presumably they were becoming more confident about expressing their feelings. Later, in her diary, Frances was to describe their regret at losing them since they were so 'beautiful' and, as Lloyd George put it, 'every word meant business'.

Lloyd George's response demonstrated how well he understood Frances, and is another example of the ruthlessness he applied to his private as well as his political affairs. He immediately wrote back in magnanimous and self-sacrificial terms, telling her that 'I must do what I thought right and that he would not stand in my way. He did not try to persuade me against it; the decision was with *me*.'[38]

This gallant and generous letter was probably only a ploy, for he followed it with another almost immediately. The second letter was very different: there was a sudden (unspecified) political crisis: something terrible had happened, and he needed her. All thoughts of Stuart Brown were dispersed, which was probably Lloyd George's intention. Frances was powerless to resist the thought that she was necessary to him. She loved him and he needed her: it was enough to make up her mind. She packed her bags immediately, and travelled to London where she placed herself 'in his hands unconditionally'.[39] 'The decision was a heart-shocking one for me,' she wrote, 'due to my upbringing and the opinions I held regarding any woman who lived with a man to whom she was not married. I held myself up to the light, so to speak, and passed judgement on myself, longing for some comfort but realising the awful things which the future might hold.'[40] A few weeks later, on 21 January 1913, they sealed the bargain.* Together alone, they solemnised the relationship on the day they both thereafter referred to as their 'marriage'. It was four days after Lloyd George's fiftieth birthday, and only three days before his silver wedding with Margaret.

* Frances is coy on the details, only noting in her diary on 21 January 1915, 'It is just two years since C. [for "Chancellor"] & I were "married"'. Her granddaughter, Ruth Longford, states in her biography of Frances that this was the date on which her relationship with Lloyd George was consummated.

11

Overloaded with Flattery

FRANCES TOOK A PURE LEAP of faith when she entered her unofficial marriage. Her fascination with and admiration of Lloyd George were so strong that she felt justified in making an unconditional commitment to him, confident in his ability to protect her from scandal and harm. In her words, 'There was something more even than [his handsome face] which distinguished him from all other men I had ever met – from all whom I ever did meet thereafter – a magnetism which made my heart leap and swept aside my judgement, producing an excitement which seemed to permeate my entire being.'[1] With the confidence of youth, it did not seem to occur to her that he might tire of her, and that if he ever gave her up she would be in a highly vulnerable position: past the age, perhaps, at which she could secure a good marriage, and without any security for her later life. She was blind too to his reputation as a ladies' man, believing wholeheartedly his assurances that his feelings were as strong and as durable as hers. Fortunately for Frances, in this at least she was right.

As soon as she returned from Scotland at the beginning of 1913 Frances began her new life at Lloyd George's side, devoting herself initially to helping him through the Marconi crisis. She could offer little in the way of practical support, although she did spend days combing in vain through newspaper reports to find some reference to the American Marconi shares offer in the hope of proving that they were available to the public. What she could offer instead was moral support. It was to her, not Margaret, that Lloyd George poured out his worries about his future. By now he recognised that he had jeopardised his entire political future by his unthinking actions. Not unnaturally, he was keen to keep as much of this as he could from his wife, and especially from Uncle Lloyd: 'Not knowing how the scandal would end he was tormenting himself, not so much for what would happen if he had to resign his office, but how he had let down his nonconformist supporters by his transactions . . . He was suffering, too, because of what old Uncle Lloyd would think of "his boy" for being so foolish when he had attained such high office and responsibility.'[2]

It is not clear what crisis, if any, occurred in January 1913, since the Select Committee had not yet reported, and there were no fresh press scoops about the Marconi affair until March.* In any case, nothing further emerged, and for the time being Lloyd George resumed normal life, going on holiday in the South of France in February with none other than Rufus Isaacs.† Meanwhile, having given up her place at Allenswood and her term-time accommodation with it, Frances was living at home again in Clapham under the eyes of her mother, which must have been even more difficult to bear at twenty-four than it had been at eighteen. Louise could not fail to notice the amount of time her daughter was spending out of hours with her new employer. Frances was close to her volatile mother, but had not confided in her while she was making her momentous choice. Soon she came to the conclusion that it was better that her mother knew the truth. If she hoped that Louise would take a tolerant view of the matter, she was sadly mistaken: 'I decided to make some confession to my mother, to seek from her some form of forgiveness or reassurance that redemption was possible, or might be. But with her strong and definite moral outlook, she turned on me the whole of her anger at the thought that

* Speculation was mounting about dealings the ministers might have had in the American Marconi company, and they were obliged to sue the French paper *Le Matin* in February/March for defamation, in order to provide themselves with an opportunity of putting their actual share dealings on the record. This was not a convincing move, since they had refused to sue several British papers for carrying similar stories, and the case was reported in the British press from 19 March onwards.

† Frances never forgave Isaacs (Lord Reading from 1914, later Marquess of Reading) for involving Lloyd George in the Marconi affair, and described him in her memoir as having 'what might be called the "cafeteria" mind – self-service only'.

her daughter could be capable of such an action, however extenuating the circumstances.'

Describing Louise as having a 'strong and definite moral outlook' is stretching the truth a little, since she seemed to be less concerned at Frances' loss of virtue than at the loss of respectability. She was incensed that Frances should sacrifice her future prospects and perhaps her reputation for such a man. Frances' excuses met with 'excoriating contempt',[3] and instead of the longed-for maternal absolution, Louise dramatically declared that she would rather see Frances dead at her feet.

Louise and John Stevenson demanded a meeting with Lloyd George to get the measure of the man, and presumably to ask him how he intended to look after their daughter. He, with typical nerve, invited them, with Frances, to dine at No. 11 – no doubt at a time when Margaret was safely elsewhere. Inevitably, perhaps, the meeting did not go well. Frances tersely records that 'it was not a success, and the attempt was not repeated'. Her parents were not won over by Lloyd George, their exact contemporary, and they took years to reconcile themselves to the situation. In time Lloyd George succeeded in charming them, at least to the point where they would accept his gifts and tickets to important state events, but for the next thirty years Louise never ceased to hope that Frances would leave him and make a respectable marriage.

In the months following her 'marriage' Frances was in an unenviable situation, living at home with parents who thoroughly disapproved of her lifestyle. She was caught between the opposing forces of her mother and her lover, ironically in much the same way as Maggie Owen had been twenty-five years previously. Lloyd George was aware of the pressure she was under, yet was as demanding and capricious as ever, both as an employer and as a lover. One Sunday he wrote to her: 'I wish you could spare an hour or two to take down a speech I am preparing this morning. Could you return with the car now? Tell Mrs Stevenson that I shall let you off a day this week to make up for it. You can get back home by 3.'[4]

One suspects that Mrs Stevenson would have seen through that flimsy excuse with ease. On another occasion Frances was torn between her mother and her lover when Lloyd George needed her, this time genuinely to work, on her mother's birthday. Birthdays were regarded as important family occasions in the Stevenson house. In a passage of her memoirs reminiscent of Maggie Owen's dejected letter of 1887 when she complained, 'My parents are angry with me one day and you another. I am on bad terms with one or the other continually,' Frances writes:

> On Sunday 29th June, 1914,* I was at 11 Downing Street in the after-noon working on a speech which L.G. was shortly to make to bankers in the City. I remember the day well, because it was my mother's birthday, and she was cross that I should have another engagement on that day ... I was upset at annoying my mother, and L.G. was annoyed with me for being upset. My mother and L.G. were never good friends and I was constantly being pulled both ways because of this.[5]

It was an eventful day for another reason, as students of the Great War will recognise, but that is to fly ahead of our story.

In 1913 a different kind of battle, and one closer to home, was more pressing: at around 6 a.m. on 18 February, a few weeks after Frances took up her new job, a bomb exploded in a house that newspaper proprietor George Riddell was building for Lloyd George on his estate at Walton Heath in Surrey.[†] The bomb, and another one which had failed to detonate, had been planted by two suffragettes, one of whom was Emily Wilding Davison. Mrs Pankhurst took responsibility, as she did for all violent acts committed in the name of Votes for Women, although she had not known of the plan in advance. She was arrested on 24 February for procuring and inciting women to commit offences contrary to the Malicious Injuries to Property Act 1861, and was sentenced to three years' penal servitude. (Her imprisonment on behalf of the perpetrators allowed Wilding Davison to go free, and stage her fatal protest at that year's Derby.)

---

* Frances' memory was at fault: the last Sunday of June 1914 was the twenty-eighth.
† The house was intended to be used by Lloyd George and his family as a weekend retreat from London; it also provided him and Frances with a convenient bolthole. It backed onto a golf course (the game was one of Lloyd George's favourite pastimes), and its only disadvantage was the ensuing lack of privacy.

Lloyd George was horrified, and assumed that the bombs were intended to cause injury to the builders working on the house. After a public statement to this effect, he received an anonymous letter from one of the women responsible:

> I write to protest against your assertion that it was intended the bombs should explode after the workmen had entered the house. The first bomb exploded at 6.5 am, the second was rendered harmless by the candle going out within 5 minutes of being lit, owing I think to the door of the cupboard in which it was placed being shut close and thus creating a lack of air . . . We intended both bombs to explode at between 5 and 5.30. I hope you will not continue to say that life was intentionally endangered after reading this. If it would enfranchise women I would willingly give myself up, but as I think my surrender would be of no use I regret for obvious reasons to be unable to sign this.[6]

In 1913 a large envelope containing red pepper and snuff was sent to every Cabinet Minister. Mrs Pankhurst wrote in her memoirs that 'the Press reported that they all fell victim to the ruse'. Actually it was Frances who opened the envelope addressed to Lloyd George, and such tactics were not going to change her mind about the violent tactics of the WSPU. When the Liberal Party seemed certain to gain office in 1906, Mrs Pankhurst and her followers adopted a policy of targeting future Cabinet Ministers to ask them whether a Liberal government would grant women the vote. WSPU members began to create disturbances deliberately in order to be arrested. Refusing to pay fines, they went to prison for brief periods, gaining more publicity for their cause. In total, 1,106 women were imprisoned between 1905 and 1914. Henry Campbell-Bannerman's Cabinet, divided on the issue of Votes for Women, did not bring forward a Bill. In response, the WSPU stepped up its campaign. Lloyd George's first personal encounter with the suffragettes had come when he was heckled while speaking at a public meeting in January 1906. He responded that he supported Votes for Women, but regretted the means they employed to further their case.

The WSPU campaign became more militant. Mass rallies were organised, and in 1908 two members of WSPU, Edith New and Mary Leigh, smashed windows in Downing Street. In October that year Lloyd George took Megan to see a mass demonstration in Parliament Square. Having witnessed a violent clash with police, he found himself in court as a witness being interrogated by Christabel Pankhurst, an encounter she was generally thought to have won.

On 6 December that year Lloyd George agreed to speak at a Votes for Women rally in the Albert Hall organised by a less militant organisation, the Women's Liberal Federation. With Margaret sitting beside him on the platform, he received a stormy reception, as he had expected. The meeting had been infiltrated by WSPU members who discarded their cloaks to reveal prison uniforms in support for Mrs Pankhurst, who was in prison at the time. They then proceeded to cause such chaos that it took Lloyd George over two hours to deliver a twenty-minute speech. At one point it was suggested that the meeting be abandoned, but according to one witness, Margaret, who had been sitting calmly through the furore, insisted that Lloyd George should not be defeated, whatever might happen.

In 1909, in a new development in the WSPU's campaign for publicity, some imprisoned suffragettes went on hunger strike. Herbert Gladstone, the Home Secretary, ordered that they should be force-fed. Outrage followed, and Lloyd George was the subject of particular vitriol, hated by Christabel Pankhurst and the WSPU because he supported their cause but refused to resign from a Cabinet that did not act to secure universal suffrage.

By 1912, when Lloyd George returned to Llanystumdwy to open the new village institute, he had grown accustomed to violent protests. He was greeted by a group of women protesters, and despite his appeals for calm, his supporters bundled them away with enthusiasm, causing mayhem, minor injury and much complaint in the press. The bombing of Lloyd George's house at Walton Heath took place six months later. To his credit, he did not take personal offence at the incident, and when in 1915 a chance came to cooperate peacefully and productively with the WSPU, he took it.

Frances was not only worried about her lover's safety and her mother's distress, her work life was full of stresses too. Naturally, her new colleagues were unaware of her true relationship with the Chancellor, but her arrival still caused considerable upset among the Treasury's civil servants.

When Lloyd George offered Frances a position in his office at the end of 1912, he was fully aware of just how unusual such an arrangement would be. Frances is often referred to from this period onwards as his Private Secretary, but that is not an accurate description of her role at the beginning. By 1913 women were employed as typists (or 'typewriters') in the larger departments, carefully segregated from their male colleagues, but the policy (administrative) grades of the Civil Service were closed to women until 1925. Even then they were largely confined to working on issues specifically relating to women, and were obliged to leave if they got married, a condition that applied until after the Second World War. The role of Private Secretary to a Cabinet Minister, then as now, was considered a job for a high-flying career civil servant.

The term is confusing, and is not well understood: all senior officials were then termed 'secretaries' of various kinds. The most senior, the heads of departments, were the Permanent Secretaries, who were served by Deputy Secretaries, Under Secretaries, Assistant Secretaries and so forth. A Private Secretary worked directly to a Minister or Permanent Secretary rather than on an area of policy. Not to be confused with the role of a modern secretary or PA, the Private Secretary typically headed an office of staff which took care of the clerical, secretarial and diary work. The Private Secretary's duties would include preparing drafts of speeches, collating information, communicating the Minister's policy directions to his department, minuting all meetings and significant conversations as well as ensuring that the Minister's office and public appearances ran smoothly. It was a position of considerable influence. In the first decades of the twentieth century a career in the Civil Service was a highly sought-after prize, an opportunity for talented young men to play their part in administering the vast British Empire. The Treasury was staffed with clever graduates determined to make their mark, and in 1913 the idea that a woman could be considered their equal would have seemed laughable. Frances was probably initially introduced to the office as a shorthand typist, and it is considerably to her credit that she achieved the role of Private Secretary later in her career.* As Chancellor of the Exchequer Lloyd George could fully justify having a large staff, and he felt emboldened to press ahead with the appointment of Frances as a secretary in his office, working directly to him but officially under the guidance of the Private Secretary.

This was not the first time Lloyd George had tried to find work for a female friend. His earlier attempt, in 1907, when he was President of the Board of Trade, had met with a firm rebuff from the Civil Service. It was deemed unseemly for a Minister to seek to find employment for a personal acquaintance or to interfere with the recruitment processes for civil servants, and John Rowland, his Private Secretary at the time, received the following beautifully crafted response from an official in the War Office:

Dear Mr Rowland,

I enclose a copy of the Regulations which govern the appointment of Lady Typists in this Office. I am afraid that even if the lady in whom Mr Lloyd George is interested possesses the necessary qualifications it is impossible to hold out any hope of early employment. The establishment is full, vacancies seldom occur, and there is a long list of qualified candidates.

We shall of course however be very happy to note her name if she satisfies the requirements which we are bound to enforce.[7]

This classic piece of official double-speak, with its clear scepticism as to the anonymous lady's qualifications, firmly blocked the Minister's intentions while implying that his relationship with the anonymous candidate was at best questionable.

* In the British Imperial Calendar and Civil Service List, Frances was not listed at all until 1916, so her status at the Treasury must have been as one of Lloyd George's personal staff only, not as a civil servant. In 1916 she does appear, listed as a Private Secretary alongside J.T. Davies and two others at the Ministry of Munitions. From 1917 on she was listed officially as a Private Secretary at both the Treasury and the War Cabinet/Cabinet – there being no official 'Prime Minister's Department' at No. 10. As for her status within No. 10, Frances herself refers to J.T. Davies as Lloyd George's 'Chief Secretary', which is more likely than A.J.P. Taylor's assertion that Davies and she were 'joint Principal Private Secretaries'. It was groundbreaking enough to appoint a woman as Private Secretary at the time. No woman has ever held the position of Principal Private Secretary to the Prime Minister.

As a relatively junior member of the Cabinet, Lloyd George had not then had the clout to impose his wishes on the impervious Civil Service machine, but as Chancellor of the Exchequer it was a different matter. He had previously suggested employing a female shorthand typist in place of the male secretary who recorded his meetings at the Treasury in longhand. This time he succeeded, and the precedent was set.

A second precedent occurred when Lloyd George appointed a Welsh-speaking schoolteacher, J.T. Davies, as his Personal Secretary in 1912.* Lloyd George's official Treasury Private Secretary was Horace Hamilton, a classic Civil Service high-flyer who ended his career as Permanent Secretary of the Board of Trade. Lloyd George generated and got through a prodigious amount of work, and needed extra support. J.T. Davies was a happy appointment, and one he never regretted.† To appoint a second member of staff from outside the Civil Service, even if she was a woman, was bound to be easier. This time there was no difficulty over the young lady's qualifications: Frances was a graduate, was fluent in French and had learned shorthand and typing at Lloyd George's request, since even in the first flush of their passion he was keen to make sure that she could be truly useful to him. Her appointment was achieved apparently without difficulty.

Once appointed, though, it was a different matter. Civil servants tend to guard their relationships with ministers jealously, and distrust anyone appointed from outside their ranks. The arrival of a young, female friend of the Chancellor's was bound to raise their hackles, and Frances records that Lloyd George's staff treated her coldly, and resented 'this intrusion by a young female into their domain'. She was conscious

---

*I have chosen to follow Frances' own terminology and interpretation of the roles of those closest to Lloyd George rather than those of later commentators, since although she wrote her memoir late in life, she was very conscious of status and rank, and is unlikely to have made errors in describing the roles of her closest colleagues.

† Davies was sometimes referred to as Lloyd George's 'Welsh Private Secretary'. It was customary for Lloyd George to have someone on his staff who could take care of the issues that arose from his constituency and his interest in Welsh affairs. These would have been outside the Treasury's scope of business – and, one suspects, the scope of its officials' interest. Both Davies and Frances were considered Lloyd George's personal staff rather than civil servants. They only crossed over in 1915, when Lloyd George was able to regularise their positions at the brand new Ministry of Munitions.

from the beginning that she would have to prove her worth, telling an audience of secretaries with feeling some years later: 'Since in the past it has been assumed that women are less efficient than men, it behoves us to rebut that theory by proving if anything that we can be even more efficient . . . in order to prove the worth of our sex and to establish our rights to equal treatment it is not sufficient for us to be merely as good as the man with whom we are competing. We must, for the sake of establishing our claim, be *better* than he is.'[8]

Frances encountered many snubs, including from the Prime Minister's secretary Maurice Bonham Carter, who went on to marry the Prime Minister's daughter, Violet Asquith. She wrote to him on behalf of Lloyd George but he insisted on writing back to J.T. Davies, unwilling to have any communication with a female secretary. 'He probably thought, with some sort of inverted ostrich complex, that by ignoring my existence I should cease to exist, officially at any rate,' wrote Frances, looking back on the incident in 1931.[9] In 1915 she wrote in wonder in her diary that 'there is jealousy in the Treasury as to who shall accompany the Chancellor [on a trip to Paris]. It is extraordinary how jealous and petty these permanent officials can be. They seem to have no sense of proportion, and magnify their little grievances while they forget the really great affairs of State.'[10]

Despite being surrounded by tensions at home and at work, Frances never regretted her decision. Her relationship with Lloyd George fulfilled her most romantic dreams, and she was too happy to feel any barbed comment or slight. Few letters survive from this period, and those that do are couched in official language to frustrate prying eyes, but Frances' memoir confirms her contentment. Lloyd George was proving a devoted lover, and they were able to spend time together almost every day. She was also fascinated by her job: 'I became immersed in my new work . . . I was more than excited – I was thrilled to find myself thus in the centre of the political scene and identified, in a very humble way, with momentous events. I did not spare myself. I worked early and late, as indeed L.G. expected everyone employed by him to do. I had no leisure: from now on I was dedicated to L.G. and his works. I saw less and less of my friends.'[11]

Frances' dreams of love and career had both been fulfilled at once, and she was wildly excited. Her duties at the Treasury may have been mundane – typing notes of meetings, answering correspondence, making sense of the piles of papers and letters Lloyd George left behind him wherever he went – but the meetings were on matters of state, the minutes of vital importance in recording and implementing government decisions, and the correspondence was at least to and from her lover. At night, she and Lloyd George would slip away for quiet dinners together at Walton Heath, and he would talk to her of politics and the great statesmen of the day. Her days as a frustrated teacher in a girls' school seemed far distant.

Thus, in 1912–13 Lloyd George began to construct the double life he was to lead until Margaret's death in 1941. He had always sailed close to the wind in matters of the heart, but now for the first time he began to form a close relationship with another woman that was likely to be, indeed was *intended* to be, as durable as his marriage to Margaret. Given what followed, it is clear that Lloyd George was serious about marrying Frances if he was ever free to do so. His feelings for this young woman were as intense as his feelings for his wife, though quite different in their nature. This relationship was not to be compared with his fling with Mrs Tim or any of his previous affairs. This time, Lloyd George had taken a mistress he wanted as a permanent part of his life.

Lloyd George was not the first Cabinet Minister to lead an irregular private life, nor the last. His actions should be placed in their context, for he was a man of his time. Gladstone once remarked that he had known twelve Prime Ministers, and all but one were adulterers.[12] Gladstone himself may not have qualified, but his 'rescue work' with ladies of the night was at best questionable. Lloyd George likewise did not have to look far to find a politician who was not true to his marriage vows. Not only had he sat in Parliament with the disgraced adulterers Parnell and Charles Dilke, but from 1908 onwards there were many others around the Cabinet table whose private lives did not bear close scrutiny. Asquith, the Prime Minister, wrote obsessive letters to Venetia Stanley, an intelligent and vivacious young friend of his daughter's, sometimes during Cabinet meetings. At the same meetings, Edwin Montagu, Chancellor of the Duchy of Lancaster from February 1915 and Venetia's fiancée, wrote to her too. Asquith's reputation for enjoying the company of attractive young ladies did not end with his second marriage, and his daughter's friends regarded him as a 'groper'. To name but a few others, Lord Curzon, appointed War Cabinet Minister by Lloyd George in 1916, conducted a long affair with the novelist Elinor Glyn during his first marriage; Viscount Milner, another member of the War Cabinet, kept his mistress, Cécile, in a house in South London and began a relationship with his wife, Violet Maxse, the wife of Lord Edward Gascoyne-Cecil, twenty-two years before they eventually married. Another famed womaniser, Lord Carson, the Admiralty Minister, married for the second time a woman thirty years his junior; Viscount Horne was known as 'Beaming Bert, that incorrigible flirt' in popular songs; and Lewis ('Loulou') Harcourt took an overdose amid accusations of impropriety with a young Etonian. Others close to Lloyd George, like Churchill and Bonar Law, took a very different view of personal morality, but it is fair to say that they were in the minority.

To the modern reader, the wonder is not that so many distinguished men behaved in this way, but that they were not exposed and disgraced. The reasons for this went beyond social convention and the sanctity of the institution of marriage, important though those factors were. Those in the public eye could also rely on the complicity of the media. Periodicals and newspapers proliferated in the early years of the twentieth century under press barons such as the Harmsworth brothers (later Lords Northcliffe and Rothermere), Max Aitken (later Lord Beaverbrook) and George (later Lord) Riddell. The Harmsworths between them owned *The Times*, the *Daily Mail*, the *Daily Mirror* and the *Sunday Pictorial*. Aitken owned the *Daily Express*, the *Sunday Express* and the *Evening Standard*, while Riddell owned the *News of the World*. They shaped and reflected public opinion, and as their influence grew, so did their leverage with men of power. They reported on their friends, but the stories were of politics and power, not private misdemeanours. Newspapers, to an extent unimaginable nowadays, abided by and reinforced the rules of high society. In practice this meant that they did not reveal the details of a prominent person's private affairs unless a divorce was involved. This self-regulation was uniform even though illicit relationships were often common knowledge around Westminster. In any case, the newspaper barons were on such intimate terms with the politicians of the day that it is inconceivable that they did not know their mistresses as well as their wives.

George Riddell was the closest of the press proprietors to Lloyd George, for not only did he own the *News of the World*, he also for a time chaired and was managing director of the *Western Mail*, an influential publication in South Wales. His diaries reveal over seven hundred discussions with Lloyd George between 1908 and his death in 1934. Many of them took place over a game of golf at Walton Heath, with Lloyd George fully aware that his views were being recorded in Riddell's diary and would often form the basis for stories in his papers. Riddell knew the Lloyd George family well and was on good terms with Margaret and Megan, travelling as part of Lloyd George's entourage on official trips. He spent far more time with Frances, though, and was among the first to know of her relationship with Lloyd George. Although they were on friendly terms, Frances was never able to relax fully in his company, writing: 'I found him at first rather forbidding, with his piercing blue eyes, gaunt figure, and his habit of cross-examining everyone with whom he came into contact. He had an insatiable curiosity, and he simply had, if possible, to get at one's private life . . . I came to like Riddell very much, and to count him as a real friend. I never quite trusted him, but when one is forewarned, one is forearmed.'[13]

It was true that Riddell was always curious to discover people's backgrounds, and in his diary he gives a colourful account of Frances' family: 'Miss Stevenson, with her wonderful history – descended from French officer who was Legion of Honour when serving under Napoleon 1, began life as a teacher in a small school . . .' This part of Frances' ancestry is not mentioned in her autobiography and so may well have been an exaggeration, although whether her own or Riddell's is unclear. It was printed in an article about Frances that appeared in 1916, and Riddell may have picked it up from there.

Unlike Frances, Lloyd George was not wary of newspaper men, and enjoyed their company. He was not averse to using their influence when it suited him, and played a part in rewarding them with peerages. He had a great deal in common with Lords Northcliffe, Rothermere, Beaverbrook and Riddell. All of them sprang from modest backgrounds, but while Northcliffe, Rothermere and Riddell were secretive about the circumstances of their upbringing, Beaverbrook, like Lloyd George, made a virtue of his childhood poverty. They were all self-made men who came to move in social circles traditionally the domain of inherited wealth. They were all exceptionally ambitious, and fascinated by power. In the early twentieth century there was less distinction drawn between journalism and politics than there is today: newspaper proprietors held political office, and politicians worked for newspapers. Beaverbrook was an elected MP who was appointed Chancellor of the Duchy of Lancaster and Minister of Information by Lloyd George in 1918; Viscount Northcliffe was appointed Director of Propaganda in Enemy Countries in 1918, and headed a special War Mission to the USA in 1917; while Viscount Rothermere was Minister for Air from 1917 to 1918. In turn, Lloyd George dabbled in the newspaper business, funding the purchase of the *Daily Chronicle* in 1918 from his controversial political fund and fancying himself as the editor of *The Times* after leaving office.

Lloyd George and the press barons had something else in common: their casual attitude towards marital fidelity. One of the reasons why extramarital relationships were not exposed in the press may well have been that people in glass houses do not throw stones. George Riddell was an intensely private man who gave little away about his private life, probably because he was anxious to conceal a brief early marriage that had ended in divorce in 1900. This was not known when he was awarded his knighthood in 1909, but Lloyd George had to fight hard to get the King to agree to award Riddell a peerage after his divorce was revealed, and in 1922 he became the first divorcee in the House of Lords. Beaverbrook was married but had many mistresses, among them the writer Rebecca West. Rothermere enjoyed the company of ballerinas, whereas his brother Northcliffe had at least four illegitimate children, three with his Irish mistress Kathleen Wrohan. He later went on to have affairs with his secretary, Louise Owen, and a writer, Baroness Betty von Hutten. Lloyd George's press-baron friends combined marriage with affairs, both casual and long-lasting. All in all, they were the last people in the world who were going to expose him for his moral lapses.

If his colleagues' example made it unexceptional for Lloyd George to take a mistress, and the complicity of the press made it possible for him to do so discreetly, it is worth asking why he should *want* to do so, given the risks involved. Margaret had always been a jealous wife. Given her proud, independent nature, Lloyd George must have known that she was not likely to be tolerant if she found out that he was keeping a mistress, especially one young enough to be her daughter.

There were certainly good reasons for Lloyd George to regularise his private life. The danger of discovery was probably less if he took a mistress than if he continued to make love to his colleagues' wives. At fifty, he may have tired of the casual flings he had previously enjoyed, and as Chancellor, he had more to lose than before if a woman exposed him. He was certainly aware of the risks, for since his relationship with Mrs Tim another brief relationship had ended badly, and in addition he had been obliged to turn to the law once more to clear his name: he was living far too dangerously.

From 1900 onwards, with the Edwards divorce case behind them and Mrs Tim having been seen off, Margaret's presence in London did have a positive effect on their marriage, for there were a few years free from jealous rows. With Margaret at hand perhaps Lloyd George did not need to seek comfort elsewhere, or it could be that he became better at hiding his tracks, but in any event, within a few years the tell-tale correspondence indicates that he was involved with another woman. The object of his flirtations was Julia Henry, the American wife of another Liberal colleague, Charles Henry, and a rare example in Lloyd George's life of an 'amour' who was not discreet. She created such scenes over a period of years that even Frances was perfectly aware of the background. As with Mrs Tim, Frances showed no jealousy towards Julia. Instead she almost felt sorry for her, well aware that Lloyd George was thoroughly fed up with his old flame's behaviour. With the confidence of a woman who knew she had nothing to fear, Frances wrote in her diary: 'I must say I think [Julia] deserves a little kindness, for [the Henrys] have both been exceedingly kind to D., only unfortunately at one time he allowed things to go too far, and is now sorry for it ... She is quite mad on him, and does not seem to have any pride or self-respect where he is concerned.'[14] But Frances was being naïve, for there was far more to it than that.

Julia Henry was a very attractive woman, tall with dark hair, who dressed expensively. In 1906 her wealthy husband Charles Henry became

Liberal MP for the constituency of Wellington in Shropshire. A substantial donor to the Liberal Party, Henry was given a baronetcy in 1911. The Henrys lived on a lavish scale, with a country house in Shropshire and another, Parkwood, near Henley-on-Thames. They also entertained in style in London at Porchester Gate, their fashionable townhouse, where Julia was determined to establish herself as one of the city's foremost political hostesses.* Lloyd George, attracted as always by the combination of political discussion, a good table and a beautiful woman, was soon on friendly terms with both Henry and Julia. He became a regular visitor to Henley, even taking his son Dick with him on occasion, and made himself agreeable to Julia. How far things went is impossible to say. Dick was convinced that they were lovers after witnessing his father pushing 'Lady J' daringly high on a swing, to the evident enjoyment of both. Julia's subsequent hysterical behaviour also implies that their relationship went beyond mere flirtation. Charles Henry, though, did not think they were lovers, and firmly took Lloyd George's side against his wife in the furore which ensued. Frances, necessarily a biased witness, took the view that whatever happened, it meant much more to Julia than it did to Lloyd George, which is almost certainly true.

In 1907 Lloyd George wrote Julia a flirtatious letter:

My Dear Mrs Henry

... How often have I meant to write but alas the cares of State have been unusually insistent & obtrusive. And moreover writing is so unsatisfactory a medium of conversation. There is so little you dare write which you would unhesitatingly say! ... There is no knowing when we can get away ... Your glowing description of your balcony with the view to be enjoyed from it is very enticing – & full of all sorts of delightful possibilities which I dare not dwell upon lest I break away from this horrid convict establishment & escape there. Mr Henry & I are off to a theatre tonight – then an all night sitting – then to Porchester Gate. But we will miss the hostess – oh so much.[15]

---

* Another prominent London hostess at the time was Domini Crosfield, the Greek wife of the Liberal MP Sir Arthur Crosfield. Lloyd George was rumoured to have had an affair with her too.

It was to Charles and Julia Henry that Lloyd George turned when he needed a car to take him home urgently on the day of Mair's operation, and when he subsequently took his sons abroad to recover from the bereavement, he met up with the Henrys in the South of France. He wrote to Margaret: 'Henry is extraordinarily kind. He is doing his best to keep me bustling about & he has taken a greater fancy to Gwilym than to any boy he has ever met.'[16]

The friendship seemed to go far beyond polite social contact. In Julia's mind at least, Lloyd George and she had a special bond, and she fell disastrously in love. Unlike Mrs Tim, the American Mrs Henry did not understand the rules of polite English society. When her behaviour became too possessive, and, more significantly, after Frances entered his life in 1911, Lloyd George took steps – none too elegantly – to end whatever relationship he had with her. Mrs Tim had accepted the cooling of their affair well, and had remained on friendly terms with Lloyd George. Julia Henry, however, reacted with undisguised fury. Surprisingly, she poured out her feelings to her husband. Perhaps recognising his wife's tendency to exaggerate, he infuriated her by taking Lloyd George's side and accusing her of overreacting. Rebuffed by both lover and husband, and outraged by their treatment of her, Julia fled back to New York. While crossing the Atlantic on the *Mauretania* in November 1911 she had plenty of time to dwell on her hurt feelings, and sent long letters to her husband in which she gave a telling account of how Lloyd George had won her over: 'You know quite well how for so many years Mr Lloyd George valued our friendship, how in the hour of his sorrow he came to us for comfort . . . You knew his attention to me, how he came to my box at the Opera, to lunch & dinner incessantly, even reading his speeches to me for my opinion. All this greatly flattered me as it would have *any* woman.'

The appeal to the intellect of this social butterfly was well calculated to flatter. Lloyd George also turned to Julia for comfort after Mair's death, and persuaded her that he relied on her for emotional support: 'He always said it was our kindness to him during his grief that enabled him to pull through. I have all his letters full of the greatest regard & gratitude.'

Then came recrimination:

I do not wish to shield myself for any wrong I have done in allowing myself to be fascinated with his company. That was my misfortune that we ever met & that he admired me, & now unfortunately as you always say we cannot job backwards, it is the present situation that has to be dealt with. Without a word to me all of a sudden he shirked coming round & the humiliation I received from his treatment would be impossible to describe. It was not a question of his coming in to see me alone he could have come back with you for dinner.

Henry himself does not escape rebuke:

... then although I implored of you not to do so you sent that letter giving him right on a matter you knew nothing about & refused to listen to, ridiculing women & their vagueries [sic] & hoped he would not allow such trivial things to upset him, & that my grievances were all imaginary ... [to] think that a man who is going to be ruler of England, one who is the idol of his colleagues & all those he comes in contact with should treat me with such discourtesy after all the kindness he has extracted is past my endurance ... I never wish to see him alone, but he owes me that respect & regard to come round with you once in three weeks or so ... I can never face England again. No harsh words or reproaches dear will have the slightest effect. I can write no further, I am too broken-hearted ... [17]

This was an extraordinary letter for a wife to send her husband. Not only did Julia confess to having a relationship with another man, but she appealed to Henry to confirm that it had actually happened. He in turn had been extremely disloyal in urging Lloyd George to disregard his wife's hurt feelings, whatever the truth of the matter, even giving Lloyd George a copy of Julia's letter. Perhaps Frances was right to imply that her lover could have been a little more understanding, given Julia's previous kindnesses to him.

Julia's letter is suffused with self-pity, but it is not only Lloyd George's rejection of her that hurt. She also minded the public humiliation of being snubbed by someone who was known to have been a friend, and who was one of the most desirable guests in the country. Hostesses across London were vying with each other to secure the Chancellor of the Exchequer to dinner, their efforts reaching almost frantic proportions in the face of his indifference. When Lloyd George began to ignore her invitations, Julia's plans to establish herself at the forefront of London society were dealt a severe blow. This was not something she took lightly, and she began to behave outrageously, in a way that annoyed both Lloyd George and indeed Frances. Many years later when he was Prime Minister, Julia was still trying to prove that she occupied a special place in Lloyd George's heart. She had also found a novel, if unscrupulous, way of explaining his absence from her salon. In 1919, when Charles Henry was dying, Lloyd George visited him at home. Frances recorded in her diary:

> Lady Henry has been complaining to everyone that D. had not been to see her husband, in spite of all their past kindness to him (D). The fact is that every time that D. has been there Lady H. has got him by himself & made a scene, she being perfectly mad about him. Last night he took Macpherson with him, so that this should not occur, but she took him aside & showed him a letter Clark (D.s secretary at the time) had written to her on the very day D.'s little girl had died in 1907 . . . She showed him this to remind him of her kindness to him, knowing well that it breaks D.'s heart to think about that terrible time or to have it referred to. D. says he thinks she is the most selfish woman he knows of. She is constantly asking people to dinner to meet D., & D. consistently refuses. She then tells people who turn up expecting to meet the P.M., that he was coming but he preferred dining alone with her.[18]

It would be interesting to know how many of her guests believed her.

Reckless behaviour of this kind was dangerous to Lloyd George. As his public profile grew, so did the risk of rumour and discovery. Indeed, soon after his appointment as Chancellor he had suffered a bruising experience at the hands of another social butterfly. Her name was Gladys Gardner.

Gladys played a far less significant part in Lloyd George's life than Julia Henry, and a bundle of half a dozen letters from her is all that survives of their dalliance. The sheer indiscretion of their author is astounding, and the serious consequences that almost certainly sprang from the relationship were perhaps the reason Lloyd George acted so decisively (not to mention heartlessly) to end the affair with Julia when she became too possessive. The background to both affairs was that Margaret did not seem to be making her presence felt in London's political circles. As her husband became ever more powerful and fêted in fashionable society, Margaret preferred, as ever, to stick to her own kind, and found her friends among the Welsh community in London. With a houseful of children, and especially when Megan was very young, she continued to regard politics and politicians as her husband's business, not hers. This was an attitude that was to persist until the family moved into 11 Downing Street in 1908.

Margaret's attitude led society hostesses virtually to dismiss her altogether and, spotting a vacancy, to feel that they could dominate or 'run' Lloyd George's social life. Politicians throughout the ages have relied on society hostesses to supply them with good dinners in comfortable surroundings and a chance to meet the 'right' people. To 'run' a public figure in this way was what many fashionable women aspired to. It was an accepted part of the political game: rising politicians, especially wealthy or aristocratic ones, had long formed allegiances and cemented friendships during weekends on country estates or over dinners in opulent surroundings, all organised by their wives. It was expected that Lloyd George would do the same, but Margaret did not even try to insinuate her way into smart social sets. As ever, she knew her husband better than anyone: Lloyd George did not operate that way, for he did not need to. His ambition, his drive and his wits were going to get him to the top, not his social contacts.

But Margaret's reluctance to entertain and be entertained gave rise to some misconceived attempts to supply for Lloyd George the kind of social advancement his wife failed to aspire to. He would be a serious trophy for an aspiring hostess, but it is hard to imagine an approach less likely to succeed than that of poor Gladys Gardner. We know nothing of her life or circumstances, except that she was unmarried and was utterly bowled over by the charming Chancellor. None of his letters, if there were any, survive, but hers tell an intriguing story.

They are all dated between 10 and 13 April 1908, and she addresses Lloyd George by the name of 'Bird'. We do not know when or how he met her, or what it was about her that made him enter into a correspondence, if indeed he replied at all to her letters, but she felt that their friendship was significant. She had visited him at the Board of Trade, planned to do so at the Treasury, and had suggested adopting the code name '400 Mayfair' to ensure discreet communication between them. The tone of the letters is coquettish in the extreme, and the conspiratorial way in which their author suggests ways of concealing their 'purely platonic' relationship lest it be misconstrued immediately invites the conclusion that she did not intend it to remain so.

Gladys begins by congratulating Lloyd George on the day of his appointment as Chancellor, referring to Mr Clark, Lloyd George's Private Secretary, who may have introduced them, and wishing he had sent word to her on the momentous day. Her letters refer to 'Mamie', a female confidante (her mother, possibly) in whom she indiscreetly confides all with regard to Lloyd George. One wonders what possessed him to allow the situation to continue beyond the first letter, but allowances should perhaps be made for the pressure on him in the immediate aftermath of his promotion. Gladys evidently felt that Lloyd George's new status was an opportunity for her as well as for him, and even – incredibly – suggests that she had better marry someone else in order to be able to keep on seeing him:

> Mamie . . . couldn't see why I wanted to marry at all, as I had everything I wanted etc but the danger 'would be that when my outlook on life & its demands became different' we would find it impossible to continue our friendship on the purely platonic grounds it is now on. That we had managed so well up to date & no one had heard a whisper (I mean the people who matter). I agreed with her – recognized the danger – hoped nothing would arise – but was prepared quite calmly to face anything that did.[19]

She then spells out her scheme, as though Lloyd George was well acquainted with it. Could he have encouraged her to think it might be possible? A more likely explanation is that he had indulged in some banter which had led, on her part, to some fantasising that had been taken all too seriously: '[I] said it was accepted fact that a statesman might have a married woman to "run him" as the saying is – & that I meant to be that woman & must be content with that – that my house should become the "most famous in the whole of Athens" – that anything that I could do to help you & your family, socially – I should do.'

Two days later, she was already beginning to devise schemes for his social advancement, and was also planning his political career:

> Lady Salomons has asked me over on Saturday . . . I will ask her to call on your wife – there is a little girl in the family about the age of yours. You see, Bird, the very fact that you don't care whether you become Premier or not will give it to you in all probability – & that is why I want to collect round you and yours the people that I should bring if I could be really with you: & the young people whom I should want your children to be friends with . . .

Lloyd George should have heeded the warning in the phrase 'if I could be really with you': Gladys was fancying herself as his mistress, and perhaps even more.

She next turns her attention to bossily establishing her status among his staff at the Treasury: 'Now: will you tell all the Secretaries at the Treasury that "Miss G—" is to be treated with consideration & put on to you at once & all that sort of thing. Now that I have found my feet I shall drop all concealment and come as Miss G—. quite simply . . . I shall probably have to get to know one of your new Secretaries – for all our sakes – so as to get him to send me answers to invitations etc. as your manners are past praying for . . .' Then she reveals the full, terrifying scope of her ambition: 'I want to go to court with a pretty spiky tiara set far back & my hair waved into little curls all round it. Diamonds are my birth stone & I love them. If anything untoward happened – to enable me to be with you – we would bust a fair amount of the Chancellor's screw on a gorgeous tiara.'

In the last surviving letter, written later the same day, Gladys has decided that Lloyd George should divorce Margaret, which she felt (wholly unrealistically) would further his career as well as enable him to marry her: 'Count Witte married a divorced woman & the English Embassy received her first – & led the way for general reception. So in return England obtained the first concessions [from Russia]. I am hungry for news & have more to give . . .'

And there the correspondence ends. Gladys Gardner plays no further part in Lloyd George's life, directly at least, if indeed she ever had. But there may have been an indirect link between the indiscreet gossip of Gladys – or someone like her – and an article that appeared in a publication called the *Bystander* on 29 July 1908. It read:

All is not going well with Mr Lloyd George in his new and exalted sphere. Not only is he having a most uncomfortable time of it politically . . . but rumour is now busy as to the existence of embarrassment of another kind, which is even less likely to prove of assistance to his career. Mr George has, of course, been overloaded with flattery of late, especially from the fair sex, which is always difficult for a man of 'temperament' to resist. The matter may, of course, be kept quiet. Also, it may not. 'Nous Verrons'.[20]

The implication that Lloyd George was having an affair is unavoidable, and this was serious enough for him to consult his lawyers. To him it was 'a foul invention of our malignant Press . . . without even a shadow of foundation'.[21] He sued the magazine, which gave in without much of a fight, publishing a retraction in September and donating three hundred guineas to the Caernarvon Cottage Hospital.

But by now rumours were circulating about the Chancellor's colourful private life, and the next time the press dared publish, the matter was not settled so easily.

12

Love and Libel

THE FOLLOWING YEAR, 1909, by which time Lloyd George's radical views and powerful position had made him plenty of enemies, the *People*, a Sunday newspaper, published an article implying that a senior politician was to be cited as co-respondent in a forthcoming divorce case which would cause his 'social and political ruin and degradation'. The article claimed that the politician's friends were trying to prevent this catastrophe, but that the wronged husband was determined to continue. A subsequent article headed 'The Price of Peace' claimed that the husband had been bought off with the enormous sum of £20,000 (the equivalent of over £1.5 million today) to ensure his silence. The editor probably thought he was protecting the paper from a libel suit by withholding the name of the accused, but there was no doubt that the articles were referring to Lloyd George. The identity of the lady in question was less easy to fathom. The *New York Times* reported that she was American, and Julia Henry therefore becomes a candidate, particularly since the husband was reported to be a 'public man of the highest position'.* But Charles Henry was on good terms with Lloyd George, and there is no evidence that the Henrys ever contemplated

---

* 'The charges against the Chancellor associated his name with that of an American woman and declared that he was on the point of being dragged into the Divorce Court . . . For weeks malignant references of the grossest nature have been in circulation regarding the family of another public man of the highest position, and in this case, also, the name of an American woman figures.'

divorce. Since the wronged husband was said to have been bought off, it was unlikely that Lloyd George's accusers could produce evidence to support the allegations. But without knowing the identity of the couple, neither could Lloyd George prove his innocence.

This charge was more serious than the rumours that had surfaced the previous year, because it involved a divorce. If Lloyd George was found to have been involved, it would mean the end of his political and public life. He summoned a formidable legal team comprising the future Attorney General Rufus Isaacs, Raymond Asquith, the son of the Prime Minister, and the renowned lawyer (also a future Attorney General) and Conservative MP, F.E. Smith, a personal friend. They advised him to sue for libel, and the case was heard on 12 March 1909. He had no defence except his denial, but he could be fairly sure that his accusers had no admissible evidence to support their claims either. It was his word against theirs, and the strongest card – indeed the only card – he had to play was the public support of a loyal wife.

For Margaret, this was a most unwelcome repetition of the events surrounding the Kitty Edwards affair. Although this time the woman involved was not named, that did not make it easier for her to face the publicity surrounding this sensational court case. What is more, her son Dick believed that she knew Lloyd George to be guilty: 'I know that my mother, a deeply religious woman, was in torment in giving support to the lie to be sworn on oath. As a woman, she had been mortally hurt by his infidelities. As a wife, she had been gravely wronged. I know exactly the extent of her conflict.'[1] Not for the first time, Margaret faced a grave choice: to support her husband and save his career, or to abandon him and face the collapse of their marriage and of his political life.

Margaret was now a mature woman of forty-two. She knew that she had married an incurable flirt, and she had been aware of at least one lengthy affair of his, with Mrs Tim. But it does not follow that she believed he was guilty in this case. Dick was not a wholly reliable witness. For Margaret to support her husband as he committed perjury, which is what their son effectively accuses him of, would have been very difficult for a woman of her deep religious conviction. Very few letters between the couple were written in the period 1908–09, presumably because they were living together at No. 11, but those that do suggest that Margaret chose to believe in her husband's innocence, and, as ever, when he appealed to her for love and support, she gave it.

12 March 1909 dawned, with Lloyd George's career resting in the balance. Margaret too faced her most public test to date. The case had attracted widespread interest, and a pack of journalists and photographers filled the courtroom. All kinds of rumours were circulating: some said that Margaret was leaving – or had already left – her husband, and it seemed that the whole press was waiting to see if she would turn up. As she stepped out of the car and took her place by Lloyd George's side, the reporters knew that the case had effectively been won. Speaking with some emotion from the witness box, Lloyd George, dressed in a black frock-coat and looking pale and agitated, said, 'The paragraphs are an absolute invention, every line of them.'[2]

By the end of the day the *People* had agreed to pay damages of £1,000. Thanks to his unswervingly loyal wife, the Welsh Wizard had survived to fight another day. He decided to use the money to build a village institute in Llanystumdwy on land donated by William George. The matter was closed, apart from one puzzling postscript which further demonstrates the risks Lloyd George was taking with his reputation as far as women were concerned. Again, this takes the form of letters from an unknown female correspondent.

On 22 March 1909, ten days after the court hearing, a Mrs M. Griffith, who gave an address in North London, wrote to the Chancellor. It was not the first time she had done so, but her earlier letter is lost. She wrote:

Dear Mr George

... [I] implore you to accede to my request & also to let me have the two photos of my little son. Surely I am entitled to a reply if it were only in respect to the photos. Must I get a solicitor to write to you before you will reply? Do not think this a threat far from it, but I want an answer & this I will have ... I know it is a critical time with you almost the eve of the Budget, & am sorry in consequence to trouble you, but my affairs to me are equally important & I do now from the bottom of my heart, I appeal to you on my knees to spare me this money . . . Or ought I to appeal to Sir G. Lewis [a solicitor] & put the facts before him. I ask you as one of your own countrywomen.[3]

Amid feverish preparations for his famous budget of 1909, Lloyd George hastened to reply to this letter, enclosing the photographs of Mrs Griffith's son. If he thought that was an end to the matter he was mistaken, for three days later she wrote a more disturbing letter:

I must write to you in reply to the letter sent with the photos & for which I thank you.

Do you think I would appeal for help did I not need it in the first place it is anything but pleasant to have to ask & the fact that my husband's earnings are 30/- does not make it conclusive that I can do without it, this remark of yours was quite uncalled for . . . instead of which you chose to insult me. The fact that that money has gone to Institutes does not affect me . . . You know in your heart that to live on 30/- pay, rent, coal, food, clothes & shoes must be a fearful struggle and to add to it a little child under a specialist for years to come . . . Through the influence of a dear old friend Mrs Guthrie Jones Dolgelly I am able to see the specialist free, but instruments & such like I must pay for. I was for 6 weeks in Liverpool attending the surgery daily. Will it touch some chord of sympathy when I tell you that every day my baby's feet (only about 10 weeks old) were put on blocks & twisted until they bled . . . so you see how welcome that £10 would be it would set us up for the year . . .

So far, this is a begging letter with a few curious elements. Why should this woman feel entitled to some share of the proceeds of the *People* libel case? Why should she send Lloyd George photos of her son when she is begging for help in relation to her baby, a girl, as she goes on to explain? There is no explanation either of why a solicitor should be involved. The next passage adds an unpleasant suggestion of blackmail to the mix:

Mr George let this be the last time I need write to you in this strain. I ask you to spare a few minutes of your valuable time & go back to the time when you first knew me, come along gradually to the present stage. Your verdict will be when you have well weighed the whole facts that you have treated me most unfairly & cruelly. Do you remember that time you asked me down to Wandsworth in reference to a berth for Mr Griffith, well I spent my last penny in fares & yet you did not as much as ask me if I had enough to take me home. I shall never forget how I felt, brokenhearted, hungry & sore. I thought then your colleague would not have dismissed me like that, he has a heart of gold, you know who I mean . . . Please don't treat me as the rest who applied to you for charity, it was unkind of you to do so in the first place. You know I don't want to have the feeling that I hate you hate everything in connection with you you'll admit I have good cause so don't dear friend refuse . . . it will be entirely between you & me if you do it . . . Mr George if you have a spark of feeling you will not keep me in suspense. Oh do it do it please, please. I shall meet you again some day. Things will be different then, in the meantime I do not want to harbour unkind thoughts & I don't want you to do so either. Heaven bless you if you do it.[4]

The letter is signed simply 'Yours faithfully M. Griffith'.

The implication is as clear as it is sordid. Mrs Griffith makes out that she appealed to Lloyd George for help in finding a job for her husband. He invited her to Wandsworth, where he was then living, to discuss the matter. Something transpired there which lifted her relationship to him above that of an acquaintance and which made it cruel of him not to have given her money to make sure she got home safely – it is not difficult to fathom what she is claiming. Furthermore, Mrs Griffith goes further, suggesting by sending the photographs that Lloyd George has a special interest in her son. There again the implication is clear. Who Lloyd George's 'colleague' is and why she should invoke him in the matter is a mystery, but it does not reflect well on the character of Mrs Griffith. There is real menace in the letter with its demand that she is entitled in some way to a share of the *People* libel damages. We do not know how Lloyd George replied, but he must have acted decisively, since Mrs Griffith does not appear to have written to him again.

There is only one firm conclusion that can be drawn from this strange episode, which is that Lloyd George was increasingly vulnerable to libel and to blackmail. He had to fight hard to keep his reputation intact, and if any attempt to link him with a broken marriage succeeded, his political career would be over. In view of these distressing near-exposures, it is not surprising that by 1911 he should be ready to reduce the risk by taking a regular mistress.

By embarking on a relationship with Frances, Lloyd George gained far more than just a regular outlet for his highly sexed nature. The object of his affections became part of his daily life, and he was able to come up with enough work reasons to make sure that he could see her at weekends as well. Frances was intelligent, hard-working and capable, and she became an indispensable part of his office, quite apart from her role in his private life. Her value to him as a secretary grew over time, reaching a pinnacle as he wrote his memoirs after leaving office. She was happy to learn new skills like shorthand to be useful to him, and there is even a suggestion in the wording of the opening line of her diary that she embarked on that at his request too, acting as Boswell to his Dr Johnson. 'I am to make a diary,' she wrote.[5] Her chosen phrase has the air of an instruction.

Frances took her work seriously, making the most of the opportunity she had been given. In 1931, when she had been working for Lloyd George for nearly twenty years, she was asked to give an address to the Association of Women Clerks and Secretaries. Her speech, published as a pamphlet under the heading 'The Private Secretary', gives a glimpse into her professional life. She emphasises the value of a good education, and recommends reading serious newspapers and periodicals daily, as well as Hansard in her own case, to be better able to assist her employer. A programme of general reading and studying languages is recommended, as are shorthand and typing. But Frances' mastery of her role shows most in the softer skills she advocates: 'Good secretaries are born, not made. To be a good secretary one must, to my mind, have gifts of tact and understanding, an intuitive knowledge of people and character . . . And as too one must be capable of summing up people quickly, so one must equally be able to conceal one's feelings and deal tactfully with tiresome people (I may add between ourselves especially in politics).' Discretion comes at the top of the list of desirable qualities:

[A secretary] holds the key very often to most important secrets. I would even go so far as to say that an employer can have no secrets from his secretary. He may sometimes think he has, but that is a delusion . . . There is perhaps no profession in which there are so many occasions when a woman might let her employer down. Most of the time her views are understood to be his views; her opinions his opinions. If she makes a mistake, it is probably her employer who will suffer. She must essentially be in complete sympathy with her employer: unless this is so she can never make a complete success of her post.[6]

Professionally, Frances was an ideal companion for Lloyd George. Personally too, there were several factors that made her virtually irresistible to him. In her, he undoubtedly saw a kind of replacement for his daughter Mair. Frances' connection with Mair had been a draw from the beginning, and in 1915 she recorded that Lloyd George 'says I have taken the place somewhat of Mair, "my little girl whom I lost" as he always calls her. He says I remind him of her & make up a little for her loss. I have always wanted to make this loss seem a little lighter to him, and he seems now to be able to speak of her with less pain than he used to.'[7]

For Frances, her memories of Mair formed part of her connection with Lloyd George, and she was proud of the fact that she helped him cope with his grief. On the back of one of his early letters she wrote a poem to Mair:

> O, cause of bitterest grief to one beloved!
> Not yet the shadows lengthened on thy way,
> When swiftly thou wert drawn to wider spheres,
> To hold more perfect sway.
> But oh! If ought [sic] the spirits wot of us –
> Still be the guardian angel for my dear,
> And let thine aureole's light reflect on him,
> To make his pathway clear!

Frances was only a year older than Mair, and it is natural that Lloyd George should have noticed the similarities between them. Less natural is the way in which he occasionally referred to himself as Frances' 'father'. It makes uncomfortable reading as he signs his letters to her as 'Your own fond old man & father', with salutations such as 'Oceans of love to my sweet little Worry from a Doting old man who is Father lover & husband all in one,' and 'fondest tenderest most eager love & affection to my girl – Papa'.[8]

In his sixth decade, Lloyd George was conscious of his age, and Frances' youthfulness attracted him strongly. In fact she looked much younger than her years, and when she gave a rare interview to the press as a secretary in No. 10 in 1922 the journalist remarked: 'Miss Stevenson looks like a mere girl, with a rosy complexion, large beautiful blue eyes, fair hair and a slim figure . . . Miss Stevenson dimpled most pleasingly. "Perhaps I am older than I look" she suggested.'[9]

Frances offered the same uncritical adoration that Lloyd George had previously received from his daughter. All the women in his life recognised that part of their role was to be his constant cheerleader, and all, to an extent, were happy to do so. From his mother and sister in Wales through to his daughters and even their friends, he demanded constant praise, especially after speeches or important public events.* 'My Dearest D,' scribbled Margaret on House of Commons notepaper in 1911, 'Ardderchog, y llais a'r delivery yn odidog [Excellent, the voice and delivery superb]. You seemed very alert & full of energy & the plea to the House was fine & what was wanted. Most amusing too.'[10] A.J. Sylvester, Lloyd George's Principal Private Secretary after the war, recalled an occasion when Lloyd George was upset not to receive a note from Megan after a speech in the House of Commons. There is no record of his ever demanding such a note from either of his sons.

Frances was an enthusiast in this respect. She attended every parliamentary appearance, listening avidly from the Visitors' Gallery and sending Lloyd George a loving note afterwards, signed 'P' (for Pussy, the Allenswood nickname that still clung to her). 'A really admirable

---

* Frances wrote in her diary in March 1934: 'We talked on the subject of self-confidence at dinner tonight. D. says he lacks self-confidence, but possesses the quality of love of approbation, which to a certain extent supplies the stimulus which lack of self-confidence needs. He said that Uncle Lloyd realised this failing in him, and for that reason sought to encourage him whenever he did well. The old man would always write him after his speeches, & if he did moderately well, the letter would begin with "Bravo" – scrawled across the page.'

little speech,' she wrote in an undated but typical note. 'You got into your stride again very soon after the interruption, were in excellent form. The House deeply interested and very pleased. I thought especially with the part about America!'[11] Her admiration of him fills every page of her letters. At the beginning of their relationship, when the glamour of his position still blinded her, she all but worshipped him. Margaret had done her share of cheerleading, but her independent spirit, together with the passage of more than twenty-five years, had worn her admiration of Lloyd George a little thin, and although she continued to support him with absolute loyalty, in this respect she did not pander to his needs as much as he felt she should have.

Lloyd George's other needs were also taken care of by Frances. Unlike Margaret, whose housekeeping skills were not her strength, Frances was good at creating comforting and cosy environments. When they dined alone she would make Lloyd George his favourite meal of fried bacon and potatoes, and while not pandering to his tendency to hypochondria, she always cared solicitously for his health and physical wellbeing. When he was working particularly hard or feeling under pressure, Frances would make him take a walk to get some fresh air, or would prepare one of her 'wonderful concoctions' of egg, port, honey and cream to 'buck him up'.[12]

The situation was not risk-free. If Lloyd George's relationship with Frances had been publicly exposed, he might not have lost his government position unless Margaret left him, but the reaction of his constituents was less predictable, and he would have faced uproar within his family. He was particularly conscious of the disappointment his behaviour would incur back home in Criccieth, for there was still no one whose good opinion he valued more than Uncle Lloyd's. Uncle Lloyd and William George did not know or care about the ways of London's smart set, but they did know and care for Margaret. Lloyd George had long since ceased to live his life according to his family's religious values, but he was anxious to avoid letting his uncle and brother know how far he had strayed from the path. He never allowed Frances near North Wales while Uncle Lloyd was alive, and his brother was among the last to know of her position in his life. 'I wanted to go to Caernarvon with him,' wrote Frances in 1917, 'but he will not take me to North Wales. He says his old uncle would see at once what our relations were, & it would upset him.[13] They could fool the world, it seemed, but they could not fool Uncle Lloyd.

But with Criccieth and Uncle Lloyd safely at a distance, Lloyd George had won himself a beautiful young companion whom he loved and who adored him in return. She was not like some of the glamorous women who had previously caught his eye, and perhaps she was of more interest to him because of that. Lloyd George's taste in women was fairly catholic, and as fame made his conquests easier, he seemed to prefer the challenge of winning over an interesting woman rather than a beautiful one. When Dick was old enough, his father would sometimes share a little of his expertise in this field. On one social occasion Dick recalled Lloyd George dismissing the more eye-catching women in the room in favour of a 'pale, dark-eyed woman in her late thirties, her hair in a severe unfashionable bun', with the comment, 'Now, she's *interesting*, she has something. She's a deep one, I'll wager.'[14] Dick also recalled his father's pride in his early conquests, made without the advantage of fame or money. Once, when Dick asked his father for a handout to take a girl out in London, Lloyd George replied with a knowing air, 'The art of courtship is a lost art . . . how would you fancy trying your hand with a girl when you've only got thruppence in your breeches and the only place you can take her is for a walk in the rain?'[15] The challenge made the conquest worthwhile. Frances appealed all the more to Lloyd George because of her subtle nature. He liked the fact that she concealed the true strength of her nature under a veneer of feminine mildness, and her inscrutability made her fascinating to him.

But what did Frances stand to gain from the relationship? Her romantic nature is the key to understanding her actions. Like Ann Veronica, the eponymous heroine of her favourite H.G. Wells novel, she believed herself to be a thoroughly emancipated modern woman. For the right cause she would be willing to break all the rules and flaunt the conventions of her middle-class upbringing, but in truth she craved love and marriage to a man who would dominate and take charge of her life. From the moment she fell under his spell, Lloyd George was her cause. The joy of having her feelings returned, together with the undoubted glamour of Lloyd George's position, was enough to sweep aside her reservations. At the same time, naïvety and youth caused her to trust absolutely in love, preventing her from seeing the vulnerability of her position.

Once they had embarked on their affair, Frances found Lloyd George to be a fascinating and attentive lover. He showered her with gifts and letters when they were apart, and he made her feel special and loved. Her feelings are captured in a pledge written in her handwriting on 11 Downing Street paper. It is highly romantic – sentimental, even – and 100 per cent Frances:

> We, the undersigned, hereby pledge our word that we give our love to each other, wholly and entirely, whatever happens; to cherish each other in sickness and in health; each one to put the other first, before all the world; to give up everything before giving up one another; in addition to this to give one another a sweet friendship and mutual understanding in the affairs of everyday life, to let none other come between the sacredness of our love, now or ever, till death do us part.[16]

It is tempting to speculate that the pledge was used by the lovers to solemnise their relationship, but the paper is unsigned, and there is no proof that it was ever shown to Lloyd George. The fact that Frances kept it with her papers, though, suggests that it had some private significance to her at least.

It would be untrue to say that Frances did not also benefit in a material way from the relationship. She had many talents and a natural flair for administration, yet she would not have been given the chance to work directly for the Chancellor of the Exchequer if it had not been for her personal relationship with him. Her role at the centre of public life was the opportunity of a lifetime, and it also reinforced her sense of working for an important cause and helping to make a difference to the world. Lloyd George flattered her by emphasising how much he relied on her: 'I cannot help wondering sometimes how he keeps up, with so many things to worry him,' Frances wrote in her diary in February 1917. 'He tells me that he could not go on without me, & I like to believe that that is true, for I love to think that I am helping him a little.'[17] Lloyd George made her feel needed, which was important to the romantic-natured Frances.

Less romantic perhaps, but still beneficial to Frances were the financial handouts that Lloyd George provided. Although she earned a good wage at the Treasury her financial situation dictated that she lived at home for the first two years. She put an end to this uncomfortable arrangement as soon as she was able, thus gaining more freedom and some respite from her mother's disapproval. From 1915 onwards Lloyd George supplemented her income – 'Are you alright for cash?' he wrote to her in April that year,[18] and he later helped her move into a larger flat in Morpeth Mansions near Westminster Cathedral. She was not a kept woman by any means, but with no private wealth of her own it is doubtful whether she could have maintained the lifestyle she enjoyed without depending financially on her lover, especially later in life.

There was a price to be paid by Frances for her relationship with Lloyd George. She knew from the beginning that she was giving up her chances of making an early, respectable marriage. She also came to realise that, despite her initial hopes of bearing Lloyd George a child, she risked giving up the chance of having children at all. Working closely with Lloyd George was a source of comfort to Frances, but it also placed an additional strain on her because of the secrecy of their relationship. The deception needed to support his double life and to maintain the myth of his untarnished personal integrity meant that Frances lived a lie. She could not easily share the truth with her friends or explain her overwhelming preoccupation with her new job. The impossibility of keeping all this to herself had prompted her in desperation to confide in her mother, but after the disastrous consequences of that confession she dared not risk another. Frances was taking a far greater risk than Lloyd George in embarking on the relationship: if their affair was discovered, he would be forgiven as long as Margaret stood by him. But Frances' reputation would be lost, and with it her chances of respectable marriage and employment. She had both less to gain and more to lose from the relationship.

Of course, that was not how Frances saw the situation. She allowed her heart to rule her head, and never doubted Lloyd George's commitment to her. For the present, she was simply content to share her lover's working life and as much of his leisure time as he could spare.

Frances and Lloyd George took scrupulous care not to be discovered, but even so they could not easily have conducted their affair without the complicity and cooperation of two loyal and discreet helpers: Lloyd George's Personal Secretary J.T. Davies and, more surprisingly, the Lloyd Georges' housekeeper, Sarah.

J.T. Davies was 'Mr Davies' at first to Frances, despite being only seven years older than her, but she later came to call him 'JT'. Unlike everyone else at the Treasury, he did not seem to resent her appointment or her closeness to the man he called his 'Chief'. JT and Frances worked closely together, and if he did not know the score from the outset, he soon realised what was going on.

JT was an easy-going man, intelligent and loyal, and free from the jealousy that plagued some of Lloyd George's other advisers. His relationship with the Chancellor had suffered a rocky start: during Lloyd George's absence from the office for a fortnight, JT had been left in charge of organising the paperwork for his return. When Lloyd George arrived back, he asked to see the most important papers first, and JT made the mistake of placing a dinner invitation from a London society hostess at the top of the pile. His Chief reacted furiously, throwing the carefully assembled bundle of papers clean across the room.[19] It was a sharp lesson to JT to think more carefully when prioritising matters for Lloyd George's attention, and one he learned well, for the two went on to become good friends.

JT seemed perfectly at ease with Frances' special status in their Chief's life. In truth, his loyalty was such that it overrode any disapproval he may have felt of Lloyd George's personal affairs. As a result, he was one of the first to be aware that Frances was the Chief's mistress. It was necessary that he should be in the know, for he was an essential part of their disguise. When Lloyd George wished to spend time with Frances by taking her away for a weekend at a country house or on official business abroad, he could not do so without rousing suspicion unless JT came too. Frances' diary is littered with examples of such occasions with JT providing cover for her presence. JT did not seem to mind at all, in fact he seems to have been charmed by her from the beginning. In May 1913, five months after they began to work together, he wrote to Frances, who was unwell, saying: 'The air seems very light with the C of E away. It would be lighter still if you were here.'[20]

JT may have been easy-going, but he was no fool. In making a

friend of Frances, and tipping her a wink, as it were, when Lloyd
George was being difficult, he won himself a powerful advocate, and
ultimately made life a lot easier for himself. Soon he felt able to tease
her about the relationship. In July 1913 Frances was ill again, and JT
wrote her a long, chatty letter revealing himself to be fully in her
camp:

> I finished at 11 o'c on Saturday night after the Chancellor's meeting at
> Dulwich. I gave him your love and he was very pleased, in fact I showed
> him your letter as he asked me if I had heard from you. I miss your
> sweet and cheery face across the table but I know that someone else
> gets that pleasure at the Hereward . . .
> The C of E is in very good form on the whole, tho' I don't see so
> much of him at the Treasury now! I wonder why! He is moving the
> Third Reading of the d—n Welsh Bill tomorrow and is going to speak
> at Caernarvon soon. Mrs Lloyd George is going down with him & she
> goes off to Criccieth and he returns – don't smile.[21]

It must have been a huge relief to Frances in an otherwise lonely period
that at least one of her colleagues understood and accepted her position. As JT became the go-between for Frances and Lloyd George in
the office, the person who helped them conceal their relationship within
No. 11 and in Criccieth was an altogether more unlikely candidate.

Sarah Jones had joined Margaret's staff as a young maid/nursemaid
for Megan in the early 1900s, and gradually extended her influence until
she was put in charge of running the whole household. With Margaret
absent for long periods it was necessary for someone else to be permanently in charge of the family's London residence, and by the time they
moved to Downing Street Sarah's authority was second only to that of
Margaret herself. Unmarried and stern, Sarah was a housekeeper of the
old school. She ruled the household with a rod of iron: the servants
and younger members of the family were terrified of crossing her.
Beneath her strict demeanour, she was utterly devoted to the family.
She had a special soft spot for Megan, whom she had nursed and cared
for from infancy, and Gwilym, the next youngest; but her heart belonged
to Lloyd George.

Sarah's devotion showed itself in a curious way, for there was no one she scolded more vigorously than Lloyd George. Like Margaret, who Sarah privately blamed for neglecting him, she took no nonsense from him. She was wholly unimpressed by his political success, and treated him like an unruly little boy even when he had become a world-famous statesman. Spoiled and pampered as a child by his mother and sister, Lloyd George had never learned to look after himself, and the details of domestic life were a mystery to him. Once when Margaret was ill he wrote home to his brother to boast that he had managed to boil a kettle. He was never able to unfasten the door of the dining room in No. 11, and if he found himself alone there, he would have to wait for someone to rescue him. Sarah would sometimes deliberately leave him in there to teach him a lesson, but to no avail. The two of them bickered and quarrelled constantly. Lloyd George took her scoldings meekly, but got his revenge by impishly baiting her to her face. A.J. Sylvester gives a glimpse of their relationship on the morning of Gwilym's wedding in 1921:

> She went up to L.G.'s bedroom earlier than usual on this particular morning, with joy in her heart and tears in her eyes, for she was fond of Gwilym. She said to L.G.: 'Ah, he was always a very good boy to me and never said a cross or unkind word to me.'
>
> 'Well,' enquired L.G., 'have I?'
>
> Sarah just looked at the Prime Minister as he lay in bed and after a pause said: 'God Almighty!' . . . and walked quietly out of the room.[22]

Frances teased him about the relationship in a letter written in 1925: 'Give my love to Sarah. She is a dear. Is she coming back with you? I know she is looking after you down there, & I would rather trust you to her than to anyone – in spite of all the insinuations you make about your relations with her (but only when I am there, as she always emphatically says!).'

Only Frances could ever think that Sarah was 'a dear'. She bossed Lloyd George like none other. Woe betide him if he embarrassed her by inviting unexpected visitors for meals. Unfortunately, he was in the habit of doing exactly that, and his amused guests would look on as he braved Sarah's anger at the door. In 1916, when Lloyd George was Munitions Minister, he dared bring the Conservative MP Arthur Lee unexpectedly back to Downing Street for dinner. Lee recalls what happened:

> ... we arrived at No. 11 only to find the house apparently deserted and no one at home but his ancient housekeeper, 'Sarah'. She was a veritable Welsh dragon; dour and cross-grained, who had been with him since the days of his obscurity and who habitually addressed him with the minimum of respect. When at last she unchained the door and L.G. informed her airily, although a little timidly I thought, that he had 'brought a friend to dinner', she broke out in a tirade, saying, 'You can't dine here; you know there's no food with the mistress away.' To which L.G. replied soothingly, 'But what about that ham we had last week, Sarah, and haven't you any potatoes?' ... she disappeared, still growling, into the basement and after some time re-appeared with the fag end of the almost consumed ham and a few half-boiled potatoes. It was not very tempting but L.G. was in such tearing spirits that we despatched it with gusto, washing it down with the only wine in the cellar – a half-full bottle of claret which had evidently been opened for some time.*

Sarah also acted as Lloyd George's valet, looking after his clothes and physically dressing him, something he could never manage on his own. Buttons, ties and laces mystified him, and he had neither the patience nor the inclination to learn how to cope with them. He preferred to be looked after by a woman rather than the customary male valet, maintaining that 'woman was sent to look after man'.[23] Even when he was Prime Minister, Newnham, the official valet at No. 10, looked after him when he travelled but at home Sarah was in charge. If he found the wrong shirt laid out on the bed, or could not put his hands on his favourite collar studs, he would explode in a furious temper. On these occasions Sarah would leave him to throw his clothes around the room, waiting calmly for the storm to pass before giving him a piece of her mind, saying, 'Great God, there you go again. I'm ashamed of you,

---

* This was an unfair reflection on Sarah's cooking, which was generally held to be excellent. On at least one occasion Lloyd George charmed a difficult lunch guest by finding out his favourite pudding in advance and deploying Sarah's skills to help win him over.

indeed I am.'[24] The two quarrelled like an old married couple, and Sarah would huff and puff about her master as if he were the bane of her life. The depth of her love for him could only be discerned through her care for him and her loyalty, hardly ever through her words. One rare exception was after his potentially life-threatening prostate operation in 1932, when Sarah was heard to exclaim, 'If he gets over this, I'll never quarrel with him again.'[25]

Over the years Sarah's fame grew back in North Wales. After she had recovered from the shock of seeing the old-fashioned kitchen at No. 11 she took to conducting guided tours of the house for visitors from Wales, pointing out its special features while giving out copious amounts of gossip. According to Olwen, visiting Sarah at No. 11 was 'a "must" for Criccieth people when they came to London; in their eyes it was probably given higher priority than seeing Buckingham Palace or Tower Bridge!'[26] She also looked after the maids and other servants, some of whom were only children when they joined the household.

We do not know how Sarah came to know about Frances and Lloyd George, but she presumably saw quickly how well Frances cared for him when Margaret was away. Margaret's tendency to neglect Lloyd George's creature comforts was something Sarah could neither understand nor forgive. Frances, with her natural gift for domestic comfort and her focus on Lloyd George's wellbeing, gradually won Sarah's approval. From there it was a small step to actively helping the lovers. She posted letters between them, helped conceal Frances' visits, and looked after Frances when she was ill. It was to Sarah that Frances turned for advice on their relationship, and Sarah respected her confidence, maintaining a complete silence as far as Margaret was concerned. Frances wrote: 'Sarah was a friend of mine from the first, and my position in Downing Street was greatly eased and abetted by her . . . L.G. was her "child" over whom she watched, unselfishly, devoted to his welfare, and often incurring the displeasure of his family by her fearless words. L.G. could depend on her help for looking after me when he wanted me in Downing Street.'[27]

As far as Margaret was concerned, Sarah was her faithful housekeeper. Neither she nor Megan had any inkling of Sarah's secret sympathy with Frances, or how she had promoted the affair. Had they done so, they would not have had her in the house. The full extent of Sarah's relationship with Frances was only revealed in 1967 with the publication of Frances' autobiography, followed by that of her correspondence with Lloyd George in 1975, but by then Margaret and Megan were both dead.

With the help of JT in the office and Sarah at home, Lloyd George's affair with Frances blossomed. The Marconi scandal had been resolved, albeit in a way that did not reflect well on any of the participants. The Select Committee delivered a report in favour of exonerating the ministers involved by dividing along party lines, and not one but two minority reports were published criticising Isaacs' and Lloyd George's actions. The crucial factor in Lloyd George's survival was the continuing support of the Prime Minister. Asquith refused to accept the resignations of his ministers, despite the fact that he did not see eye to eye with Lloyd George on a number of issues. There has been some puzzlement since as to why he should have been so loyal to his troublesome lieutenants. John Grigg, Lloyd George's principal biographer, revealed that Asquith knew of the existence of the shares bought on behalf of the Liberal Party, and therefore had no choice but to defend his colleagues. To admit that Lloyd George and Isaacs had been wrong to buy the shares would be to admit that he too, as leader of the Liberal Party, was in the wrong. Indeed, if either had been permitted to resign, Asquith risked bringing down his own government. If this was indeed so, then what looked at the time like magnanimity could, after all, have been self-preservation. Once more, Lloyd George had survived a career-threatening scandal.

With the shadow of scandal removed and restored to a powerful position within his party, Lloyd George must have felt unstoppable. The long session of 1912 had seen two major Bills close to his heart pass through the House of Commons: the Home Rule Bill, intended to solve the growing tensions in Ireland; and, at long last, the Welsh Church Bill which would finally deliver disestablishment in Wales. Lloyd George did not rest on his laurels, but persuaded his party that the next social reform to tackle was to secure fair working and living standards for those who worked the land, at the expense of those who owned it. The Bill he proposed gave the state unprecedented powers over land management, and on 22 October he announced the establishment of a Ministry of Lands.

Not only did he fail to get the Bill through the House of Commons, however, but another crisis diverted his attention, as the House of Lords sent back the Home Rule Bill for an unprecedented third time. With Ireland edging ever closer to civil war, this debate was in turn cut short by the calamitous descent into armed conflict in Europe in 1914. The land campaign, and indeed normal life, were suspended.

For Frances the crisis began on 29 June 1914, the day she incurred her mother's displeasure by working on her birthday. Torn between her mother and her lover, Frances was working miserably in the outer office in the Treasury when a red box arrived from the Foreign Office. Lloyd George was having his customary afternoon nap, and when he awoke Frances took the box in to him. Inside was a telegram announcing that the Archduke Franz Ferdinand of Austria and his wife had been assassinated at Sarajevo. Lloyd George studied the message and looked up: 'This means war,' he said.

13

A Family in Downing Street

FIVE WEEKS LATER, on 4 August 1914, Lloyd George sat at the long table in the Cabinet Room of 10 Downing Street late at night, distractedly doodling triangles and circles on the back of a War Office telegram. With him sat Prime Minister Henry Asquith, Foreign Secretary Sir Edward Grey and Home Secretary Reginald McKenna. Finally Big Ben chimed 11 o'clock, the hour at which the ultimatum issued to Germany earlier that day expired. The diplomatic efforts of the past five weeks had failed, and Britain was at war.

The solemn mood inside No. 10 was not necessarily shared by the general population. Frances, for one, welcomed the beginning of the war. Not only did it mean a rush of work as Lloyd George went about the urgent task of raising finance to pay for it (Frances was always happiest when busy), but she felt passionately that Britain had a duty to stand and fight side by side with France. This was partly a reflection of her love of the country. It was also characteristically idealistic. Frances saw war in terms of honour and glory. She had not seen the suffering of armed conflict for herself, and did not count the cost, like the more experienced Chancellor of the Exchequer, in financial or human terms.

Lloyd George had taken longer to make up his mind whether or not to support the war. In his cautious attitude he was much closer to the peace-loving, nonconformist Margaret than to Frances. Margaret was less ready to contemplate sacrificing Britain's youth, much less her own sons, unless she could believe it was in a just cause. From Criccieth, along with Uncle Lloyd, she had been urging her husband to do all he could to prevent war. He wrote to her on 3 August:

> I am moving through a nightmare world these days. I have fought hard for peace & succeeded so far in keeping the Cabinet out of it but I am driven to the conclusion that if the small nationality of Belgium is attacked by Germany all my traditions & even prejudices will be engaged on the side of war. I am filled with horror at the prospect. I am even more horrified that I should ever appear to have a share in it but I must bear my share of the ghastly burden though it scorches my flesh to do so.[1]

The same Welsh background made both Margaret and Lloyd George the champions of small nations like Belgium. Frances did not fully understand his initial hesitation or his eventual reasons for supporting war, because she could not look at the world through her lover's Welsh eyes.

While Frances spent long hours at the Treasury helping Lloyd George in his work and soothing his leisure hours, Margaret's life had changed too. Margaret was forty-seven years old, and as fond of Criccieth as ever. Even so, she had been living in 11 Downing Street for nearly six years, and had managed to create a family life there, despite a somewhat discouraging start. At first she had been despondent at Lloyd George's promotion to Chancellor of the Exchequer, because it meant moving house for the third time in a year. Mair's death was still fresh in their minds, and they had been living in their new home in Chelsea for only a few weeks when, in April 1908, Lloyd George came home to announce, 'You will have to start packing all over again. We are going to move into No. 11 Downing Street!' Margaret was aghast. 'What? Move into that dirty, dingy street, and leave this pretty, clean house I love!' – not, perhaps, the response he had been hoping for.

Her impressions of her new home were far from favourable:

> The sun hardly seems to penetrate its narrow precincts, but apart from this drawback, both No. 11 and No. 10 ... if viewed solely from the exterior, look most unimposing places in which to house Great Britain's principal government officials, so my criticism on hearing that one of

these was to be our future dwelling was not really so unmerited as it sounds . . . Looking back through the years I often wonder what my feelings would have been if, when we moved into No. 11, I had been allowed to glance forward into the future, and to glean the knowledge therefrom that we were destined to make our home in Downing Street for the next fifteen years.

Asquith, Lloyd George's predecessor as Chancellor, had preferred his own London house to No. 11, and the place had been let to a tenant. As a result, Margaret arrived to find a dark, neglected house connected by a labyrinth of winding corridors to No. 10 and the offices on Whitehall. The only thing she liked about it was that the main reception rooms looked out on the spacious back garden. But at least her new home was modernised. When she accepted an offer of a tour of No. 10, she found that the Prime Minister's residence had no bathrooms, while in its attic 'there were a sufficient number of foot-baths stored away to pave Downing Street from one end to the other!' Characteristically, Margaret's thoughts flew straight away to the practical difficulties of cleaning such a house: 'Small wonder that the annual event of spring cleaning was regarded with awe and dread both above and below stairs during the Victorian era, when we consider the labour entailed and the difficulties that must have been experienced by the domestics in moving out from their established positions the wardrobes and the large beds!'[2]

Her own house was easier to manage, and was also more comfortable to live in, being more of a private residence than a working office like No. 10. Downstairs, there were a fine dining room and a large, well-proportioned drawing room which only needed fresh upholstery and a thorough cleaning to make them ideal for entertaining. On the first floor Margaret had her own sitting room, and in addition to bedrooms for the family of six and their live-in staff, she was able to mark out a schoolroom for the six-year-old Megan, which she shared with Gwilym and Olwen during school holidays. Margaret was especially proud of the fact that she had two modern bathrooms in her new house – and one of them had a tiled floor, quite an innovation at the time. She soon had the house arranged to her satisfaction, and, with her Welsh staff, set about creating a Welsh family home at the very heart of the political establishment.

This was the first time Margaret had not been able to keep her life with the children separate from Lloyd George's political world, and she now found herself living in the maelstrom of her husband's working life. Although he had an office in the Treasury and spent most of his days there or at the House of Commons, the close proximity of No. 11 meant that he often used it for meetings and for entertaining. It was a shock to Margaret to discover that not only was she expected to produce meals for visitors at very little notice, but also to provide china and glass for dinners and receptions at No. 11. She would occasionally resort to hiring tableware if a particularly large party was expected, but she had to abandon her customary frugality and buy a much larger stock of plates, glasses and cutlery.

As numerous residents of 10 and 11 Downing Street have attested, it is difficult to maintain a balance between public formality and privacy when living in an official residence. To Margaret, this did not come naturally. She was by nature highly unpunctual, and found it difficult to adapt to the new regime of rigid mealtimes and the endless stream of official guests. In her haste to attend to the children in the morning, she frequently wandered around in her nightgown. Her daughters' warnings fell on deaf ears, even after she was rushing out of the bathroom one morning and collided sharply with the rotund form of the Chief Whip, who was staying with them. The incident embarrassed him far more than it embarrassed Margaret, who told the children gaily that she simply bounced off him.

It was more difficult to avoid embarrassment when unexpected guests arrived and needed feeding. Downstairs, Sarah ruled the kitchen with her customary strictness and economy. There would be food enough for those who were expected, but extra guests posed a real problem. Lloyd George often invited colleagues and advisers to dine at No. 11 on the spur of the moment, incurring both Margaret and Sarah's wrath, and nearly landing himself in trouble on one occasion when he pressed Herbert Samuel, the Jewish Postmaster General, to lunch. Margaret had to hiss at him in Welsh, 'It's *pork* for lunch!' whereupon the hospitable Chancellor abruptly ceased to urge his friend to stay.

Margaret grew accustomed to sharing her dining table with officials, politicians and businessmen, for Lloyd George was not exaggerating when he told Julia Henry that he 'talked shop at every meal'.[3] He was working at a furious pace, and was reluctant to break off for lunch or dinner. Eventually it occurred to him that he could also make use of the first meal of the day, and he began to invite guests to join the family for breakfast. From then on, his business breakfasts became an almost daily forum for informal discussions of the issues that were on his mind at the time. He would select his guests for their ability to add a point of view or a different perspective, and the talk would inevitably be 'shop'. These breakfasts hardly suited Margaret, since they put even more pressure on her already overburdened morning schedule, but she took them in her stride along with all the other sudden changes to her life. It was taken for granted that the family, and any personal guests they had staying, would be included at mealtimes, which made for sometimes eclectic gatherings of politicians, businessmen, Welsh preachers and visiting family. Guests and family alike would gather for breakfast at 9.15 prompt, and Margaret kept a family atmosphere as far as she could: 'We preferred everything to be done in as informal a way as possible, so when the maids had finished serving the tea and coffee and hot dishes they withdrew, in order that we might talk undisturbed.'[4]

Also present at breakfast (the early start was described by Olwen as 'agony'[5]), as at every meal, were the children, who listened avidly to the wide-ranging discussions. The price to pay for their inclusion was total discretion, and Margaret impressed on them the importance of never repeating what had been said. Olwen once received a stiff rebuke when she was heard saying that Asquith, who had earned himself the nickname 'Old Squiffy', had fallen asleep after drinking too much. Even the talkative Megan had to learn never to repeat what she heard at mealtimes.

For Margaret, life was turning out very differently to how she had expected. Her public duties inevitably kept her for longer periods in London, and as a result of Lloyd George's political success she was drawn into the highest political and social circles. She grew accustomed to being presented in court to the King and Queen, occasionally even attending events at Buckingham Palace alone to represent her husband, and she attended many official and semi-official dinners when Lloyd George was out of London or giving speeches elsewhere. She was well equipped temperamentally to cope with the demands of her new life, but the strain did occasionally show. Despite her pride, her unflappable nature and her calm, practical approach to life, she was not from the same stable as previous occupants of No. 11. There was no sharper contrast than that between Margaret and her predecessor and new neighbour at No. 10, Margot Asquith.

Margot, Herbert Asquith's second wife, was born in Scotland into the wealthy and aristocratic Tennant family. Striking, clever and vivacious, she had unwittingly captured Asquith's heart while he was still married to his first wife, Helen, and married him three years after Helen's death, in 1894. Margot prided herself on her wit, and considered her husband's career her own. She did not hesitate to interfere in politics, and was wholly unapologetic if her actions made things worse for her husband, as they frequently did. She was at the centre of a group of upper-class intellectuals known as 'the Souls' who wrote to each other freely and gathered in country houses for Saturday-to-Monday parties with the ease of lifelong familiarity. From her new home in 10 Downing Street, Margot dominated London society.

In her relationship with Lloyd George, Margot veered between contempt and admiration before finally settling for the former. She was kinder towards his wife, but regarded her as too low down on the social ladder, and too Welsh, to merit much attention. She patronisingly described Margaret as 'a very homely, intelligent, little servant of a woman with a heart of gold and no ambition or rise in her'.[6] Megan was 'a clever little girl dressed like our coachman dressed his children on Sundays'[7] – not a remark that was likely to produce warm feelings between Margot and Megan's mother. But if Margaret minded her exclusion from the social set that included not only Margot Asquith but Clementine Churchill and the wives of her husband's other Cabinet colleagues, she did not show it. She steadfastly – almost stubbornly – clung to her familiar world of Wales and the Welsh, and although she made many friends in England, they were rarely of the fashionable society kind, with the notable exception of Queen Mary, with whom she shared a passion for gardening.

Margaret continued to employ only Welsh-speaking servants even in No. 11, and she refused to employ a butler, as was expected of her, preferring her guests to be greeted by her long-serving parlourmaid on the grounds that women needed to earn a living as much as any man. More stubbornly, she refused to alter her style of dress to suit her new position.[8] Lloyd George seemed content on the whole with Margaret's household management, and shared her scornful views on fashionable society, but her lack of personal vanity did grate on him. There may have been financial reasons why she did not spend money on her wardrobe in the early days of her marriage, but later on, when their income increased, she still did not dress well. Olwen commented in her memoirs that this was a contentious issue between her parents:

> Father used to say to her, 'Why don't you wear that blouse I gave you?' I remember how proud he was of her when she was presented at Court. She had a lovely white dress with a long train lined in pale green chiffon, and the people of Caernarvon had embroidered the train with a leek in white and silver. Father was standing in the drawing-room with some friends when Mother was ushered in. She looked beautiful. Her hair had been styled specially for the occasion and her cheeks were pink with excitement. Father was so overwhelmed when he saw her that his face went absolutely crimson. He was so proud of her; it was a shame that there were so many occasions when she wouldn't please him in this way.[9]

Lloyd George would often bring home expensive presents of hats or jewellery for Margaret which she was reluctant to wear. She had never been vain or cared about clothes, and her religious views encouraged her towards simplicity in dress, but her stubbornness might also have had something to do with her husband's enthusiastic appreciation of the more glamorous women with whom he was surrounded. Her unwillingness to compete with them only underlined her special – and permanent – status in his life.

Despite the tensions, and whatever he chose to tell Frances, Lloyd George and Margaret were still close, and there were happy times for the family in No. 11. Visitors commented on the comfortable atmosphere Margaret had created in the house, as indeed she did when the family eventually moved to 10 Downing Street. There, Riddell described a typical dinner party as a 'wonderful sight. So far as the food, service, and appointments were concerned, it looked as if a small suburban house-hold were picnicking in Downing Street – the same simple food, the same little domestic servant, the same mixture of tea and dinner. And yet with all that, an air of simple dignity and distinction pervaded the room – no affectation, no pretension, nothing mean, nothing ignoble.'[10] The letters between Lloyd George and Margaret during this period reflect the warmth of their relationship, and would have horrified Frances had she seen them. 'I am so delighted to know you are coming up tomorrow,' wrote Lloyd George to Margaret in March 1914. 'In spite of occasional sulks &c. I cannot do without my round little wife. I am so disappointed you were not in the House last night. By common consent, I scored the greatest Parliamentary triumph of my life.'[11]

Margaret remained unhappy about living in London. She was less worried about the children's health now that they were older, but she still preferred country air. Fortunately, the Chancellor's salary could stretch not only to maintaining Brynawelon in Criccieth, but also to setting up a modest home in Brighton, where they escaped as often as duties permitted. Brighton was chosen not only for the quality of the air but also because it was close to Roedean, where Olwen was enrolled. This house, which they gave up when the Walton Heath house was built in 1913, was Margaret's bolthole when the pressures of London became too much.

The children, on the other hand, seemed to thrive in the environment of No. 11. Dick and Gwilym, away at Cambridge and Eastbourne College respectively, were less present in Downing Street, but Olwen and Megan regarded it as their home. Their father's position was bound to make things difficult for them at times, and both found themselves occasionally shunned by girls whose parents disapproved of Lloyd George's politics, but it was a small price to pay for the excitement of life at No. 11. Olwen was sixteen when they moved in, and was old enough to enjoy being in the centre of the political world. This was, to her, 'the compensation of living in Downing Street where everything was happening and everybody who was anybody came to visit us',[12] and although, unlike her younger siblings, she never considered a career in politics, she grew up to be highly politically aware, and was the only one of Lloyd George's children to remain an active Liberal for the rest of her life.

Olwen was thrilled by the historical events happening around her, and relished the occasional perks her father's position could bring. In 1910 she was allowed to watch the funeral procession of King Edward

VII from the windows of the Foreign Office, and was excited to spot the Kaiser among the European heads of state passing below. Since her parents' protectiveness meant that going to university like her brothers was not an option for her, she studied useful social skills like cookery and languages. She spent a year in Dresden learning German and another in Paris improving her French at a select establishment for young ladies, returning to Downing Street or Criccieth in the holidays. It was a happy time for her, and one she looked back on with nostalgia later in life: 'The last year before war broke out in 1914 seemed a wonderful year, full of excitement and parties. We were always doing something or going somewhere, and we of the younger generation seemed to be living for the enjoyment we could get out of it. It was almost as if we knew that some of us did not have that much longer to live.'[13]

Olwen was twenty-two when the war began, and still lived at home in Downing Street, where the restrictions of sharing a house with her parents were just beginning to chafe. Her father was particularly strict, and once made her accompany him to a Salvation Army pageant as punishment for being caught creeping into the house from a dance at five in the morning. She was old enough to be aware of her father's reputation, and if he tried to come down too hard on her for staying out late, or to lecture her on her choice of friends, she would occasionally snap and say, 'That's nice, coming from you!'[14]

On the whole, however, Olwen's relationship with her parents was close and affectionate. She frequently accompanied her father to meetings or to the House of Commons, adopting the family habit of sending him approving little notes after his speeches. She became accustomed to seeing famous people in the drawing room at home, none more famous perhaps than the young Edward, Prince of Wales. The reason for his frequent visits to No. 11 in 1911 was a scheme conjured up by Lloyd George himself. He had persuaded the new King, George V, to hold a ceremony at Caernarvon Castle to invest his eldest son as Prince of Wales. The investiture was to be held at Caernarvon rather than Cardiff because it was at Caernarvon, tradition had it, that the first Prince of Wales was presented to the people in 1301.

Lloyd George had been Constable of Caernarvon Castle, a largely ceremonial role, since 1908. As well as benefiting him locally by bringing the full pageantry of monarchy to the heart of his constituency, he saw the investiture as an opportunity to give a nod to the House of Lords and to draw a line under his very public past feuding with the King. Likewise, recognising the momentum behind Lloyd George's political career, the King's agreement was given partly to ease his relationship with his hot-headed Chancellor. A date was set – 13 July 1911 – and Lloyd George set about organising every detail.

At the climax of the ceremony the King would invest the Prince with a sword, a coronet, a ring and a gold rod, known as the Golden Verge. Having pledged his loyalty to the King, the new Prince of Wales would receive an address from the Welsh people delivered by Sir John Rhys, Principal of Jesus College, Oxford. The Prince's response contained several phrases in Welsh, and unsurprisingly the young man was terrified. Lloyd George offered his services as a personal tutor, and for months before the investiture the heir to the throne would make his way twice a week to 11 Downing Street for Welsh lessons. Not only did Lloyd George teach him the Welsh phrases he had to master, he involved the whole family in the process so that the future Prince of Wales was surrounded by fluent Welsh-speakers, playing the part of the crowd or the chorus according to his tutor's commands. Lloyd George's powers of oratory were legendary. In the days before artificial amplification changed the nature of public speaking, he could address a crowd of 2,000 people, and make himself heard at the back of even the largest halls. Standing at the end of the long dining room in No. 11, the shy young Prince would repeat the phrases over and over again until Lloyd George, standing at the other end, could hear them clearly.

As dawn broke on 13 July, people had already begun to swarm into Caernarvon, the town's inhabitants swelled by passengers from 150 special trains that had been laid on for the occasion. The sun beat down on the crowds that filled every vantage point around the castle as the guests of honour arrived. The royal family was accompanied by the Prime Minister and various members of the Cabinet, Welsh Members of Parliament, Lords and prominent Welsh dignitaries. Inside the castle a green carpet had been laid, with the royal dais in the centre, covered by a canopy of green and white silk under a gold figure of St David. Gentlemen-at-arms wearing crimson uniforms stood at its four corners, watching over the oak thrones stamped with the royal arms, awaiting the royal party. Invited guests inside the castle were entertained by a

Welsh choir in scarlet cloaks, and the arrival of the Prince was heralded by trumpeters in gold tunics. Lloyd George greeted the King at the gate of the castle and handed him the key – the traditional duty of the Constable – but otherwise he deliberately kept himself out of the limelight to avoid upstaging the principal players. In any case, he did not have to push himself forward: everyone knew that the event was masterminded by him. The seventeen-year-old Prince looked nervous, but spoke the words he had rehearsed across the drawing room at 11 Downing Street with confidence.

The event was a resounding success. Lloyd George had provided a splendid pageant for his constituents' entertainment, and had put together a magnificent celebration of Welsh history and culture. Due credit was given to him, the *South Wales News* describing him as 'the greatest democrat of modern times ... to whom Welsh Nationalism owes more than to any other man. [The people of Wales] will recognise him as one of themselves, as one who was once a youth in a poor cottage home, and has earned his title to stand before Princes, not by virtue of privileges, but by virtue of his own personal worth.'[15] After the investiture Lloyd George received a letter from the Prince of Wales in which he wrote, 'It was chiefly due to the valuable lessons you gave me in Welsh that the answers to the addresses were such a success. I really did feel what I said.'[16]

As they grew accustomed to being one of the most famous families in the country, there was one member of the Lloyd George household who relished the spotlight far more than the others. Megan spent her formative years, from six to twenty, living in 11 and 10 Downing Street. Already a precocious and much-indulged youngest child, she took naturally to being the centre of attention, and delighted in performing to a crowd.* She had a lively imagination, a wicked sense of humour and an uncanny gift for mimicry.

Before she was sent to Allenswood at the age of ten, Downing Street was Megan's personal playground. At first she found a willing playmate

---

* When Winston Churchill visited Criccieth on board the Admiralty yacht the *Enchantress* he ordered that the ship's spotlight be trained on Megan's bedroom window at Brynawelon in salutation.

in the youngest member of the Asquith family. Anthony Asquith, having inherited his mother's rather prominent nose, was nicknamed 'Puffin', and he was Megan's equal in daring and in mischief-making. She later recalled: 'I fell in love with the sweet, pixie-like boy next door. We became inseparable and kept running through the intercommunicating doors from one house to the other, romped rather noisily up and down stairs, and played hide-and-seek in the vast warren of rooms in the two houses.'[17]

To the children's delight, Margot Asquith had installed an electric lift at No. 10. This was cutting-edge technology at the beginning of the twentieth century, and it was more impressive than reliable. It held a particular fascination for Puffin and Megan, who behaved as though it had been installed for their own amusement. One day while they were riding up and down it came to a halt between floors. The children could not make themselves heard, and when their absence was noticed a full-scale search of Downing Street was conducted for fear of a kidnap plot. The hunt had reached Horse Guards Parade, and both families were distraught, before an enterprising servant thought to examine the lift and discovered the children. On another occasion they went missing again, and the servants began to search for them, trying not to disturb an official lunch that was taking place in No. 11 at the time. Olwen describes what happened next:

> The meal progressed, when suddenly someone happened to look up through the glass cupola above the dining-table. There was a narrow gallery running round the cupola, and two small figures were seen creeping stealthily along the ledge. They had climbed out of a window to get on the roof, and were intending to walk over the roof to No. 10 and climb in through another window there.
>
> We thought that any minute one of them would slip and crash through the glass dome on to the dining-table! Luckily it didn't happen. One of the family made an excuse to leave the table, and the children were quietly and gently removed from the roof. Father's wrath afterwards was quite predictable.[18]

After that, Puffin was deemed to be a suitable playmate for Megan no longer.

Olwen describes Megan as a child as 'pretty, intelligent, lively and full of fun, but thoroughly spoiled by all the family'. She was closer to her father than any of her older siblings, partly because he naturally saw in her a replacement for Mair, and partly also because he was able to spend much more time with her at No. 11 than he had done with the older children when they were living at a distance from Westminster. He would frequently break off from his work to climb the stairs to the schoolroom to check on his youngest child or to whisk her away for a walk or drive. It is little wonder that Megan fell behind in her schoolwork.

Of all the children, Megan was closest to Lloyd George in terms of temperament. As well as being a natural performer, she inherited his drive and ambition. She occasionally irritated her siblings by 'showing off' in front of company, encouraged by her devoted father, but she was also very close to her mother. Megan was raised as a Calvinistic Methodist, and like Margaret she was a true believer. Like her mother too, she was steadfast in her opinions and rarely changed her mind about anything or anyone, which was to prove the source of much unhappiness to her in later life.

Since her parents were both busy, Megan was alone for much of the time, and often retreated into her own imaginary world, sometimes assuming the character of one of the women around her. On one occasion a visitor arrived at No. 11 for breakfast and was astounded to see Megan open the door wearing the parlourmaid's cap and apron. She introduced herself as the maid, and gave an impassioned account of her morning duties.[19] At other times she would answer the telephone and pretend to be 'Miss Evans, the Chancellor's Secretary'. The family happily humoured her, and Lloyd George would sometimes pretend to consult his 'secretary' on important matters. As the Chancellor's little girl, Megan received a lot of attention from the press, who found her as charming as visitors to No. 11 did. She grew to enjoy her public profile to such an extent that she boasted to Olwen, 'I am in the papers much more than you!' Criminals, replied the down-to-earth Olwen, also got their names in the paper.[20]

Megan was twelve years old when war broke out in 1914, bringing the happy times to an abrupt end. The war was to have a profound effect on every member of the Lloyd George family. Dick and Gwilym soon enlisted, and Margaret's maternal anxiety was shared by the rest of the family, especially after they were both sent to France in December 1915. Dick, by now a qualified engineer, joined the Royal Engineers. He was involved in the action on the first days of the battle of the Somme, and suffered badly from trench fever and from trauma. Gwilym was initially appointed ADC to a General, but later engaged in active service also. Both had risen to the rank of Major by the end of the war.

Back at home, Olwen joined the Voluntary Aid Detachment in Criccieth and was set to work in the local emergency hospital, while in London Megan sold flags to raise money for the war effort. Olwen later joined her brothers in France, working for the British Red Cross. She complained that she saw precious little of France for she was confined to the station at Boulogne, running the reception area for the hospital trains. She took every opportunity to gather information on her brothers' whereabouts to allay Margaret's anxiety. Occasionally there would be a chance to socialise, but there was no opportunity for a lasting relationship with any of the young men who passed through Boulogne. They were bittersweet encounters: 'Young officers I knew who were passing through would take me out for a few hours. We almost forgot the war as we talked about home and our friends. I knew some very nice young men who escorted me for an evening and afterwards took me back to the villa where I was staying. Our escorts were never allowed in, so we had to say goodnight at the door. Many of them were killed while they were still little more than boys.'[21]

After a year Olwen returned to London to continue her Red Cross work there. It was a fortuitous homecoming, for soon after she arrived back in Downing Street, Margaret announced that the son of some Welsh friends of hers was coming to tea. Tom Carey Evans was a doctor and a captain in the army, and Olwen describes their meeting as 'love at first sight for both of us'. The young couple were able to spend some time together in London and Criccieth when Tom returned from Gallipoli on leave. On the day his new orders arrived, he made his intentions clear. The war hastened many marriages, but after her experience in Boulogne Olwen hesitated. She did not give Tom an answer at once, afraid of giving her heart to a man she might never see again. The parting in spring 1916 was difficult, but by the time Tom's birthday came around in June, her mind was made up.[22] She cabled him her answer: 'Happy Birthday. Yes. Love Olwen'. Their marriage was happy, and lasted for thirty-one years until Tom died suddenly in 1947 at the age of sixty-three. In his will he wrote, movingly, that his estate was 'bequeathed free of duty unto my wife, Olwen Elizabeth Carey Evans, absolutely, to whom I owe an unpayable debt for my blissful married existence'.[23]

With her children growing up Margaret had more time on her hands, and began to overcome her shyness about getting involved in public life. At first she suffered from a shortage of confidence, or perhaps a consciousness of her lack of formal education. In 1895 Lloyd George wrote her an encouraging letter: 'You have more brains than you give yourself credit for. Mrs Freeman was telling Towyn Jones on Monday that you were the very essence of commonsense. She never met anyone so thoroughly sensible. That is exactly my opinion. You have the most valuable intellectual faculty – sound judgement & if you have transmitted it to the children I shall be more content than if they have inherited all the troublesome powers I may be endowed with.'[24]

Margaret herself confessed to being nervous when she first started addressing meetings, but as she grew more experienced, her confidence increased. 'You must make a good speech one of these days,' wrote her husband in the same year. 'That will surprise them. I am sure you can do it. You have any quantity of brains of a very good quality if you only set them to work. THINK – that is what you must do.'[25] By 1899 her speeches were being reported in the press, and Lloyd George was able to write from Canada: 'I felt proud of my old Mag & her speech in the Guardian was so pat, sensible & to the point. Just fel hi ei hunan [Just like her].'[26]

A distinction needs to be drawn here between politics and public life, for while Margaret was increasingly being drawn into the latter, she did not consider the former to be her *métier*, and unlike the meddle-some Mrs Asquith, adopted a strict policy of non-interference in her husband's political work. This is not to say that she did not participate in politics, far from it. In private she was firm in her opinions, and she did not hesitate to join in the political discussions in her drawing room. She also frequently sat behind the grille of the Ladies' Gallery in the House of Commons to listen to her husband speak in order to provide him with the praise and appreciation he constantly sought. As Lloyd George's career took him away from his constituency for longer periods she began to represent him on platforms in North Wales, and in time became a formidable campaigner both for him and for Megan. In Margaret's mind, though, politics remained primarily her husband's domain. Voluntary work of all kinds – for her chapel, for the Red Cross, for the National Lifeboat Institution and for countless other local and national charities – was the field in which she played an increasing role, and which during the war she made fully her own.

With the outbreak of war Margaret was asked whether she could do something to help the Welsh troops. This was a cause close to her heart. Lloyd George had already used his influence to ensure that Welsh regiments were created, so that recruits from Wales could fight side by side, speaking their own language, and he had gone on to enrage the War Office by demanding that nonconformist ministers be assigned to these regiments, not just Anglican priests. By 1915 Margaret had two sons enlisted in Welsh regiments, and it was a natural step for her to lead a campaign to ensure that they, and all other recruits from Wales, received whatever home comforts could be provided. Thus the Welsh Troops Comforts Fund was created, led from No. 11 not by Lloyd George, but by Margaret.

The first recruit to her new fund was Olwen, who returned from Criccieth to help out. Supported by an able committee, Margaret set up a formidable network of women all over Wales, especially those who had husbands, fathers, brothers or lovers in the armed forces, who formed branches of their own to carry out the Fund's work. The concept was simple: the women knitted scarves, balaclavas and socks, and raised money to buy chocolate and cigarettes. These were all sent to Margaret at No. 11 to send on to the Welsh troops in France. What began as a trickle of parcels soon became a torrent, taking over a whole room in No. 11. Margaret set her helpers to work opening the parcels, sorting their contents and repacking them in larger boxes which would be despatched to France and beyond, wherever Welsh soldiers were serving. Lloyd George had a childlike fascination with parcels, and could not resist poking about in them. Margaret was obliged on more than one occasion to admonish him sharply for untying a carefully wrapped package to examine a pair of khaki socks.

Margaret also used her influence to raise money for the Fund from the wealthy people she now knew, some of whom gave her gifts to sell in lieu of cash. Lord Rhondda's donation of a heifer caused her some amusement, but its sale raised £150 for the Fund. She spent a day selling saving certificates from a tank in London, and was the first woman ever to be allowed to sell flags on the floor of the Stock Exchange. By the end of the war she had collected over £200,000, the equivalent of more than £7 million today, to provide comfort for the troops and assistance for their dependants at home. Raising money was an onerous task, but ensuring that it was spent wisely and appropriately was an even greater one, which Margaret worked at tirelessly. The practical, down-to-earth nature of the scheme reflected her own character. Its success brought her recognition which she did not seek, but which sealed her reputation both in Wales and nationally. The work was to prepare her for the greater task she faced when two years later she moved next door to No. 10, where, in the words of her brother-in-law, 'Maggie showed the world what a home-loving Prime Minister's wife could do.'[27]

14

Secrets and Smokescreens

As Margaret set about forming the Welsh Troops Comforts Fund, her husband's relationship with his mistress was flourishing. Frances too was busy during the war, but while Margaret's work took her away from No. 11 and from Lloyd George, Frances' brought her into closer contact with him. The lovers took every opportunity to spend time together whenever Margaret and the family were looking the other way. During the summer, when Margaret was based in Brynawelon, the opportunities were greater, and Frances recorded in her diary in September 1914: 'I returned from Walton Heath this morning with C.,* after the happiest fortnight of my life. Have been correcting Saturday's speech for publication. The family have returned from Criccieth, and I go home.'[1]

Lloyd George was under tremendous pressure, and this made him irritable at times, even with Frances. An undated letter from this period bears witness to a lovers' tiff:

My darling little girl

I am deeply grieved I spoke so sharply to you this morning & I apologise to you from the bottom of a contrite & loving heart. It was in addition to other faults a distinct breach of faith after the promise I gave

---

* In Frances' diary, Lloyd George is sometimes 'C' for Chancellor and sometimes 'D' for David. After he became Prime Minister he was 'D' from then on. In her memoir he is 'LG'.

you not to worry you. Forgive me darling – because I love you with an inexhaustible affection & tenderness & I care not one jot for the past.

Ever your own,

D.

The letter does not reveal the cause of the quarrel, but something from the past had clearly come between them. Could it have been something to do with Lloyd George's other women? The rumours of his womanising persisted, even though it appears that he was too wrapped up in his new love for Frances to look elsewhere. Early in 1914 he was obliged to send a letter to the *Liverpool Daily Post* protesting his innocence when he was reported to have had dinner in Paris with the celebrated (and beautiful) actress and singer Edna May. 'Perhaps I might as well remind you of what the second paragraph was,' he wrote. 'It stated that I had been seen dining in a restaurant in Paris in the company of Edna May. As a matter of fact, she happened to be one of a large company – but so was her husband. This most important fact is omitted . . . if [the writer] knew it and deliberately omitted it then he must be a downright blackguard.'[2]

Yet Frances had absolute faith in the strength of Lloyd George's love, and her diary reveals her to have been untroubled by his previous dalliances. She believed herself to occupy a unique position in his life, and if anything was sympathetic towards her less fortunate rivals. She certainly felt sorry for Julia Henry, and was even prepared to be magnanimous when Mrs Tim made an occasional appearance: '[Lloyd George] was so busy all day that I scarcely saw him. In the evening he took Mr. & Mrs Timothy Davies out to dinner, she being downhearted as she had not seen him for a long while. I think he is very kind & nice to her, and I would not have it otherwise.'[3]

By 1916 she was a little less happy about his continuing friendship with Mrs Tim, but she tolerated the situation as long as Lloyd George was open about their meetings:

Had a terribly busy day – all of us hard at it from morning till night. D. managed to find time, however, to go to tea with Mrs. Timothy Davies. He does not go there often, but he says she has been a good friend to him, and he does not wish to appear to neglect her. He always

tells me when he is going, so I don't mind so much. I don't care for
her so much – she is too pretentious & I don't think she is very sincere.
However, I don't like to think badly of D.'s friends, as I like to think
that he has good taste![4]

As Frances worked in Lloyd George's office and had access to his diary,
it is difficult to envisage how he could have concealed his visits to Mrs
Tim from her, but he was adept at turning situations to his advantage,
and Frances was prepared to believe his every word, even when he was
on shaky ground. Returning from a trip to Paris in 1915, he proudly
presented her with a gift: 'C. has brought me back the sweetest little
brooch – diamonds – & a big sapphire – from Paris. He said he spent
all his spare time walking the streets to find something to bring me home.
It gives him such intense pleasure to give presents and he was so pleased
with this one. It was sweet to watch him.'[5]

This was naïve even by Frances' standards. When she first met J.T.
Davies at the Treasury in 1913 he was about to get married, and one of
her first tasks was to buy him a wedding present from Lloyd George:
'Will you go to Carrington's Regent St & buy something nice to give
him for me,' he wrote. 'Ask them to send it to the Treasury for me.'[6]
Despite this and other examples of Lloyd George's habit of delegating
personal matters, Frances always steadfastly believed that his presents
to *her* were bought personally, and marvelled at how he could find time
in his busy schedule to visit shops. After describing her Parisian brooch,
she goes on to display further credulousness:

> He was very annoyed yesterday, however, over a paragraph in the
> Sunday papers to the effect that 'Mr Lloyd George, after a hard day's
> work in Paris, drove to the Latin quarter in the evening to see what
> life there during war time was like'. C. was furious, as he never went
> near the Latin quarter the whole time he was there, & he says it is
> exactly as if a Russian paper made the announcement that 'M. Bark,
> (the Russian finance Minister) while in London, after a hard day's
> work, spent his evening in Leicester Square.[7]

Frances could on the one hand believe that Lloyd George had spent his
evenings 'walking the streets' to buy her presents, and on the other that

those wanderings had not taken him anywhere near the notorious Latin quarter. It was fortunate for him that his mistress was not the suspicious type.

Could the cause of the quarrel referred to in his undated note have been *his* jealousy? Frances did not have much past history with men, but we know that Stuart Brown, who had proposed to her in Scotland over Christmas and New Year 1912–13, had not given up hope of marrying her. He renewed his suit in November 1914, using his sister Dorothy as a go-between. Dorothy asked Frances whether her feelings for Stuart had changed at all. Her reply was sympathetic but unrelenting: 'I told her that I had not changed my mind. I cannot explain how things really are, but feel that I am doing right in refusing to see him, since he may forget & marry someone else. I am sorry he is unhappy.'[8]

Unreasonable as it may have been, Lloyd George was acutely aware of how attractive his young mistress was, and became jealous of any man who paid her attention. Frances knew this, and although utterly devoted to him, she was not above reminding him occasionally that she had other options. During these first years of their 'marriage' there was no real prospect of her being unfaithful, but tension existed nevertheless, as each judged the other by their own standards. Frances, confident in her first love, was certain of Lloyd George's fidelity, whereas he was not so sure of hers. By early 1916 he was warning her against 'naughty' behaviour when they were apart, and he would continue to refer semi-jokingly to her flirting with other men behind his back.

Frances calculated that Lloyd George made twenty-two major speeches between January 1913 and November 1914. She had worked on every one, gathering and checking information, working on drafts and proofreading. When he spoke in the House of Commons she would be there to provide moral support and to send the expected little note of praise afterwards. There is no record of whether she and Margaret ever attended the same parliamentary occasions, but there must have been a good chance that they did.

Working side by side with her lover every day of the week and most weekends, Frances was truly happy. Lloyd George was working long hours under tremendous pressure, but Frances could be with him and help ease his burden. Even though the time they could spend together privately was limited, the stimulation of working together in a time of national crisis was some compensation, and forged a strong bond between them.

For his part, Lloyd George was managing to divide his time between family and Frances without much difficulty. The heavy demands of his position made it easier for him to spend time away from home even when Margaret was in London, and he was adept at covering his tracks. As for Frances, he showed himself again to be a master at handling her. Whenever he had to – or chose to – spend time away from her he would point to his neglect of his family, or the unbearable pressure of his work, and Frances immediately and unquestioningly fell in with his plans. If he felt he had to put in an appearance in Wales, he would tell Frances that spending time with Margaret in Criccieth was 'duty', a façade he had to maintain for the sake of his career. This had the advantage of being true, but it was not the whole truth, for he was extremely fond of his family and enjoyed a close relationship with his wife even during these first years of his relationship with Frances. He needed, and wanted, them both.

This required careful handling of Frances so that she would not make more demands on him than he could fulfil. In his letters he made it clear to her that she was closer to him than anyone else, and came first in his heart (though never in his life). For example, in August 1915 he wrote her a carefully worded letter to excuse the fact that he was delaying seeing her privately for two days after returning from a holiday in Criccieth. Addressed to 'My own sweet little Pussy', it is supremely skilful in its manipulation of her. He begins by making a declaration of love in the strongest terms: 'I am longing to be back with you. I am becoming more intolerant of these partings month by month. I cannot live now without my darling. I know that better even than I did weeks ago. It is either you or nothing for me Cariad.' He then enlists her sympathy by claiming to have had a miserable time in Wales before coming to the point:

Now Pussy I have made up my mind to disappoint myself – & you. I have two days of most important & trying work in front of me – conferences & decisions upon which the success of the Department depend & I must reserve all my strength for them. I know you will agree. Wednesday we can go to Walton. Meanwhile help me to restrain myself – or I am lost for my passion for you is a consuming flame – it burns up all wisdom prudence & judgement in my soul. Help me cariad bach annwyl aur [dear little golden love].*

I feel as if during the last two months I have not given my very best to the terrible task entrusted to me. My future depends entirely on it. What is much more important – the nation's future depends on it. The distracting events of the past few weeks have half paralysed me & I must pull myself together. I cannot do so without your wise help. You are everything to me now. My failure or success will depend entirely on you. You possess my soul entirely . . .

Oh I do want to see you – I want you & no one & nothing else.

Your own D. – for ever[9]

The romantic, naïve Frances thrilled at his words and swallowed them whole. She seemed happy with her lot, providing she received constant reassurance that Lloyd George's heart belonged to her alone. By way of compensation, her exciting new job kept her occupied, and the thrill of being at the centre of political life had not faded. The war must have had an effect on her state of mind too: it was more natural to live one day at a time when the future was uncertain. She took on some Red Cross work on top of her already heavy schedule as a way of 'doing her bit', and generally kept herself busy when Lloyd George was elsewhere.

On 17 January 1915, two years after their secret 'marriage', Frances wrote an ecstatic entry in her diary:

I fear my diary has got very behindhand. The last three weeks have been so busy and happy that I have not had the opportunity for writing things down. C. returned from Wales on Dec. 29th and from then till now I have been with him at [Walton Heath], coming up every day to town, & going back in the evening. It has been like an idyll, but alas! came to an end yesterday, when the family returned from Criccieth, & I returned home. The longer we are together, the more our love and

---

* In his letters to Frances, Lloyd George often strings together Welsh endearments, usually involving the words 'cariad' (love/darling), 'bach' (little/dear), 'aur' (gold), 'cusan' (kiss) and 'mel' (honey). It is doubtful that she understood them, but no doubt she got the drift.

affection seems to increase, so that it is all the more difficult to part. But we have resolved not to be miserable at parting, for 'my true love hath my heart, & I have his' and happy memories will buoy us up till 'the next time'.[10]

The happiness she felt was to be short-lived. Within a few weeks the consequences of their idyllic fortnight together became apparent, as she began to suspect that she was pregnant. By the end of February she was feeling very ill, and there follows a significant gap in her diary, which she resumes on 11 March with the words, 'The last fortnight has been too dreary and unhappy to write of.'[11]

The published form of her diary is heavily edited, since Frances was still alive at the time of its publication, but from the original manuscript it is possible to piece together what happened during those miserable days. In late February she told her mother that she was pregnant. It seems that at first she envisaged keeping the child, and furthermore that she believed Lloyd George was as happy as she was: 'C and I have wanted for so long to have a child, and we thought this week that our wish was about to be realised.'[12]

Unlikely as it seems that Lloyd George would have contemplated the risk involved in having a child with Frances at this stage of his career, she nevertheless chose to blame her mother for what followed: 'But when I told Mama of what was going to happen she was terribly upset and is still. She says she would rather see me dead than that such a thing should happen. She has raised all sorts of issues to persuade me, but behind it all is the spectre of respectability which haunts her with horrible pictures of what can happen to "disgraced" women.'

Between Louise's conventional outlook and her mistrust of Lloyd George, and Frances' extreme romanticism, there was no room for understanding:

[Mama] does not think it possible for a woman to give a child to the man she loves, but who is unable to marry her, and still be happy and willing to face the criticism of the world. She does not understand that if anything happened to C my only chance of happiness would be for me to have someone to remind me of him, and to whom I can devote my life. She can only think of the wickedness of it, his wickedness she calls it, and will not understand that our only fault is that we love each other too well and that where love is, the greatest trials can be sustained.

Even allowing for Frances' distress and her emotional condition, she was being staggeringly unrealistic. She goes on to claim that it is her mother's view of the world that is distorted:

> If she would only look at things clearly and judge the facts fairly! But she will not – there is one part of her which has never come out into the clear light – which may not do so, in case the futility of conventions should be revealed and the crippling bonds of middle-class routine be weakened. She does not understand that I would be proud to have his child and would be willing to suffer for it, nay I should glory in suffering, rather than die childless – I would suffer so that the child should not. I would spend my life so that he might be happy and I would brave the coldness of the world, for I know there are some friends who would stand by me, and I should not be entirely alone.

Frances eventually faces the fact that her dreams will come to nothing this time: 'But it is not to be. I fear if I insisted upon this, she would be so upset that people would see what had happened and I cannot be responsible for the ruin of C's career.'

In implying that she could have gone ahead and had Lloyd George's child if not for her mother's emotional state, Frances was surely deluding herself. There would be many things that might have given the game away, chief among them her advancing pregnancy, but her mother's tears would surely not in themselves constitute evidence to connect it with her employer.

Had Frances asked Louise to help her hide the pregnancy? It was not unusual for mothers to hide their daughters' disgrace under the guise of an unexpected late pregnancy, and for grandparents to raise their grandchildren as their own. Could that have been the strategy that Frances devised, but that Louise's outrage made impossible? But Frances' declared willingness to face the criticism of the world suggests that she envisaged having the child openly, without subterfuge, concealing only the identity of the father.

The passage that follows in Frances' diary makes it clear that she was in a state of considerable mental turmoil: 'And then too, my love for Mama makes me hesitate from hurting her too much. I hate myself for inflicting this upon her, and I fear that the wound is a deep one. C. says that in love lies do not pass for such, just as in war killing is not called murder. But the long and short of it is, that much as I love Mama and Dada, I love C better and will never leave him, and am impelled to put everything else subordinate to his love.'

Again, this is a curious passage. Frances does not explain the connection between her mother's hurt and Lloyd George's justification of lying when love is concerned. Could she have lied to Louise about the circumstances of her pregnancy? Is it possible that despite the risks, she and Lloyd George had been trying for a baby – or at least not taking precautions? Later in life Frances told her daughter Jennifer with feeling that 'precautions are never one hundred percent reliable', and her granddaughter's interpretation, that the precautions Frances was taking at the time did not work because she did not really want them to, has a ring of truth about it.

Whether or not the pregnancy was accidental, it became clear to the distraught Frances that she could not continue with it:

But the idea of our love child will have to go for the time being. I fear too, that I shall not be able to stay at home after this, for Dada does not yet know what has happened and I do not know what his attitude will be. I dread hurting him, but one thing is certain. I cannot give C up.

I can't help <u>hating</u> myself for making Mama so miserable. The thought haunts me all day long, and I would do anything to prevent it. But what <u>can</u> I do? Some years ago Harold Spender [a journalist who acted as Lloyd George's unofficial press man] said to C 'You are the most lonely man I know.' I think I have changed all that now, & I cannot think that I have done wrong. I am not vicious or evil, and my only fault, in this matter and his, is love. 'Love justifies many audacities'. I think the justification for these audacities is the length of love's duration & I know C. and I belong to each other for ever. I should be so happy were it not for the fact that I am causing unhappiness to two people whom I love and who have been so good & loving to me.[13]

Frances' troubles were far from over, as she now had to deal with the consequences of her decision. Previous commentators have variously suggested that she might have suffered a miscarriage, or miscalculated her dates and found that she was not pregnant after all, but her use of the words 'our love child will have to go' can surely only bear the meaning that she intended to bring the pregnancy to an end, as she later confirmed privately, telling her daughter that she had had not one but two abortions in the early years of her relationship with Lloyd George.

The trauma of ending the pregnancy she had longed for was difficult enough for Frances, but the practical arrangements for doing so were also far from easy. Abortion and self-induced miscarriage had been illegal in England since the passing of the uncompromising 1861 Abortion Act, and would remain so until the 1960s. Marie Stopes, the pioneer in England on this issue, set up her first Mothers' Clinic in London in 1921, having published her controversial book *Married Love* in 1918. In the preceding decade, for women in Frances' situation there was simply no legal way to get help or even to get reliable information on either contraception or abortion. Sympathetic family doctors were extremely difficult to find – even in the 1920s, most who were prepared to talk about birth control insisted on speaking to the husband alone, and advising an unmarried woman was out of the question. A study in 1914, a year before Frances' dilemma, found that 100,000 women a year in England with unwanted pregnancies took drugs or used other means to induce miscarriage rather than seek medical help.

The Church and state continued to hold all contraception and abortion to be sinful and therefore forbidden, but the fall in the population numbers suggests that the illegal practice of birth control was nonetheless spreading. Common practice included the use of sheaths and douches for contraceptive purposes, together with the use of sponges soaked in vinegar or other acidic fluids. By 1914, fairly reliable rubber sheaths were sold in barbers' shops or via carefully-worded newspaper advertisements, as were some forms of rubber caps. For working-class women who could not afford these measures, home-made pessaries of lard, margarine, flour, cocoa-butter and quinine had been used as a last-ditch measure since the 1890s. For those who took their religion seriously, abstinence was the only sanctioned alternative to endless childbearing, although coitus interruptus and variations of the rhythm method were also in use. Unless couples were prepared to risk prosecution, abstention or withdrawal were their only options to prevent conception.

Induced abortion or miscarriage was considered to be a perfectly valid alternative, and there is considerable evidence to suggest that even as late as 1937 working-class women at least did not consider self-induced miscarriage before twelve weeks to be the same as abortion; some did not even know that it was illegal. Traditionally, it was thought that a foetus could only be *aborted* after the 'quickening', which happened at the end of the third month. Before then, if women took measures to end a suspected pregnancy, it was talked of in terms of bringing on a late period, or of 'making themselves regular' again. Measures in common use included jumping down stairs, taking hot baths, drinking gin and, for the more desperate, swallowing violent purgatives like penny royal or using compounds of aloes and iron, phosphorus from the ends of matches and slippery elm. Advertisements appeared in the press for pills for women to 'restore regularity', but these carried a double danger. Not only were they dangerous, but unscrupulous vendors sometimes followed up an order with a blackmail demand, threatening to expose their customers for inducing a miscarriage. Backstreet abortionists used salves and potions or inserted instruments like knitting needles to bring the pregnancy to an end. In the days before reliable antiseptics were available, this was a grim prospect. For those with the means to pay for it, a doctor might be bribed, or a clinic in another country might be an option, but there was no escaping the deception and sordidness involved.

Frances was, understandably, not forthcoming in her diary about which course of action she chose, for what she was doing was both illegal and shameful. The whole subject of sex was still strictly taboo in respectable Edwardian households. The typical middle-class girl of the time was often in complete ignorance of the facts of life until her wedding night. Marie Stopes herself had been married for a year before she realised that her husband was impotent, and she claimed her marriage was unconsummated. Olwen Lloyd George herself was to walk down the aisle in 1917 without any advice at all on the subject.

When she later asked her mother to explain this omission, Margaret replied, 'Oh, well, you were marrying a doctor, so I thought it was all right.'[14]

Frances was not quite in this category. Perhaps her French mother was more forthcoming, or perhaps she had picked up some useful information at university. In May 1915 she wrote in her diary of an old college friend who 'on her marriage day knew absolutely nothing of what was expected from a wife to her husband on marriage. The consequence was that she was frightened & unhappy, & the revelations which came to her that day did not tend to make the first 48 hours of their wedding go as smoothly as would have been the case had she been more prepared.'[15]

As well as the need for emotional support, there may have been more practical reasons why Frances confided in her mother at the time of her 'marriage' to Lloyd George, and why she did so again when she was confronted with a pregnancy. The way in which she expresses her decision – 'the idea of our love child will have to go' – as if she could end the pregnancy just by changing her mind about it, suggests that she did not think of her action as abortion *per se*. But the wording is consistent with the prevailing idea that a woman could put an end to a pregnancy before life had taken hold. Frances had an additional motive for secrecy in that she risked utter disaster if her identity, and through that the identity of the child's father, ever became known. She needed help to end her pregnancy, and since her mother was her only confidante, it is likely that Louise had to come to her daughter's rescue.

Whatever means she chose to terminate her pregnancy, Frances found the episode highly distressing, and was ill and depressed for some time afterwards. Her parents were furious with Lloyd George, and tried every argument to get her to leave him. She was reaching the end of her tether:

> They do not understand – they will never understand – they do not see that our love is pure and lasting – they think I am his plaything & that he will fling me aside when he has finished with me – or else they think that there will be a scandal and that we shall all be disgraced ... I fear that in the end I shall have to leave home, for they will never

cease to urge their views upon me, & it will be almost intolerable. Besides which, they will never speak of C. except in unfriendly & contemptuous tones & that I will not endure.[16]

With sympathy in short supply at home, Lloyd George installed Frances at Walton Heath, where she was nursed back to health by Sarah.

Lloyd George himself was prone to hypochondria, and according to Frances always imagined himself to be ill if someone commented that he did not look well. As a consequence he was particularly squeamish when those close to him were ill. The rare exception had been when Margaret suffered her miscarriages, after which he was unusually caring. In Frances' case, it was the same:

> C. insisted that I should come down here & have absolute rest for a few days & be free from worrying surroundings. I agreed to this all the more willingly as I could see that C. was making himself ill through worrying about me – several times I thought he was on the point of breaking down; but he has been better since I have been down here & have shown signs of recovering. I do not think I can ever repay him for his goodness to me the last fortnight or three weeks. He has been husband, lover & mother to me. I never knew a man could be so womanly & tender. He has watched and waited on me devotedly, until I cursed myself for being ill & causing him all this worry. There was no little thing that he did not think of for my comfort, no tenderness that he did not lavish on me. I have indeed known the full extent of his love.[17]

Frances dwells on her own guilt to such an extent that she fails to see the guilt evident in Lloyd George's behaviour. He had fulfilled the Stevensons' worst expectations and put their daughter through a dangerous and shameful experience. But her love was so strong that she saw only the praiseworthy aspects of his behaviour. The effect of the episode was to bring them closer together than ever before, but it had driven home the reality of their situation. Frances wanted badly to bear Lloyd George's child, but could no longer pretend to herself that it was possible for her to do so without endangering his career. He was discovering the danger inherent in his double life and the disadvantages of choosing a single woman as his mistress, since such incidents could not be passed off discreetly. Out of these realisations came a bizarre scheme to provide them with additional cover – by arranging for Frances to get married to someone else.

The plan seems to have been entirely Lloyd George's brainchild. On a purely intellectual level, it made sense. The lovers had been shocked out of their complacency by Frances' pregnancy, and there was a considerable risk that she might fall pregnant again in future. Given her professed desire for children and Lloyd George's fondness for his own, any arrangement that would allow her to bear his child respectably, if not honestly, would be a good thing. Added to this, if she married a tolerant and worldly husband who would not place too many demands on her and who would respect her relationship with Lloyd George, it would make their relationship more acceptable to those who needed to know; they would be 'playing the game'.

The obvious first step was to find a man who was willing to marry Frances and to comply with the conditions attached. He would have to assume the outward appearance of a husband, to shield Frances from gossip and suspicion, but agree to refrain from interfering with her relationship with Lloyd George in any way. The delicate issue of whether Frances would be 'married' to her husband in the same way that she was 'married' to Lloyd George was left unanswered, but given her devotion to her lover, it would seem unlikely that normal marital relations were to be part of the deal (Frances said later in life that she thought sex was 'overrated'). The option of finding a husband who was ignorant of the true relationship between her and Lloyd George was dismissed early on. Lloyd George fully understood the difficulties Frances would face in managing such a situation – her husband would be bound to demand more from her than she wanted to give – and he found both the possibility of her giving way and the alternative of lying distasteful. He decided that Frances' husband would have to know the truth from the outset.

What could possibly motivate anyone to take on this role? One possibility was to find a man who was genuinely in love with Frances, and who would want her hand in marriage at any price. The other was to find a man whose ambition was strong enough for him to accept the deal offered in return for the professional advancement Lloyd George could give him. The latter option was deemed best, and luckily there was a suitable candidate available.

The man to whom Frances was briefly engaged was William Hugh Owen. Their relationship was entirely one of convenience, on her side at least, and does not merit a mention in her autobiography. She also expunged all mention of him from her diary before it was published; but from the unpublished manuscript and her correspondence with Lloyd George emerges a partial but decipherable account of the attempt to find a respectable and compliant sham-husband for her.

Captain Billy Owen served in the Royal Engineers, coincidentally the same regiment as Dick Lloyd George. A Welshman, he was assigned a government job, as liaison officer between the Ministry of Munitions, a new department created in 1915 and headed by Lloyd George, and the War Office. Little is known of his early life, apart from the facts that he worked as the stationmaster at Holyhead before joining up and that he played hockey for Wales. The first mention of his name in connection with Frances occurs in a letter from Lloyd George in August 1915. The casualness of the reference indicates that the plan had been discussed between them, and also – more surprisingly perhaps – with J.T. Davies, who appeared to be the go-between sent to sound out Owen on the subject: 'I've had a talk with D[avies]. His view is that O. is moved by a consuming desire to get on. That is the line. I believe he would do it unconditionally. There is peril & pollution in any other course. I love my *pure* little darling.'[18]

Frances would have known Owen through her work, and the two liked each other – but not enough to rouse Lloyd George's jealousy. Over the next few weeks Lloyd George managed to bring them together to test the proposed relationship when Owen spent a weekend at Walton Heath. This trial run was clearly satisfactory, for an 'arrangement' was agreed upon and an engagement was formed between Frances and Owen. It seems that Frances was prepared at first to go along with the marriage, but she soon reconsidered: 'I cannot marry Owen. I have told him so & broken off the engagement. It did not last very long!'

Her reasons? Not that she herself was unhappy at the thought of marrying another man, but that Lloyd George disliked the idea. 'D. was making himself miserable over the idea of my belonging to someone else even in name. Several times he had cried & sobbed as a child when speaking of it, begging me all the time to take no notice of him. But I could not bear to give him pain, & I know that he is relieved now that I have broken it off.'[19]

The scene Frances paints of a distraught Lloyd George arranging her marriage to another man while imploring her to ignore his tears is farcical. But even if she was taken in by his blatantly manipulative behaviour, she had clearly thought about the practical implications of the proposed marriage, and realised that whatever agreement she had with her husband, tying the knot with another man would inevitably weaken the bond between her and Lloyd George. Also, in contemplating the marriage her contempt for Owen had grown: 'I must be free to be with [Lloyd George] always, & marriage I know would forge new bonds. Owen is very upset, but wishes to be friends still. He is very weak, and a very little satisfies him.'[20]

In October 1915 Frances was about to move out of her parents' house and set up her own home for the first time. The stated reason was that her parents were moving to Wallington in South London, and she would need a flat in town to avoid the daily commute, but this was no doubt the excuse she needed to escape her mother's constant vigilance. Frances found a small but highly convenient flat to rent at 41A Chester Square, Belgravia, a smart address and, more importantly, within walking distance of the House of Commons. She maximised her freedom by sharing it with Mary Phillips, formerly a teacher at Allenswood, who returned to the school in 1916 and was thus absent for much of the time. Frances enjoyed furnishing the flat and making it comfortable.* The two friends could afford servants to look after them, and they enjoyed a lively social life when Mary was not at school and Frances could not be with Lloyd George.

Perhaps Frances was reluctant to give up this freedom, or perhaps she realised how much easier it would be – even without a husband –

---

* She was helped financially by Lloyd George, at least to the tune of some furnishings including a Napoleon clock and two candlesticks which he bought her in France. He may or may not have subsidised her more directly as well.

to carry on her relationship with Lloyd George now that they had a convenient bolthole near Westminster. Either way, she was rapidly going off the idea of marrying Owen just as he, it seems, was forming a serious attachment to her, or at least an attachment to the benefits that marrying her would bring.

On 11 October he wrote her a letter that suggests he was not going to let her slip away easily:

My dear Miss Stevenson
The right to address a more intimate salutation is one I would fain possess. As it is my pen almost committed me, but fear of incurring your displeasure coupled with the thought that the state of, well, shall we say 'benevolent neutrality' which you now graciously extend to me hardly warranted such a liberty deterred me. Some day – well some day you may feel disposed to extend to me the privilege.[21]

In some alarm, it would seem, Frances wrote back to pour more cold water on his ardour, and to repeat her decision not to proceed with the engagement. In reply she got a curious letter from Owen, using the 'more intimate salute' that he had not dared to use previously, suggesting that a third party (Lloyd George, or J.T. Davies on his Chief's instructions, perhaps?) may have tried to resurrect the plan:

My dear Frances
. . . As you say, the present state of affairs is very unsatisfactory and cannot be allowed to continue indefinitely . . . Please do not think that I write in a spirit of recrimination but rather with a desire to put to you the matter from my point of view . . .

You say that, first of all having agreed with you that our engagement should be at an end I subsequently said that I came to this agreement against my will. A brief review of matters will explain my position. Your letter breaking off our engagement was couched in very definite language . . . You did not then suggest that any action of mine had caused you to write, but very decidedly stated that 'you could not proceed with the arrangement that we had come to at Walton Heath because you were fully convinced that such an arrangement would only bring unhappiness to all concerned etc.' . . .

Subsequently, however, a remark let fall by one for whom I in common with you have the deepest regard, generated the hope that some action of mine upon which you had placed a wrong construction had influenced you in arriving at the decision you had taken. Your letter strengthens this hope, for it implies want of keenness on my part. Such is not the case. My apparent inattention during the days immediately preceding the rupture was due to causes entirely beyond my control . . . All I ask is that you give me a chance to explain.[22]

Owen got his chance, and the relationship was resumed on a cautious footing, fully encouraged by Lloyd George, who had undergone one of his characteristic changes of heart. 'D is now on the marriage tack again,' wrote Frances. 'He says that there are many advantages to be gained by marriage <u>provided that Owen understands clearly</u> what <u>our relations are</u>, & promises to respect them. Am dining with Owen tonight to discuss the matter.'[23]

Lloyd George was particularly worried about the threat of discovery at this time. He wrote defiantly to Frances: 'There is much satisfaction in "doing" the world! I have defied it for 25 years – treated it with contempt, spat upon its tinsel robes, and I have won through. If you pay homage to it in certain things, you can defy it in others as much as you like.' But his words were a gesture to hide the fact that he had decided that he could not risk letting Frances drive down with him to Walton Heath any longer. Their custom had been for him to signal her to leave the Treasury office in Whitehall a few minutes before him, and to be picked up at the far side of the House of Lords, away from prying eyes, but from now on she travelled alone by train.

In resurrecting the marriage plan, Lloyd George was taking care of Frances, protecting her reputation and giving her the respectability of a good marriage. Yet there was something deeply distasteful about the scheme. Although there were benefits for Frances, in the main the advantage was all his: the marriage would add another smokescreen to hide his relationship with Frances, and would lessen the risk of scandal if she fell pregnant again – all without sacrificing his first place in her life. For Owen also, the advantage was clear: he would be doing his 'Chief' a great favour, and could expect to be rewarded. The price demanded was that he would at best have to share Frances with Lloyd George, and at worst that he would have to accept a purely platonic relationship with her – at least until such time as Lloyd George moved on to another mistress or put an end to the affair. Since it seems that Owen was keener in his pursuit of Frances than was strictly necessary, perhaps he thought this would inevitably happen, and that he would then take the Chief's place in her life. If so, he was a poor judge of the female character. Frances, with her taste for powerful men, was unlikely ever to fall for such a submissive specimen as him. But this was wartime, and people did not dare think too far ahead. The long-term complications of such an arrangement might not have seemed to matter very much when young men were leaving for France every day, never to return.

But what of Frances? She was certainly in a position to gain from marrying Owen. Quite apart from hiding her true position from the world, it would mean an end to awkward questions from inquisitive friends, and it would also have been a relief and comfort to her mother, making Frances' life at home much easier. The main advantage, though, was that she could finally have Lloyd George's children without threatening his career. For many women this alone would have been a decisive factor, but Frances proved oddly ambivalent about the idea. Looking back on this period in early 1916, she wrote in her diary:

[D] said he has been thinking, all the way to Chester Square, of how he wished he could marry me. But we both agreed that we must put that thought out of our minds, for it only leads to bitterness and discontent, and sometimes to injustice and folly. However, he has sworn to marry me if he ever finds himself in a position to do so, & I am content with that. Not that I wished him to promise it, for I am happy as we are – we have our little home now, where we can spend many evenings together in solitude – and how sweet the evenings are! The only thing we lack is children, but I often think that if I were married & had children, then I should not be able to keep in touch with D.'s work to the extent that I do now, & perhaps should be less happy. At present all our interests lie together; he does nothing but what I know of it; I almost know his very thoughts. I don't suppose I should see nearly as much of him if I were married to him.[24]

In other words, she could only contemplate having children with Lloyd George if it was openly, in marriage. Even then, she was a little hesitant about the prospect, for if she was married to Owen she would be expected to give up her job, and then how could she retain her main advantage over Margaret by being part of her lover's all-important work? Frances' priorities were clear: Lloyd George held the first place in her life, and he would come first, ahead of any children.

In the end, whatever Frances' reservations might have been, the scheme was scuppered by Lloyd George himself. The renewed engagement had lingered on until November 1915, when Frances made a seemingly decisive entry in her diary: 'I have come to the conclusion that D. needs all my energies and devotion, and I think that marriage might bring an element of worry and unhappiness into his life, even on the most favourable terms (to him). Owen & I are therefore not engaged & I have not seen him for some time.'[25]

Yet Frances was still keeping up the pretence of an engagement in public, even to her family. With any serious idea of marriage between them put aside for good, the astonishingly compliant Owen was yet happy to act the part of Frances' devoted fiancé. He accompanied her and Lloyd George on a trip to Eastbourne in January 1916, and kept up contact with her to the extent that a rumour was started in May 1916, apparently by Frances' flatmate Mary Phillips, that the couple were about to marry. It is most unlikely that Mary was ignorant of the true state of affairs, and it is difficult to envisage the circumstances that could have led her to commit such a blunder. Congratulations flooded in from friends and acquaintances, and Frances must have been highly embarrassed as she had to explain that no wedding was planned. And yet she *still* did not break off the public appearance of an engagement. She maintained a fitful correspondence with Owen throughout the rest of the year, and only formally ended the engagement in February 1917, much to her family's disappointment. It seems that they had believed the engagement was genuine. Her mother's letter is full of concern:

> My darling,
> I was very sorry to get your letter this morning but not surprised. I have known all along that you did not care sufficiently for Owen to marry him – the pity is that you ever engaged yourself to him.

However, I am quite of the opinion that it is quite right not to go on with it if you feel as you say – I must admit that I had looked forward to your being married to a good man who really cared for you, & that I am sure Owen does – however, least said, soonest mended . . .

I have known that your heart was not in this engagement for some long time, but as you did not say anything to me I did not like to force your confidence, but you must know my darling, how much your happiness is to both Dada and myself.

Will you be coming home before Saty, I should like to see you. Muriel was very upset.[26]

Owen was subsequently posted to Canada, and ended the war as a Ministry of Munitions official for purchasing ships in Canada. He married in 1919, and played no further role in Frances' life.

In May 1915, prompted by lack of success on the war front and by First Sea Lord Admiral Lord Fisher's resignation on 15 May over the disastrous Dardanelles campaign, Asquith had finally given in to Lloyd George and others who had been urging the formation of a coalition government. Bonar Law, Balfour and other leading Conservatives were appointed to the Cabinet, and Asquith's close ally Viscount Haldane and Winston Churchill cast out to make way for them. In addition, Lloyd George had been seeking a bigger role in the management of the war, and was ready to resign if he did not get it. The role he eventually secured, Minister of Munitions in charge of equipping the armed forces, might have seemed like a demotion, but he felt it was of crucial importance to the success of the campaign, and was even willing to step down from his position as Chancellor to do the job, which both Uncle Lloyd and Margaret thought unwise. A deal was brokered with Asquith which allowed him to take the job for a limited period of time, while Reginald McKenna filled in for him at the Treasury, on the understanding that Lloyd George would eventually return to his job as Chancellor. Much to Margaret's relief, the deal included staying on at No. 11.

The first two members of staff of the new Ministry of Munitions were Lloyd George's faithful lieutenants J.T. Davies and Frances. As they looked around their new quarters at 6 Whitehall Gardens, two removal men arrived and attempted to take away the only furniture in the room. It was to be the first of many battles the two of them would fight together.

Shortly after taking up his new job, at the end of an exhausting day, Lloyd George decided to cheer up his two weary troops by taking them with him as he dined with friends and then went on to see J.M. Barrie's new play *Rosy Rapture, the Pride of the Beauty Chorus*. During the last act JT was called out, and on his return to their box he quietly passed a message to Lloyd George. There was nothing unusual in this, and it was only after the play had ended, when Lloyd George asked Frances to return with him to No. 11, that she began to suspect something was wrong. Once there, he broke the news to her that her younger brother Paul had died of his wounds in France at the age of nineteen. Frances was numbed by the news, and Lloyd George was care itself as he took her back to her parents' house to find them 'in desperate need of comfort',[27] her father weeping openly for the first time in front of his daughters.

Paul's death was a bitter blow to the Stevenson family. He had won an exhibition to St John's College, Oxford, having won a gold medal for Greek and Latin composition at his school, Christ's Hospital, and as soon as war broke out he had joined up and obtained a commission. He was sent to France in March 1915, and was killed before he had the chance to return home on leave. Frances' naïvety about war is revealed by the fact that she had convinced herself that someone as blessed and golden as her brother could not simply be taken away so abruptly. His death brought it forcibly home to her that when her lover spoke of the sacrifice necessary to win the war, he was not doing so rhetorically.

Paul's death, on top of her pregnancy, made 1915 the most difficult year of Frances' life so far. Her mother was distraught, and gave her clearly to understand that she would have preferred any of her daughters to be sacrificed in Paul's place. Frances' diary is silent for weeks afterwards, with one exception when she recorded Paul's memorial service at his old school:

A year ago today we were down at Christ's Hospital for the last prize-giving that Paul would partake in as a member of the school. We were so proud of him & of all the honours that fell to him. Today we have been taking part in a Memorial Service for him & others of the 23rd London, who have fallen recently in France. Even now it seems incredible that he is dead – that he will never return. It is the first time that I have experienced the death of one who was dear to me, & the hopelessness of it all has thrown a shadow over my life that I do not believe can ever disappear. The nobility of his death takes away some of the bitterness, and the many tributes that we have received from all who ever knew him. But all our hopes and plans have come to nothing, though I know he would have wished for no better end than this. He was so terribly eager to get to the firing line, but I did not worry about him, for it seemed to me that he at least would come safely back, that death at least would spare one so promising & so dear and necessary to us. The shock came cruelly, & has numbed my brain, & the consolation seems to be little for so terrible a loss. They say that time will heal the wounds, & leave only pride instead of grief, but how can we ever do anything but miss him and need him more and more as the years go on?[28]

The manner in which Frances was told of her brother's death is significant, in that it provides further evidence that JT was in on the secret of her relationship with Lloyd George. Indeed, it was becoming known to an increasing number of people, most of whom were happy to play the game. One of these, and by now a key member of Lloyd George's inner circle, was George Riddell, whose insatiable curiosity soon unearthed Frances' secret. But there were also those who did not approve of Frances' role in Lloyd George's life. One of those was Lucy Masterman, wife of Lloyd George's political colleague Charles Masterman, who had been house guests at Criccieth during the summer of 1911 when Lloyd George had so impressed the young Frances. In August 1916 Frances accompanied Lloyd George to a private showing of films taken of the brutal Somme battle. She was becoming used to moving in the highest government circles, and was, as ever, keen that her special status in Lloyd George's life be tacitly acknowledged: 'There were few people there, most of them well known people. Most of them exceedingly kind and nice: all except Mrs. Masterman, whom D & I both thought rather aloof and cold. Probably she disapproves of our relations, for she most surely knows, & what would be winked at between a celebrity & a society woman must not be tolerated between D. & his private secretary!'[29]

The danger inherent in the affair becoming more widely known was that Margaret would find out. The evidence shows that she did seem to be aware – or at least to suspect – when her husband developed a lasting relationship with another woman, like Mrs Tim, for example. Whether she knew the precise nature of those relationships is less clear, but with the passage of time it seems that – with painful difficulty – she accepted the inevitability of Lloyd George's attraction to other women, and believed that while he might flirt with other women, she alone held a permanent place in his life.

It was only a matter of time before Margaret began to suspect that Frances was the current object of her husband's attentions. It is unclear when the idea first occurred to her, but it is highly unlikely that she was fully aware of how deep the affair ran. It is inconceivable that she would have accepted her husband keeping a mistress. She still bridled at any suggestion of Lloyd George's infidelity, and in March 1916 a row ensued when she caught him speaking to Frances on the telephone. Frances gleefully recorded in her diary: 'D. got into trouble the other day at [Walton Heath]. Mrs. Ll.G. was outside the door while he was talking to me on the telephone, & took him severely to task. "I know very well whom you would marry if anything happened to me," she said. D. tried to laugh it off, but he says she knows very well that his affection for me is real.'[30]

While the first part of this passage is very credible, the second is less so. Clearly, Frances was recording Lloyd George's version of events, and he was only too happy to assure her that even Margaret accepted that she was a permanent part of his life. But while Frances rejoiced at the evidence that Lloyd George was serious about her, Margaret's words actually reveal the extent of her confidence that he would never leave her during her lifetime. 'I know very well whom you would marry *if* anything happened to me': these are not the words of an insecure woman, or one who thinks her husband is in love with someone else. Margaret knew full well that her husband's political ambitions ruled out a divorce. She also knew that he needed her, and still loved her. But her words also reflect an awareness that Frances, if not a threat, had caught Lloyd George's eye. His reaction in 'laughing off' the incident was entirely typical of his behaviour when cornered. He was behaving as he always had done when Margaret accused him of flirting, and she cannot be blamed for failing to realise that this time his feelings for the other woman were more lasting.

The war entered a particularly difficult phase during the long, grim months of the Somme stalemate, but Lloyd George was winning his battles in the Cabinet, and weapons and ammunition were finally reaching the front in the required numbers. One surprising development that helped him achieve this task was the cooperation of Mrs Pankhurst.

The WSPU campaign of violence had continued unabated through the first seven months of 1914, but when war broke out in August, Mrs Pankhurst immediately ended it. All imprisoned suffragettes were freed, and the organisation offered its services to Lloyd George, who badly needed workers to fill the factories he had had built to supply the army with munitions. Mrs Pankhurst was far-sighted enough to see that the war could offer women opportunities, and Lloyd George was not one to let an advantageous proposal pass by. He offered women work in munitions factories on equal pay, and Mrs Pankhurst put the full weight of WSPU behind the recruitment campaign. By July 1916, 340,844 women were working in national factories.

At the same time, all was not well at 10 Downing Street. The Prime Minister, able and active in peacetime, was badly equipped for the demands of leadership in war. Unable to make decisions with the necessary speed, over-fond of drink, and fatally distracted by his love life, Asquith was losing his grip on his government and his party. By contrast, Lloyd George, who was liable to ruffle the feathers of his colleagues in peacetime, was proving highly capable at the Ministry of Munitions. His energy seemed endless, and he was prepared to challenge military leaders if he felt they were mistaken. His success as Minister of Munitions further established him as a man of action, a minister who could achieve tangible results and one of the most effective politicians in the House of Commons. His pragmatism enabled him to involve businessmen (his so-called 'men of push and go') in producing military equipment. The same pragmatism led him to conclude by summer 1915 that a compulsory recruitment scheme was essential to increase numbers in the armed forces. The Cabinet was divided, but Lloyd George's voice was a powerful influence during the crisis of winter 1915 that led to the introduction of partial conscription early in 1916.

The Easter 1916 rising in Ireland served to remind the country that the war in Europe was not the only issue at hand, and Asquith asked Lloyd George to take the lead in handling the crisis. A few weeks later, in June, the war effort was dealt an unexpected blow when the ship carrying Lord Kitchener, the Minister of War, was sunk and all aboard were lost. Lloyd George had been due to travel with Kitchener, but due to the Irish situation he was forced to cancel his plans at short notice. Now he was the obvious man to replace Kitchener. For the next five months, during some of the darkest days of the conflict, he was Minister of War, a role that only served to heighten his unease at Asquith's performance as Prime Minister.

The events of the second half of 1916 have caused controversy ever since, with supporters of Asquith believing that Lloyd George conspired to force him out of office and grab power himself. Those who are less mistrustful of Lloyd George take at face value his assertions at the time that he did not seek the premiership. He would, he claimed, have been prepared to continue to serve under Asquith if only he had been given the autonomous responsibility for the war he sought as chairman of a streamlined War Committee. Asquith's pride, and the power-blindness that invariably affects those who have been in office for too long, led him to reject this option, and in doing so he fell from power after nine years in No. 10.

5 and 6 December 1916 were tumultuous days for Lloyd George's inner circle. The tension between Lloyd George and Asquith over the size of the War Committee (which by now had ten members and tended to argue fruitlessly over every detail of the war) reached a head on the fifth. Lloyd George prepared a letter of resignation, but an uneasy compromise was agreed between him and Asquith. An article in the following day's *Times*, which told the story in embarrassing detail, with Lloyd George as its hero, blew the concord apart. Asquith wrongly suspected that the newspaper's proprietor, Lord Northcliffe, and Lloyd George were plotting to undermine him. He reneged on the compromise agreement, and Lloyd George promptly resigned.

It became evident to Asquith that he could not hold together a government without Lloyd George. The Conservative leader Andrew Bonar Law, Colonial Secretary in the Coalition Government, informed the King that he could not provide an alternative, and that he believed Lloyd George was the man for the job. As these momentous events unfolded on 6 December, Lloyd George, technically a backbencher again, waited in the War Office with Frances. She described it as 'a *terrible* day – we were all sick with excitement and suspense'. Finally, at 7.30 p.m. the King called for Lloyd George, who went to the Palace to accept his invitation to form a government. It was by no means certain that he could do so, for the Conservatives on the whole were no friends of his, and Asquith still commanded significant loyalty within the Liberal Party. The attractions of power, though, together with the genuine need to put personal squabbles aside in the interests of winning the war, meant that on the afternoon of 7 December Lloyd George confided to Frances, 'I think I shall be Prime Minister before 7 o'clock,' his high spirits replacing the modesty with which he had previously protested, 'I'm not sure I can do it. It is a very big task.' His prophecy turned out to be true. By evening he was Prime Minister, with Bonar Law as his Chancellor, Arthur Balfour as Foreign Secretary, and the aristocratic Lord Curzon serving the man he referred to dismissively as the 'little Welsh Attorney' as Lord President.

Whatever doubts Lloyd George had felt the previous day, the momentum was simply unstoppable. The day's events swept away his reservations and catapulted him, together with Margaret and Frances, into the harsh limelight of No. 10 in the middle of an unprecedented, brutal conflict.

15

Two Wives at No. 10

Aᴼᴛᴇʀ ꜰᴏʀᴛʏ-ᴇɪɢʜᴛ ᴏꜰ ᴛʜᴇ most pressured hours of his life, Lloyd George finally had time on 9 December to write home to his brother and family. The letter is brief, but speaks volumes: 'Presided over my first War Cabinet. Found it embarrassing to be addressed as Prime Minister by all the members. Completed my list except one or two small ones I am holding over ... Love to all. Tell Uncle Lloyd that he is responsible for putting me in this awful job.'[1]

At the hour of his political triumph, Uncle Lloyd was not far from the thoughts of the new Prime Minister. But while the reactions among Lloyd George's London associates ranged from astonishment to disbelief, his family had never doubted that he could achieve the highest position of all. For Uncle Lloyd, the news merely confirmed what he had always known – that Lloyd George was born to lead the country. The old man reacted with quiet satisfaction: 'Y mae'r dyn yn fwy na'i swydd' (The man is greater than the office he holds). [2]

It is unlikely that Margaret or Frances had much time to reflect on their change of circumstance. They were both caught up in the domestic and political upheaval caused by the change of leadership, quite apart from the need to support and sustain Lloyd George at this most crucial time. The circumstances of his promotion were far from ideal. The Liberal Party had been torn apart, and he had two formidable opponents to face. Asquith was once again sitting on the backbenches after nearly nine years as Prime Minister, leader of the Liberal Party still and fully expecting to be summoned back to the Palace within weeks. Sitting next to him was Winston Churchill, disgruntled at having been thrown out of the Cabinet at the insistence of its Tory members. However much Lloyd George sought to work with Asquith rather than against him, warring factions had developed among supporters of the two men, with MPs and even officials loyal to their 'Chiefs' holding the other side in contempt. There are some who take the view even now that Lloyd George split the Liberal Party to satisfy his personal ambition. As if to underline his precarious situation, his greatest ally was Bonar Law, leader of the Conservatives, while his own party sat opposite him in the House of Commons. It would be some time before he could feel secure in his new position.

When it was established that Lloyd George would succeed in his first vital task of forming a coalition government of senior Liberal, Conservative and Labour ministers, the mood in Asquith's camp was one of sheer incredulity. Political events move quickly at times of crisis, and it can often take longer for the reality to sink in to those involved. When Margaret kindly and properly sent a note to Margot Asquith urging her to take her time in moving out of 10 Downing Street, Mrs Asquith delayed and delayed again, fully believing that she would be moving back in before long. Perhaps too she could not bear the fact that the homely little neighbour she had patronised was going to take her place.

Lloyd George's supporters were jubilant. While their Chief felt the full weight of the responsibility resting on his shoulders, officials in the War Office were drawing up a spoof schedule for the handover of power, written in military jargon and triumphantly lampooning the man who had been ousted from No. 10:

The Lloyd Georges will relieve the Asquiths at 10 Downing Street to-morrow 7th inst., under arrangements enumerated below.

An advance party consisting of Mrs Lloyd George and Megan will arrive at the junction of Whitehall and Downing Street at 10 a.m. where they will be met by Mrs Asquith and [her daughter] Violet. No arms will be carried by either party.

The Lloyd George advance party will proceed to view the premises at 10 Downing Street. Every facility for this inspection will be afforded by the Asquiths who will hand over all dixies, toast racks, ablution benches etc and take receipts therefor . . .

Members of the outgoing Government will assemble at the National Liberal Club, Athenaeum or other places within the meaning of the act, where they may continue their debates which will no longer be reported.[3]

Lloyd George immediately set about tackling his most urgent priorities, giving himself a firmer grip on the premiership with a *tour de force* speech to the House of Commons, establishing a War Cabinet of just five members, and rejecting an opportunistic offer by Germany of peace on unacceptable terms. Meanwhile, life had changed altogether for the women in his life.

Margaret was not pleased at the prospect of moving house yet again – even next door – and it may have been to her secret satisfaction that Mrs Asquith waited six weeks before moving out. Margot had not particularly enjoyed living in No. 10, which she regarded as an uninviting house in an unfashionable part of town:

> 10 Downing Street ought to be as well known in London as the Marble Arch or the Albert Memorial, but it is not. Although I lived there from April 1908, till December 1916, I nearly always had to tell my driver the way. I was taken to Down Street, Piccadilly, when I was sleepy or unobservant; or there was a risk of the children and umbrellas being thrown into the streets by the taxi-man opening the door suddenly from his seat and asking me where Downing Street was. This historic house is in a quiet cul-de-sac off Whitehall and of such diffident architecture that the most ardent tourist would scarcely recognise it again ... It is an inconvenient house with three poor staircases, and after living there a few weeks I made up my mind that owing to the impossibility of circulation I could only entertain my Liberal friends at dinner or at garden parties.[4]

But that did not mean she was happy to move out.

At the end of January 1917, Margaret and Megan walked into their new home by the garden gate that linked it with their old one. Although Margaret had grumbled when she had moved into No. 11, she was sorry to leave it eight years later. No. 10 was even less comfortable, with a hall porter guarding the entrance instead of the familiar maidservant, and chauffeurs sitting on the ground-floor windowsills waiting for their masters, alongside messengers and visitors waiting for admission to the Prime Minister's office. In stark contrast to the security around 10 Downing Street in the twenty-first century, Margot Asquith complained in her diary:

> I never knew what prevented anyone coming into this house at any moment: some would say after lunching with us that nothing had. There was a hall porter who looked after our interests when visitors arrived, but he was over-anxious and appeared flurried when spoken to. Poor man, he was never alone; he sat in his hooded chair, snatching pieces of cold mutton at odd hours; tired chauffeurs shared his picture paper, and strange people – not important enough to be noticed by a secretary or a messenger – sat watching him on hard sills in the windows; or if he were left for a moment, the baize doors would fly open and he would find himself faced by me, seeing a parson, a publican or a protectionist out of the house. But our Porter was not a strong man, and any determined Baronet with hopes of favours to come about the time of the King's birthday could have penetrated into No. 10.

Margaret still harboured dread memories of the unmodernised No. 10 with attics full of antique hip baths, so it was with relief that she found that Mrs Asquith had installed two or three bathrooms. She set about allocating rooms and creating a home in what was her eighth London address. Megan still needed a schoolroom when she was at home during school holidays, and Margaret had now become so immersed in her own work and vast correspondence that she too needed a study, although, with typical modesty, it was hardly grand: 'Economy in space being important I finally selected a small room on the first floor that was really a passage way to and from the other and larger apartments, but it served quite well for my purpose.'[5]

Margaret was not the only woman who was now installed in No. 10 because of her connection with Lloyd George. He had brought with him from the War Office his two indispensable private secretaries: J.T. Davies, who now became the Principal Private Secretary to the Prime Minister, and Frances Stevenson. Frances thus became the first female Private Secretary to work in No. 10, and although the more senior role went unquestioningly to her male colleague, she could take pride in the important position to which she had risen. Her office was adjacent to the Cabinet Room on the ground floor, which placed her at the heart of the new administration. Members of the Cabinet, foreign visitors and other important guests often loitered around her desk to finish a conversation, to prepare themselves to meet the Prime Minister, or simply to pass the time of day with his attractive secretary.

Amid the upheaval of the first few days of Lloyd George's premiership, Frances set about organising his office. To her horror, she found that Asquith had employed only one typist, a situation she quickly corrected with the help of Mrs Hoster's secretarial school. One person alone could barely cope with opening the mail that arrived for Lloyd George each day, let alone deal with it efficiently. Lloyd George was a phenomenally hard worker who generated vast quantities of correspondence, far more than his predecessor. Frances was used to this, and noted with amusement that serious political and governmental correspondence was intermingled with letters from the public, and that her job – as every Private Secretary to a Cabinet Minister will know – involved dealing with all manner of enquiries, sane and not so sane. 'We have any amount of letters from these men,' she complained in her diary, 'thinking that they can stop the war if only they can get the P.M.'s ear. One of these men who wrote demanding to see D., & followed the letter up with a call, signed himself "Rabbi Ben Ezra" and stated that he had been a caterpillar until 11.30 a.m. Easter Monday, at which time he had emerged from the chrysalis!'[6] Frances was so busy that she did not have time to record a word in her diary from 7 December 1916 until 9 January 1917.

No. 10 as Frances found it was incapable of adequately serving the needs of Lloyd George, who demanded far more from his staff than had his predecessor. It was not just the volume of work he created that required a larger support staff. Lloyd George changed the way in which the Prime Minister conducted his business with the creation of two new entities: the Cabinet Secretariat, a collection of expert advisers and specialists working to support the newly reconfigured War Cabinet, and, closer to home, the Prime Minister's Secretariat. This consisted of equally bright officials whose job, according to Frances, was to 'keep an eye on the Government departments, to maintain a liaison with the heads of these departments and keep the Prime Minister informed of important items'.[7]

The Secretariat was hurriedly formed during the first days of Lloyd George's premiership, and because of the confined space of No. 10 it was housed in huts in the garden, soon acquiring the nickname 'the garden suburb'. Its creation was bitterly resented by the Civil Service, but Lloyd George relied on it for advice on key issues, drafting speeches and checking facts as well as keeping him informed of all the political gossip. Frances worked closely with the new Secretariat, and there was so much to do that the first few weeks passed in a blur of activity. She was well aware how unpopular Lloyd George's personal staff were among government ministers and civil servants, but by now she was used to facing such opposition. With the full backing of the Prime Minister as well as four years' experience at the heart of government, as Frances made her way through the crowds that had assembled outside 10 Downing Street to catch sight of the new Prime Minister and self-consciously entered through the famous front door, her position had never been so secure.

For six weeks Frances settled into No. 10 while Margaret and Megan lingered next door. With their arrival she found herself working under the same roof as her rival, and in closer proximity to her lover's family than she had been since 1912. The situation can hardly have been comfortable for either Frances or Margaret, and the intense jealousy Frances felt shows clearly in her uncharacteristically spiteful account of Margaret's domestic arrangements. No. 10 was then still run as a large private house, although with more offices than No. 11. The ground floor consisted of the Cabinet Room and staff offices, the first floor had a large dining room, Margaret's study and various reception rooms. The family slept on the second floor, with the servants' bedrooms at the top of the house.

Frances watched demurely as her rival moved in, giving vent to her feelings only in her diary, which she filled with examples of Margaret's selfishness and lack of attention to Lloyd George's needs:

D. has been very unhappy this week owing to the change from No. 11 to No. 10. They did not bother to get a comfortable room ready for him & the first night he came down to my office to work after dinner. The second night he did not go up to dinner at all as he & Mrs LL.G. were not on speaking terms. She had closed the bedroom windows on the quiet, thinking that the room was cold, but knowing that he always gets a headache when he sleeps with closed windows. He was furious when he found out, as it has made him feel seedy all day. She does not study him in the least – has hung up some hideous family portraits painted by some cheap artist, though he has had them taken down more than once before. In fact, the whole house is hideously uncomfortable at the present moment, quite unworthy of a Prime Minister & very irritating to him, for he has a keen sense of what is beautiful & artistic & what is not.[8]

Margaret had been married to Lloyd George long enough to know his taste in furnishings, but it was simply not her style to fuss too much about household decoration. The same was true at Walton Heath, where Frances also observed her neglect of her husband's creature comforts: 'The old woman who looks after the house, though a very good sort, does not know how to make the place comfortable, & Mrs Ll.G. does not bother, or does not know how either.'[9]

In her autobiography, with the benefit of hindsight and from the more comfortable position of a widow, Frances was kinder to Margaret, but the references to her neglect, her parsimony and her failure to understand Lloyd George's needs still crop up. Describing Walton Heath, she wrote:

L.G. now had a house within a stone's throw of the golf club – a house furnished from left-overs from L.G.'s former houses – lacking in comfort and adequate heating. I remember that there was no heating at all in the spare bedroom, which used to get horribly damp when unoccupied . . . The house was looked after by an old Welshwoman who would cook L.G. simple meals but did not believe in luxuries! When I suggested that L.G. might sometimes be given cream with his food as it would be good for him, she replied that she could not include that extravagance in her account to Dame Margaret.[10]

Frances fails to note that Margaret was at that time running three establishments on Lloyd George's salary – Brynawelon in Criccieth, Walton Heath and 10 Downing Street, and while their income was greater than at any time in their marriage, it was not limitless.

Frances' resentment of Margaret had been growing for some time. There is a sideswipe at her alleged frugality in a diary entry of April 1915: 'She always wakes up when it is a question of money. As someone once put it, "As far as she is concerned, she would rather go without food than pay for it." '[11] A more charitable entry in November of that year noted that Margaret was ill and alone, and that she and Lloyd George were miserable because their sons had left for France.

A year later, with Frances' affair with Lloyd George established more firmly, her jealousy towards Margaret spilled out in a vitriolic outburst in her diary:

> Little Miss Davies – typist – was also there, & D. & I tried to make her feel at home, as Mrs Ll.G. had been rude to her in the morning, & she had been very upset by it. It is extraordinary how everyone dislikes Mrs LlG. Mr J.T. Davies was talking to me about her this morning: he says that sometimes when he is feeling particularly unfriendly to her, he tries to find some redeeming feature about her which will compensate for all her unlovely qualities. But it is impossible to find one. I have often felt the same too. She is simply a lump of flesh, possessing, like the jellyfish, the power of irritating.

We are not told how 'little Miss Davies' incurred the displeasure of a woman who was notoriously difficult to offend. There is little evidence that Margaret was ever rude to anyone, let alone members of her husband's staff. We can be sure, however, that Frances would have noted every instance that came to her attention. JT was firmly in Frances' camp when it came to the Chief's private life, although he got on well with Margaret. His comments can be read, as Frances intended, as a conspiratorial confession that he too disliked Margaret, but they can also be interpreted as an attempt to get Frances to feel less antagonistic towards the older woman.

Frances was not an unkind person, and she goes on to chide herself for being so bitter:

> But I am being very nasty. I try as much as possible to refrain from commenting upon her, as she has good reason to dislike me. But she has no pride. D. has told her time & again that he does not want her in London, that he would much prefer her to live in Criccieth – when she has been making a fuss about me. I am sure I would not want to remain with a man who showed so plainly that my presence was not wanted.[12]

This last passage is an extraordinary insight into Frances' relationship with Lloyd George. Is it possible that he was so lacking in loyalty to his wife of twenty-nine years that he could discuss her in these terms with his mistress? The alternative is hardly more attractive: that he was capable of lying to Frances, the woman he claimed he loved, telling her that he was urging Margaret to live in Criccieth, while his letters to his wife still contained affectionate appeals for her to spend more time with him in London.

Was Frances naïve enough to believe him? The answer, it seems, is yes. The closer she became to Lloyd George, the more she resented his family. Despite her compassionate nature there seems to have been no room in her heart for sympathy for her lover's wife, who had welcomed her into her home and whose trust she was so comprehensively betraying. The most likely explanation is that in order to overcome her scruples at the beginning of the affair, Frances had allowed herself to believe that Margaret had effectively broken the marriage contract with Lloyd George by neglecting him. Although Frances regarded herself as a modern woman, at heart she still carried the traditional values of her 'essentially Victorian upbringing'. Before she consented to live with Lloyd George, she had to persuade herself that they were 'married' in the moral sense, and that his previous marriage with Margaret was morally if not legally invalid.

Lloyd George understood this. He was a superb judge of character, and in his private life as in his political career he used his knowledge of people's values and characters to inspire them, manage them and manipulate them. 'His first method would be to try to get inside [people's] minds,' wrote Frances in later years, 'and ... having found that out, his path was easy.'[13] The evidence in Frances' diary suggests that he told her what she needed to hear – that his marriage was a sham. Frances would not have been the first woman or the last to believe her lover's assertions that his marriage was already dead when they met, that he was only staying because of the children or his career, and that his wife tacitly understood and accepted the situation. If she truly believed that there were no bonds of affection between Lloyd George and Margaret, and that it was only fear of scandal that bound them together, then it is understandable that she should have come to resent the woman who claimed so much of Lloyd George's time, and who – to Frances' increasing chagrin – was publicly recognised and lauded as his wife.

One thing is certain: there was no lack of pride on either side. If Margaret had known the full extent of Lloyd George's relationship with Frances from the beginning, given her views on marriage and fidelity, we can be sure that she would have left him. But if Frances had been aware of Lloyd George's true relationship with Margaret – loving and enduring as it was – her jealousy would have been even greater, and it is doubtful if she would have stayed either. Both women tolerated the situation because each believed that she alone held first place in Lloyd George's heart. Such was the balancing act that Lloyd George would have to maintain for thirty years.

The years in Downing Street saw the start of a long and painful feud between Frances and the Lloyd George family, a feud that blighted all their lives and that was kept alive long after Margaret's death. The situation caused both Margaret and Frances great unhappiness, yet neither was willing to confront Lloyd George or bring their relationship with him to an end. The rights and wrongs of the situation will have as many interpretations as there are people to judge it. The question at this stage is just how did Lloyd George sustain the situation, especially with his wife and mistress spending each day under the same roof?

If, in order for Lloyd George to persuade Frances to become his mistress, he had to convince her that Margaret was a bad wife to him, he needed to keep up the complaints against her once the relationship was established. In doing so, he was treading a very thin line. At times Frances hankered after an acknowledgement of her position. There are hints in her diary that she felt it was fundamentally unfair that Margaret should get all the glory when it was she, Frances, who really took care of Lloyd George and shared his innermost thoughts. Lloyd George was working hard to keep Frances happy, and convincing her that he was encouraging Margaret to stay at home in Criccieth was part of the pretence. Similarly, he was still dangling the prospect of marriage in front of her, somewhat cruelly given his determination never to divorce Margaret. Both pretences had the effect of giving Frances the impression that she was his 'true' wife, and that he barely tolerated Margaret and did not want her at No. 10. Lloyd George's strategy may not have been honourable, but it succeeded in preventing Frances from stepping out of line or confronting Margaret, however strong the temptation.

It was not just Margaret about whom he complained to Frances. An entry in her diary as early as January 1915 records him grumbling to her about his whole family:

C. is not very well today. He has been working very hard, but personally I think he is suffering from too much 'family'. He was very upset on Monday because not one of them had remembered that it was his birthday on Sunday. They did not think of it until Sir George Riddell came in at 7.30 in the evening & wished him many happy returns, & then it suddenly occurred to them. He always remembers their birthdays, however busy he is, and goes to a lot of trouble to get them something that will please them – he takes a delight in doing it.* 'They take me for granted,' he said to me rather bitterly. 'They treated me as someone who must be just tolerated because I provide money for everything they want. But they don't seem to remember that it is through me that they have their education and position and that if it were not for me they would get very little notice taken of them.'[14]

Whether or not this is accurate, it shows once again how necessary it was for Lloyd George to be the centre of attention. He needed to feel that he was the first priority in his home, and was quick to descend into self-pity if his family ever strayed from the mark.

Essentially, Frances' priority was Lloyd George, while Margaret and

---

* After his death, Frances recalled that actually Lloyd George could never remember his wife or his children's birthdays.

the other members of his family were increasingly living their own lives. Dick and Gwilym, aged twenty-eight and twenty-two, were on active service in France. Olwen was twenty-four and living at No. 10 until her wedding to Tom Carey Evans, helping Margaret with her war work. She was proudly wearing the engagement ring she had chosen from a selection that Tom had asked his sister to pick out, unaware until many years later that she had inadvertently chosen the most expensive.

Megan, aged fifteen, was away at Garrett Hall School in Banstead during term time, but returned to 10 Downing Street for holidays. She alone of the children was too young to be aware of her father's relationship with Frances, and as a consequence she alone remained on friendly terms with her former teacher. As the older ones came to understand the situation they adjusted their own relationships with Frances, whom they nicknamed 'Flossie'. Dick and Gwilym did not have to deal with the daily reality of the relationship, since they had left home. Both managed to remain on civil terms with Frances, although Dick found it difficult to do so, being more sensitive to the pain his father's behaviour caused Margaret. Olwen, who was living at No. 10, resented Frances' influence over her father and complained bitterly in her memoir that she used to 'carry tales' to Lloyd George about the family. She described Frances as 'possessive and avaricious beyond words', but the memoir was written many decades later, when she had inherited the running feud with Frances from her mother, and this could have coloured her memories of the early years in No. 10.

In one respect, Olwen was right: Frances did occasionally betray some resentment towards Lloyd George's children. After only a few weeks in No. 10 she wrote another scathing diary entry betraying her jealousy not only of Margaret, but of the children as well:

> T.P. O'Connor has written an article in The Strand magazine. I wonder whether these people, when they write these articles, really believe what they say, or are simply writing what they think they ought to say? T.P. talks about the beauty of D.'s family life! T.P. must know D. well enough to realise the conditions of his home life. Of course D. is fond of his children, but as he himself said to me when I made the same remark in defence of someone else: 'Every animal is fond of its young.'

Lloyd George was exceptionally fond of his young, and it was probably the strength of his attachment to his children that prompted this outburst. Next came a rare criticism of Lloyd George himself:

> As a matter of fact, he & Olwen are continually at loggerheads & yet he is always pleased when the papers make a fuss of her, simply because she is his child. Of course D. is very clever in the way he <u>pretends</u> at being the happy family man when people visit him at home. He makes me very angry sometimes, but he tells me that it is necessary – it is very useful to him in his public life. I do not believe it is as necessary as all that . . . I think it is a good deal the result of D.'s kindly nature too & the fact that he wants to play the game by his wife & not to hurt her feelings in public. I can understand that, but I think he rather overdoes it, & it hurts me when I read articles like T.P's where they hold him up to be the model family man. It amounts to hypocrisy.[15]

Frances' love of Lloyd George largely blinded her to his faults, but she was less indulgent towards Megan. Frances had been very close to her when she was younger, but by now the girl's closeness to her father had become a threat. Frances turned a critical eye on her former pupil, taking a sideswipe at Margaret even as she paid Megan a backhanded compliment:

> Sat next to Megan at the Mansion House Lunch. She is an amusing little person, but is getting rather artificial. D. thinks she is growing selfish, but that is not her fault, for she has not been taught to be unselfish. I think she is wonderfully unspoilt, considering the way she has been brought up. Many children would have been unbearable. She informed me that her mother 'reminded her of a character out of Dickens'. 'But this is only for your ear!' she added.[16]

Megan was unaware of the relationship between her father and Frances at this stage, and the memory of instances like this – with worse to come – when she had talked freely to Frances about her mother, increased her sense of betrayal when she realised the truth, and led to a passionate, bitter and lifelong hatred of Frances.

At other times, the family's intrusion into Frances' rare private moments with Lloyd George irritated her. Her account of a weekend at Walton Heath gives a flavour of how difficult it was at times for her to steal a few hours with him:

I went down on Saturday to look after D. during the weekend. (Mrs Ll.G. being at Criccieth.) He wanted absolute rest & arranged that Olwen & a friend who was staying with her should remain at Downing Street. However, his family with their usual consideration for him (!) wished otherwise. Dick [recently married] & his wife arrived without any warning to lunch on Sunday morning, having borrowed the official car for the purposes of motoring down. Then they got on the telephone with Olwen & arranged that she & her friend should come down in the afternoon. The whole thing was done without D. being consulted as to what he would like or what he intended to do. He was perfectly furious, for not only did it disturb the whole of his Sunday's rest, but as he said, they never think about him or consider him in any way, but simply use his house & garden & car when they think they will. I saw he was very upset by the whole thing, & tried to soothe him by saying that it was most natural for them to come & pay their father a visit on the spur of the moment; but I honestly think the whole thing was engineered & done a good deal out of spite, as they knew very well that he would not be there alone. However, they all cleared off after tea.[17]

But Lloyd George's grievances against his family were rare, and the impression he gave to others was of a happy family life. In February 1916 George Riddell recorded dining with the Lloyd Georges:

We discussed the conduct of married people in public. L.G. says no couple are entitled to indulge in public demonstrations of affection until they have been married twenty years; until that period has elapsed they cannot be sure that they will not have a violent disagreement which may terminate their relationship. He added, 'We have been married for twenty-eight years, so we are justified in making a public demonstration.' Whereupon he kissed 'Maggie bach', as he calls his wife.[18]

This is not the behaviour of a man who is unhappily married.

Could Frances really have believed that Lloyd George's marriage was a sham when she was in such close contact with his family that she knew he was still sharing a bedroom with Margaret? Her jealousy would seem to indicate that, at some level at least, she could see that Lloyd George needed his wife. She was not jealous of Mrs Tim or Julia Henry, as she knew that Lloyd George was not emotionally engaged with either of them. With Margaret it was different, and Frances, who was not prone to violent emotions, began to hate her. Despite his protestations about the need to preserve an outward show of respectability, Frances sensed that Margaret occupied a special and non-negotiable place in Lloyd George's life.

What of Margaret's feelings as she shared her home with Frances? There is nothing to suggest that she objected to the arrangement when Lloyd George became Prime Minister, and it is hard to establish exactly when she became aware of the affair. The only time we know that she referred directly to her rival was when she confronted him in March 1916 after overhearing him on the telephone to Frances. On 15 January 1917 Lloyd George believed Margaret knew about the affair. Frances recorded in her diary: 'D returned from W.H. very fit after the weekend, though we had both been very miserable without each other. D. said he would have sent for me, "only," he said, "considering that she knows everything that is going on. It is not right to try her too far." '[19]

Olwen wrote in her memoirs that 'it was not until after I married [in June 1917] that Mother ever mentioned Father's infidelities to me',[20] but that does not prove that Margaret knew about the affair with Frances at that time. Olwen, however, states: 'As far as the family was concerned, [Frances] was just another employee and we never discussed her. Mother certainly never mentioned her, but she quickly realised what was going on.'[21] Frustratingly, she does not offer any explanation of how she knew that Margaret 'quickly' became aware of the affair if she never mentioned Frances. As Olwen goes on, it becomes clear that the family were able to discuss Frances only after many years: 'Probably Megan was the last of the family to become aware of the relationship between Frances and Father . . . As the years went by, Mother was able to joke about her, which was a very good thing; by then I don't think it hurt her any more.'[22]

There were people in Margaret's immediate social circle who knew all about Lloyd George's relationship with Frances and who could easily have betrayed the secret to her, wittingly or unwittingly. George Riddell, for example, hosted weekends at his house for Lloyd George and Margaret as well as for Lloyd George and Frances, and friends of Margaret's like Lucy Masterman were uncomfortable in Frances' presence. Another frequent visitor to No. 11 and No. 10 was Winston Churchill, who had stayed with Margaret at Brynawelon with his wife Clementine. Churchill was a man of the world, and his mother, the glamorous American socialite Jennie Jerome, married three times and was rumoured to have had over two hundred lovers. Perhaps in reaction to his upbringing, Churchill took a very different view of his own wedding vows, and was one of the few public figures at the time who did not take a mistress. Although he was close to Lloyd George, it would appear that Churchill did not approve of his private life. Frances was a little puzzled if not hurt by Churchill's coldness towards her and his refusal to acknowledge by word or deed her significance in Lloyd George's life. Churchill was an enthusiastic fan of Margaret's, and she was fond of him. It would seem that he was uncomfortable with Lloyd George's mistress because he was on such good terms with his wife.

Despite the general acceptance of private adultery among the press, the aristocracy and politicians alike, a significant minority of those around Margaret and Frances felt unhappy about the situation. Friends of Lloyd George who knew both women were in a tricky situation. Some, as we have seen, took Margaret's or Frances' side, but others tried to be friends with both – usually to Frances' private scorn. Sir Vincent Evans, a prominent Welsh journalist, earned a blatantly unfair rebuke from her for maintaining good relations with Margaret:

I think he is one of the greatest humbugs I know. He loses no opportunity of advertising himself, chiefly through the reflected glory of the Lloyd George family, attaching himself to them in public whenever possible. He knows all about D. & me, & aids & abets us whenever necessary, & for this he knows that he is on D.'s right side, & it gives him extra chances of being in D's company – which fact (being in D's company) he never omits to make public. On the other hand, he trundles Mrs Ll.G. about to all kinds of functions, and gets himself photographed and talked about in connection with her. He makes flowery speeches about her virtues, & assiduously makes a fuss of her, knowing that by this means he gets on her right side, which is also useful on occasions.[23]

Frances denounces Evans as 'a repulsive personality', despite the fact that he was only playing along with the pretence that her affair with Lloyd George made necessary. During her years in No. 10 her diary betrays a growing sense of impatience with the situation. She was more necessary to Lloyd George than ever, both personally and professionally. As she saw it, Margaret served only to make his life more uncomfortable, yet she received all the public acclamation due as his wife.* This had been the understanding from the beginning, but Frances grew to resent it bitterly. Prior to December 1916 she had grown accustomed to taking her place at Lloyd George's side on private occasions – dinner parties, weekends in country houses, snatched evenings at Walton Heath – and it must have been tempting at times to forget Margaret's existence. But as soon as she entered No. 10 it was no longer possible to ignore the fact that Lloyd George had his 'official' wife at his side.

Occasionally – inevitably perhaps – someone would offend Frances' sense of her own position, and she would take revenge in her diary. One such incident occurred when Harold Spender overstepped the mark by actually treating her like Lloyd George's secretary:

> Harold Spender is writing a book about D., & I am looking out some material for him. I do not know what the book will be like. Personally I think Harold Spender himself is a frightful bore, & D. himself, though he likes him, says he is one of the most tactless persons he has ever come across. His latest example of tactlessness, though perhaps he is not to blame for it, has been to ask me if I would get Mrs Lloyd George to dictate to me anecdotes about D.!!! I hope he will suggest the same thing to Mrs. Ll.G.[24]

---

* In retaliation, perhaps, Frances gave a few interviews to journalists who were intrigued by a young female secretary in No. 10. Riddell warned her that she should not draw attention to herself, and the interviews ceased.

With an increasing number of people in the know, Margaret certainly *could* have known about Frances from quite early on. She knew that Lloyd George was fond of Frances, even that he was carrying out a flirtation with her, but there is nothing to suggest that she was fully aware of the situation. Given her jealousy and her religious beliefs, if she did know, it is difficult to believe she would have stood for Frances' presence in No. 10 for a moment.

It should be remembered that Margaret was sexually quite naïve. Lloyd George had been the only man in her life, and the sexual rules of high society were as different from her Methodist upbringing as could be imagined. She was reluctant to speak about sexual matters even when her daughter was about to be married, and thus far, every time she had been confronted with her husband's infidelity she had chosen to believe in his innocence and had stood by him. With the possible exception of the affair with Mrs Tim, she had seen Lloyd George clear his name every time he had been associated with sexual scandal, and she had, with apparent sincerity, stood by him in a court of law to protest his innocence. By the time she moved into No. 10, Margaret had been giving Lloyd George the benefit of the doubt for nearly thirty years. There is no evidence that any of his less public indiscretions ever reached her ears, so it is at least possible that Margaret still believed that, however much he flirted with pretty girls, he was essentially faithful to her. This would explain how she put up with Frances' presence in No. 10. In later years, when Margaret certainly did know the truth, she could not stand to have Frances anywhere near her. Lloyd George's staff had to prevent them from meeting, bundling Frances out of the back door as Margaret entered by the front door. It is difficult to believe that Margaret could have been tolerant of the affair at first, only to become more sensitive about it later on.

During the first hectic weeks of Lloyd George's premiership, family life in No. 10 took on a new rhythm. 1917 was to prove to be the family's most eventful and testing year yet.

16

The Family at War

As was their invariable custom, Margaret and Megan spent Christmas 1916 at Criccieth; not even Lloyd George's recent elevation to the premiership was considered reason enough to break the habit. As was also customary by now, Lloyd George chose to stay in London, citing the pressure of work (with some justification) as his excuse. As soon as his wife had left he hastened down to Walton Heath to spend a week with Frances, and they saw in the New Year together.

Frances needed his attention badly, for she had not had an easy time over the past weeks. Lloyd George had been preoccupied with his work and had not been able to offer her moral support as she struggled to cope with her new job and her emotionally taxing new working environment. During the first few months of 1917, the new Prime Minister was still under considerable pressure: food shortages were beginning to bite as German U-boats took their toll on merchant shipping bound for Britain. Lloyd George appealed for voluntary rationing, and passed emergency agricultural measures through the House of Commons. At the same time he was tackling unrest in Ireland and the continuing clamour for universal suffrage at home. Revolution in Russia in March would bring hope that a powerful ally would redouble its efforts against Germany, but the toppling of the Tsar brought internal strife and was to eliminate Russia as a combatant. Lloyd George was working day and night. The strain made both him and Frances short-tempered, and their relationship was suffering, but at its core their love was as strong as ever. Lloyd

Two wartime weddings: Olwen marries Tom Carey Evans on 19 June 1917 with Megan as bridesmaid and Margaret, who hated having her photograph taken, as a stern mother of the bride. Lloyd George cut short a Cabinet meeting to give Olwen away, taking just a few hours off for the wedding.

Dick and Roberta McAlpine in 1917. Prime Minister Lloyd George looks happy and relieved: he had just heard that America had joined the war.

Public duty: Margaret on the platform with Lloyd George at the 1917 Birkenhead Eisteddfod – Eisteddfod y Gadair Ddu (the Eisteddfod of the Black Chair). Frances was in the audience.

Lloyd George inspecting the troops in the trenches in France.

The other woman in Downing Street: Lloyd George's Private Secretary and mistress, Frances Stevenson, at her desk.

Above A rare photograph of Frances looking straight at the camera. Her contemporaries often noted her petite mouth and the softness of her expression.

Right Firm friends and roommates – for the present: Frances and Megan in Paris during the 1919 Peace Conference.

Lloyd George carried Frances' portrait with him always, disguised to look like a pocket book.

Lloyd George, 'the doyen of the Peace Conference', with Italy's Premier Vittorio Orlando, France's Georges Clemenceau and US President Woodrow Wilson. The 'big four' met daily during the six-month conference.

The tangled web: Chequers, c.1921. Lloyd George, his hand on Margaret's shoulder, stands between French Prime Minister Aristide Briand and Marshal Foch. Megan looks away, far right. Behind, Frances looks happy standing next to Philippe Berthelot, with whom she had 'a rather exciting flirtation'.

Chequers in 1921: the house was gifted to the nation for the use of the Prime Minister, and Lloyd George was the first beneficiary. Frances acted as hostess when Margaret was absent, which eventually opened Megan's eyes to her relationship with Lloyd George.

Megan, still her father's little girl, with Lloyd George at Brynawelon.

THE LLOYD GEORGE FAMILY DICTATE THEIR MEMOIRS.

Lloyd George featured in hundreds of cartoons. This one by David Low from March 1929, portraying the many phases of his public career, (ironically) depicts a female secretary helping him with his memoirs.

Two separate headquarters: Brynawelon, the house Lloyd George and Margaret built in Criccieth in 1908, was her domain, while Bron-y-De in Surrey was his.

George now carried with him in his breast pocket a leather-bound photograph of Frances disguised as a notebook, and the week together at Walton Heath was all that was needed to restore harmony between them.

Frances was by now twenty-eight years old, and had been Lloyd George's mistress for four years. Watching from her outer office as he worked over breakfast, lunch and dinner, with meetings in between and paperwork to finish at night and in the early morning, she was fully aware of the pressure on him, and he did not have to explain why he was tired when they snatched time together. She was not sparing herself either. 'D's speech yesterday seems to have made an enormous impression,' she wrote in late February after Lloyd George's powerful performance in the Commons paving the way for passing emergency agricultural measures. 'He himself was very pleased with it, but was very tired afterwards. We both went down to [Walton Heath] after it, but were both too tired to enjoy each other's company, as I had been up till 2 the night before over the speech.'

Their closeness was if anything cemented by the crises they had weathered. Lloyd George's political difficulties had been played out in public, but Frances' troubles were of a private nature. She was still traumatised by the events of March 1915, when her pregnancy had been terminated, and was struggling to come to terms with her sense of personal morality. Later the same year she had been asked by a friend to be godmother to her daughter, which caused some bitter heart-searching:

My little god-daughter Nancy is to be christened today. I have undertaken to be her guardian on the strict understanding that it shall not involve any religious teaching, but only the responsibility for her moral and material welfare. I scarcely know whether I am fit to undertake even the former of these two; many people would think I am not. But I do not, oh I do not think that I am wicked & unfit to help in the upbringing of a child. Surely my experiences have made me more fit for this: for knowledge is safety.[1]

It is likely that Frances' second abortion happened a year or so after the first. We do not know for certain, but she was ill in April/May 1916, and there is a gap in her diary lasting until July. Lloyd George was worried about her, and wrote her a passionate letter on 5 June, after she had left to convalesce at the coast, headed by a scribbled pencil note warning her not to leave the letter lying around. Its tone suggests that she had suffered an emotional blow, and that her illness was accompanied by depression:

My darling

I miss you so much although you have only been gone just a few hours that I feel I must open up some communication – however imperfect – with you. I love you so dearly. My heart throbs with tenderness for you. You are all in all to me & I could not now even exist without you. This morning was dark & cloudy – & this evening bright and shining – to all that dwell in this city – & yet to me it is just the other way about. The sun set for three days at 3 o'clock this afternoon after a brilliant morning.

Enjoy yourself my little cariad bach ANWYL, ANWYL [dear, dear little love]. Lean on me. I will carry you through the Gates of Hell if necessary – not inside though darling – but carry you out into the fair blue land outside.

Pussy do be good. Don't get miserable. I would rather you got naughty (within decent limits of course). Dont get too near the cliffs – but inhale the ozone & look now & again to the east where there is a longing loving heart beating & waiting for you.

Ever & Ever

Your own fond old man & father[2]

When Frances eventually resumed her diary, it was clear that her illness had caused her to re-evaluate her whole life with Lloyd George:

It is a long time since I kept a record. I lost heart after being ill: was very depressed and rundown for a long time, & D. & I had constant quarrels, & got out of tune with each other. I was sick at heart and had no courage to face the future – the result of my illness – & D. sent me down to Walton Heath to recuperate. I was feeling very bitter & sore with things in general, when one night I had a dream. I dreamed that D. had been killed, & the horror that that filled me with drove out every other feeling. I knew then that I loved him better than anything in the world, & that if he were dead nothing else would matter. It is extraordinary what a difference this dream made to my mental attitude. That is all past, however & we are now just as we always were.[3]

As with the first abortion, as soon as Frances had physically recovered, her relationship with Lloyd George continued on an even closer basis than before. From December 1916 she was a constant presence, working downstairs even as he spent time with his family at No. 10.

The beginning of 1917 was an anxious time for Margaret too. Uncle Lloyd was now eighty-two years old, and his health was causing serious concern. Around his eightieth birthday he had begun to suffer 'some internal weakness that gradually sapped his strength',[4] and by 1917 the family knew that he was fighting bowel cancer. It was not until February that Lloyd George was able to make his first visit home to Wales as Prime Minister. His meeting with Uncle Lloyd must have been a joyful one to both of them, for although he had long since ceased to consult his uncle in any meaningful way about political matters, he never forgot how much he owed him. Although neither knew it, it was to be their last meeting.

Uncle Lloyd's physical strength was failing, but he remained sharp of mind until the very end. He was still preaching every Sunday in Berea, but as they gathered in chapel on the bitterly cold afternoon of 11 February 1917, his congregation already suspected that, after fifty-seven years of devoted service, Richard Lloyd was ready to give his last sermon. His choice of text was the 23rd Psalm: 'Ie, pe rhodiwn ar hyd glyn cysgod angau, nid ofnaf niwed; canys yr wyt Ti gyda me; dy wialen a'th ffon a'm cysurant' (Yea, though I walk through the valley of the shadow of death, I will fear no evil; for thou art with me; thy rod and thy staff they comfort me). No heart was left untouched that afternoon as the faithful of Berea listened for the last time to their beloved Richard Lloyd.

Shortly after Lloyd George and Margaret had returned to London, Uncle Lloyd took to his bed and his condition deteriorated rapidly. Margaret hastened back, but Lloyd George could not abandon an important planned trip to France. On 28 February, with Margaret at his bedside, Uncle Lloyd uttered his last words, 'Iesu Grist' (Jesus Christ), and passed away. 'He has been more than a father,' wrote Margaret. '. . . Lloyd George owes everything to him.'[5]

Even Frances, who had not met Uncle Lloyd since her first visit to Criccieth in 1911, understood how much he meant to her lover. She had written in her diary a few days before his death that Lloyd George had been 'very worried all the week about his old uncle, who is very ill and not expected to live. I think D. will be very upset when the end comes, for he often says that he owes everything to him & that it is he who has kept him up to the mark during the whole of his career, writing him every day a letter of encouragement . . . Uncle Lloyd's interest in D. never flags nor does his enthusiasm diminish, & it must have been a wonderful thing for the old man to see his boy Prime Minister.'[6] Frances was on hand to comfort Lloyd George when the news reached him, and he leaned on her for emotional support: 'D. is very upset and will be until after the funeral has taken place. It is a great strain for him coming at this time. He will miss the old man very much, and he says that I am his only devoted friend now – that I shall have to fill the old man's place. God knows I will try. D. needs so much someone who will not hesitate to give him everything, & whose sole thought & occupation is for him.'[7]

Lloyd George was very upset, but to call Frances his 'only devoted friend' was an exaggeration in view of the way in which Margaret had cared for Uncle Lloyd. Frances, as ever, took it at face value. She was correct in observing that Lloyd George needed 'someone who will not hesitate to give him everything', but failed to recognise that in his family, he had been surrounded by such people from the day he was born.

Even the war could not prevent Lloyd George from travelling back to Criccieth for the funeral on 3 March. Uncle Lloyd's fame as Lloyd George's mentor had spread far beyond Criccieth. A few days before his death he had been listed in *The Times* as a distinguished invalid,[8] and the press flocked to Criccieth much as they had done for Mair's funeral nine years previously. The day of the funeral was grey, with spots of rain falling as the procession made its way up the hill to the cemetery above the town. Yet again, Lloyd George walked with his brother and Gwilym behind the hearse while Margaret and the women of the family stayed behind in Garthcelyn. Crowds gathered in respectful silence along the route but, according to Uncle Lloyd's wishes, the funeral was simple and private, and less than a hundred gathered at the graveside.

'Here was the most highly placed man in the world's greatest Empire,' reported *The Times*, 'burying his foster-father and uncle, the village cobbler.' Lloyd George 'stood with his head bared, and the expression on his face was the index to his feelings . . . [Uncle Lloyd] was a man who might have made the same mark on the world as his foster-son but he preferred to let his light illumine his own small circle.'

Messages of condolence flooded in from friends, acquaintances and politicians the world over: 'My most sincere sympathy in your sad personal loss,' wrote Herbert Asquith. 'He was a splendid example of the best type of British citizen.' Aristide Briand, the French Prime Minister, sent his 'profound condolences and my warm sympathy with you in the sad loss you have suffered'.[9]

Richard Lloyd was buried next to his sister Betsy in the Criccieth cemetery. Both of them would be famous long after their deaths for the part they played in the life of Lloyd George.

Back in London, Frances was not the only one to feel that she needed to help fill the gap in Lloyd George's world. Megan, by now fourteen years old, adored her father with a fierce intensity. He in turn allowed her to feel that she occupied an unrivalled position in his life. She was 'bach y nyth' (a colloquial North Wales term meaning the youngest child, literally 'the smallest in the nest'), the pampered younger daughter and, furthermore, the child who most resembled Lloyd George himself. She modelled herself on him, and in return he drew her more and more into his political life. It was after discussing the matter with Megan over tea that he took the gamble of leaving the Treasury to take on the Munitions job in 1915 – although we can be fairly sure that he was seeking affirmation from her at best, since he rarely needed anyone's advice on political matters. Nevertheless, a decision of that magnitude could not be taken without talking to Megan, and she began to adopt his interests in politics as her own.

In keeping with the way in which young ladies were raised, Megan was an innocent girl, and did not suspect the truth of her father's relationship with Frances. Consequently, she saw no reason not to maintain her friendship with her former tutor. Back in 1915, Frances had returned Megan's affection, writing in her diary, 'she is a dear child, and very sweet when she is away from the other female members of her family'.[10] By May 1917 her opinion had become rather coloured by her resentment of Margaret, and she was noting (as we have seen) that Megan had become 'rather artificial'. Lloyd George regarded his daughter as a delightful child and a prodigious talent, no doubt seeing some of his own youthful characteristics in her. He boasted proudly to Frances whenever Megan said something clever or amusing, and made time to spend with her when she was home from school. As the youngest, Megan was also indulged by the other members of the family, even to a degree by her more level-headed sister Olwen. Megan was accustomed to being the centre of attraction, and saw no reason why she should not command her sister's attention at all times. This became an issue when Olwen fell in love with Tom Carey Evans. She insisted on accompanying the young couple on their outings, completely oblivious to the fact that she was playing the gooseberry, and was outraged when she was eventually told she had to stay at home.

Lloyd George was acutely distressed when in March 1917, only days after Uncle Lloyd's death, Megan fell ill with measles. He terrified himself with the thought that he was about to lose her, as he had lost Mair. She made a full recovery, but the episode made her parents even more over-protective. At the same time, Lloyd George and Margaret were worried about their sons in uniform. On the whole, since Dick and Gwilym had left for France Margaret had succeeded in concealing her feelings, maintaining her calm demeanour, but her anxiety broke through when Gwilym returned unexpectedly from the front, and was perplexed to find her collapsed in fits of uncontrollable laughter. She had convinced herself that his sudden return could only be for one reason: Dick had been killed, and Gwilym was sent to break the news to her. Her laughter was in fact hysteria born of relief that Dick was still alive.

At the beginning of 1917 Dick had been hospitalised with trench fever, and while he was recovering in the Red Cross hospital in Bath he met the eighteen-year-old Roberta McAlpine, daughter of the construction magnate Sir Robert McAlpine. She had spent part of her childhood in North Wales, which presumably gave them something in common, and within a few weeks the two had fallen in love and were engaged. Unexpectedly perhaps, this was not altogether to his parents' liking. They worried that Dick had committed himself too soon after the breakdown of his earlier engagement to a Welsh girl, Dilys Roberts. Lloyd George also fretted, somewhat selfishly, that a marriage between his son and the daughter of a wealthy businessman would damage his reputation in Wales, giving the impression that he and his family had moved too far away from their roots. Frances wrote in her diary: 'It will not be a very popular marriage in North Wales. It is too like a piece of business & the North Wales people especially will not forgive [Dick] for giving up a Welsh girl.'[11] Nevertheless, Dick was determined, and the wedding day was set.

The bleakness of the war situation contributed to Lloyd George's downcast mood. In the spring of 1917 the Allies were at crisis point. To address the German U-boat campaign to starve Britain into submission, Lloyd George had battled hard to win support for the idea of using the Royal Navy to escort merchant shipping bringing vital goods to Britain. The convoy was now in place, and imports were finally reaching their destination, but the outcome of the war depended on whether America would enter the war before Europe was overcome and Britain finally ran out of food. On 6 April, the day before Dick's wedding, came the welcome news that America, finally goaded beyond tolerance by German attacks on her ships, had declared war.

It was the best news Lloyd George had received since moving into No. 10, and the family set off for Bath in celebratory mood. The wedding was held in the splendour of Bath Abbey, with a fully recovered Megan acting as bridesmaid. The only member of the family who could not be there was Gwilym, who was at the front. Lloyd George, conscious of his public image, was nervous of any displays of extravagance, but since he was the father of the groom and not of the bride, his influence was limited. *The Times* reported that Roberta wore 'a dress of white charmeuse with an Empire tunic of silver lace and semi-court train attached by crystal and diamante ornaments'.[12] She carried a bouquet of lilies of the valley and wore her father's gift of a string of pearls. After the ceremony, the wedding breakfast was held in the nearby Empire Hotel. There, Lloyd George did manage to exert some influence, and the guests were denied any alcohol. In 1915 he had tried to persuade the nation to abstain from drinking for the duration of the war, but had failed miserably.* He could not break his own pledge publicly, and the wedding was dry.† Dick and his new wife spent their honeymoon in Cornwall, while Lloyd George and Margaret stayed for a short two-night holiday in the West Country.

Frances had long since ceased being friendly with the older Lloyd George children, and there was no question of her attending the wedding. These times when Lloyd George was with his family were difficult for her, but she did not complain. Indeed, she comes across as admirably self-reliant in the way in which she would take herself off for a few days at the seaside with a sister or a friend, or spend a weekend at the country house of a friend of Lloyd George's who understood her position. Her social life was active even though she worked hard, and she often went to parties or dinners without Lloyd George. She formed friendships with other men too, which could on occasion cause trouble between them.

Although Frances missed her lover when he was away, she had his letters, and in them ample proof that he was missing her too. What she minded more was when they were in the same place but unable to meet because of his hectic schedule. Even though she saw him every day in London they had to maintain a strictly business relationship in the office, and there were days on end when Frances had to be content with just that. Without his daily letters and reassurance of his affection she felt depressed and lonely, and there was often tension and fractiousness between them when they could not get together at her flat or at Walton Heath. Early April 1917 was one such time. Frances barely saw Lloyd George for a week, so the weekend before the wedding he made a special effort. Frances wrote that they drove down to Walton Heath and had 'two hours of bliss together'.[13] Her gratitude was immense, and peace was restored: 'D. saw I was rather down & lonely, & it was sweet of him to suggest it, for he was very tender & kind & bucked me up

---

* He had persuaded George V to set an example, prompting the King's butler to nail a crêpe wreath on the door of his wine cellar, but there is little evidence that anyone else responded to his appeal.

† Or so he thought. Dick's son Owen was told that 'there was apparently a small room at the reception to which various McAlpine uncles retreated at intervals, returning with heightened colour and raised spirits'.

again. I feel as though I ought not to mind when he is busy & cannot pay me very much attention, but I suppose I am only human and I get depressed. But he soon puts me right again.'[14]

At this difficult time, it was not just Frances who craved reassurance. By the end of April the strain was showing on Lloyd George too. Throughout his premiership he showed remarkable resilience, both physical and emotional. 'My husband is fortunate for he never has worried, not even during the most anxious days of the war,' wrote Margaret in the 1930s. 'He always did his best – his uttermost. If things went wrong after that – well, he could not help it.'[15] Lloyd George's ability to project optimism and strength of purpose was part of what made him an excellent war leader, and was a major factor in maintaining the country's morale. But his self-belief and mental buoyancy needed to be constantly fuelled by the devotion of his women. He had to feel that he came first, and that they were absolutely committed to fulfilling his needs. In 1917 mere praise was not enough. With Margaret busy with her war work and with organising Olwen's wedding, Lloyd George asked Frances to give him the most absolute commitment of all: that she would die with him.

This extraordinary conversation took place on Sunday, 22 April. Lloyd George had been in France, trying unsuccessfully to get France and Italy to agree to negotiate a separate peace with Austria. He had been advised not to travel, and indeed the Germans had made a serious attempt to sink the ship on which he was meant to be crossing the Channel, sending no fewer than five destroyers to attack him, of which three were lost. Lloyd George had escaped unharmed, having chosen to wait for a daytime crossing, but an anxious Frances urged him not to risk his life by travelling abroad again. They had a loving reunion, with Frances writing, 'I do not think that we have ever loved each other so much. D. says that ours is a love that comes to very few people and I wonder more & more at the beauty & happiness of it. It is a thing that nothing but death can harm.'[16]

Death was on their minds, understandably given the war, the specific threat to Lloyd George's life and the age difference between them. Frances looked younger than her twenty-eight years, but Lloyd George at fifty-four was feeling his age. His hair, a reliable indicator of his physical condition, had turned grey, although it was still capable of darkening again when he was feeling particularly fit,* and while he had not yet developed the white mantle of hair that characterised him in later life, he was looking older and more worn. Frances, on the other hand, was in the prime of her youth. Photographs taken at the time show an unlined, pretty face, her hair fashionably bobbed and waved and an air of youthful energy. Lloyd George could expect to die long before her.

Their conversation turned to his death, and the loneliness Frances would feel when he was no longer there. Her diary entry continues: '. . . even death has no terrors for me now, for D. asked me yesterday if I would come with him when he went. He begged me not to stay behind, but for both of us to go together, and I promised him to do so, unless I have any children of his to claim me.' The request may have been Lloyd George's, but it was Frances' fear of the future that was assuaged by the pact, for she goes on: 'So, I am not afraid now of the misery if D. is taken away, for then I shall go too & his end will be my end, and until then everything is happiness, if our love stays.' Frances does not reveal how she intended to follow Lloyd George in death, but, strange as it seems, the pact comforted rather than disturbed her: 'I am so happy now that we have decided this, for sometimes my heart would stop beating with terror at the thought of life without D.'[17]

For his part, Lloyd George certainly was not going to offer Frances the comfort of going together if by any chance she died first. She did not expect him to: 'I hope by any chance I will not go first, for I know his misery would be great, and he could not leave his work, which is a great one.' There was no more chance of Lloyd George committing suicide if Frances died than of his divorcing Margaret to marry her. His unswerving focus on his work and his duty was never questioned by Frances, nor indeed by any of the other women in his life.

Bizarrely, the pact is recorded in a matter-of-fact way by Frances in the middle of a long diary entry. She apparently did not see any injustice in a man of fifty-four asking a woman of twenty-eight to end her life for him. For her, it was the confirmation she needed that she and

---

* George Riddell once accused him of dyeing it. Margaret remarked that even when he was young he had a grey streak in his hair when he was working hard, which disappeared as soon as he was able to relax.

she alone would be with Lloyd George for eternity. At a time when men they knew were dying every day, with no end to the misery in sight, it was what she wanted to hear.

It is impossible to know how serious they were about the pact. Frances does not mention it in her autobiography, nor does she refer to it again in her diary. But she also over time ceased to refer to Lloyd George's promise to marry her if he could, and she certainly meant to hold him to that. She probably put the agreement to the back of her mind, and when Lloyd George actually died there is no suggestion that she ever contemplated joining him in death. By then, though, Lloyd George was an old man, and their relationship had changed beyond measure.

Olwen had been living at No. 10 since her engagement to Tom Carey Evans in June the previous year, and the young couple had not set eyes on each other for over a year. Finally Tom had been able to get leave from Mesopotamia, where he was stationed, but then Lloyd George received a dreadful message: Tom's ship had been torpedoed, and it was not known whether he had survived. It had been Olwen's nightmare to fall in love with someone who did not come back, 'a myth who wasn't there';[18] that was why she had hesitated before accepting Tom's proposal. Lloyd George decided not to tell her the news until he knew whether Tom was coming back or not. As the days passed Olwen began to suspect that something was wrong, and just as she was getting frantic with worry, a coded telegram arrived for her. There were advantages to living in No. 10, and Lord Carson, First Lord of the Admiralty, who happened to be taking lunch there that day, was able to interpret it. Tom had escaped with only his life and the uniform he was wearing. A few days later, only four days before his wedding day, he arrived in London safe and sound.

The wedding was an altogether more Lloyd George kind of affair than Dick's marriage a few weeks before had been. This time Lloyd George and Margaret had no misgivings about their child's choice of partner. The two families were old friends. Tom grew up in Beddgelert, near Lloyd George's constituency, and his family readily agreed that a low-key wedding would be best. At 1 p.m. on Tuesday, 19 June, Lloyd George brought to a close a meeting of the War Cabinet, saying that he had 'an important engagement this afternoon', and joined the family for lunch. Olwen was too nervous to eat, and was pale with nerves as she dressed in a simple gown of white satin with a chiffon train, lined in shell pink. It was less elaborate than most wedding gowns, even in wartime, but photographs confirm that it suited her beautifully. After lunch she drove with her father in his Rolls-Royce from Downing Street to the Castle Street Baptist chapel. The service was bilingual, with one Welsh hymn and one, especially composed for the occasion by the Rev. H. Elvet Lewis, sung in English. The bride was attended by Megan, serving as bridesmaid for the second time that year. Despite the family's attempt to downplay the occasion, there was inevitably public interest in the wedding of the Prime Minister's daughter, and as the bride and groom left the chapel, wounded soldiers from Millbank Hospital formed a guard of honour and a group of young female munitions workers presented Olwen with flowers.

The reception at No. 10 was informal, with a fake wedding cake made out of white card substituting for the real thing. Lloyd George could only take a few hours off, and he returned to work as soon as the wedding breakfast was over. Olwen and Tom spent their honeymoon in Cornwall, with a few days in Wales before Tom's recall. Olwen returned to No. 10 to live, and was overjoyed to discover before long that she was expecting a baby. The child was born in Criccieth on 25 April 1918, two months after Roberta had presented Lloyd George and Margaret with their first grandchild, Valerie. Margaret was with Olwen for the birth, and immediately sent word to London. Lloyd George was thrilled, especially since the new arrival was another little girl. 'To all my sweethearts at Brynawelon – great and small,' he wrote, 'good luck to the dear little recruit that has arrived to reinforce the Brynawelon garrison. Sarah woke me up at 3 am with the good news. I was delighted, and especially delighted that Olwen has started her family with a little girl. She can reserve the boys for Granny – Grandpa prefers the little girls. Well done Llwydyn bach. Fondest love from old Grandpa.'[19]

Olwen wanted to call the baby Margaret Lloyd. Margaret senior was delighted, and encouraged Olwen to move quickly to register the name, for she knew what was coming next. Sure enough, a few days later a letter arrived from No. 10: 'Have you fixed upon your name for the little one? Ask Llwydyn to give her a pretty Welsh name like Gwifid

["Honeysuckle"].[20] Margaret chuckled and said, 'Well, too late, old boy. She's called Margaret.'[21]

Whatever crisis he might be dealing with, Lloyd George never missed a National Eisteddfod in Wales. This most important of Welsh gatherings happened at a different location each summer, and it is difficult to overstate its significance as the expression of Welsh culture in all its different manifestations. The main prize is awarded for poetry in traditional Welsh strict-metre, a fiendishly complex system of metre and rhyme which few can master. Poets submit their entries under pseudonyms, and the identity of the winner is kept strictly secret until the climax of the ceremony, when they reveal themself by getting to their feet at the bidding of the Archdruid. The prize is a chair, symbolising the role of court bard, historically the prize on offer. Lloyd George had adopted the habit of speaking at the Eisteddfod on Chairing day (Thursday), which had become known as 'Lloyd George day'. It was one of the principal ways in which he connected annually with Wales.

In 1914 the war began shortly before the Eisteddfod was due to be held in Bangor, and the festival was postponed. It was eventually held in 1915, but the decision was controversial, since many leisure activities and events had been postponed for the duration. The following year the Eisteddfod again took place amid accusations of unpatriotic behaviour. Lloyd George made his appearance as usual, and used the occasion to tackle the subject head-on. It was one of his most memorable speeches, a *tour de force* of oratorical power. He spoke to the heart of Wales, but his speech resonated out to the whole country with its message of defiance, pride and hope:

> Why should we not sing during war? Why, especially, should we not sing at this stage of the War? The blinds of Britain are not down yet, nor are they likely to be. The honour of Britain is not dead, her might is not broken, her destiny is not fulfilled, her ideas are not shattered by her enemies. She is more than alive; she is more potent, she is greater than she ever was. Her dominions are wider, her influence is deeper, her purpose is more exalted than ever. Why should her children not sing? I know war means suffering, war means sorrow. Darkness has fallen on many a devoted household, but it has been ordained that the best singer amongst the birds of Britain should give

its song in the night, and according to legend that sweet song is one of triumph over pain. There are no nightingales this side of the Severn. Providence rarely wastes its gifts. We do not need this exquisite songster in Wales; we can provide better. There is a bird in our villages which can beat the best of them. He is called Y Cymro [the Welshman]. He sings in joy, he sings also in sorrow; he sings in prosperity, he sings in adversity. He sings at play, he sings at work; he sings in the sunshine, he sings in the storm. He sings in the daytime, he sings also in the night. He sings in peace; why should he not also sing in war? Hundreds of wars have swept over these hills, but the harp of Wales has never been silenced by one of them, and I should be proud if I contributed to keep it in tune during the war by the holding of this Eisteddfod today . . .

I make no apology for advocating the holding of the Eisteddfod in the middle of this great conflict, even although it were merely a carnival of song, as it has been stigmatised. The storm is raging as fiercely as ever, but now there is a shimmer of sunshine over the waves, there is a rainbow on the tumult of the surging waters. The struggle is more terrible than it has ever been, but the legions of the oppressor are being driven back and the banner of right is pressing forward. Why should we not sing? It is true there are thousands of gallant men falling in the fight – let us sing of their heroism. There are myriads more standing in the battle-lines facing the foe, and myriads more behind ready to support them when their turn comes. Let us sing of the land that gave birth to so many heroes.[22]

There was no more criticism.

The following year the Eisteddfod was held in Birkenhead, which was home to a large Welsh community. Margaret and Megan accompanied Lloyd George to stay with Lord Leverhulme at his nearby Port Sunlight mansion. On Thursday, 6 September, Lloyd George and Margaret took their positions on the platform for the chairing ceremony. It was to be one of the most dramatic and moving occasions in the history of the Eisteddfod. The afternoon's events led to the 1917 Eisteddfod becoming known as Eisteddfod y Gadair Ddu – the Eisteddfod of the Black Chair.

The chair that year was to be given for an ode on the subject 'The

Hero'. After Lloyd George had given a speech on the subject of small nations, the Archdruid proclaimed that the winning poet was 'Fleur de Lys'. The crowd waited expectantly to see the identity of the winner, but no one stood to claim the chair. The Archdruid asked twice more before making the solemn announcement that 'Fleur de Lys', the poet Hedd Wyn, had died in action in France.* The poet's parents stood on the platform alongside Lloyd George and Margaret as their son's chair was draped with black linen, a gesture that came to symbolise the horrific loss of Welsh youth during the Great War.

Lloyd George spoke once more at the Eisteddfod the following day before leaving for Criccieth, still affected by the emotion of the occasion. George Riddell, who accompanied the party, wrote in his diary: 'As we neared our destination the PM began to recite Welsh verses with much emphasis and feeling – all the time holding his wife's hand as if they were a newly married couple.'[23]

In a curious postscript to this event, Frances wrote in her autobiography that she too was at the Birkenhead Eisteddfod and attended the dramatic ceremony – although she wrongly refers to it as the crowning ceremony, and also gets the date wrong. Confirmation comes in the form of a letter from Gwilym on 18 September, in which he wrote to Frances, 'I am glad you like the Eisteddfod. I wish I could have been there as I'm awfully keen on the singing.'[24] Lloyd George's Welsh supporters would not have been pleased to know that his mistress was one of his entourage. Perhaps he felt more confident in taking Frances along because the Eisteddfod was held just across the border in England. It could not have been a comfortable situation for either Frances or Margaret, but it was not uncommon. The two women were thrown together from time to time on trips like these. Indeed, as we shall see, Frances even sometimes accompanied them on working holidays while Lloyd George was Prime Minister, a situation Margaret would surely not have tolerated had she known the full extent of her betrayal.

---

* Hedd Wyn was the bardic name of Ellis Humphrey Evans (1887–1917), a shepherd from Trawsfynydd in North Wales who was called up in 1917 and had joined the Royal Welch Fusiliers. He was killed during the battle of Pilkem Ridge on 31 July, having posted his winning poem home.

Frances returned to London when Lloyd George and Margaret left for Criccieth, but she was summoned to his side there on 13 September, when he was ill and missing her. He proposed that she and her sister Muriel should stay at the Marine Hotel in Criccieth and arrange to meet him secretly, using the valet Newnham as a go-between. If she did indeed go, it would have been her first visit to Criccieth since the summer of 1911.

In general, Frances was seeing very little of Lloyd George in 1917, and her low spirits were probably responsible for the gap in her diary from May to November that year, although it is possible that a section or notebook has been lost. But when Frances resumed it, it was to record the happiest week of the year, 'one of the most interesting and exciting incidents in my life', when she accompanied Lloyd George on an official visit to Rapallo.[25]

The trip was hastily arranged when Lloyd George received a message asking him to intervene in Italy, where German advances were causing great concern. Frances persuaded him to include her as the only woman in what was quite a large party – 'indeed, he did not need much persuading, for I think he had already made up his mind before I asked him'.[26] They spent a night in Paris to break the journey, and she noted with sorrow that it was hardly recognisable as the bright city she had visited before the war. Apart from a few early-morning walks, the conference was all business. It is unlikely that she and Lloyd George were able to spend much private time together, surrounded as they were by delegates, but they were at least away from his family and the tensions of No. 10.

The conference was Frances' first opportunity to observe the leaders of other European countries in person, and she made notes recording her opinion of everyone she came across. But she was also a genuinely useful and hard-working member of the team, which may well have paved the way for her inclusion in the secretariat that accompanied Lloyd George to the peace conferences after the Armistice.

Frances' diary breaks off once more on 9 November when Lloyd George paused for two days in Aix-les-Bains to prepare a critically important speech he was due to give in Paris three days later. In it he called for unity of command among the Allies, a highly controversial policy that was not fully carried out until after the near-disastrous events of the following spring. Nevertheless, Frances watched adoringly as Lloyd George used his famous powers of oratory to the full. 'There never was such a leader,' was her verdict.[27]

As the year 1918 dawned there was little good news on the war situation, but Frances was able to take satisfaction in seeing her name in the New Year's Honours list, awarded a CBE 'for services in connexion with the war'. The Orders of the British Empire had only been created in 1917, and 25,000 OBEs would be awarded within the first four years, along with peerages and knighthoods on a scale never before witnessed, some for far less honourable reasons than Frances', although the honours scandal that was to overshadow Lloyd George's last few weeks in office was still far distant.

In March, German forces made their most concerted effort yet to break the Allies' line of resistance. They smashed through the defences, and for a heart-stopping few weeks it seemed that there was no holding them back. At No. 10, a map in the Cabinet Room showed the British line marked in red, and every day Frances watched as it was redrawn further and further back. By April the enemy had reached Bethune. This was of particular significance to Frances, since her brother Paul had fallen near the town and was buried there: 'They will soon be trampling over his grave,' she wrote.[28] The thought that her brother's sacrifice could have been in vain was almost too much to bear. In a daze she made her way home, not to her flat but to her parents' house in Wallington. She did not consciously decide to do so, nor could she remember how she made the journey. It was the closest she ever came to breaking down under the pressure.

As it happened, the night of Frances' crisis was the night the German advance was halted. From the summer of 1918 onwards the Allies, reinforced by American resources, gradually assumed the ascendancy, and Lloyd George was able to tell Frances privately that victory was just a matter of time. But during 1918 a second deadly killer was sweeping through Europe: the influenza epidemic that killed as many people as fell on the battlefields. In September Frances was ill with an inflammation of the kidneys, and was being looked after by two nurses in George Riddell's rented country house, Danny Park in Sussex.

Normally fairly robust in health, Lloyd George was worn out from four years of worry and hard work. His hair was by now nearly white, although, to his immense satisfaction, it was not thinning. He had travelled to Manchester to receive the freedom of the city when he was struck so severely by the deadly 'flu infection that Newnham, the No. 10 valet, reported to Maurice Hankey, the head of the Cabinet Secretariat, that it was 'touch and go'.[29]

It took a fortnight for Lloyd George to recover his strength sufficiently to travel to Danny Park, and when he did so Frances was shocked at how gaunt he looked. She would not have been able to nurse him through his illness, but neither was Margaret, who had also succumbed to the epidemic and was confined to bed in Brynawelon. She hid her illness from her husband so that he would not affect his own recovery by worrying about her, and he was distressed when he learned about it later in a newspaper report.

With the war situation improving by the day, Lloyd George turned his attention to his own political position. The coalition had been assembled only for the duration of the war, and as soon as it was over a general election would have to be called. As the Liberal Prime Minister of a mainly Unionist government, and still facing considerable opposition from his party colleagues, it was not going to be easy to hold on to power.

On Sunday, 10 November 1918 came what Margaret called 'the most dramatic moment of our life in No. 10'.[30] She had gone with Lloyd George to Walton Heath for the weekend, and that afternoon she went out for a drive. As she walked back into the house, Lloyd George met her and said, 'Don't take off your hat, we're going back to Downing Street.' He did not explain, and presumably such changes of plan were commonplace, for Margaret did not question why they had to return at such short notice. When they reached Downing Street, Winston Churchill and General Smuts of the Imperial War Cabinet were waiting, and they sat down to dinner together. Nothing of any note was discussed, but Margaret sensed excitement in the air: 'Suddenly a message came for my husband, "You're wanted on the telephone from the War Office," and he went immediately. The three of us that were left never spoke a word. Mr. Churchill paced restlessly up and down the room. General Smuts and I sat in silence. He was not gone many minutes, but to us sitting there it seemed an age.'[31]

Lloyd George returned jubilantly to announce, 'They're going to sign.' Terms had been successfully imposed on the German leadership: the war would be over in a matter of hours. Margaret allowed herself a rare moment of self-satisfaction: 'I felt proud at that moment that I had been able to help him even a little in bringing the war to a successful end and the country out of its dark hour.'[32]

Finally, after over four years of war and the loss of 956,703 soldiers, 40,000 of them young men from Wales, and countless more wounded, the Armistice was signed in the early hours of 11 November 1918. When the news was delivered to Lloyd George, the relief brought with it no sense of triumph, initially at least. 'I am feeling like a man who has been in a big thing that is over,' he had told Riddell at Walton Heath. 'He is at a loose end; he does not know what to do. I feel like that. I have had a terrible time during the past four and a half years.'[33] But after he had informed the Cabinet, the good news began to sink in, and a group of bystanders in Downing Street were surprised to see the Prime Minister, his white hair fluttering in the wind, flinging the door of No. 10 open, waving his arms and shouting, 'At 11 o'clock this morning, the war will be over!'[34]

Before long a large crowd had gathered outside No. 10, blocking the entrance to Downing Street and beginning to fill Horse Guards Parade. They appeared to Harold Nicolson, who viewed the scene from the windows of the Foreign Office, to be numbed: too shocked and relieved to utter a word. Lloyd George next emerged through the garden door of No. 10 and walked over to the gate to Horse Guards Parade. 'Two secretaries who were with him urged him on,' wrote an eyewitness. 'He opened the door. He stepped out into the Parade. He waved his hands for a moment of gesticulation and then again retreated. The crowd rushed towards him and patted him feverishly at his back . . . Having regained the garden enclosure, Mr Lloyd George laughed heartily with the two secretaries who had accompanied him. It was a moving scene.'[35]

Frances watched from the window of her office as the crowds gathered, and heard the bells of London ring out the news. She felt flat and low, without quite knowing why. Thoughts of loss and bereavement filled her mind, and she was relieved to find that Lloyd George was feeling rather depressed too, which they both put down to the sudden lifting of such long-standing anxieties. Lloyd George went immediately to the House of Commons, where he read out the Armistice conditions and uttered the famous words, 'Thus at eleven o'clock this morning came to an end the cruellest and most terrible war that has ever scourged mankind. I hope we may say that thus, this fateful morning, came to an end all wars.'

A thanksgiving service was held in St Margaret's, the church opposite the Palace of Westminster, after which Lloyd George returned to Downing Street to dine quietly with Churchill, the Conservative MP F.E. Smith and General Sir Henry Wilson. Outside, the crowds celebrated into the night, and eventually even the tired Prime Minister could not resist joining in. He and Margaret ran upstairs to Olwen's bedroom, overlooking Downing Street. Leaning out of the window, they waved to the crowds and enjoyed the ecstatic reaction. Margaret was overcome with relief. She wrote to Olwen, with characteristic restraint: 'It's been a wonderful evening.'[36] In her possession was a new bracelet, beautifully made of diamonds and sapphires. It had been delivered anonymously to No. 10 with a note saying simply, 'To the Wife of the man who won the War.'[37]

17

Diverging Paths

AFTER THE ARMISTICE, the world did not change overnight. The long-anticipated end of the conflict seemed rather anticlimactic: guns fell silent, but the soldiers did not come home, food was still scarce and, for politicians keen to take advantage of the good news, it was straight into a hectic general election. Having ensured the survival of the British Empire, Lloyd George turned immediately to his own political survival.

The 'Coupon Election' of 1918 was a unique and particularly divisive election. On the face of it there was little that could stop 'the man who won the War' from also winning the votes of a grateful electorate. But the situation was complicated by the fact that Lloyd George was at war with his own party, and headed a coalition which depended on Conservative support to keep it afloat. Asquith was still nominally leader of the Liberal Party, and was not ready to stand down to make way for his former Chancellor, but neither did he command a sufficient following in the country to pose a serious threat to Lloyd George. Neither Lloyd George nor the Conservative Party could be sure of winning an election alone, and concluded that the only way to stay in power was to fight on as a coalition. The Labour Party, confident that the recent extension of the franchise to all men and women over thirty would strengthen its support, decided to break free and withdrew its members from the government, but in essence the coalition remained intact.

The practical arrangements were hammered out between No. 10 and Conservative Central Office: 150 'Lloyd George Liberal' candidates were to be given the coalition's official sanction by means of a letter of endorsement from the Cabinet (the so-called 'coupon' that lent its name to the election) and would, on the whole, be allowed to fight the election without opposition from Conservative candidates. Conservative candidates in all other constituencies would also fight on a coalition manifesto. This left the 'Asquith Liberals' – those who would not join the coalition, who made up the official opposition in the House of Commons – out in the cold. Each Liberal candidate had to make up his (or, for the first time, her*) mind whether to apply for a coupon or to place himself in official opposition to Lloyd George, who because of the war was at the height of his power and popularity. For many this was a painful personal decision, and Frances recorded in her diary how dismayed Lloyd George was at the schism within his party. His distress was heightened when he had to deny the coupon to many long-standing personal friends – most notably perhaps the hapless Tim Davies, who subsequently lost his seat.

The election was held on Saturday, 14 December 1918, and the result was a landslide for the Coalition. Five hundred and fifty 'coupon candidates' were returned, made up of 133 Lloyd George Liberals, 335 Coalition Unionists (Conservatives) and ten Coalition Labour MPs. The Asquith Liberals were routed – the ultimate humiliation was Asquith himself losing his seat – returning only twenty-eight Members overall. The Labour Party, with sixty-three seats, became the largest opposition party for the first time in history, since Sinn Féin won seventy-three seats, but refused to take them up, signalling how problematic the issue of Ireland was going to be during the forthcoming Parliament.

Lloyd George now had the mandate he wanted to negotiate peace and create the 'fit country for heroes to live in' he had promised to build.[1] For Frances, the election campaign had been fraught – she had mistakenly sent an endorsement to the opponent of the Coalition Liberal candidate in Swansea, showing how difficult it was to distinguish between Liberal candidates and earning herself a rare rebuke from Lloyd

* There were seventeen female candidates in 1918. The first female MP, Constance Markievicz, a Sinn Féin candidate, was elected at the Coupon Election but did not take up her seat. The first female MP to be introduced to the House of Commons was the Conservative Nancy, Viscountess Astor, in 1919.

George. The campaign had been enlivened for her when she was invited to John (later Lord) Reith's house to hear a radio broadcast for the very first time. The programme was, naturally, one of Lloyd George's election speeches.

Lloyd George had worked hard to secure his victory, but even on the eve of polling day he was uncertain of how this most unpredictable of elections would go, writing to Margaret, 'The factors are so uncertain that I cannot form any estimate.'[2] He was not the only one who had worked hard. Margaret had thrown herself wholeheartedly into the campaign, no longer confining herself to working on her husband's behalf in Caernarvon Boroughs, but embarking on nationwide tours. A grateful Lloyd George could not thank her enough: 'You have done brilliantly. Your tours have been the feature of the campaign. You have been flitting about though so much that I found it impossible to know where to write you.'[3]

Margaret had played an important role in the election, and was fast becoming as popular in the country as her husband.

In January 1919 the eyes of the world turned to Paris, where world leaders were gathering to decide how to proceed after the most devastating conflict in history. Weeks of negotiation had gone into deciding who should form part of Lloyd George's British Empire delegation, and as a consequence he led a group of no fewer than fourteen delegates, accompanied by over two hundred clerks, military staff and aides. Lloyd George, Margaret and Megan arrived in Paris a few days before the official opening of the conference, and were given the use of a splendid apartment on rue Nitôt, lent to them by a wealthy Parisian. Balfour, Lloyd George's Foreign Secretary, occupied the flat above, and the apartment was well equipped for entertaining, with a cook/housekeeper in residence and a piano in the drawing room.

The remainder of the British delegation was allocated the Hôtel Majestic, just down the street, as both accommodation and office space. The latter was at a premium, as A.J. Sylvester, who later became Lloyd George's Private Secretary, was to discover when he was given a bathroom as an office. Scores of telephone lines were installed with direct-dial access to London, a daily flight was arranged between Paris and London, and maids, waiters and officials were brought across from

Britain to look after the delegates. The hotel became a home from home as the delegation dug in for the six months it would take to produce the peace treaties. Even the food was brought across from Britain to replace 'the more intricate and mysterious dishes of the French Restaurant'.[4] The Majestic became as British as fish and chips, with a branch of Lloyds Bank in the foyer. Among the scores of military and clerical staff was one member of the delegation whose presence was non-negotiable. Frances moved into her room at the Majestic alongside her colleagues from No. 10. It was to be the highlight of her professional career, and a profoundly happy time for her.

There was plenty of work for Frances to do, but not as much as there had been during the war, and the relaxed atmosphere in Paris was a pleasant contrast to grey, wartime London. As the international delegations settled down to their work, Frances found herself working alongside the leading politicians of the world. President Woodrow Wilson of the USA arrived with his 'Fourteen Points' and a vision for a League of Nations. Georges Clemenceau, the French Prime Minister, had already won a tactical victory in locating the conference in Paris, and was determined not to give ground on any other issue either. Vittorio Orlando, Italy's emotionally charged Premier, Billy Hughes, the Welsh-speaking Prime Minister of Australia, and numerous other world leaders met daily, producing reams of minutes, papers and memoranda. As the conference progressed, the most powerful nations formed a 'Supreme Council' which met several times daily to confer on major decisions. To cut through the bureaucracy, as well as to ensure strict security, officials were excluded, so Lloyd George spent a large proportion of each day in private conference with Wilson, Clemenceau and Orlando. In between meetings he returned to the apartment in rue Nitôt, where Frances and JT had set up an office.

Security was a major concern even at a conference of allies, and the British delegation became aware that their telephone conversations with the Foreign Office in London were being intercepted. There was an urgent need to develop an unbreakable code. As officials struggled to devise one, Lloyd George had an idea: why bother with a new code when he had one already at hand? He gave his instructions to JT, who telephoned Ernie Evans, Lloyd George's Welsh Secretary at No. 10, and passed the necessary information across in Welsh. The other delegations never succeeded in breaking the new, impenetrable British code.

Lloyd George was not the easiest employer, and with so many complicated issues on his mind, it took all of Frances and JT's ingenuity to keep the flow of letters, papers and decisions going. Sylvester said of Lloyd George that 'like most men of genius, he was unmethodical'.[5] He would not sit down with his secretaries to deal with issues systematically; he enjoyed the game of making it difficult for them to focus his attention on matters he did not consider urgent. Male secretaries followed him to the lavatory or rode with him in his car to meetings to snatch a few uninterrupted moments. It was fatal to leave a letter with him, for he would lose it or put it aside for months. At his worst he would let his secretaries talk for a few minutes and then get up and leave the room without a word.

Nevertheless, Paris was more enjoyable for Frances than No. 10. She had plenty of time with Lloyd George, and had time at last to reflect on how far she had come. 'Who would have thought,' she wrote in April, musing on a trip to Paris she had made in 1905, 'when I made the same visit with [her French cousin] Suzanne one morning before breakfast 14 years ago, that I should one day be coming there with the Prime Minister of England, after a terrible war!'[6] Occasional walks around the city provided the lovers with the opportunity for intimate conversation: 'There is nothing to compare with these little walks with D when we unburden our hearts to each other & feel that we are about 10 years old!'[7] Amidst the hard work, Frances and Lloyd George were able to spend plenty of time together, walking, taking day trips out of Paris at the weekends, enjoying picnics and even dining together with friends who knew better than to gossip about their relationship. After the strain of the war years, the six months spent together in Paris were a golden opportunity for Frances and Lloyd George to renew their romance. She grew accustomed to spending time with him privately every day, and missed him desperately when he occasionally had to return to London to avert political crises at home. She would ring London constantly for news of his speeches, and wrote miserably in her diary, 'it is desolate without him, & I don't enjoy my freedom a bit'.[8]

Lloyd George's womanising reputation was international, as Frances was to discover, and his fondness for women was legendary among the delegates – not that any of the other main leaders led exemplary private lives.* Frances felt so close to her lover that she could laugh at the rumours, recording with amusement in her diary:

> P.M. lunched today at Mr Balfour's flat to meet with Queen of Rumania, & according to everybody, was on his best form. D. says she is very naughty but a very clever woman, though on the whole he does not like her. She gave a lengthy description of her purchases in Paris, which included a pink silk chemise. She spoke of meeting President Wilson on his arrival. 'What shall I talk to him about?' she asked, 'the League of Nations or my pink chemise?' 'Begin with the League of Nations,' said Mr Balfour, 'and finish up with the pink chemise. If you were talking to Mr Lloyd George, you could begin with the pink chemise!'[10]

On one occasion when they went for a drive to Fontainebleau, Frances wrote: 'We took along one of the girls from the Majestic, "the Peach", & D. flirted with her to his heart's content. However, he was quite open about it & I think it did him good, so that I did not mind.'[11]

As with Mrs Tim, provided that he did nothing behind her back, Frances was not inclined to make a scene about Lloyd George's flirtations. Doubtless, this was one of the characteristics that appealed so strongly to him. She also tended to blame the women for paying Lloyd George so much attention, rather than him. Occasionally she would betray some irritation, as with the wife of one of the delegates at Paris:

> Spent a very happy day wandering about the woods, though was annoyed by Mrs Clement Davies, who expected D. to pay a lot of attention to her, & I was cross in consequence. She is a most self-satisfied person, talks a lot & loves the sound of her own voice. Of course all women are fascinated by D. & he in turn is nice to most of them, &

* Woodrow Wilson married Edith Bolling Galt, his second wife, in 1915. Washington wags circulated the joke, 'What did Mrs Wilson say when the President asked her to marry him? Why, she fell out of bed in surprise!' Vittorio Orlando kept a Sicilian princess as his mistress. Georges Clemenceau's first marriage did not last long, he had many affairs, and in 1919 'he complained sardonically that, just when he was too old to take advantage of it, women were throwing themselves at him'.[9]

once having started they expect him to go on. The silly ones get their heads turned immediately & there is no doing anything with them. It is most amusing to watch. But I got rather angry with Mrs C.D. having had rather too much of that sort of thing lately. However D. & I made it up in the evening.[12]

Lloyd George was expected to respond to a pretty woman's advances, and there were plenty of opportunities in Paris in the spring of 1919. The delegates were engaged in serious business, but the war was over, and there was no need to be serious during their leisure hours. Day trips and dancing were perfect ways to express the release of tension after over four years of war.

Margaret's presence in Paris had cast only a brief shadow over the lovers' freedom, as to Frances' relief she returned to London on 8 February. Megan, however, stayed on. Nearly seventeen now, Megan was at a loose end. She was too old for school, but still young enough to be her father's adored pet; old enough to want to join in the fun in Paris, but young enough to be oblivious to what was going on between Frances and her father. Having been brought up on 'politics for breakfast, lunch and tea',[13] Megan found the heady mix of international politics and dancing at the Majestic irresistible. She had never been abroad before, and was determined to have a wonderful time.

At first Megan dutifully stayed at rue Nitôt under her father's watchful eye, but her privileged position as the Prime Minister's daughter, together with her vivacious personality and her artless love of attention, made her the conference 'pet'. Members of the delegation were only too happy to break off from their work to take her on picnics or to lunch, and she was soon living at the centre of a social whirlwind. Megan, never a systematic or disciplined person, kept a diary only for the first few days of the conference, but in it she describes her hectic social life, and also reveals how she was often chaperoned by Frances:

Met Lord Reading [the former Rufus Isaacs] on the way to the restaurant. When he saw me he immediately rose and leaving a friend came over to talk to me. 'Well, how are you?' 'Oh, splendid, thanks.' 'With whom are you lunching today?' 'I am sorry, I am lunching with Miss Stevenson and Mr Davies.' 'What a pity. I have been thinking of getting at you this morning. Please remind me, we will arrange something another day. We will go out together.'

Went to restaurant – Botha, Hughes, Smuts, C.I.G.S., Maharajah of Bikaner & son, Sinha among people there. Very jolly lunch. First of all prevented from coming in by a waiter but saved by Foreign Office man.

Went to the Louvre. Went up a quaint 'moving staircase', a very ricketty [sic] affair altogether, down which Miss Stev. refused to come.[14]

In her autobiography Frances writes that it was difficult to 'add the duties of a chaperone to those of a secretary',[15] but she does not complain of any awkwardness in the situation. She was used to being around Lloyd George's children – it was only Margaret who ever upset her – and seemed untroubled by their presence. Megan regarded her former tutor as a kind of honorary older sister, and it soon occurred to her that rather than stay with her Tada, it would be far jollier to share Frances' room at the Majestic. Frances had become such a good secret-keeper by this time that even sharing a room with Megan did not threaten to expose her double life. But was it wise of her to become so close to her lover's daughter? With hindsight it was this friendship, and the complete trust that Megan placed in Frances, that made her feel so bitterly betrayed when her eyes were finally opened. Frances did not realise that she was sowing the seeds of a lifetime's enmity.

Frances and Lloyd George were often accompanied by Megan, and by Gwilym and Olwen when they visited their father, on their day trips out of Paris. In her autobiography, Frances describes how they would go on tours of the battlefields:

Every Sunday during the dreary January of 1919 we drove through towns and villages which were unrecognisable but for the sign-boards which indicated their names: through country intersected with trenches and rusty barbed-wire entanglements and swathes of poppies. The language of Gwilym, who had had enough of these scenes under the terrible conditions of active warfare, and who was inclined to resent having to give up his weekend to this kind of entertainment, became on one or two occasions unprintable. But for L.G. it seemed almost an obsession and he gloried in it.[16]

If Frances' recollection of the dates is accurate, it is possible that Margaret was also of the party, adding further weight to the presumption that Frances' relationship with Lloyd George was as yet unknown.

Dances at the British delegation's HQ became the focal point of the conference's social life. Nevertheless, it was less than six months since hostilities had ceased, and Frances was conscious that it was not appropriate for the fun to go too far: 'People rather resent this invasion of the Majestic on Saturday nights, & steps are to be taken to put a stop to it, otherwise the thing will become a scandal.'[17] This, though, did not stop her from waltzing in the 'very pretty dresses' she had brought from London as a 'tonic'.[18] Her diary gives the impression that she loved the dances almost as much as Megan did, but felt guilty about letting herself go so soon after the war. She also felt guilty about the male attention she attracted as one of relatively few young females in the delegation: 'The Saturday evening dances there are great fun, but I do not say much to D. about it, as he gets rather jealous.'[19]

In an account she published anonymously later, Frances described the dances in more detail:

> They were simple scenes, these Saturday nights, but how attractive and unusual! The large hall downstairs was approached by a flight of steps which led down to the dancing floor, and often these steps would be thronged by higher officials of the Conference who came to watch the dance. Mr. Lloyd George would come for a short time to contemplate the bright scene; Lord Milner, Lord Robert Cecil, Lord Curzon were often spectators; I have seen Mr. Balfour studying the jazz band with a rapt intentness, entirely oblivious of everything else . . . there were very few members of the Conference, whether high or lowly, who did not at some time or other appear on these occasions.[20]

Megan shared none of Frances' scruples, and threw herself into the social scene at the Majestic so enthusiastically that it was jokingly suggested that the hotel should be renamed 'The Megantic'. Tales of her late-night escapades soon reached her father, and he decided (to Frances' relief) to enrol Megan in a finishing school in Paris, where she could be more closely supervised.

For the first time in many years, Frances was relatively carefree. She was thirty years old, but looked much younger, and occupied a position at the very heart of the conference. The attention she enjoyed in Paris was a balm after years of being kept in the background. Famous men like John Maynard Keynes and T. E. Lawrence sat in her office passing messages to Lloyd George, Augustus John invited her to parties (which a jealous Lloyd George forbade her from attending), and Nancy Astor made a friend of her. She was fêted as Lloyd George's unofficial wife, dining with him at discreet dinner parties, accompanying him on weekend day trips and being treated with gallantry by the great and the good. On one occasion she accepted an invitation to the opera and arrived to find, to her horror, that the red carpet had been laid out, and that it was Lloyd George himself who was expected, not his 'secretary'. But there were plenty of powerful, attractive and eligible men who paid her the most flattering attention for her own sake, and Lloyd George's jealousy was not entirely unprovoked.

In March, she records in her diary that she went to the opera twice with Edmond Harmsworth, the son of Lord Rothermere and heir to the Daily Mail Group, who was acting as Lloyd George's ADC in Paris. She described him in her diary – 'much nicer nature [than his father] I should imagine, but still rather cold & calculating' – in a way that suggests she was not emotionally engaged, despite signing off by saying he was 'extraordinarily handsome, & I like him'.[21] Later that month, during a game of golf at St Cloud, Frances roused Lloyd George's jealousy by walking with Harmsworth rather than with him, and that seems to have been the end of the relationship: it was not important enough to Frances to risk antagonising her lover, and she records a few weeks later that Harmsworth had left Paris and would probably not return.

After Harmsworth's departure, another suitor appeared, or rather reappeared, in Frances' life. In May Lloyd George left Paris briefly to visit Welsh troops stationed on the Ancre. Frances writes, 'Everything seems desperately lonely when he has gone,' but her loneliness did not last long, for the next day she writes warmly: 'Went to lunch at Armenonville with Bertie Stern, who has just come to Paris & says he is going to have a good time, which means he is going to give other people a good time. He is a most generous & thoughtful person & the best host I have ever met.'[22]

Colonel Albert Stern was an unmarried Jewish businessman. He had been a banker before the war, but had displayed more entrepreneurial skills while working for Lloyd George at the Ministry of Munitions, helping to develop the first tanks for use in battle. By 1917 he was head of the Mechanical Warfare Division, and on friendly terms with both Lloyd George and Frances. He was excellent company, wealthy enough to entertain the Prime Minister in style, and was knighted in recognition of his service in 1918. Frances liked him very much, and her diary in 1916 and 1917 is littered with references to weekends spent at Stern's 'beautiful' house near Worthing, drives in the countryside with Lloyd George and Stern, and lunches where he introduced her to fascinating characters such as Arthur Conan Doyle.[23] In November 1916 she wrote an animated account of an evening out on the town with him:

> Col. Stern took a party including Mr. Davies & me to dine & to a concert last night. Very amusing. Up till now we have seen only the official side of Col. Stern – his 'Tank' side, occasionally playing the role of host on very respectable lines. We had heard rumours of another side. Last night we had a glimpse of it – of 'Bertie Stern' of the Smart Set. I enjoyed it, though I'm glad I don't belong to them. Am beginning to feel, however, that I can deal with them effectively. They are very entertaining, & I like the glitter & light and laughing, but I'm glad I don't go <u>home</u> to it! However, Col. Stern is one of the least frivolous of them, though he seems to have a considerable reputation! He is not quite sure how much I know about him![24]

By April 1917 Frances was seeing so much of Stern that her mother, who had still not given up hope that her daughter would leave Lloyd George and find herself a respectable husband, harboured hopes of a wedding: 'Mamma told me that she had heard that I should marry Colonel Stern. Was never more surprised in my life. I hope he does not want anything of the sort, as he is quite a good pal, and besides I am quite sure he knows of the relations between D. & me. He has several times invited us down to his house together.' She goes on, however, to think about Stern's character in a way that implies she was at least considering her mother's suggestion:

I like him, though he has an unloveable side, but he is most kind and considerate. But it is always a question of how deeply these qualities penetrate – whether they are merely on the surface and displayed from a point of view of diplomacy, or whether they are genuinely spontaneous and natural. I have never found Col. Stern lacking for one moment in them so, unless he is extraordinarily clever, I am inclined to assume that they are natural – and indeed I prefer to do so, for it is bad for me to be continually looking for a hidden motive in every kind action, though public life rather tends towards fostering this attitude.[25]

Frances was experienced enough to know that some people courted her because of her influence with Lloyd George rather than for herself alone, but she dismissed this possibility in the case of Stern. Perhaps out of fear that rumours would spread, though, she did not see him as often thereafter. It was barely a fortnight later that she and Lloyd George made their extraordinary suicide pact, and rumours of Frances' relationship with Stern may well have contributed to Lloyd George's possessiveness at that time.

When Stern arrived in Paris, Frances found that the rumours about their relationship had taken hold: 'One of his friends asked me the other day why I did not marry him. "One excellent reason," I replied, "is that he has never asked me." But all the same I think he might ask me if he did not know perfectly well that I would not leave D.'[26] Despite this, she lunched, played tennis and danced with Stern (admittedly with Lloyd George present most of the time) on two of the following four days. On 24 May she actually discussed marrying Stern with Lloyd George: 'D & I had a long talk. I know Stern would marry me if I gave him the slightest encouragement & if he thought I would leave D.'

Unlike the Billy Owen plan, marrying Stern would mean Frances breaking off her affair with Lloyd George: Stern would demand full commitment from his wife. But she was not entirely immune to his charms, and could see the advantages a good marriage would offer:

It is a great temptation in a way for although I don't love him, we are good friends & I know he would be very kind to me. It would mean a title & wealth, whereas now I may find myself old & friendless &

having to earn my own living, if anything should happen to D. People will not be as anxious to marry me in 10 years' time. On the other hand, I know I should not be happy now away from D. & no-one else in the world could give me the intense & wonderful love that he showers on me. He was very sweet about it & says he wants to do what is best for me. But I can see that he would be unhappy if I left him, so I promised him I would not.[27]

Two days later, she records the end of the story: 'D. told me this morning that he had definitely made up his mind that he could not let me leave him. So that is final, & I am very glad. I need not worry about it any more. It would be very foolish to spoil for material prospects the most wonderful love that ever happened.'[28]

First in 1912, when Frances thought of marrying Stuart Brown, then again in 1915 with Billy Owen, and now in 1919 with Stern, Lloyd George had employed the same tactic of pretending to consider letting her go, putting her needs ahead of his, and then dramatically declaring his love in a swift reversal that ended up with her wrapped around his little finger again. This time Frances had a serious offer in hand, a marriage to a man she liked a great deal that would secure her future, but as soon as Lloyd George took a firm stance she put aside the 'material prospects' that had seemed so compelling two days previously, and accepted his decision without resentment.

What this episode does demonstrate is the extent to which Frances was worrying about her future. She was alive to the possibility that Lloyd George could die before Margaret, and that she might never be able to marry him. It was a bleak prospect, and one that made the alternative of becoming Lady Stern seem quite attractive. In the end the romantic in Frances' nature won out over the materialist, and Bertie Stern's wealth and respectability proved insufficient to wean her away from Lloyd George.

Despite the atmosphere of gaiety and mild decadence surrounding the Peace Conference, there was a very solemn side of life to be seen by those who ventured out of Paris to the battlefields beyond. The mud was barely dry on the Vimy Ridge, and it was only a three-hour drive from the centre of Paris to the fields where the battles of Paschendaele and the Somme had claimed so many lives. On 15 April Frances made the journey to see her brother Paul's grave, with her new friend Nancy Astor for company. It was a difficult day for Frances, reawakening bitter-sweet memories of the brother who had gone 'straight from the school-room to the battlefield'.[29] As if to further emphasise the fragility of life, on the way back from a picnic at Fontainebleau with the Churchills on the anniversary of Paul's death, a cyclist fatally collided with a lorry in front of Frances' eyes. The coincidence of the date and the sudden shock of witnessing her first death created a phobia in Frances' mind where driving was concerned. At first she was merely a nervous driver, but in time her fear increased and she gave up driving altogether, being nervous even of sitting in a car as a passenger.[30]

Towards the end of June the tortuous negotiations of the conference reached their conclusion, terms were put by the Allies to the Germans and the Peace Treaty was drawn up. The signing ceremony was arranged for the twenty-eighth in the Salle des Glaces at Versailles. Lloyd George ensured that Frances received a ticket, but her excitement at witnessing such a historic event was dulled both by the crush in the room, which kept her at a distance from the main event, and by the awareness that it marked the end of her happy time in Paris. She vented her irritation at the crowds in her diary, but nevertheless thrilled at the spectacle and at the sense of history being made. Many people hoped that the Treaty of Versailles would bring about the end of war itself. Lloyd George was not so optimistic. 'We shall have to do the whole thing over again in twenty-five years at three times the cost,' was his prescient comment.[31]

While her husband was in Paris, preoccupied with foreign negotiations, what of Margaret? With Megan in school in Paris, Margaret was free of family commitments for the first time since Dick's birth, and as the children became more independent, she had time to devote to her public work, which had increased dramatically since she had become the wife of the Prime Minister. She was now a well-known public figure, much in demand for speaking engagements across the country. During her last days at No. 11 she had agreed to launch a second fundraising appeal in connection with the war, this time on behalf of the British and Foreign Sailors' Society, for which she raised £70,000 (£2.75 million today). She was amused to note that the appeal was so successful that her postbag at No. 10 was bigger even than the new Prime Minister's.

Margaret's efforts for her Welsh Troops Fund were so successful that the Fund had a balance of £30,000 at the end of the war. She decided that the money should be used to help the children of those who had not returned, and she continued to raise money long after the war was over. She also worked diligently for the British Red Cross Society, the Ivory Cross, the YMCA and YWCA, the Middlesex Hospital, St Bartholomew's Hospital, the Jewel Fund and the Unwanted Babies Fund. In addition, she helped found the Criccieth branch of the Women's Institute, and was President of the Criccieth Lifeboat Association.

Margaret has often been portrayed as politically inactive, or as largely confining her political activities to North Wales. It is true that her focus was on raising children during the first years of her marriage, but in a newspaper article she wrote in 1934 she states unequivocally that she was actively involved in her husband's career very early on:

> ... there were only a few years, and those right at the beginning [of our marriage], before my husband had entered politics and while he was still occupied entirely with his legal practice, during which I did not actively share his work.
>
> In those early days, home and the children took up all my time, but as soon as he began his political career I began to help him. I started by canvassing with him at election time in Criccieth, North Wales, where we lived and were well known, for we had grown up there.
>
> Then I began to address meetings, just occasionally at first because I was nervous – more often as my nervousness left me. The next step was to take a hand at organising during election time, but I still only worked in my husband's constituency.
>
> It was not until three elections had passed and my youngest son was six years old and well out of the baby stage, that I began to do political work in other parts of the country. Megan was not born then, and the other four children were old enough to be left.[32]

If Margaret's memory is accurate, this places the beginning of her political work at around 1899. Her account is slightly at odds with that of her son Dick's, which like Olwen's memoir states that she only began to help Lloyd George in the constituency when he joined the government in 1905. Perhaps they were too young to realise the extent of her involvement, for further evidence of Margaret's early political activity comes from a profile of her in the nonconformist Welsh journal *Y Gymraes* (The Welshwoman) in June 1904 (translated from the Welsh):

> She has been of incomparable assistance to her husband in his public work. When she accompanies him on his election trips her presence on the platform always ensures the crowd's hearty applause . . . She is not fond of speaking, and left to herself she desists, but when the call comes, she is sure to have something worth saying and is certain of a hearing. We heard of her charming the audience to such an extent that they cheered many times, they worked themselves up into a frenzy, and it is said that her husband took fright and threatened to keep her at home lest she take the oratorical laurels away from him.[33]

By the time she had been a Cabinet Minister's wife for three years, Margaret was more heavily involved in politics. She had long been associated with local campaigns on traditional Liberal issues such as temperance, but by 1908 she was ready to take to the national stage, standing for election to the Executive Committee of the Women's Liberal Federation. Her election address includes a revealing passage:

> You are naturally right in supposing that I am deeply interested in Liberal work in the progress of those Liberal principles which my husband and his colleagues in the Cabinet are fighting so hard to advance. I have not hitherto taken a very active public share in them, but I believe that I now may be of use, and that especially in Wales I can help to rouse the women to support both the Government and the great cause of their own enfranchisement.[34]

Margaret's support for the enfranchisement of women might have developed late in the day, but it was not a passing fancy. Despite her disapproval of the militant tactics employed by the suffragettes before the war, she maintained steady support for women's suffrage through her membership of the WLF, which did much to compel the leaders of the Liberal Party to support the cause. In a draft of a speech she gave to the Welsh Temperance Society celebrating the enfranchisement of women, she writes: 'People say that woman has been given the vote. I would rather say that woman has earned the vote. The victory was won by the women in munition offices, camps . . . I read that in the past few weeks our armies have often marched forward under cover of darkness. Under cover of the war woman has marched forward to her political emancipation.' She goes on to counsel the new voters to use their power wisely:

> Power is one thing to possess, political wisdom is quite another thing. Women have won the right to vote. We must now see that they vote right. Political power without political wisdom is a great danger (Bolshevism is a case in point). As women will have so large a share of political power in Britain it is of the utmost importance to take all the means in our power not simply to <u>organise</u> but also to educate them. I hope also that women will not only study how to vote but study the problems which have to be solved so as to bring an original & fresh contribution to the discussion.[35]

Margaret had found a political voice of her own, and it came as no surprise to her family that she should be asked to stand for Parliament no fewer than ten times between 1910 and 1920 – nor that she refused each time, for however active she might be behind the scenes, the front line of politics was not for her. In a refreshingly frank article entitled 'Petticoats Behind Politics' written for the *Daily Chronicle* in 1926, Margaret explained her views on women in the House of Commons:

> It is on account of the stressful side of politics that I am doubtful whether there will ever be an overwhelming majority of women M.P.s in our House of Commons. Taking women in the bulk, they are physically not as strong as men . . . to give one concrete example only in proof of my statement that they are not as strong physically as men, – women are not employed in the mines. It is generally realised that such labour is beyond their strength, and not a woman's job. It is this physical handicap that, to my mind, will prevent our sex from having a majority in the House of Commons. Here and there, it is true, may occur isolated examples of women Leaders who, through the sheer force of their personalities, triumph over their physical disabilities. This fact is evidenced by some of the clever women M.P.s at present in the

House of Commons, but generally speaking such women Leaders have attained to their positions because they possess the vivid personality that crushes all obstacles, and carries its Owners triumphantly to the desired goal . . .

She goes on to reflect on her own experience:

I shall doubtless call down vials of wrath on my defenceless head if I divulge a private inclination of my own, and say that I do not believe in young married women having political careers. I am even so old fashioned as to unabashedly declare that I consider that they have a more important 'career' to hand in the bringing up of their children. For the benefit of those superior Critics who designate such a 'career' as being hum-drum, and beneath the super-intelligence of the modern woman, I would add that it takes all a woman's super-intelligence and beyond to be an understanding and successful wife and mother.[36]

Time and time again in her public statements Margaret stressed the importance of placing the family first. Frances Stevenson, her staunchest critic when it came to domestic management, might not have agreed, but the devotion of Margaret's children and grandchildren tells a different story. Lloyd George fully supported his wife's priorities, telling Riddell: 'She is full of courage, and she never hankered after society. She kept me to the simple life. That was a great advantage . . . it is well to have a wife whose interests are centred entirely in her modest home.'[37] Riddell confirmed the comfort of the home Margaret created in Criccieth: 'This is a comfortable villa, such as a prosperous tradesman might have. Everything is comfortable, but there are no frills. L.G. is very adaptable. When one sees him here, one would never imagine that he had ever lived under any other conditions.'[38]

Luckily for Margaret and for Lloyd George, her greatest challenge – being the wife of the Prime Minister – occurred when the children were grown and all but Megan had left the family home. She had been living in Downing Street for eight years, but moving into No. 10 was a different matter altogether: 'As soon as my husband became Prime Minister,' she wrote, 'I realised that I must help him as I had never helped him before.'[39] Margaret worked long hours, without sparing herself. She would often start the day by helping Lloyd George host a breakfast party, often followed by meetings, receptions and dinners until midnight: 'From the moment when I first put on my hat in the morning, I never had a second to take it off until I went to bed at night.'[40] Her engagements often took her away from London, and she had to rely heavily on Sarah to manage the household during her absence.

As the Prime Minister's wife, besides running her own war charity and organising Lloyd George's work in Caernarvon Boroughs, Margaret had an increasingly large number of letters to deal with. Attending to the post with the help of her secretary was her first job of the day, as she wrote in an article in the *Sunday News*: 'This was a heavy task to get through, apart from anything else, as my usual daily post-bag seldom averaged less than sixty letters per morning, and generally a great deal beyond that number. Still, I managed somehow to read every one of those letters.'[41]

At first Margaret tried to accept every invitation to open bazaars and attend charitable functions, but eventually she realised the impossibility of the task, although she still attended three or more functions a week throughout her husband's time in office. Her sense of duty was as strong as her work ethic, a fundamental part of both her religion and her character. Nothing was allowed to stand in her way if she had given her word that she would be at an event: once, on the way to a bazaar in North Wales, she broke her arm as she helped to crank the car's engine. Nevertheless she carried on, performed her duties and only complained of the pain when the event was over. She was anguished if she could not fulfil a promise, and hated letting people down. When she had to cancel an engagement to speak to the Baptist Union conference in Birmingham because of illness, she made a point of apologising publicly the following year:

> We are advised on high authority to make peace with our adversaries quickly. My first duty this afternoon is to make peace with my friends of the Baptist Union. I made a promise to attend your meeting last year at Birmingham. It was an engagement among a number of other engagements I failed to keep because I had a slight breakdown. I now apologise for any inconvenience I may have caused you. Having, I hope, made peace, let me say that it is a real pleasure to me to be here today . . .[42]

This was not the flowing oratory that won Lloyd George the attention of his audiences, but it was heartfelt and simple, and Margaret's audiences loved her for it. 'I am not a talker,' she once said. 'I leave that to other members of my family.'[43] While her husband would work on a speech for weeks, Margaret preferred to make a few notes and then speak from the heart. On a rare occasion when she did put some work into preparing an address, noting down headings and jotting notes underneath them, no sooner had she ascended the platform than she discovered her piece of paper was lost, and she had to extemporise as usual.

Margaret may not have shone as brightly on a platform as her husband, but few could match her ability to host a gathering and make every guest feel welcome. These were hard-working, austere times, quite unlike the gaiety of pre-war London, but they suited Margaret well, for she was not a frivolous person. In her 1927 *Sunday News* article she recalled: 'there were no late Balls, nor a number of social parties to attend, but instead there were a number of official duty functions, and charity dinners in the evening. At that period we neither gave dances nor went to any. In any case, even had you felt like dancing, there was no time to indulge in the pastime. Your entire day was spent in hard work . . . I generally ended up somewhere about midnight, which made nearly a 15-hour day.'*[44]

Downing Street guests spoke of Margaret's naturalness and warmth, and she had an ability to put everyone at their ease, from aristocrats to Welsh serving girls in London chapels, who proudly told their mistresses that Mrs Lloyd George had spoken to them. Her quiet, digni-fied bearing was better suited to looking after her guests than to taking the lead in social events, which in any case Lloyd George did naturally, and when he was present she happily took a supporting role.

Margaret's willingness to let her husband take centre stage was part of her philosophy when it came to being the wife of a politician. In every marriage where one partner is a public figure, the other has to

---

* In the unedited version of the article she goes on to say: 'It amuses me when I listen to some of the Socialists volubly clamouring for an eight hour day for the working classes, as they express it, and think of the length of my own working day when we lived in Downing St.'

reconcile him or herself to a secondary position in public. Political spouses have interpreted their role in many different ways, but few occupants of 10 Downing Street can have been as different in their approach as Margaret Lloyd George and her predecessor, Margot Asquith. While Margaret believed that she should not interfere in politics, Margot would frequently write to members of her husband's Cabinet, causing him untold political embarrassment. Asquith's career was his wife's. Margaret, by contrast, believed that she had a separate, parallel role to her husband's, helping him by concentrating on non-controversial and domestic matters, and allowing him to take the lead in public. As she wrote in her *Daily Chronicle* article:

> I so often hear the following speech spoken concerning some well-known Public man, 'Oh yes, x was made politically by his wife!' Speaking personally, I do not believe in that theory. A wife may assist her husband in his career, but if he possesses the divine spark of personality . . . then that personality will be the spur to ultimately win him through in his career. It is true a wife may materially assist her husband in this aim by seeing that his home atmosphere is as peaceful and restful as possible, and by giving him every opportunity when there, to relax . . . The wife who has her husband's career really at heart will have sufficient sympathy with his aims, and ideals, to submerge her own personality in his. There is a vast difference between merging and submerging. The former entails a total obliteration, whereas the latter is a submerging in order to create a wider mental Isthmus for the husband and wife.[45]

Margaret praises Gladstone's wife Catherine for her restraint in public, and continues, in a passage that was crossed out: 'Of very different calibre to this is Lady Oxford [as Margot Asquith had become]. Her chief characteristic is to superimpose her own personality.' The crossing-out is in a hand suspiciously like her husband's, and Lloyd George might well have felt that the comment was unnecessarily provocative. The same hand softened a critical passage about Lady Astor later in the article, and deleted some negative remarks about the Labour MP Margaret Bondfield, the first female Cabinet Minister. Margaret was, though, allowed to say: 'Speaking personally, I consider it a mistake for a wife to interfere in her husband's career, and to seek to lead him. Such a policy tends to make the man appear a fool and the woman becomes the bear-leader!' Of that, Margaret could never be accused.

Considering Margaret's background, her role model in public life was an unexpected one: she had become an admirer and friend of the Queen's.

Queen Mary, born Princess Mary of Teck, had a sheltered childhood, but from her mother, who worked hard for charity, she learned to sympathise with the working classes. People commented on her shyness, but she was intelligent, alert and had a sense of the ridiculous – not unlike Margaret Lloyd George. She had been engaged to marry Queen Victoria's eldest grandson Albert Victor, Duke of Clarence, but he died in January 1892, a few weeks before the wedding, and the following year Mary married his brother, the Duke of York, who became King George V in 1910. Queen Mary was not an immediate hit: people found her stiff and forbidding, and she was manifestly not in tune with the smart set, disliking small talk and gossip. But she played a central role in developing and administering wartime charity – it was said that during the war she undertook three times her normal number of engagements. In her fundraising and hospital visits she would have found a natural point of contact with Margaret. Both were naturally conservative, lovers of tradition who were slightly out of keeping with the twentieth century.

Her own public work gave Margaret a rare insight into Queen Mary's position. She knew from experience how physically tiring it was to be constantly on show, and admired the graciousness with which the Queen carried out her difficult role:

Persons who imagine that the wife of a Prime Minister, or for the matter of that, the wife of any public man, leads a pleasure seeking easy going existence are entirely mistaken in their ideas. Just as those who use the catchphrase 'As happy as a King, or a Queen!' employ it in all ignorance of the vast responsibilities that Kingship, or Queenship, entails.

Queenship indeed in these days at least, necessitates practically complete self-forgetfullness [sic]. For instance, no matter how fatigued Her Majesty, Queen Mary may be feeling by the performance of her numerous public functions, yet to the members of the public she invariably contrives to display that charming smile that warms them, by its subtle expression of an understanding appreciation of their pleasure.[46]

In Margaret's view the wife of the Prime Minister should desist from independent political activity, and she therefore cut down on her own political campaigns. Until Lloyd George left office, her public and political work was strictly in support of him. Her reticence in public was well known, and journalists regarded it as 'unthinkable to approach Mrs. Lloyd George for any inside information . . . she was too profound of self respect and the honour of her soul to purvey matters for social and political gossip'.[47] This did not mean, however, that she gave up her political views, and those who knew her well were accustomed to hearing her speak her mind without holding back. Lloyd George would have done well to listen to her in 1922 when, with his mind on resignation, he accepted a contract to write his war memoirs for £90,000, the equivalent today of over £3.5 million. He was vehemently attacked in the press for profiting from the war, and was forced to announce that the money would go to charity. 'I did tell you not to take the money for the book didn't I?' wrote Margaret. 'That's a feather in my cap. You can write another book to make money, but not on the war. I could not touch a penny of it.'[48]

George Riddell's diaries record numerous examples of Margaret's outspoken opinions. For instance, after the Coupon Election of 1918 when Lloyd George and he were discussing the composition of the government, she burst out with: 'It is a pity that the PM accepted any assistance from Beaverbrook and Rothermere at the election. I am sure he did not need it. I don't trust them or like their ways. The PM does best when he goes his own way and keeps clear of all these wire-pullers and people who want nothing but to grind their own axe.'[49]

Margaret was a confident woman, even if her public reticence could sometimes be mistaken for shyness. When it came to Lloyd George's constituency, Welsh matters or natural Liberal territory like temperance, she felt able to take decisions on behalf of her husband. On one occasion in his absence she received a delegation of Cardiff dignitaries in Downing Street. The Lord Mayor explained that since Lloyd George had achieved such political success, it was unsuitable for him to represent a constituency such as Caernarvon Boroughs, and that they felt he had now earned the honour of representing Cardiff. Dick tells the story: 'Well, that did it. The explosion that followed the belittling of Snowdonia shook these Cardiff bigwigs to their marrow. Eyes blazing, and scorn filling every syllable, my mother told the dumb-founded Deputation just what she thought of them . . . It was a two-fisted, bilingual knock-out.'[50]

Margaret was tested to the limit during the war years. As well as enduring the strain of constant hard work and responsibility, she worried about her sons in uniform as much as any mother. She confessed that it was a relief to have such a busy life to take her mind away from the dangers her sons were facing: 'a day crowded with appointments left me with no time to think of my two sons at the front'.[51] With Lloyd George focused on the war situation, she helped ease the burden by looking after his constituency. Despite what he might say to Frances, this increased Lloyd George's dependence on his wife. He might turn to another woman for romantic love, but it was Margaret he consulted on political matters.

During the Coupon Election, Margaret came into her own as an effective and popular political campaigner. As Lloyd George fought vigorously across the country, he placed his faith – and his political future – in her hands, entrusting her to make sure the voters of Caernarvon Boroughs returned him to Parliament. Olwen recalled: 'I think it was this election which really proved her worth, and showed the people of Wales and beyond that she was a forcible character in her own right. With characteristic energy, she toured the countryside speaking at meetings, and in her hands his Caernarvon seat was safe.'[52]

She organised the campaign herself, preparing for Lloyd George's visits and addressing meetings in his absence. Her unassuming style and readiness to roll up her sleeves during the war had made such an impression that she was heavily in demand far beyond the boundaries of Caernarvon Boroughs. During the campaign she spoke for nineteen candidates besides her husband, fourteen of whom won their seats: they were so grateful that they clubbed together to buy her a silver tray in appreciation. She could now truly describe herself as a politician: 'I am, in fact, my husband's second in command.'[53]

Even in Downing Street, though, Margaret put her domestic duties first:

I had a large staff to manage and a lot of entertaining to arrange, I had my own full share of social work, and at the same time I had always to be ready to help my husband, and even to be his deputy as often as possible at minor engagements when his presence was required more urgently elsewhere. In addition, I had to watch his health as I always have watched it – to see that he had the right kind of food at the right time so that he could carry on.[54]

Lloyd George might complain to Frances that his wife did not study him, but her own version of events is significantly different. Her articles are littered with references to making sure that he was comfortable: 'my first duty was to him – to keep him in good health and to secure for him, as far as possible, rest and quiet, and freedom from petty worries'.[52] She also refers to her attempts to get him to leave London at the weekends to get some rest and peace at Walton Heath: 'We tried to get away to Walton Heath every week-end, but often he did not arrive there until seven o'clock on Saturday evening, and was obliged to be back in town by Sunday night. Any leisure he did have he spent quietly at home.'[55]

Reading Margaret's words, it is impossible not to wonder if she suspected that her husband may not have been quite as busy as he claimed, and that the reason for his short weekends and lack of leisure time might have been his desire to spend time with Frances. Margaret was a straightforward and truthful individual, and it is unlikely that she was painting a picture of a happy home life which she knew to be false. But she was referring only to those periods when she was in London. She was frequently absent, and at those times it was Frances who provided him with comfort. Margaret undoubtedly cared about Lloyd George's welfare when she was with him, but did she ever wonder how he managed without her? Frances commented: 'Mrs. Ll.G. is watching [Lloyd George] like a hawk. She is an extraordinary person. She goes away for weeks & does not bother about him, but when she comes back she is on the watch all the time. Most inconsistent.'[56]

One domestic detail does ring true: Margaret might not care about her own wardrobe, but she did care about her husband's. 'I don't know if all busy men are the same or if the tendency is confined solely to politicians,' she wrote, 'but if I did not attend to it I believe my husband would never have any new clothes. I doubt if he has even been inside a shop in years, much less bought anything. When he needs a new suit I have to remind him. Of course, he does the actual choosing of the material himself, but the rest is left to me or to Megan, now she is grown up. All his shopping – the buying of his ties and socks and shirts we do between us. If it were left to him it would never be done.'[57]

Margaret was particularly busy while her husband was in Paris in 1919, for she had new family commitments in the form of her two little granddaughters, Margaret Carey Evans and Valerie Lloyd-George. While Dick was away in uniform, Margaret spent a great deal of time with Roberta and Valerie at their home in Llanystumdwy. She was the fondest of grandmothers, and was only too happy to add 'Nain' (Granny) duties to her list of activities. These, of course, kept her from accompanying her husband on his foreign engagements more often, but that suited them both quite well.

With the Treaty of Versailles signed, Lloyd George and Frances said goodbye to Paris. For Frances, it was a sad homecoming. She did not relish sharing Lloyd George with his family again. 'We left with many regrets,' she wrote. 'D. hates returning home. He has been well looked after in Paris – has had every comfort – the best food – the best attendance. He has been able to entertain at will. When at Downing St., or Walton Heath it is another matter. There is never enough to go round & what there is, is very inferior.'[58] But if Lloyd George was sad to leave Paris, there was a big consolation prize waiting for him.

Lloyd George's triumphant return with the peace terms signed was avidly anticipated in London. The government had discussed marking the occasion by lining the streets with troops, but this had been rejected by Winston Churchill. Lloyd George was therefore expecting a low-key reception, but the spontaneous scenes at Victoria Station were no less impressive than the government's aborted plan. An excited crowd gathered, and a red carpet had been rolled out along the platform, ending at the very point at which he would alight from his special train. Margaret, Olwen and Tom were escorted through the crowd to wait at the edge of the red carpet. There was even more excitement to come when, in an unprecedented move, the King decided to welcome his Prime Minister home personally. To the delight of the people who thronged the station, the King and the Prince of Wales arrived shortly before the train.

The King invited Lloyd George to travel with him in his open carriage to Buckingham Palace. Excited spectators threw flowers and even a laurel wreath, which landed on the King's lap. He handed it to Lloyd George, who later gave it to Frances as a memento. Margaret, Olwen and Tom followed in the official car while Frances, reverting seamlessly to her official role as private secretary, made her own way home. At the Palace, Margaret was taken in to join her husband while Olwen and Tom waited in the car in the courtyard. When the Queen realised they were there, she sent a footman to invite them in. Tom tried to excuse himself, for he was wearing his well-worn, shabby uniform, but Olwen would not let him, and in they went to be greeted by the King and Queen, the Prince of Wales and Princess Mary.

Back at Downing Street, reporters and cameras pressed against the car as a tired Prime Minister made his way into the house. For Margaret and Frances, the homecoming marked the beginning of a new dynamic to their relationship, as Frances' position at Lloyd George's side became impossible to ignore. World peace had been restored, but the war in No. 10 was about to begin.

18

Disillusionment

Frances came back from Paris with a heavy heart, for it would not be as easy for her to spend time with Lloyd George back at No. 10 with his family close at hand. Barely a week after their return, Lloyd George went to Criccieth for a fortnight's holiday. Frances was left behind, feeling that 'everything is so dreary when he is not here, & time hangs so heavily'.[1] She managed the occasional telephone conversation with him, but the separation was even more painful for having come after the happiest spell of their six-and-a-half-year relationship. A rare surviving letter from Frances shows how much she missed him:

> My own darling man,
> It was just heaven to hear your voice today, & it has given me the necessary courage to keep up my spirits till you return. I really have been trying to be cheerful, but I cannot help counting the time, which is a very bad plan; for I try all sorts of ways to try & make the days seem shorter, but all I do only seems to have the reverse effect . . . I want you to have all the rest you can, sweetheart, but oh! I do miss you so dreadfully, & I get such awful fits of loneliness . . .[2]

This is the passionate language of a young lover, unlike the more measured tone she uses in her diary, but there is no doubting the sincerity of her feelings or her faith in his love as she writes: 'It frightens me, now, cariad, when I realise how you are all in all to me, & how nothing,

nothing in the world matters to me but you. Is it not a terrible thing to have staked your all like that on one person? It would be, but I know that that person is mine, & that he will not fail me, & that I can lean on him, & trust in him, & that he is my father & lover & brother & friend. You are all that to me, my beloved, and much more.'[3]

Apart from the fact that she was missing Lloyd George badly, it must have seemed very dull to Frances to be back at her desk at No. 10 without the sense of national crisis that had supplied the adrenalin previously. It was a painful contrast to the excitement and glamour of the Peace Conference, and her low mood manifested itself in outbursts of vitriol against Lloyd George's family. Seeking a new out-of-London bolthole that provided more privacy than Walton Heath could offer, Margaret had chosen a house called The Firs, set back from the road between Esher and Cobham in Surrey. It was larger and more comfortable than Walton Heath, but was surrounded by woods and lacked a view, something Lloyd George regarded as essential. Margaret was officially in charge of furnishings and decoration, but while she was with Lloyd George in Wales Frances was able to exert her influence, for instance preventing the hanging of a portrait of Dick's wife Roberta in the entrance hall. 'How everyone dislikes her!' wrote Frances. 'I have never heard a single person say a good word for her, not even D., who usually finds <u>some</u> good points about everyone.'[4] It seems that Frances had taken a dislike to Lloyd George's attractive young daughter-in-law.

To Frances' private satisfaction, Lloyd George did not immediately take to his new house:

D's first impressions of the Cobham house were not very good. It was wet & cold & they had not even bothered to light a fire for him, & even when he asked for one they were hours making it – & when they had made it it was not worth looking at. That is how he is always served. So that he is not very favourably impressed. However, I think it will be very nice, if only they make it warm. He would not even have had a room of his own if J.T.D. & I had not insisted on the billiard room being turned into a dining-room, & the latter being made into a study for D.[5]

After being treated as Lloyd George's unofficial wife in Paris, Frances was even more conscious of the indignities she endured in London, where Margaret's presence meant that she was frequently obliged to pretend she was just a secretary. Occasionally she even had to endure working holidays with her lover and his wife. In August–September 1919 Lloyd George had been persuaded to take a long break: the strain of the previous three years was taking its toll on his health. Riddell organised a house in Brittany, and as usual a large group of colleagues and officials travelled with Lloyd George and Margaret to keep the Chief occupied. Frances was of the party, but apart from a slightly disapproving reference to the choice of destination (which probably means that it was chosen by Margaret) she says little about the early part of the trip in her autobiography. Things livened up for her when Margaret went home and Frances took centre stage, playing the piano at Lloyd George's favourite impromptu concerts in the evenings. On his return he went back to Criccieth for more rest, and Frances' diary is silent again from July to November.

Even after the signing of the treaty in Paris there were countless foreign policy issues to be settled, and the situation was tense as the government struggled to decide its relationship with the new Bolshevik state in Russia. All in all, Lloyd George took part in thirty-three international conferences between 1919 and 1922. Closer to home, the Irish situation became critical as relations between the British government and the Sinn Féin Parliament (the Dáil) established after the 1918 election deteriorated. Violence was spreading, and an army of volunteers, the infamous Black and Tans, was sent to Ireland. They entered enthusiastically into the fray of shootings, executions and reprisals, and it seemed the situation was fast getting out of hand.

The industrial unrest that broke out before the war resumed with even greater vehemence. The cost of living in Britain more than doubled between 1914 and 1918; by 1920 it was three times as high as it had been at the outbreak of the war. A diminished market for goods led to job losses, and those who had employment did not see why they should accept lower wages now that the war was over. Housing was in desperately short supply, and the majority who were suffering pointed angry fingers at the few who had done well financially out of the war. The gulf between rich and poor widened, but the poor were now organised, and had trade unions and Labour MPs to represent them. These were spurred on by the success of communism in Russia, and amid rising unemployment and widespread dissatisfaction, the government worried that the tide of revolution would soon reach Britain.

The initial popularity of the coalition that had delivered victory soon faded, and the government seemed slow and incompetent as it failed to address the pressing need for reconstruction. Lloyd George made strenuous efforts to keep all the plates spinning, holding on to his War Cabinet for as long as possible. Eventually it had to be disbanded, and he reluctantly reverted to an expanded Cabinet with its diminished capacity for quick decisions and decisive action. Lloyd George was also spending most of his time on foreign policy, which he enjoyed, and was not devoting enough energy where it was needed at home.

Politically, he looked increasingly isolated. The Coalition Liberals had rejected the idea of closer cooperation with the Conservatives, and the pressure of office prevented Lloyd George from establishing the strong party machinery they needed as an independent movement. A small group of Asquithian Liberals, having lost their general in the election, still refused to make peace with their former colleagues, and sat on the opposition benches, calling themselves Independent Liberals. Their resolve was strengthened by the return of Asquith to Parliament as MP for Paisley in 1920.

There were positive developments amid the gloom. Lloyd George succeeded in passing some of his land reform measures, for instance facilitating local authorities to purchase land for smallholdings for returning servicemen. Also, the long-awaited Welsh Disestablishment Bill finally made its way onto the statute books in 1919. An independent Church in Wales came into being the following year, but Lloyd George had long since lost his enthusiasm for the issue, which seemed to belong to a past age. Much more pressing was the need to fulfil his promise of a 'fit country for heroes to live in'. The war might be over, but there was still urgent work to be done.

In London, social life resumed with a vengeance after years of restraint. Frances, her confidence boosted by her Paris experience, made the most of it. She had made new friends in Paris, and became a regular guest at the Astors' house and at the Conservative MP Philip Sassoon's fashionable dinner parties. Sassoon was rich, amusing and socially very ambitious. He realised that the way to Lloyd George's heart was to pay attention to his secretary. Frances wrote of an early encounter in her diary:

> P. Sassoon came down to Cobham with D. & Sir George Riddell & me today & we played golf at St. George's Hill. Had a very jolly day. He is quite good company. Very ambitious though, which he admits. D. has asked him to come to Paris with us after Xmas purely D. says because he has been nice to me! He certainly has, & very attentive – almost embarrassing, in fact. He seems to be fabulously rich, but is clever also & can be most amusing.[6]

Sassoon's tactics evidently worked, for by the following year Lloyd George had appointed him his Parliamentary Private Secretary. Nancy Astor was furious. She was engaged in a social battle with Sassoon over whose house the Prince of Wales – the ultimate social prize – preferred. The dispute eventually caused Frances to end her friendship with Lady Astor. Firmly in Sassoon's camp thereafter, she entered a smart social scene. Her diary is full of dances, dinners and trips to the theatre or the opera, sometimes with Lloyd George but often on her own. Frances might have turned down opportunities to marry titles and wealth, but she was gaining social status nevertheless, even becoming friends with the royal princes themselves.

Frances' first encounter with the future King Edward VIII came at a dance thrown by a Mrs Rupert Beckett. Earlier in the day she noted in her diary that the Prince of Wales was due to be present, adding, 'I have never actually spoken to him & don't suppose I shall tonight for that matter. But it will be interesting to see him there.'[7] To her delight she was able to record the following day: 'Was introduced to the Prince, who was very charming & said he was glad to meet me as he had heard such a lot about me!' She noted that he was 'a dear thing, with beautiful eyes, but such a boy'.[8]

At an intimate dinner thrown by Sassoon soon afterwards not only was she seated next to the Prince, but in private conversation he pleased her by implying that he fully understood her relationship with Lloyd George:

Did not know till I got there that the Prince of Wales was to be there. Just 8 of us. I sat between the Prince and [Chancellor of the Exchequer] Sir Robert Horne. Was simply shaking with fright at first, but that soon vanished & we got on quite well. He is a really nice boy, & most amusing when his shyness wears off. He must know about D. & me, because he said: 'Mrs Lloyd George does not spend much time in London, does she?' with a meaning look. I said: 'No; she preferred being in Criccieth,' & let him infer what he liked.[9]

This was recognition indeed. Frances felt comfortable among her new friends precisely because they treated her as Lloyd George's mistress rather than his secretary. She got to know Mrs Dudley Ward, the Prince of Wales' own mistress, and became so familiar with the royal family that she was able to write in rather blasé terms after returning from a weekend party, 'Played tennis with Prince Henry. Prince Albert is great fun.' Frances thus fulfilled one of her childhood ambitions, 'to play with the little princes'.

She was able to fulfil a second ambition when, in 1921, she published a book. *Makers of the New World* was a compilation of pen portraits of the famous statesmen she had met in Paris she had written for the *Sunday Times*. The book was published anonymously 'By One who Knows Them'. It received mixed reviews, but the author was complimented in the *Times Literary Supplement* for having 'an undoubted gift for concise and caustic character-etching'.[10] It was also notable for the adoring tone of its comments on Lloyd George, 'the doyen of the Peace Conference': 'More than once the Conference might have broken up in confusion had it not been for his gifts of mediating between angry forces . . . It needed all the magnetism of an unusual personality to keep these conflicting elements in any sort of concurrence.'[11]

One relationship in Frances' life during this period went a little further than friendship, and was enough to make Lloyd George very jealous. This time it was a gallant Frenchman who dared to flirt with her, and she was by no means immune to his charms. Philippe Berthelot was the charismatic Secretary General of the French Foreign Ministry, and future Foreign Minister. In his mid-fifties and married, with his clever mind, striking dark looks and eye for interesting women, he seemed almost like a French Lloyd George. It was Lloyd George who

sat Berthelot next to Frances at a dinner to celebrate Megan's eigh-
teenth birthday during an international conference in San Remo in
1920. She 'fell quickly under his spell', writing that Berthelot 'wooed
me mentally, weaving an exquisite web from mind to mind, speaking
no word of love, but taking infinite pains and being entirely indifferent to any onlookers'.[12]

Frances found herself seriously interested in another man for the
first time since meeting Lloyd George. Indeed, of all her male admirers,
Berthelot was one of the few who came close to tempting her away
from him, no doubt because he offered the same near-irresistible combination of mental brilliance, prominence, and a flattering interest in her.
It would have been both impractical and unwise for her to meet
Berthelot privately – and there is no evidence to suggest that she ever
tried to do so – but they exchanged flirtatious letters, and Lloyd George
would most certainly have been jealous if he had read her description
of Berthelot in her memoirs: 'He was profound, amusing, cynical,
erudite, provoking. No Englishman could possess this especial power
of attraction: no Celt would be able to subordinate himself so completely
to the task. The Frenchman is supreme in this art, and Berthelot was
a master.'[13]

Over the following months Frances and Berthelot were thrown
together regularly at international gatherings, and she was both flattered and slightly embarrassed by his pointed gallantry. He 'exercised
an uncanny fascination', and she confessed that she was 'in love with
his mind'.[14] She was fully sensible of the risk inherent in the situation:
'It would have been exciting to see more of him, but dangerous from
many points of view,' she writes in her diary. Even though Lloyd George
had persisted in flirting with other women, she still feared his jealousy
and did not want to risk her position and her life with him. She does
not make reference to the fact that Berthelot was married. If she was
aware of it, perhaps she had become inured to any feelings of guilt
where adultery was concerned.

Berthelot was a persistent suitor, sending Frances teasing, ardent
letters and gifts. She received a pendant shaped like a Norman cross, a
copy of the *Vie des Martyrs* and 'a quaint old Indian necklace, which
Berthelot says is "sans valeur", but which I have reason to think is not'.[15]
The relationship remained innocent enough for Frances to include it

in her memoirs, from which she carefully excluded the more sensational details of her life, and she even seems a little proud of having attracted the attention of such a fascinating and prominent man.

Frances was content to enjoy this flirtation without taking it too seriously, until she picked up some gossip among French reporters that '*Berthelot a fait une déclaration à Miss Stevenson*' (Berthelot has declared his love to Miss Stevenson). This made her alive to the danger of her position, and she pulled back. In her letters to Berthelot, which have not survived, she seems to have succeeded in tactfully conveying the message that she was not interested in an affair, for in May 1921, when he was in London for a conference, she wrote in her diary, 'I like him much better than I did, since he has ceased to be sentimental, and is just friendly and interesting.'[16] They remained on friendly terms thereafter.

Curiously, Lloyd George's jealousy was at its worst when the most intense period of the flirtation was over. Perhaps Frances hid more carefully how much she liked Berthelot while he was actually wooing her, or perhaps Lloyd George too had heard the rumours. As usual when Frances was showing dangerous signs of independence, Lloyd George acted decisively to bring her to heel, in this case sabotaging her only attempt to entertain Berthelot. In 1920, with Lloyd George's financial help, Frances had moved into a larger flat in Morpeth Mansions near Westminster Cathedral, a short walk from Downing Street. Two days after noting that he had 'ceased to be sentimental' Frances invited Berthelot, who was in London with a French delegation, to dinner there with Philip Kerr and Muriel Beckett. She also invited Lloyd George, but he had refused to attend, implying that he did not approve of the plan while stopping short of forbidding it outright. Frances went ahead regardless, for once choosing to ignore his displeasure.

In the grip of jealousy Lloyd George could be childish and manipulative, and in his response to Frances' dinner party he was both. Kerr and Berthelot were involved in a meeting with him on the evening of the party, and he deliberately prolonged it until 9 p.m. Frances' male guests did not arrive for dinner until nearly 9.30, and only Berthelot's determined efforts at sparkling conversation prevented the evening from being ruined. Two days later the French delegation left London suddenly. Frances found a farewell note from Berthelot on her desk, but the last word belonged to the French Prime Minister Aristide Briand, who also left her a note, saying, '*Les Conférences Interalliées ne sont pas les champs des batailles les moins dangereux*' (Conferences between the Allies are not the least dangerous battlefields). Frances showed this to Lloyd George, and wrote in her diary, 'I think there is a double entendre and D. thinks so too. I think he is rather glad B. has gone.'[17]

The correspondence between Berthelot and Frances limped on for a few months, but eventually, starved of opportunities to meet, he faded out of her diary and out of her life. Her last mention of him was sadly to note his death in 1934. 'Poor Philippe Berthelot is dead,' she wrote. 'I once had a rather exciting flirtation with him, chiefly through the medium of letters . . . He was without exception the most fascinating conversationalist I have ever met.'[18]

Despite the celebrations and the resumption of a thriving social life in London, the dark undercurrent of unrest that was running through the country boded ill for the Coalition government. Millions of newly enfranchised electors began to feel that they deserved better, and that 'the man who won the War' was spending too much time abroad. Margaret was by now more fully involved in politics, and used her profile to protect her husband as best she could while he was away at international conferences. 'Coalition much *criticised* these days,' she wrote in notes for a speech in 1919. She goes on to remind her audience of the Coalition's successes:

> As political memory is so short let us remind ourselves of some achievements:
> *War ended victoriously*
> *Peace Conference achievements*
> *League of Nations*
> *Abolition of Conscription*
> *Provision made for pensions etc*
> *Extension of franchise*
> *Education*
> *Housing*[19]

When she spoke on behalf of her husband, Margaret did not shy away from contentious political issues. Her public and political work was fully recognised by her grateful husband, and in May 1919 he wrote her one of his most appreciative letters: 'I have watched with gratitude, appreciation & admiration the way you have filled my place in my absence. I am proud of it. You are doing it with unostentatious dignity & efficiency.'[20]

Lloyd George's pride led him to seek official recognition for Margaret's public work the following year, when he nominated her for the DBE for public service: 'I signed, yes, today, your D.B.E. This is the greatest & the highest of all. You wear on State occasions a gorgeous sash across your chest.'[21] Maggie Lloyd George would henceforth be known as 'Dame Margaret', and such was the respect she commanded that her title became universally recognised.

As well as her public duties, Margaret had domestic ties to keep her at home. In 1919 Olwen's husband Tom Carey Evans was appointed Residency Medical Officer to the state of Mysore, in India. Olwen was happy to follow him out to Bangalore, but they decided that at eighteen months old, their daughter Margi was too young to face the uncertainty and discomfort as they settled into their new life. Fortunately, there was a warm welcome for her at No. 10, where she frequently had a playmate her own age in her cousin Valerie. Riddell recorded the warm family atmosphere: 'L.G. is much taken up with his little grand-daughter, Margaret. At meal-times he takes her on his knee and feeds her with tit-bits, and is perpetually walking hand-in-hand with her about the house. She is a dignified, clever little creature . . . Full of fun with his wife and children.'[22]

Margaret was still unwilling to enter any kind of formal political career, but there was one cause that could override any objection, and that was Criccieth. In 1919 she was persuaded to stand for election to Criccieth's Urban District Council, and came top of the poll. Now, not only was she in demand as a speaker and political organiser, she was also serving as a councillor in her home town, a role she was to hold, re-elected annually, until her death twenty-two years later. Her first meeting took place on 22 April 1919. The Council's Clerk who took the chair to open the meeting was none other than her brother-in-law William George. Margaret was appointed to the General Purposes Committee, the Library Committee, the Advertising Committee, the Harbour Committee and the Housing Committee. Among the items of business at Margaret's first meeting were a vote of congratulations to Major Christian of Swyddfor, Criccieth, who had been awarded a medal 'for bravery on the battlefield in France', and the arrangements for the welcome home of returning Criccieth soldiers and sailors which was to take place the following day.

The Council was elected annually, and met on the last Monday of the month, with 'special' and 'extraordinary' meetings in between. Margaret could not attend its meetings when she was with Lloyd George in London, and the number of absences recorded in the minute book during her first years in office are a good indication of how often her public (and marital) duties took her away from Criccieth. In her first year she attended only six meetings out of twenty, and her attendance would remain sporadic at best throughout the 1920s, becoming more regular only in the following decade. But her busy schedule as the wife of the Prime Minister did not prevent her from taking an active interest in local matters, and her committee work involved her in such issues as ensuring that the water supply was kept clean, that mail deliveries were made on Sundays, and, most importantly for a seaside resort, that the Criccieth Bathing Tent Licences were properly awarded each year.

The town was proud of the Lloyd Georges, and Margaret's fellow councillors understood when she needed to be elsewhere, for instance when she missed the meeting on 30 June 1919 to welcome her husband home from the Paris conference. The Council minutes record: 'From the Chair a cordial vote of congratulations was passed to the Prime Minister, the Rt Hon David Lloyd George of Bryn Awelon Criccieth on his return to 10 Downing Street London from France, having after many months of enormous strain, brought about the Peace of the World after the Great European War', and a telegram was despatched to London to that effect.

Margaret's presence in No. 10 was duly reflected by an increase of bile in Frances' diary, and it was inevitable that members of the inner circle should notice the tension between the two women. Lloyd George was worried enough about gossip to insist that Frances should travel separately from him when they moved between London and the country. His fears were confirmed the following year when Robert Horne, the Chancellor of the Exchequer, found it necessary to give him a warning, which Frances recorded in her diary: 'Another very heavy day. D. worried by all sorts of things. He really has too much to do. Horne has been telling him that people are talking about us, and that we are too reckless. He said someone asked him the other day how long it would be before there was a bust-up in Downing St? Meaning I suppose D. & Mrs Ll.G.'[23]

Frances never really minded the gossip, as long as it stopped short of public exposure, and by now she regarded Lloyd George's family with something approaching contempt. She was blind to the enduring connection between Lloyd George and Margaret, preferring to interpret his domestic grumbling as proof that the marriage was a burden to him. Frances alone of Lloyd George's staff, as far as we know, found Dame Margaret difficult and unhelpful: 'D. & Mrs Ll.G. on very bad terms. D. is giving a big weekend party at Cobham, including the American Ambassador & Mrs Davies, and Mrs. Ll.G. instead of helping, is doing all she can to hinder D.'s arrangements. She simply hates him to enjoy himself & will not lift a finger to make the Cobham house comfortable.'[24] Similarly, in February 1920 she wrote: 'D. has at last gone off to Cobham (7 o'clock). His family are down there, so that explains his reluctance. Also, he has arranged a meeting tomorrow evening at 6.0 to give him an excuse to come up again. I feel really sorry for him, as he needs a weekend rest so badly, & would take it if it were not that he cannot stand being there with that crowd.'[25]

She was careful to hide her feelings from 'that crowd' when circumstances threw her together with Lloyd George's children. Whatever suspicions the family might harbour, they did not yet shun Frances' company. Dick, living in North Wales, spent less time in London than his younger siblings, who had regular contact with their father – and with his secretary. Olwen no longer corresponded with Frances, but she was on friendly enough terms to play golf with Riddell, Lloyd George and Frances as late as January 1920, only a few weeks before Frances wrote so dismissively of the family.[26] During the Paris conference Frances had spent a great deal of time in the company of Gwilym Lloyd George, and their relations remained warm. Gwilym joined the party when his father took a group including Frances for a short holiday to Lake Lucerne in Switzerland in the summer of 1920. Frances recorded that he was an amusing member of the party, and attributed his good mood to the fact that he had just become engaged. Through 1919 and 1920 Frances was even on continuing good terms with Megan, who wrote an affectionate letter to 'Dear Puss' in the summer of 1920: 'Scuse the notepaper, but the house doesn't boast any better . . . It has relieved me considerably to let off steam about the weather and people in general to you. Thank you for being – I hope – a patient – and sympathetic listener . . . Au revoir, Megan.'[27]

Frances might have been patient, but we must assume that she was not particularly sympathetic to Megan by this time, although her diary is silent from March 1920 to April the following year. During that period a significant event heralded a change in circumstances for both Frances and Margaret. It was to bring both good and bad fortune to the Lloyd George family.

Chequers, an impressive country house on 1,200 acres of land in Buckinghamshire, forty miles from London, was built when Elizabeth I was on the throne. In 1917 it was owned by the Conservative MP Arthur Lee. He and his American wife had no children to inherit the estate, and decided to give it to the nation for the use of the sitting Prime Minister.* A trust was established to endow the running costs of the estate, and provision was made for the Lees to be, effectively, tenants in their own house during their lifetime. Lloyd George accepted the gift in the genuine expectation that he personally would not benefit during his time in office. 'Your offer in regard to the Chequers Estate is most generous and beneficent,' he wrote to Lee, 'and one for which PMs of England in the future will have much to thank you . . . I have no doubt that such a retreat will do much to alleviate the cares of state which they will inherit along with it, and you will earn the grateful thanks of those whose privilege it is to enjoy it.'[29] After a change of

---

* Lee explained his reasons in the preamble to the Trust Deed: 'It is not possible to foresee or foretell from what classes or conditions of life future wielders of power in this country will be drawn. Some may be, as in the past, men of wealth and famous descent; some may belong to the world of trade and business; others may spring from the ranks of the manual toilers. To none of these in the midst of their strenuous and responsible labours, could the spirit and anodyne of Chequers do anything but good . . . Lastly, the better the health of our rulers the more sanely they will rule, and the inducement to spend two days a week in the high and pure air of the Chilterns and woods may, I hope, result in a real advantage to our nation as well as to its chosen leaders.'[28]

heart in 1920, the Lees decided to hand the house over immediately, writing in the visitors' book on their last night: 'Tonight, we leave this dear place, with a sense of loss which cannot be measured.'[30] They almost certainly did so to allow Lloyd George to use it for international gatherings and for his own comfort before leaving office.

On 8 January 1921 the Prime Minister held his first weekend party at Chequers as a combined leave-taking for the Lees and a housewarming for himself. A dinner was held to mark the signing of the Chequers Deed of Settlement. Margaret was consulted about the guest list, so Frances was excluded. Megan was cast in the role of hostess for the evening since Margaret was in North Wales, and only arrived the following morning. Her characteristic refusal to be impressed by her unexpected elevation to the status of landed gentry led her, inadvertently, to offend Lady Lee. Not only was Margaret absent as the Lees made their departure on the night of 8 January, but when Lady Lee, tiring of waiting for Margaret to contact her in grateful appreciation, arranged a meeting to 'hand over', Margaret made a few enquiries as to housekeeping and failed to thank her at all. Margaret was not usually so graceless, but to her Chequers, like No. 10 and No. 11, was only another official, and therefore temporary, residence.

Lloyd George was of the same mind as his wife, and was not fond of the house. Grateful though he was for the Lees' generosity, according to Frances and others he was never entirely happy there. Frances attributes this to the fact that the house was built in a hollow, and lacked a view. Lloyd George also preferred new houses, and seemed uncomfortable within the aged walls of Chequers. In this he was not helped by the strange behaviour of his favourite dog, a Chow named Chong. Whenever he entered the Long Gallery, the library on the first floor which runs almost the whole length of the northern side of the house, Chong would bark frantically, staring fixedly at a corner of the room. This convinced Lloyd George that the house was haunted. Frances, though, loved Chequers, describing it as a 'splendid home . . . perfect in all its appointments'.[31] She was more comfortable there than either Margaret or Lloyd George, and there is a suggestion in a letter Lloyd George wrote to her in April 1922 that she sometimes went there on her own when he was away.[32] Frances' familiarity with Chequers, and the staff's tacit acceptance of her role in Lloyd George's life, was her delight, but it would also be her downfall as far as cordiality with the Lloyd George family was concerned.

With Megan continuing to regard Frances as a kind of substitute older sister, the two spent a lot of time together, particularly when Megan, liberated from any educational establishment since her refusal to return to her Paris school in January 1920, accompanied her father abroad. On their journey to the conference at San Remo in April 1920, the two women shared a cabin. They both suffered badly from seasickness, and Newnham, Lloyd George's valet, caused great hilarity when he solemnly reported to Lloyd George that 'the young ladies [were] still in the perpendicular'.[33] Megan regarded Frances as a trusted confidante, completely unaware of how one-sided the confidences were. But the innocence that had protected her from discovering her friend's secret was eroded as she learned more about the world and its ways. She had turned eighteen in April 1920, and was spending time in London with a cosmopolitan social set. Perhaps she picked up a rumour, or perhaps her increasing independence led her to spend more time with her father. Whatever the cause, she began to be suspicious and to look for signs that all was not as it seemed between her father and his secretary. Frances became aware of Megan's scrutiny in May 1921 when they lunched with Lord French, who mentioned that he had been a guest at Philip Sassoon's house over Easter together with Frances. Megan, on his other side, 'pricked up her ears . . . She knew her father was there. She is a little too clever, but not clever enough to do her father in, which she is constantly attempting. One of these days they will come to grips over something & then there will be a row.'[34]

Megan was clearly on to something, and a few days later Frances recorded how her former pupil was desperately trying to make sure that her parents spent time together:

D. entertaining the Crown Prince of Japan at Chequers today. Mrs Ll.G. was down at Criccieth & did not want to come up, so D. did not over-persuade her & thought she was not coming. Megan however, who is playing her mother off against D. & me, telephoned her mother all day Friday and yesterday morning told her that D. insisted on her coming up! So she got into the next train & came, much to her disgust & very angry with D. at making her come. I am left high & dry, everyone else having gone away for Whitsun. However it is the fortunes of war, & cannot be helped. D. frightfully angry with Megan, but of course he hasn't much of a case![35]

Frances had long since begun to regard Megan – together with every other member of the Lloyd George family – as an enemy, but though her jaundiced account paints Megan as an irritating meddler, through it we can see the actions of an anguished young girl who, beginning to suspect that her parents' marriage is not as solid as she had thought, tries through any means possible to bring them together again.

It was inevitable that Megan's growing suspicions would harm her close relationship with her father, and a few days later Frances records that she was making light of a suspected Irish terrorist attack on Chequers: 'Megan takes a contemptuous view of the whole affair; says it is only a practical joke, and thinks her father is making a great fuss about nothing! Lady Greenwood is furious with her, especially since M. informed her that she "considered father was becoming quite impossible: it was time someone taught him a lesson".[36] Megan had always been her father's most loyal supporter, in private and in public. Even though she was not the only one to note that Lloyd George was becoming difficult as his years in office were taking their toll on both his health and his behaviour, it would have been inconceivable for her to criticise him in front of others a few years earlier.

Finally, after months of watching and noting every nuance of her father's relationship with Frances, Megan received what she considered to be definitive proof of their affair. The occasion was a weekend at Chequers at the beginning of July 1921. Megan, continuing her policy of trying to make sure that either she or her mother was always present to 'chaperone' Lloyd George, turned up unexpectedly in the late morning. As the party gathered over lunch, a butler who had not noted her arrival brought Frances a note from Lord Riddell, asking if he could come down for the night. Frances consulted Lloyd George and replied that Riddell was most welcome. This was highly unfortunate. Megan, as Lloyd George's daughter, should have taken precedence over the other ladies present, and most especially over her father's secretary. The hapless butler had unconsciously but incontrovertibly demonstrated that Frances was regarded as much more than a secretary – that she was treated as no less than the official hostess when the family was absent. It was the proof that Megan was looking for.

It seems that Frances did not realise the significance of the gaffe at first, noting lightly in her diary that Megan 'resented things being in my hands & was very cross and rude'.[37] With all pretence of friendship over, she went on to give full vent to her feelings: 'Everyone noticed how bad-tempered she was. Her frivolous life is taking from her charm and looks. No one seems to have any control over her or to be responsible for her comings & goings. She just goes wherever she pleases & does what she likes – avoids her father when she has something else to do and resents finding me there when she condescends to turn up.' But with hindsight Frances realised how damaging the incident had been.

Megan's disillusionment with her father was in proportion to her former admiration, and she could not contain her disappointment. It was only a few days later that Horne issued his warning to Lloyd George about his and Frances' 'recklessness', and according to Frances' diary he went on: 'Megan also has been talking to people about me & criticizing her father, thinking I suppose that she would put a stop to it in that way, & not realising that all she would succeed in doing is to discredit her father. But I don't think she would stop at anything to obtain her ends. D. told Horne that he would rather go out of public life than do without me, & that if it came to the point he would do that.'[38]

Frances was conscious of the risk of exposure, and her bitterness towards Margaret now extended to the youngest member of the family. On meeting Margot Asquith at a royal garden party, Frances was agreeably surprised at how well they got on, with Margot, perhaps unintentionally, pleasing Frances by commenting unfavourably on Megan: 'She does not approve of Megan, says she is disappointed in her – says she dresses badly & altogether has not improved. That is what most people say, though judging by the papers one would think she is the most charming & beautiful & wonderful girl that ever existed. The comments one hears, are far from complimentary, & D. is getting a little worried, as to the way she behaves.'[39]

Initially, Megan assumed that Frances was a passing fancy of her father's, and that if she applied some pressure he would give her up. She would have been horrified if she had known that Frances had been a fixture in Lloyd George's life for the past eight years. Other members of his family – Olwen for one – might have suspected that the affair was going on, and were prepared to accept it tacitly, but Megan's reaction was less predictable. She was closer to her father, and had enjoyed far more of his attention, than his older children. Megan also felt doubly betrayed: Frances had been her governess and her friend. Megan had thus unwittingly been the cause of Frances' introduction to Lloyd George, and of the subsequent problem in her parents' marriage. Megan, like her mother, did not want to cause a scandal that would drive Lloyd George out of office: her love for him was too deep to destroy him in that way. It was also too deep – ultimately – to be soured by the revelation she now faced, and in the time-honoured way, finding that she could not hate her father, she focused her hatred on his mistress instead.

19

'Dame Margaret is the Star'

'WHEN ARE YOU GOING to Cardiganshire?' Lloyd George asked his wife at the end of a letter written on 31 January 1921. It was not a casual enquiry. Cardiganshire in mid West Wales was on his mind a great deal at that time.[1]

The events that led to the Cardiganshire by-election on 18 February 1921 began when Lloyd George decided to help his Welsh Private Secretary, Ernest Evans, to win a seat in Parliament. There seemed to be no end in sight to the rift in the Liberal Party, and with Asquith back in the House of Commons, Lloyd George's need for supporters in the House had never been greater. Evans, a Welsh-speaking Calvinistic Methodist from the Liberal heartland of West Wales, was a contemporary of Dick Lloyd George's at Cambridge who had joined Lloyd George's 'Garden Suburb' in 1918. He was a talented young man of the kind that Lloyd George liked to have around him, and the plan to get him elected as Member for Cardiganshire had been hatched some years earlier.

By 1920, Lloyd George had decided that he would *create* the need for a new Member in the constituency by persuading the sitting MP, Matthew Vaughan-Davies, to accept a peerage. He then let it be known to the Liberal Association that Evans was his man. This did not go down well with the notoriously independent-minded people of Cardiganshire, who sensationally rejected Evans in favour of Llewelyn Williams, former MP for the neighbouring Carmarthen Boroughs, who had lost his seat in 1918 and who had turned from a supporter to an outspoken opponent of Lloyd George's when conscription was

her knowledge of the vernacular, and she has had much success in the villages. In all future elections, feminine influence and appeals are bound to become more prominent, but this is probably the first election in which women on both sides have played a more important part than the men, both on the platform and in the work of organisation.[12]

On election day, 18 February, Margaret returned a third time to conduct a polling-station tour, ending with a visit to the nervous candidate's campaign headquarters in Aberystwyth. Her last-minute plea was published that day in the *Cambrian News*: 'I am greatly impressed and encouraged by the magnificent reception which the people of Cardiganshire have given me since I came into the county as a personal representative of the Prime Minister,' she wrote. 'Whilst I am confident that the electors will support Mr Lloyd George by voting for Captain Evans, I make this last appeal through the "Cambrian News" to the electorate that they will not be over confident, but leave no stone unturned to secure the election of Captain Evans.'[13]

The election hinged on whether the Liberals or the Coalitionists could get more voters to the polling station, not an easy task in a constituency of scattered and remote rural communities. The Coalition summoned no fewer than 250 vehicles to the area, from as far afield as Manchester and London, to ferry voters to the polls, while the Liberals had only fifty vehicles at their disposal. Every vote counted, and Margaret, seemingly tireless, gave more than fifteen speeches, looking 'perfectly fresh & . . . as placid and serene as usual' at the end of the day.[14] Early the next morning she caught a train to London and joined Lloyd George at Chequers to await the result.

George Riddell described the scene as the news came through:

The result expected every minute when I arrived. Mrs LG has been working like a Trojan in the constituency, delivering fifty-eight speeches in a fortnight. While LG and I were walking in the park, Mrs LG came running out breathless, to tell him that Evans had won by a majority of 3,500. He was delighted and said that if the result had been the other way it would have been a serious personal set-back. He warmly embraced Mrs LG, bestowing several hearty kisses upon her and telling her that she had won the election.[15]

Lloyd George had been spared a painful and damaging political blow, and the credit belonged to his wife. 'CAPTAIN EVANS owes his victory more to the indefatigable efforts of MRS. LLOYD GEORGE than to any other factor,' announced The Times.[16]

Unsurprisingly, other Coalition candidates were keen for Margaret to replicate her Cardiganshire success on their behalf. Three weeks later she campaigned in a by-election in Yorkshire, but on that occasion was unsuccessful. Nevertheless, Lloyd George was well aware of her importance as an electoral asset, and in March 1921 he jokingly said that 'he had once been quite a great man, but now it was his wife who was the great one, and he was only a second fiddle, existing to arrange her political meetings and cut press notices out of the papers'.[17] In June he wrote to Olwen: 'As you may have perceived from the papers your mother has completely eclipsed me as a public performer. I am already a back number & a drudge. Dame Margaret is the star. She is having a remarkable success. England has never seen before a swell quite of her sort – simple, unostentatious – talking plain . . . common sense without frills – & Englishmen like it. The contrast to her predecessor [Margot Asquith] helps!'[18]

During the last years of Lloyd George's premiership, Margaret and he worked together, a married couple who understood each other perfectly and, after thirty-three years of marriage, felt deep affection for each other. Whatever their private differences the marriage was essentially strong, and whenever Lloyd George was in trouble Margaret supported him. Her behaviour is very unlike that of a suspicious wife. Yet if Megan knew of his affair with Frances by the summer of 1921, it is probable that Margaret too had pretty accurate suspicions by that time: after all, Olwen claimed that Megan was the last of the family to learn the truth. But Megan left no diary or letter to suggest that she had told Margaret her father's secret, and it is possible that she kept it from her mother in an attempt to protect her.

We do know, however, that Margaret had suspected Lloyd George of infidelity before. Each time she had confronted him, demanding the truth before accepting his protestations of innocence. In Frances' case her behaviour was significantly different. For years after the alleged overheard telephone conversation in 1916 she did not confront him. She did not object to Frances' role in Lloyd George's working life or to her constant presence in their home, and even accepted that Frances would accompany them on working holidays. She also left Lloyd George alone in London for long periods of time, whereas in Mrs Tim's case her suspicions had brought her permanently to London. Margaret allowed her children to socialise with Frances, and in Megan's case to regard her as a friend. This suggests that Margaret's knowledge of the affair did not come until after the Paris Peace Conference, or even later. Here we must acknowledge the distinction between knowledge and suspicion. In Mrs Tim's case, Margaret had proof that something was going on, and acted immediately. In Frances' case, it is likely that she only suspected a relationship and, in the absence of proof, continued to give Lloyd George the benefit of the doubt. A photograph of the two women together at Chequers proves that Margaret's tolerance of Frances' presence extended to 1921 or beyond. Suspicion but not proof: that is the most likely explanation of Margaret's uncharacteristic failure to confront her husband.

Margaret was sanguine enough about her husband's relationship with his secretary to put up with an extraordinarily awkward situation during Lloyd George's late-summer holiday in 1921. Whatever her reasons, at this stage at least she was not prepared to cause a row over Frances. That did not mean she was going to make life easy for her rival. Neither woman has left a frank record of what happened, but Frances' diary gives glimpses into a holiday that proved to be a very unhappy one for her.

The strain of office was taking its toll on Lloyd George, and 1921 was a particularly testing year. His hair, though still abundant, was less grey than white, and the lines on his face were getting deeper. The Cardiganshire by-election had demonstrated how his support had eroded even in his own heartland, and he was struggling to hold the Coalition together in the face of rising unemployment, time-consuming international negotiations, and the persistently worrying Irish problem. The Coalition had been severely weakened in the spring by the resignation of the Chancellor of the Exchequer, Andrew Bonar Law. Law was Lloyd George's closest political ally, and his main link with the Conservative Party upon whose support he depended. Bonar Law resigned on health grounds, but Frances for one suspected that the deteriorating political situation and the constant opposition of Lord

Beaverbrook's newspapers were the main contributing factors.[19] By summer Lloyd George was exhausted, and his doctor, Lord Dawson, ordered him to take a lengthy holiday. In answer to Lloyd George's protests, Dawson replied: 'Nonsense . . . a holiday *must* last a month at least to be any use to you. The first week you will be quite certain that things cannot go on without you; the second week you will be a little less certain. The third week you will have come to the conclusion that they can; and the fourth week you will not care a damn whether they do or not. That is when you can feel quite sure that your holiday has done you good.'[20]

Lloyd George had planned a motoring holiday with Frances on the Continent, but Dawson found him a house in the Highlands of Scotland where he would have a total break from politics. Flowerdale House was situated by the sea in Gairloch, looking across to the Isle of Skye and surrounded by spectacular scenery. The house had no telephone, and was a four-hour drive from the nearest railway station. The only connection with the outside world was via a single telegraph wire operated by the local postmistress. It was, on the face of it, an ideal spot for an overworked politician to relax.

Margaret and Lloyd George arrived on 1 September. The house was not large, but by this time Lloyd George travelled nowhere without a sizeable staff, and they were joined by Lord Riddell and a party of colleagues and friends, the ever-present JT – and Frances. At various times General Macready, Sir Alfred Mond, Sir Hilton Young, Lord Birkenhead and Winston Churchill dropped in to talk business, and the practical difficulties of travelling there did not deter a deputation of London Mayors bent on discussing unemployment with the Prime Minister. Lloyd George managed to fit in an audience with the King and a full Cabinet meeting in Inverness Town Hall during his month's 'rest', so there was no need to convince Margaret that he needed his secretaries with him. In turn, even Frances had to acknowledge that Margaret 'had her hands full' looking after all the visitors. The party quickly outgrew the house, and some visitors were sent to a local hotel, but it seems that Frances stayed in the house throughout, a situation that was not comfortable for either her or Margaret.

The holiday was not a success. It rained every day. In between meetings and business the guests tried to make the best of it, playing golf and walking the hills. There was alarm when an abscess in his jaw caused Lloyd George's face to swell and threatened to poison his blood. The local dentist balked at treating the Prime Minister, and Margaret sent for Lord Dawson. On his advice a dentist from Inverness was summoned, put the Prime Minister to sleep and extracted a tooth. Adding a touch of surrealism to the scene, as Lloyd George woke up after the operation he heard Madoc Davies, a musician friend of the family, playing 'Men of Harlech' on the piano to rouse his spirits.

As Lloyd George recovered, Frances developed a temperature. She was not the only one to suffer from the effects of the inclement weather, and Dawson stayed on with a houseful of patients on his hands. Diagnosed with influenza, Frances was ordered to stay in bed, and was isolated from the rest of the house for some days. She might not have been able to talk privately to Lloyd George before, but now she could not even see him, and she felt lonely and miserable. To cheer her up, Lloyd George sent her a few light-hearted notes, but they reveal the tension in the household: the lovers were being closely watched:

> My own darling little girl
> I am so sorry you have got this beastly cold. We have both had bad luck. But I am pulling through mine & you will sooner get through yours. I shall miss you so much. You are my heart's sunshine & even when I cannot talk to you I like to know you are there shining through the storm clouds.
>
> Get a good steaming dish of Allanbury. Insist on its being hot. Pile clothes on until you perspire thoroughly – then sleep dreaming of an old man who loves you more than anything or anybody in the world & would gladly if need be give them all up for you.[21]

And again:

> My sweet
> I heard the doctor's report & it gave me joy. I have been increasingly enquiring about you & I do miss you so much.
>
> Police very vigilant today so cannot write but my love is beyond all police supervision.

He signed off another note with four scrawled cartoons showing how his face had recovered, and how his mood had lightened after receiving her letter. Finally, he wrote of his disappointment that she was still not well enough to rejoin the others, but reassured her: 'You are more deeply rooted in my heart than ever – no gas or forceps can take you out. Except with the last drop of my blood. There are billions of my little girl coursing through my veins – sometimes normally sometimes septically with a quick pulse & a very high temperature.'

Frances needed all the moral support he could offer. She was prone to feel the loneliness of her position when deprived of his company, and this time, weakened by illness, she descended into depression. She could generally endure the indignity of her situation with equanimity, but living cheek by jowl with Margaret at Gairloch was too much for her. In her own words: 'One morning, suffering from the depression which influenza drags in its wake, I was ruminating on my equivocal position in the house party, some of whose members inevitably regarded me with disfavour; and dwelling on my sins in general, I decided to settle down and have a good cry.'

Her consolation came from a surprising direction:

> I was in the middle of it when the door opened and in walked Lord Dawson. He was a marvellous psychologist, and took in the position at once. He could sum up in a moment what was the trouble with anyone, and prescribe the right treatment. I said I would like to go home, but he said that was impossible, and would not help L.G. at all. I was soon feeling that my troubles would quickly disperse, and I was filled with gratitude to Lord Dawson.[22]

Lloyd George was not the only one who appreciated that Frances could be relied upon to suffer any indignity as long as she felt she was needed.

Once Lloyd George had recovered from his dental treatment, work picked up once more and Frances rejoined a busy office. As September drew to a close she and Margaret left Scotland, Margaret returning to Wales and Frances going to view some land in Surrey that Lloyd George was thinking of buying. Lloyd George saw them both off fondly, writing to Margaret: 'I miss you so much. I very nearly came with you & should have done so but for Dawson's express orders.'[23] Whatever the tensions, it seems that the affection between Lloyd George and Margaret was so deeply rooted that not even his passionate love affair with Frances could destroy it.

On his return from Gairloch, Lloyd George focused on the situation in Ireland. In October an Irish delegation headed by Michael Collins and Arthur Griffith arrived in London for a conference to consider the fate of Ulster. Many weeks of frustrating talks and negotiations followed. Lloyd George not only had to convince the Irish, but also to maintain support within his government. Collins came to respect his skill as a negotiator, but his greatest admiration was for Margaret, as he told his biographer Hayden Talbot: 'Sure, I've seen with my own eyes what a good wife can do for her husband. Cunning as a fox they say the Welsh Wizard is. Clever and artful and full of guile. But I'll let you into a secret. He'll never live to see the day when he'll outsmart that quiet little wife of his. She's a jump ahead of him all the time and has all the wisdom of Eve in keeping that fact very much to herself. A lucky man is the Welsh Wizard!'[24]

In an attempt to resolve the matter one way or another, Lloyd George imposed a deadline of 6 December. A treaty was drafted in which the British government recognised Southern Ireland as a free state but, crucially, retaining the British Crown as head of state. A controversial safeguard was included, allowing the six northern counties of Ulster to opt out. Determined to get agreement, Lloyd George used the ultimate threat: if the treaty was not signed, hostilities would resume within three days. His gamble paid off, and in what was considered at the time to be the greatest triumph of his political career, in the early hours of 6 December the Irish delegation signed. Lloyd George was hailed as 'the solver of the insoluble'. He fully understood that peace had been won at a hefty price, telling Frances that Michael Collins signed the treaty 'like a man who was signing his own death warrant'.[25] He was not mistaken. The following year, Collins was shot.

Immediately after the signing, Lloyd George took the treaty into Frances' room, where she was patiently waiting. It was a little before 3 a.m., and he was 'exhausted but triumphant'.[26] He handed her the precious document and bade her to keep it safe, so she locked it in a despatch box. Over twenty years later she was amused to find the box, still locked and with the signed treaty inside, among Lloyd George's papers after his death. No one had asked to see it during the intervening years.

Unfortunately for the over-strained Lloyd George, his political troubles were to increase over the following year. The Prime Minister who had been fêted after the war was now struggling to hold together a crumbling coalition in the face of social and industrial unrest, and growing tensions in his Cabinet and in his own party.

There was no single issue that brought matters to a head in the summer of 1922. Rather, it was a combination of factors that finally pushed the creaking Coalition over the edge. In foreign policy, where Lloyd George's genius had reigned since 1916, his grip seemed to be faltering. A World Conference held in Genoa in April–May to agree on issues of repatriation and reparations called. 'If this conference were to fail,' wrote Lloyd George to Frances, 'I should like to take Pussy to an obscure island in the South Seas where there are no cables letters or newspapers & then come back in 5 years – with the kittens – & see what had happened.'

Megan's relationship with her father was still strained, and for the first time in her life, it seems, she was prepared to rebel against him. Her rebellion took the form of a young man called Stephen McKenna, playboy novelist and nephew of Reginald McKenna, whom Frances described as 'one of the most inveterate of L.G.'s Liberal foes'. Tired of education and lacking a career, Megan spent her time helping her parents with their public duties and indulging her love of dancing and theatre. Inevitably, given that she was the lively, attractive daughter of one of the most famous men in the world, she was fêted in the smartest social circles. In the midst of this social whirl, she met Stephen McKenna.

Stephen was, at thirty-four, fourteen years older than Megan, but that did not mean he was more grounded. He had been called to the Bar, but did not practise law. During the war he had been excused active service on health grounds and had carried out some intelligence work instead. After the war he preferred writing novels and having affairs to pursuing a career; he was known as a womaniser and a heavy drinker. His novels, of which he wrote fifty in total, were racy, popular and ephemeral, written in slang and reflecting a somewhat louche attitude. It is doubtful that his intentions towards Megan were serious (in the end he never married, dying a bachelor at the age of seventy-nine), but she set her heart on marrying him.

When Margaret and Lloyd George were told of her plans, they were horrified. The unfortunate family connection might have been over-looked, but they had no wish to see their pet younger daughter married to a seducer and, worse, a drinker. A series of rows ensued, with Megan hopelessly outnumbered – even Olwen in India concluded that McKenna was 'a thoroughly bad hat'.[27] Megan could not marry without consent until her twenty-first birthday, so she grumbled and raged without coming close to changing her parents' mind.

It is not certain when the affair began, but Megan's mood and her anxiety to return to London during the World Conference at Genoa in spring 1922 imply that it was under way at that time. In a letter to Frances written from Criccieth shortly before the conference, Lloyd George wrote that Megan 'is only concerned to get through this three weeks deportation'.[28] The implication that she regarded her forthcoming trip to Genoa as a punishment suggests that her parents may have been using the trip to separate her from her lover. If so, it was an effective scheme, for the conference went on longer than the three weeks orig-inally planned. Megan arrived in Genoa with her parents on 8 April, and did not return home until 19 May.

Accounts of the Genoa conference offer a tantalising glimpse into Lloyd George family life. For the duration of the conference Lloyd George and Margaret lived together – the longest continuous spell they had spent under the same roof for many years – in the Villa D'Albertis, on a hillside overlooking the city.* It was a beautiful setting, but the atmosphere was tense as Lloyd George was depending on the confer-ence to restore his political fortunes by reminding the country of his mastery of international affairs. From the start, the conference was beset by problems, and in the end the United States declined to send a dele-gation at all, while the French and Russian delegations were not headed by their leaders, Poincaré and Lenin, as Lloyd George had hoped.

---

* Margaret wrote to Thelma Cazalet, a close friend of Megan's, with considerable amuse-ment: 'I enclose specimens of how I am addressed here, so that you will not forget your-self when I return. I was actually called the Queen of England one day. So be on your guard.'[29]

Nevertheless, with over twenty-five countries represented, hopes were high that a solution could be found to the complex issues of repatriation and reparations in Europe.

According to A.J. Sylvester, Lloyd George worked 'like a Trojan'.[30] Frances was prevented from attending by an unspecified illness. This did not lighten his mood, and he wrote long, yearning letters to her throughout the conference, alternating between endearments and detailed accounts of political developments. 'I have had a simply diabolical day of work & worry,' he wrote on 26 April:

> The Conference is trembling on the edge of a precipice & I am doing all I can to save it – & I am just now very tired & wishing – oh so much – that my little girl was here to help me bear up.
>
> I am still sanguine. Post is going. If we stay here long you must come here. Can't bear it any longer – my own life & joy.
>
> Fonder than ever of you. Need you here more than ever. More resolved than ever that you are mine & I am yours.
>
> Ever & Ever
>
> Your weary old Man[31]

The momentum of the conference came to an abrupt halt on 16 April, when it was announced that the Russian and German delegates had reached an agreement in secret. This was a significant blow, running counter to the spirit of openness Lloyd George had tried to establish, and from then on the chances of achieving significant advances diminished. As negotiations limped on there were occasional days off for the delegates to relax, and Margaret and Megan accompanied Lloyd George up into the hills around Genoa to walk and picnic, accompanied by other politicians, two or three members of staff and journalists. On one occasion they dined aboard Lord Birkenhead's yacht, and played cards after dinner. Both Margaret and Megan ended up losing money, with an ebullient Lloyd George parading his winnings with childlike satisfaction.

A.J. Sylvester spent a great deal of time with Margaret and Megan, and his diary records a typical scene:

> It is Sunday evening 6 o'clock. I am in the room which was formerly my office but which events have compelled me to convert into a confer-

ence room. Dame Margaret is perusing the illustrated London papers which arrived this morning. Sunshine is streaming through the windows; church bells are ringing. Next door, type-writers are clicking, in the Grand Saloon, L.G. is with Dr. Wirth the German Chancellor. Megan is quietly smoking a cigarette in the next room to them, smoking it surreptitiously. To-night we are feeding early, and then going to the Seamen's Rest (Presbyterian) evening service.[32]

Before going to chapel, Lloyd George had time to dash off a quick letter to Frances:

I am off to Kirk! No time to write . . . Your letter cheered me greatly. They always do. They are so well written & so full of life & interest apart from the sweet affection they breathe. They breathe into my nostrils the breath of life. That is why I am still a living man . . . I am not done yet, although beset by enemies on all hands. Many more enemies open & secret than friends – at least that is the case here. When I return I will satisfy you as to my state of health! Longing to reassure you on that point – my own sweetheart.[33]

But all was not well between Megan and Lloyd George. At the beginning of May, her behaviour began to alarm him: 'Domestic crises in addition to the International perplexities,' he wrote. 'Megan is getting very sick of this place. Worrying her mother for permission to return to London.' We can infer that her reason for wanting to leave Genoa was Stephen McKenna. She was prepared to use any ammunition to get her way, including causing trouble about Frances, now recovered and keen to join the delegation: 'It wouldn't do for you to come the moment they go,' Lloyd George continued. 'On the other hand if you came whilst they are here Megan is quite capable of taking advantage of that to say she insists upon returning because you are here. That would create a first class scandal as the place is a hotbed of gossip & rumour. I have never been so perplexed before what to do. I want you here more than ever because my troubles are greater. On the other hand the danger of your coming are greater. What am I to do sweetheart? Do talk it over with J.T. & make up my mind for me. I am utterly incapable of decision.'[34]

They decided on caution, and Megan at least had the satisfaction of ensuring that Frances was separated from Lloyd George for one of the longest periods of their relationship.

On his return to London Lord Riddell, who went to meet Lloyd George at Victoria, noted sombrely: 'A big crowd on the platform and outside the station, but I thought the former not very representative or enthusiastic.'[35] The failure weighed heavily on Lloyd George's mind, and in August, further saddened by news of Michael Collins' murder, he chose the spot on the bank of the river Dwyfor in Llanystumdwy where he wanted to be buried. He was not yet sixty, but was feeling tired and disheartened. His thoughts turned frequently to resigning, and he began to prepare for life after office, signing a contract to write his war memoirs and building a house for himself at Churt in Surrey.

In the summer a furious row erupted over Lloyd George's alleged abuse of the honours system. This was as much a symptom of his diminishing authority as it was a cause of his eventual downfall, but it was to overshadow the remainder of his time in office, and to damage his reputation to the current day. The controversy began over the nomination of Sir Joseph Robinson, a South African financier recently found guilty of fraudulent practices, for a peerage. This was seized upon by outraged peers as proof that honours were being awarded as reward for financial donations to political parties. Despite Robinson's voluntary withdrawal from the list of nominations a debate was held in the House of Lords on 17 July. In a sense the Lords' outrage was unjustified, since the practice of awarding honours for this reason was as old as the honours system itself. The 'sale' of honours extended across the political spectrum, and there were no laws on the statute books to prohibit it. Lloyd George had not sought to reform the abused system, but nor, arguably, had he used it excessively. The reason for his downfall was that he had created an environment in which the political establishment was prepared to use the practice against him, and, crucially, that a damning trail of evidence had been allowed to exist.

Lloyd George had always been disdainful of the House of Lords. His non-establishment background, unprecedented among British Prime Ministers, led him cheerfully to ignore the unwritten rules that meant his predecessors took into account social status and respectability when nominating individuals for a peerage. Lloyd George did not care who he sent to the Upper House. The King had at first raised nothing more than a genteel eyebrow at the list of nominations presented by his Prime Minister, but nominating a known fraudster was a step too far.

The case against Lloyd George was by no means unequivocal, and a large number of honours were awarded for proper reasons. Lloyd George asserted that he was not personally involved in compiling the list of names for nomination, which came from among supporters of the Conservative Party as well as from his own supporters, and proceeds were divided equally between the two parties. However, and this was a major contributory cause to the row, the Conservatives' share went into general party funds, whereas Lloyd George absolutely refused to hand over his share to the bitterly divided Liberal Party, which was still under the leadership of Asquith. Instead he set up his own political fund, reputedly amassing a sum as large as £1.5 million (£59 million today) during his premiership. This smacked of personal gain – although there is no evidence that it was intended as such – adding to the furore.

During the July debate in the House of Lords, the Duke of Northumberland publicly revealed the existence of the fund, and claimed that the money had been acquired 'during a period when there has been a more wholesale distribution of honours than ever before, when less care has been taken with regard to the services and character of the recipients than ever before, when whole groups of newspapers have been deprived of real independence by the sale of honours and constitute a mere echo of Downing Street, from where they are controlled'. More devastatingly still, he produced a letter setting out the going rate for knighthoods (£12,000, which could be paid in instalments) and baronetcies (£35,000).*

On the same day, Lloyd George was faced with a debate on the issue in the House of Commons. He acknowledged that the sale of honours was a disreputable practice, but argued that the proportion of honours awarded for political service was no higher under the Coalition govern-

---

* The author of this letter was not named. One candidate was the notorious honours broker Maundy Gregory, who in 1933 was charged under the 1925 Honours (Prevention of Abuses) Act. Modern equivalents of the sums mentioned are £370,000 for a knighthood and over £1 million for a baronetcy.

ment than any other. Surely, he told the House, this was preferable to the American system, where the steel trusts supported one party and the cotton people another, and the fact that someone had donated money to a political party should not rule them out from receiving an honour. 'The worst of it,' he said, 'is you cannot defend it in public, but it keeps politics far cleaner than any other method of raising funds.'[36] Furthermore, he argued that he had not personally been privy to any discussion as to the size of political donations, and that the list of nominations for honours was drawn up by party officials and merely approved by him, a point that was reinforced by Frances in her autobiography: 'Any requests or recommendations for honours were sent straight to the office of the Whips, who drew up the final honours list for submission to the Prime Minister, who then presented it to the King for approval. I didn't know – I was never interested in – whether any question of payment arose.' Her protests are rather weakened as she goes on to confess, 'I knew that payments *were* made, as I suppose everyone did: details were given in a later, impassioned debate in the House of Commons,' and she ends on a naïve and over-optimistic note: 'The custom was an old one, and like so many other old political customs I imagine it is dying out, or is perhaps already dead.'[37] Riddell was more forthcoming in his diary, recording a conversation in which J.T. Davies said: 'They have done well this time with honours. Everyone has had to pay up – whatever his qualifications.'

Lloyd George had offended the political and social establishment in countless ways, and as his parliamentary support crumbled the honours scandal became a convenient stick with which to beat him. He was obliged to set up a Royal Commission to examine the issue and it recommended that all nominations should be put to an independent Political Honours Scrutiny Committee.

It was therefore a damaged Prime Minister and a discredited administration that faced a potentially devastating international débâcle at the end of August 1922. The Chanak crisis was brought about when the Turkish leader Kemal Atatürk ended the Greco–Turkish War by defeating the Greek army at Smyrna (modern-day Izmir, in Turkey). The Cabinet immediately called on France, Canada and other Allied countries to help twelve battalions of British troops defend the neutral zone between the Turks, Constantinople and Europe while the British commander, Lieutenant-General Sir Charles Harington, shored up his defences at Chanak. Despite the evident lack of support from the other Allies, Lloyd George decided – wrongly – that the people of Britain would rather face another war than see the Dardanelles fall into Turkish hands. The final stage of every overlong premiership had come: the Prime Minister could no longer judge the mood of the nation.

After exhausting diplomatic options, Lloyd George and Winston Churchill, the Colonial Secretary, went into Frances' room next to the Cabinet Room and Churchill dictated a telegram to the Dominion governments, effectively seeking their support should Britain declare war on Turkey. Frances could not bear the thought of another conflict less than four years after the end of the Great War: 'I was horrified at the unwisdom of the message, conveying as it did the prospect of renewed warfare on a grand scale. L.G. and Churchill took the draft back into the Cabinet Room, where the meeting was in progress. Shall I send L.G. in a note warning him against such an action? I thought. But then again I thought, he will never agree to such a telegram being sent. The next thing I knew was that the telegram had gone.'[38]

War was fortunately averted when Harington took matters into his own hands, ignoring a telegram from the Cabinet ordering him to set the Turks a deadline, and threatening them with 'all the forces at our disposal, naval, military and air'.[39] He negotiated an international conference with the Turks, and was hailed as a hero by the British press, in contrast to the warmongering Prime Minister.

After a domestic scandal and a foreign policy blunder such as these, Lloyd George's days in Downing Street were numbered. 'The man who won the War' was no longer the people's hero. It was clear that the Coalition could not continue, but the end was to come sooner than anyone anticipated.

20

Alone into the Wilderness

IN THE AUTUMN OF 1922, Margaret, Frances and Lloyd George were feeling the strain of nearly six years in 10 Downing Street. Lloyd George appeared to be mentally prepared to give up the premiership, and had talked about resigning on at least two occasions, to allow the Coalition to be led by a Conservative Prime Minister to shore up its crumbling parliamentary authority. 'D. is becoming more & more anxious to get out of Office,' Frances had written in her diary on 3 February 1922, 'partly because it is becoming irksome to get so much criticism for all his efforts, partly because he thinks it is better to retire gracefully than to wait till people begin to sling mud, & partly because he wants to get a little rest and then to write his book. His family, too, are becoming very troublesome and he will be more independent when he is out of office.'[1]

In June, Lloyd George came up with an alternative career. Hearing that the press baron Lord Northcliffe had finally succumbed to mental illness, Frances wrote excitedly: 'D. says he would not mind resigning if he could become Editor of The Times at a decent salary & with a decent contract.'[2] In September he wrote to Margaret, 'I really cannot stand this much longer. I don't believe my nerve & spirits can sustain the constant wear & tear.'[3] He described himself two days later as 'a beetle in a glass case or a tiger in a menagerie. There is no nerve relaxation for me.'[4] In each case he hesitated to stand down, proving, as so many politicians have found, how difficult it is to relinquish power voluntarily.

The end, when it came, was swift, and not at the time of his choosing. In a dramatic and unprecedented backbench rebellion, Conservative Members of Parliament turned against their pro-Coalition leadership, including the party leader Austen Chamberlain, and looked around for an alternative. Their opportunity came when the former Conservative Chancellor Bonar Law wrote a letter to *The Times* which was critical of the government's approach to the Chanak crisis. This was seized upon as a sign that Law was well enough to return to the political fray, and he immediately became the focus of the rebellion. Law and Lloyd George had remained on good terms, with Lloyd George grumbling in a letter to Margaret in September, 'I lunched with Bonar today. He cheered me up as usual by telling me I looked very much older than he did & as to the political situation it was so bad as to be quite irretrievable.'⁵ Politics proved stronger than personal loyalty as, under great pressure from his own party, Law sided with the rebels against the Coalition he himself had founded with Lloyd George. A meeting of Conservative backbenchers was convened for 19 October, when it would be decided if they would continue to support the Coalition or bring about its downfall.

A direct threat of this kind brought out the fighting spirit in Lloyd George. He gave a speech on 14 October at the Manchester Reform Club, appealing to the people of the country for support. It was one of the best speeches he had made in recent years. He set out his defence of the government's actions during the Turkish crisis and then turned his fire on his political enemies, notably attacking the outspoken Lord Gladstone, son of the Grand Old Man, as 'the best living embodiment of the Liberal doctrine that quality is not hereditary . . . There is no more ridiculous spectacle on the stage than a dwarf strutting before the footlights in garments he has inherited from a giant.'⁶ Having entertained his audience, he adopted a statesmanlike tone for the climax, portraying himself as the hero of international affairs even as he stated that he would personally welcome the opportunity to stand down. It was Lloyd George at his best:

> I shall play no personal or party game. I place the national security and prosperity above the interests of any party and . . . if in consequence of that I am driven alone into the wilderness, I shall always

recall with pride that I have been enabled, with the assistance of loyal colleagues, in the dark hour of this nation's history to render it no mean service . . . I shall be prouder than all of the fact that it was given me, in the last days and weeks of my premiership to invoke the might of this great Empire to protect from indescribable horror men, women and children by the hundred thousand who were trusting to the plighted word of France, Italy and Britain as their shield and their defence, and who are thanking God at this hour that Britain, Great Britain, has kept faith.

As the Conservative backbenchers gathered on the morning of 19 October, Lloyd George strolled with seeming casualness into his office. He was nearing his sixtieth birthday, and had been in the Cabinet for seventeen continuous years. Dressed as usual in grey trousers and a black morning coat, and with the pince-nez he now needed suspended on a black silk ribbon, the Prime Minister based himself in the Cabinet Room with Frances, and only his enquiry on entering J.T. Davies' room, 'Any news?', betrayed any awareness on his part that the day had any particular significance.[7] It was JT who received the phone call with the news that the Tories had voted decisively to end the Coalition, and effectively to bring down the government.* 'That's the end,' said Lloyd George as he left the room. A little later, Frances was with him in the Cabinet Room when Austen Chamberlain burst in, declaring, 'We must resign, L.G. Baldwin has carried the meeting.'[8] It was indeed the end: the end of the Coalition, the end of Lloyd George's premiership, and, although no one would have predicted it at the time, the end of his time in government for ever.

By all accounts Lloyd George accepted his fate with equanimity and good grace. As those around him struggled to come to terms with the news, he seemed relieved, even elated. His first word to J.T. Davies was 'Rhyddid!' (Freedom!), and Maurice Hankey, bumping into him shortly afterwards, recalled that he was 'positively cheerful'.[9]

Lloyd George went to the Palace to tender his resignation to the

---

* To this day the name of the Conservative Party's committee of backbenchers, the 1922 Committee, commemorates this occasion, on which the party's backbenchers brought down the Coalition and installed a Conservative Prime Minister.

King, and Frances telephoned Riddell to give him the news. Riddell made his way to No. 10 to find Lloyd George sitting by the fire in Frances' room planning a speech he was to deliver in Leeds. It was business as usual – almost – for Bonar Law had agreed to become Prime Minister, but wanted to be elected leader of the Conservative Party first, replacing Chamberlain who had resigned with Lloyd George. The process was to take four days, and Lloyd George stayed on in No. 10, his thoughts immediately turning to the general election that was bound to follow.

For Margaret, the four-day delay was a chance to start packing up. She had lived in Downing Street for fourteen years, six of them in No. 10, and although she had never loved the place, there was a lot of work to be done in arranging their move. First, they would need a place in London to stay, temporarily at least. Luckily, Sir Edward Grigg, one of Lloyd George's Private Secretaries, offered them the use of his house, 86 Vincent Square, as a stopgap. An obviously harried Margaret wrote to Olwen in India: 'We are very busy packing to go away . . . I have never seen such a lot of rubbish collected in all my life. The general election will be a rest after this. I can't see myself oping [sic] these cases if I live to be a hundred. I leave here for Cric. & B'dawelon after this. We have taken a furnished house, it is Sir Edward Grigg's & Tada is in such a fever haste to get there but I am not going until I return from Wales.'[10] The change had come suddenly, and Margaret had not adjusted emotionally to the thought of Lloyd George being out of office. She could not believe that after seventeen years her husband was just a backbencher again, and clung to the belief that the change was temporary, just as Margot Asquith had done in 1916: 'I hope we shall have a house of our own by then,' she continued, 'or back in No. 10 perhaps. I can't see Bonar Law lasting *too* long.'

This was not the line Margaret took in public. On 20 October, less than twenty-four hours after Lloyd George's resignation, she took time to give an interview to the *Daily Sketch*. The piece was somewhat ironically entitled 'Mr Ll. George a Husband Again', and the interviewer, Edith Shackleton, was lavish in her praise for Margaret's calm demeanour and quiet, domestic confidence. 'Dame Margaret's sincere face' is lyrically praised as bearing 'the beatific look of women who still know how to put children to bed and cure a man's sore throat'. Despite the emotional turmoil and physical upheaval that surrounded her in No. 10, Margaret presented a collected, measured face to the world: 'Yesterday was so dramatic that many people may have wondered how he felt at the end of it. But he did not sit up and go over things again. He went to bed early and slept well, and to-day is well and cheerful. He hasn't forgotten how to be plain Mr. Lloyd George.'

When asked for her own feelings, Margaret seems wistful as she reflects on her time in Downing Street, betraying a little regret at their hasty departure:

'It is a long time we have been here,' went on Dame Margaret, looking out through the long windows to the yellowing trees across the Horse Guards Parade. 'My daughter Megan can scarcely remember any other London home than a Downing Street one. I suppose it is the busiest term of office any Prime Minister has ever had.' 'Or any Prime Minister's wife,' I suggested, for Dame Margaret has shouldered countless dull duties and reigned during a period when glitter and gaiety were rare.[11]

While her mother gave calm interviews in the drawing room, Megan wrote to her sister describing the scene upstairs in Downing Street:

We are packing as hard as ever we can. The mess is indescribable – books, papers, photos, caskets, over-flowing waste paper baskets, men in aprons, depressed messengers, abound in rooms in the house in vast numbers . . . Newnham walks about with the air of a man whose sufferings are so intense that he hopes he may not have long to live. He stays on with B L of course; his only reason for not resigning is that he may be here, when we come back, if ever we do!*

She goes on to give an account of the political atmosphere surrounding the change:

The crisis came about, as I expect you know, very suddenly – with the exception of Father, stunned everyone. No one was expecting Bonar

* Newnham, the No. 10 valet, later told Olwen that Downing Street was 'like the grave' without Lloyd George, 'no fun at all'.

to act as he did . . . Tada had wonderful receptions both at Manchester & Leeds & made wonderful speeches in both places. The people are absolutely with him, altho' very tired of the government, more particularly because of its being a coalition than anything else.[12]

Megan loved her father too much to be objective about either his popularity or his political authority, and her faith in him was stronger than ever. She could not imagine a time when Lloyd George would not dominate the political landscape, in or out of office: 'Whatever happens, Tada will be the power. He will be tremendous in opposition – & Bonar knows it.' But while it was true that the crowds in Manchester and Leeds had been enthusiastic, the subsequent election was to prove that Lloyd George's electoral appeal had been smashed.

There was another woman packing up in Downing Street. Frances left no diary entry to describe the events of October 1922, and strangely makes no reference in her memoirs to her feelings on leaving No. 10, but the night before Bonar Law took office, Maurice Hankey's deputy Tom Jones recalls seeing her in her office burning papers, 'looking sadder than I have ever seen her'.[13] When it came to the moment of departure, he noted again that 'Miss Stevenson . . . could hardly conceal her sadness at parting with No. 10.' Frances, it seems, did not share the family's confidence that Lloyd George would soon be back.

Lloyd George was on great form as he made his farewells in Downing Street on 23 October. He had the assembled staff in gales of laughter as he play-acted his imagined return to No. 10 heading a deputation of Welsh MPs. Then, after making a final visit to the King in the afternoon, he and Gwilym headed for Churt. He had done his best to secure the future for his most loyal supporters. The civil servants would be posted to new roles, but his own personal staff's employment ended with his premiership. With his own future uncertain, he could not take them with him, and his private secretaries had to look around for alternative positions even as they packed up their desks in Downing Street. A.J. Sylvester, a relatively recent addition to Lloyd George's inner circle, was surprised and pleased to be asked to stay on at Downing Street to work for Bonar Law. For J.T. Davies, this was not an option. JT had worked for Lloyd George for a decade, and had his eye on a vacancy on the board of the Suez Canal Company. The 'Chief' had promised it

to him, and despite a last-minute hitch, Davies finally got his director-
ship, and a knighthood as well.*

Frances was in the most difficult position of all. No other employment could compete with working at her lover's right hand in Downing
Street. To her gratification, her professional ability was recognised when
Sir Warren Fisher, Head of the Civil Service, offered her a permanent
position. She was also flattered to receive a letter from a female colleague,
who wrote ecstatically: 'It's been a splendid thing for all of us humble
secretarial rank & filers to have had you at the top. The height at which
women keep their professional flag flying & never once to be lowered
matters awfully, I think, in what are still rather pioneer days, & the
record of your fine running will, I hope, go down in history.'[15] But
nothing could persuade her to leave Lloyd George: her future was bound
up with his.

At first this meant helping to set up his new office opposite the
House of Lords at 18 Abingdon Street, just a few doors down from
where the Asquithian Liberals had their headquarters. Frances immersed
herself in the administrative detail at which she was so capable. Lloyd
George's immediate concern was the impending general election, which
was to be held on 15 November, but Frances also had to deal with the
more long-term opportunities that came his way, mainly offers of
contracts from newspapers. Although she does not admit to any distress
at leaving Downing Street, the strains of the sudden change in her life
show in her description of the new office:

> L.G. had been in office for seventeen years, with all the aids to living
> that that implied, officials to help him, messengers to wait on him,
> secretaries to look after him, an official residence to live in. At one fell
> swoop, all this was removed . . . I soon discovered that the work in our
> new office was going to be more than I could manage, for I was the
> only secretary left out of the little band at Downing Street, and now
> that the resources of official departments were no longer at our
> command the work really became very heavy indeed. One of L.G.'s

---

* Lord Curzon could not accept that a mere civil servant had been given such a privileged role, and said that he regarded the appointment as 'the greatest piece of nepotism
since Caligula appointed his horse to be a consul'.[14]

weaknesses was that he was quite incapable of comprehending how much work one person could do in a given time, however willing, nor could he grasp how long any given job would take . . . I struggled on through the spring and summer in an endeavour to cope with an almost overwhelming variety of responsibilities.[16]

Frances' sense of isolation was increased by the fact that Lloyd George was as preoccupied as ever with politics during this period. He had many reasons for campaigning vigorously during the general election, not least that his son Gwilym was standing as a candidate in Pembroke, the first of his children to follow him into politics. Former allies who only weeks previously had worked together in coalition were now pitted against each other. Bonar Law, who retained an affection for Lloyd George, was nevertheless obliged – albeit hesitantly at first – to attack his former Chief. He made 'tranquillity' his motif, deliberately contrasting his own steady style with the crisis-loving, dramatic Lloyd George. Lloyd George, in turn, even now could not bring himself to seek a reconciliation with Asquith (who was not inclined to make friends either), and instead stood for re-election at the head of a loyal faction of 'Lloyd George Liberals' under the banner of the 'National Liberal Party'. The Labour Party, which had steadily been gathering strength, was intent on exploiting the division within the Liberal ranks to become the official opposition party.

Lloyd George normally relished a fight, but the previous years had left their mark, and although he drew huge crowds wherever he went, he was not able to conjure up his usual oratorical magic. Privately he acknowledged that he needed a spell out of office to regain his strength: the electorate agreed with him and returned Bonar Law to Downing Street with a respectable majority of seventy-two. Law won 342 seats, and the official opposition was Ramsay MacDonald's Labour Party, with 142 seats. Lloyd George and Asquith were obliged to continue their squabbling, with only sixty-two and fifty-four MPs respectively. If this was not enough of a blow to Lloyd George, the results in Wales sharply reflected his diminished stature. Out of thirty-five seats, the Welsh Wizard could command only eight. His one consolation was that they included Pembroke: Gwilym could sit beside his father on the backbenches.

And so, veering between plans to set up a new party of the centre and seeking a half-hearted reconciliation with Asquith, Lloyd George set off into the political wilderness, taking Margaret, Megan and Frances with him. A holiday in the sun was required to restore everyone's strength, and Lloyd George and Frances set off together for Algeciras, where they spent the New Year. They enjoyed a fortnight there with only JT for company before Frances returned to England, making way for Margaret and Megan, who arrived on 7 January 1923. A stream of political friends joined him, among them Riddell (despite changing his allegiance to support Bonar Law in the election), the deposed Conservative leader Chamberlain, and Lord Birkenhead. It was with these companions, and not with Frances, that Lloyd George celebrated his sixtieth birthday on 17 January.

With Lloyd George fully expecting to return to power, he was not able to be more open about his relationship with Frances, nor did she expect him to be. She must have wondered what life now had in store for her, yet she betrayed no hint of doubt that her position in his life would remain the same. She was consoled by a series of passionate letters from Spain in which he wrote freely of his love for her, his passion seemingly undiminished by ten years of unofficial 'marriage':

> My own love,
> The effect of our week's separation has been to deepen the conviction of my heart that I cannot do without you my girl. But as that convic-tion was already rooted so deeply in my soul that no fingers can tear it out it seems superfluous cruelty to inflict these days of longing pain upon me to teach me something I already know so well . . .
>
> This place is too far from everywhere that matters. I never discov-ered that – at least it never bothered me much – as long as my sweet-heart was here. I measure all distance by my distance from her. Abroad for me means far away from Pussy.[17]

Frances felt that their love had been renewed by the time spent together: 'I cannot grumble at not being with you on your birthday, after the beautiful time we have had together, but I have been thinking very lovingly of you all day, my darling, instead. It is only just over a week since we parted, but it seems like a hundred years.'[18] She had paused in

Paris on her way back to London, and used her time there to catch up with her Versailles contacts and pass on the political gossip to Lloyd George. 'The Paris letter was so valuable as a report,' he wrote, 'that I mean to keep it.'[19] Encouraged, Frances picked up political snippets whenever they were apart, acting as Lloyd George's eyes and ears wherever she went.

As well as gathering intelligence, Frances had another absorbing task to attend to: establishing Lloyd George's new house at Churt in Surrey. The sixty-acre estate between Hindhead and Farnham that Frances had hurried back from Gairloch to view in 1921 had since been cleared of pine and bracken, and the hilltop became the site of a comfortable house, well positioned to take advantage of the view over the South Downs. This view had nearly been Frances' undoing. She had been looking for land to buy for Lloyd George for some time, with strict instructions to find a position for a house that had a good view and that faced south. The day on which she first visited Churt was clear and bright, and she was enchanted. She wrote enthusiastically to Scotland, and after sending Margaret to view the site, Lloyd George agreed to its purchase. Sadly for Frances, the weather was not as clement when Lloyd George finally stood on the hilltop himself, and the view was obscured by mist. Worse, he found to Frances' chagrin that it faced due north. Ignoring her distress, he laughed and promptly named the house Bron-y-De, literally 'Breast of the South', but here used in its secondary meaning, 'south bank' or 'slope'.

From the beginning it was clear to everyone else, if not to Margaret, that Bron-y-De was Frances' domain. She supervised the building of the new house from beginning to end, and staffed it carefully: 'Don't forget your dragon was hired for the end of April,' wrote Lloyd George early in 1922 when the project was delayed – Frances was not about to engage female staff who could tempt her lover's roving eye. He goes on to tease her, 'Your descriptions of the place are thrilling. It was a lucky find. The often[er] I see the place the better I am pleased with the *Southern aspect*.'[20]

The house was designed by Philip Tilden, who had impressed Lloyd George with his work at Port Lympne for Philip Sassoon. It was built quickly, so quickly in fact that six months after its completion, alterations were already in progress. In the interest of speed, the ground floor was completed in brickwork, with the upper storey incorporated into a mansard roof of timber and quick-drying plaster. The house had two wings, connected on the ground floor by a paved loggia. The main architectural feature of the front, a striking second loggia on the upper floor, was added during the alterations. Inside, the house was comfortably furnished with wooden furniture, including a traditional three-part Welsh dresser (cwpwrdd tridarn) sitting alongside a dining suite made from holly from the grounds. The dining room was panelled with oak, also from the estate, and comfortable chairs were grouped around the fireplace in the spacious, book-lined study. A portrait of Uncle Lloyd by Christopher Williams hung over the fireplace in the inner hall, and in Lloyd George's bedroom stood the small table at which he made his first speech in a chapel in Penmachno.

Frances claimed in her memoirs that Margaret and Megan 'felt keenly' the change from official residences to private homes.[21] If so, Margaret took remarkably little interest in the development of her husband's new house. She felt excluded from the process of building it, and wrote derisively to Olwen: 'The only part of the house facing de [south] is the front door, the dining room, drawing room & all good bedrooms face north west, so pen ol [backside] & not bron [breast] is the best name for it.'[22] These were unusually catty remarks from the easy-going Margaret, indicating that she was feeling upset and jealous. For once, Frances seemed to be getting the upper hand.

Margaret was going through a difficult time in the early 1920s. In addition to the physical and emotional strains of public life, she was actively engaged in raising her granddaughters, of whom there were three after Olwen gave birth to Eluned (named after the late Mair Eluned) in 1921. While this was by no means a burden – there can hardly have been a more willing and devoted grandmother – when Megan was later invited to visit India, a hint of loneliness entered Margaret's letters: 'I shall miss [Megan] terribly. I shall be very lonely, perhaps Dick will lend me Valerie for a while.'[23] Margaret was otherwise keen for Megan to take the trip, for she had her reasons for wanting her daughter to leave London for a while.

Megan's relationship with her parents was further strained when they insisted she ended the affair with McKenna. Under pressure, she gave him up, although she continued to hope. This may be why Margaret took her to join Lloyd George in Algeciras in January 1923. There are many hints in the letters the family wrote from Spain to indicate that tempers were frayed. Margaret confided to Olwen that Lloyd George was as much to blame as Megan:

> Tada has been very severe on her lately, once at Seville when the child had done nothing, we were at a Hotel she knew no one there & could not talk Spanish. One night or rather morning he asked her when she went to bed & she said about midnight & he flew at her & asked what she had been doing. She said I went to write a p.c. & then I went to my room to write an account of what she had seen during the day at Seville. He never said well that's alright, you know he never will admit that he has made a mistake, since then Megan is not very happy.[24]

'Not very happy' was an understatement. The next morning Riddell found Megan red-eyed from weeping: 'We returned to Algeciras [from Seville], going part of the way by train,' he wrote in his diary. 'I saw Megan had been crying. She intimated that she had had a terrible row with her father, with whom she was not on speaking terms, but did not disclose the cause, except to intimate that he had been very irritable. LG came into the railway carriage, but soon disappeared into the next compartment, evidently not caring to remain in the same carriage as his daughter. In fact he seemed very short with everybody except Mrs LG.'[25] The row was serious enough for Lloyd George to mention it to Frances in a letter: 'Megan & I are not on speaking terms. Bad row – not over you this time.'[26]

Megan travelled home by land rather than accompany her father by boat, arriving a day after him. Her absence from London seems to have done the trick, for she wrote to a friend that she had given up all hope of marrying McKenna.

On 20 May 1923, Bonar Law, whose voice had diminished to a whisper over the preceding months, resigned. He had been diagnosed with cancer of the throat, and within six months was dead. The Lloyd George family were truly sad, for Law had been a friend for many years, despite being of so different a temperament to the ebullient and short-fused

Lloyd George. He was succeeded as Prime Minister and leader of the Conservative Party not by Lord Curzon, to Lloyd George's private satisfaction, but Stanley Baldwin.

This development was significant, for out of office did not mean out of public life for Lloyd George. The shock of his fall had now diminished, and he was able to take stock of his situation realistically. 'We'll pull through,' he wrote to Frances from his summer break at Criccieth. 'We are passing through the worst time – immediately after the fall. But it is nothing to Asquith's,' he went on to console himself. 'He retired an accepted failure – without a triumph to redeem his fame.'[27] Lloyd George regarded his greatest personal triumphs as 'the war & Home Rule', and it was true that his achievements had not been entirely eclipsed by the honours scandal. No one was prepared to write off the Welsh Wizard at the relatively young age of sixty, least of all himself. Soon he would step back into the limelight with a highly effective reminder of the power, global fame and sheer magnetism he commanded.

In the meantime, the Wizard was being rather short-tempered. Not only was he finding it difficult to keep the peace between his wife, his daughter and his mistress, but now that he was out of office he was constantly exposed to the stares and comments of curious members of the public. When he was Prime Minister he travelled by special train, and was accompanied everywhere by drivers, police officers and a sizeable entourage. Now, as a private citizen, there was no barrier between him and the world. The change bothered him, not because of personal vanity or loss of status. For one of the most famous men in the world, whose distinctive appearance meant that he was instantly recognisable, the lack of privacy he endured was a real problem. Nowhere did he feel this as acutely as in Criccieth. Brynawelon was not designed with privacy in mind, and with Criccieth full to bursting with summer visitors, Lloyd George constituted a major attraction. On 14 August he was writing to Frances from his bed, where he did most of his paperwork, when he noticed a crowd of people sitting on the wall surrounding the house, staring at him. On that occasion he kept his sense of humour, writing in a postscript, 'Crowds now on the wall looking at me – in bed. Only just discovered it. Had they known what I was doing.'[28] The next day, his patience was wearing thin: 'This is no place for me. Overlooked all day by visitors – some actually invading the grounds, and I dare not go outside. Snapped by endless cameras. Requests for autographs etc etc. Churt is the place for me.'[29]

Frances too was nearing exhaustion. The emotional strain of supporting Lloyd George through his exit from No. 10 was beginning to tell on her, and to make matters worse, it was now open warfare between her and the family. 'Love me, my darling,' she pleaded, '& don't let yourself be influenced by anything *they* say about me.'[30]

Partly to relieve her feelings, she had begun to write a novel while she was in Paris. The plot follows a familiar scenario: a young woman (Ann or Delphine) forms a relationship with an older, married politician (Mike) who cannot abandon his public duty for her. Ann probably speaks for Frances when she says: 'A child of her own! How sadly the words came from her lips. An infinite longing . . .'[31] Frances gives Ann a happy, if unconvincing, ending when Mike finally sacrifices his career for her. The novel is written in a romantic and sentimental style, and Frances abandoned it after two drafts or so.

Lloyd George was playing a skilful hand at this time, for he was able to keep both Frances and his wife happy. 'Dearest D,' wrote Margaret after his departure from Criccieth, 'Very glad of your letter saying you missed me. Life is not worth living unless someone misses you, & for you to miss me, well it makes me happy.' This may lack the passion of Frances' letters – Margaret was never as fluent in expressing her feelings on paper as her better-educated rival – but it speaks of deep affection between her and Lloyd George. She continues: '. . . I saw 40 of your ladies from the constituency here today. We had a meeting & I gave them tea. They were charmed with Brynawelon, & the sun WAS shining all day!!!'[32]

Margaret was not the only one working hard on Lloyd George's behalf. Frances had been shouldering the burden in Abingdon Street alone for too long, and when help came, in the shape of A.J. Sylvester, it was not altogether welcome.

A.J. Sylvester, at thirty-four, was a little under a year younger than Frances. He had left school at the age of fourteen, to work as a clerk in Burton-on-Trent, where his father was a brewery farm worker. Like Lloyd George, Sylvester was supported by his family as he studied in his spare time, in his case shorthand and typing, achieving top speeds in both. By the age of twenty he had moved to London, where he took a number of clerical jobs, including a stint working on the official record of debates in the House of Lords. He became one of the most proficient shorthand typists in the country: in 1910 and 1911 he was a member of the British international speedwriting (typewriting) team which competed at the Business Efficiency Exhibition at Olympia.

During the war Sylvester worked at the Admiralty, where he worked closely with Maurice Hankey as a stenographer. In 1915 he became the first person to take a shorthand note of a Cabinet committee meeting, and in due course Hankey, now Secretary to the War Cabinet, appointed him as his Private Secretary. This role brought him into close contact with Lloyd George. After the war Sylvester continued to serve Hankey, becoming a full civil servant. He was awarded the OBE in 1918 and the CBE in 1920. In 1921 he joined the staff at No. 10 as Lloyd George's Private Secretary. He kept notes of events and conversations, writing them up for publication in 1947 in an uncritical book called *The Real Lloyd George*. He also kept a diary, parts of which were published in 1975 as *Life with Lloyd George*, which gives a detailed account of Lloyd George's last years.

After Lloyd George's fall from office, Sylvester had stayed on at No. 10. He was finding it hard to fit in with his fellow civil servants, most of whom were high-flying graduates, and with the political staff, who could not forget his allegiance to Lloyd George. With Frances nearing collapse, the staff at Abingdon Street needed to be expanded. More urgently still, Lloyd George had accepted an invitation to visit the United States and Canada, and needed a male member of staff to accompany him. The solution seemed obvious, and Sylvester was invited to leave No. 10 and rejoin Lloyd George.

Sylvester was fully aware of the relationship between Lloyd George and Frances, and when negotiations relating to his salary and pension had been resolved he made one further demand: that he should be given the title of 'Principal Private Secretary', placing him in a senior position to Frances. He was wise to insist on the distinction, for however much Frances might protest that they were equals, it would have been impossible for Lloyd George to continue much longer with a female secretary running his office, and besides, it would have been very uncomfortable for Sylvester to join the staff as anything other than the most senior official given the relationship between his boss and his closest colleague. But his title caused a rivalry between him and Frances that was to last throughout the twenty-three years of their professional partnership and beyond. Frances still felt the injustice of it when writing her autobiography forty-five years later. In it she pointed out that she was by then a graduate with ten years' experience at the top of the Civil Service, while Sylvester was 'the last comer to the secretarial staff at Downing Street'.[33] The comment is followed by an unflattering anecdote, and though Frances swallowed her pride and worked with Sylvester, she never shared with him the easy camaraderie she had with J.T. Davies.

Sylvester's first job was to organise the forthcoming visit to North America. It was no mean task. As soon as it was known that Lloyd George was making the trip, thousands of invitations poured in from all corners of the United States and Canada. Sylvester had very little time to put together an itinerary that would satisfy the demand. To complicate matters, Lloyd George was taking Margaret and Megan with him, but not Frances, so the whole administrative burden fell on Sylvester's shoulders.

As well as Sylvester, the party that left Southampton on the *Mauretania* on 29 September included William Sutherland (a trusted adviser and Lloyd George's former Parliamentary Private Secretary), a messenger and Sarah Jones to look after Lloyd George's personal comfort. From their arrival in New York, as they sailed up the Hudson accompanied by boatloads of cheering Greek and Jewish well-wishers, the trip was a triumph.* A hundred or more journalists, a Welsh choir and a massive crowd were waiting to glimpse the famous man. As they travelled by special train they were forced by well-wishers to make unscheduled stops, with Lloyd George making fifteen or more speeches a day. He visited the White House, was hailed as 'the quintessence of democracy' in New York, greeted by 3,000 people on Toronto station, and inducted into the Sioux tribe in Minneapolis, given the name 'Wambli Nopa' meaning 'two eagles': one for war and one for peace. Of particular personal significance was his visit to the home of his hero,

---

* Four groups of Americans were particularly enthusiastic about Lloyd George: the Welsh (naturally); the Greeks, who felt he had saved them from the Turks; the Jews, who now had a homeland thanks to the British settlement of Palestine; and the large Irish population, who saw him as the architect of Home Rule.

Abraham Lincoln in Springfield, Illinois. He also laid a wreath on Lincoln's tomb on which he wrote, 'In humble and reverent homage to the memory of one of the world's greatest men'.[34]

Margaret and Megan had never been to the United States, but they found that they were already famous there, and were made as welcome as Lloyd George himself. On occasions when he was feeling the strain, Margaret stepped in to deputise for him, making at least four or five speeches during the trip, and she was in demand to give interviews to satisfy the curiosity of the American public. 'In his earlier years,' wrote one journalist, '[Lloyd George] used to submit every important speech to his uncle. The role of censor is now played very effectively by Dame Margaret.'[35] She also said that she envied America its Prohibition,* and when asked about the hectic pace they were keeping, gave a tactful answer: 'You keep us going pretty fast. But it is just kindness, isn't it?' Reporters wrote approvingly of her 'gracious motherliness', and described every detail of her appearance. They wrote in amazement that she sometimes 'gave as many as twenty speeches a day during the war to raise money for her Welsh Troops Fund'.

Margaret tried to keep a record of the trip, but she was not a diligent diarist. Nor were her observations particularly insightful: Niagara Falls were 'impossible to describe'; the White House, where she took tea, was a 'beautiful house ... pictures of past Presidents, full sized Abraham Lincoln ... Very characteristic Roosevelt'; and Woodrow Wilson 'had to be wheeled about. His brain & voice v clear.' Her enthusiasm was reserved for the kitchen of the train on which they were travelling. She found the galley 'most marvellous', with an ice safe, a big stove and ingenious cupboards.[36]

Despite Lloyd George and Margaret's popularity, without doubt the heroine of the trip was Megan. It was to emerge during the visit to America that she had inherited some of her father's star quality. Sylvester noted in his diary that 'the crowd often clamoured for Megan', and a caption to a photograph in the *Daily Sketch* reads: 'Megan, surrounded by naval and military officers, was the pet of the party.'[37] She was as

---

* AJ recalled that he had 'never seen so much secret drinking anywhere as ... in the USA during Prohibition. Even young boys carried hip flasks and shared the contents with their girl friends.'

happy in the limelight as her father, and began to be more confident in dealing with the press: 'Women reporters interviewed Miss Megan Lloyd George,' wrote the *Daily Express*, 'who answering their questions, said: "I have no aspirations. I am not in love. I do not want a career. I am twenty-one years old, and my only ambition is to be with father. I do not smoke cigarettes, but I have no censure for those who do." '[38]

For Lloyd George and Margaret, the trip was politics on a vastly different scale to anything they had experienced before. In all, during the six-week visit they travelled 6,000 miles. Lloyd George addressed a quarter of a million people, and hundreds of thousands more heard his voice over the airwaves. He spoke at public events in twenty-two cities, and made impromptu speeches at over forty stations along the way. They received a particular welcome in towns like Scranton, Pennsylvania, home to a large Welsh community, where the Mayor declared a holiday, the schools were shut, and the Lloyd Georges were mobbed at a public reception.

Modern technology made it possible to communicate with people on a scale Lloyd George had never thought possible. Early in his trip he refused to make use of the loudspeakers that had been installed in the Montreal Arena so that a crowd of over 10,000 people could hear him speak. The organising committee had to threaten mass resignation and a public scandal before he relented. He had never in his life resorted to artificial amplification, but when he was pressured into doing so he became an instant convert. He was equally impressed by his first personal experience of radio, listening in his train carriage to the Mayor of Ottawa welcoming him while he was chugging along many miles away from the city. After his return home, he described the wonders of the new technology:

I . . . had experience of another machine. I do not think you have it here, but it is a machine which I think is going to revolutionise public speaking. It is called the Radio or Broadcasting. I had quite a remarkable experience over there where I used it. I delivered a speech at Chicago, and the following morning I had a telegram from Texas saying, 'Listened to your speech last night.' That was about 1,200 miles away . . . In future, instead of going to a hall to address a meeting, you will just sit in your own library, and you will deliver your speech and take a puff at your cigar any time when you think applause should come. There are really great developments in front of us.[39]

While radio was a novelty that came late in Lloyd George's political life, for Megan it would shape her career as she became one of the star broadcasters of her generation, able to transmit her vitality and quick-wittedness from a studio with ease. It was, however, too late for Lloyd George to change his style of communicating, and although he made many radio broadcasts in later years, he was never able to captivate his listeners in the way that he could when speaking in front of a live audience.

It is possible that Megan's career as a radio performer and as a politician began on this trip, for although she did not speak in public, numerous articles and photographs show her relishing the enthusiasm of the crowd. In Ottawa, the visit of the Lloyd George party coincided with one from the Prince of Wales. He opened a ball held in his honour by dancing with Megan, and no princess could have been as well received as she.

Behind the scenes, all seemed well between Margaret, Megan and Lloyd George, although the latter was indulging in the kind of behaviour that had caused Riddell and Dick to believe that years in office had left him arrogant and demanding. He was missing Frances, who had taken a holiday herself in Paris and Florence. Lloyd George was travelling constantly, and had time to write only one letter to Frances from America. In it, he gives a flavour of the hectic pace of the tour:

My own darling girl

This is the first chance to get one word through to the girl of girls for me – the one & only girl of my heart. I have literally not one minute to myself. It has been a terrible experience although a triumphant one. Literally one triumphal procession. Had I been their own general returned victorious from the Wars they could not have been more enthusiastic. Crowds everywhere. Every little station on the route with great gatherings come to see & cheer.

I have already spoken 40 times & I have still 12 days to go. Tonight I have a meeting of 10,000. I have addressed 75,000 through a megaphone . . .[40]

Frances did not forget her permanent commission as Lloyd George's eyes and ears, cabling him (or rather, cabling Sylvester with news intended for Lloyd George) almost daily. If she missed a day she received a rebuke, as happened on 27 October:

> FOLLOWING FROM SYLVESTER DISAPPOINTED NOT RECEIVED WIRE WIRE NEWS URGENTLY WASHINGTON CHIEF EXCEL-LENT FORM[41]

Occasionally, Sylvester would send on brief, mis-spelt endearments from Lloyd George:

> NEW WORLD AMAZING SUCCESS GAR IA DIGEED [i.e. gariad i gyd – all love] SYLVESTER[42]

Due to the difficulty of predicting his movements and the risks involved in writing to him while he was with his family, Lloyd George received only one letter from Frances during the trip. It contained the usual mixture of endearment and political gossip that he loved:

> I am so afraid that what you see over there will make you dissatisfied with what is over here, & that the charming people you are meeting may distract your love from me – No, I don't really think that – I know you do not change . . .
>
> I had lunch with the Pertinaxes yesterday,* & they were very charming . . . Pertinax was in London in July, & asked to see Baldwin but was told that it was no longer a Lloyd George regime, & people who could go to the Foreign Office were not allowed to come to Downing Street for information. It looks as though Curzon is running this government at present, but the French do not expect it to last long.[43]

Lloyd George arrived at Southampton on 9 November a giant once more, restored in stature and reputation as one of the world's great statesmen. The trip had taught him, Margaret and Megan what a formi-

---

* 'Pertinax' was the French political journalist André Géraud. Frances had become friends with him during international conferences to which he accompanied Briand and Berthelot.

dable political team the three of them made. It was a lesson they never forgot, and from then on when public duty called they put their private differences aside to present a united front. The next time they campaigned together it would be Megan, not her father, who was the star of the show.

21

Megan

MEGAN LLOYD GEORGE at twenty-one was an unusually privileged young woman. With her dark, wavy hair cut short in the fashionable 'flapper' style, she stood only five feet two inches. She was not considered a beauty, but she stood out in a crowd because of the striking blue/grey eyes she had inherited from her father, and her lively, gregarious and attractive personality. Along with his eyes she had inherited Lloyd George's love of performing, his impatience, his enjoyment of a good political fight and his radical views. From her mother she took a love of gardening, bad timekeeping, a quick temper and a fierce sense of loyalty. The combination made for a fascinating and volatile mix.

From early childhood Megan had idolised her father. She was accustomed from her infancy to sharing his successes, listening avidly to his musings and living at the heart of the political establishment. Lloyd George was more than a father to Megan, he was her hero and her mentor as well, and her friend Thelma Cazalet described her relationship with Lloyd George as 'almost telepathic'.[1] Megan once said that she had tried to form a friendship with Herbert Asquith's daughter Violet, but had failed to overcome the latter's hostility, born of her devotion to the memory of her father. 'If she'd only known,' Megan had said. 'Nobody could sympathise more than I could.'[2]

Megan's life is often interpreted solely in relation to the dominance of her father's influence. As a result, her mother's equally strong influence, even in politics, is overlooked. While Megan's personal and political relationship with her Tada inspired and complicated her later life, her relationship with her mother was more straightforward: A.J. Sylvester asserted that she 'adored her father, but she adored her mother even more'.[3] Megan's erratic schooling meant that she had spent most of her childhood with her mother. Margaret loved to have a child around, and her two miscarriages, and the loss of Mair shortly afterwards, magnified the love and affection surrounding Megan throughout her early life.

Megan alone of the Lloyd George children was living at home when the relationship with Frances was uncovered. Unlike her elder siblings, Megan had no career or family of her own to distract her from dwelling on her double betrayal, and she was in the unhappy position of seeing the full extent of her mother's humiliation. Megan was not pragmatic like Olwen or easy-going like Gwilym, nor was she patient enough to follow her mother's lead and wait for the affair to blow over. Her feelings were exacerbated by the frustration of her social position: as a not particularly well-educated young lady, she had little to occupy her time while she waited for a suitable young man to come along. She had plenty of time to brood on her father's betrayal and her mother's pain, yet she could not bring herself – quite – to confront Lloyd George. Instead she concentrated her ire on her former friend. This may not have been logical – it was Lloyd George, not Frances, who had betrayed Margaret – but it is understandable. It was the one way in which Megan could hold on to her love for both her parents.

That is not to say that Megan's relationship with her father was easy. As we have seen, she tried again and again to cause trouble, but failed even to dent her father's relationship with Frances, let alone bring it to an end. There was constant friction between Megan and Lloyd George, and those who were frequently in their company noted their bickering and mutual antipathy.

After two unhappy years, Megan's loyalty to Margaret – together perhaps with a less consciously acknowledged jealousy of Frances – led her to seek an escape. Her opportunity came via an invitation from the Viceroy of India, Lord Reading (the former Rufus Isaacs), to make a long visit to Delhi. Megan was missing her sister Olwen, and this was an opportunity both to see her and to get away from the tension at home for a few months. She would leave at the end of November 1923.

Olwen had been living in style in India since her husband Tom's appointment as the Viceroy's personal physician, with homes in Delhi and Simla, but after a while she found it difficult to adjust to the idleness imposed on her. She had servants to take care of domestic duties, and nothing to do except socialise with other British wives. She was lonely when Tom was away accompanying the Viceroy on his frequent regional tours, and she missed her family. She had already returned to England for a visit in September 1921 when her second daughter Eluned, born in March that year, was old enough to travel, making the long trip home to collect her eldest, three-year-old Margi, and take her back to India. While she was in London, Olwen once more became Megan's confidante. 'It's been great to have had you home,' wrote Megan. 'It'd [sic] done me an awful lot of good in more ways than one – mental, moral and physical – and you've cheered us all up enormously. You've been an awful brick! I am not likely to forget all the little things you have done that count for so much.'[4] At that time Megan was still struggling with her feelings for McKenna, which goes some way to explain the unhappiness hinted at in her letter. Had Olwen stayed longer, with her customary good sense she might have helped Megan deal with the other strains in her life.

In 1923, when Olwen was expecting her third child, Margi succumbed to a near-fatal bout of dysentery. Olwen described the episode as 'a shattering blow', reminding her of her sister Mair's death, and it brought to a head her dissatisfaction with life in India. Tom managed to secure early retirement from the India Medical Service, and the family returned home together once Robin, born in September, was old enough to make the journey. They reached London on 25 November, and settled into the family's London residence, 10 Cheyne Walk in Chelsea.* This prompted a rather catty comment from Frances, who wrote to Lloyd George, 'Olwen arrived safely yesterday – I suppose Cheyne Walk will be turned into a nursery now. Whatever you do, *keep them away from Hindhead* [Churt]!'[5] Only two days later, Megan sailed for Delhi.

---

* The Lloyd Georges had stayed only a few weeks at Edward Grigg's house in Vincent Square before finding a London home of their own in Cheyne Walk. In the summer of 1927 they moved again, to a more spacious house, 2 Addison Road in Kensington, where Margaret was able to indulge her love of gardening.

When Megan arrived she at once joined the Viceroy's party on a Christmas visit to Burma. She was an immediate hit, and was persuaded to extend her stay, sitting out the hot weather at Simla in the foothills of the Himalayas, ignoring her father's grumbles ('I miss your joyous little presence so much'[6]). She indulged her love of theatre by taking part in a production by the Simla Amateur Dramatic Society, dressed in traditional Burmese dress for a Festival of Lanterns pageant, and attended a fancy dress ball as an early Victorian lady, with hair to match. Lord Reading wrote to Margaret that Megan 'is having the most wonderful time in Simla and seems to enjoy every minute of it . . . She has a splendid capacity for enjoyment – it is attractive and refreshing to see her.'[7] Her visit was further extended so that she could join the Viceroy's tour of Kashmir, and it was not until 6 December 1924 that she finally returned to Britain. Her year in India was a success, it seems, not only in driving all thoughts of McKenna and other unsuitable young men from her head, but also in bringing to an end her frivolous life in London.

During Megan's absence, British politics had been turned on its head. Unlike his predecessor as Prime Minister Bonar Law, who had enjoyed a good relationship with Lloyd George, Stanley Baldwin seemed to regard him as a political timebomb, a 'big beast' to be feared. Shortly before Lloyd George's return from North America, Baldwin announced a programme of protection measures for trade, aimed at solving the unemployment problem. Law had promised not to introduce such measures, and Baldwin's policy u-turn obliged him to call an election on 6 December. Free trade was a cornerstone of both Asquith and Lloyd George's political philosophy, and was the one issue that could bring the two men together again. Lloyd George accepted Asquith's leadership once more, although he withheld all but £100,000 of his political fund, and the Liberal Party fought the election as a united front. The Tories remained the largest single party, with 258 seats, but Labour won 191 seats and the revived Liberals 159, which meant that Baldwin had no overall control, and could not remain Prime Minister.

Asquith was determined not to enter another coalition, and as a consequence Ramsay MacDonald became Britain's first Labour Prime Minister on 22 January 1924. He was in office by grace of Liberal votes, but did not acknowledge the debt – according to Lloyd George he behaved 'like a jealous, vain, suspicious, ill-tempered actress of the second rank'.[8] MacDonald and Lloyd George clashed on the floor of the House, Lloyd George scornfully deriding the Prime Minister's woolly statements on France's continuing occupation of the Ruhr. Amid worsening economic conditions and attempts by the government to set up a trade agreement with Russia, the end of MacDonald's brief administration came when the *Worker's Weekly*, a British Communist paper, published an appeal to soldiers not to fire on demonstrating workers. The editor, John Campbell, was charged under the Incitement to Mutiny Act, but the action was withdrawn, leaving the government vulnerable to charges of Communist sympathies. On 8 October 1921 the Conservative Party put down a vote of censure in the House which the Liberals, frustrated and goaded by Labour's unfriendly attitude, supported, toppling the government. The general election on 29 October was dominated by accusations in the press of a left-wing conspiracy (most notoriously the 'Zinoviev letter', later exposed as a forgery, urging British Communists to prepare for armed uprising). The result was a Tory landslide. Baldwin returned to power with 419 seats, while Labour held on to 151. The Liberals were routed, left with only forty MPs, the beginning of Lloyd George's long conviction that the three-party electoral system was unfair. Gwilym lost his seat, as did Asquith, who accepted a peerage but stayed on as party leader. Lloyd George became the main Liberal spokesman in the House of Commons.

Talk of lowering the age of enfranchisement for women from thirty to twenty-one, meaning that younger women could stand for election to the House of Commons, galvanised Megan into action. She enrolled as a part-time student of politics and modern history at King's College London, and gradually took a more prominent role in national politics. The focus of her political activity in the mid-1920s was her father's resurrected Land Campaign, which proposed that the unjust and ineffective landlord system should be replaced by state ownership of agricultural land and a leasing system to give tenant farmers greater security. While both Megan and Olwen did their bit, appearing on platforms and at fundraising events, Olwen had no interest in a political career. But it was becoming obvious that Megan was destined to follow her father and her brother to the House of Commons.

According to the *Daily Mirror* in 1933, 'Megan Lloyd George [was] probably the most carefully trained politician, man or woman, who has sat in Parliament since the days when certain families bred their eldest sons for Parliament as a horse is trained for the racecourse.'[9] 'So now for politics,' her father wrote to her in 1924, '– the greatest and most varied stage in the world.'[10] Megan evidently agreed, and apart from a bout of appendicitis that brought her anxious father hurriedly back from a trip to Italy, she concentrated her efforts on developing her speaking skills and building up a support base in Wales.

With the probability that women's suffrage at twenty-one would become law in the near future, Megan began to consider which seat she might contest at the next general election. It was rumoured early in 1928 that she would put her name forward for Pontypridd, but it was unlikely that she could win a seat in South Wales, which was fast becoming a Labour stronghold. Instead, in March – before the Franchise Bill giving her the vote was passed – she entered the race for the Liberal nomination for Anglesey.

The island of Anglesey, lying off the coast of Caernarvonshire and sheltered by the Snowdonia mountain range, is both geographically and culturally a little apart from the rest of Wales. Known outside Wales as a holiday destination for the urban dwellers of North-West England and as a stopping-off point for ferries to Ireland, it is omitted with tedious regularity from maps of the British Isles. The Welsh know Anglesey (Ynys Môn) as 'Mam Cymru', the mother of Wales. Erstwhile home to the druids and last stronghold against the invading Roman armies, it has provided Wales with more than its share of poets and writers. In 1928 Anglesey's people were farmers or worked in the docks of Holyhead, and spoke mainly Welsh. With high unemployment and widespread poverty, it was a natural target for the Labour Party, and could no longer be considered a safe Liberal seat. But the retiring Member, Sir Robert Thomas, had a majority of over 5,000, which was a good starting point for his successor.

Megan was a strong candidate. There were around five million new voters in 1928, and it was not clear how they would affect the political balance. As a result, all constituencies were keen to put forward a candidate who appealed to young women, which Megan clearly would. Secondly, her name counted for a great deal. Lloyd George's constituency,

Caernarvon Boroughs, in which Megan had been born, lay directly across the Menai Straits from Anglesey, and she could count on a wide network of supporters. Thirdly, Megan was already a national figure, with a high public profile and considerable experience of politics for her age. It was a promising combination.

Megan was not without strong competition. Ellis 'Willie' Roberts, a barrister born in Anglesey, believed that he had been promised the nomination, and campaigned vigorously against her, as did Lawrence Williams, a colonel from Parciau. While being her father's daughter was generally helpful to Megan, there were some who disapproved of Lloyd George because of his readiness to work with Tories and his refusal to join forces with Asquith after the end of the Coalition. Megan's youth and gender were also not unmixed blessings. Her reputation as a socialite did not go down well in rural North Wales, and neither did the more traditional voters like the thought of a female MP. No female Member had ever represented a Welsh constituency, and Megan would have to fight hard if she was to be the first.

With the selection meeting scheduled for 24 May, Megan and Margaret headed for Wales. Lloyd George knew what he was doing in sending Margaret along as Megan's minder, as she was an experienced public speaker who enjoyed unrivalled popularity throughout Wales. He himself stayed away, presumably to avoid giving the impression that he was interfering in the selection process, but he was far from inactive, dispensing feedback and advice at every turn. 'A word for the big M. first,' he wrote on 30 March. 'Your speech at Penrhyn Hall was excellent. In spite of the success of the little M. the old girl is not by any means on the shelf yet. She has the knack of getting straight to the point. She is what is known at the Bar as a good verdict getter.'[11] He went on to voice his concern over Megan's schedule. With his customary preoccupation with her health, he protested that it was too much to ask her to speak at Llanelli on the South Wales coast, a three-day round trip from Anglesey, immediately before giving a crucial speech at Amlwch in the constituency:

I am very anxious about her programme, next week more especially. Llanelly is a sad blunder & I am most unhappy about it . . . A tired person cannot do justice to herself. R J [Thomas, the retiring MP] . . .

knows Megan but with a cruel selfishness & conceit he insisted on her coming because it inconvenienced him to put it off. I can assure you his conduct has put him finally off my register of friends . . . He has shown himself quite ready to risk not only Megan's chances but her health in his own interest. I begged him to postpone & [said] that I would pay all loss. He said his Committee would not agree. Bunkum – if he had urged it they would have done so . . .

All you can do now is to see that her health does not suffer. You ought to go with her. She will beg you not to. Take my tip & go.

Insist that she must not stay for the night meeting. She won't get to Aberystwyth by 8. Get her to rest in the train with a slightly open window otherwise the stuffiness will poison her blood.[12]

Lloyd George was longing to throw himself into battle on behalf of his youngest daughter, but contented himself with sending Margaret his thoughts on speeches: 'When you speak either privately or publicly – you M. no. 1 – you ought to call attention to the unexampled training Megan has had. She has come in direct contact with the leaders of all the political parties – Libs. Cons. & Labour & heard them all discuss public affairs.'[13] Occasionally his barrage of advice was irksome, and he had to apologise: 'My darling M's,' he wrote, 'Just a word to say that when I scolded so unreasonably & violently the other day it was only because of my concern for the success of the little M. You are both doing well – very well & I don't care one hoot what happens. I shall be quite happy about it.'[14]

Megan and Margaret campaigned steadily through April and May, amid claims of unfair tactics and malicious gossip. After the temperance-loving nonconformists of Anglesey had been shocked by a false report in the *Daily Mail* that Megan had attended a 'pyjama bottle party' thrown by the Hon. David Tennant, it took a full denial and much local reassurance to calm the situation. Two days before the selection meeting, Lloyd George wrote his final words of counsel: 'I only want to write you to wish the best [of] luck on Thursday. It seems according to all accounts to be a "cert". You have no cause for nervousness or anxiety about your speech. I know you will do well. So don't worry about it my sweet.'

However much of a 'cert' he thought it was, Lloyd George could not resist pulling one more string to ensure Megan's selection:

I have caused it to be hinted to Walter Jones for use <u>after</u> the vote that if E.W.R. [Ellis 'Willie' Roberts] behaves decently I will do my best to help him to find a constituency to fight. But I have warned him that this must on no account be used <u>before</u> the vote as an inducement for him to withdraw.* But it will be helpful with several good fellows who had promised him already before you came out . . .

You have fought a splendid fight & I am prouder of you & the old girl than ever.[15]

Megan faced a stormy selection meeting, with her rival candidate Colonel Williams unwisely launching a vitriolic attack on her: 'The first farmer in the world had tenure conditionally, and when the condition was violated he was turned out of the Garden of Eden. It was owing to a woman. Let me tell you she was a young woman too.'[16] Nevertheless, when the votes were counted Megan became the Liberal candidate for Anglesey, with a margin of forty votes over her nearest rival.

Lloyd George was jubilant:

HWRE! HWRE!! [Hurrah! Hurrah!!] The estimate I made this morning of the division is not far wrong. I'll show it to you. You two Megs! did it all yourselves against great odds. A fortnight ago you'd have had a majority of three. Three weeks ago you would have been beaten. A month ago you had no chance.

Hallelujah. Hallelujee!![17]

The following year, 1929, a general election was called for 30 May, and this time both her parents were able to campaign for Megan, attending meetings and speaking from platforms as well as accompanying her on her tours of the constituency. Amid scenes of jubilation, Megan Arvon Lloyd George was elected MP for Anglesey, with an increased majority over her predecessor. She was paraded through the streets of Llangefni on the shoulders of her supporters in a celebration similar to that which followed her father's election to the House of Commons for the first time in 1890. Megan was twenty-seven, the same age as he had been

* In fact this did not prevent Roberts from claiming during the general election campaign the following year that the vote at the selection meeting at Anglesey had been rigged.

then, and few doubted that she had an equally glittering career ahead of her.

Stanley Baldwin was out of No. 10 and Ramsay MacDonald back in, but there were still only fifty-nine Liberal MPs in the House of Commons and the main political debate was between the Conservative Party with 260 seats and Labour with 288. Megan was one of only thirteen female MPs, and the only Liberal among them. Two years later, when Megan's close friend Thelma Cazalet was elected as a Conservative MP, she noted that 'there was still something slightly freakish about a woman M.P. and I frequently saw male colleagues pointing me out to their friends as though I were a sort of giant panda'.[18] Megan, however, was not averse to the attention.

Wary of making her much-anticipated maiden speech before she was fully ready, Megan concentrated at first on her constituency. Frances, writing in her diary in 1934, noted cattily: 'We discussed (D & I) Megan and her fondness for her constituency & for running about there so busily. We decided that it satisfied her innate appetite, which she has had ever since she was a small child, for appearing all the time as it were upon a stage, & being the centre of attraction.' Implausibly, given Lloyd George's love of an audience, she went on: 'D. says that he has never had any such desire, & I do believe him, to the extent that he is still shy, as he says he always has been, of the actual public appearances, & not of the speaking & all that that involves, but rather of the glances and notice of strangers – he says his Uncle was just the same, to the extent that he could not bear to see a stranger enter his congregation.'[19]

The same was most certainly not true of his daughter. Megan loved the celebrity of being an MP. According to Cledwyn Hughes, who met her as a young boy and who was to be one of her main political opponents as well as a friend in later life,* she came across as 'brisk, cheerful and pretty'. She had the attractive quality of being happy in her own skin, a quality she inherited from the quietly self-possessed Margaret, not from her more sensitive father.

*

* Hughes, the Labour candidate, would win Anglesey from Megan in 1951.

As Megan settled into her new role, she relied heavily on her mother's help. Having looked after her husband's constituency for over twenty years, the routine of garden fêtes, village hall meetings and ribbon-cutting was long familiar to Margaret. At the time of Megan's election, Margaret was sixty-two years old. Since leaving No. 10 she had not been able to relax into private life, and she was still a major figure nationally even if she did spend most of her time in Wales. This had its positive aspects, such as being able to help her daughter find her feet in politics. It also had a negative side.

In 1925 Margaret had mislaid a pearl necklace, a gift from Lloyd George, on her voyage home from Algeciras. This was entirely typical: she was forever putting things down and losing them, but in this case the item was valuable, and word got out. The left-wing *Daily Herald* estimated the value of the necklace as £1,000 (£42,016 today). Margaret immediately asked the paper to publish the correct value of around £600, which it did. But the *Herald* spotted an opportunity to make mischief, and on 1 April it published an editorial attack on the leaders of the Liberal Party, using Margaret's necklace as proof that Lloyd George had betrayed his class:

'Killed by its leaders.' That is the epitaph which Mr. Arthur Ponsonby suggests on our Book Page to-day as suitable for the Liberal Party, and the theft of Mrs. Lloyd George's thousand-pound pearl necklace illustrates how they killed it . . . the existence of the Labour Party depends upon its success in prevailing upon Labour leaders not to take the same disastrous road.

The two men who have done more than any others to kill Liberalism are Lord Oxford and Asquith and Mr. Lloyd George. Their chief mistake was allowing themselves to be enticed into a social atmosphere altogether different from that in which their early lives had been passed.

They exchanged simple tastes and habits for the luxurious ways of the rich. They adopted the cynical tone of the Class which had so long been accustomed to rule, and which regarded, with amused contempt those over whom it ruled . . . They saw that their interest lay in keeping things as they are.

And now the people who believe in Liberalism as a religion, who trusted their leaders wholeheartedly and felt sure they would never go over to the enemy, read about Mrs Lloyd George's thousand-pound pearl necklace with a bitter smile and say to themselves: 'So it was for this that we chose them to lead us and set them in high places – in order that they might win for themselves and their families social advancement and leave us in the lurch . . .'[20]

– and so on, for another six paragraphs. Margaret was incensed. She had once told Lord Riddell, 'I don't believe in taking attacks and abuse in a resigned, humble way,'[21] and now she was about to prove it. The accusation stung because it was both credible and damaging: Lloyd George and Margaret were living in comfort, with three capacious homes. They took foreign holidays and enjoyed a lifestyle that would have been unimaginable to their parents. However modest their income might be compared to their rich friends – the Philip Sassoons and Lord Readings of the smart set – it was still a fortune in the minds of the constituents of Caernarvon Boroughs. But Margaret felt the injustice of the charge keenly: despite the material wealth they had gained over the years, she and Lloyd George could not truthfully be accused of forgetting their roots. She might wear a valuable pearl necklace, but she was still very much the farmer's daughter from Criccieth. Being accused of betraying her own people infuriated her, and she retaliated in a letter printed in the paper:

Sir, in to-day's 'Daily Herald' you make an offensive attack on me, or rather on Lord Oxford and my husband, in connection with the report that I had lost a necklace supposed to be valued at £1,000.

I have already contradicted the report as to the value, and publicity has been given to that contradiction in every paper except yours. It suits you rather to repeat the mis-statement. If you are curious as to the real value of my lost necklace I can enlighten you. It was not worth one-fortieth, and probably not one-fiftieth of the gift made to your leader when he was Prime Minister, by one of his capitalist friends.*

I have no recollection that at the time of that princely gift, or since, you have rebuked Mr Ramsay MacDonald as you do Lord

---

* Margaret is referring to the gift to Ramsay MacDonald of a car, together with an income of £30,000 to support it.

Oxford and my husband on the proof that transaction gave of the betrayal of his class, and the abandonment of the simple tastes of his youth.

If that example of your partiality as a censor does not suffice, I can quote a few more from your own political household which are much better illustrations for your theme than my over-valued necklace. Most of my pearls were given me from time to time by my husband, out of his earnings as a journalist since he left office. Is it a crime for him to earn high fees for writing? If he is to be arraigned for this offence, many of the most prominent Socialist leaders – ex Ministers and others – ought to be in the 'dock' with him. In fine, had you not better cleanse your own stable first before you undertake to sweep the dust on the Liberal floor?[22]

One suspects that the *Herald* wished it had directed its attack at a more docile target.

Publicly, Margaret and Lloyd George seemed to work and live in unison, and only those close to them glimpsed the private battle that raged between them in the first years after leaving Downing Street. Perhaps she expected him to give up his mistress when he no longer needed her services as a secretary so badly, or perhaps she felt the indignity of her situation more deeply as time went on, but the uneasy truce that had existed between them when Lloyd George was in office shattered soon after his fall.

Margaret, for all her ease in public situations, was a private individual who did not leave much evidence of her thoughts and feelings behind, but as it became clear that Frances was a permanent fixture in her husband's life, her opposition to the relationship hardened. The first sign was that Frances was no longer tolerated on trips abroad, and after Gairloch she and Margaret were never to sleep again under the same roof. While we cannot say with certainty that Margaret imposed a ban on Frances' presence, it is unlikely that Frances brought the practice to an end, since if Lloyd George needed or wanted her with him, she would have endured any amount of unpleasantness to be at his side. A quarrel in 1924 prompted Lloyd George to write an extraordinary letter to his wife: 'You talk as if my affection for you came & went. No more than the sea does because the tide ebbs & flows. There is just as much water in it . . . You like me better sometimes when I am nice to you. So do I you when you are nice to me. But if at the worst moment anybody is not nice to you I am as murderous towards him as Patrick Mahon [a notorious murderer]. I would readily hit them with an axe.'

Margaret was feeling neglected and insecure. If Frances was more than a passing fancy, where did that leave his wife? On previous occasions when she had tackled him over his philandering, Lloyd George fought back fiercely, using cold, legalistic language and implying that she was as much to blame as he. This time it was different. Margaret was hurt, not angry, and Lloyd George responded by reassuring her that his love for her was genuine and her position in his life unchallenged. He couldn't resist going on to defend himself, albeit in a teasing tone:

> You say I have my weakness. So has anyone that ever lived & the greater the man the greater the weakness. It is only insipid, wishy washy fellows that have no weaknesses. Would you like to marry Tim [Timothy Davies]!! He is sober & sternly good in all respects. Would you like to swap me for Tim? Don't let's quarrel by letter. You must make allowances for the waywardness & wildness of a man of my type. What if I were drunk as well? I can give you two samples you know of both the weaknesses in one man & the wives do their best under those conditions. What about Asquith & Birkenhead? I could tell you stories of both – women & wine. Believe me hen gariad I am at bottom as fond of you as ever. Ond paid tynny y rhaff yn rhy dyn [but don't pull the rope too tight] . . .[23]

Lloyd George's method of 'handling' Margaret is still masterly. First he holds up to her the example of a husband who is dull and unstimulating, then he goes on to cite two others who are both promiscuous and drunk. Since drunkenness was a sin worse even than infidelity in Margaret's book, the effect is to downplay his womanising and to persuade her that in comparison with other men he is not such a bad husband after all. However hurt Margaret was by her husband's relationship with Frances or by rumours of other infidelities, she remained, in public at least, his loyal wife. But that loyalty was severely tested in October 1926, when they faced one of the biggest crises of their married lives.

Lloyd George was fascinated by newspapers, perhaps more than any Prime Minister before him. He read them avidly, noting earlier than his political contemporaries how influential they were becoming, and in 1918 the Lloyd George Political Fund had enabled him, via a consortium, to acquire the *Daily Chronicle*. In 1926 his son Gwilym, who had lost his seat in the House of Commons in the 1924 election, was the Managing Director of the paper. The Chairman, Charles McCurdy, decided that they needed a woman to join the board, and, with Lloyd George's active acquiescence no doubt, Frances was invited to take the position.

This placed Gwilym in an invidious position. He had hitherto juggled his loyalty to both of his parents by not making an issue of his father's relationship with Frances. He was perfectly pleasant to her when they were thrown together at Churt or London. He did not seek out her company, but neither did he object to it like his sisters, and Frances had begun to regard him as her only friend in the enemy camp. It was all the more surprising therefore when he voiced his strong objection to her appointment as a director of the *Chronicle*. Frances – probably accurately – attributed this to Margaret and Megan's influence. It seems that Lloyd George had made a bad error of judgement. Mistaking Gwilym's easy-going acceptance of Frances for approval, he had put him in the position of having either to oppose Frances' appointment or to be seen by all to be working happily alongside her. Even if Gwilym himself could have contemplated agreeing to this, Margaret, Olwen and Megan reacted furiously, and he felt he had no option but to resign from the *Chronicle*.

Lloyd George came out fighting. If Gwilym would not sit on the same board as Frances, then he would see if his other son would do so instead. Dick, earning his living variously as an engineer and a farmer, was always short of cash, and the £2,000 salary was a strong incentive to him to side with his father. But once again Lloyd George had miscalculated. Dick eagerly accepted the offer, then realised that Gwilym was no longer on the board, and Frances was. Believing that his father was acting 'out of pique to annoy Gwilym, but probably out of fear of his girl friend and desire to placate her ... [so that] she would therefore no longer feel that she was an Outcast in Isolation',[24] he changed his mind and turned down the position.*

For the first time, Lloyd George's whole family was united against Frances. According to her they were all 'incensed', and they decided to confront him. The only account of this incident is given in Frances' autobiography, in which she claims that they wrote a letter, signed by all of them, demanding that Frances should be removed from Lloyd George's secretariat. If not, they threatened, he would be exposed. This letter has not survived – rather curiously, in view of the number of people involved in its authorship and of Frances' habit of keeping a record of anything that cast Margaret in a bad light – and is not mentioned by Dick or Olwen in their memoirs. According to Frances, Lloyd George responded with 'a terrible letter to Dame Margaret, upbraiding her and the children for attacking him and offering her a divorce, which he said he would welcome'.[25]

If this is true, it was a significant moment in the marriage, for Lloyd George had never before admitted the possibility of divorce. But *is* it true? Not only is there a lack of evidence for the jointly-signed family letter, there is also no surviving letter from Lloyd George to Margaret mentioning a divorce. What does exist is an angry letter from him to his wife:

Your Criccieth letter had nothing to do with the unhappy break with G. He never mentioned that subject to me either during the quarrel or before. On the contrary he seemed to be on the best of terms with the person he now pretends to you was the cause of the quarrel. They always – & up to the last moment chatted & chaffed together.

However I know now too well what has been going on the last few days. G. in his new mood of ranting hysteria has told three or four persons all the details of the 'family councils' which have taken place. It appears that my children are following the example of the children of Noah by exposing their father's nakedness to the world. It is not the reputation of Noah that has suffered. But his children have gone down the ages as first class skunks for turning on the old man . . . As

---

* Forced to concede defeat, Lloyd George went on to sell the *Chronicle*. Everyone concerned, including family members and Frances, made a healthy profit.

to G: I have offered him good terms & I do not propose to recede from them whatever the consequences. I will be neither bullied nor blackmailed . . .

I must tell you how deeply pained I am to learn that you & Megan have turned against me. I have been for some time sick of public life. I work hard – very, very hard – & get nothing but kicks. I have been contemplating clearing out & writing my book in retirement . . . I am an old man. I mean henceforth to enjoy the leisure which is my due.[26]

While there is no doubt that this is a strong letter, it falls somewhat short of Frances' description. Lloyd George accuses his family of disloyalty and ingratitude, and petulantly threatens to leave politics and retire. He touches on one of his main grievances, that his family relies on him financially without acknowledging the debt, and demonstrates how critical and unsympathetic he could be towards his sons, in contrast with his affection and support for his daughters. But he does not so much as hint at a divorce; does not ask Margaret if she wants one, and certainly does not say that he would welcome one. He forbears from mentioning Frances' name directly and, passing over the cause of the quarrel rather quickly, uses his retirement from public life as a diversionary tactic. Furthermore, he does not mention receiving a letter from his family, but implies that he has heard of their threats indirectly through a third party. If this is the letter that Frances recalled in her memoirs, the reality is rather tame.

Another mystery surrounding this letter is that it was not kept with Margaret's papers or in Lloyd George's children's collections. It was found in Frances' papers, both in draft and as a typescript. Lloyd George's explanation to Frances when he showed her the letter he had supposedly sent his wife was that Margaret had returned it to him. Frances took this to mean that she had accepted that Frances was a permanent part of Lloyd George's life. But it could also mean that it was never sent, merely written and shown to Frances as evidence of a row with Margaret and to gloss over the fact that he had backed down over her appointment to the board of the *Chronicle*. This may sound unduly manipulative, but when Frances' memoir was published in 1967 Olwen was outraged by its account of the 'divorce' letter, and wrote to the *Evening Standard* to set the record straight:

As the only surviving daughter of the late Lloyd George I do not wish to enter into any unnecessary controversy about a life that was by its nature controversial. But I must point out an error of fact which concerns my mother, Dame Margaret, and the children. The letter referred to . . . in which 'Dame Margaret and all the children are alleged,' etc., was never, to my certain knowledge, sent, or even considered. I ought to know as one of the alleged signatories. In addition, such a letter would have been wholly out of character to my mother's calm and dignified behaviour in such a personal matter.[27]

We will probably never know for certain, but it seems likely that both letters were conjured up by Lloyd George to keep the peace with Frances.

This altercation takes its significance not only from the fact that it was the first occasion on which the family showed itself to be united in its disapproval of Frances, but because it came just as Lloyd George, finally, grasped the leadership of the Liberal Party. There could not have been a time when he was less likely to retire from politics, making his family's threat of exposure more potent and his own threat ineffectual. After four years of painful negotiation with the Liberal Party under the leadership of Asquith, Lloyd George's criticism of the government's handling of the General Strike in May 1926 put him at odds with the Liberal Shadow Cabinet. Amid false rumours that Lloyd George was about to defect to Labour, Asquith took the opportunity to rid himself of a formidable rival by expelling him from the party. In the resulting test of strength between the two former political giants, on 8 June Lloyd George was narrowly elected Chairman of the Liberal MPs – effectively the party leader in the House of Commons – but Asquith still clung to the leadership. Weakened by a stroke on 12 June, it was not until 15 October that he finally resigned in favour of his former colleague and political nemesis.

As Lloyd George took the reins of the Liberal Party, Frances was still hoping that he would regain office and take her back to No. 10. She was thirty-eight years old, and there was no escaping the fact that her professional life was considerably less interesting than it had been in the past. She found her new existence 'a little dull',[28] and her diary fell into neglect; there may have been little of interest to write. The thrill of setting up a home for her lover at Bron-y-De had faded, and since she could not accompany Lloyd George on foreign trips, she had more time to herself than at any time since her 'marriage' thirteen years previously. Her official home was still her flat in London, but she could not have afforded the flat in Morpeth Mansions, overlooking Westminster Cathedral, without Lloyd George's financial help. In 1919 the Scottish-born American millionaire Andrew Carnegie had awarded Lloyd George £2,000 (worth £17,400 today)per annum in his will in appreciation for his role in winning the war. With a mistress, a wife and houses in Criccieth, London and Churt to maintain, the extra income no doubt came in handy.

Frances shared the flat in Morpeth Mansions with her sister Muriel. Muriel was twenty-four in 1926, the same age as Megan, and Lloyd George, who liked the company of young people – young women especially – had taken an interest in her from her early teens: Muriel was quite unlike her sister. Frances, light-haired and pretty, favoured their father's side of the family, while Muriel, dark in hair and complexion, had inherited the striking looks of the Armaninos. Their personalities were also quite dissimilar. Nervy and prone to depression in her childhood, Muriel had developed into a 'passionate, intense, neurotic and demanding' young woman.[29] In later life she became 'a forceful woman with a very damaging tongue'.[30] Frances loved her sister, although she was a little afraid of her sharp comments. But the ties of common childhood were strong, and the two sisters shared a similar sense of humour. Muriel's early ambition was to be a writer, but instead she became secretary to Leonard Rees, the editor of the *Sunday Times*, in 1922. Rees knew Frances – he commissioned the articles from her that became *Makers of the New World*, and she may have fed him snippets of political gossip from No. 10, no doubt with Lloyd George's full cooperation – and so it is possible that she had a hand in securing Muriel the position.

Frances still acted as Lloyd George's Private Secretary, and was now also his literary agent, negotiating with newspapers and publishers and taking 10 per cent of his journalistic fees in lieu of a salary. Lloyd George was a prolific writer, and with confidence high that he would return to office, his opinions were highly sought after. To Frances' surprise and delight, her earnings from that source amounted to £3,000 (around £126,700 today) in 1923, far exceeding her expectations.

Bron-y-De became the centre of operations for Lloyd George, who much preferred it to working in London. The house was large enough to accommodate guests, and since A.J. Sylvester and other members of staff frequently stayed overnight, the fact that Frances had her own bedroom there could be passed off discreetly. It was quietly accepted that while Lloyd George based himself at Bron-y-De, Margaret's realm was Brynawelon, although she too had a bedroom at Churt, with their London house as 'neutral territory'. Even William George, who had been kept in the dark with regard to his brother's private life, accepted as a matter of course that the heads of the family should have their separate headquarters. William George was no fool, and his reading of the situation was not far wrong: 'This did not mean, of course, that there had been anything in the nature of a separation between them. On the contrary, it was well understood between them that either would at all times be welcome at the other's place of abode – a privilege not infrequently exercised by both. But generally speaking, each one had enough of their own particular concerns to keep them fully occupied.'[31] When Margaret visited Bron-y-De, Frances had to leave, sometimes at very short notice, but otherwise she and Lloyd George lived together when he was at Churt, maintaining appearances when necessary and breaking off from work to plan improvements to the house and farm.

This represented a new level of domesticity in Frances' relationship with Lloyd George. Instead of snatching time together when other commitments allowed they were now able to develop habits and routines in a way that had only been possible on brief holidays before. It was like a delayed start to married life. In April 1925 Lloyd George wrote a reflective letter to Frances from Madeira, where he was holidaying with Margaret. Its meaning bears several interpretations, but it points to a change in their relationship in 1922:

Although I have no delusions as to the past – none – neither have I any regrets. It is all to me like a previous existence. A new birth came in October 1922. A new tenderness & a new clear & firm purpose came to us both. Before that – to use a legal term applicable to the law of domicile – there was a certain <u>animus revertendi</u>. More marked in your case than mine – naturally. Since then we have definitely settled our domicile. Your love is henceforth my country & mine is yours.

So we have a right to expect loyalty & patriotism to our new domicile. We did not quite feel it was due before. I love you more tenderly than ever – in a different way altogether. I cannot think of life apart from you now.[32]

This letter was written at a time when Lloyd George was feeling his age, which perhaps explains why he wanted to establish 'loyalty & patriotism' in their relationship. The term '*animus revertendi*' literally means 'intention to return', and A.J.P. Taylor suggests in his edition of Frances and Lloyd George's letters that this refers to the fact that each expected the other to end the relationship in its earlier years. From 1922 onwards, Lloyd George is saying, they committed irrevocably to each other.

While she was in Downing Street Frances had longed for a quiet life in the country with her lover, but when it actually came about the rural existence was not enough to keep her fulfilled. The age difference between them was beginning to show. 'You talk about the time being nigh when I shall be called back,' he wrote to her from Criccieth in June 1925. 'My thoughts have been all the other way – about retiring somewhere from the confusion & din & worries.'[33] Lloyd George sensed Frances' boredom, and he began to worry that she was flirting, or worse, with other men. Frances looked younger than her age, and was still capable of turning heads. The teasing references to infidelity that were part of the couple's erotic vocabulary began to take on a more urgent tone in his letters.

This may be why during Lloyd George's annual summer visit to Criccieth in 1925, Frances was persuaded to take a holiday with Muriel at the Welsh spa town of Llandrindod Wells. Did Lloyd George want her to be relatively close at hand, as a guard against bad behaviour? He would be sure to hear about it if she misbehaved in Wales. He knew all too well how elderly and staid the company in Llandrindod would be, and was more than happy for his mistress' charms to be wasted on dullards. For her part, Frances was conscious that her slim figure was filling out, and she was determined to lose weight on her holiday. It suited her to visit a spa where weight-loss and other 'cures' were catered for. In the event, her holiday was enlivened by a surprise encounter with Mrs Tim. Lizzie Davies arrived at the same hotel as Frances, pointedly refused to speak to her, and left after only one day. Lloyd George wrote to Frances, 'You could not expect her to be cordial could you?'[34]

Mrs Tim's appearance was Frances' only amusement, but Lloyd George seemed racked with jealousy. At first he merely teases: 'Give my love to Muriel, & tell her not to flirt too much but that *all* the flirting that is permissible to the party must be done by her.'[35] He enclosed a sprig of white heather picked at the top of Treceiri hill to remind her of their walk there together during the summer of 1911. A few days later, he returns to the theme of infidelity: 'do leave the flirtations to Muriel . . . I am getting more & more jealous of your fascinations. I want them all to myself – my own cariad. I want your thoughts your dreams – your naughty impulses – every one of them. You have captured mine to the last particle of mischief.'[36]

Frances enters into the spirit of the exchange by teasing him that she has made a conquest of an entire family – a father and his two sons were in love with her. She takes care to let Lloyd George know that the sons are only sixteen and twenty, that she is 'quite impartial' to their father, and had been befriended by his wife. Muriel has 'been quite a success, & one married man is completely gone on her'. Surprisingly, she goes on, 'The Stevenson family seem to have an attraction for married men!'[37] Could she have become so inured to the immorality of her position that she made light of it in this way?

Lloyd George's references to Frances' flirting continued through each separation. A different, more serious tone enters his letters from the summer of 1928: 'Now keep out of mischief my sweet heart. I know how difficult it is for you to resist temptation. You are [an] enticing little devil & you know it & you like to exert your power & to enjoy the rewards. Don't – I beg of you. I promise to be good if I feel confident that you are.'[38] His fidelity, in other words, is conditional on hers.

Margaret had never given Lloyd George cause to worry about her fidelity, despite her frequent separations from him. Frances was in a very different position, and his letters betray real mental turmoil as he alternates between his need to believe that she is faithful and his suspicions that she is not: 'Continue to write me my own girl – who is not & never has been naughty – my girl who thro' life has resisted temptation! Oh you little d—l [devil]. I'll pay you out – in person & scrag it out of you.'[39]

The following year, 1929, his tone is more plaintive as he returns to the hotel in Rapallo that they had visited together in 1917: 'Do you remember it. Of course you do. Oh you little devil! No more hanky panky – please my little darling. I beg of you.'[40] Frances could not allow the suggestion that she had been unfaithful to pass unanswered: 'You shouldn't tease me about it. I wasn't nearly as naughty there as you think!'[41]

If Frances did flirt with other men when Lloyd George was looking the other way, it was no more than fair retaliation. Her lover was again applying double standards. Frances was single and could expect neither marriage nor children from him, but he felt that she should conduct herself with absolute fidelity, as if she were his wife, while he was free to be unfaithful as he pleased.

As time went on, two things became apparent: firstly, Lloyd George's wilderness years were going to be longer than Frances and he had assumed. He might still be a major force in politics, but for that very reason, rivals like Baldwin and Asquith were determined to keep the giant in his cave. The second was that the passage of time had not altered the fact that he intended to remain married. Where did that leave Frances? As tensions built up between them, his constant suspicion may have led her to conclude that she had nothing to lose by playing him at his own game if a sufficiently attractive man presented himself. Unfortunately for Lloyd George, that was exactly what had happened.

22

New Loves

THE MAN WHO NOW ENTERED Frances' life was Thomas Tweed. He had been a Liberal Party official since the war ended, and began to work closely with Lloyd George's private office when Asquith appointed him Chief Organiser to the party in 1926. When Lloyd George took over as party leader later that year, Tweed worked on the Land Campaign. The following year, Lloyd George appointed him as Secretary to the party's Organising Committee, a body set up to rebuild support at constituency level. Both these roles brought him into constant contact with Lloyd George – and with Frances.

Thomas Frederick Tweed was born in Liverpool in 1890, which made him more than a year younger than Frances. His father was a provisions merchant, and Tweed grew up to be an 'ardent socialist of the extreme type'.[1] According to one account he was sent to prison in his teens for holding a meeting which had been banned by the police. Clever, eloquent and politically active, Tweed abandoned socialism for Liberal politics in 1910. He attended the Liverpool Institute, where he joined the 1st Cadet Battalion of the King's Liverpool Regiment and graduated through Liverpool University's Officer's Training Corps. The *Eccles and Patricroft Journal* states that he was a Company Commander of the special police during the great Liverpool dock strike of 1911, and was hospitalised after leading a baton charge on a looting mob.

That same year Tweed was appointed Liberal Agent for Eccles in Lancashire, having served as an election agent for the party during the two elections of 1910. He married Ann Louise Hatton in 1912, and they had a son and a daughter, Fred and Wilma. Tweed was twenty-two when he married, and believed his wife was twenty-six. She was in fact nine years older, and her deception was to have far-reaching consequences.*

When the war began, Tweed enlisted in the 16th Lancashire Fusiliers in the 2nd Salford Pals, where he was put in charge of B Company. He personally signed up most of the 120 men under his command, all of whom came from Salford and Eccles. In November 1915, B Company was sent to France. 'Our lives were suddenly changed from the well-ordered discipline and security of the training camp to the hurly burly of strife and sudden death,' wrote Tweed in a letter home to the *Journal*.[2] On 1 July 1916, the most disastrous day in British military history, B Company went into action. On that day, over 19,000 men were killed and 37,000 wounded. It was the first day of the Battle of the Somme.

For days British artillery had targeted the German machine gun positions and the barbed wire that lay between the opposing armies' trenches. B Company was to be part of the second wave of troops. Their orders were to go over the top at 8 a.m., half an hour after 'Zero' hour, when the first wave of soldiers left their trenches, and to march through the enemy lines to take the town of Thiepval. After a tense night 'Zero' hour came, and Tweed and his men watched from their trench as their comrades walked slowly towards the enemy. They saw the German machine guns that should have been destroyed start spitting their deadly fire.

The British Generals' rigid adherence to the battle plan that day in the face of the artillery's catastrophic failure has been described many times. Tweed's orders were not revoked, and he had no choice but to order his men straight into heavy enemy fire. By the end of the day nearly a hundred of the 120 men of B Company were dead or missing. Back in Eccles, a whole community was cast into mourning. Unable at first to get a clear picture of what had happened and who had survived, the *Journal* sent out a forlorn plea:

Relatives of the men in the 2nd Eccles company, who may receive letters descriptive of the fighting in which the battalion took part are asked

---

* Ironically, Tweed gave his age as twenty-five on his wedding certificate, so he too was lying about his age.

to supply information in order that a recording may be preserved. The list of casualties will make melancholy reading, but Captain Tweed in a letter to a friend in Eccles . . . refers to the unexcelled heroism of the men from Eccles who died for their country and the recollection of how they did their duty, he adds, brings tears to his eyes.[3]

On 21 July the *Journal* published Tweed's account of the battle. The men were cheerful and excited as he led them out to the front line. The noise of the artillery bombardment was 'indescribable': 'the sky was lit up as if it were day as far as the eye could see, and the earth shook and vibrated as if by an earthquake', he wrote. Five men were killed by shells before they reached their assembly trench. As the order came to go over the top,

the machine gun opened up again. Some, like young Grindley, were killed getting over, and rolled back into the trench, but through the perfect storm of lead the company went on. Ignoring the rain of death that whistled about them, they kept running from shell hole to shell hole, on and on. Pals of years' association dropped, others fell riddled with bullets, never to rise again. But the cry was always 'On!' . . . To the last Eccles Pals fought and died. My heart is too full to give further details. Their gallantry, their calm courage when they were hit and knew they were beyond hope – I never heard a murmur of complaint from any of the wounded. They died like very gallant Englishmen and Eccles while mourning their loss should be very proud of its heroic company.

'Most of my men I personally persuaded to join the colours,' Tweed wrote in a 'Message to Relatives' in the *Journal* on 4 August,

and I felt the burden of responsibility for their welfare, as a matter of both honour and duty, and now so many of them have made the supreme sacrifice. I wonder with what feelings their loved ones regard myself . . . The men died, as a soldier would wish to die, with their faces all towards the enemy, some of the bodies have been recovered and buried with all reverence, but some have not yet been found, but wherever they are or wherever they lie buried . . . the ground in which they are laid is hallowed and made sacred by the greatness of their sacrifice.[4]

Tweed's courage and leadership at the Somme earned him the Military Cross, and the *Journal* announced his promotion to Major in September. 'Few officers,' it proclaimed, 'have gained a greater popularity with their men, all of whom speak in the highest terms of their leader.'[5] He was subsequently promoted to Colonel – the youngest in the British Army, it was said at the time – and remained on active duty until he was sent back to Britain in April 1918 on medical grounds.

Tweed returned to England a wounded man, both physically and emotionally. In order to survive, it would seem, he had learned to put a distance between himself and anything that could affect him emotion- ally, which included his family. In the aftermath of the war he decided that since his wife had deceived him over her age she had nullified their wedding vows, and he was therefore at liberty to have as many liaisons as he wanted. He continued to live in the same house as his family, and to support them financially, because he was 'not the kind of man to walk away from an obligation',[6] but he no longer felt the need to play the role of husband and father. Just as he had done his duty in the trenches, obeying orders he knew to be wrong, Tweed went through the motions of doing his duty by his family, but withheld his emotional engagement.

The Great War cast a long shadow over the 1920s. Civilians who had joined up for the duration clung to their military titles long after returning to normal life, and Colonel Tweed, as he was known, did likewise. His war record, and his Military Cross in particular, made him stand out, as did his striking black hair and swarthy complexion, while his private unhappiness and the cynical attitude he cultivated only added to his glamour. Frances had never met anyone like him.

Tweed worked in the Liberal Party office in Abingdon Street, but spent a great deal of time at Churt consulting and assisting Lloyd George, who was soon won over by his capability and his blunt forth- rightness. Few people dared speak their minds in front of Lloyd George, but Tweed did not hesitate to challenge him, another factor that impressed Frances. 'He was a man of strong Liberal principles,' she wrote in her memoirs, 'and a splendid war record – and sometimes uncompromising in character. There were often clashes between Colonel Tweed and L.G. on principles and tactics, for the former was fearless in expressing his opinions; but the common cause of Liberalism usually settled their differences'.[7]

During 1927 Frances and Tweed worked closely together. In April that year, a piece appeared in the *Evening News* entitled 'Colonel Tweed at Close Quarters by One Who Knows Him':

Last Spring, Colonel Tweed left Manchester for London in order to undertake the organisation of a thorough-going campaign to popularise the new Liberal land policy, and it is a tribute to his personality that though during the Coalition period he was one of its bitterest opponents, Mr Lloyd George had no hesitation in appointing him to such a position on his staff. His work [as] Chief Political Officer to Mr Lloyd George will stand him in good stead in his new position, for no one knows better than does Colonel Tweed the conditions of Liberalism throughout the country, and the state of its machinery.[8]

There is no record of when Tweed and Frances crossed the line between being colleagues and becoming lovers, but two letters he wrote in August 1928 when he was on a cruise in the Baltic suggest that the affair had been going on for some time. 'Darling,' he wrote, 'There is no real need for visible tokens of our love – you are with me at all times and sometimes I feel your presence so overwhelmingly that I expect to see you by my side when I open my eyes.'[9] He offers tantalising glimpses into the affair:

I wonder if you can recall and place the odd pieces of the jigsaw – Cambridge and a starless night – wind and snow at Lynton – Red Chimney Pots and Cocktails – Riversmeet – the Grey and Red of the Howard – Victory and defeat at Barnstaple – a funny little teashop near Beaux Art – Churt and thrown kisses before a door closes – ivory flesh and love lit eyes – and over all harmony and an abiding peace and one man's – your man's – great thankfulness for your love and the wonderful happiness you have brought him. Good night my beloved. You are very near to me tonight.

Tweed's second letter is even more explicit: 'From now on every mile and every minute brings me nearer to holding you in my arms again – at least nearer to your physical self – because you have never been away from my side, when the sun goes down and in the morning I have stretched out my arms and almost felt the warmth and sweetness of your body within them.'[10]

Lloyd George's suspicions were justified: Frances was indeed sleeping with another man. This, her only sexual transgression as far as we know, was not a passing fancy. Frances was in love with Tweed, and their relationship was to have serious consequences affecting the rest of their lives. Tweed's reputation as a cold-hearted seducer does not tally with the warmth and tenderness of his letters to Frances. Could he have been seriously in love with her? It would seem possible from the next passage of his letter: 'In a curious sort of way, I have almost enjoyed this forced severance because it has quickened my realisation of what your love means to me. I never realised quite so vividly my rich happiness and the joyous promise of the years which are yet to come, as much as I do at this moment when hundreds of miles of land and water separate us and yet we are together. I am very much in love with you my sweetheart, my love, my wife and darling.'

His *wife* and darling? Tweed was married, but not to Frances. Tweed appears to believe that he and Frances had a future together. Did he think that she would leave Lloyd George for him, or that they would manage to carry on their liaison indefinitely behind his back? Both seem highly unlikely. Lloyd George may have been distracted by his political activity at this time, but he still found time to monitor Frances' movements closely and to be suspicious of her. He may also have been difficult to live with, more so at the age of sixty-five than ever, but he could offer Frances more security and comfort than his comparatively impecunious rival. In any case, in Tweed Frances had found herself a second lover who, like Lloyd George, had no intention of divorcing his wife. Her chances of becoming Mrs Tweed were little better than her chances of becoming Mrs Lloyd George.

To cover her infidelity, Frances went as far as to hint to Lloyd George that Tweed was carrying on an affair with her sister Muriel, an alibi he was more than ready to believe. 'Apologise for me to Muriel for taking Tweed away,' wrote Lloyd George in January 1929; and again, 'Muriel returned in time to have a few evenings with Tweed so she'll be happy.'[11] This complicated lie took on an even more bizarre twist when in later years Muriel left her job at the *Sunday Times* to work as Tweed's secretary, and really did have an affair with him.

Frances' motives and state of mind during this period are difficult to fathom. What is clear is that she succeeded in concealing her affair with Tweed from Lloyd George, and from all but a few people around her, for quite some time. The suggestion has been made that Lloyd George did know of the relationship, and sanctioned it in order to provide cover for himself if his own affair with Frances ever came to light. Frances, though, was never enough of a cynic where love was concerned to entertain such an arrangement. A more likely explanation is that, having led a double life for such a long time, she had become a very good liar, and was able to deceive those around her without difficulty. We know that she had a rare ability to conceal her innermost feelings, and that she had grown accustomed to keeping her private life utterly secret. She knew how to arrange secret assignations and to communicate with a lover privately. Having concealed her relationship with Lloyd George from the world for so long, she was successful in concealing her relationship with Tweed from him.

As Frances celebrated her fortieth birthday on 7 October 1928, her private life had never been more complicated. She had been Lloyd George's mistress for fifteen years, and had aborted at least two babies. She desperately wanted children, and the chance was fading as time passed. Her affair with Tweed was known to at least two members of their inner circle: her sister Muriel and A.J. Sylvester, who observed all the comings and goings with his usual detached cynicism. Frances was treading a hazardous path, but instead of leaving one or other of her lovers, she chose instead to raise the stakes sky-high by having a child.

The identity of the father of Frances' daughter Jennifer remains unproven, and has given rise to much speculation and controversy. Frances spent time alone with both Lloyd George and Tweed during January 1929, when the child was conceived. Was this sheer luck, or good planning on her part? The circumstances of her pregnancy give little away.

Frances had been prepared to be on her own over Christmas 1928, for Lloyd George was intending to go to Criccieth. But in the event he succumbed to a bad dose of 'flu in December, and as a result they spent five weeks together at Bron-y-De. On 13 January Lloyd George left with his family for a trip to Genoa. Frances had already departed for her own holiday in Torquay; the date of their separation is, as we will see, fairly crucial.* The only evidence comes from their letters, which are not reliably dated.

The first, from Frances to Lloyd George, was dated 15 January. She complains of tiredness and says, 'I am missing you so sorely – all the more because we have been so constantly together lately.'[12] The next letter is from Lloyd George. It seems to have been written on 16 January, and begins: 'Just one week of the chasm between my sweetheart & myself already bridged.'[13] If the letter really was written on the sixteenth, it would appear that they parted around 9 January, in which case it is somewhat strange that there are no letters before the fifteenth. A later letter from Lloyd George dated '22nd January – Tenth Day' makes more sense, and points to their parting on 12 January, the day before the family trip began.

With Lloyd George out of the country, Frances set off for Torquay. Her letters to Lloyd George describe her comings and goings at the Palace Hotel, first with Muriel and then with her best friend at the time, Felicia Brook, who was herself conducting an affair with the married politician Charles McCurdy. The letters are warm and loving, and continue throughout January and into February. There is nothing in

---

* A.J. Sylvester believed that the 'flu was an excuse to allow Lloyd George to stay at Churt, citing as proof some engagements that appear in Lloyd George's diary during the weeks he was meant to be bedridden. He also believed that Frances and Tweed had ample opportunity to meet during this period, and claimed that Lloyd George left the country several days before 13 January, although his diary shows meetings on 10 January, so this is unlikely. In an unpublished memo entitled 'Secret and Strictly Private. Lloyd George, Frances Stevenson and Tweed' written after the publication of Frances' memoirs in 1967, and a further memo written after Frances and Lloyd George's letters were published in 1975, Sylvester set out all the evidence he had to confirm his belief that Tweed was the father of Frances' daughter, including the physical similarities between them. He claimed that Lloyd George was not happy when he heard of Frances' pregnancy, and that Frances' letters were part of an elaborate deception to conceal the truth. Sylvester was an old and angry man when he wrote his memo. This does not mean that his memory is wrong, but he did have a tendency to see what he wanted to see.

them to suggest that Frances had left Torquay. In 1931, though, A.J. Sylvester wrote, 'there was a good deal of suspicion that Tweed was down in Devon' with Frances.[14] This was confirmed by Muriel, who later told Frances' daughter that during Lloyd George's absence Frances had been on holiday with Tweed at Lynmouth, North Devon, eighty miles from Torquay.

The letters between Frances and Lloyd George during January 1929 seem as loving and warm as ever, with Frances professing her loneliness without him ('I am storing up love and affection & tenderness to lavish on you when you come back to me, my own darling, whom I love & adore'[15]). Lloyd George, on the other hand, continued to suspect her of infidelity from time to time ('Keep off naughtiness my sweet'[16]). But on 22 January he wrote her a long letter in which he reveals not only that he knew she was hoping to become pregnant, but that he was keen for her to succeed: '. . . I shall be expecting an interesting wire from you next Monday week. You know what I mean. If the usual thing happens wire "transactions". If not then "no transactions". I am hoping for the latter. Monday may be premature. If so wire me on the critical date.'[17]

There can be little doubt as to his meaning: Frances' menstrual period must have been due on 'Monday week', 4 February. He was hoping that it would not arrive, indicating that she was pregnant. Even if the wire read 'no transactions', he appears convinced that a pregnancy would happen sometime soon, for he goes on: 'I do hope my darling you are having a real rest. You will need all your nervous reserves the next few months. We shall have a trying time.'[18] He sounds excited and eager for the child he assumed he was to have with Frances. What would he have said if he had known that she was secretly with another man at that very time?

Frances was at her most reassuring as she wrote back: 'Yes, my darling, I will wire you on Monday week, & I very much hope it will be "no transactions". I have a feeling that it may be so, but then I have had that feeling so often before. Only, although I feel so much better in myself, I still feel very lazy, & sometimes I think my eyes are a little tell-tale. However, we mustn't be premature. I have so often been disappointed.'[19]

She has 'often been disappointed', so they must have been trying to conceive for some time. Frustratingly, she does not hint at why Lloyd George had changed his mind about having a child with her, or at how they planned to explain the arrival of a baby in the life of Miss Stevenson. Eight days later, she is still hopeful: 'There are no "transactions" yet, cariad, but there are still two days to go, & I am not letting myself be unduly excited in case of a disappointment. But I do most passionately hope that the longed-for thing may happen. It would just put a seal and crown upon our love & be a marvellous fulfilment.'[20] This appears unambiguous: the child she hopes she is carrying is Lloyd George's.

A few days later she is protesting her fidelity, much as she usually did: 'I am afraid perhaps you are a little jealous, from what you say in your letter. Let me tell you at once, cariad, there is absolutely no grounds or need for it, & I do hope you will dispel at once any fears you may have on that account . . . I don't feel the least inclined to flirt with anyone, & have not flirted with anyone.'[21] Her reason for emphasising this point becomes clear as the letter continues: '& I expect you have had my telegram by now & will know that the most wonderful thing, the thing we have been longing & hoping for, has really happened this time. But I will tell you about that in a minute.' Oddly, there follows a paragraph about her friends and their movements before she returns to the subject:

And now for the great news. It really <u>has</u> happened this time, my love, & I am so thrilled about it – & hope that you will be too. I told you that I thought it <u>might</u>, as I had a curious lethargic feeling, & on the other hand I thought that might be due to Torquay air. But now it seems that it wasn't only that. But I feel extraordinarily well (only a little lazy) and very rested & very fit in mind. I have been loving you so tremendously, my darling, so very completely & tenderly . . . you really can depend upon me to love & cherish you 'till death do us part'. You are my husband, & my little child, & you will never cease to be. Do not doubt me, my darling; it upsets me when I think you are doing so, and under the present circumstances I want all your love and trust.[22]

If Frances suspected that her child might not be Lloyd George's, she certainly hid it well. She could not allow a hint of doubt to enter his mind. Her choice of words is very deliberate, and with their echo of the marriage service they convey a renewing of her commitment to their relationship. If she had ever thought of running away with Tweed, it would seem that her pregnancy had put an end to it. She wanted Lloyd George to support her child and to accept it as his own.

We lack evidence as to how Frances managed to conceal the pregnancy. Loose clothing and the discretion of the Bron-y-De staff can only have gone so far. Until the end of May Lloyd George was caught up in the general election campaign. In August he retired to Criccieth to rest, and Frances, nearing the end of her pregnancy, went away, no doubt to conceal the unmistakable signs. Family tradition has it that she went to France, returning to London for the birth.

Jennifer Mary Stevenson was born by caesarean section, probably in a private clinic in Welbeck Street, London, on 4 October 1929. On her birth certificate, her mother's name is given as Louise Frances Stevenson. This has sometimes been interpreted as an attempt to conceal her identity, but it was in fact Frances' real name. She was known by her middle name from childhood, presumably because her mother was also called Louise. The father's name is left blank.

The child spent the first few months of her life in a nursing establishment which she calls a 'baby farm', where she was regularly visited by her mother. She was then taken to Frances' flat,* where a wetnurse and a nanny had been employed to take care of her. Anyone who asked was told that Miss Stevenson had adopted a little girl, and as far as the world was concerned, Jennifer was Frances' adopted daughter from that point onwards. For Frances to have succeeded in bearing a child with no scandal attached, and with no disruption to either of the affairs she was conducting, was no mean feat.

Whether or not he was actually her biological father, Lloyd George certainly treated Jennifer like a daughter. He taught her to call him 'Taid', Welsh for grandfather, and doted on her for the rest of his life. Tweed, on the other hand did not take an interest in her, and she believes she only met him once, if at all. Jennifer loved Lloyd George and was

---

* Frances moved to a bigger flat in Morpeth Mansions when Jennifer was born. She sold the lease to Winston and Clementine Churchill in 1930, and was most embarrassed when they arrived unannounced to measure for furniture when her hair was in curlers.

loved in return, and as far as she is concerned he was her father in the only sense of the word that counts for anything. 'I do not think there will ever be certainty in this matter,' she says, 'but I would prefer to be the child of someone I loved and respected, and who loved me and enjoyed my company, than of someone I may, or may not, have met on one occasion. Publicly, I refer to LlG as my stepfather, which he was, legally; but when other people speak of him as my father, I do not contradict them.'[23] It would be Tweed, however, and not Lloyd George, who remembered Jennifer in his will.

Frances was silent on the issue of her daughter's paternity for many years, but when Jennifer was fifteen, after Lloyd George's death, Frances told her that she could finally reveal that she was Tweed's daughter. She later repeated this to her future son-in-law, Michael Longford, when Jennifer announced their engagement, adding that she and Tweed were 'secretly married' at the time of the birth. Muriel too was firmly of the view that Tweed was Jennifer's father, as, eventually, was A.J. Sylvester, who claimed that J.T. Davies could back him up since he 'knew to the day when Tweed slept with Frances'.[24] This might all be convincing if it were not for the fact that, to protect Lloyd George's public career, it was necessary to convince anyone who wanted to know that he had not fathered an illegitimate child.

What about the possible fathers themselves? Lloyd George never acknowledged Jennifer as his own child, not even in private correspondence with Frances. When eventually he was challenged on the subject, he claimed to have a letter in his possession in which Tweed took responsibility for Jennifer, but he failed to produce any such letter, and we cannot know if it ever existed. Tweed left no word on the matter either. He had once told Muriel casually that 'If Frances wants a kitten to play with, I don't mind giving her one,'[25] but he took little or no interest in Jennifer. Then again, nor did he take much interest in the children of his official marriage.

Attempting to trace a physical resemblance is highly subjective, and the evidence here is equally unclear. Muriel thought that Jennifer not only resembled Tweed, but had inherited some of his mannerisms. This is confirmed by Sylvester, who wrote in a letter to Olwen in later years: 'by the time she had reached her teens, Jennifer had developed some of Tweed's characteristics to a marked degree. So much so that, to me, who knew Tweed very well indeed, they were unmistakable. Her confor-mation, the face and her complexion, the sagging of the shoulders, the slouch, and the somewhat gangling gait, to mention a few.'[26] Jennifer herself believes that she resembles Lloyd George, but acknowledges that he and Tweed were not dissimilar physically. A surprising witness emerges in William George, Lloyd George's brother, who on the first occasion he met Jennifer was told that she was the adopted daughter of Miss Stevenson. On the way home the unworldly but shrewd William showed that he was not taken in, commenting wryly to his son that Jennifer was the spitting image of Megan at the same age: 'Mae hi r'un ffunud a Megan yn ei hoed hi.'[27]

In the absence of any other reliable evidence, we must look at the dates. The facts as we know them are as follows. Frances and Lloyd George were together for some weeks over Christmas and New Year 1928–29. They parted (most probably) on 12 January, and were apart through the rest of January and into February. During that period Frances and Tweed spent some time together, but we do not know when, and on 3 February Frances sent her telegram to Lloyd George to announce her pregnancy. It has always been assumed that Frances was faithful to Lloyd George sexually during their time together over Christmas, but she could easily have arranged assignations with Tweed. All that is certain is that she did not sleep with Lloyd George after 12 January, and that by the time he returned from Italy she was pregnant. Jennifer was born on 4 October, which suggests that she was conceived in January. The ques-tion is whether it was before Lloyd George left, or after. If we assume that Jennifer was a full-term baby, she could well have been conceived around the third week of January, when Frances was not with Lloyd George, but with Tweed. A further biological clue points to the same conclusion. Frances was expecting her 'transactions' on 4 February, more than three weeks after Lloyd George's departure for Italy. This makes it unlikely that she could have conceived before 12 January.

So why did Frances seem so confident and happy in telling Lloyd George that she was pregnant, and why did she suspect the first signs of pregnancy as early as 17 January? She was actively trying for a baby, that much is clear, and had been disappointed 'many times' before. In other words, she was hoping for, and looking for, signs of pregnancy. The tiredness she reported was not in itself evidence of anything, although it would have seemed so retrospectively. We must however take into account that this was 1929, when the details of the menstrual cycle, conception and pregnancy were not as well understood as they are today.

With so many unsafe assumptions involved in each theory, there can be no certainty on this matter. The only conclusion that makes sense is that while Jennifer *could* be the daughter of either Lloyd George or Tweed, she is more likely to be Tweed's, although Frances allowed Lloyd George to believe otherwise throughout his life.

Frances was playing a dangerous and complex game. We have only her letters to Lloyd George as evidence of her state of mind during these years, as she either did not keep her diary at this time, or later destroyed it. She toyed with the idea of inserting a chapter on her 'adopted' daughter in her autobiography, but Jennifer was insistent that if Frances could not tell the truth she should say nothing, and the chapter was omitted.

It is not surprising that Frances should keep the more sensational details of her life out of her diary. She wrote it as a record for posterity of what she and Lloyd George wanted remembered. It was never a spontaneous, private document, and was always intended for publication – although not perhaps in its unedited form. Ann Parry, a Welsh secretary who joined Lloyd George's staff in 1931, wrote an account of her life in which she revealed that Lloyd George was not only aware of the existence of Frances' diary, but would often dictate to her what to record in it: 'It was obvious that Miss Stevenson was keeping a diary because many times I heard [Lloyd George] say to her, "Put that down," and, "Make a note of that." ' The diary was never intended to be a frank record of Frances' life.

Frances' motives for having an affair with Tweed are unclear, but it is significant that their relationship coincided with her decision to have a child. If she was determined to have Lloyd George's child and his child only, she would not have embarked on a physical relationship with Tweed at the same time. When Jennifer asked her later in life how she knew that Tweed was the father, Frances replied that she had 'taken precautions', the implication being that she had done so with Lloyd George. However, her 'precautions' had proved ineffective on at least two occasions in the past, and as Lloyd George was hoping she would become pregnant, he for one was not aware of any such precautions. On this subject, we must conclude, Frances was not a reliable witness.

Is it possible that Frances was sleeping with Tweed with the express intention of becoming pregnant by him, or at least to provide a plausible 'cover' should Lloyd George be accused of fathering her child? The fact that she continued her affair with him after Jennifer's birth argues against this theory. It would also have been out of character, for however determined Frances was to have a child, the cynicism needed to use Tweed in this way is not consistent with her character. It is more likely that she felt a genuine passion for him, and pursued the relationship because she was frustrated by professional tedium and resented having been wrongly suspected of infidelity by Lloyd George in the past. In love with both men, it would seem that she let fate decide which would father her child.

Life with Lloyd George was becoming more difficult as he got older, which may have been one reason why Margaret preferred to live apart from him for most of the year. The strain of leading the Liberal Party was taking a heavier toll on him than it would have done on a younger man, and he gave serious consideration to giving up at least twice in 1927. In February, Frances wrote: 'D. is most anxious to resign the Chairmanship of the Party. He finds the duties attached to it becoming more & more irksome. He hates having to get up in the House with a cantankerous group of Liberals behind him, most of them looking unpleasant & disgruntled & hardly ever giving him a cheer . . . I don't know what to advise – I always think it best on these occasions for him to follow his own instinct – it is rarely wrong.'[28]

She returned to the same theme in August: '[D] is in a mood now to retire from politics & write his book. I do not think he will do this. He has had these moods before, & now he is less able to leave the Party to itself . . . D. says he wants to leave the Party to get on without him for the present & see how [his probable successor Herbert Samuel] can manage. I don't think he will be allowed to do it, however. Besides, things are going so much better now, it would be a pity.'[29]

However much Lloyd George hated the thought of her with another man, he was not prepared to be faithful to Frances in return. Much has

The Lloyd George family campaigning. Lloyd George was the foremost orator of his generation, Margaret became an accomplished political campaigner, and Megan became a star broadcaster after entering Parliament in 1929.

Frances, Nanny and Jennifer, bound for a holiday in Portugal in 1934 with the captain and Mrs A.J. Sylvester (wife of Lloyd George's Principal Private Secretary). Lloyd George was there to see them off. *Below*, Jennifer with 'Taid', who adored her.

Frances with her lover Thomas Tweed, hard at work in Lloyd George's office.

Lloyd George and Tweed, his Chief Political Officer.

Above 11 December 1932: the support network unravels. Margaret arrives in Churt with Olwen, Tom and Megan to tell Lloyd George that Frances has been unfaithful. A.J. Sylvester (left) looks on in trepidation.

Jennifer with Taid at Bron-y-De: 'I could not help asking myself who was the bigger baby,' Sylvester commented.

Jennifer with Frances on her first day at school in 1941. Her relationship with her mother was difficult.

Above Dame Margaret Lloyd George, the most famous woman in Wales.

Right Megan with her married lover Philip Noel-Baker. Margaret, on her deathbed, made Megan promise to give him up.

Margaret's funeral in January 1941. Members of the Home Guard pulled her coffin on a simple farm cart through the streets of Criccieth. Lloyd George's wreath bore the message 'I fy nghariad – Dei' (To my love – Dei).

Above Open warfare: Lloyd George's eightieth birthday, January 1943. Olwen and Megan attended the celebratory lunch, reluctantly tolerating Frances' presence, but she was excluded from the official photographs.

Mrs Lloyd George – after thirty years by his side. Lloyd George and Frances on their wedding day, 23 October 1943. His children did not attend.

Right Full circle. Lloyd George's coffin leaves Tŷ Newydd, his Llanystumdwy home, on 30 March 1945. His boyhood friend Robert Evans sits alongside, on the same farm cart that had borne Margaret's coffin four years previously. Lloyd George was buried alone by the banks of the river Dwyfor.

Frances, Countess Lloyd-George of Dwyfor. On her passport she gave her occupation as 'widow'.

Megan Lloyd George MP, Frances' rival as guardian of Lloyd George's memory.

The Prince of Wales and the Duchess of Cornwall unveil a statue of Lloyd George in Parliament Square on 25 October 2007. He stands between Winston Churchill and General Jan Smuts, both of whom served as members of his Cabinet.

been said, written and assumed about his relations with women during the last period of his life, not least by members of his own family, for example in Dick's account of his father's 'harem' at Churt. More reliable, though not wholly objective, evidence comes from members of Lloyd George's inner circle, A.J. Sylvester in particular. Sylvester's jealousy, not only of Frances but of anyone who was close to Lloyd George, made his comments shrewish at times, and he was more relied upon than liked, but he was a keen observer. He seems to have understood and accepted his Chief's womanising habits early on.

In a fragment of a diary he started in 1924 but gave up soon afterwards, Sylvester records a brief affair between Lloyd George and one of his typists, Miss Cheek. He first suspected the affair when Lloyd George spent a night alone at Bron-y-De with Miss Cheek in December 1924. There was clearly tension in the office, because in the second week of that month Sylvester wrote cryptically that he had 'dealt with Miss Cheek and told her she could stay if she could do as she was told'. On 18 December Lloyd George failed to attend a fundraising event and went instead to his London house to work on a speech alone with Miss Cheek. Sylvester recorded that he turned up at the house at 9 a.m. the following morning to find that Miss Cheek had stayed all night – and that the speech was nowhere near finished. Miss Cheek then accompanied Lloyd George on a visit to Scotland – to help with his speech.[30]

Miss Cheek appears to have been but a brief diversion, and one of many. It would have been impossible for Frances to be unaware of what was going on; she knew her lover far too well. Although she was a less jealous woman than Margaret, she did suffer pangs of frustration at Lloyd George's behaviour, and was wary when a new female was introduced into his circle. If it had been left to her, all his female staff would have been like the 'dragon' she had employed as his housekeeper at Bron-y-De. It may well have been for that reason that Frances took against Ann Parry before she had even met her, and showed surprising hostility towards the Welshwoman before she joined the staff.

Ann, born in Anglesey the year after Frances, had been the secretary of Sir Robert Thomas, Liberal MP for East Denbighshire, but found herself unemployed when Sir Robert gave up his seat in 1931. Lloyd George had a Welsh secretary on his staff at all times, to help with constituency matters and to ensure that everyone who wrote to him in

Welsh received a reply in the same language. The previous incumbent, Gareth Jones, had resigned, and Ann was ideally qualified to fill the vacancy. Frances had reason to dislike the idea of a woman her own age becoming secretary to Lloyd George: Ann shared his Welsh roots, and could speak to him in the language that Frances had never mastered. Frances was well aware of the fact that it was Margaret's Welshness that bound Lloyd George firmly to his wife, and she regarded a new, younger version as a threat.

Not only did Lloyd George appoint Ann as his Welsh secretary, he also suggested that she be put in charge of Bron-y-De. When Frances was told, she was furious, and told Lloyd George that if Ann was in charge, she would not go near the place. Lloyd George backed down, and Ann took charge only of the library and the very productive apiary at Churt. She was an unassuming, almost painfully shy woman, whose devotion to Lloyd George and respect for 'Miss Stevenson' quickly disarmed Frances. The two women developed an 'almost sisterly friendship', according to Ann,[31] and she never gave Frances cause to be jealous or resentful.

By the 1930s Lloyd George's whole family knew that he was a serial womaniser, even if they did not know the details of most of his liaisons. An exception was his relationship with his daughter-in-law Roberta, which if true, was the least forgivable of all his dalliances.

Roberta Lloyd George was not a happy woman. As the years passed, the differences in age, background and temperament between her and her husband Dick began to work their way between them. Their son Owen would write: 'My father, a most loveable man, was very easy going, enjoyed the good things of life, and from quite an early age drank more than was good for him. My mother, ten years younger, had a very strong personality and a quick temper . . . there were, undoubtedly, rows over money, which unhappily ran through my father's fingers like water.'[32] The marriage had been in trouble for some time when, in 1931, Roberta finally left Dick. Their divorce came through in 1933, and she married again the same year.

The allegation that Lloyd George had an affair with Roberta dates to the very end of the marriage, but is no less shocking for that. It stems from two sources: Frances and A.J. Sylvester. Many years after the event, Frances told Jennifer that the affair had taken place when Dick and

Roberta accompanied Lloyd George, Margaret and Megan on a cruise to South America in December 1927 and January 1928. Sylvester, who went with them, wrote a detailed account of the trip in his memoir *The Real Lloyd George*, but if he saw anything untoward he did not record it.

The confirmatory evidence, if such it is, is provided by Sylvester's diary. In the late 1920s it is clear that Roberta had developed a much closer relationship with her father-in-law, and she became a regular visitor at Bron-y-De. Roberta also had none of the family's reservations when it came to Frances, and the two became friends. In June 1931 Sylvester made a diary entry which is suggestive, but not explicit: 'Unexpectedly got through a whole batch of work with L.G. Roberta phones. He leaves with her for Churt at 1 p.m. . . . Frances told me this morning that she knew what he was up to as he had apparently put his underclothes in his little dispatch box. She seems to accept these expeditions now, as a matter of course.'

The following month Lloyd George suddenly fell ill. Tom Carey Evans, Olwen's husband, was summoned, and diagnosed a prostate condition that needed an immediate operation. The family rallied together: Gwilym arrived to help nurse his father, while Dick went to Criccieth to bring his mother back to London. Sylvester wrote in his diary:

> Dick then spoke to Roberta, who was at home . . . She had spoken to LG on the telephone yesterday and L.G. had been 'short with her'. But that might be according to plan, as Frances was there. It was quite clear from the conversation Dick had on the phone with Roberta that he could not know anything. If only he knew! It was only by the grace of God that she was at home and not in London. She is coming to town tomorrow, but do not think L G will see her. There is great prejudice against her. Carey and Gwilym speak very frankly about her because they know of her attentions.[33]

Sylvester seems to be absolutely certain of the relationship between Roberta and Lloyd George – and certain too that Dick was in complete ignorance. If he was right, the relationship was a well-established fact within the family, who blamed Roberta, not Lloyd George, for it. Later Sylvester gave another hint when he wrote:

'Frances said that . . . when L.G. was taken ill Carey went for him and told him that he had brought all this on himself through his relations with Roberta, that it was her disease which was making her like this, and that she was as hot as hell. She had been off her head already.' The family were demonising Roberta, in order perhaps to excuse their father.

Lloyd George's operation was conducted at home. Margaret hid her anxiety during the operation itself by working quietly at her embroidery, while Megan prayed in her room. When it was all over, however, Dick arrived and Margaret 'just fell into his arms and wept with sheer thankfulness'.[34] Frances was nowhere to be seen. From the moment Margaret arrived from Criccieth, she had been banished from Addison Road. Her only consolation was that Roberta was also banned. Meanwhile, Sylvester devoted a lengthy diary entry to whether Lloyd George wanted to see Roberta but was afraid to say so because of Frances, or truly did not want to see her.

As Lloyd George recovered, matters came to a head. Olwen confronted Roberta, telling her bluntly 'that it was the talk of the place and everybody knew!' Sylvester and Frances discussed what to do about the situation:

> . . . without doing anything very definite it was thought best to go slow. Frances was to try to see [Roberta] and advise her not to try to see L.G. . . . she herself had not even seen him . . . In the course of this discussion Frances said that the week before L.G.'s illness, Roberta had planned to go away with L.G. She had actually had it in her mind to go with him to Switzerland, which of course was impossible and unthinkable . . . Instead it was planned they should go to Churt. Frances says that L.G. did not want to go; I know he did not, but Roberta insisted. He did not want to be naughty at any rate, and she made him so. That is the reason why, when Frances told him on Tuesday that Roberta had been asking about him, and whether he wanted to see her, he said 'Good God, no.' He thinks Roberta is the cause of his trouble. She did no doubt accentuate it; but she was not the only one.[35]

Extraordinarily, it appears that Frances shared the general view that Lloyd George's relationship with Roberta had brought on his condition, and was aware that he had agreed to spend some time alone with Roberta only the week before. Her attitude carries the implication that as far as Lloyd George was concerned the relationship was over, but Roberta was still pursuing him. In her quasi-sympathetic attitude towards Roberta, Frances was behaving magnanimously, as if to a rival she had seen off. She may also have believed that any physical aspect of their relationship could not continue, for Sylvester gleefully records, 'Carey says this will stop all his "rogering" for a long time, although he is such a wonderful fellow with such vitality.'[36] Frances could stop looking over her shoulder for a while. After the operation, the references to Roberta fade from Sylvester's diary, and once Dick's marriage collapsed, there was little further gossip about Lloyd George and his daughter-in-law.

The evidence of a flirtation, inappropriate as that may have been, is strong. But was it an affair? Frances thought Lloyd George was being 'naughty', although it was at Roberta's insistence, not his, but she remained friends with Roberta for many years after the events of 1931, which seems strange if she thought that Lloyd George had slept with her. Both Sylvester and Frances had reasons for thinking the worst of Lloyd George: Frances because it would justify her own infidelity, and Sylvester because he felt threatened by anyone who became close to Lloyd George. But Sylvester had assumed that Frances was having an affair with Berthelot some years previously: perhaps he consistently mistook flirtation for something more? There was considerable jealousy among Lloyd George's staff, and resentment of Roberta could also have distorted the picture.

The current Earl Lloyd George, Owen, Dick and Roberta's son, regards it as unthinkable that his mother should have had an improper relationship with his grandfather. He points out that in 1931 his parents' marriage was virtually over, and with Roberta's own father suffering from illness, feels it was natural for Roberta to seek advice and comfort from Lloyd George. Margaret, Roberta would have assumed, would not be sympathetic since she was much closer to Dick. He remembers that there was a great deal of jealousy and possessiveness among Lloyd George's staff but neither his mother, father nor stepfather ever alluded to an affair in his presence.[37] The picture is not clear. A flirtation is credible, an affair less so. The only firm conclusion we can draw is that Lloyd George's reputation as a ladies' man was getting him increasingly into trouble.

Frances soon had more than Roberta on her mind as she fretted, still banished from Lloyd George's bedside. The separation was difficult for both of them, and Lloyd George asked his son-in-law Tom to arrange for Frances to visit him. This necessitated removing Margaret from the house, and Tom succeeded in persuading her to go for a drive to get some fresh air. In her absence, Frances was smuggled into the house to visit the invalid. On Margaret's return she asked a nurse who had left the splendid bouquet of flowers which lay by his bedside, to be told innocently that 'Miss Stevenson' had paid a visit. Margaret exploded, and turned on Tom so fiercely that he told Lloyd George he would never intervene in family politics again. Frances was barred once more. On key occasions, Margaret was still firmly in charge.

23

Crises Public and Private

'M Y DEAR LG,' WROTE THE physician Lord Dawson in September 1931, when the sixty-eight-year-old Lloyd George was recovering slowly from his ordeal, '. . . How wonderfully well you have done, though no doubt you realise that recovery is a tedious process and when the "slump" days come, not without discouragement.'

Dawson had known Lloyd George intimately for many years, and did not shy away from personal issues. His letter gives Lloyd George frank advice about his still-active sex life: 'About sex – perhaps I can help you a bit – strictly the nearer you can keep to abstention for many months the better – but if the Pauline view about "burning" obtrudes itself,* come what may, the wise plan is to keep to well tried love. In this way you avoid the emotional stimulus which any new goddess must promote and to the patient's detriment. This view, I think, fulfils the dictates of statesmanship!'[1] There were no secrets between doctor and patient, and Dawson knew full well that Lloyd George not only had a mistress but was still pursuing 'new goddesses'.

A.J. Sylvester, who witnessed him getting out of his bath in 1931, wrote admiringly in his diary: 'There he stood as naked as when he was born with the biggest organ I have ever seen. It resembles a donkey's more than anything else. It must be a sight for the God's [sic] – or the women – in erection! No wonder they are always after him; and he after them!'[2]

---

* i.e. That it is better to marry than to burn.

Sylvester took a practical view of Lloyd George's womanising, but betrayed some irritation when it interfered with the smooth running of the office or the farm. Usually he commented without judgement on his Chief's habits: 'He was now always going round his orchard, counting thousands of small apples forming on the trees and making a computation of his crop. The truth is that he was after two girls on the estate.'[3] But the Chief's womanising sometimes caused extra work – one farm manager left because 'he did not like the moral atmosphere of the place'.[4] Above all, Sylvester was frustrated when Lloyd George's obsession with women distracted him from serious political work: 'If L.G. gave his mind to thinking out how he could best help his country, instead of thinking cunt and women, he would be a better man.'[5]

Most of Lloyd George's affairs were merely physical, and Frances accepted them with a degree of equanimity. Jennifer once commented that she didn't like a particular bust of Lloyd George because it made him look lecherous. 'Oh, that,' her mother said, 'that was absolutely accurate.'[6] Frances was even able to joke about his reputation. On a trip to Morocco in 1935 she ran into Winston Churchill and his son Randolph while she was on her way to tea with the local chieftain's harem. ' "Can't Randolph go too?" asked Winston with a twinkle in his eye. I shook my head. "They won't even let L.G. go," I replied. This seemed to amuse him a great deal.'[7]

This aspect of Lloyd George's character seemed to become more exaggerated over time. According to Jennifer's daughter Ruth, 'Frances found herself often coping with distraught young secretaries or farm workers. She was later to say that at least Lloyd George always took no for an answer, but the trouble sometimes arose because young girls did not know how to say no to this enormously famous and distinguished elder statesman who was also their employer.'[8] Even Margaret came to regard his affairs with a certain degree of tolerance. In family gatherings the adults would turn to Welsh when discussing them, which they did 'fairly often',[9] since none of the grandchildren were brought up to speak the language.*

---

* Olwen comments in her memoir that it must have been a sadness to Margaret that none of the grandchildren spoke Welsh but she never mentioned it – it was, she says, simply not fashionable then.

Still, Lloyd George was acutely aware of the need to keep Margaret and Frances on side, and he hid his liaisons from them as far as possible. With other men he was less bashful, and would sometimes acknowledge his reputation as a ladies' man with a wink. In 1937 Lloyd George took Frances on a trip to Jamaica. They enjoyed a good holiday together, which 're-cemented the ties' between them, according to her. She left Jamaica on 8 January to make way for Margaret, and unusually Lloyd George was left by himself with only Sylvester as a companion until she arrived six days later. He spent the time working on his memoir, *The Truth About the Peace Treaties*, and writing an article for the *Strand Magazine*. To Frances, he wrote lovingly: 'Where are you? I always seem to be looking out for you & on the point of calling you & when I remember I am so sad. I have worked with frenzy in order to forget . . . At first I could not realise it. The empty room – the vacant chair on the balcony . . . I turn round to boast that I have written so many words & there is no Frances to hear me. I seize my pad once more & write savagely to forget – but I cannot.'[10] 'I shall never forget that balcony,' wrote Frances in reply. 'It has imprinted itself on my heart.'[11]

The following year, Lloyd George revealed to Finney, his chauffeur, and Sylvester that he had had a more amusing distraction. 'I claim that the writing of that article was a feat of concentration,' he told them proudly. 'I wrote that article whilst sitting on my balcony, beneath which there were numerous half-naked beauties bathing in the pool below. So concentrated was I on my job that the result was that article. I give myself a 100 percent for concentration.' 'God forgive the thoughts that ran through my mind,' wrote Sylvester. 'He took days to write that article and no fresh belle went into that pool without his noticing her.'[12]

In Lloyd George's mind, truth was a relative concept. Megan's friend Thelma Cazalet offered a shrewd insight into his character: '[Lloyd George] is extra-many-sided; and that is why the average person who is only two- or three-sided himself finds it hard to understand a man who has at least a dozen different sides to his nature. He is the most sincere and insincere man I have ever met; he is the most grateful and ungrateful man I have ever met . . . he is a man of the moment – I don't believe he ever really looks back or looks forward. That is why he is nearly always so full of vitality and happiness.'[13]

*

The timing of Lloyd George's illness had been particularly unfortunate for him politically. In 1931 the country was experiencing an economic crisis, with over 2.7 million unemployed and trade figures falling, and it was suggested that Ramsay MacDonald's Labour government would have to give way to a National Government combining all three major parties to turn the situation around. It looked as if Lloyd George might at last get his long-awaited chance to return to government, or if he refused to serve, to be a formidable leader of the opposition in the House of Commons.

The excitement among his political staff grew, but their hopes were to be dashed. On 26 August 1931, while Lloyd George was recuperating from his prostate operation, the National Government was formed under the leadership of Ramsay MacDonald, with the support of Baldwin and Herbert Samuel, who was acting leader of the Liberal Party in Lloyd George's absence, and who now became Home Secretary. The boat had sailed without him.

When the National Government had been formed, it was intended that normal party politics should be resumed as soon as the economic crisis had been resolved and the national budget balanced. But Baldwin was determined to force an early election over tariff reform.* With MacDonald's grudging support, the Liberals were under pressure to agree. Lloyd George, struggling to exert his influence from his sickbed at Churt, was adamant that Samuel should not back down to Tory pressure, but eventually he did so, and on 27 October a general election was called. Lloyd George, still weak and in poor health, found himself estranged from the leaders of the Liberal Party. He fought on as best he could, portraying himself as the champion of free trade, and Gwilym and his brother-in-law Goronwy Owen resigned their ministerial posts in solidarity. The three of them plus Megan formed a group of their own, the 'Lloyd George Liberals'. The man who only weeks before had anticipated a triumphant return to power now cut a lonely figure. He

---

* Conservatives were still in favour of taxes on imported goods to protect British industry. MacDonald was pressured by his party to agree to an election to win a mandate for stronger measures to tackle the economic crisis, and a breakaway group of Liberal MPs, headed by Sir John Simon and calling themselves the 'Liberal National Party' declared themselves in favour of tariff reform too. To Lloyd George, a staunch free-trader, this was treachery, and he would never forgive Samuel for giving way.

had only three supporters in Parliament, and was entirely reliant upon his wife and family to ensure his re-election as MP for Caernarvon Boroughs.

Margaret rose to the occasion superbly. 'Dame Margaret has been working very hard both in the Boroughs and for Megan in Anglesey,' A.J. Sylvester wrote in his diary. 'Here she is loved, admired and is the uncrowned queen.'[14] Invalided at Bron-y-De, Lloyd George did what he could, recording a message to his constituents on gramophone records, and trusting that his wife could carry the election. The result, an overwhelming victory for the National Government,* was disappointing, but Lloyd George held on to his seat with a 5,387 majority and a higher percentage of the vote than in 1929. When the news came through, Lloyd George wired his constituency chairman: 'Thankful the peaks of Snowdonia remain above the deluge.'[15] Margaret's campaigning had paid off.

Lloyd George was extremely frustrated at being out of action during this highly volatile period. He was now the longest-serving MP, the Father of the House of Commons, but that was no consolation for a man who less than a year ago had harboured realistic expectations of the premiership, or at least of a Cabinet position. During this rare extended period of physical weakness he was grateful to Frances for her care and companionship. 'I am so thankful you were with me thro' the most trying time of all,' he wrote, 'the first days of anxiety & apprehension & that horrible night of intense agony. Your wonderful calm & your marvellous gentleness of spirit fragrant with affection kept me up without giving way. I never thought it possible I could have faced it all without a tremor of panic. But I did & it is all due to my treasure of a girl helpmate.' Without a hint of irony, he went on: 'All the doctors speak of my constitution as a prodigy & claim it as a triumph for a careful – otherwise a virtuous life.'[16]

As soon as he was well enough, Lloyd George departed on a two-month winter journey to Ceylon with Margaret, Gwilym and his wife

---

* The National Government won 554 seats, comprising 473 Conservatives, thirteen National Labour, thirty-five Liberal Nationals and thirty-three Liberals. Labour became the official opposition party with fifty-two seats and they were joined by the four 'Lloyd George Liberals'.

Edna, and Megan. This was the longest period he had spent with his family for some years and there was bound to be tension, with Megan in particular, who was no longer his devoted little girl. 'Megan has not bothered much about me,' wrote Lloyd George plaintively to Frances.[17]

Megan was twenty-nine years old, a Member of Parliament of two years' standing, and not inclined to offer her father the constant devotion and pampering to which he was accustomed. She had matured into a young woman who combined the strongest characteristics of both her parents. She was as self-centred as her father, commanding the attention of any group in which she found herself and determined to get her own way. It was remarked that she could 'charm the birds out of the trees, exactly like her father', yet she could also 'lash out with a tumbling torrent of words that stung like a whiplash'.[18]

From her mother Megan had inherited a passionate, almost obsessive dedication to Wales, which was second only to her devotion to God. Megan considered her faith to be a private matter, and although it dictated her daily life through her habit of spending the morning alone in prayer, she did not like to talk about it. This routine, coming as it did from a religious conviction that Lloyd George simply could not understand, put her on a collision course with her father. The difference in their outlooks was exacerbated by Megan's casual attitude towards timekeeping and her dislike of hard work, products no doubt of her somewhat undisciplined upbringing. Her nieces and nephews, of whom she was very fond, recalled how exasperating Megan could be. She expected the drivers among them to be at her beck and call, and she could never be on time for anything. She also invariably lost anything she had in her hands, a trait she had inherited from Lloyd George.*

---

* Megan's niece Margaret recalled a typical trip: 'She invited me and my sister Eluned to go to Stratford-on-Avon . . . We set off by train. She had forgotten that we had to change at Leamington Spa and, on being told that we had to, could only put on her hat back to front three times, whilst we practically hurled ourselves and the luggage out of the train. On the journey home Aunty Megan remembered she had left one of her dresses in the hotel where we had stayed. At Leamington Spa Eluned and I had to leave the train and put through a phone call to the hotel for her. When we arrived at Euston she went to the Lost Property to report some other article she had left on the train, and left her handbag on the counter.'

But while he saw this in himself as a sign of preoccupation and hard work, in his daughter he regarded it as sheer disorganisation.

Lloyd George woke early, and usually worked for a few hours before breakfasting at nine. He was at his best early in the day, and expected his companions to be at his service for a walk before breakfast. Megan preferred solitude and prayer, but did not offer an explanation of why she would not join him. Her father, talking to Sylvester, concluded that she was 'selfish'. 'He said to me as we sat alone in the drawing-room what a peculiar girl she was . . . Although he often begged her to be up early she was never up before eleven o'clock to go for a walk with him. Even though he was probably absolutely alone and dependent upon her.'[19] Frances, naturally, was less kind. With all pretence of friendship long vanished, she wrote in 1934: 'But why had Ll.G. done what he has done with Megan? An old woman in looks at 32, a mess of nerves so spoiled & impossible that no-one can live with her – that is the result of his upbringing of her.'[20]

Megan's refusal to dance to her father's tune was partly a reflection of the fact that they now spent most of the time apart, and she had developed her own lifestyle and habits. It was also partly because of her desire to assert her independence. If Olwen was the least dazzled by Lloyd George of all his children, Megan was easily the most enthralled. She had grown up in her father's world, and when she followed him to the House of Commons it was inevitable that she would be in his shadow.* Throughout her early career she struggled to reconcile her admiration of her father with her desire for an independent political identity. Sylvester noted her dependence on Lloyd George, and wondered if she would manage to make anything of her career when he was no longer around: 'I like Megan, and she is attractive, but she is a very difficult person to manage. She is clever in a certain kind of a way, but so self-centred that I wonder how far she will get when she is left to herself, and has not the reflex action of her father. He, too, is terribly self-centred.'[21]

Frances also observed the contradictions in Megan's behaviour, and for once acknowledged Lloyd George's part in driving his children away:

* Gwilym also suffered from this, to a lesser extent. He was known in his constituency as 'Ask my Dad'.

He is bitter about his children, saying that they all now take the line that he is more of a hindrance than an asset to them, after having benefited by all he has given them. Megan is the worst of them all in this respect, being rude and indifferent to him in private, & in public taking any reflected glory there may be, and playing the 'little daughter' most prettily. They all spend the minimum of time with him, for which he is not sorry. Perhaps they know this and it influences their behaviour. There is always something to be said on both sides![22]

When she was first elected, Megan devoted herself to her constituency. Lloyd George, who had never felt the same way about Caernarvon Boroughs, remarked that one might just as well criticise the Holy Ghost as say anything against Anglesey in Megan's presence.[23] She was arguably more in touch with Wales than he in the 1930s, and certainly spent more time there, although when a particularly Welsh issue cropped up they still sometimes conferred and campaigned together. In Westminster her profile was high, not only because of her famous name, but because as an attractive young female MP she was something of a rarity: she and her friend Thelma became known as the 'Dolly Birds of Westminster'.[24] Megan chose not to try to emulate her father's mastery of the Commons chamber, but he monitored her infrequent speeches carefully, praising her to Margaret in 1935: 'I have just read her speech in Hansard. It is first rate. It is a real debating speech & therefore a real parliamentary achievement. I cannot tell you how pleased I am with it.'[25]

He was also quick to remonstrate with Megan for not attending debates and speaking in them more frequently. 'I am very disappointed not to have had a word from you,' he wrote to her the following year. 'It cannot be your absorption in your Parliamentary duties, for I am disappointed to find that you have not yet taken any part in the Debates. You really ought to do so. It's a first-class mistake, because you are neglecting a great opportunity, and no-one can do it better, and very few as well, when you choose to do so.'[26]

Megan was fostering her speaking talent – different from, but no less powerful than, her father's – in broadcasting studios rather than in the chamber. She had witnessed the power of radio on her father's trip to North America in 1923, and had shared his wonder that in this way his words could reach many thousands. Broadcasting, Megan realised, was the way to communicate directly with the people. She became one of the most regular and best-respected broadcasters of her generation.

As early as 1929, shortly after the BBC lifted its ban on politics on the radio and before she had spoken for the first time in the House of Commons, Megan became the Liberal contributor to *The Week in Parliament*, a ten-minute address by a female MP which was broadcast on Wednesday mornings. As the only female Liberal MP, for reasons of political balance she was guaranteed a slot, but nevertheless she had a genuine gift for broadcasting. In 1933 she responded on radio to a speech by Oswald Mosley, the leader of the British Union of Fascists, from 1935 onwards she was a regular contributor to the BBC's *Week at Westminster*, and during the Second World War she was a panellist on the popular new programmes *The Brains Trust* and *Any Questions?*. Megan's infectious *joie de vivre*, her unaffected, natural style of speaking and her ability to put a point across all worked well on radio, and in time on television as well. She had a rare ability to paint a picture in words to convey the atmosphere of the House of Commons. 'It isn't going to be easy to tell you about this week in Westminster without planting both my feet into it,' she said in her address on 12 September 1942, 'but I will walk as delicately as I can. The House pretty well ran through the gamut of all the emotions at one time or another. There was more than a dash of temperament about it. It was angry, good-humoured, sympathetic, intolerant, solemn and hilarious – all in the twinkling of an eye.'[27]

Megan's lack of interest in House of Commons debates perhaps reflected her dislike of detailed preparation and her lack of mastery of facts and figures. It certainly did not reflect any lack of ability in public speaking. She was a popular figure on platforms throughout Wales, and could excel in front of mass meetings as well as smaller gatherings; her performances were 'electrifying'.[28] In 1948 a witness described her speech at a Liberal rally in the Albert Hall as 'chemical communication – she was sucking in their feelings and spraying them back'.[29] It was a description that could have been applied to Lloyd George in his heyday.

Lloyd George had always regarded Megan as his little girl, and would never stop seeing her in that light. He veered between over-protectiveness and complaints that she did not work hard enough. In 1935 he admonished Margaret for giving Megan a negative account of a meeting in Anglesey. 'L.G. delivered a devil of a lecture to Dame Margaret and me this morning,' wrote Sylvester in his diary, 'saying that as a consequence of the pessimistic information given to her last night Megan had not slept at all. He went on: "It is no good telling the little girl (she is thirty-four) of the difficulties in Anglesey when she is ill. Tell her the things which will help her in the fight." '[30] On the other hand, Lloyd George was not above reminding Megan that he was still helping to pay for her upkeep. Since Megan's fuse was as short as his, this was bound to cause friction between them. 'Could not anyone have a personality of their own?' she demanded after one argument.[31] Sometimes squabbles would occur over seemingly trivial incidents, as on the last evening of their trip to Jamaica in 1937. A.J. Sylvester tells the story:

At 7.25 p.m. Megan arrived and, raising her cocktail glass, she said to LG: 'Well, Tada, thank you very much for a most delightful holiday.' Dame Margaret drank to that toast, and I did also. L.G. said nothing. Megan went out. As soon as she had disappeared, he turned and showed his great disapproval of her lateness. When Megan presently returned, he opened 'fire' on her: 'If you had intended to drink my health,' he said, 'and thank me for your holiday, you might at least have been here at seven o'clock instead of being twenty-five minutes late. You have never thought me of sufficient importance to be on time.' Then working himself up into a fit of anger, and with his face red and his eyes steely grey he proceeded: 'you have never once been up to have breakfast with me . . . still less to walk with me before breakfast, which you know I like to do.' Then with venom he added: 'But your mother has always been there. That is what I would have expected of her. But then she is a lady and you are not.'

Megan's face went white with rage, and her eyes filled with tears.[32]

The cause of the tension between father and daughter was not simply their different attitudes to punctuality or politics, it was also bound up with their underlying battle over Frances. After the showdown over the *Chronicle* in 1926, Margaret and the family may well have accepted that Frances was a permanent feature in Lloyd George's life, but that did not mean that Megan was going to forgive her for her betrayal. When Megan had first found out about the relationship she spent some years trying to drive a wedge between her father and his mistress. She did not succeed, but she was an accomplished campaigner who had learned from both her parents that important battles took time to win. In 1932 came the opportunity she had been waiting for.

Bron-y-De, Lloyd George's main home through the 1930s, was built on an elevated piece of ground with a commanding view, and was surrounded by seven hundred acres of farm and woodland. Its north-facing aspect was not designed to catch the warmth of the English sun, and the atmosphere was distinctly frosty as Margaret, Olwen, Tom and Megan made their way from Criccieth to join Lloyd George there for a weekend in December 1932. The visitors had come for more than a family reunion: they had news to impart that would have such an impact on Lloyd George that they feared for his health.

On the second day of their visit the family gathered in the study for a routine press photograph, for even on a private weekend there was no respite from the demands of public life. Lloyd George sat in his favourite armchair in the handsome book-lined room, in front of an ornamental screen by the brick fireplace. His hair was white, though still flowing in abundance to his collar, and he was dressed with characteristic care in a dark three-piece suit and tie. Only the practical studded boots revealed his country location. Otherwise he might still have been in his study in No. 10 or about to give a speech in the House of Commons. In the photograph he looks intently at his wife. Margaret, grey-haired now, her figure rounded by age and childbearing, gazes steadily back at him from the sofa facing the fire on which she sits with Megan. Behind them, perched on the arms of a chair, sit Olwen and Tom, surveying the scene with anxious expressions. AJ completes the party, standing by the fireplace. There is little sign, except in the tension visible in Olwen's face, of the crisis that had engulfed the family the previous day when Margaret broke the news to her husband that Frances had taken another lover.

Frances had been betrayed by Rowlands, a maid who had originally been employed by Margaret at Addison Road and who Frances had ill-advisedly offered a job at Morpeth Mansions. In 1931 Frances decided that dividing her time between London and Churt was not productive, and that she would see more of Jennifer if she found somewhere close to Churt, and moved to Heathercourt, a house in Worplesdon, twenty miles or so from Bron-y-De. Rowlands did not want to leave London, and transferred her services, together with her allegiance in the ongoing family battle, to Olwen and Tom Carey Evans, who were living in Wimpole Street. Sometime in late summer, Rowlands told Olwen that Colonel Tweed paid Frances regular, secret visits. Olwen realised the significance of the revelation: Lloyd George demanded complete loyalty from all his family, advisers and staff, and most of all from the women in his life.

The meeting at Bron-y-De constituted the most serious crisis of Lloyd George's personal life: his trust in his mistress had been betrayed and possibly destroyed. At first he could not accept the truth. He tele-phoned A.J. Sylvester and summoned him to Churt early the next morning. On arrival, AJ was met at the door by Tom, who cautioned him, 'Watch out!' Alone with Lloyd George in his bedroom, AJ was issued with an entirely unnecessary reminder: 'Now your first duty you owe to me!' He was then asked what he knew of Frances' relation-ship with Tweed. AJ, who was often resentful of Frances' hold over Lloyd George, confirmed the affair, adding the devastating news that there was 'a good deal of suspicion that Tweed was down in Devon when L.G. was away on the yacht', a broad hint that Jennifer's pater-nity was doubtful. It is far from certain that by the time of the confronta-tion at Bron-y-De the affair between Tweed and Frances was still continuing. Sylvester believed that they were still seeing each other throughout 1932,* but he was not in Frances' confidence, and could have been mistaken.

---

* In December 1932 Sylvester wrote in his diary: 'It was [Frances'] custom, whenever she was in London to go about with Tweed and often she would return to the office after having seen [Lloyd George] away to dinner, in order to pick up Tweed who ordinarily went away early but always stayed late when she was there ... The whole office knew about it.'

After the photographic session with his family, Lloyd George quizzed Sylvester for the second time. Sylvester noted: 'L.G. was terribly upset. I have never seen him so weighed down with grief in my life.' Lloyd George took a painting of Jennifer out from a drawer in his bedroom and asked Sylvester if he could see any resemblance to Tweed in the child. 'I do not think Tweed is the father,' he told Sylvester, hastily followed by, 'but at any rate I am not the father.'[33] Always alert to the possibility of scandal, even after receiving a body blow such as this, Lloyd George was careful to deny paternity himself, but he could not bear the thought that Jennifer was Tweed's. There followed a confused conversation, with Lloyd George demanding to know if Sylvester saw any physical similarities between Lloyd George and his children by Margaret, almost as if he were doubting his wife's fidelity as well as his mistress's.

Although the exchange was rambling and incoherent, it is clear that Lloyd George was facing up to the possibility for the first time that he was not Jennifer's father. If he had previously believed that she might not be his child, he must logically have suspected that there was another man in Frances' life. The revelation of her lover's identity might still have been a shock, but not the blow Lloyd George evidently suffered on this occasion. Sylvester ended his account of the day by noting that '[Lloyd George's] mind is never still. He is always doing.' Indeed he was. True politician that he was, he was working out how to respond to the situation and turn it to his advantage.

The following morning, Sylvester arrived at the London office ahead of Lloyd George. When he saw Frances, he realised that she must have spoken to Lloyd George the night before. Her eyes were 'as red as ferrets', as if she had been crying all night. Sylvester filled her in on what had happened. He also spoke to Tweed, telling him that 'he seemed to have made a mess of things'.[34] Tweed's nonchalant reaction irked Sylvester, who tried to impress on him the seriousness of the situation: 'I said that I had never seen L.G. so upset about anything before. Tweed said that they could either have met openly or secretly and F. would not tell L.G. because he would have been annoyed. They had not covered anything up.'[35]

Tweed's calmness revealed a very cool head, for by any standards he had 'made a mess of things', and had most definitely 'covered up' the liaison, or tried to. His job, as well as his relationship with Frances, hung in the balance. As Riddell, who with his talent for nosing out gossip soon caught up with events, wrote the following year, 'It was the most extraordinary thing that . . . L.G. who has had so many affairs, with whom no woman seemed to be reckoned safe . . . now finds out that his own mistress has been seduced, in his own house, almost by one of his paid men. What retribution!'[36]

Frances spent the rest of the day in tears, largely ignored by Lloyd George while Tweed came and went from his office. Sylvester was taken to task for speaking to Tweed, but was otherwise deliberately favoured by Lloyd George that day in order to further wound Frances. For a couple of days Lloyd George froze Frances out of his life and spent time instead with his family. We have no record of what passed between them, but the rather surprising outcome was clear: Lloyd George was not going to break off his relationship with Frances, nor was he going to punish Tweed by throwing him out of his job. Lloyd George was devastated, but he could not face life without Frances. At sixty-nine years old, such was his dependence on her that he had no option but to accept the unhappy situation, much as Margaret had done over the preceding twenty years. Outwardly, life continued much as before. The private drama that resulted in and ensued from this meeting was played on a purely domestic stage, hidden from the world at large by the discretion of the players and the codes of conduct that conspired to keep such things out of the public domain.

This seems extraordinary, given how jealous Lloyd George had been when Frances was suspected of flirting in the past. Now that she had committed the triple sin of having a relationship with another man, taking a lover from among his own staff, and, perhaps worst of all, of casting a doubt over Jennifer's paternity, could he really forgive her? And if he could forgive Frances, could he also forgive Tweed?

Lloyd George was not given to acting precipitately, and both Frances and Tweed were very important to him. Tweed had been a key member of his staff for a year, was good at his job, and furthermore was privy to the details not only of Lloyd George's political situation, but also of his financial and private dealings. There is a suggestion in Sylvester's diary that Riddell thought Lloyd George feared the consequences if Tweed turned against him ('Lord R said that the reason why L.G. had not got rid of Tweed was that he feared that T. would tell all the noncon-formists about his carryings on'[37]), and in due course Sylvester received direct proof that Tweed was considering using his knowledge to threaten Lloyd George. In 1935, after a quarrel with Lloyd George, Tweed was explicit in talking to Sylvester: 'T's face assumed the most extraordi-nary contortions I have ever seen . . . He said that he had got to the end of his tether . . . he knew a lot about L.G.'s relationship with R. [Roberta, possibly] and he would let these Freechurchmen know about it; that would bust L.G.'[38] In June of the same year, Sylvester recorded another conversation with Tweed: 'He told me in detail of his personal position and his thoughts with regard to L.G. and the future, about which he made no bones. He said he had told J.T. that if anything happened to L.G. the trustees [of the political fund] would not be allowed to divide up the fund between the family. Tweed intended to see that he got his share.'[39]

Sylvester also records his suspicion that Tweed was keeping notes, with a view to writing a book about Lloyd George. In fact, unlike Sylvester himself, who did exactly that, Tweed wrote a successful novel instead, based on his experiences of working with Lloyd George and his travels in America. *Rinehard*, published in 1933, is a political fantasy in which a newly elected US President is involved in a car accident which changes him into a 'divine madman' who then proceeds to change the world through bold political action. One of the novel's characters, the President's secretary and former mistress Pendie Malloy, is loosely based on Frances.[40]*

Whatever passed between Lloyd George and his Political Organiser, Tweed remained on his Chief's staff until his sudden death in 1940. Whenever Lloyd George toyed with the idea of dismissing Tweed, some-thing (or someone) stayed his hand. In 1936 he told Sylvester, 'I do not know what to do with Tweed. His agreement has expired. It would suit

---

* *The Times* described *Rinehard* as 'an attempt to suggest in pseudo-fictional form . . . what a really statesmanlike President of the United States might achieve if prepared to take all power and responsibility into his own hands', and concluded that it 'can hardly fail to stir the imaginations of all interested in world problems'. There was speculation at the time that the book's author was in fact Lloyd George. It was later made into a film, *Gabriel over the White House*, starring Walter Huston, which made Tweed a considerable amount of money.

me if Tweed found another job. On the other hand, he is a good politician and useful in counsel.'[41] Furthermore, while Tweed occasionally criticised Lloyd George in a 'reckless and indiscreet' way,[42] according to Frances the two men remained, on the whole, on good terms. In 1940 Tweed wrote Lloyd George a warm letter of congratulation on the fiftieth anniversary of his election to Parliament, ending: 'And amongst those anonymous millions who have not forgotten twenty five years ago and whose regard and affection is undimmed by neither time nor the fortunes of politics, please include one who in humble duty signs himself, T.F.T.'[43]

But what of Frances? Lloyd George was deeply upset by her betrayal, but it seems that he could not, or would not, face the future without her. He had been living apart from his wife and family for ever longer periods of time over the previous decade. After what had passed between them, he could not rely upon his wife and daughters to pander to his needs as he grew older. Frances may have been essential to his comfort, but that did not mean that he could easily forgive and forget. After the revelation of 1932, he showed again his masterly understanding of Frances' character by neither forcing her to choose between him and Tweed nor casting her away from him. Had he done either, she would probably have fled straight to Tweed. Instead, to all outward appearances he accepted her affair and carried on as before. And so Frances stayed.

The fact that Lloyd George forgave her publicly does not mean that he behaved well towards her in private. Her diary falls silent for an extended period after the crisis, and there are no surviving letters between her and Lloyd George until January 1934, when he writes, curiously, 'I was so pleased to read that you meant to be a good girl. I know you will be happier. The double life is full of worry & apprehension which wrecks the nerves.'[44] This is followed by a second letter in which he says, 'Got your 2nd letter. So pleased with it *all*. I know I can trust you not to betray your promise.'[45] This suggests that Frances may have made him a promise to give up Tweed and/or other men for good.

Frances did not leave a detailed record of the nature of their relationship during the years that followed, but the evidence of others suggests that it was at times turbulent and tense. Sylvester recorded numerous quarrels between them, and this is echoed in Jennifer's recollections of her childhood. She remembered her mother returning home from Bron-y-De in tears, on one occasion refusing to go back for a few days. This could well have been in April 1934, when Sylvester recorded that there was 'domestic upheaval' when Frances left 'in a huff',[46] or else in 1937–38, when the relationship seemed particularly precarious.

In November 1936 Sylvester wrote that Lloyd George was behaving 'like a madman',[47] never letting Frances out of his sight. When Frances dared to have lunch at the Savoy with an old admirer of hers, Sir Thomas Jaffrey, who had once proposed to her, Lloyd George arranged to have lunch there too. He sat facing her across the restaurant, keeping his eyes fixed upon her and silently toasting her, much to Jaffrey's embarrassment. This appears to be proof of Frances' claim to Sylvester that 'she could not be out of his sight a fraction of an instant without his calling out and looking slyly around for her. His suspicions are at once aroused. She said that he had held her down by force in an endeavour to get her to confess to things she had never done. But she now had her remedy. When she found herself at the end of her tether, whatever he said or did could not hurt her any more than she had already been hurt. He had been so cruel to her and had said such terrible things in the past.'[48] This is probably a reference to his accusations of her affairs with other men; indeed, any man with whom she had contact was suspected. Even Dyer, Lloyd George's long-standing and loyal chauffeur, was not above suspicion, and on at least two occasions Lloyd George entered Frances' room late at night to check that she was alone. By June 1938 she was nearly at breaking point, so much so that when Lloyd George postponed his Whitsun visit to Criccieth she blurted out to his dismay that she 'had thought she could just last out until then'.[49]

Lloyd George struggled to make sense of Frances' betrayal. He could not understand what had led to it, and this had knocked his confidence. When Dick was younger Lloyd George had counselled him on the subject of women like the expert he undoubtedly was, but when his grandson Owen was fifteen he seemed less sure, telling him, 'Well, I am five times your years but I feel sure I know no more about women than you do now.'[50] He was self-doubting also in conversation with Sylvester in 1937: 'women were funny creatures. You thought you understand them, but you did not . . . He had known Frances for twenty-five years. He had seen more of her during that time than any other woman, because she was with him in his work, and yet even now he did not profess to understand her.' This he followed with the comment that 'Tweed had ruined her life.'[51] This was presumably because the affair had driven a wedge between Frances and Lloyd George.

The closest Lloyd George came to acknowledging this unhappy state of affairs in his letters to Frances was in 1937, after their relatively happy holiday together in Jamaica. After Frances left to make way for Margaret, Lloyd George wrote to her: 'We have trodden the cinders of hell these last few years – both of us. I more than I can [tell] you. Perhaps also you more than you have revealed to me. Often my heart has been chilled with despair & despondency & I foresaw nothing but a gloomy future with no ray of consolation. Work is only a distraction & I have worked like a maniac to divert my thoughts from poignant memories that sting. Let there be a second spring.'[52] But it was not to be. For many years it was probably true that falling in love with Tweed had ruined Frances' life: it had certainly soured her relationship with Lloyd George and made her very unhappy.

Frances still felt passionately about Tweed, and it was difficult for her to keep her promise to stay away from him. She could not avoid him completely, for they still worked together. She continued to 'look out' for him, and warned him on at least one occasion when his job was under threat. A few months after making her promise to Lloyd George, she heard that Tweed had suffered a heart attack. In an entry later torn from her diary, she poured out her feelings:

My darling T.F.T. is very ill, ill unto death. If he dies I do not think I shall be able to bear the scent of the gorse and the lilac, when another spring comes round. All day long, I have been walking about, trying to staunch the wound at my heart and to relieve my agony. I have never before had to bear pain like this, but I knew it must come one day. People do die, and those who love them live on. But what agony in between.

My little Jennifer came to me, and puzzled at seeing traces of tears, looked at me very searchingly, and said:– 'Grown up ladies don't cry do they, Mummy?[53]

Five days later she wrote with relief: 'Better news of my darling. It looks as though he would live, but it will be a long business. The fierce pain at my heart has lessened, & the grip of panic has loosened.'[54]

That Frances was still in love with Tweed is confirmed by a second deleted passage, written in October 1934:

Saw the back of my [?] T.F.T. disappearing down the corridor & my heart bled with longing. It is dreadful to be in the same building and not to see or speak to him, but it is better for him that I should be firm, & if I am strong & [illegible] I may [?] get my reward. Yet will I? My heart tells me that in this life, there are no rewards [several words illegible] the only thing to do is to take what you want with both hands and pay the price afterwards. That is the only transaction Fate really understands.[55]

She was evidently still dreaming of a future with Tweed, even if she had to 'pay the price' of an uncertain future. But this melodramatic outburst did not change her decision to stay with Lloyd George and the security he offered. Furthermore, by 1934 she had an additional reason for staying away from Tweed: he had started a relationship with her sister Muriel. If Frances found it 'dreadful' to work in the same building as Tweed, how much worse must it have been to know that he was making love to her own sister? Yet somehow she endured his affair with Muriel, and also found a way to see and talk to him without seriously threatening her relationship with Lloyd George.

Tweed's health had not been strong since the Great War, and in 1940, at the age of fifty, he fell ill and was taken to Hendon Cottage Hospital. Frances was desperate to see him, and used a visit to see Jennifer (who was at boarding school) as an excuse to get away from a suspicious Lloyd George. She therefore saw Tweed two weeks before his death, which came suddenly as he was apparently recovering. He was found by a nurse sitting up in bed with his still-burning pipe in his mouth.[56]

Tweed was well known in political circles, and in her grief Frances cut out and kept the tributes to him that appeared in the newspapers. 'He was as cool a man as I have ever known,' wrote the author of the *Evening Standard*'s 'Londoner's Diary'. 'Nothing upset him.'[57] The *Manchester Guardian* described him as 'an original among political organisers' who was yet 'more than a political organiser. He was himself a politician, a Radical through and through . . . insatiably curious about life and politics.'[58] Lloyd George issued his own tribute, in which he wrote that Tweed 'had an unusual mastery of the political issues of the day and an exceptionally sound and penetrating political instinct'.[59]

The final act of the extraordinary drama between Frances, Tweed and Lloyd George was yet to be played out, for Lloyd George could not resist celebrating his ultimate triumph over his rival. Tweed's funeral was held at the Golders Green crematorium, and Frances braved Lloyd George's disapproval to attend, along with Muriel. Sylvester went to pay his respects to his former colleague, and noted that both women looked very upset. It was going to be an ordeal for Frances: not only was she saying a final goodbye to the lover she adored, but she knew she was bound to meet his wife and children for the first time as well. In addition, Olwen had asked Sylvester to reserve two seats for her. He guessed who her companion was going to be, and describes the scene that followed:

> No sooner had we taken our seats than L.G. entered, with Lady Carey Evans; they took their seats on the left-hand side. Never have I seen him attend a funeral service thus. He is always most particular about his attire on all occasions. Today must have been a studied insult to the dead, and intended to persecute the living in the person of Frances. He wore a blue suit, a blue overcoat, a blue hat, with a dark tie that was not even black. His face was white – knowing him, he was het up. He sat in the front seat, well towards the left: as he looked towards the pulpit on the right he could see Frances in the second row and watch her every movement and reaction.[60]

Frances endured Lloyd George's scrutiny during the service, and was composed enough to meet Louise Tweed and her children, who acknowledged afterwards in a letter that she shared 'equally with us our grief'.[61]*

---

* In his will, Tweed left Frances £2,000 and Jennifer £500. This caused quite a stir, and it was reported in the newspapers that he had done so 'in compensation for an investment advice that resulted in a loss'. It is tempting to speculate that this was Tweed's apology to Frances for causing so much trouble.

Later there was a bitter quarrel with Lloyd George when he took her to task for grieving for Tweed, and she complained to Sylvester that he was 'literally persecuting her to death'.[62] Sylvester's verdict was damning: 'What was the motive for this extraordinary behaviour? Jealousy. He is eaten up with it.'[63]

Jealousy and work were Lloyd George's twin obsessions in the later years of his life, and his work now included not only politics, but also his farm. At Bron-y-De he had fertilised and irrigated some very unpromising land at great cost to produce some satisfactory crops, mainly fruit. His growing interest in his agricultural experiments meant that during the 1930s Margaret was spending more time apart from him than ever before. She too had her jealousy to contend with – although it was better controlled than her husband's – and she too immersed herself in her work. She was elected Chairman of Criccieth Council in 1931: the topics for discussion at her first meeting in the chair included the later despatch of mail in the evening, proposals to erect a wireless aerial, and the annual awarding of bathing tent licences. At the end of her term she sought re-election as a Councillor, and claimed in her election address that during her chairmanship 'several improvements have been carried out, which have already proved to be of benefit to the town, and great attractions to summer Visitors, and I believe that some of them at least will in the near future bring some measure of relief to the ratepayers'.[64]

In her sixties, Margaret was still politically very active, representing her husband in Caernarvon Boroughs while also helping Megan in Anglesey. Lloyd George depended on her judgement, as well as her instinct for local affairs, in constituency matters. 'Here is another begging letter,' he wrote in 1936 on receiving a letter from Moriah chapel. 'I would like you to find out from Lloyd Jones what they expect. I must not give anything which if published will bring down on me requests from every quarter. I might give them £20 as a special donation. Do you think that would do?'[65] Margaret was involved in all aspects of his political life in Wales, even interviewing candidates for the position of Welsh Secretary on his staff. Her fame in her homeland had not diminished: she was a member of the Gersedd and had been awarded an honorary law degree by the University of Wales. She spoke at Liberal fundraising meetings and fêtes as President of the Women's Liberal Federation of North and South Wales, and she loved attending meetings – something Lloyd George himself hated. Whenever she was in London she would attend the House of Commons to hear her husband speak. After each performance she would loyally send him the little note he expected, congratulating him on his mastery of the House.

One of the trickier challenges she faced was to explain to supporters in Caernarvon Boroughs why her husband chose to spend so much of his time elsewhere. Margaret held the fort well in his absence, but inevitably there was clamorous demand for Lloyd George when he did visit his constituency. During his infrequent stays in Brynawelon, Margaret organised a programme of appearances for him to satisfy his constituents, and was blamed by him for forcing him to attend 'all sorts of silly little functions which he dislikes and yet cannot very well refuse', as Frances put it.[66] In doing so, she probably saved his political life many times over.

When she was not working, Margaret had her beloved garden to tend, and her skill in coaxing plants and flowers to grow was legendary. Megan, who shared her interest in gardening, would help her select seeds from the annual catalogues that arrived in Criccieth, and she was justifiably proud of the resulting display. Thelma Cazalet, who received regular letters from 'Aunt Margaret', remembered that 'every one of them contained a passage about flowers. A peasant woman had given her a bunch of camellias in Italy in April; she had cut a bowl of wallflowers every week from her garden at Criccieth in January; she had a fuchsia in her garden there at Christmas. Compared with flowers, politics were trivialities.'[67] Margaret would take cuttings from any source, including bouquets she was presented with at events, from which she could always produce a viable plant. Once, on holiday in the South of France, she gathered up some twigs that had been discarded after a magnificent hedge had been pruned and announced her intention to line the drive at Brynawelon with one just like it. Her husband was so confident that the dry twigs would not produce a living hedge that he said he would give her half a crown for each one that took hold. His offer cost him dearly, and as Margaret enjoyed the spectacle of her thriving new hedge, she was presented with a piece of jewellery in addition to her winnings to mark her achievement.

Brynawelon was a maelstrom of activity when Lloyd George made his annual summer visit, but when he was not there Margaret presided over a calmer, more relaxed family home. The house had been in her name for several years, and it was hers in spirit as well.[68] William George, who knew his brother and his sister-in-law as well as anyone, noted the contrast in their philosophies of life: 'To Dafydd, life was a battle, and he was never happy unless he had somebody or something to fight. On the other hand, "Peace and plenty" were Maggie's ideals, and she was never happier than when settled down in her comfortable home in Criccieth with her gardens and grounds in front of her and her children and grandchildren bustling around her.'[69]

In Criccieth, Margaret was surrounded by friends, neighbours and family. She ran Brynawelon with the help of Sarah and one or two maids,* with a gardener and his wife living in a cottage in the grounds. She spent evenings of happy companionship with her brother and sister-in-law, playing bridge, telling jokes and solving crossword puzzles. The impression given is that she was perfectly content with her life, and that she was more missed by Lloyd George than he was missed by her. Olwen believed this to be true, adding that in her view, Margaret's feelings for her charismatic husband were ultimately destroyed by his infidelities: 'During the whole of their married life, I never heard her run him down in any way, although I think in the end the deep love she had felt for him had just faded away. In contrast, Father, I am quite certain, loved Mother deeply right to the end of her life. He wanted them both – Mother and Frances.'[70]

Lloyd George's need for Frances was a bitter element in Margaret's otherwise happy later years. Margaret's easy-going nature made her less active than her husband in seeking time together, and he still occasionally pleaded for her to visit him. When she did, or when he made the journey to Criccieth, they were at ease in each other's company, and he was happy to see her when she came to hear him speak or attended an event with him. They travelled abroad together frequently, and Margaret would take over the task of looking after

---

* Sarah had been in charge of Lloyd George's London house in Addison Road after leaving No. 10, but eventually moved to Criccieth to look after Brynawelon for Margaret and Megan.

him physically, cutting his nails and pandering good-naturedly to his hypochondria, which increased with age. The fact that they now occupied separate bedrooms did not affect their closeness, and did not strike Lloyd George's staff as indicative of a rift between them. Separate bedrooms were not unusual for married couples, and Lloyd George maintained a similar arrangement with Frances, admittedly for different reasons.

The snapshots we have of Lloyd George and Margaret together at Criccieth and Churt show them to be a happy couple despite their unorthodox living arrangements. At Criccieth they went mushrooming together before breakfast, while at Churt he would take her to the orchard and lift the protective nets over the cherry trees to allow her to feast on her favourite fruit. They enjoyed entertaining together: Margaret would sit at the head of the table at Criccieth since Lloyd George was so bad at carving, or so she said. He enjoyed the fact that his wife could hold her own with any guest, listening contentedly as she swapped reminiscences of the Boer War with Field Marshal Smuts. They also entertained together in style at their London house, hosting a joint coming-out dance for their granddaughters Valerie and Margi in 1936, and entertaining King Edward VIII there at an evening reception in the same year.

Lloyd George and Margaret retained a warm relationship with the King, who they had befriended when he was Prince of Wales. This made it all the more painful that Lloyd George was in Jamaica with Frances during the crucial period of the constitutional crisis in 1936, when Stanley Baldwin led the government in opposition to the King's intention of marrying a divorced woman, Mrs Wallis Simpson. Frances believed that the crisis was deliberately forced by the government to coincide with Lloyd George's absence. Megan and Gwilym kept him abreast of the situation, Sylvester booked return passages, and Frances packed their bags. But before they could leave, a message came to say that it was all over: the King was going to abdicate. 'The woman Simpson is not worth the price the poor infatuated King was prepared to pay,' was Lloyd George's verdict.[71] 'Like so many others,' wrote Frances, 'we listened to his abdication speech with wrung hearts.'[72]

At Christmas, Lloyd George sent a message to the former King. It read:

Best Christmas greeting from an old Minister of the Crown who holds you in as high esteem as ever and regards you with deeper loyal affection, deplores the shabby and stupid treatment accorded to you, resents the mean and unchivalrous attacks upon you and regrets the loss sustained by the British Empire of a monarch who sympathised with the lowliest of his subjects.[73]

In return came this reply:

Very touched by your kind telegram and good wishes, which I heartily reciprocate. Cymru am Byth [Wales Forever]. EDWARD[74]

Lloyd George frequently grumbled about his wife, but he rarely lost sight of her positive qualities, her courage and her strength of character. He told Sylvester, 'she is the best of the bunch and when we were on the point of having a frightful row she stepped in and said: "I will have none of it," and I always remember that.'[75] When he went too far, Margaret would rein him back, and he respected her more for standing up to him than he did the more compliant Frances. On one occasion he accused the whole family of disloyalty, a bizarre claim given their collective silence on the subject of his private life. Margaret would have none of it, telling him sharply 'not to talk to her about disloyalty, that no family was more loyal'.[76]

Frances was alert to any sign of tension between husband and wife, and faithfully recorded in her diary every outburst from Lloyd George on the subject of his ungrateful family. 'He is bitter about his children,' she wrote in 1934, 'saying that they now all take the line that he is more of a hindrance than an asset to them, after having benefited by all he has given them.'[77] The old accusation of lack of supportiveness was also levelled at Margaret. Lloyd George grumbled to A.J. Sylvester that she 'never helped me in my work. In the early days she did not even help me in the constituency as she does now. She was always at Criccieth and I was in London.' He did not rehearse all the reasons why it had been impractical for Margaret and her young brood to be in London in the early years of their marriage, except to hint that the children came first with her, saying to Sylvester once that 'there were two kinds of wives: those who give up everything to their children, and those who give up everything to their husbands. My wife belongs to the former.'[78] Lloyd George was a fortunate man, for in fact he had one of each type.

Inevitably perhaps, rumours spread from time to time regarding Lloyd George's personal morality. Megan often got the blame for these from Frances, although there is little evidence to support her accusations. It was still vitally important to protect Lloyd George's good name, for it was widely expected, not least by himself, that his long-predicted return to power would happen one day. He was cultivated or feared by the leaders of the other parties, and invited abroad by heads of state and government. Adolf Hitler felt the force of Lloyd George's charisma when he entertained him at Berchtesgaden in 1936, and world leaders such as Gandhi made their pilgrimages to Bron-y-De, where Lloyd George remained for long periods of time, relying on Megan and Gwilym to keep him abreast of Westminster gossip. It was a serious matter, therefore, when rumours concerning Jennifer's paternity surfaced in 1937.

The news that a whispering campaign against Lloyd George had started in his constituency reached the ears of A.J. Sylvester soon after his return from Jamaica in February 1937. People were talking about Lloyd George's 'immoral life', he was told, saying that he had taken Frances with him to Jamaica, and that there was a child.[79] This was the event that Lloyd George and Frances had feared: he was being linked publicly for the first time with Jennifer. Lloyd George came up with his defence, which he outlined to Sylvester. He had been accused of misdemeanours many times before, he said, and had always won his case in court. As usual, he intended to come out fighting, and would bring criminal charges against anyone who made allegations against him. Frances was essential to his work, and he could not have completed his six-volume *War Memoirs* (published 1933–36) without her help:* 'She knows French. She knew Foch, Briand, Clemenceau, Bonar and all the ministers – Smuts, Henry Wilson, Curzon, Austen Chamberlain, Winston, in fact all the members of the Cabinet.'[80] He went on to say that it was ridiculous to accuse him of fathering

---

* Frances also helped Lloyd George write *The Truth About the Peace Treaties*, which would be published in 1938.

Jennifer, since he had had a serious operation six years previously, and he had a letter from Tweed claiming responsibility for the child. In any case, the Statute of Limitations, whereby a man could only be identified as the father of a child within the first three years of its life, meant he was in the clear legally.

In truth, Lloyd George's arguments did not amount to much of a defence. The fact that he had been cleared before did not mean that he was not guilty this time, and it was the nature of Frances' relationship with her boss, not her competence, that was at issue. His operation in 1931 would not have affected his ability to father Jennifer in 1929, and it is difficult to believe that even he would have risked that argument in court. Finally, the fact that he never actually produced the letter from Tweed which would conclusively have settled the matter of Jennifer's paternity seems a little suspicious.

But the legal efficacy of his argument was not the deciding factor, and he knew it. 'I will meet anybody in the Caernarvon Boroughs,' he said. 'I will guarantee they won't kick me out there. The old girl will stand by me.'[81] Despite everything, the partnership between Lloyd George and Margaret was still rock-solid, and his enemies could spread all the rumours they liked: as long as he had his wife's support, he would live to fight another day.

Sylvester loyally conveyed all the arguments to the right circles, and to end the rumours once and for all, Lloyd George arranged for Sylvester's home movies of Margaret, Megan and himself in Jamaica to be shown in Criccieth at Easter, reinforcing the image of a united family on the very trip that had sparked the rumours. Fortunately, the audience did not know that Sylvester had also taken a film of Lloyd George with Frances in Jamaica a few days before his family had arrived. Lloyd George had, it seemed, got away with it again.

There was no suggestion at the time that Megan was behind the rumours; indeed, throughout the 1930s Lloyd George and Margaret were more worried about their eldest son than their youngest daughter. Dick had divorced Roberta and married his second wife, June Calvé, but his financial situation had not improved, and he approached his mother for help several times. Margaret could never refuse him, and eventually he persuaded her to underwrite all his debts, thus putting her own financial security at risk. As a result, the strained relations between Lloyd George and Dick gradually gave way to no relationship at all. Dick's health began to deteriorate, and his alcohol dependency grew worse; he was reduced at one stage to persuading his young son to empty his post office account so that he could retire to a nearby pub. Margaret helped him when she could, and kept his problems to herself, without confiding even in William George, from whom Dick also became estranged.

As time went on, Margaret found equilibrium in her relationship with Lloyd George. She was able to accept their close but parallel lives, and was even heard to make the occasional joke about Frances. Her life was punctuated by pleasant holidays and enjoyable public appearances. Frances herself bore witness to the fact that Lloyd George made a genuine effort to ensure his wife's comfort, writing in a draft of her autobiography a fairly objective assessment of her rival's life:

> What surprises me is that not one of the children (except perhaps Gwilym) who were after all intelligent people, seemed to realise that they owed a certain amount of consideration for their father. They were prepared to use their mother against him. It was a form of blackmail. She was not unhappy. LG would have blamed himself if that had been so. He considered her – went to enormous lengths to be sure that she had all that was due to her as his wife – except of course himself. He gave her lovely presents (but this, I believe, is customary when husbands are unfaithful to their wives) and humoured her to an extent which was almost? undignified.[82]

Frances never could or never would understand the respect that underpinned Lloyd George's relationship with Margaret, nor what he owed her for her constant support in public.

Margaret began to spend less and less time away from Criccieth. This earned her some gentle teasing from her family. Lloyd George would urge visitors to refer to Criccieth as a village rather than a town in front of her, in order to enjoy the outrage on her face as she corrected them. In 1938, with the tension in Europe temporarily easing, A.J. Sylvester recorded a telephone conversation between Olwen and her mother: ' "Things are much better this morning." "Why?" inquired Dame Margaret, "Have you been ill?" "No, no," said Olwen, "I mean in the international situation." "Phew . . . that thing," said Dame Margaret cynically, as much as to say that we in *Criccieth* have much more important things to think about than the foreign situation.'[83] Lloyd George roared with laughter when he heard the story.

War was indeed on the horizon, and Lloyd George was watching the situation anxiously, still half-convinced that his country might yet need his service. He had committed a serious public relations blunder in 1936 when, after visiting Hitler with Megan in tow, he described him in a newspaper article as 'a magnetic, dynamic personality'. As the German Chancellor's ambitions became more apparent, Lloyd George's remarks were interpreted as appeasement, and the chances of a triumphant return to power receded even further.

On 24 January 1938, Margaret and Lloyd George celebrated their golden wedding anniversary. Fifty years had passed since their hurriedly-arranged union in Pencaenewydd chapel, and in that time their lives had changed beyond recognition. The event attracted international interest, and an 'official' celebration was planned to take place in Cardiff on 1 March. Lloyd George invariably spent January in warmer climates, and it was decided that the family would gather in Antibes in the South of France for their own private celebration on the day itself.

Lloyd George had been ensconced in Antibes since early January, working on *The Truth About the Peace Treaties* with Frances. She noted with excitement that they were staying in the same hotel as the Duke and Duchess of Windsor, but they do not seem to have met socially with the former King on this occasion. Sylvester had stayed behind to escort Margaret as far as Paris, and on 11 January Frances returned home just as Margaret and Megan left London. She had not had an easy time with Lloyd George, who had monitored her every move, suspecting her of being unfaithful with the former Liberal MP Victor Finney. Lloyd George's jealousy had become so fierce that even Sylvester came under suspicion, despite the fact that Frances held him in contempt.*

---

* Frances and Sylvester's relationship was not helped by the fact that he admired Margaret and took her side. On a note covering a newspaper article on Margaret in 1934 he wrote: 'It bears out in the strongest possible language my own feelings about Dame M. She was a great woman: it puts Frances in her place.'

When Frances and Sylvester bumped into each other by chance in Folkestone on 12 January, they agreed not to mention the meeting to Lloyd George in case it inflamed him further. Sylvester wrote in his diary, 'he is absolutely mad if Frances is even seen speaking to anyone else. He is mental on matters of sex and therefore has no understanding. A man and a woman could not possibly in his view be friends without sexual intercourse. He judges everyone by his own standard.'[84]

The accusation against Frances and Finney was, if anything, even more bizarre, and shows the unbearable pressure Frances was under and the extent to which Lloyd George's jealousy controlled her life. Finney had gone to Antibes to try to persuade Lloyd George to take a more active interest in the Council of Action, a non-party vehicle for promoting Lloyd George's ideas. Lloyd George had invited a senior civil servant to lunch, and asked Frances to take Finney elsewhere so he and his guest could talk more freely. Frances, wary of provoking a quarrel, said she would only go if Lloyd George promised not to accuse her of flirting, or worse, later. Sylvester reports what happened that night:

Finney was in the salon with L.G. and Frances and presently L.G. went to bed. At the same time Finney wished him good-night and made his exit. In a few moments, however, Finney came back into the room. L.G. had gone into his bedroom, which adjoined. Finney in a very confidential tone asked Frances to ascertain whether it was advisable for him to return home; he did not want to outstay his welcome. When Frances went into L.G.'s bedroom, she opened the door suddenly and found him with his ear to the door trying to listen. The fact that Finney had spoken very softly only aroused L.G.'s deepest suspicions. There was a hell of a row. Frances said that either she or Finney would go home next day. Finney went![85]

As Frances retreated from Antibes, Margaret and Megan arrived to take her place, shortly to be joined by Dick and June, Gwilym and Edna, and Olwen and her eldest daughter Margi. Sylvester had ensured that there was plenty of favourable publicity surrounding the event, and reporters descended on the South of France in droves. Margaret gave many interviews, and Lloyd George took the opportunity to pay tribute to his wife to the *News Chronicle*:*

> She is a woman of serene courage. She never fusses or fumes. Such qualities are an invaluable help to a politician living amid the stresses and strains and excitements of continuous Parliamentary life. She has played a very great part in my political career. I think I can say she is deservedly popular in North Wales. When I could not be there she held the constituency for me. I regard my wife – and I am a fairly good judge – as an excellent speaker. She rarely speaks for more than five minutes; but what a rich store of common sense she compresses into those five minutes.[86]

The morning of 24 January began with Margaret and Lloyd George opening presents from around the world and the telegrams that 'poured in in shoals'.[86] The family had bought a silver-gilt loving cup as a tribute, engraved with their names, a Welsh dragon and a line of poetry.

Later in the day the whole party was invited to lunch by Winston and Clementine Churchill, who by coincidence were staying at a nearby hotel. Winston and Lloyd George made generous speeches about their long friendship and political partnership, and the press took photographs in the hotel garden. In the evening the family gathered for dinner. Their private dining room had been filled to bursting with flowers, and the evening progressed merrily, with toasts in champagne from the loving cup and fireworks in the hotel gardens. Over a nightcap in Lloyd George's sitting room, there was much hilarity as Olwen dressed in her father's clothes to impersonate him, with Gwilym, in a grey evening dress, playing the part of his mother. Margaret later said that she had never laughed so much in her life.[88]

Throughout the day Sylvester had been fielding telephone calls from

---

* At the Cardiff event to mark their anniversary Lloyd George made a memorable and entertaining speech, the only public speech he ever made on the subject of his marriage. To gales of appreciative laughter from his audience, who knew them both well, he said: 'Marriage is a wonderful institution which enables two people of entirely different temperaments to live together in perfect harmony for fifty years. One of us is contentious, impatient, intolerant and aggressive – that's my wife. The other of us is long-suffering, easy-going, mild of manner, never saying an unkind word about anyone – that's me!'

domestic and international newspapers until he was absolutely exhausted. He entered into the spirit of the celebration, but allowed himself one caustic comment in his diary: 'The world has paid tribute to L.G. and Dame Margaret on their golden-wedding day. What would it think if it knew that for the greater part of every year, L.G. lives with another woman?'[89]

Back in England, the other woman might well have echoed the same sentiment, for while Lloyd George celebrated his fiftieth anniversary with his wife, Frances celebrated their twenty-fifth anniversary on her own.

24

Private Sorrows

Frances may have been apart from Lloyd George on their twenty-fifth anniversary, but her loneliness was greatly eased by having her daughter in her life. By 1938 Jennifer had grown to be a clever, blonde-haired nine-year-old with an independent mind and enough charm to wrap her 'Taid' around her little finger. Her home was an attractive modern house built on land adjoining the Bron-y-De estate. Frances had decided shortly after moving to Heathercourt that the twenty-mile journey to and from Bron-y-De was impractical, and had bought land in Churt so that she could have a home nearby and be able to visit Jennifer at odd times during the day. Over the years she bought more land as it became available, and Jennifer could walk the mile between her home and Bron-y-De over land that was owned either by her mother or by Lloyd George.

The house was called Avalon (pronounced in the Welsh way, with the emphasis on the second syllable), after the legendary resting place of King Arthur in the Welsh version of the tale. Jennifer moved in on 9 March 1935. Avalon was Frances' second attempt at building her own home. The first, an ambitious barn conversion with a magnificent two-storeyed reception hall, proved too expensive to run, and was let instead. She had definite and radical views on how her daughter's new home should look, and the result was a contemporary and aesthetically pleasing one-storey house with a flat roof, surrounded by gardens and with a magnificent, polished copper front door in which visitors could see their reflections.

There were two Scottish servants, Margaret and Rose Cameron, and Jennifer was looked after by a nanny/governess called Marjorie Hackett. Miss Hackett taught her to read and write, but was also fond of using the back of a hairbrush to discipline her. Jennifer was beaten at least once a week for telling an untruth, for misbehaving, or just because a beating was due. It was not uncommon at the time for nannies to behave in this way, nor did parents always object, but Jennifer was left feeling resentful, and developed a lifelong hatred of injustice. By her own admission, she also became a more efficient liar as a result.

Jennifer's early childhood was solitary. She spent time at Bron-y-De with her mother and with Lloyd George when they were there, but had little opportunity to play with other children. Eventually she found a playmate and substitute sister in Elizabeth Mary, the daughter of Elsie and John Morris, Lloyd George's solicitor. Frances' situation made it difficult for her to form close friendships at a time when any hint of a lack of respectability was frowned upon, but Elsie had been divorced after marrying disastrously at the age of seventeen, and Frances felt comfortable with her. John Brook, Jennifer's other little friend, was the son of the unmarried Felicia Brook and Charles McCurdy, and the three children made an innocent, perfectly matched trio of social outcasts. Jennifer recalled, 'I found it difficult to get on with normal children from normal families, but in fact rarely needed to try.'[1]

Jennifer was educated at home until September 1936 when, just before her seventh birthday, she was sent to St Ursula's in Grayshott as a day girl for a term, and then as a weekly boarder. In her second year she became a full boarder, and adapted easily to her new environment. Her holidays were spent in London or at Avalon, where she was looked after by one of her aunts, by Elsie Morris, or occasionally by the servants alone while her mother looked after Lloyd George. Jennifer writes in her autobiographical notes of a solitary but not necessarily lonely child-hood, during which she created her own world and her own routine independent of Frances.

Frances, having fulfilled her long-held ambition to have a child, took great care over the arrangements for Jennifer's wellbeing. What she was not able or willing to do was to change her life so she could be more present in her daughter's. Being constantly at Lloyd George's side to help him in his work and to look after his needs was a non-negotiable condition of her relationship with him, leaving no time for Jennifer unless he was away with his family. Frances spent all day with Lloyd George, and slept either at Avalon or at Bron-y-De, where she had her own bedroom and bathroom. Jennifer would join them for lunch, and talk to Frances in the afternoon while Lloyd George slept. When she was old enough, Frances walked back with her halfway before returning to Bron-y-De to take tea with Lloyd George.

Jennifer's time alone with Lloyd George was usually just before lunch, when the two of them would inspect the fruit trees in the orchards and exercise the dogs. She treasured these walks when she had him to herself, and according to Sylvester, Lloyd George 'worshipped' Jennifer in return. Always fond of children, and of little girls in particular, Lloyd George was a loving and larger-than-life figure in Jennifer's life. With her he was as unselfconscious as a child himself, playing with a hosepipe to 'make rain for Jennifer', and getting a thorough wetting himself in the process. 'I could not help asking myself who was the bigger baby,' was Sylvester's comment.[2] On another occasion he delighted Jennifer with a sardine sandwich that 'swam' through the air, and risked Nanny's displeasure by hiding cherries in his pocket, pretending that he sensed 'a little mouse' as Jennifer retrieved them. He took an interest in Jennifer's education, and his experience of being a parent showed: 'Taid enjoyed educating me, liked giving me all kinds of information, introducing me to books and music and jokes, and never spoke down to me. He also tried to make me think – that was more difficult. I still regret the stupidity of some of my efforts, but he was never irritated with me; when he laughed, it was not in a hurtful way; his criticisms were constructive; and I knew he enjoyed talking to me, and with me.'[3]

Jennifer developed into an independent-minded child, quiet and a little shy in company, but a keen observer of all around her. Despite her mother's frequent absences, she had ample opportunity to observe Frances' relationship with Lloyd George, and was overheard once observing to another child that she did not have a father, but did have a godfather. 'My godfather,' she said, 'is very strict with my Mummy, but he is not strict with me.'[4]

Frances also adored Jennifer, but since she was not her primary carer, the relationship was more distant than either would have liked. She worried about her daughter's future, writing to Lloyd George that

Jennifer 'will have lots of strange things to learn as she grows up, poor darling, and we shall have to give her all the love and tenderness we can to compensate for any shocks she may have to suffer! But I agree with you that she *has* all the attention and love & tenderness we can possibly lavish on her, so she ought to grow up without any inferiority complex, I think.'[5]

This letter, written when Jennifer was only twenty months old, suggests that Frances assumed that the truth about her daughter's illegitimacy was bound to come out. She had encountered a fair degree of scepticism already. When Tom Carey Evans, one of the less gullible members of the family, was told that Jennifer was her adopted daughter, he responded, 'Well, you can tell that to the Marines!'[6] If, however, Frances was aware of the dangers ahead, it is strange that she did not come up with a more plausible story to tell Jennifer when, as was inevitable, the child began to ask questions.

Until she started school, Jennifer had accepted her unconventional childhood as perfectly normal. At the age of eight she moved to Penrhos College, near Colwyn Bay in North Wales, and when her classmates started asking questions she told them she had never had a father. This worried the headmistress, who wrote to Frances that she thought Jennifer should be told a little more about her own background. Frances told Jennifer the rather flimsy cover story that she was the child of missionary parents who had given her to Frances' care and then died in China. Jennifer happily relayed the story to her friends, and was not surprised that Frances never mentioned her 'parents' again.[7] It seems that she accepted the story at face value, but at the same time vaguely believed that Frances was in fact her natural mother.

Frances, however, had been jolted from her complacency by the headmistress' letter, and realised that the world would need a better explanation in due course. It was at this time that she took John Morris' advice and legally adopted Jennifer, a common device at the time to disguise illegitimacy. In future Jennifer could answer all questions about her parentage by saying simply that she was 'the adopted daughter of Miss Frances Stevenson'. In order for her to use this line, though, Jennifer would have to be told that Frances had adopted her. The way in which Frances allowed this to happen shows how deeply ingrained the habit of concealing details of her private life had become to her. When Jennifer was eleven she found a folder labelled 'Jennifer's file' in a cupboard in her room at Avalon. Inside it she found a certificate of adoption with her name on it. It seemed that the file had been placed there deliberately for her to find, for if Frances had wanted to hide the document, she would surely not have left it in Jennifer's bedroom. Frances used the same means of communicating with Jennifer several times, reinforcing the distance in their relationship.

With unfortunate timing, Jennifer asked her mother about the adoption when they were at lunch with Lloyd George at Bron-y-De. Frances was furious – or pretended to be – and told Jennifer that she should not have looked at the file, presumably because any discussion of her parentage had to be conducted safely out of Lloyd George's hearing. She did talk to Jennifer about it later, and this time assured her that she was her natural daughter, but refused to give any further information, saying that she had promised Taid that she would not tell Jennifer who her real father was until she was sixteen. She would not hear another word on the subject until after Lloyd George's death, four years later.

Much as Frances had longed for a child, Jennifer was never given first place in her life. Shortly after her birth she reassured Lloyd George, 'My feelings of tenderness towards you have increased so much during the last few weeks. I feel that you too are my baby.'[8] Although Jennifer was constantly reassured that she was loved, Frances left her to be with Lloyd George whenever he needed her. Jennifer felt that Taid came first with Frances, and when Taid went away, would ask her mother why she wasn't going too. Frances was frequently torn between spending time with her lover and her child, but it was as natural for her to favour her lover as it was for Margaret to choose her children. 'My little love,' wrote Frances in 1944, 'now I have something to say that you will not like, my sweet, and neither do I. Taid has begged me not to leave him next weekend . . . and I can see that he will upset himself if I do come to Oxford [where Jennifer was then at school] next Saturday. Will you be very tolerant and forgiving, my darling, if I do not come?'[9]

Jennifer had to make sense of some very mixed messages. She was told that she was the natural daughter of Frances, but had to call herself 'adopted' in public. Frances said that she loved her, but was frequently absent, and always preoccupied by Lloyd George's needs. She was taken to lunch by Lloyd George in London restaurants, and even to Paris, much to his family's disapproval. They visited Versailles, the scene of his triumph at the peace conference nearly twenty years before, and he introduced her to the French Prime Minister, Léon Blum; but when the press photographed them visiting Napoleon's tomb, the resourceful Sylvester prevented them from discovering her name.

Jennifer grew up to be resistant to any demonstration of physical affection from her mother. She was a highly independent child, mature from years of constant exposure to adult conversation, but shy to the point of silence in company. Frances taught her not to draw attention to herself in front of visitors, in order to avoid awkward questions, but with her customary reticence she did not explain this to Jennifer, who wrongly concluded that her mother was ashamed of her. Jennifer once said that she assumed people would be disappointed when they met her because she was not beautiful and charming like her mother. She tried her best to blend into the background, which gave the impression that she was reserved and uncommunicative. In truth, she had inherited a great deal of Frances' liveliness and charm. Sadly for her, the ambiguity of her parentage denied her the opportunity to show her attractive personality.

When Lloyd George and his family returned from Antibes, it was at a time of rapidly escalating political crisis in Europe. Despite his reputation for appeasement, the elder statesman who had negotiated the peace at Versailles frequently warned against an over-trusting attitude towards Germany. It did not help that his old political enemy Neville Chamberlain had taken over the premiership from Baldwin in May 1937. There were few politicians Lloyd George held in deeper contempt than Chamberlain, and in his now more frequent interventions in the House of Commons he allowed it to show.

In March 1938 Germany annexed Austria, and at Munich in September it was agreed that Germany should take the disputed parts of Czechoslovakia in return for a non-aggression agreement. Chamberlain hailed the deal on his return to the UK as 'peace for our time'. Lloyd George's warnings to pay attention to what Adolf Hitler was doing, not what he was saying, had fallen on deaf ears. Chamberlain was never going to take advice from a man he hated and feared, and the British public, only twenty years after the end of the Great War, was in no mood to contemplate another. In March 1939 Hitler occupied the remainder of Czechoslovakia. Poland was next in line. The invasion took place on 1 September, and two days later Chamberlain announced that Britain was once more at war with Germany.

Frances and Lloyd George were driving from Bron-y-De to London on Sunday, 3 September when they heard the declaration of war on the car radio. Back at home in Avalon, nine-year-old Jennifer listened to the same announcement on the radio. It was a solemn moment, but the tension was broken when a visitor's bull terrier made them all laugh by standing to attention when the National Anthem sounded.

The following morning there began a protracted debate between Lloyd George and the government over the handling of the war. There was no prospect of him joining any government that was headed by Chamberlain, and he had plenty of scope – and credibility – to criticise from the backbenches. In May 1940, after a disastrous campaign in Norway, Chamberlain's government was on the point of collapse. Megan was sitting in the chamber of the House of Commons listening to a weakened Prime Minister face a devastating attack from the opposition when she realised that one crucial voice was missing from the debate, and ran to find her father. Lloyd George entered the chamber, caught the Speaker's eye, and what followed was the most effective twenty-minute demolition of a Prime Minister those assembled had ever heard. 'The Prime Minister must remember that he has met this formidable foe of ours in peace and in war. He has always been worsted,' thundered the Welsh Wizard. 'He is not in a position to appeal on the grounds of friendship. He has appealed for sacrifice. The nation is prepared for every sacrifice so long as it has leadership, so long as the Government show clearly what they are aiming at and so long as the nation is confident that those who are leading it are doing their best. I say solemnly that the Prime Minister should give an example of sacrifice, because there is nothing which can contribute more to victory in this war than that he should sacrifice the seals of office.'[10] Within two days, Winston Churchill had replaced Chamberlain as Prime Minister.

Churchill gave the appearance of being anxious to have the seventy-seven-year-old Lloyd George in his Cabinet, and made the offer several times. The answer, after some hesitation, was 'no'. Frances believed that

Lloyd George never intended to accept, although he consulted his friends on the matter, and even underwent a medical examination to see if he was fit for office.* He was already feeling weakened by the cancer that was eventually to kill him, and after so many years of waiting for his country's call, he was unequal to the task. It is said that Churchill was privately relieved when he received Lloyd George's refusal, and offered him the post of Ambassador to the United States, which Lloyd George also turned down.

Frances had been waiting for eighteen years for the chance to return to the excitement and stimulation of government. She was baffled by Lloyd George's decision, and quarrelled badly with him, accusing him of failing in his duty to his country. In 1941 she recalled: 'He sat in this window, silent, for many an hour for many days after Hitler had attacked Russia, and what was going on in his mind I could not fathom.'[11] In October 1940 she was still urging him to look after his health in preparation for his triumphant return to office: 'Your time will surely come, & the great thing is to keep fit until that time arrives.'[12] At the same time she indulged herself occasionally in her diary, or with friends, by reminiscing about 'the great days – D. Prime Minister . . . & all the glory & excitement of the post-war days'.[13] But with hindsight she realised that Lloyd George's vitality was already being sapped by his final illness, and her frustration slowly gave way to the knowledge that he would never return to Downing Street. Frances was fifty-one, and her role from then until Lloyd George's death would be as his companion and nurse, although this was never openly acknowledged between them.

---

* He explained his decision in a letter to Jennifer: 'Darling Jennifer, . . . You want to know why I have declined to join the War Cabinet when I was given the Offer. I have asked Mummy to give you my reasons when you meet this weekend. But I can give you just a hint – for yourself alone. You are not to repeat it to anyone else except of course, your Mummy.

1. I do not believe in the way we entered the war – nor in the methods by which it has been conducted. We have made blunder after blunder and are still blundering. Unless there is a thorough change of policy we shall never win.
2. I do not believe in the way or in the personnel with which the War Cabinet is constituted. It is totally different to the War Cabinet set up in the last War. It is not a War Directorate in the real sense of the term. There is therefore no real direction.

I am convinced that unless there is a real change in these two matters it would be a mistake for me to join up with the present lot . . .'

Meanwhile, Jennifer was so happy at Penrhos College that she occasionally worried that her life there was only a dream, and that she would wake up and have to return to real life. When the North Wales building was commandeered to accommodate government officials, the school was evacuated to Chatsworth in Derbyshire. Living on the famous Chatsworth estate thrilled Jennifer, but it was so cold that she caught a near-fatal dose of pneumonia, and was transferred by her mother to a school in Oxford.

Frances oversaw the building of a vast air raid shelter in the grounds of Bron-y-De. It was dug sixty feet under the surface, and was so big that Sylvester compared it to Piccadilly underground station. It had several rooms, one of which was furnished as a bedroom for Lloyd George, complete with telephone.* Lloyd George, it was rumoured, had been afraid of bombs during the Great War, and when the German raids on London began in September 1940 he decided to head for Criccieth, which meant leaving Frances behind, and embarked on his longest stay in North Wales for many years. Frances did not seem to mind, and jokingly referred to the bombs as 'fireworks'.[14]

The task of looking after Lloyd George now fell to Margaret. It was not a happy time for her. Sylvester wrote, 'Megan told me that Dame Margaret had had a terrible time with L.G. in Wales. That he thought of nothing but air raids, that he had got them completely on his mind, and that they were afraid he would make himself really ill.'[15]

Criccieth was not immune to the effects of the war. German bombers on their way to attack Liverpool and the industrial North of England droned noisily overhead, William George took in two families of evacuees at Garthcelyn, and Olwen's house in Porthmadoc Road was similarly put to use. His son William, who was of the same pacifist persuasion as his great-uncle Richard Lloyd, refused to register for the army despite its being almost certain that he would have been rejected on medical grounds. Margaret was of the view that he should take the medical exemption and be free to practise his profession as a solicitor in the

---

* A total of nineteen bombs were dropped on the farm during the war, according to Owen Lloyd George, who believes that they were intended for the nearby army town of Aldershot. Lloyd George, however, thought that the Germans were deliberately targeting him, and slept each night in the shelter.

family firm, which he would not be allowed to do as a conscientious objector.[16] He did not take her advice, but she bore no grudge, and when he consulted her on whether he should remain a member of Criccieth Council, she and Lloyd George both advised him to stay in office as long as the law allowed him to.

Margaret's war work was focused on North Wales, this time as an active Council member and as Chairman of the Red Cross Society. Once again she experienced the fear and anxiety of war when the younger members of her family joined up: her grandsons Owen, David, William, Robin and Benjy all saw active service, and all survived. Margaret did her bit nationally over the airwaves, broadcasting an appeal in Welsh, for instance, for volunteers to join the Women's Land Army.

Olwen, who had had more faith in the government's ability to nego-tiate peace than did her father, had not believed that war was immi-nent, and August 1939 had found her, Tom and their two sons in Switzerland on holiday. They raced for Boulogne, and caught the last boat for England before the frontiers closed. Olwen's seventeen-year-old daughter Eluned was on a school trip to Canada. Olwen cabled her to come home immediately, but then, because of the presence of German U-boats in the Atlantic, she was persuaded by Tom to tell her to stay where she was. Eluned was separated from her family for nearly seven years, during which time she met and married a Canadian, Bob Macmillan, and had her first child, whom she named Margaret after her sister and her grandmother.

Olwen stayed in London for much of the time during the war, and threw herself into the war effort, galvanising support for a Service Club for Welsh troops in the capital. Premises were found in Gray's Inn Road, and Olwen, like her mother before her, proved a very effective fundraiser. As Chairman of the Ladies' Committee, the work of trans-forming the premises into a comfortable overnight hostel for Welsh servicemen fell to her. She scrubbed floors, washed dishes and painted furniture, and ran the club with flair and efficiency. Many young men in uniform had never left home before, let alone been to London, and Olwen realised that providing them with a warm, friendly Welsh atmos-phere and good home cooking was a much-needed morale booster. Her efforts were recognised in countless letters of thanks from the families of servicemen across Wales.

Megan was much occupied with her role as MP during the war years. She had been working hard, and two letters from her doctor to Lloyd George in September 1939 suggest that she was suffering from nervous exhaustion. Amid the disruption to normal life, she saw an opportunity to make advances in the campaign for social reform. In particular she pressed ahead with her campaigning for women's rights, becoming a prominent figure on the Women's Power Committee, which advocated equal pay and working conditions for women. She joined Olwen as one of the founders of the Welsh Services Club in London, and also became the first female Church Commissioner in Wales and campaigned in the House of Commons to give the Welsh language recognition in law courts. By the end of the war she had been elected Chairman of the Welsh parliamentary party of the Liberal Party.

Megan had been a bridesmaid no fewer than five times, but she was no closer to getting married herself. A.J. Sylvester had commented to Lloyd George as early as 1931 that her selfishness meant that no man would want to marry her, to which Lloyd George replied that she 'had made up her mind to celibacy when she took up a political career. She liked the company of men and wanted to be the centre of attraction.'[17] The following year he commented that Megan 'would never allow anybody to dominate her now'.[18] Nevertheless, he had given Megan a converted barn on the Churt estate to live in when she found the right man to marry. The barn stood empty, used occasionally by Olwen and her family.

It was clear to those who knew her that Megan was deeply affected by her close relationship with her father, and they sometimes concluded that she had not found a man to measure up to him. But Megan had in fact found a man she wished to marry. With excruciating irony, he was not free to marry her: Megan was having an affair with a married man.

Shortly after her first election victory in 1929, Megan was in the House of Commons when she bumped into a fellow MP and they sat on a bench in the Lobby to talk. Her companion was Philip Noel-Baker, Labour Member for Coventry, and he later claimed that he fell in love with her there and then. By the late 1930s Megan felt the same way, but unlike Frances and Lloyd George, Megan's love for Philip did not bring her lasting happiness.

Born in 1889, the son of Canadian industrialist and Liberal MP J. Allen Baker, Philip was a high-flyer. He was President of the Cambridge Union, and in 1912 he was selected for the British team at the Stockholm Olympics. He won a silver medal in the 1,500 metres at the Antwerp games in 1920, and captained the athletics team both there and at the 1924 games in Paris. Because he was raised as a Quaker, he did not volunteer for active service in the Great War; instead he co-founded and commanded the Friends' Ambulance Unit in France and Italy. In the early months of the war he met a nurse called Irene Noel, and they married in 1915. After the Great War Philip served in the Peace Conference at Versailles as Lord Robert Cecil's Private Secretary, and afterwards he became one of the founding members of the League of Nations Secretariat. When Irene, who was ten years older than Philip, inherited a 1,500-acre estate in Greece called Achmetaga from her father, he hyphenated her name to his, and was known thereafter as Philip Noel-Baker.

From 1924 to 1929 Philip was Professor of International Relations at the London School of Economics, and his many published works included *The Geneva Protocol for the Pacific Settlement of International Disputes* (1925) and *Disarmament* (1926). 'I have only one real concern in public affairs – peace,' he wrote to Megan in 1953. 'My father made me care for almost nothing else, before I was twenty, & I always felt he left me a legacy & mandate to carry out when he died . . . There is only one subject on which I have always been accepted in many countries as a recognized authority – disarmament & international institutions. I'm better equipped by knowledge, work & experience than anybody else.'[19]

In 1929 Philip was elected as Labour MP for Coventry. He was one of many brilliant, Oxbridge-educated politicians hoping for ministerial office, but was disappointed to be appointed PPS to the Foreign Secretary, Arthur Henderson, instead. Nevertheless, by the time he sat on a bench in the Lobby with Megan, he had already made a name for himself as an intellectual and an international athlete, and it seemed only a matter of time before he ascended higher up the political ladder.

But Philip would not feature in Megan's life again for many years, for in 1931 he lost his seat, and for the next five years he worked mainly abroad, including a year as a lecturer at Yale. By 1936 he was back in England, and had a second chance at politics when he was selected as the Labour candidate for a high-profile by-election in Derby. During the campaign, in which Philip was supported by the Liberals, Lloyd George made a memorable and highly theatrical speech to the voters: 'Scan the firmament and you see the clouds gathering, darkening, deepening, lowering . . . You may give a judgement that will clear the skies . . . Mr Noel-Baker does not pay lip-service to peace – he has it coursing through his veins. If he is returned on Thursday, it will not merely be a victory for peace in Derby, it will give heart and hope to people who were broken, weary and faint.'[20]

Philip was returned to the House of Commons on 9 July 1936. In 1942 he joined the government as a Junior Minister for War Transport, and in 1945 he was appointed Minister of State in the Foreign Office. He was in government continuously until 1951 when Labour lost power. He was Chairman of the Labour Party in 1964, and in 1977 he was made a life peer. His international peace work was recognised in 1959 when he was awarded the highest accolade of all, the Nobel Peace Prize. In Philip, Megan might well have felt that she had met a man who could compare with her beloved Tada.

Seven years after their first meeting, Philip and Megan renewed their acquaintance, and before the end of the year they had become lovers. Their relationship was mutual and passionate. They met daily at the House of Commons, borrowed Thelma Cazalet's room at the Dorchester hotel on Thursday afternoons, and spent weekends at her country house, Raspit, near Sevenoaks. The lovers' need for discretion was very real: Megan confided only in her two best friends, Thelma and Ursula Norton-Griffiths (who disapproved of Philip from the start), and eventually in Olwen and her mother. Philip was a married man, and although divorce was no longer an absolute barrier to public life, it was still not to be taken lightly. For Megan the risks were even greater: the nonconformists of Anglesey on whose votes she depended would be horrified if she was exposed as the mistress of a married man.

We can only guess at the crisis of conscience that Megan went through before embarking on this relationship. None of her numerous earlier affairs (as far as we know) were physical, and none of the men were married. She was distraught at her father's affair with Frances, and had witnessed for herself the pain it had caused her mother. Sexual relations outside marriage were strictly forbidden by the Calvinistic Methodist Church of which she was a devout member, and involvement in a divorce case would endanger, if not end, her parliamentary career. Why would Megan take such a risk? The answer, it seems, was love.

In 1936 Megan was thirty-four years old. She had been an MP for seven years, and had become a public figure and a popular broadcaster. A man would have to be very accomplished indeed to impress a woman who had been raised in Downing Street, and Philip Noel-Baker came close to her ideal. He was ideally suited for her in all ways but one: his marriage, and that was not happy. As Thomas Tweed had done to Frances, Philip protested to Megan that he had married too young under the pressure of war, and to an unsympathetic older woman:

> I was 25 when I married; 10 years younger; young for my years, inexperienced & immature in every way, especially socially; under a tremendous nervous strain . . . the war meant separation for more than 3 years. That didn't help. I was flung straight from 1918 influenza into the Peace Conference, where I worked desperately hard . . . That no doubt was the start of processes which have led to the situation of today, where I am often told: 'Of course, you never were a lover in any way; you didn't begin to understand anything about it'. There has always been a total loss of everything that marriage might have meant & ought to have meant.[21]

The letter was written in 1955, and while it may smack of post-justification, it indicates that Philip and Irene had their problems before Megan came along. Their physical relationship was not successful, and Philip indulged in several close friendships with other women – 'platonic philanderings', as Irene called them, although whether they were entirely platonic is doubtful. Philip was good at giving others the impression that he enjoyed the company of women only up to a point: his secretary, Patricia Llewellyn-Davies, called him 'a romantic puritan',[22] and was not sure that his relationship with Megan was ever consummated. But Philip's letters to Megan indicate that their relationship was physical, and Wilfrid Roberts, with the insight of a fellow MP and a man, considered him to be 'a serious philanderer'.[23]

Megan fell deeply in love, and by 1938 Thelma Cazalet was convinced that she would accept a proposal from Philip, whom they called 'the greyhound' in recognition of his athletic prowess, regardless of the consequences. Megan's biographer Mervyn Jones believes that Megan wanted children, and at the age of thirty-six was running out of time. There is no evidence to back the theory, but it may explain why Thelma felt she should intervene to try to persuade Philip to leave Irene and marry Megan. She and Megan were very close, and she would not have interfered without Megan's agreement. Astonishingly, it emerged that Philip and Megan had not discussed marriage, or his divorce. Philip later protested, wholly unconvincingly, that he was not even sure that Megan would have accepted him:

> Thelma told me that I ought to cut all the Gordian knots, & take the risks . . . She had no doubts, & she tried . . . to get rid of mine. I don't need to tell you how my mind went with hers along that road . . . And yet I was quite certain that for you the cutting of the Gordian knots would never do. I was absolutely certain you would be deeply, absolutely, unalterably against it, & that you wouldn't easily forgive me if I even tried to make you take that path. Was I wrong my angel? . . . I don't believe so . . . I had to go on loving and trying to help you . . . Trying to give what a husband sh'd give . . .[24]

The matter was left unresolved, and soon the war came to worry and distract. Megan was not well in the autumn of 1939, and might have been unable to take such a momentous decision even if Philip had proposed to her. Her illness took her home to Criccieth, where it was not safe for her lover even to write to her, and she had plenty of time to reflect. Eventually she could not hold out any longer, and allowed Philip to write to her under cover of typewritten envelopes. In one of her own letters, at Christmas 1939, she wrote a heartfelt postscript: 'Never love me less.'[25] The words struck Philip deeply, and were to haunt him for many years to come.

During the troubled year that followed, Philip and Megan did discuss marriage. In his letters he repeatedly referred to the time when they would be married: 'Soon I shall be perfect, if you persevere! Or I should be, if I had you always with me! That's why, of course, I want to marry you, as I said last night! . . . I want to marry you for a thousand other reasons too – because I want to dance with you & play with you &

swim with you, & lie still & talk & talk & talk with you in the sunshine.'[26] But then he would write the opposite, offering to give her up for her own good: 'If you ever find anyone who would look after you as I should, I hope you will marry him very quick . . . I want you above everything to be absolutely free. You *do* know that, don't you?'[27] A month later, he writes as if they were engaged: 'When we're married, I'll develop a special technique of lying down & looking up at [the profile of your nose] so as to get it exactly as I got it this afternoon.'[28] And again: 'I think when we are married we shall have to arrange a private line between two rooms in our house, to which no one can possibly listen, & on which we can have long political & business discussions. It seems that I concentrate on the *talking* rather better when I can't see you!'[29]

What was going on? Philip was in danger of sounding very much like Lloyd George in his early letters to Frances. On the one hand he was making it very clear to Megan that he loved her and wished to marry her, while on the other he was writing as though there was an insuperable barrier to their marriage and offering to leave her for her own good. His own explanation, written much later, was that he was so insecure that he did not believe that Megan wanted to marry him, and would not be able to bear the rejection if he proposed and she turned him down. He also felt that she was 'a woman of destiny',[30] and would do better with her own name than if she took his, with all the scandal that would have involved. He counted himself as 'one of a large number', and expected that Megan would marry someone else as soon as she felt like it. He asserts that he tried during this period to offer her all that a husband would, only in secret.

There are gaping holes in this self-serving apologia. There was no insuperable barrier to his marrying Megan, and the decision as to whether she would do better as a Lloyd George than as a Baker was not his to take for her. He had been told categorically by Thelma, Megan's closest friend, that he should propose, and if he had no intention of leaving his wife, he was simply being cruel in dangling the prospect of marriage in front of Megan. He could not in fact offer her 'what a husband sh'd give', for in continuing the relationship he deprived her of the opportunity to have children. In his version of events, Philip is a sensitive soul who did his best to support his famous mistress rather than subject her to public humiliation and censure. Another view would be that he was too much of a coward to make the break with his rich wife, an incurable flirt who could not commit to one woman, and that he callously led Megan on for many years.

At the end of 1940 Megan had not given up hope that Philip might leave his wife and marry her. Time, disappointment and a lengthy separation had not succeeded in breaking the bond between them. Her Criccieth convalescence would certainly have tested the strength of her feelings, since Olwen and Margaret both came to know about her relationship with Philip, and disapproved strongly. The affair imposed a serious strain on Megan's relationship with her mother. Matters were to come to a head in one final confrontation at Margaret's deathbed.

After the golden wedding celebrations in 1938, Margaret had returned to Criccieth with some relief. Although she still enjoyed visiting her husband, she was quite content for someone else to have the troublesome task of looking after him as he became more difficult both temperamentally and physically, and was reconciled to the idea that Frances was his permanent companion. Her national profile was still high, and she made several radio broadcasts appealing for volunteers to join the war effort. There was no better way of conjuring up memories of the sacrifices made during the Great War, or of victory, than to put Dame Margaret on the airwaves.

There were, however, signs that Margaret was getting older. She had broken her wrist in an accident in 1932, and in April 1930 she and Megan had been badly shaken when a five-year-old boy was killed after running into the road directly in the path of the chauffeur-driven car in which they were travelling. Throughout the 1930s there are increasing references to her ill-health in Frances' diary and Lloyd George's letters, but it was an accident that hastened Margaret's final illness. On 26 November 1940, after she had chaired a meeting at the Memorial Hall, Margaret was pouring tea in the library at Garthcelyn when the telephone rang in the next room. As she hastened to answer it, she slipped on a mat and fell heavily to the floor. She was seventy-four, an age at which any fall could be serious. Lloyd George was staying at Brynawelon at the time, although he was confined to his room with a cold. His Rolls-Royce took Margaret to the hospital in Porthmadoc for an x-ray, which found that her hip was fractured, although a full recovery was predicted.

After a short stay in hospital Margaret was sent home to recover in bed. Cheerful and optimistic that she would soon be up again, she was advised to move as much as possible without putting her weight on her legs, and her grandchildren were pressed into service to help her with her exercises, throwing her a balloon so that she could hit it back to them.

With Margaret apparently recovering well, Lloyd George left to spend Christmas at Churt. But early in the New Year news came from Criccieth that she did not seem to be getting better, and Lloyd George immediately sent a bone specialist from Liverpool to examine her. Frances, with slightly uncharacteristic generosity towards Margaret, felt that he should return to Criccieth to see his wife, but it was bitterly cold, with heavy snows falling across the country, and he decided against making the journey.

Towards the end of January Margaret's condition deteriorated, as the month she had spent in bed increased the strain on her heart. She had been suffering from heart problems for some time, and according to Sylvester, Lord Dawson, whom Lloyd George also sent to tend his wife, attributed this to Lloyd George himself: 'L.G.'s treatment of her and his carryings-on had no doubt worried her and this would undoubtedly aggravate her trouble and speed the end.'[31] There may have been some truth in this, for as far back as 1933 Tom Carey Evans had advised his mother-in-law to live separately from Lloyd George for the sake of her nerves.[32]

It quickly became clear that Margaret was dangerously ill, indeed that she was dying; but there was one issue she needed to resolve before it was too late. She was desperately worried about Megan's relationship with Philip Noel-Baker. A lifelong Calvinistic Methodist, she believed that her daughter's soul was in danger. As she lay in bed, she begged Megan to make her a solemn promise to give Philip up. Megan could not refuse her mother's wish. She gave her word, and she did not take the promise lightly, though there was no sign that the relationship was cooling. Sometime after 18 December she told him that their affair was over.

Margaret's decline was rapid, and Dr Prytherch, the family physician in Criccieth, decided to send for Lloyd George on 18 January 1941. The following day Lord Dawson set off for Criccieth by train, accompanied by A.J. Sylvester. Lloyd George preferred to be driven in his Rolls-Royce by Dyer. He was accompanied as far as the Midlands by Frances, who then returned to London, and by his secretary Ann Parry, who was on her way to Anglesey for a holiday but readily agreed to travel with Lloyd George to take care of him until he could meet up with Sylvester.

When Sylvester and Lord Dawson reached Bangor, they found that the exceptionally heavy snow meant there was no road open between there and Criccieth. They were obliged to spend the night at a hotel, where they met up with Tom Carey Evans, who was also unable to reach Brynawelon. Lloyd George and Ann, meanwhile, were driving up a hill in Denbighshire when a WRAF stopped them to warn Dyer of a hazard ahead. Unfortunately, in the struggle to get the car restarted, the snow chains broke, and they had to proceed without them. At Cerrigydrudion, a village between Llangollen and Betws-y-Coed a little under forty miles from Criccieth, the car plunged into a deep snow-drift and could go no further.

Ann was able to arrange transport for the three of them to the nearest hostelry, the White Lion, where, despite a shortage of fuel, a fire was lit in Lloyd George's bedroom. After a frustrating night, Sylvester tried to organise a special train to take Lloyd George to Criccieth the following morning, but the snow was still too heavy. It fell to Lord Dawson to inform him later that morning that Margaret had suffered a heart attack, and had died at 10.20 a.m.

Lloyd George reacted calmly at first. Ann Parry, standing beside him as he received the news, did not realise at first what he had been told. He replied to Dawson that he had been expecting the news, but when Sylvester took the receiver, Lloyd George sobbed: 'She was a great old pal.' He then asked Sylvester to join him as soon as he could: 'I want your companionship.'[33]

To everyone's intense frustration, the weather continued to make travel impossible, and Ann Parry was left to look after a distraught Lloyd George by herself. He became very unwell under the strain: 'I was so concerned that I sat in his room all that night, of which he was unaware I thought, until Frances Stevenson told me some time later how touched he was by this.'[34] They were obliged to stay in the White Lion for another agonising night, during which Ann hardly slept: 'For me, during those three days, there was no rest, for the Press were on the telephone day and night, and I could snatch only a few minutes' rest at a time, lying on my bed in my fur coat. It was too cold to undress and my bedroom was icy.'[35]

Eventually the weather eased, and arrangements were made by Sylvester for Dick, Gwilym and their wives to take a train from London to Corwen, where they would meet Lloyd George and travel on together to Criccieth. In order to get Lloyd George to Corwen, a crowd of forty local well-wishers, deeply moved by the famous statesman's predicament, cut a passage through miles of snowbound lanes: 'Just wide enough for his car to pass through, the deep snow piled on both sides so high that only the sky was visible,' according to Ann. 'It was like passing through a white tunnel – an eerie sensation.'[36]

Margaret's sons were grief-stricken. Dick travelled from London full of bitterness against his father, and determined to have his say about the way in which his mother had been treated. When he saw Lloyd George, though, his face 'an awful colour', all thoughts of rebuke evaporated and the father fell into his son's arms. When the party arrived at long last at Brynawelon, Megan could not contain her grief, and Sylvester wrote, 'The scenes I witnessed between members of the family were most pathetic.'[37] Lloyd George sought comfort from Olwen by asking if Margaret had asked for him at the end. Olwen wrote, 'I hadn't the heart to tell him the truth, so I held his hand, looked him straight in the eye and told him that she had. He cried, but seemed to be comforted.'[38]

The funeral, a private service, was held on 24 January 1941. Two local ministers conducted the service, and with the snow still deep on the ground, the coffin was taken to the cemetery on a traditional farm wagon, pulled by sixty-five members of the Home Guard, each carrying a wreath. As they passed through Margaret's beloved town, a crowd of her neighbours and friends gathered to pay their respects to Criccieth's first lady. It was fifty-three years to the day since she had travelled by coach with her father from Mynydd Ednyfed to Pencaenewydd to become Mrs Lloyd George. As Margaret was laid to rest beside her daughter Mair in the family vault near her childhood home of Mynydd Ednyfed, the sun shone briefly. Her husband, standing between his two sons, wept. On the grave stood a wreath of red carnations and lilies bearing the simple message 'I fy nghariad – Dei' (To my love – Dei).[39]

The family mourned Margaret amid seemingly endless gifts of flowers and food. Thelma Cazalet rushed to Criccieth as soon as she could, and was greeted emotionally by Lloyd George – '[He] threw his arms about me, burst into tears and sobbed out that he would never forget my coming at that moment.'[40] Tributes flowed in from friends, acquaintances and admirers, and newspapers published glowing obituaries: Dame Margaret was 'one of the most lovable and beloved of women' according to the *Caernarvon Herald*;[41] 'no Minister of the Crown had ever had a more completely worthy wife than Dame Margaret', wrote the *Daily Sketch*.[42]

Megan's wreath had borne the message 'To my beloved head gardener from her grieving and ever-devoted under gardener,'[43] and Margaret's love of flowers was so well known that the list of floral tributes at her funeral filled a twelve-inch column in the *Caernarvon Herald*. Hundreds of messages were received from around the world, including from the King and Queen, Queen Mary, the Princess Royal, General Smuts, President Roosevelt and McKenzie King, the Prime Minister of Canada. The last word goes to her friend and admirer Winston Churchill: Dame Margaret was a 'great woman, who embodied all that is most strong and true in the British race'.[44]

Margaret's sudden death came as a devastating shock to Lloyd George. He had been convinced that he would die before his wife, and according to Sylvester he was 'a changed man'.[45] Lord Dawson hastened to warn Frances that she must expect to see Lloyd George suffer some remorse.

Frances, showing great sensitivity, withdrew from Bron-y-De to allow Lloyd George and Megan to comfort each other and to plan a memorial garden for Margaret in Criccieth. But one thing was clear: Lloyd George was now free to make good his promise to marry her. Frances was determined to make sure that he would, whatever his family might think. The fight, as Sylvester put it, was now on.[46]

25

Till Death us do Part

MARGARET'S DEATH CHANGED everything. Lloyd George's lifeline back to Wales and his constituency was severed. His marriage, the bedrock on which he had built his public career and the one factor that maintained the balance between his first family and his second, was gone. He was seventy-eight years old, and the relationships he had so carefully built up to support him in public and in private had, at a stroke, been blown wide open.

Megan inherited Brynawelon from her mother, and, somewhat hastily, Lloyd George informed her on the day after Margaret's funeral that he would not continue paying his allowance towards the house's upkeep. Megan was outraged, and Sarah Jones, who had been Lloyd George's ally for forty years, vowed never to speak to him again. Lloyd George was not to know that Megan had suffered a double bereavement, and was grieving for both her mother and her lost lover. It was the first, unheeded sign that Megan expected life to go on much as it had before, and would resist any attempt to change things after her mother's death.

Frances may have acted sympathetically at the time of Margaret's death, but it was not long before she began to assert herself more firmly where the family was concerned. She desperately minded the fact that she had to leave Bron-y-De whenever Margaret or Megan were there, and now that Margaret was dead, she saw no reason to do so any longer. In April, only three months after Margaret's funeral, Sylvester was reporting friction: 'There is a terrific row in progress between L.G. and

Megan. Since Dame Margaret's death, Frances remains at Bron-y-De during the weekend. Megan saw her there the other day and, as a consequence, just ignored her father and refused to speak to him.'[1]

At around the same time, Frances, clearly expecting that Lloyd George would fulfil his promise to her now that he was finally in a position to do so, told Jennifer that they were going to be married. Jennifer was eleven, old enough not to be surprised by her mother's news, and she was pleased, since her relationship with her Taid remained close. Nothing happened for more than a year, but when the anniversary of Margaret's death had passed (the traditional 'decent interval') and Lloyd George had still not made a move, Frances took matters into her own hands. She asked Sylvester to look into the procedure of marriage in a Baptist chapel, and he sent her a memo with some information in March 1942.

Lloyd George had aged rapidly after Margaret's death, and, much preoccupied with the war situation, was looking pale, his leonine head and neck shrunken. He did not know that Frances had asked for the information, nor did Sylvester discuss it with him. Was it possible that he did not intend to renew his proposal to Frances after keeping her waiting for twenty-eight years? The family were certainly not expecting him to remarry. Olwen wrote: 'Perhaps we should have anticipated it, but if we thought about it at all we probably expected them to continue living as before.'[2] Maybe Lloyd George too thought that Frances would be happy to carry on as they were. Perhaps he felt that her affair with Tweed had negated their agreement, or that Frances, having had a child, was less concerned about marriage. Either way, he was soon to be disabused.

Lloyd George was more worried about another family battle that was looming on the horizon. Two years previously he had astonished everyone by buying a house in his native village of Llanystumdwy. Tŷ Newydd (The New House) was an attractive manor house set on the hill above the village and surrounded by farmland, which Lloyd George announced he was going to cultivate in the same way he had developed Bron-y-De. He did not divulge his reasons for wanting a house in Llanystumdwy, a mile or so from Criccieth where his wife was then living. Did he intend to persuade her to leave Brynawelon, or did he want somewhere that he could stay independently of her? If so, how would he explain that to his conservative, chapel-going constituents? He could not possibly take

Frances and Jennifer to Llanystumdwy while Margaret was alive, nor did he seem anxious to leave Bron-y-De. His intentions were still unclear when, the year after Margaret's death, there were signs that he was planning to occupy Tŷ Newydd. The farm manager came to Churt to receive instructions, and a wagon of furniture arrived at the house.

In May 1942, Frances asked Sylvester to 'commit an indiscretion', by letting Megan know that Lloyd George and she were contemplating marriage. Her reasoning was that she believed Lloyd George was holding back from proposing because he was frightened of Megan's reaction. Frances grossly underestimated the depth of Megan's hatred of her as she blithely told Sylvester, 'I do not see how she could quarrel about it now not having quarrelled over other things. I do not think she would like it, but I do not think she would break off relations . . . He is so frightened of saying anything to her himself. I think I am perfectly justified in taking things into my own hands. Everyone in the neighbourhood is expecting it. I have no doubt his intentions are all right, but you know how difficult it is for him to make up his mind to do anything these days. I would like to jog it on a bit.'[3]

Frances must have been intensely frustrated with Lloyd George's inaction, and Sylvester was put in an invidious position. He did not refuse her, but balked at telling Megan himself. Instead he asked Miss Brady, a shorthand typist on Lloyd George's staff, to let Olwen know what was afoot, confident that she would alert the rest of the family. Sure enough, the following day Sylvester received a phone call from Megan, in a state of distress. In her mind, the issues of moving to Tŷ Newydd and marrying Frances were entwined, and she regarded both as an insult to her mother's memory. A month later she had not calmed down, and Lloyd George was simultaneously reassuring both her and Frances, and playing for time. Sylvester observed the situation with calm detachment: 'I have seen L.G. in many a wangle, but never one like this,' he wrote. 'He is playing a deep game between Megan and Frances. One of them must be disappointed one day.'[4]

In July Frances succeeded in getting Lloyd George to say that he meant to marry her 'on his own initiative',[5] and she took to wearing a new diamond ring on her engagement finger. Her campaign faltered in the autumn, though, when Lloyd George announced that he wanted to wait two years after Margaret's death before getting married again, after which time, Frances told Sylvester with considerable over-optimism, she did not think he would 'bother about Megan'.[6] The following month she confessed to Sylvester that 'L.G. [was] not quite frank' about his intentions.[7] By now Frances was realising how strong the opposition really was: Lloyd George had talked to Gwilym about the marriage and even he – the only one of his children who was friendly with Frances – had expressed reservations. A second marriage would not be popular with his constituents, Gwilym said, and Megan would simply not accept it.

Having failed to bring his children around to the idea, Lloyd George tried to persuade Frances to drop it: they had lived together for nearly thirty years, and had grown accustomed to being discreet. Why change things now? Frances reacted angrily, reminding him of all the marriage opportunities she had given up for him. ' "That is all done with," L.G replied. "Honourable people think you should do it," Frances had said. "There are no honourable people," L.G. had said.[8] Sylvester, who recorded Frances' account of the conversation in his diary, concluded that Lloyd George was trying to get out of the marriage. Frances was not prepared to give way: she craved respectability, and had hoped for nearly three decades that she would one day be married; and she could not afford to give in on this issue even if she had wanted to. She could reasonably expect to outlive Lloyd George by decades. To live on as his widow would mean respectability, recognition and financial security. To live on as his former mistress was quite another thing, and not what Frances thought she deserved after nearly thirty years of devoted service. The shrewd Lord Dawson was probably right when he said to Sylvester that Frances would have married Lloyd George even on his deathbed.

The battle of wills intensified towards the end of 1942 as Frances commissioned Sylvester to investigate 'Plan B', a register office wedding. She consulted John Morris, who advised her to leave Lloyd George in order to force his hand. This, though, was a step too far. 'L.G. is an old man,' she said. 'I do not like to bring pressure on him.'[9] In December Dawson was asked by Frances to talk to Megan, and reported back that she was irreconcilable. She kept coming back to the same thing – her mother. Frances could not understand why Megan felt so strongly, telling Sylvester, 'You cannot talk to Megan like a normal being. She did not understand. She was not a normal woman. She had this mixture of sex and religion which created the most extraordinary obsession in her.'[10] What Frances did not know was that Megan was struggling with her own feelings after giving up her married lover. She had kept her promise to her mother, and had stopped seeing Philip. Philip in turn had not left Irene, the one thing that could have enabled them to be together, and Megan believed that the affair was over for good. To see Frances, the mistress who had made her mother unhappy, marry her father and achieve the happy ending Megan herself had been denied, was too much to bear. Megan's grief, disappointment and hatred of Frances made her unpredictable and volatile.

January 1943 was approaching, the second anniversary of Margaret's death, after which Lloyd George had promised to marry Frances. That month also saw his eightieth birthday, and Sylvester was busy fielding requests for interviews and arranging a family party to mark the occasion. Since Margaret's death, Megan and Olwen had refused to go to Bron-y-De at all if Frances was present, and they were in a quandary about the birthday party, telephoning Sylvester and Lord Dawson for advice. In December, Dawson had met Frances at Lloyd George's request to give his professional view on the proposed marriage, and reported back that he had found her to be 'an extremely well-preserved woman, who would be acceptable in any place or circumstance', and that he had been won over by her arguments for the marriage. 'What she wanted,' according to Dawson, 'was the name.'[11] In addition, Frances had made it clear that the marriage would not affect Jennifer's status in any way – in other words, that Jennifer would not take the name 'Lloyd George', which had been one of Megan's strongest objections. But shortly after this meeting Lloyd George became so upset at his daughters' decision not to attend his birthday party that Frances offered to 'put the whole idea of marriage off', for the time being at least.[12]

In light of this, Dawson strongly urged Megan to make a gesture of reconciliation by agreeing to attend a birthday lunch with Frances present. He went on to spell out to her the simple truth that Lloyd George was now an old man who needed Frances more than ever: 'Now I want you to listen to me,' he told her, possibly prompted by Frances. 'I both understand and sympathise with your feelings and especially those which surround your mother's memory, but I am sure she would wish nothing but that the evening of your father's life should be made as smooth as possible. He is in need today of physical care and is likely in this respect to become more dependent in the future. Miss S. fills this role and there is no one else at once fitted, available and acceptable for this duty.' He referred to the apparent abandonment of the plans for Frances and Lloyd George to marry: 'If it be a fact that what you feared is off, as it appears to be, it must in justice be said she has now made a great sacrifice and from what she said to me I think she has made things easy and put aside the bitterness of her disappointment . . . From my deep attachment to you I do urge you on the next suitable occasion to make that gesture and make it generously and you will never regret it.'[13]

Sylvester gave similar advice to Olwen, urging her to think how badly she would feel if Lloyd George died in his sleep the night after his birthday without having seen her. Both daughters had been given the impression that the wedding idea had been wholly abandoned, and as a result, at the last minute, the whole family gathered at Bron-y-De for the first major family occasion to take place without Margaret. Over lunch, dominated by a huge birthday cake sent by the *Daily Mirror* and with the BBC playing almost continuous tributes to Lloyd George, they read messages of congratulations from the King and Queen, Queen Mary, the Prime Minister and other world figures. It took the office weeks to answer the hundreds of cards and telegrams. Frances was present at the lunch, but tactfully withdrew when a photographer recorded the toast.

The day passed off as successfully as possible under the circumstances, but Frances had only suggested postponing, not cancelling, the wedding. By Easter she was again thinking of marriage, and when Jennifer asked her why Taid did not marry her, she urged her to ask him herself. This Jennifer duly did, and the embarrassed laugh with which Lloyd George answered the question signalled that she had touched a nerve. In the summer Frances confided to Ann Parry that plans were afoot, and enlisted the help of Thelma Cazalet in breaking the news to Megan. Frances disliked Thelma, as she disliked many of Margaret's supporters, but she was enough of a politician to use every means at hand to bring Megan around. Thelma insisted that Lloyd George should ask her to do this himself (perhaps the antipathy ran both ways), and asked Olwen to go with her to see Megan. The interview was as unpleasant as she had feared. There seemed to be no softening on Megan's part, but by now Frances had the upper hand. On her birthday, Lloyd George asked if she would like a wedding ring as a gift, firm plans were made, and a date finally set. They would be married on 23 October.

In an attempt to avoid the press furore that would follow if news of the wedding leaked out, Sylvester managed all the arrangements for a quiet wedding at Guildford Register Office. Ann Parry was sent to London to order a cake and flowers, which were not easy to come by in wartime, and for discretion's sake paid for them with her own cheques. A few days before the wedding, Lloyd George steeled himself to tell his family. He spoke to Olwen, who by now felt that it was a matter for her father to decide. When she in turn informed Megan there was another scene, and it became clear that neither daughter was willing to attend the wedding. There was no question of Dick attending – war work and ill-health prevented it – but Gwilym and Edna agreed to be present. They would be the sole representatives of the family.

On the eve of the wedding, Lloyd George was keeping up a strange pretence that, despite making all the arrangements, Sylvester knew nothing of what was to happen the following day. They were talking politics together when Megan came on the telephone. Lloyd George took the call in another room, and after a long interval Frances went to check that all was well. She returned to ask Sylvester to intervene, worried that Megan would make her father ill. Sylvester found Lloyd George thoroughly upset in the middle of a furious row with Megan. Her threats included that she would leave public life, that she would have nothing more to do with her father, and even that she would 'do away' with herself.[14] Sylvester took the receiver, and heard Megan's sobs. 'I felt sorry for her in many ways,' he wrote, 'but it is the old, old question.'[15] Megan had not forgiven Frances, and never would.

This time Lloyd George was not to be deterred. He recovered from the upset of the conversation with Megan, and he and Frances spent the night before their wedding, unromantically, in the Bron-y-De air raid shelter. The following morning Gwilym telephoned Sylvester to say that he was detained in London on ministerial duty and could not, after all, be at the wedding, but would come down to Churt for lunch afterwards. Sylvester privately thought that Megan had persuaded him to change his mind.

The wedding group left Bron-y-De at 11.15 a.m. on Saturday, 23 October. Dyer, who brought the car to the front door, had no idea where they were going, and only the couple and their witnesses, Muriel and Sylvester, set off for Guildford. Frances, who still did not like Sylvester very much, had asked Ann Parry to be the second witness, but at the insistence of Lloyd George she had been asked to stand down in favour of his Principal Private Secretary.

The wedding was a simple and quiet affair. Sylvester had ensured that the room was filled with flowers, which pleased both Frances and Lloyd George greatly, and the couple took their seats in front of the Registrar's desk, with Muriel and Sylvester on either side. The groom was eighty years old, the bride had just turned fifty-five. Frances had had her hair cut short in middle age, and wore it tightly permed. She still looked younger than her age, and was dressed in a neat, undressy belted tartan dress with short sleeves. Lloyd George looked smart in a pinstriped three-piece suit, a gleaming white shirt and striped tie. They repeated their vows 'in clear and definite tones',[16] and signed the register with a special pen. After requesting that the flowers should be sent to a local hospital, the wedding party departed, Lloyd George looking 'immensely happy' according to Sylvester, 'gay and handsome' according to Frances. They drove back to Churt, calling at the farm office, where Frances was introduced for the first time as 'Mrs Lloyd George', the title she had long waited for. 'The whole countryside was bathed in sunshine, as was my heart,' she wrote in her memoirs, 'and a deep contentment possessed me; contentment, but not the thrills of the usual bride. Our real marriage had taken place thirty years before.'[17]

In their absence Bron-y-De had been decorated with flowers by Ann Parry, and a bottle of champagne was opened as soon as the newly married couple appeared. The office staff presented Frances with a pair of Sheffield-plated tureens, and were kept busy for the rest of the day fielding phone calls and messages from friends, dignitaries and journalists. To Lloyd George's delight, Jennifer had been allowed home from school and was waiting to greet him. She was told she could help answer telephone enquiries from the press – on the strict understanding that she would pretend to be a secretary, and on no account reveal that she was Frances' daughter. Her status, as well as her name, had not been changed at all by the wedding.

The following day William George was obliged to read in the newspaper that his brother had married again. It was the first he had heard of Lloyd George's plans. Later, Owen, son of Dick and Roberta, was at home when his stepfather arrived with the evening papers. 'Well, your Taid has made an honest woman of her at last!' he announced. Owen recalls, 'It may sound incredible now but I had to ask my stepfather what he meant; I was so naïve that even at the age of nineteen I had not realised that this affair had been going on for thirty years.'[18] His cousin William, Gwilym's son, exclaimed, 'Good God, Jennifer's my aunt!'[19] Sylvester's response to the press comment was to note: 'He has lived a life of duplicity. He has got clean away with it.'[20]

There was no sign of any rapprochement from Brynawelon. In November, Frances wrote to Megan in a vain attempt at reconciliation:

> I hope you will read this letter through as it is written in all sincerity to ask if you will not reconsider your attitude towards your Father's marriage with me . . . I am depriving you of nothing in becoming his wife – neither of his affection nor of any material benefits now or in the future . . . Even if you cannot see your way to burying the past as far as I am concerned, I hope you will make this concession to him and so establish yourself even more firmly in his heart.[21]

Megan did not reply.

Owen Lloyd George, visiting his grandfather, noted that Lloyd George had aged dramatically in two years and had 'lost a lot of his fire'.[22] He had lost none of his interest in international affairs, but Frances was alarmed by his fascination with listening to propaganda broadcasts from Germany: he would never miss the notorious Lord Haw-Haw's broadcasts, which were intended to lower British morale. He would sit silently for hours at a time, and instead of being the life and soul of the dinner table as before, he would sink into a meditation. He did not seem to be unwell, but Frances was worried, and called a doctor to examine him in the autumn of 1944. The doctor's diagnosis of bowel cancer was confirmed by Lord Dawson. Given Lloyd George's age and infirmity it was felt that nothing could be done, so Frances chose not to tell him what was wrong. Instead she redoubled her efforts to make his last months as comfortable as possible. Even the envious Sylvester had to acknowledge that Lloyd George was 'marvellously looked after by Frances'.[23] Dawson also noted that Lloyd George was happier, an improvement he attributed to the success of his second marriage.

At around the same time the house in Llanystumdwy, which had been remodelled by the architect Clough Williams-Ellis, was completed, and Lloyd George announced his intention to spend a few weeks there with Frances. This was going to be most uncomfortable for Megan, who was still not speaking to her father, but although he had taken pains to avoid meeting her since the wedding except on formal occasions in the House of Commons, he could not be dissuaded. Sylvester could see that he was nervous of his family's reaction, but nevertheless he set off with Frances on 19 September, and arrived that evening at his new home, back where his journey had begun. Frances was not aware of any particular purpose to the visit – indeed, it is entirely possible that Lloyd George himself was not – but she noted that he had seemed very reluctant to leave Bron-y-De. He changed his mind about departing several times, and had to take a long, lingering look at his beloved library before he was finally ready to leave. It seems that a deeply buried instinct within him had signalled that it was time to go home to die in Wales, for he would never return to Bron-y-De.

Tŷ Newydd had been designed for Lloyd George's comfort, with a library featuring a large bay window looking out on the mountains and the sea. He and Frances quickly established a routine of walks around Llanystumdwy, where he delighted in showing her all the familiar haunts of his childhood, and drives out in the mountains of Snowdonia. Despite his weakness, Lloyd George made a few public appearances, delighting his constituents. Relations with the family were less easy. Frances caused unwitting offence when she accompanied Lloyd George to a service at Margaret's chapel, Seion, and actually sat in Margaret's pew. It was tactless at best, and demonstrated louder than words how alien the new Mrs Lloyd George was to the society in which she found herself.

William George went to see his brother at Tŷ Newydd and received him at Garthcelyn, but he was 'more and more saddened at each of these visits'. 'Strangely enough,' he wrote in his memoir, 'for the first time in our joint history, we did not have much to say to one another . . . the past, both his and mine, was obviously dead to him.'[24] Megan's reaction when Sylvester telephoned to say that her father wished to see her was 'acid', but she agreed to let him visit Brynawelon, provided he came alone. Lloyd George, 'just a shrunken old man, looking very delicate and feeble', rang the doorbell and was reunited with his daughter. Within minutes they were walking in the garden arm-in-arm as if they had never quarrelled. Sylvester, meanwhile, was trying to coax Sarah to greet her old master, but found her harder to persuade than Megan. 'I will not go,' she said. 'He stopped my money.' By the end of the visit, however, she had agreed to shake hands, and they had a pleasant talk in Welsh. She said afterwards that he had looked so altered that she could not help but be civil.[25]

On the same day, good news came through on the war front, with British patrols reaching German soil. Lloyd George turned his thoughts to the peace negotiations that would have to be conducted after the war. He was passionate on this subject, and felt that he could make a real contribution based on his experiences at Versailles. At the same time, the end of the war would mean a general election, and he was not sure that he had the strength to fight another campaign.

Sylvester had agreed to accompany Lloyd George to Criccieth for two weeks, and had not prepared for a longer trip. But it gradually became clear that there was no end to the visit in sight, and that he was expected to stay indefinitely. Any hope that Lloyd George would return to government had now faded away, and Sylvester was concerned that cutting himself off from Westminster in this way would prove fatal to his future career. Dressed in unsuitably light clothing, he became more and more agitated about his personal situation, and finally agreed with Frances that he would split his time between London and Llanystumdwy. He was assured by her that he would be looked after when his services were no longer needed, a promise he later claimed was inadequately fulfilled by the granting of a month's salary for each year of service, a bequest of £1,000 and a failed attempt to get him a knighthood.

While Lloyd George was still alive, Sylvester was loyal and active on his behalf. He set about securing an uncontested election in Caernarvon Boroughs. The local Liberals were happy to re-nominate him, even at the age of eighty-one, but warned that the electorate had changed a great deal in the nine years since the last general election. There were countless new voters in Caernarvon Boroughs, some public servants and military personnel stationed there for the duration of the war, others evacuated from English cities. These new voters could not be counted on to support the great Welsh statesman, and the local Labour and Conservative parties refused to grant Lloyd George a 'walkover'. Lloyd George badly wanted a platform from which he could advise the government on how to approach the peace – even he recognised that he could do no more – but he did not want to risk ending his spectacular political career by losing an election. There was an obvious but unpalatable answer: could Lloyd George, scourge of the House of Lords, be persuaded to take a peerage? Sylvester made discreet enquiries, and Churchill replied that he would be happy to oblige with a nomination. Only one question remained: would Lloyd George himself agree?

Lloyd George's family had no doubt that the lifelong rebel who held the Upper House in contempt would never accept a peerage. His daughters quickly dismissed rumours of an impending announcement, and were shocked to find that their father was considering it. This was one of the most difficult decisions of his long career. Accepting a peerage would give him a platform from which to play whatever part he could in the peace negotiations. In addition, a peerage would allow him to bow out of his political career with honour, with no need to fight another general election or, worse, to admit that he could no longer do so.

The opposite view was also compelling: his daughters felt that Lloyd George would be betraying his roots, his class and his integrity by accepting a peerage. Like Pitt the Elder, he would be seen to have made a self-serving u-turn, and instead of the respect he deserved, he would end his career in ridicule. He could easily make his views on the peace process known through newspaper articles, they felt, and no one in his immediate family seemed to want to be burdened with a hereditary title, least of all his eldest son Dick, who was in no fit state to support it. Lloyd George was nearly eighty-two years old, and in frail health. Would it not be better for him to retire from politics altogether?

He could not decide. He consulted widely – even Ann Parry was asked what she thought – before the messenger from Churchill arrived in Criccieth to receive his answer, and he had to make his choice. Frances and William George were the final witnesses to his agonising. Frances was quietly thrilled at the thought of becoming a countess, although Jennifer firmly believes that the only title she really wanted was 'Mrs Lloyd George'. Seeing him make himself unhappy over it, Frances said, 'If you have any doubts about it, why not send a telegram refusing – that would be an end of the matter.'[26] But finally Lloyd George could not accept that he no longer had a part to play in public life, and the telegram was sent, 'Gratefully accept'. Frances confessed that her heart beat a little faster.[27]

Megan and Olwen were extremely upset. In their minds, the only possible explanation was that Frances had persuaded their father in order to get herself a title, and nothing that Lloyd George or William George said could alter their view. It was yet another reason to hate their father's wife. The announcement was made on 1 January 1945, and Jennifer described the effect on Lloyd George's spirits as 'a kind of resurrection'.[28] The peerage was made official on 11 February: Lloyd George was gazetted as Earl Lloyd-George of Dwyfor,* and Frances, the schoolteacher with the bohemian background, was henceforth a countess.

Among the letters that poured in when the news became public were a number accusing Lloyd George of putting Frances' social status ahead of his principles. Some were so unpleasant that Jennifer burned them without showing her mother. Others were kinder, including some from Lloyd George's grandchildren, who were too young to understand their grandfather's reservations: 'Long live the House of Dwyfor!' wrote Valerie.[29] There was one person in particular who was delighted, and who fully understood how long Frances had waited for social rank and respectability. Frances wrote to her mother, Louise: 'I cannot really believe it is true – it seems more like a fairy tale to me.'[30]

His last big decision taken, Lloyd George settled down to his apples and his books in Tŷ Newydd. There, in his last home, his strength faded away, and it became apparent that he would never take his seat in the

---

* The hyphen was necessary, according to the Garter, because the surname on Lloyd George's birth certificate was simply 'George'. In order to be known by the name he had adopted for himself as a teenager, he had to link the 'Lloyd' and the 'George' together formally.

House of Lords, or see the Palace of Westminster again. He became bedridden shortly after his eighty-second birthday in January 1945, and with Ann Parry's help, Frances took good care of him, working together in friendship, as Ann put it, 'sharing the pain and the privilege of smoothing the path of a famous man'.[31] Dr Prytherch wrote in glowing terms to Lord Dawson:

> [Lloyd George] is comfortable and placid and extremely well looked after. His wife is doing a grand job of work. She has done so for the last six months, and latterly, with his loss of control, this is not an easy task, but she is doing it with all the devotion he deserves, and she is doing it unstintingly and extremely well, and he calls for her constant presence. One cannot say more than that he is one of the best cared for patients I have ever had.[32]

Frances was in constant attendance at her husband's side, but her devotion was tested when, in the spring, Louise Stevenson became seriously ill. Frances could not bring herself to leave Lloyd George, not even to see her mother for the last time. She wrote her father a heart-wrung letter but did not leave Llanystumdwy. Louise died on 13 March, and Frances was not even able to attend her funeral.

Frances was skilled at presenting a calm face to the world, and with her husband in decline, it was more important than ever that she should not succumb to her emotions. This was not apparent to the fifteen-year-old Jennifer, who had been taken ill with appendicitis while staying at Tŷ Newydd, and was there throughout her Taid's last illness. Jennifer was close to Louise and, probably upset at missing the funeral herself, berated her mother for lack of feeling. Pushed beyond endurance, Frances struck her. It was the only time she ever did so, and Jennifer, realising for the first time that her mother's cool demeanour did not mean that she was not deeply distressed, felt ashamed that she had not recognised the immense pressure Frances was under.

A few weeks earlier, on 21 February, Dr Prytherch had released a bulletin to the press to alert the nation that Lloyd George's condition 'must cause some anxiety to his family, his friends and the nation at large'.[33] An army of newspaper reporters arrived in Llanystumdwy, and inundated Lloyd George's staff with requests for information. Despite the relentless progress of the tumour in his abdomen, of which he was seemingly unaware, Lloyd George continued to impress his doctors with his ability to rally his strength, for instance when Megan made one of her rare visits to Tŷ Newydd: 'Undoubtedly,' wrote Dr Prytherch to Lord Dawson, 'we are dealing with a remarkable mind and constitution.'[34]

Faced with her father's imminent death, Megan had at long last been persuaded to drop her objection to being in the same room as Frances. Sylvester, who was keeping the whole family informed, wrote to Owen that 'Megan's attitude to Frances has undergone a radical change and she is now polite!'[35] It was only a temporary concession, but it was nevertheless welcome. Olwen was staying with her sister at Brynawelon, and was a frequent visitor, along with William George and his family.

When, on 26 March, the end drew near, the family gathered together in the library at Tŷ Newydd which had been converted to a bedroom so that Lloyd George could gaze out over the mountains for as long as possible. All feuds and quarrels were put aside, for the time being at least. Megan took her father's right hand, Frances his left. Olwen stood behind Megan, and Jennifer and Ann Parry stood at the foot of the bed. Sylvester was also present, standing further back with Sarah Jones, but William George had found the scene too emotional to bear, and was waiting downstairs with Tom Carey Evans. As the interval between Lloyd George's breaths grew longer and longer, it was clear that the end was near. At 8.35 p.m. Prytherch felt for his pulse one last time, and let it be known that Lloyd George had died. He was surrounded in death, as in life, by the women who loved him.

The funeral was held on Good Friday, 30 March 1945, which was a chilly, overcast day. Churchill had rung Gwilym to discuss arrangements, assuming that Lloyd George would be buried in Westminster Abbey, but Gwilym told him that Lloyd George had already chosen the site of his grave. He would not be buried at the Abbey or any other conventional resting place, but on the banks of the river Dwyfor, the spot marked by the stone on which he used to sit to listen to its waters. Margaret had made her wishes equally clear: 'You can if you like, but not me,' she was reported to have said.[36] Even in death, Margaret preferred to be with her children. The Prime Minister bowed to Lloyd George's wishes, and arranged to have his old friend's four uniformed grandsons flown back to Wales for the funeral, a kindness that was greatly appreciated by the family.

The days between Lloyd George's death and the funeral were spent by Frances in a haze of activity. She told Jennifer that she felt she had been 'knocked off her perch',[37] and she seemed emotionally unprepared to carry on without the lover who had dominated her life for over thirty years. Tributes flowed in from the four corners of the earth. Lloyd George was 'a giant among giants', said General Smuts. According to Sir Archibald Sinclair, who had become leader of the Liberal Party in 1935, he was 'the great prophet and champion of [the Liberal] cause . . . He served the people faithfully in peace; he led them valiantly in war.'[38] 'We have lost our most distinguished member and Wales her greatest son,' said Aneurin Bevan. Churchill abandoned the affairs of state to work until 4 a.m. on his eulogy to his friend and mentor. On 28 March he delivered it to a hushed House of Commons: 'As a man of action, resource and creative energy he stood, when at his zenith, without a rival . . . He was the greatest Welshman which that unconquerable race has produced since the age of the Tudors . . . we ourselves, gathered here today, may indeed be thankful that he voyaged with us through storm and tumult with so much help and guidance to bestow.'[39]

The funeral arrangements were made, not without squabbling, and on the day itself the whole family, including Jennifer, stood around the coffin in the library at Tŷ Newydd for a short, private service. Having bidden farewell to Lloyd George the husband, father, brother and grandfather, they prepared to accompany Lloyd George the statesman to his grave. Owen, arriving from Italy only an hour before, had seen that the lanes surrounding Tŷ Newydd were thronged with people. More arrived with each passing minute, until the narrow lane to the village was lined with mourners and the riverbank crowded on both sides.

The coffin was lowered onto the same simple farm cart that had borne Margaret's four years earlier, and a single shire horse was saddled up to make the short journey down to the riverbank. It was covered with wreaths, among them one from the garden of Highgate, Lloyd George's boyhood home. Beside the cart walked his grandsons Owen, David, Robin and Benjy, with the rest of the family walking behind, Frances first and Megan at a considerable distance. An old man rode on the cart as it made the final journey. He was Robert Evans, Lloyd George's childhood playmate by the river in Llanystumdwy.

The scene at the graveside was unforgettable, and there are many accounts of the congregation's heartfelt singing, and of people perched on trees and buildings to get a better view. Men in uniform stood next to newspaper reporters, family friends and members of the public who had come to pay their last respects. As the coffin was lowered into the ground the crowd fell silent, and Lloyd George went to his resting place accompanied only by the gushing sound of the Dwyfor in full spate. Frances and Megan stood at the graveside, again at a distance from each other, both looking emotional and strained. Ann Parry felt indescribably sad. 'Something big had gone out of our lives,' she wrote.[40]

Peace and harmony did not last long, as Megan and Olwen refused to go back to Tŷ Newydd for tea after the funeral. William George did go, and as he was preparing to walk back to Criccieth, Frances surprised him by presenting him with Lloyd George's silver-topped walking stick. He later wrote touchingly in his memoirs: 'And so, should a friend ask me as he sees me flourishing the stick on my walk, "Where did you get that handsome stick from?" I reply proudly, "I got this stick in remembrance of my late brother." '[41] As he was to discover when his brother's will was read in Brynawelon later that night, despite all the sacrifices he had made over the years, it was the only remembrance he was to receive.

Lloyd George's will deepened the rifts within his family after his death. Bron-y-De was left to Gwilym, with the outer ring of the farm left to Megan during her lifetime. Tŷ Newydd and all personal chattels and documents were left to Frances – there was no need to leave her any land in Churt, since she already owned Avalon and the adjoining farmland. Olwen was left some cottages on the estate, and Ann Parry was given one as well; but Dick received nothing, and an earlier bequest of £5,000 was withdrawn on the grounds that he had been given significant financial assistance during Lloyd George's lifetime. This would have been a devastating snub under any circumstances, but Dick was incandescent with rage that his father had taken a hereditary peerage, yet had left his heir nothing with which to support the title. His indignation was heightened by the memory, two years previously, of coming face to face in a London pub with a man who was his physical double.

Dick struck up a conversation and discovered that the stranger was an illegitimate son of Lloyd George's,* and that, unlike his legitimate offspring, he received a pension of £400 a year for life.

Much bitterness followed, with unjustified accusations made against Frances for having influenced Lloyd George during his last days. Eventually Dick resorted to legal challenge, which failed. Frances showed great magnanimity in later years by doing what she could to help her stepson.

As Lloyd George was buried, the war in Europe was drawing to a close, but the domestic war in Criccieth still raged furiously. Megan did not wait long before resuming hostilities. The day after the funeral, she gave vent to her feelings to the rest of the family. 'Megan made no secret of her deep-seated hatred of Frances,' wrote William George (Junior) in his diary. 'It was hatred like a spider's web within which she sought to entrap anyone who associated with Frances.'[42] She went on, with venom in her voice, to issue her uncle and cousin with an ultimatum: 'It's either her or me, and that goes for you too, William.' William George Senior was adamant that he was not going to be bossed around by 'bach y nyth' (the smallest in the nest), and continued to be civil to Frances and Jennifer. But shortly after the funeral Jennifer came face to face with her stepsister at the end of a film showing at the Memorial Hall. In front of everyone, to Jennifer's astonishment and distress, Megan cut her dead.

Tradesmen were told that if they supplied Tŷ Newydd, they would not be supplying Brynawelon any longer, and even the loyal Dr Prytherch was put under pressure to choose which of the two households he wanted as his patients (he would have none of it, and continued to look after Frances while she was in Criccieth). It was inevitable that others should be dragged into the dispute, and two camps gradually emerged, with Megan and Olwen at the head of one, and Frances and Ann Parry heading the other. Jennifer called it 'a guerrilla war',[43] and wrote an angry and upset account of each incident in her diary (which she later destroyed) to relieve her feelings. At a memorial service in

---

* Possibly the son of the Caernarvon widow 'Mrs J', who would have been the same age as Dick and who was reputed to have received an annuity.

Caernarvon to which Ann accompanied Frances, the Chairman of the North Wales Women's Liberal Federation closed her address by pointedly saying that she 'could not let this occasion pass without paying tribute to the memory of the late Dame Margaret Lloyd George who, as a young woman, had joined forces with David Lloyd George, and for several decades had encouraged, upheld and inspired him on his tempestuous journey through life'.[44] It was yet another reminder to Frances that the world did not recognise her role in Lloyd George's life.

Frances wished to establish a permanent, physical memorial to Lloyd George in his native village. She conceived a plan to build 'an agricultural centre for young people',[45] which in her view was the kind of practical memorial he would have wanted, in the middle of Llanystumdwy, on eleven acres of land she donated from the Tŷ Newydd estate. A committee was formed which included William George, the University of North Wales in Bangor was consulted, and plans drawn up, but Frances had underestimated the extent of the family's disapproval. They withheld their support and, as a result, Winston Churchill and other dignitaries declined to contribute to the appeal to finance the venture. A magnificent pair of iron gates was donated by the Borough of Caernarvon, but they led only to an empty site as plans for the college were gradually scaled down and finally mothballed. In the meantime, Ann Parry made her home in Llanystumdwy and carried on looking after Lloyd George's effects as curator of a small museum that had been founded when Frances donated his awards to the village. Even that transaction was problematic, with Frances having to resort to a solicitor's letter to retrieve awards that Megan had in her possession but which properly belonged to her. Eventually, Ann ventured to suggest that since the agricultural centre's site was standing empty, a permanent museum would be an equally suitable memorial. Her proposal was taken up enthusiastically, a larger collection was gathered together, and the museum now stands in Llanystumdwy as a tribute to the memory of the village's most famous son.

The bad feeling between Frances and the family did not ease with the passage of time. After Frances had arranged to have a protective ornamental enclosure put up around Lloyd George's burial place, with gates to allow access to the grave itself, she wrote to his children enclosing a key to the gates. She received no acknowledgement. Megan in particular was never to relent in her determination not to forgive Frances, who acknowledged in time that 'nothing [could] eradicate [her] original offence against the family'.[46] Many years later, in her autobiography, Frances had the good grace to write as her final comment on the feud, 'Looking at the case quite dispassionately, it was I who was to blame, not Megan, in the first place, and I suppose she was entitled so to regard it.'[47]

Recognising that she could never conquer Megan's antipathy, Frances concluded that she should not stay in Wales, and returned to Avalon. 'You have left the battlefield after winning the war,' was William George's comment.[48] Back in Churt, where she lived with her sister Muriel as a companion, any rumours there might have been concerning the irregularity of Frances' earlier life had been entirely cancelled out by her newfound respectability as Dowager Countess Lloyd-George, and she was in demand to open fêtes, chair charitable committees and act as President of the local Horticultural Association. She became a devout Anglican, and took her social duties to heart: it was the life that had been predicted for her when her grandmother had said that she would marry a clergyman and have ten children. But when an invitation came for Frances to open a fête in aid of the League of Moral Welfare, Muriel and Jennifer roared with laughter.

Megan, meanwhile, continued with her political career as best she could after the loss of the man who had been her political mentor as well as her father. The post-war years were turbulent politically, and she lost her Anglesey seat in 1951, having become intensely frustrated as her attempts to move the Welsh Liberal Party to the left to address the challenge from Labour failed. She finally broke with the Liberals in 1955 and joined the Labour Party, where her mature sympathies lay. There were those who attributed her decision to her relationship with Philip Noel-Baker, for their estrangement had lasted only until 1946, after which they resumed their affair. Megan returned to Parliament in a by-election in 1957 as the Labour Member for Carmarthen in South-West Wales. She won the seat at four successive elections, but despite her famous name (or perhaps because of it) she was never offered a ministerial position. Thelma Cazalet, who was not as close to Megan in her later years, wrote that the end of Megan's life 'did not match the exuberance of its beginning'.[49] Her political and personal lives were both to end in disappointment.

Philip Noel-Baker was still married to Irene when he persuaded Megan to rekindle their relationship, but his wife was not in good health, which gave Megan some hope. The two were lovers throughout the 1950s, and Philip wrote Megan a detailed letter explaining why he had not asked her to marry him when they first fell in love. He continued to protest his love for Megan, and his intention to marry her, right up until his wife's sudden death of a heart attack early in 1956. He spent some weeks in Greece sorting out his wife's affairs, then returned to Britain. Megan's friends confidently expected that, after the usual passage of time, he would marry her. Instead, in June 1956 he wrote her a devastating letter retracting all his earlier proposals and making it brutally clear that he would never marry her:

> My beloved, I must so start, tho' I know that it will grate on your ears ... I must now tell the truth, as I've always meant to tell it to you & never succeeded ... [When she died] I suddenly found, in an instant, that I loved Irene far more & far more deeply than I knew. I suddenly found that a knowledge of her wonderful qualities, & of her true nobility, was deeply embedded in my heart and mind ... I was unconscious of this, or nearly all of it, until Feb. 8th; then it swamped my life. It doesn't mean that I love you any less ... It does mean that I can't now give you what I would like to give, & would try desperately to give if it were any good. It does mean that when I am with you, or think of you, there is always present another dark, unhappy, very powerful train of thought, sometimes conscious, sometimes subconscious, but never absent. It does mean that I understand that I am now confronted by problems, & beset by anxieties & troubles, that I must face & resolve alone – & that I have no right to seek to see you, or to take from you any of the precious gifts of life & love & companionship & wisdom that you have given me with such prodigal generosity for so long.[50]

Megan was distraught. She continued to see Philip politically, but their love affair was over. A few years later a lump in her breast, left unheeded for too long, proved cancerous, and she died in 1966 at the age of sixty-four. Megan never made her peace with Frances, who returned to their former battleground at Criccieth to attend her funeral. Frances was not invited, nor did she feel welcome, but for reasons she did not explain she felt that she should be there to pay her final respects to her former pupil, former friend and implacable enemy.

The funeral was held on a sunny day, and the private service took place in Brynawelon's garden, which was at its loveliest. Cledwyn Hughes, newly appointed Secretary of State for Wales, was there, as was Gwynfor Evans, who would win the by-election in Carmarthen that was held as a result of Megan's death, becoming the first ever Plaid Cymru MP. Ursula Norton-Griffiths and her son Jeremy Thorpe were there, but Philip Noel-Baker stayed away.

Megan's obituaries all commented on her father's influence. In *The Times*, Dingle Foot wrote: 'Her likeness to her father has frequently been remarked. At times it seemed almost uncanny. There were the same eyes, the same gestures, the same inflections of the voice and, in large degree, the same mastery of the spoken word.'[51] Another tribute mentioned a book presented to Megan in which she was described as 'a true daughter of the Welsh Wizard: she bewitches friend and foe alike'.[52] She died as she lived, forever in her father's shadow.

Megan's death was the end of a chapter in Frances' life. While Megan was alive, she held back from publishing her papers, perhaps unwilling to provoke her stepdaughter. Things were bad enough as it was. But she pressed on with her plans for a memorial, determined to stand her ground as Lloyd George's legitimate widow. Olwen and Megan boycotted the official opening of the museum in Llanystumdwy on 28 May 1960, with Olwen telling the *Sunday Express* that 'they would be letting the family down' if they attended.[53] A few weeks later they both ignored Frances at the unveiling of a statue of Lloyd George in Cathays Park, Cardiff.

When Megan died, all fear of confrontation, as well as any hope of reconciliation that might have existed, were buried with her. The feud continued, albeit with some of the heat taken out of it. In 1970, when Frances was eighty-one years old, a service was held at Westminster Abbey to mark the unveiling of a plaque to Lloyd George by the Prince of Wales. The Liberal leader Jeremy Thorpe gave the address and the lessons were read by Harold Wilson and the Prime Minister, Edward

Heath. According to Frances, the singing was 'heavenly', but the family were a 'blot on the proceedings': Olwen 'was throwing her weight about and looked awful'. Later, in a broadcast to mark the occasion, Frances described Olwen as 'revolting with a face like a Cheshire cheese going mouldy, and full of giggles'.[54]

Having lost the private battle for the acceptance of Lloyd George's family, Frances decided to fight for public recognition instead. Her memoirs were published in 1967, revealing for the first time publicly that she had been Lloyd George's mistress for thirty years. 'The writing of this book has been good for my soul,' she wrote.[55] It was not the full story, though, for at Jennifer's request she omitted all references to her daughter.* The publication created a sensation – not least in Criccieth, where it revealed for the first time (after her death) the important part Sarah Jones had played in their early relationship. It was the first undisputed revelation of Lloyd George's irregular private life, and was well received – 'a frank story, artlessly dignified in the telling, and deeply interesting' according to the *Times Literary Supplement*.[56]

If Jennifer expected that as time went on Frances would be free to acknowledge her adopted daughter as her own, she was to be mistaken. Frances recorded a television interview with Fyfe Robertson in the late 1960s in which she discussed her life with Lloyd George. On the day of the broadcast a neighbour who knew that Frances' television was black and white invited Jennifer to watch the interview on her own colour set. Frances let her go without a word of warning of what she was about to hear. At the very end of the interview, Frances was asked a seemingly innocent question: had she ever regretted not having a child? As Jennifer sat in her neighbour's house, she heard her mother deny her very existence, saying, 'Lloyd George was my child.'

In 1971 more of Lloyd George's papers were published. Frances had sold all the papers in her possession (including her own diaries, although she later claimed that this was unintentional) to Lord Beaverbrook in 1950. She received only £15,000 for them, but Beaverbrook promised to form a committee of Lloyd George's former colleagues in government to revive the Lloyd George Memorial Fund as part of the bargain.

---

* Frances gave her ten-year-old granddaughter a copy of the book, curiously inscribed with Charles Kingsley's words 'Be good, sweet maid, and let who will be clever.'

Beaverbrook failed to form the committee, but Frances' diary, with all references to Jennifer carefully edited out, was published, and was hailed as a fascinating historical document. In an interview she gave to the *Liverpool Daily Post* to mark the publication, Frances said: 'I would have liked a large family. But in my day you did not have children unless you were married.'[57] Four years later, A.J.P. Taylor's edition of Frances' correspondence with Lloyd George announced Jennifer's existence to the wider world. Jennifer was astounded: it was the first time she had ever thought that 'Taid' might have been 'Father'.

The publication of Frances' story was the final shedding of the secrecy that had surrounded her private life for so long. With it, she achieved all that she had wanted: she had Lloyd George's name, and, in addition, public recognition of the part she had played in his life. Thereafter she gave many interviews to broadcasters and historians, defending her husband's memory and being consulted as an expert on his life and work. She even denoted her occupation as 'widow' on her passport.

Frances died on 5 December 1972, at the age of eighty-four. After six decades of devotion to Lloyd George and his memory, her journey was finally complete.

EPILOGUE

Frances outlived nearly all of those who had been close to her husband. Megan was quickly followed by William George, who died after a short illness in January 1967, only four weeks before he would have reached the age of 102. Within a month, Gwilym succumbed to a heart attack, and Dick followed in May 1968. But one member of the family lived on: Olwen, who never forgave her stepmother.

Olwen and Tom retired to North Wales in 1945. They bought Eisteddfa, a house on a hill overlooking Pentrefelin, the nearest village to Criccieth along the Porthmadoc Road. It had belonged to Tom's family, and he had spent holidays there as a child, but he would not enjoy living there for long. He was suffering from angina, and died suddenly in 1947 at the age of sixty-three. Olwen stayed on at Eisteddfa, close to her youngest son Benjy and his family. She raised money for local charities, wrote her memoir (published in 1985), and gave interviews about her famous family. She was, to the last, her parents' daughter, a staunch Liberal and a patriotic Welshwoman with a broad North Wales accent when she spoke in Welsh, while her surprisingly proper English accent was the outward sign of her extraordinary upbringing. She was awarded a DBE in 1969 for 'services to Wales', although unlike her mother she never used the title. Whenever she called at the Post Office to collect her pension, she would say 'Thank you, Father,' in recognition of the fact that it was he who introduced the old-age pension in 1908.

Olwen ended her days as the 'grand dame' of Eisteddfa. She learned to drive late in life, and as she approached her nineties she could still be seen pottering along the road to Criccieth to an event or committee meeting in her car. Her sons feared that she was a danger to herself and others, but Olwen was a determined old woman, and would not be told to slow down. Eventually, after a slight accident which grounded her for a few weeks, Benjy conspired with her doctor to deny her an insurance certificate, and the residents of Criccieth heaved a sigh of relief. Olwen died at the age of ninety-eight in 1990. She is buried with Tom in Pentrefelin, and a plaque to her memory can be seen on the Lloyd George family grave in Criccieth.

Of the women in Lloyd George's life, Olwen was survived only by Jennifer Stevenson. Jennifer's loss of her 'Taid' at the age of fifteen had a profound effect on her. Her relationship with Frances had been difficult for many years, but it deteriorated sharply after Lloyd George's death. After fifteen years of putting Lloyd George first, Frances was finally ready to be a mother, but her efforts were clumsy and inept. She turned to Jennifer to fill the gap in her life, and overwhelmed her with attention. Jennifer had developed an independent personality, and it was a case of too much too late. She had grown up in confusion as to whether she officially existed or not, and was not prepared to play the dutiful daughter now that her mother had time to give, although she tried hard not to let her resentment show.

Whatever her DNA might say, Lloyd George was the father in Jennifer's life, and she inherited his radical social views. After graduating from St Andrews University, she trained as a teacher with the intention of specialising in areas of deprivation. As part of her training she researched the lives of residents on a housing estate in Bristol. With typical thoroughness and commitment, she went to live with a family on the estate for a few months. Her observations are recorded in an extraordinary and shocking book, *Wellington Road*, which was published in 1962. Her account is startling in its raw description of the squalor and casual immorality she encountered, but it is also typically Jennifer: its impact comes from the fact that she passes on her observations without judgement, keeping herself and her opinions out of the picture. In adulthood, Jennifer was wholly unlike Frances. She became a Christian in her twenties, and there was little likelihood of her choosing a life as morally ambiguous as her mother's.

In January 1955, partly to escape Frances' oppressive attention, Jennifer accepted a teaching post in Tanganyika, East Africa. Frances paid her a Christmas visit, and as the Dowager Countess Lloyd-George, she was invited to lunch with Jennifer at the Governor's house. The Governor,

Lord Twining, was a kind but domineering man, and to Jennifer's private amusement Frances was appalled that the whole household revolved around him. The visit was fortuitous because Jennifer met Michael Longford, a twenty-eight-year-old civil servant in the Colonial Office who was serving as the Governor's private secretary. Over lunch they both decided, separately and silently, to marry; ten days later they were engaged. Jennifer was married in 1956, wearing a beautiful wedding dress Frances had brought over from England. She had to sell her grand piano to pay for it, a fact she hid from her daughter. It was a happy union that produced three children.

When the family returned to the UK after Tanganyika was awarded independence in 1961, tensions surfaced between Frances and Jennifer over Frances' well-intentioned attempts to interfere in her grandchildren's upbringing. Money was also a source of contention. It flowed through Frances' hands like water, and she sold a large number of her Lloyd George mementoes over the years to make ends meet. Jennifer confessed that, although she learned to get along with her mother over the years, she preferred the company of her Aunt Muriel, who did not feel she had to dominate or dictate.

Towards the end of Frances' life, Jennifer visited her regularly, occasionally escorting her on one of her 'official widow' functions. Frances lived with Muriel in Farm Cottage on the Churt estate, having sold Avalon in the early 1960s. When she died, Jennifer was first on the scene to close her eyes. As she kissed Frances goodbye, it was the first time in her life that she had touched her mother 'without some inward reluctance'.[1]

Lloyd George once wrote to his brother that 'the biography of living persons is not a thing to be encouraged. Personally I hate it in my own case, as I feel confident I shall be a much more interesting person dead than alive. Apart from that, the story is not complete; you cannot have the necessary perspective.'[2] And so we will leave Jennifer's story at the time of her mother's death, in the hope that someone will complete it in years to come.

'Like many men of genius,' wrote Frances of her husband in 1948, 'the friendship of women was a necessity to him, and he could persuade each one of them, even the most intelligent, that she alone really understood him. He compelled unreasoning and passionate adoration. He charmed and was irresistible. His voice alone was a seduction.'[3] He loved women as much as women loved him. 'Lloyd George was very frank about liking women,' according to Frances. 'Though he preferred women who were good conversationalists he liked them to be womanly. He loved them to be dressed in soft fabrics, silks, satins, anything that had a rustle.'[4] 'Many of his friends,' wrote Olwen, 'felt he should be protected against women; they flocked round him and often threw themselves at him.'[5] Everyone who came into contact with him noted the hypnotic effect he had on the opposite sex, and this amused Frances as much as it annoyed Margaret. 'I was unable to stay to hear the end of a speech as we were all turned out of the Ladies' Gallery at 7.30 in accordance with an absurd rule to that effect,' wrote Frances in 1934. 'The Sergeant at Arms found difficulty in getting us out, & he said to me as I went: "I wish you would get your man to sit down before 7.30. I always have the greatest difficulty in getting the ladies out of the Gallery if he is speaking!" '[6]

It was Lloyd George's good fortune that he was able to share his life with two outstanding women. Margaret, despite her thoroughly Victorian upbringing, was politically adept and carved out a public career independently of her husband. Her life fell into three phases. In the first, she married and raised her family. In the second she stepped forward, sharing the limelight to support her husband and work alongside him. Finally she became a public figure in her own right, pursuing her own causes and wielding considerable national influence.

Frances, despite her Edwardian views on female emancipation, was far more in Lloyd George's shadow than Margaret. She left university craving the freedom to choose her fate. She loved the man of her choice, and sacrificed conventional goals such as marriage, family and respectability for many years. But she was never the liberated woman she aspired to be in her youth. She became financially and emotionally dependent on Lloyd George. He dominated her life, and she had no real freedom of her own.

Frances was Lloyd George's soulmate, whereas Margaret was his consort and his wife. Frances kept him happy, but Margaret kept him up to the mark. She never let him get away with anything, and he respected her for it. Margaret connected with Lloyd George in a way that Frances never did. In 1934, Frances had been Lloyd George's mistress for more than twenty years, yet she still failed to understand the way in which he looked at the world: 'D. very angry because a Welsh Broadcasting Committee had been treated de haut en bas by a B.B.C. official (not Sir John Reith, but a subordinate),' she wrote in her diary. 'He always rises in wrath when anything like this happens, having an inferiority complex about his race. He says he can understand the hatred of English officials abroad, with their air of self-satisfaction & their contempt of "lesser breeds".'[7] Frances puzzled at his 'inferiority complex'; Margaret would have shared his outrage.

Lloyd George believed every word he said to both his wives. If he had not been honest, the edifice would have come tumbling down – they were not stupid women, and could see through pretence. They were both first in his heart, but in different ways. This ability of his to compartmentalise and tap into different facets of his soul at different times led people to conclude that he was devious and untrustworthy. A kinder and no less valid interpretation would be to compare it to acting. A good actor believes what he is saying at the moment he says it, even if it contradicts what he has said in a play the night before. Lloyd George was sincere about his feelings for both women. He was 'very dependent' upon Frances, yet his affection for Margaret came and went 'no more than the sea does because the tide ebbs & flows'. He reached into different parts of his heart when he was with each woman, and each believed in his sincerity.

Megan was the third groundbreaking woman in Lloyd George's life. She learned politics at his knee, and never broke free of his influence. Her father was the dominant figure in her life to the end, and after his death she was as much the professional widow as Frances. All three women were pioneers. Margaret was the first female JP in Wales, and Frances the first female Private Secretary to a Prime Minister. Megan went further than either of them, and her career shows how far women's lives had changed. Margaret never considered a profession: she was trained for marriage, and entered public life only because of circumstance. Frances started out with ambitions of independence and professional achievement, but her advancement did not rely on her professional ability alone. Megan, on the other hand, had a career, and one for which she passed up many chances of marriage (albeit not to the man she loved). Her private life mirrored that of Frances, but her professional life was very different. She was the first woman MP ever to be elected in Wales, and one of only fourteen female Members in the House of Commons. By the time of her death female politicians had ceased to be a novelty.

Lloyd George encouraged each of them to make the most of her potential. He was interested in women, not just sexually attracted to them, and urged the women he loved to take opportunities – as long as they did not conflict with the comfort and companionship he needed. He supported suffrage because it was self-evident to him that women should be treated equally to men in terms of voting and rights of citizenship. He had grown up in an 'equal' society in which women ran businesses and were breadwinners alongside men. His grandmother Rebecca and his mother Betsy, both widowed, held the family together. They were capable women, broad-minded despite their lack of education, lacking only the opportunities that they secured for Lloyd George and his brother. Lloyd George honoured their memory as he strove to extend those opportunities to women of all backgrounds.

Not many women had cause to berate Lloyd George for treating them badly. He made clear to his lovers that while he would not divorce his wife, they could count on his respect and loyalty as long as they stuck to the roles he had assigned them. The exception was Margaret herself. He did not make clear to her the limits of his commitment, and that his personal interpretation of the wedding vows excluded sexual fidelity. The discovery of this side of his character was painful to her, and ultimately damaging to their relationship. But he did marry for life, and he put her first, even if it was at the head of a lengthy line. That he loved Frances too is beyond doubt, even if he treated her badly at times. Tom Carey Evans, a wise man who knew Lloyd George well enough not to be in thrall to him, spoke the truth about many great men and women when he said that he preferred to view Lloyd George through a telescope than a microscope.

He may have been difficult to live with and chronically unfaithful, but however much they resented each other, the women in Lloyd George's life did not leave him, even after social taboos had loosened and made it possible for them to change their rules of engagement with him. His charisma and the extraordinary force of his personality held them in an iron grip. Margaret and Frances both suffered great pain because of him, but they also lived extraordinary lives because of their association with Lloyd George. Their stories exemplify both the pain and the privilege of loving and living with a great man.

ACKNOWLEDGEMENTS

My thanks go to the many people who helped me piece together the story contained in this book: to Michael Sissons and my editors at Harper Collins – Richard Johnson, Robert Lacey and Arabella Pike; to the staff at the National Library of Wales, the House of Lords Records Office, and the Caernarfon Record Office for their patience and help in sifting through thousands of boxes of original documents; to BBC Wales for permission to read and quote from transcripts in their archive; to Avis and Robert Ronald at A&R Booksearch for tracking down many out-of-print books for me; to Elana Cheah for her painstaking work; to my colleagues and friends at Hanson Green for their forbearance over the past three years; to Glyn, Menna and the staff at the Harbourmaster Hotel in Aberaeron for their warm welcome during my research trips to West Wales; to Keith Simpson MP and Sir Martin Gilbert for their helpful suggestions; to Graham Jones at the National Library of Wales for sharing with me his unrivalled knowledge of the Lloyd George archives; and to Lord Morgan of Aberdovey and Mr Stuart Lavery, both experts in their fields, for helping me make sure of my facts. Any errors or omissions that remain in the book are, of course, mine and mine alone.

A special thank you to those who shared with me their memories of Lloyd George, Margaret, Frances and Megan: Earl and Countess Lloyd George and Mrs Greta George, who were extremely generous hosts; Dr W.R.P. George, who sadly died during the writing of the book but who was an inspiration to me during the final months of his life; Mrs Jennifer Longford and Ruth Nixon, who gave up a great deal of their time to talk to me; and also Robbie Lloyd George, Lord Tenby, Mrs Margaret Barratt, David Carey Evans, Robin Carey Evans, Lord Hunt and Anita George. Thank you also to the many individuals who wrote to me suggesting that a parent or grandparent could have been an illegitimate child of Lloyd George's – sadly no evidence came to light to substantiate the vast majority, but they certainly confirmed that Lloyd George's reputation was well known in North Wales.

And last but not least, my thanks to my husband William, who has never failed to encourage and support me since I began to work on this subject. Both his political insight and his experience as an author have been invaluable resources for me to have 'on tap', and I am grateful to him for the considerable good humour and understanding he has shown during the writing of this book.

NOTES

David Lloyd George's diary is in the William George Papers, National Library of Wales, reproduced by permission of the National Library of Wales.

Frances Stevenson's diary is in the Frances Stevenson (FLS) Papers, House of Lords Records Office, reproduced by permission of the Parliamentary Archives acting on behalf of the Beaverbrook Foundation.

A.J. Sylvester's diary is in the A.J. Sylvester Papers, National Library of Wales, reproduced by permission of the National Library of Wales.

Correspondence between David Lloyd George and the Lloyd George family is in the Brynawelon Group, William George Papers and Earl Lloyd-George Papers, National Library of Wales, reproduced by permission of the National Library of Wales.

Correspondence between David Lloyd George and Frances Stevenson is in the Lloyd George (LG) Papers and Frances Stevenson (FLS) Papers, House of Lords Records Office, reproduced by permission of the Parliamentary Archives acting on behalf of the Beaverbrook Foundation.

Jennifer Longford's unpublished autobiography is in the Frances Stevenson Papers, National Library of Wales, reproduced by permission of the National Library of Wales.

INTRODUCTION

1 Lord Boothby interview, *At Home*, BBC Wales 1963
2 Frances Stevenson, BBC interview April 1970
3 Frances Stevenson, 'The Private Secretary', p.5, Ruth Longford Papers
4 Parry, p.50

CHAPTER 1: Hewn from the Rock

1 George, W., *Richard Lloyd*, p.3, quoting from an article in *Yr Ymwelydd*, 1915
2 George, W., *My Brother & I*, p.9
3 Ibid., p.3
4 George, W.R.P., *The Making of Lloyd George*, p.39

5 Ibid., p.43
6 Ibid., p.45
7 Ibid., p.60
8 Elizabeth George to Mr Goffrey, William George Papers 7974

CHAPTER 2: The Cottage-Bred Man

1 George, W., *Richard Lloyd*, p.31
2 *Lord Riddell's War Diary 1914–1918*, p.274
3 'In the Days of my Youth', DLG, reprinted in *Tit-Bits*, December 1916, Caernarvon Records File
4 George, W., *My Brother & I*, p.10
5 'In the Days of my Youth'
6 George, W., *Richard Lloyd*, p.87
7 FS Diary, 12 February 1934, FLS/5/2
8 George, W., *My Brother & I*, p.92

9 DLG to William George, 21 August 1895
10 'In the Days of my Youth'
11 George, W., *My Brother & I*, p.17
12 DLG Diary, 8 February 1884
13 Mrs Greta George in conversation with the author, August 2005
14 George, W., *My Brother & I*, p.74
15 D.R. Daniel Memoir, p.9, Daniel Papers
16 FS Diary, 10 April 1934 (this and all following quotations translated from Welsh)

CHAPTER 3: Love's Infatuated Devotee

1 George, W., *Richard Lloyd*, p.71
2 Viscount Gwynedd, *Dame Margaret*, p.232
3 Rowland, p.22
4 McCormick, *The Mask of Merlin*, p.31
5 George, W.R.P., *The Making of Lloyd George*, p.100
6 DLG Diary, 12 November 1881
7 George, W., *Richard Lloyd*, p.101
8 DLG Diary, 24 April 1886
9 George, W., *My Brother & I*, pp.110–11
10 DLG Diary, 9 May 1880, George, W.R.P., *The Making of Lloyd George*, p.97
11 Ibid., 25 January 1880, George, W.R.P., *88 Not Out*, p.18
12 Ibid., 26 March 1880, George, W.K.P., *The Making of Lloyd George*, p.93
13 Ibid., 29 March 1880, ibid.
14 Ibid., 17 June 1880
15 Ibid., July 1880, George, W.R.P., *The Making of Lloyd George*, p.99
16 George, W.R.P., *88 Not Out*, p.22
17 DLG Diary, 31 December 1880
18 Ibid., 9 and 10 May 1880, George, W.R.P., *The Making of Lloyd George*, p.97
19 Ibid., 24 September 1883
20 George, W.R.P., *The Making of Lloyd George*, p.106
21 George, W.R.P., *88 Not Out*, p.24
22 Ibid.
23 DLG Diary, 25 November 1883, George, W.R.P., *The Making of Lloyd George*, pp.115–16
24 Ibid., 18 June 1884
25 Ibid.
26 Ibid., 23 March 1885, George, W., *My Brother & I*, pp.94–5

27 George, W.R.P., *The Making of Lloyd George*, p.136

CHAPTER 4: Maggie Owen

1 DLG Diary, June 1885, George, W.R.P., *The Making of Lloyd George*, p.138
2 Ibid., May 1885, ibid., p.136
3 Ibid., 17 June 1885
4 Lloyd George, R., *Dame Margaret*, p.36
5 DLG to Margaret Owen, 30 December 1885
6 DLG Diary, 7 Jan 1886, George, W.R.P., *The Making of Lloyd George*, p.138
7 Ibid., 4 February 1886, ibid.
8 Ibid., 7 February 1886, ibid.
9 Ibid.
10 Ibid., 15 Feb 1886, ibid., p.139
11 Ibid., 27 June 1886, ibid.
12 Ibid., 22 July 1886, ibid.
13 Ibid., 25 August 1886, ibid., p.140
14 Ibid.
15 DLG to Margaret Owen, postmarked 28 August 1886
16 DLG Diary, 1 October 1886, George, W.R.P., *The Making of Lloyd George*, p.141
17 Ibid., 20 June 1886, George, W., *My Brother & I*, p.131
18 Ibid., 11 November 1886, George, W.R.P., *The Making of Lloyd George*, p.141
19 Ibid., 13 November 1886, ibid.
20 DLG to Margaret Owen, 19 November 1886
21 DLG to Margaret Owen, 23 November 1886
22 Margaret Owen to DLG, George, W.R.P., *The Making of Lloyd George*, p.145
23 DLG to Margaret Owen, 8 December 1886
24 DLG to Mr Thomas, 26 January 1887
25 DLG to Margaret Owen, Thursday 1 a.m., William George Papers 4615
26 DLG to Margaret Owen, undated, but written early in 1887, clearly not in 1886 or 1885 as has been asserted by other biographers, because it is addressed to 'dearest Miss Owen', which dates it after November 1886,

and because in DLG's pocketbook, in which he kept copies of all his letters, it follows the letter to the jeweller in January 1887. A postscript to the letter reads: 'You will probably get your ring straight from Birmingham by this morning's post. It will afford you another opportunity to show your grit.' NLW

27 DLG to Margaret Owen, no date, William George Papers 4615
28 DLG to Margaret Owen, Wednesday evening 10 p.m., ibid.
29 Dame Margaret LG interview, April 1940, Morgan Humphreys Collection

CHAPTER 5: Mrs Lloyd George

1 DLG Diary, 27 March 1887
2 Ibid., 22 March 1887, George, W.R.P., The Making of Lloyd George, p.146
3 DLG to Margaret Owen, postmarked 25 September 1886, Morgan, Lloyd George Family Letters, p.65
4 Lloyd George, R., Dame Margaret, p.72
5 DLG Diary, 30 March 1887
6 Ibid., 3 April 1887
7 Ibid., 30 August 1887, Morgan, Lloyd George Family Letters, p.19
8 DLG to Margaret Owen, postmarked 18 July 1887
9 DLG to Margaret Owen, 6 August 1887, Grigg, The Young Lloyd George, p.71
10 George, W.R.P., The Making of Lloyd George, p.149
11 DLG Diary, 3 September 1887, Morgan, Lloyd George Family Letters, p.20
12 George, W.R.P., The Making of Lloyd George, p.149
13 DLG Diary, 5 October 1887
14 Ibid., 1 November 1887, Morgan, Lloyd George Family Letters, p.21
15 Ibid., 8 November 1887, ibid., pp.21–2
16 William George Diary, 3 May 1891, George, W.R.P., The Making of Lloyd George, p.175
17 DLG Diary, 9 January 1888, George, W., My Brother & I, p.99
18 Ibid., 10 January 1888

19 George, W.R.P., The Making of Lloyd George, p.149, DLG Diary, 19 January 1888
20 Ibid., 20 January 1888
21 Ibid., 24 January 1888
22 Richard Lloyd Diary, 24 January 1888

CHAPTER 6: From Wales to Westminster

1 DLG to D.R. Daniel, 24 January 1887, Daniel Papers
2 DLG Diary, 3 February 1888, George, W.R.P., The Making of Lloyd George, p.151
3 Margaret LG to DLG, undated, William George Papers 4820
4 Carey Evans, p.28
5 George, W.R.P., 88 Not Out, p.30
6 Margaret LG to DLG, undated, William George Papers 4821
7 Du Parcq, Volume 1, pp.86–7
8 Lloyd George, R., Lloyd George, pp.42, 232
9 Carey Evans, pp.63–4
10 Dame Margaret LG interview, April 1940, Morgan Humphreys Collection
11 Du Parcq, Volume 1, p.95
12 William George Diary, 7 April 1890, George, W.R.P., The Making of Lloyd George, p.169
13 Grigg, The Young Lloyd George, p.84
14 George, W.R.P., Lloyd George: Backbencher, p.2
15 Ibid.
16 Richard Lloyd Diary, 11 April 1890, George W.R.P., The Making of Lloyd George, p.170

CHAPTER 7: Kitty Edwards

1 Lloyd George, R., Dame Margaret, p.228. Lloyd George's words quoted in an unidentified newspaper article in 1938 at the time of their golden wedding anniversary
2 Caernarvon and Denbigh Herald, 2 May 1890, ibid., p.98
3 Grigg, The Young Lloyd George, p.97
4 Du Parcq, Volume 1, p.101
5 George, W.R.P., Lloyd George: Backbencher, p.7

6 George, W.R.P., *The Making of Lloyd George*, pp. 173–4

7 Mary Ellen George to William George, 21 April 1891

8 George, W.R.P., *Lloyd George Backbencher*, pp.15–16

9 Margaret LG to DLG, undated, William George Papers 4825

10 Margaret LG to DLG, undated, ibid. 4829

11 Margaret LG to DLG, undated, ibid. 4827

12 DLG to Margaret LG, 23 June 1890

13 Ibid.

14 *Daily Star*, 12 January 1938

15 Rowland, p.85

16 Margaret LG to DLG, undated, William George Papers 4824

17 DLG to Margaret LG, undated, Morgan, *Lloyd George Family Letters*, p.65

18 Ibid.

19 DLG to Margaret LG, 11 November 1895

20 DLG to Margaret LG, 18 February 1896

21 Grigg, *The Young Lloyd George*, p.247

22 DLG to Margaret LG, undated, ibid., pp. 247–8

23 'RFL' to DLG, undated, Lloyd George Correspondence, 22520E

24 'Kate' to DLG, undated, Lloyd George Papers, National Library of Wales

25 Ibid.

26 25 November 1890, NCW 20407C, No. 141

27 27 November 1890, ibid.

28 Lloyd George, R., *Lloyd George*, p.62

29 George, W.R.P., *Lloyd George: Backbencher*, p. 209

30 W. George Diary, 11 October 1896, ibid., p. 210

31 R.O. Roberts to DLG, 12 October 1896, ibid. p.211

32 K. Edwards to DLG, postmarked 15 February 1894, S.T. Evans Collection

33 Margaret LG to William George, George, W.R.P., *Lloyd George: Backbencher*, p. 223

34 Ibid., p.229

35 *Times* Law Reports, 17 and 20 June 1899

CHAPTER 8: Mrs Tim

1 Lloyd George, R., *Lloyd George*, p.54

2 DLG to Margaret LG, 24 July 1924

3 Lloyd George, R., *Lloyd George*, p.60

4 DLG to Margaret LG, 27 May 1897, Rowland, p.129

5 Carey Evans, p. 63

6 DLG to Margaret LG, 28 May 1897

7 DLG to Margaret LG, 6 August 1897

8 Richard Lloyd Diary, 13 August 1897

9 DLG to William George, 13 August 1897, George, W.R.P., *Lloyd George Backbencher*, p.244

10 DLG to Margaret LG, 19 August 1897

11 DLG to Margaret LG, 20 August 1897, Rowland, p.130

12 DLG to Margaret LG, postmarked 21 August 1897

13 DLG to Margaret LG, 21 August 1897

14 Carey Evans, p.1

15 DLG to Margaret LG, 4 March 1896

16 DLG to Margaret LG, 23 December 1897

17 Sylvester, *The Real Lloyd George*, pp.63–4

18 Lloyd George, R., *Lloyd George*, p.48

19 DLG to William George, 9 July 1898

20 Carey Evans, p.16

21 Ibid., p.9

22 DLG to Margaret LG, 11 February 1896

23 Ibid.

24 DLG to Margaret LG, 29 July 1896

25 DLG to Margaret LG, 26 May 1897

26 DLG to Margaret LG, 11 August 1897

27 William George Diary, 6 January 1898, George, W.R.P., *Lloyd George Backbencher*, p.280

28 Margaret LG to DLG, 10 August 1898

29 Margaret LG to DLG, dated 'Thursday evening'

30 DLG to Margaret LG, 13 August 1898, Morgan, *Lloyd George Family Letters*, pp.113–14

31 DLG to Margaret LG, dated 15 August 1898

32 DLG to Margaret LG, dated 20 August 1898

33 Grigg, *The Young Lloyd George*, p. 244 dated 8 September 1898, DLG to Margaret LG, 8 September 1898

34 Margaret LG to DLG, 'Friday', Grigg, *The Young Lloyd George*, p.244

35 Margaret LG to DLG, 11 September 1898
36 DLG to Margaret LG, 12 September 1898
37 DLG to Margaret LG, 13 September 1898
38 DLG to Margaret LG, 18 September 1898
39 Grigg, *The Young Lloyd George*, p.219, AJS Diary, 6 October 1933
40 Timothy Davies to DLG, 20 November 1918, LG Papers, LG/F/94/3/76
41 DLG to Margaret LG, 7 January 1899
42 Margaret LG to DLG, 22 September 1899
43 DLG to Margaret LG, 23 October 1899

CHAPTER 9: Mair

1 Camplin, Jamie, *The Rise of the Plutocrats*, quoted Wilson, p.43
2 Ibid., p.53
3 Margaret LG, 'Petticoats Behind Politics', *Sunday Herald*, 12 June 1927
4 DLG to Margaret LG, 27 April 1892
5 Mary Ellen George to William George and Richard Lloyd, 1 July 1897
6 Du Parcq, Volume 2, p.218
7 Carey Evans, p.20
8 Ibid., p.66
9 DLG to Margaret LG, 17 March 1902
10 DLG to Margaret LG, 23 May 1902
11 DLG to Margaret LG, 24 May 1902
12 *Daily Argus*, 19 December 1901
13 Ibid.
14 Ibid.
15 Carey Evans, p.21
16 Ibid., p.26
17 DLG to Richard Lloyd, 13 November 1907, George, W., *My Brother & I*, p.213
18 Lloyd George, R., *Dame Margaret*, p.106
19 D.R. Daniel Memoir, p.13
20 Watkin Davies, p.279
21 Lloyd George, F., *The Years that are Past*, p.27
22 FS Diary, 10 March 1934, FLS/4/9
23 DLG to William George, 4 May 1891
24 *Daily News*, 30 November 1907
25 George, W.R.P., *88 Not Out*, p.39
26 R. Lloyd Diary, George, W., *My Brother & I*, p.215

27 *The Years that are Past*, p.31
28 *Y Cymro*, 5 December 1907
29 Press report, unattributed, Lloyd George Papers
30 Unattributed newspaper article, Lloyd George 2 Papers, 22519E
31 HRH Queen Alexandra to DLG, Lloyd George Papers
32 Herbert Lewis Diary, 3 December 1907, Grigg, *Lloyd George: The People's Champion, 1902–1911*, p.126
33 Unattributed newspaper article, Lloyd George 2 Papers, 22519E
34 D.R. Daniel Memoir, p.12
35 George, W., *My Brother & I*, p.219
36 DLG to Margaret LG, 4 December 1907
37 *The Years that are Past*, p.49
38 George, W., *My Brother & I*, p.218
39 DLG to Margaret LG, 5 January 1908, Morgan, *Lloyd George Family Letters*, p.150
40 D.R. Daniel Memoir, p.13
41 FS Diary, 10 March 1934, FLS/4/9
42 George, W., *My Brother & I*, pp.217–18
43 Lloyd George, R., *Dame Margaret*, p.50
44 D.R. Daniel Memoir, p.64
45 Asquith to Lloyd George, 8 April 1908. NLW
46 Sylvester, A.J., *The Real Lloyd George*, p.50
47 Rowland, p.226 quoting from Lucy Masterman's memoir

CHAPTER 10: Frances

1 29 April 1909, Parliamentary Debates
2 Rowland, p.221
3 Ibid., p.222
4 George, W., *My Brother & I*, p.27
5 *The Years that are Past*, p.40
6 Ibid., p.27
7 Ibid., p.32
8 Ibid., p.34
9 Ibid., p.20
10 Ibid., p.39
11 Longford, R., p.10
12 *The Years that are Past*, p.30
13 Longford, R., p.8
14 *The Years that are Past*, p.22
15 Ninette Stevenson to FS, FLS /1/1
16 Grigg, Vol. 3, p.80

17 Carey Evans, p.68
18 Margaret LG to Mrs Woodhouse, 18 July 1911, FLS/1/14
19 Olwen LG to FS, 28 July 1911, FLS/1/2
20 *The Years that are Past*, p.42
21 DLG to Margaret LG, undated, Morgan, *Lloyd George Family Letters*, p.156
22 *The Years that are Past*, p.43
23 Frances LG, BBC interview, 28 April 1970, NLW FA1/7
24 DLG to Megan LG, 7 August 1911, Morgan, *Lloyd George Family Letters*, p.157
25 Olwen LG to FS, 4 October 1912, FLS Papers
26 *The Years that are Past*, pp.44–5
27 Ibid., p.50
28 *The Years that are Past*, p.48
29 FS to Sian, November 1912, FLS/6/19
30 *The Years that are Past*, p.51
31 NLW MS 22515C
32 FS Diary, 20 November 1914, FLS/4/1
33 Ibid., 24 May 1921, FLS/4/7
34 *The Years that are Past*, p.50
35 Ibid., p.52
36 Ibid.
37 Ibid., pp.52–3
38 Ibid., p.53
39 Ibid., p.55
40 Ibid., p.56

CHAPTER 11: Overloaded with Flattery

1 *The Years that are Past*, p.42
2 Ibid., pp.53–4
3 Ibid., p.56
4 DLG to FS, undated, FLS/1/2
5 *The Years that are Past*, p.70
6 'An anonymous woman' to DLG, 12 November 1913, LG Papers, LG/C/10/2/25
7 Mr A.E. Widdows to Mr J. Rowland, 22 June 1907
8 Frances Stevenson, 'The Private Secretary', p.8, Ruth Longford Papers
9 Ibid., p.7
10 FS Diary, 25 January 1915, FLS/4/1
11 *The Years that are Past*, p.58
12 *ST Weekly Review*, 28 September 1975
13 *The Years that are Past*, pp.58–9

14 FS Diary, 15 November 1915, FLS/4/2
15 DLG to Julia Henry, 16 August 1907, Grigg, *Lloyd George: From Peace to War*, p.87n
16 DLG to Margaret LG, 28 December 1907
17 Julia Henry to Charles Henry, 21 November 1911, Grigg, *Lloyd George: From Peace to War*, p.87
18 FS Diary, 28 November 1919, FLS/4/11
19 Grigg, *Lloyd George: The People's Champion*, pp.183–4 (and all quotes following)
20 Ibid., p.182
21 DLG to Sir Luke Fildes, LG Papers, LG I/2/1/8C

CHAPTER 12: Love and Libel

1 Lloyd George, R., *Lloyd George*, p. 112
2 *People*, 14 March 1909
3 M. Griffith to DLG, 22 March 1909
4 M. Griffith to DLG, 25 March 1909
5 FS Diary, 21 September 1914, FLS/4/1
6 Frances Stevenson, 'The Private Secretary', pp.4–5, Ruth Longford Papers
7 FS Diary, 18 February 1920, FLS/4/5
8 DLG to FS, 5 June 1916, MPD, p.16; August 1918, FLS/6/1; 2 May 1922, ibid.
9 *Saturday Night*, Women's Section, Toronto, 23 September 1922, LG F/93/1/2
10 Margaret LG to DLG, undated, 22515 NLW
11 Longford, R., p.15
12 FS Diary, 10 March 1917, FLS/4/4
13 Ibid., 1 February 1917, ibid.
14 Lloyd George, R., *Lloyd George*, p.59
15 Ibid., p.32
16 FLS/6/26
17 FS Diary, 1 February 1917, FLS/4/4
18 DLG to FS, 6 April 1915, Taylor, A.J.P. (ed.), *My Darling Pussy*, p.7
19 *The Years that are Past*, p.58
20 J.T. Davies to FS, May 1913, FLS/1/2
21 J.T. Davies to FS, 7 August 1913, ibid.
22 Sylvester, *The Real Lloyd George*, p.49
23 DLG to FS, 20 August 1925
24 Sylvester, *The Real Lloyd George*, p.49
25 Ibid., pp.48–9

26 Carey Evans, p.39
27 *The Years that are Past*, pp.72–3

CHAPTER 13: A Family in Downing Street

1 DLG to Margaret LG, 3 August 1914, Morgan, *Lloyd George Family Letters*, p.167
2 *Sunday News*, 7 August 1927
3 Grigg, *Lloyd George: From Peace to War*, p.409
4 *Sunday News*, 21 August 1927
5 Carey Evans, p.40
6 Clifford, p.187
7 Ibid., p.467
8 *Sunday News*, 28 August 1927
9 Carey Evans, p.72
10 *Riddell Diaries 1908–23*, p.188
11 DLG to Margaret LG, 11 March 1914, Morgan, *Lloyd George Family Letters*, p.166
12 Carey Evans, p.47
13 Ibid., pp.61–2
14 Ibid., p.71
15 *South Wales News*, 13 July 1911, NLW Ex 566
16 Carey Evans, pp.54–6
17 Jones, M., p.18
18 Carey Evans, p.42
19 Ibid., p.43
20 Ibid.
21 Ibid., pp.82–4
22 Ibid., p.85
23 Ibid., p.169
24 DLG to Margaret LG, 19 November 1895
25 Grigg, *The Young Lloyd George*, p.226
26 DLG to Margaret LG, 24 September 1899, Morgan, *Lloyd George Family Letters*, p.122
27 George, W., *My Brother & I*, p.102

CHAPTER 14: Secrets and Smokescreens

1 FS Diary, 21 September 1914 FLS/4/1
2 DLG to Sir Edward Russell, *Liverpool Daily Post*, 27 January 1914, Rowland, pp.314–15
3 FS Diary, 25 April 1915, FLS/4/1
4 Ibid., 9 February 1916, ibid.
5 Ibid., 8 February 1915, ibid.

6 DLG to FS, Taylor, *My Darling Pussy*, p.3
7 FS Diary, 8 February 1915, FLS/4/1
8 Ibid., 20 November 1914, ibid.
9 DLG to FS, 8 August 1915, FLS/6/19
10 FS Diary, 17 January 1915, FLS/4/1
11 Ibid., 11 February 1915, ibid.
12 Ibid., 23 February 1915, ibid.
13 Ibid.
14 Carey Evans, p.94
15 FS Diary, 10 May 1915, FLS/4/1
16 Ibid., 11 March 1915, ibid.
17 Ibid.
18 DLG to FS, 23 August 1915, FLS/6
19 FS Diary, 5 October 1915, FLS/4/2.
20 Ibid.
21 Billy Owen to FS, 11 October 1915, FLS/1/3
22 Billy Owen to FS, 20 October 1915, ibid.
23 FS Diary, 23 October 1915, FLS/4/2
24 Ibid., 8 February 1916, FLS/4/3
25 Ibid., 24 November 1915, FLS/4/2
26 Louise Stevenson to FS, 7 March 1917, FLS/1/4
27 *The Years that are Past*, p.80
28 FS Diary, 12 June 1915, FLS/4/1
29 Ibid., 4 August 1916, FLS/4/3
30 Ibid., 12 March 1916, ibid.

CHAPTER 15: Two Wives at No. 10

1 DLG to William George, 6 December 1916
2 George, W., *Richard Lloyd*, p.161
3 FLS Papers, NCW D3
4 Asquith, M., Volume 2, p.77
5 *Sunday News*, 21 August 1927
6 FS Diary, 23 April 1917, FLS/4/4
7 *The Years that are Past*, p.101
8 FS Diary, 1 February 1917, FLS/4/4
9 Ibid., 19 November 1916, FLS/4/3
10 *The Years that are Past*, pp.68–9
11 FS Diary, 4 April 1915, FLS/4/1
12 Ibid., 11 November 1916, FLS/4/3
13 Frances LG, Introduction to Thomson, *David Lloyd George: The Official Biography*
14 FS Diary, 21 January 1915, FLS/4/1
15 Ibid., 9 February 1917, FLS/4/4
16 Ibid., 29 April 1917, ibid.
17 Ibid., 28 May 1917, ibid.

18 *Lord Riddell's War Diary 1914–1918*, p.155
19 FS Diary, 15 January 1917, FLS/4/4
20 Carey Evans, p.63
21 Ibid. p.68
22 Ibid.
23 FS Diary, 21 April 1917, FLS/4/4
24 Ibid., 19 May 1917, ibid.

CHAPTER 16: The Family at War

1 FS Diary, 16 May 1915, FLS/4/1
2 DLG to FS, 5 June 1916, *My Darling Pussy*, pp.15–16
3 FS Diary, 26 July 1916, FLS/4/3
4 George, W., *Richard Lloyd*, p.161
5 *The Times*, 1 March 1917
6 FS Diary, 24 February 1917, FLS/4/4
7 Ibid., 1 March 1917, ibid.
8 *The Times*, 17 February 1917
9 Ibid., 5 March 1917
10 FS Diary, 6 December 1915, FLS/4/2
11 Ibid., 9 April 1917, FLS/4/4
12 *The Times*, 9 April 1917
13 FS Diary, 2 April 1917, FLS/4/4
14 Ibid.
15 Margaret LG interview, 'How do You Help Your Husband?', *Daily Express*, 1934, AJS Papers C25
16 Ibid.
17 Ibid.
18 Carey Evans, p.85
19 Ibid., p.100
20 DLG to Margaret LG, 26 April 1918
21 Carey Evans, p.101
22 Grigg, *Lloyd George: From Peace to War*, pp.416–17
23 *Riddell Diaries 1908–23*, p.197
24 Gwilym LG to FS, 18 September 1917, LG Papers, LG I/3/2/11
25 *The Years that are Past*, p.119
26 FS Diary, 5 November 1917, FLS/4/4
27 *The Years that are Past*, p.121
28 Ibid.
29 Hankey Diary, 22 September 1918, ibid., p.594
30 Margaret LG, 'How do You Help Your Husband?', *Daily Express*, 1934, AJS Papers C25
31 Ibid.
32 Ibid.

33 *Lord Riddell's War Diary 1914–1918*, p.380
34 Harold Nicolson quoted in Rowland, p.460
35 Ibid.
36 Carey Evans, p.101
37 AJS Diary, 11 November 1941

CHAPTER 17: Diverging Paths

1 Lloyd George, speech at Wolverhampton, 24 November 1918, quoted in *British Political Facts*, p.267
2 DLG to Margaret LG, 13 December 1918
3 Ibid.
4 Stevenson, F., *Makers of the New World*, p.161
5 Sylvester, *The Real Lloyd George*, p.40
6 FS Diary, 21 April 1919, FLS/4/11
7 Ibid.
8 Ibid., 16 April 1919, FLS/4/11
9 Macmillan, p.38
10 FS Diary, 10 March 1919, FLS/4/11
11 Ibid., 13 March 1919, ibid.
12 Ibid., 11 May 1919, ibid.
13 Jones, M., p.43
14 Ibid., p.39
15 *The Years that are Past*, p.149
16 Ibid., p.160
17 FS Diary, 23 March 1919, FLS/4/11
18 *The Years that are Past*, p.158
19 FS Diary, 17 May 1919, FLS/4/11
20 Stevenson, F., *Makers of the New World*, pp.176–7
21 FS Diary, 12 March 1919, FLS/4/11
22 Ibid., 16 May 1919, ibid.
23 FS Diary, 26 July 1916 and 23 October 1916, FLS/4/3
24 Ibid., 15 November 1916, ibid.
25 Ibid., 14 April 1917, FLS/4/4
26 Ibid., 16 May 1919, FLS/4/11
27 Ibid., 23 May 1919, ibid.
28 Ibid., 25 May 1919, ibid.
29 Ibid., 15 April 1919, ibid.
30 Author conversation with Jennifer Longford 2006
31 Watt, R., p.11
32 Margaret LG, 'How do You Help Your Husband?', *Daily Express*, 1934, AJS Papers C25
33 *Y Gymraes*, June 1904, Olwen Carey Evans Papers 79

34 Margaret LG, Election Address to the Executive Committee of the Women's Liberal Federation, Lloyd George Papers 1, 20473E, 3050

35 Margaret LG, Speech to the Welsh Temperance Society, ibid., 20472C, 3019

36 Margaret LG, 'Petticoats Behind Politics', *Daily Chronicle*, 6 December 1926

37 Lloyd George, R., *Dame Margaret*, p.185

38 Ibid., p.188

39 Margaret LG, 'How do You Help Your Husband?'

40 *Sunday News*, 4 September 1927

41 Ibid.

42 Margaret LG, Speech to the Baptist Union, Lloyd George Papers 1, 20472C, 3034

43 Lloyd George, R., *Dame Margaret*, p.223

44 *Sunday News*, 4 September 1927, unpublished section, Lloyd George Papers 1, 20472C

45 Margaret LG, 'Petticoats Behind Politics'

46 *Sunday News*, 4 September 1927.

47 'London Letter', *Caernarvon Herald*, 24 January 1941

48 Margaret LG to DLG, August 1922, LG Papers, LG I/I/2/144

49 *Riddell Diaries 1908–23*, p.252

50 Lloyd George, R., *Dame Margaret*, pp.186–7

51 Margaret LG, 'How do You Help Your Husband?'

52 Carey Evans, p.103

53 Margaret LG, 'How do You Help Your Husband?'

54 Ibid.

55 Ibid.

56 FS Diary, 20 February 1920, FSD p.202

57 Margaret LG, 'How do You Help Your Husband?'

58 FS Diary, 29 June 1919, FSD p.187

CHAPTER 18: Disillusionment

1 FS Diary, 5 July 1919, FLS/4/11

2 FS to DLG, 10 July 1919, FLS/6/1

3 Ibid.

4 FS Diary, 12 July 1919, FLS/4/11

5 Ibid., 21 July 1919, ibid.

6 Ibid., 20 December 1919, FLS/4/11

7 Ibid., 17 December 1919, ibid.

8 Ibid., 18–19 December 1919, ibid.

9 Ibid., 12 February 1920, FLS/4/5

10 *Times Literary Supplement*, 4 August 1921

11 Stevenson, F., *Makers of the New World*, pp.4–5

12 *The Years that are Past*, p.177

13 Ibid.

14 FS Diary, 23 November 1934, FLS/5/2

15 Ibid., 1 May 1921, FLS/4/7

16 Ibid.

17 Ibid., 5 May 1921, ibid.

18 Ibid., 23 November 1934, FLS/5/2

19 Margaret LG, Speech notes, NLW 20472

20 DLG to Margaret LG, May 1919, Jones, Graham J., 'Dame Margaret in Cardiganshire', p.110

21 DLG to Margaret LG, 'Wednesday', 18 August 1920, ibid.

22 Lloyd George, R., *Dame Margaret*, p.188

23 FS Diary, 6 July 1921, FLS/4/7

24 Ibid., 29 November 1919, FLS/4/11

25 Ibid., 28 February 1920, FLS/4/5

26 Ibid., 24 January 1920, ibid.

27 Longford, R. pp.150–1

28 Major, pp.11–12

29 Ibid., p.86

30 Ibid., p.104

31 *The Years that are Past*, pp.179–80

32 DLG to FS, 19 April 1922, FLS/6/1

33 *The Years that are Past*, p.176

34 FS Diary, 10 May 1921, FLS/4/7

35 Ibid., 15 May 1921, ibid.

36 Ibid., 24 May 1921, ibid.

37 Ibid., 4 July 1921

38 FS Diary, 6 July 1921, FLS/4/7

39 Ibid., 22 July 1921, ibid.

CHAPTER 19: 'Dame Margaret is the Star'

1 All details of the 1921 by-election appear in Jones, Graham J., 'Dame Margaret in Cardiganshire'

2 *The Times*, 24 January 1921

3 DLG to Margaret LG, 9 February 1921

4 *Cambrian News*, 11 February 1921

5 Ibid., 18 February 1921

6 Ibid., 11 February 1921

7 *Welsh Gazette*, 10 February 1921, ibid

8 *Cambrian News*, 18 February 1921

9 *Morning Post*, 15 February 1921, quoted in Jones, Graham J., 'Dame Margaret in Cardiganshire', p.115

10 DLG to Margaret LG, 14 February 1921

11 *The Times*, 11 February 1921

12 Ibid., 16 February 1921

13 *Cambrian News*, 18 February 1921

14 John Herbert Lewis Diary, 18 February 1921, 'Dame Margaret in Cardiganshire', p.116

15 *Riddell Diaries 1908–23*, pp.337–8

16 *The Times*, 21 February 1921

17 Cazalet-Keir, p.58

18 DLG to Olwen Carey Evans, 3 June 1921, 'Dame Margaret in Cardiganshire', p.39

19 *The Years that are Past*, p.185

20 DLG to Margaret LG, 19 August 1921

21 DLG to FS, August 1921, FLS/6/1

22 *The Years that are Past*, p.186

23 DLG to Margaret LG, 21 September 1921, Morgan, *Lloyd George Family Letters*, p.194

24 Gwynedd, *Dame Margaret*, p.183

25 *The Years that are Past*, p.190

26 Ibid.

27 Jones, M., p.52

28 DLG to FS, 15 March 1922, FLS/6/1

29 Cazalet-Keir, p.48

30 Sylvester, *The Real Lloyd George*, p.83

31 DLG to FS, 26 April 1922, *My Darling Pussy*, p.45

32 AJS Diary, 7 May 1922

33 DLG to FS, 7 May 1922, FLS/6/1

34 DLG to FS, 30 April 1922, ibid.

35 *Riddell Diaries 1908–23*, p.368

36 Grigg, Vol. IV, p.141, quoting from Davidson, J.C.C., *Memoirs of a Conservative*, p.29

37 *The Years that are Past*, p.114

38 Ibid., p.206

39 Rowland, p.580

CHAPTER 20: Alone into the Wilderness

1 FS Diary, 13 February 1922, FLS/4/7

2 Ibid., 22 June 1922, ibid.

3 DLG to Margaret LG, 6 September 1922

4 DLG to Margaret LG, 8 September 1922

5 DLG to Margaret LG, 6 September 1922

6 Rowland, p.581

7 Sylvester, *The Real Lloyd George*, p.99

8 *The Years that are Past*, p.207

9 *Riddell Diaries 1908-23*, p.378

10 Margaret LG to Olwen Carey Evans, 25 October 1922, Morgan, *Lloyd George Family Letters*, p.197

11 *Daily Sketch*, 21 October 1922

12 Megan LG to Olwen Carey Evans, 25 October 1922, Morgan, *Lloyd George Family Letters*, p.197

13 Jones, T., *Whitehall Diary*, 19 October 1922, Volume I, p.214

14 Sylvester, *The Real Lloyd George*, p.100

15 Jean Scott to FS, 27 December 1922, FLS/1/13b

16 *The Years that are Past*, p.210

17 DLG to FS, 14 and 18 January 1923, FLS/6/2

18 FS to DLG, 16 January 1923, ibid.

19 DLG to FS, 28 January 1923, ibid.

20 DLG to FS, 4 May 1922, FLS/6/1

21 *The Years that are Past*, p.214

22 Margaret LG to Olwen Carey Evans, undated, Morgan, *Lloyd George Family Letters*, p.201

23 Ibid.

24 Ibid.

25 *Riddell Diaries 1908–23*, p.385

26 DLG to FS, 25 January 1923, FLS/6/2

27 DLG to FS, 15 August 1923, ibid.

28 DLG to FS, 14 August 1923, ibid.

29 DLG to FS, 15 August 1923, ibid.

30 FS to LG, 15 August 1923, ibid.

31 Longford, R., p.77

32 Margaret LG to DLG, August 1922, LG Papers, LG I/I/2/44

33 *The Years that are Past*, p.212

34 Sylvester, *The Real Lloyd George*, p.131

35 *Daily Despatch*, 20 October 1923

36 Margaret LG Diary of the trip, Lloyd George Papers 1, 20472C

37 *Daily Sketch*, 15 October 1923

38 *Daily Express*, 6 October 1923

39 Sylvester, *The Real Lloyd George*, p.121

40 DLG to FS, 22 October 1923, *My Darling Pussy*, p.72

41 AJS to FS, 27 October 1923, FLS/1/26

42 Ibid.

43 FS to DLG, 9 October 1923, FLS/6/2

CHAPTER 21: Megan

1 Cazalet-Keir, p.52
2 Jones, M., p.70
3 A.J. Sylvester quoted in ibid., p.47
4 Carey Evans, p.127
5 FS to DLG, 26 November 1923 FLS/6/2
6 Jones, M., p.61
7 Carey Evans, p.139
8 Jones, M., p.62
9 *Daily Mirror*, 28 November 1933
10 DLG to Megan LG, 2 October 1924, Morgan, *Lloyd George Family Letters*, p.204
11 DLG to Margaret LG, 30 March 1928
12 Ibid.
13 DLG to Margaret LG, 26 April 1928
14 DLG to Margaret LG, 17 April 1928
15 DLG to Megan LG, 22 May 1928
16 *Leeds Mercury*, 24 May 1928, Jones, M., p.75
17 DLG to Megan LG, 24 May 1928
18 Cazalet-Keir, p.126
19 FS Diary, 19 October 1934, FSD pp.283–4
20 *Daily Herald*, 1 April 1925, p.581
21 Lloyd George, R., *Dame Margaret*, p.180
22 *Daily Herald* letter and Margaret's response, LG Papers, LG/H/167
23 DLG to Margaret LG, 24 July 1924
24 Lloyd George, R., *Lloyd George*, p.220
25 *The Years that are Past*
26 DLG to Margaret LG, October 1926, *My Darling Pussy*, pp.105–6
27 *Evening Standard*, 6 November 1967
28 *The Years that are Past*, p.220
29 Longford, R., p.110
30 Longford, J., p.2
31 George, W., *My Brother & I*, p.289
32 DLG to FS, 14 April 1925, *My Darling Pussy*, p.81
33 DLG to FS, 3 June 1925, ibid., p.82
34 DLG to FS, 20 August 1925, FLS/6/2
35 DLG to FS, 11 August 1925, ibid.
36 DLG to FS, 18 August 1925, ibid.
37 FS to DLG, 21 August 1925, ibid.
38 DLG to FS, 12 September 1928, FLS/6/3
39 DLG to FS, 14 September 1928, ibid.
40 DLG to FS, 22 January 1929, ibid.
41 FS to DLG, 23 January 1929, ibid.

CHAPTER 22: New Loves

1 *Evening News*, 1 April 1927
2 *Eccles and Patricroft Journal*, 25 February 1916
3 Ibid., 14 July 1916
4 Ibid., 4 August 1916
5 Ibid., 29 September 1916
6 Muriel Stevenson, according to Jennifer Longford
7 *The Years that are Past*, p.220
8 *Evening News*, 1 April 1927
9 Thomas Tweed to FS, 9 August 1928, Longford, R., pp.95–6
10 Ibid., 14 August 1928, p.96
11 DLG to FS, 31 January and 5 February 1929, FLS/6/3
12 FS to DLG, 15 January 1929, *My Darling Pussy*, p.111
13 DLG to FS, 16 January 1929, FLS/6/3
14 AJS Diary, 11 December 1932
15 FS to DLG, 21 January 1929, FLS/6/3
16 DLG to FS, 25 January 1929, ibid.
17 DLG to FS, 22 January 1929, ibid.
18 Ibid.
19 FS to DLG, 23 January 1929, ibid.
20 FS to DLG, 1 February 1929, ibid.
21 FS to DLG, 4 February 1929, ibid.
22 Ibid.
23 Longford, J., p.4
24 AJS Diary, 26 April 1932
25 Longford, J., p.1
26 AJS to Olwen Carey Evans, 4 October 1975, AJS Papers, E2
27 Author conversation with Dr William George, 2005
28 FS Diary, 3 February 1927, FSD p.249
29 Ibid., 18 August 1927, FLS/4/8
30 AJS Diary, 18 and 19 December 1924
31 Parry, p.50
32 Lloyd George, O., p.31
33 AJS Diary, 26 July 1931
34 Ibid.
35 Ibid., 2 August 1931
36 Ibid., 26 July 1931
37 Private information from Lord Lloyd-George

CHAPTER 23: Crises Public and Private

1 Longford, R., p.106
2 AJS Diary, 25 June 1931 and 5 August 1932

3 Ibid., 3 June 1938, Sylvester, *Life with Lloyd George*, p.210

4 Ibid., 8 June 1937, ibid., p.182

5 Ibid., 29 October 1940

6 Longford, J., p.31

7 *The Years that are Past*, p.245

8 Longford, R., p.135

9 Lloyd George, O., p.21

10 DLG to FS, 11 January 1937, FLS/6/5

11 FS to DLG, 16 January 1937, ibid.

12 AJS Diary, 21 November 1938

13 Cazalet-Keir, pp.49–50

14 AJS Diary, 25 October 1931

15 Ibid., 28 October 1931

16 DLG to FS, 10 August 1931, FLS/6/4

17 DLG to FS, 26 November 1931, *My Darling Pussy*, p.155

18 Gwynfor Evans and Clem Thomas, quoted in Jones, M., p.104

19 AJS Diary, 30 December 1931

20 FS Diary, 2 May 1934, FLS/4/9

21 AJS Diary, 22 December 1931

22 FS Diary, 9 March 1934, FLS/4/9

23 Parry, p.58

24 Price, E., *Megan Lloyd George*, p.21

25 DLG to Margaret LG, 18 December 1935, Morgan, *Lloyd George Family Letters*, p.211

26 DLG to Megan LG, 1 December 1936

27 *The Week in Westminster*, 12 September 1942, BBC Archives

28 Patricia Llewellyn-Davies, quoted in Jones, M., p.104

29 Ibid.

30 AJS Diary, 6 November 1935

31 Ibid., 5 September 1936

32 Ibid., 16 February 1937

33 Ibid., 11 December 1932

34 Ibid., 12 December 1932

35 Ibid.

36 Ibid., 6 October 1933

37 Ibid.

38 Ibid., 25 June 1935

39 Ibid., 28 June 1935

40 *The Times*, 3 March 1933

41 AJS Diary, 23 September 1936

42 *The Years that are Past*, p.233

43 Thomas Tweed to DLG, LG Papers

44 DLG to FS, 14 January 1934, FLS/6/5

45 Ibid., 15 January 1934, ibid.

46 AJS Diary, 11 April 1933

47 Ibid., 23 November 1936

48 Ibid., 13 December 1936

49 Ibid., 3 June 1938

50 Lloyd George, O., p.21

51 AJS Diary, 9 January 1937

52 DLG to FS, 24 January 1937, FLS/6/5

53 FS Diary, 18 May 1934, Longford, R., p.113

54 Ibid., 23 May 1934, *My Darling Pussy*, p.210

55 Ibid., 19 October 1934, ibid., p.211

56 *Evening Standard*, 1 May 1940

57 Ibid.

58 *Manchester Guardian*, 1 May 1940

59 DLG Statement on Thomas Tweed, LG Papers G/28/2/20

60 AJS Diary, 3 May 1940

61 Longford, R., p.142

62 AJS Diary, 3 May 1940

63 Ibid.

64 Margaret LG, Election Address, Carey Evans Papers, p. 85

65 DLG to Margaret LG, 1 February 1936, Morgan, *Lloyd George Family Letters*, p.211

66 FS Diary, 23 May 1934, FSD p.274

67 Cazalet-Keir, p.48

68 George, W., *My Brother & I*, p.289

69 Ibid.

70 Carey Evans, p.68

71 DLG to Megan LG, 9 December 1936, Morgan, *Lloyd George Family Letters*, p.213

72 *The Years that are Past*, p.258

73 Sylvester, *The Real Lloyd George*, p.232

74 Ibid.

75 AJS Diary, 14 January 1937

76 Ibid., 20 May 1936

77 FS Diary, 9 March 1934, FLS/4/9

78 Ibid., 14 January 1937

79 Ibid., 17 February 1937

80 Ibid., 23 February 1937

81 AJS Diary, 23 February 1937

82 Longford, R., pp.135–6

83 AJS Diary, 30 September 1938

84 Ibid., 12 January 1938

85 Ibid.

86 *News Chronicle*, 12 January 1938

87 AJS Diary, 24 January 1938

88 Ibid.

89 Ibid.

CHAPTER 24: Private Sorrows

1　Longford, J., p.12
2　AJS Diary, 4 April 1932
3　Longford, J., p.16
4　FS to DLG, August 1935, FLS/6/5
5　FS to DLG, 30 July 1932, *My Darling Pussy*, p.182
6　Interview, Robin Carey Evans, August 2005
7　Longford, J., p.2
8　FS to DLG, 20 November 1931, FLS/6/4
9　FS to Jennifer Stevenson, 18 June 1944, NLW FCF 1/2
10　Rowland, pp.771–2
11　*The Years that are Past*, p.268
12　FS to DLG, 6 October 1940, FLS/6/5
13　FS Diary, 11 June 1936, FLS/4/10
14　FS to DLG, 23 September 1940, FLS/6/5
15　AJS Diary, 17 September 1940
16　George, W.R.P., *88 Not Out*, p.204
17　AJS Diary, 30 December 1931
18　Ibid., 4 April 1932
19　Philip Noel-Baker to Megan LG, 19 July 1953
20　Jones, M., p.111
21　Philip Noel-Baker to Megan LG, 5 October 1955
22　Jones, M., p.120
23　Ibid.
24　Philip Noel-Baker to Megan LG, 24 July 1953
25　Jones, M., p.136
26　Philip Noel-Baker to Megan LG, 28 June 1940
27　Philip Noel-Baker to Megan LG, 11 July 1940
28　Philip Noel-Baker to Megan LG, August 1940
29　Philip Noel-Baker to Megan LG, 6 August 1940
30　Philip Noel-Baker to Megan LG, 5 October 1955
31　AJS Diary, 19 January 1941
32　Ibid., 11 August 1933
33　Ibid., 21 January 1941
34　Parry, p.52
35　Ibid.
36　Ibid.
37　AJS Diary, 21 January 1941
38　Carey Evans, p.162
39　*Caernarvon and Denbigh Herald, North Wales Observer*, 24 January 1941
40　Cazalet-Keir, p.47
41　*Caernarvon and Denbigh Herald, North Wales Observer*, 24 January 1941
42　*Daily Sketch*, 21 January 1941
43　Olwen Carey Evans Papers, 96
44　AJS Diary, 26 January 1941, Sylvester, *Life with Lloyd George*, p.288
45　Sylvester, *The Real Lloyd George*, p.294
46　AJS Diary, 9 February 1941

CHAPTER 25: Till Death us do Part

1　AJS Diary, 24 April 1941
2　Carey Evans, p.166
3　AJS Diary, 6 May 1942
4　Ibid., 9 June 1942
5　Ibid., 16 July 1942
6　Ibid., 23 October 1942
7　Ibid., 17 November 1942
8　Ibid., 23 November 1942
9　Ibid., 30 November 1942
10　Ibid., 11 December 1942
11　Ibid., 18 December 1942
12　*The Years that are Past*, p.271
13　Lord Dawson to Megan LG, 15 January 1943, Longford, R., p.155
14　AJS Diary, 25 October 1943
15　Ibid., 22 October 1943
16　Ibid., 23 October 1943
17　*The Years that are Past*, p.272
18　Lloyd George, O., pp.79–80
19　Longford, J., p.26
20　AJS Diary, 25 October 1943
21　FLG to Megan LG, 7 November 1943, Longford, R., p.156
22　Lloyd George, O., p.80
23　AJS Diary, 9 August 1944
24　George, W., *My Brother & I*, p.291
25　AJS Diary, 21 September 1944
26　*The Years that are Past*, p.274
27　Ibid.
28　Longford, J., p.27
29　Valerie Daniel to DLG, LG Papers, LG I/3/1/23
30　*The Years that are Past*, p.277
31　Parry, p.74
32　Dr Prytherch to Lord Dawson, 26 February 1945, Sylvester, *Life with Lloyd George*, p.339

33 AJS Diary, 21 February 1945
34 Ibid., 26 February 1945, Sylvester, *Life with Lloyd George*, p.339
35 Lloyd George, O., p105
36 Parry, p.88
37 Longford, J., p.28
38 *The Times*, 27 and 28 March 1945
39 Lloyd George, R., *David and Winston*, pp.245–6
40 Parry, p.75
41 George, W., *My Brother & I*, p.296
42 George, W.R.P., *88 Not Out*, pp.277–8
43 Longford, J., p.33
44 Parry, p.76
45 *The Years that are Past*, p.282
46 Ibid., p.283
47 Ibid., p.284
48 Ibid., p.282
49 Cazalet-Keir, p.52
50 Philip Noel-Baker to Megan LG, 22 June 1956
51 *The Times*, 17 May 1966
52 Ibid., 16 May 1966
53 Longford, R., p.197
54 Ibid., p.208
55 *The Years that are Past*, p.285
56 *Times Literary Supplement*, 9 November 1967
57 *Liverpool Daily Post*, 13 August 1971

EPILOGUE

1 Longford, J., p.34
2 DLG to William George, 19 May 1917, Rowland, p.638
3 Frances LG, Introduction to Thomson, *David Lloyd George: The Official Biography*
4 *Liverpool Daily Post*, 13 August 1971
5 Carey Evans, p.63
6 FS Diary, 30 November 1934, FSD p.294
7 Ibid., 7 November 1934, ibid., p.288

BIBLIOGRAPHY

Manuscripts
National Library of Wales
BBC Archives
Brynawelon Group
Olwen Carey Evans Papers
William George Papers
Earl Lloyd-George Papers
A.J. Sylvester Papers
Frances Stevenson Papers

Parliamentary Archives
Lloyd George (LG) Papers
Frances Stevenson (FLS) Papers

Caernarfon Record Office
Gwynedd Archives

Books
Asquith, M., *The Autobiography of Margot Asquith*, Volumes I–II, Thornton
   Butterworth, London, 1920–22
Beaverbrook, M.A., Baron, *The Decline and Fall of Lloyd George*, Collins,
   London, 1966
Butler, G. and D., *British Political Facts 1900–2000*, Macmillan, Basingstoke, 2000
Campbell, J., *Lloyd George: The Goat in the Wilderness*, Jonathan Cape,
   London, 1977
Campbell, J., *If Love Were All*, Jonathan Cape, London, 2006
Carey Evans, O., *Lloyd George was my Father*, Gomer Press, Llandysul, 1985
Cazalet-Keir, T., *From the Wings*, Bodley Head, London, 1967
Clifford, C., *The Asquiths*, John Murray, London, 2002
Davies, D., *The Problem of Girls' Education in Wales*, Association for
   Promoting the Education of Girls in Wales, Liverpool, 1887

Davies, D., *Christian Schools: Christianity and Education in Mid-Nineteenth Century Wales*, Evangelical Library of Wales, Bridgend, 1978

Davies, J., *A History of Wales*, Penguin, London, 1993

Douglas, R., *The History of the Liberal Party 1895–1970*, Sidgwick & Jackson, London, 1971

Du Parcq, H., *The Life of David Lloyd George*, Volumes I–IV, Caxton Publishing Co., London, 1912–13

Garrison, W.E., *The Disciples of Christ, A History*, Christian Board of Publication, St Louis, 1948

George, W., *Richard Lloyd*, Western Mail a'r Echo, Caerdydd, 1934

George, W., *Atgof a Myfyr*, Hughes a'i Fab, Wrecsam, 1948

George, W., *My Brother & I*, Eyre & Spottiswood, London, 1958

George, W.R.P., *The Making of Lloyd George*, Faber, London, 1976

George, W.R.P., *Lloyd George: Backbencher*, Gomer, Llandysul, 1983

George, W.R.P., *88 Not Out: An Autobiography*, Gwasg Dwyfor, Penygroes, 2001

Gilbert, M., *The First World War*, Weidenfeld & Nicolson, London, 1994

Grigg, J., *The Young Lloyd George*, Eyre Methuen, London, 1973

Grigg, J., *Lloyd George: The People's Champion, 1902–1911*, Eyre Methuen, London, 1978

Grigg, J., *Lloyd George: From Peace to War, 1912–1916*, Eyre Methuen, London, 1985

Grigg, J., *Lloyd George: War Leader*, Eyre Methuen, London, 2002

Gwynedd, Viscount, *Dame Margaret*, Allen & Unwin, London, 1947

Harris, J., *Private Lives, Public Spirit: Britain 1870–1914*, OUP, Oxford, 1993

Hattersley, R., *The Edwardians*, Little, Brown, London, 2004

HMSO, *British Imperial Calendar and Civil Service List*, London, 1912–20

Jenkins, R., *Gladstone*, Macmillan, London, 1995

Jenkins, R., *The Chancellors*, Macmillan, London, 1998

Jones, E. (ed.), *The Welsh in London*, University of Wales Press, Cardiff, 2001

Jones, Graham J., 'Mair Eluned Lloyd George (1890–1907)', *Caernarvonshire Historical Transactions*, Volume LX, 1999

Jones, Graham J., ' "Auntie Pollie": Mrs Mary Ellen Davies (1861–1909), Sister of Lloyd George', *Caernarvonshire Historical Transactions*, Volume LXV, 2004

Jones, Graham J., 'Dame Margaret in Cardiganshire', *Ceredigion*, Volume XIV no.3, 2004

Jones, Graham J., 'Lloyd George and Dame Margaret, 1921–41', Lecture to the Friends of the National Library of Wales, NLW, 2006

Jones, M., *A Radical Life: The Biography of Megan Lloyd George, 1902–66*, Hutchinson, London, 1991

Jones, T., *Whitehall Diary*, Volumes I–II, OUP, London, 1969

Kavanagh, D., and Seldon, A., *The Powers Behind the Prime Minister*, HarperCollins, London, 1999

Lloyd George, D., *War Memoirs*, Volumes I–VI, Nicolson & Watson, London, 1933–36

Lloyd George, D., *The Truth About the Peace Treaties*, Volumes I–II, Victor Gollancz, London, 1938

Lloyd George, F., *The Years that are Past*, Hutchinson, London, 1967

Lloyd George, O., *A Tale of Two Grandfathers*, Bellew, London, 1999

Lloyd George, R., *Lloyd George*, Frederick Muller, London, 1960

Lloyd George, R., *David and Winston*, John Murray, London, 2005

Longford, R., *Frances, Countess Lloyd George: More than a Mistress*, Gracewing, Leominster, 1996

McCormick, D., *The Mask of Merlin*, Macdonald & Co., London, 1963

McLaren, A., *A History of Contraception from Antiquity to the Present Day*, OUP, Oxford, 1990

MacMillan, M., *Peacemakers: The Paris Peace Conference of 1919 and its Attempt to Change the World*, John Murray, London, 2001

Major, N., *Chequers: The Prime Minister's Country Home and its History*, HarperCollins, London, 1996

Martindale, H., *Women Servants of the State 1870–1938: A History of Women in the Civil Service*, Allen & Unwin, London, 1938

Mervyn Jones, R. and Ben Rees, D., *Liverpool Welsh and their Religion*, Modern Welsh Publications, Liverpool, 1984

Morgan, K.O., *Wales in British Politics*, University of Wales Press, Cardiff, 1963

Morgan, K.O., *David Lloyd George: Welsh Radical as World Statesman*, University of Wales Press, Cardiff, 1963

Morgan, K.O., *The Age of Lloyd George: The Liberal Party and British Politics, 1890–1929*, Allen & Unwin, London, 1971

Morgan, K.O. (ed.), *Lloyd George: Family Letters, 1885–1936*, University of Wales Press, Cardiff, and OUP, London, 1972

Morgan, K.O., *Rebirth of a Nation: Wales 1880–1990*, Clarendon, Oxford, 1981

Nicolson, J., *The Perfect Summer: Dancing into Shadow in 1911*, John Murray, London, 2006

Owen, F., *Tempestuous Journey: Lloyd George, his Life and Times*, Hutchinson, London, 1954

Pankhurst, E.S., *The Suffragette: The History of the Women's Militant Suffrage Movement 1905–1910*, Sturgis & Watson, New York, 1911

Parry, A., *Thirty Thousand Yesterdays*, Gee & Son, Denbigh, 1977

Price, E., *David Lloyd George*, Gwynedd Archives Service, Gwynedd County Council, 1981

Price, E., *Megan Lloyd George*, Gwynedd Archives Service, Gwynedd County Council, 1983

Price, E., *Lloyd George Y Cenedlaetholwr Cymreig: Arwr Ynteu Bradwr*, Ceredigion, 1999

Pugh, M., *Women and the Women's Movement in Britain, 1914–1999*, Macmillan, London, 1992

Riddell, G., *Intimate Diary of the Peace Conference and After, 1918–23*, Victor Gollancz, London, 1933

Riddell, G., *Lord Riddell's War Diary 1914–1918*, Nicolson & Watson, London, 1933

Riddell, G., *The Riddell Diaries 1908–23*, Athlone, London, 1986

Rose, K., *King George V*, Weidenfeld & Nicolson, London, 1983

Rowland, P., *Lloyd George*, Barrie & Jenkins, London, 1975

Soames, M., *Clementine Churchill*, Cassell, London, 1979

Stedman, M., *The Salford Pals*, Leo Cooper, London, 1993

Steinbach, S., *Women in England 1760–1914*, Weidenfeld & Nicolson, London, 2004

Stevenson, F., *Makers of the New World by One Who Knows Them*, Cassell & Co., London, 1921

Stevenson, F. (ed. A.J.P. Taylor), *Lloyd George: A Diary by Frances Stevenson*, Hutchinson, London, 1971

Stevenson, J., *A Social History of Britain: British Society 1914–1945*, Penguin, Harmondsworth, 1984

Stopes, M.C., *Married Love*, Fifield, 1918

Sylvester, A.J., *The Real Lloyd George*, Cassell, London, 1947

Sylvester, A.J. (ed. C. Cross), *Life with Lloyd George*, Macmillan, London, 1975

Taylor, A.J.P. (ed.), *Lloyd George: Twelve Essays*, Hamish Hamilton, London, 1971

Taylor, A.J.P. (ed.), *My Darling Pussy: The Letters of Lloyd George and Frances Stevenson, 1913–1941*, Weidenfeld & Nicolson, London, 1975

Thomson, M., *David Lloyd George: The Official Biography*, Hutchinson, London, 1948

Watt, R., *The Kings Depart*, Weidenfeld & Nicolson, London, 1969

Wilson, A.N., *After the Victorians*, Hutchinson, London, 2005

Wrigley, C., *Lloyd George*, Blackwell, Oxford, 1992

INDEX

P.S.

Ideas,
interviews
& features . . .

About the author

About the book

Read on

Intertwined Lives and Lifelong Relationships:

Ffion Hague talks to Sarah O'Reilly

In your introduction you write that your original intention was to write a biography of Margaret, who has always been as compelling a figure to you as Lloyd George. When in your life did you first come across her?
I grew up in Wales and it is quite impossible to do so without hearing quite a bit about Lloyd George and his family! I visited Llanystumdwy as a child and wandered around 'Highgate' and the museum there and so I suppose I registered Margaret as someone who had an interesting life from that point onwards. I also remember enjoying the BBC drama 'The Life and Times of David Lloyd George' very much in the early eighties when I was twelve or so. Lisabeth Miles's portrayal of Margaret was very unaffected, warm and very Welsh so that only increased my interest in her.

Can you tell me a little bit about the landscape of your childhood? What sort of things did you learn about your country in the writing of this book that you hadn't known before?
My childhood was very musical and I was always surrounded by books. I was raised a Welsh-speaker like Margaret (though in Cardiff, not in North Wales). I'm very, very proud to be Welsh and the book helped me learn umpteen new things about my own heritage. I was able to research the origins

of the Calvinistic Methodist Church, and post-devolution, learn more about the struggle for home rule in the 1890s when most people think of Welsh Nationalism as a late-twentieth-century issue.

One thing in particular I found scandalous was the new fact I uncovered that Lloyd George had taken both his wife and his mistress to the Birkenhead Eisteddfod in 1917. Every Welsh-speaking schoolchild learns about the 'Black Chair Eisteddfod' in school and the thought that Lloyd George could be sitting on the platform with Margaret while his mistress was in the audience at such a seminal and solemn occasion really shocked me!

Where was the book written? How important, generally, are your surroundings to you when writing?
I'm quite practical about writing – I have to be since I am working at the same time – and I found myself trying to fit in a few hours on the book in the strangest of places. I'm not very superstitious or particular about my surroundings. As long as I have my books, some quiet, and an endless supply of tea, I can write almost anywhere but the majority of the book was written in my study in Yorkshire, looking out on a glorious scene of fields, birds, sheep and horses.

Margaret's voice, indeed her 'take' on events, is not preserved in a diary or memoir. ▶

6 I'm very, very proud to be Welsh and the book helped me learn umpteen new things about my own heritage 9

Intertwined Lives . . . *(continued)*

◄ How did this affect your attempts to understand and write about her life and character?

The lack of primary material such as a diary or memoir is a considerable disadvantage when you write about someone's life. I suspected that no-one had taken a good look at her life before and that there might be some new material to uncover. I was delighted to find I was right. Margaret left behind hundreds if not thousands of letters which give an account of her day-to-day existence in her own words. I also found a number of newspaper articles she had written herself and read all the interviews she gave which all helped build up my understanding of her character. I was able to include a lot of new information about her in the book, including her letters from the 1890s, her newspaper articles and her strong self-defence against false accusations in the press over her lost pearl necklace. I also researched her time as chairman of Criccieth Council. The majority of these have never featured in a book before so it was exciting to discover them and to be able to reproduce so many of Margaret's own words. It just took a bit more of an effort.

Writing about a subject's private life can be a difficult area to negotiate. How did you decide what to put in and what to leave out of your biography? Were there things you deemed you couldn't publish in your book? If so, what were they?

I took the view when writing this book that I had to be honest in presenting the material

I discovered in its totality. I also felt, of course, that I had to avoid speculation and exaggeration at all costs and so the only material I excluded was information I could not verify. With regards to the delicacy of the subject, I did think very carefully before embarking on the book for that very reason. However, all the material I used was put into the public domain by the Lloyd George/Longford family themselves. The women in the book had a choice whether to preserve their letters and papers or destroy them and keep their stories private. All my female subjects decided to give or sell their papers to a public source or bequeath them for others to do so. It was their choice that their stories should be told and I did so in good conscience. Even the letters relating to Mrs Tim and Mrs Griffiths, for instance, are now in public libraries, letters that Lloyd George could easily have destroyed if he had wanted to. Sometimes, I wonder if these letters were kept, then what on earth did he see fit to destroy?

> ‘ It was exciting to discover and to be able to reproduce so many of Margaret's own words ’

How did you go about capturing Lloyd George's charm and charisma on the page? Was this a challenge you were conscious of when writing?
My general policy was to let him speak for himself as far as possible. His words were always carefully chosen – he was not one to speak or write at random – and I've included as many quotations as the text could bear. We may not be able to hear his voice (although recordings do exist) but we can get an impression of the force of his ▶

All rights reserved

◄ personality through his letters, speeches and newspaper articles.

Did you fall for Lloyd George's charm when researching his life, or did your feelings for him alter over the course of writing your book? I wonder how you felt, for instance, about his prevarications over marrying Frances after the many sacrifices she made for him.
I tried hard to understand the viewpoint of every character in the book, including Lloyd George. In the case of the second marriage, he was caught in a real bind, not wishing to tear his family in two, but Frances's determination was more than equal to the task! With regards to his charm, I felt it strongly as I was writing, but what surprised me more was how much I grew to admire him as a politician through learning more about his originality of mind and his social radicalism. He was not only The Man Who Won the War, but also introduced old-age pensions, national insurance, health insurance and female suffrage as well as brokering peace in Paris and in Ireland. That's quite a record by any standards.

Many biographers write about the strange ways in which their subjects come to play a central role in their own lives and thoughts, sometimes eclipsing their own daily lives. Did you experience this?
Not really. I suppose I had too many characters to write about for that to happen, but I did start seeing parallels everywhere as I was writing, and there were some strange

coincidences. For instance, I was writing about the famously hot summer of 1911 in the summer of 2006, which was the hottest summer on record since. I was also writing about the honours scandal of 1922 during the later incarnation of the same debate in 2006 – I hope those factors helped me get the atmosphere right.

Looking back on the experience, what were the most and least satisfying aspects of writing the book?
The most satisfying aspect was the research itself – especially when I was able to uncover a new line of evidence about one of the women or read a letter that had never been published before. I also enjoyed meeting members of the Lloyd George, George and Longford families and, through them, feeling that I was almost in direct contact with the subjects of my book. The least satisfying thing was having to cut so much out of the final version of the book to keep the overall length down and the endless false finishes, thinking 'That's it – finished' and then discovering that there was a whole new piece of work to be done.

What's next? Do you have another book in mind?
Yes – I can't wait to start properly. I'm sworn to secrecy on the subject at the time of writing, but it will be another story of intertwined lives and lifelong relationships, which I find fascinating. ∎

> ❛ I tried hard to understand the viewpoint of every character in the book, including Lloyd George. ❜

Author photograph © Caroline Forbes

LIFE
at a Glance

BORN

Cardiff

LIVES

North Yorkshire

CAREER TO DATE

Eclectic. I started off as a civil servant, worked as a director of a national charity, moved into head-hunting and now have a portfolio of commercial consultancy and not-for-profit positions as well as writing.

A Writing Life

When do you write?
Whenever I have a few hours, but preferably from early in the morning to mid-afternoon.

Where do you write?
At my desk in my study in Yorkshire, at my desk in our London flat, or anywhere else.

Why do you write?
I suppose it has never occurred to me not to write. Writing is part of my every day, and has been as far back as I can remember.

Pen or computer?
Computer.

Silence or music?
Silence. I've always felt I should have music playing in the background but for some reason it doesn't work for me.

How do you start a book?
With a good idea.

And finish?
Good question. I don't really think a book is ever finished but it gets to a point where you think it's ready for publication.

Do you have any writing rituals or superstitions?
No, but I find it hard to write if I haven't got a mug of tea at my elbow.

Which writer has had the greatest influence on your work?
There isn't one writer I can single out as an influence but my writing is more influenced by writers of previous ages, rather than contemporary ones.

What are your guilty reading pleasures?
I love Harry Potter! ■

Ffion Hague talks to Jennifer Longford

What do you think about all the various theories about how you came to be born?
My mother never talked about all that. She told me once that no contraception was secure but that was about it. What I believe is this: at the beginning of 1929, LG was missing power and he had to face up to the fact that he probably wasn't going to get back into power. LG told my mother she could have a child – it was with his permission. LG said to my mother she could have a child, providing she never said who the father was. She kept her word even after he was dead. I would have expected her to talk about it then, but there you are!

Did she never drop as much as a hint?
Well, she told Michael, who was my fiancé at the time, that she was married to Tweed, which wasn't true, of course. But no, Frances never discussed my relationship with LG after his death – although she talked about him a lot. That was partly because she lived with my aunt, who had also been Tweed's mistress, and was absolutely sure I was Tweed's daughter and it was easier for my mother never to contradict it. But she did say occasionally, just at the end, 'Your father said this', meaning Lloyd George, not Tweed. She also left a note for me to find with the same thing in it. She still didn't mention his name and the note with that in it was left for me to discover, just as all kinds of other things were. Her wedding certificate, for instance, which put her down as a spinster;

she left me that to find too, and my own adoption certificate which proved that she was my natural mother. She left me things to find, then it wasn't quite her fault if I found them.

How did you feel about your mother's secretive attitude towards you as you were growing up? And did that change after Lloyd George's death?

She wanted Ruth to write her biography and to tell the truth – everything she hadn't put in her own memoir. I can't begin to tell you what she wrote about me in the first draft of her autobiography. I was absolutely enchanting, couldn't tell a lie and all sorts of things – absolute nonsense!

Anyway, I can't remember who I was supposed to be at that stage but I read it and said, 'You either tell the truth or you don't say anything at all' and so she cut me right out. Well, I mean, she wasn't going to tell the truth! The book was my fault, I accept that, but what was really hard was when she was interviewed by Fyfe Robertson some years later. They'd just invented colour television and we hadn't got one, but a person who worked for us did – she did the cleaning and cooking, etc, she was a very nice woman. She lived next door but two to us and so she invited me round to see it in colour. I was sitting there and the last thing Fyfe Robertson asked my mother was, 'Did you mind not having a child?' That, I think, was the ▶

❝ Frances never discussed my relationship with LG after his death – although she talked about him a lot ❞

11

Ffion Hague talks to . . . *(continued)*

◄ last question, and it took her by surprise. It was not something that had been worked out, and she just said, 'Lloyd George was my child'.

I felt I had been absolutely wiped out. She hadn't warned me that would be in the film. It was easier for her just not to say, but I really was taken aback by that. It wasn't that she didn't like me. When Lloyd George died she wanted me to be her child again, but at fifteen, it was too late for that.

Why is your mother not buried with Lloyd George?
Well, she was widowed for over 27 years before she herself died. She never asked to be buried with LG – I don't think she would have wanted to go back to Wales.

What was your relationship with Lloyd George like?
I loved him very much and I think he loved me. He always made time for me – I thought he was wonderful. He could teach me things and make it seem like a game. I would think we were just playing but really he was educating me.

Later on, I remember he was very possessive. When he had his eightieth birthday, I think, some people wrote to him to congratulate him and said they were looking forward to his ninetieth and I thought, 'I don't think I am!' That sounds terrible, I know, but he had become so possessive and he didn't like me going to the cinema with anybody – not even with another girl, I mean. I could see life was going to be difficult. But as a child he was the perfect grandfather.

Were you aware of Frances's relationship with Lloyd George as you were growing up? Were you surprised when they got married?
I didn't know my mother had been Lloyd George's mistress until after he died, but I wasn't at all surprised when they married – it was my idea! Even after Dame Margaret's death he didn't mention marrying Frances. It was I who said one day on a walk – I can remember exactly where I was, at Bron-y-De down the hill, on the way from the garden into the farm just off a stile – and I said, 'When are you going to marry my mother?' and he laughed in that sort of laugh people make when they're embarrassed. He arranged the marriage straight away after that. He'd always promised her, he knew there was no way out, and he wasn't going to say, 'I'm not going to' to me. And that was that.

Were you at the wedding?
No, I was only allowed to answer the telephone. The office was very busy with calls when the news got out and when people rang up, I was told to say I was the secretary. I was never allowed to take part in anything like that until he was dying – I was at the foot of the bed when he died, that was allowed.

What was Frances's life as a widow like?
She was very, very lucky that she married him. Dame Margaret had died only two ▶

❛ I loved Lloyd George very much and I think he loved me. He always made time for me – I thought he was wonderful. ❜

13

Ffion Hague talks to . . . *(continued)*

◄ years before and might well have gone on. In Surrey, if you're a dowager countess you can get away with anything, but if you've been someone's mistress for thirty years – no, it doesn't do at all!

Occasionally, we laughed about it. She was asked to address the League of Moral Welfare and we thought that was very funny. People didn't realise her history, and when she published her autobiography there were people who were absolutely horrified. People who she knew very, very well had no idea she'd been Lloyd George's mistress – really great friends. In the end, they forgave her but they never mentioned her book, never.

How much did you know about Dame Margaret when you were growing up?
Nobody spoke a kind word about her in my presence. I always thought she was a terrible nuisance, a bore. That, I suppose, was the attitude of those around me. I never realised until I read your book how intelligent she was. Your book is the only one that is completely fair both to my mother and to Dame Margaret.

How did you meet your husband, Michael Longford? He was private secretary to the governor of Tanganyika, wasn't he?
Yes, he was – my mother had come out to Africa, where I was teaching, and for Christmas we went on holiday to Lushoto, which was cooler. The governor, Sir Edward Twining, went there also because it was so hot in Dar es Salaam. Someone we knew

offered to take us shopping and halfway down to town we passed a big lodge. Our friend said, had we signed the governor's book? It never occurred to us to sign the governor's book – my mother didn't throw her weight around, ever. But they insisted and so we went to the lodge and signed the book. They saw who she was and the next day we were invited to lunch.

Michael apparently decided he wanted to marry me straight away but I took at least half an hour to make up my mind. While we were having lunch the governor said, 'He's an interesting man, intelligent, musical and unpunctual' and I thought, 'That'll do for me!' And it did, very well.

How would you like to be remembered?
I don't mind how I'm remembered. Possibly LG's daughter, possibly not. We don't know and it doesn't matter. ■

> ❛ I don't mind how I'm remembered. Possibly LG's daughter, possibly not. We don't know and it doesn't matter. ❜

If You Loved This,
You Might Like . . .

My Darling Pussy: The Letters of Lloyd George and Frances Stevenson, 1931–1941, edited
by A.J.P. Taylor
These letters chronicle the intense attachment between Lloyd George and his mistress; not surprisingly, they are more passionate than political.

Lloyd George Was my Father
by Olwen Carey Evans
With a title that nods to the old music hall adage 'Lloyd George knew my father', this is the autobiography of Lady Olwen Carey Evans, the third child of David Lloyd George.

Life with Lloyd George: The Diary of A.J. Sylvester, 1931–45, edited
by Colin Cross
A.J. Sylvester's work remains a unique source of information on David Lloyd George and his complex personal life.

A Radical Life: The Biography of Megan Lloyd George, 1902–1966
by Mervyn Jones
The first full life of the youngest – and favourite – daughter of Lloyd George, a radical, eloquent campaigner for her father's ideas, who spent thirty-one years as an MP and was an early supporter of equal pay for women and a separate parliament for Wales. ■